To my good friend Trevor Simpso

People move in and out of each other's lives
on the other. You find you are made up of
have touched your life... and you are more because of it; ...
would be less if they had not touched you!
John Ward
Sept 98

BEWARE OF THE DOG AT WAR

An Operational Diary of

49 Squadron

Spanning 49 Years 1916 - 1965

by

John Ward

The picture featured on the cover is an original oil painting by the author, John Ward.
It depicts Lincoln Cathedral with the Hampden, Manchester, Lancaster, Lincoln and Valiant bombers as operated by 49 Squadron.

This book is dedicated to all those who served with

49 SQUADRON
ROYAL AIR FORCE
BOMBER COMMAND

ISBN - 0 9532252 0 8

British Library Cataloguing in Publication Data.
A catalogue for this book is available from the British Library.

Published by :
John Ward and Ted Cachart as:
JoTe Publications. 4 Cottage Close. Heage. Belper. Derbyshire. DE56 2BS
Telephone 01773 853181

Printed by:
Esparto Digital Ltd. Slack Lane. Derby. DE22 3DS

First published December 1997
Reprinted March 1998
Reprinted August 1998

FOREWORD

I suppose the question is why should I, someone born several years after the events, wish to produce a book about a World War Two Bomber Squadron? I readily admit to being totally unqualified to accurately describe 'what it was like' to be a member of a wartime bomber crew... for I am of the succeeding generation... part of that future for whom the war had been fought.

My small part in this story began in the early 1960's, when my family moved out of Lincoln to live in the tiny but rapidly expanding village of Cherry Willingham. I attended primary school in the neighbouring village of Fiskerton where the school buildings were very different from the modern ones I had experienced in Lincoln. I was later to learn that Fiskerton School was actually housed in a former RAF Officers' Mess and that our assembly/dining hall had been in the Sgts' Mess.

At weekends and school holidays, in the company of friends, we walked across the fields adjoining Cherry and the old Fiskerton airfield, where many happy, adventurous, youthful hours were spent amongst the slowly decaying RAF buildings. Dares were always made as to who would enter the dark cavernous hangars alone... where daylight penetrated through only the merest of cracks. We would climb the steeply inclined iron steps in order to venture precariously out onto the roof of the old control tower... where the wind always blew strongest. A favourite haunt was the static water tank; here many species of newts had established their homes... in fact I remember our class going there once for a nature lesson.

Tramping back home across the fields for tea... the tops of our Wellington boots chaffing bare legs, with socks having disappeared to toe ends for the hundredth time. It was then that the conversation would often be of Lancasters... those huge black bombers, with engines on fire, its valiant crew desperately trying to make base... such were childhood images.

At such an early age, my imagination and naive curiosity must have been fired. Endlessly I sought facts and knowledge from various sources. My parents, their friends, relatives... anyone who was old enough to remember the war received a deluge of questions. I listened intently to their memories of long summer evenings with scores of bombers visible, slowly circling the city, gradually gaining height before heading out for Germany. They spoke of Lincoln High Street bustling with uniforms of every nation... airmen on push bikes... airmen in buses and lorries and airmen on foot, walking back to base.

Lincolnshire folk had listened from the sanctuary of a warm bed to the heart wrenching sound of a damaged aircraft limping back in the early hours. Morning's first light would reveal the harrowing sight in a farmer's field of a burnt out wreckage, marking where one more crew didn't quite make it.

Gradually it became clear to me what the significance of Fiskerton airfield (and the many other such airfields) meant from the human perspective. At 12 years of age, the Christmas present I received from my parents was 'Bomber Squadrons of the RAF' by Philip Moyes.

FOREWORD

That first book, now very worn from use, takes pride of place amongst my collection of Bomber Command related books. Over the years, I have read and researched extensively on the subject but 49 Squadron... Fiskerton's squadron, always retained a very special place in my heart.

It wasn't until 1987, when the 49 Squadron Association was invited to a reunion at Fiskerton, that I would at last have direct contact with the unit. Unfortunately the reunion was by invitation only and having no bona fide reason for access, my contact with the squadron was from the fringe only. My extreme frustration was relieved by a fortuitous chance meeting with Eddy and Pat Coward; Eddy's elder brother had been killed on ops from Fiskerton. He in turn introduced me to former 49 Squadron pilot Ernie Webb, with whom I immediately felt a rapport. The following year, Ernie invited me along to the squadron reunion at the Pathfinder Club in London. I was overwhelmed by the warmth of the reception I received. After being introduced to secretary, Tom Gatfield and Chairman 'Uncle Will', I chatted for hours with 'my heroes'... for me the night could have lasted a week. Perhaps I was intoxicated by the atmosphere but at some point during the evening, I asked the Association if they would like me to compile a book about 49 Squadron wartime activities. The enthusiasm shown was extremely encouraging... I was committed!

I decided to use a chronological diary format for ease of reference by veterans, historians and the casual reader. In the text I have referred to a crew by the pilot's name, this is for reasons of brevity and there is certainly no lack of respect implied towards the other crew members. Where a crew is shown to have 'Failed to return', they have been listed as either killed, P.o.W., evader or missing. Whilst the first two categories are self explanatory, the other two may need some clarification. Evader means an airman who managed to avoid being captured by the enemy and gained sanctuary in a neutral country or returned back to Britain. Sadly, the official term 'missing' means an airman whose body has never been found but is now acknowledged as dead, has no known grave, but is remembered for evermore, by name, on the Runnymede Memorial.

Of the 'failed to return' Lancaster crews; I have recorded how many operations each crew (pilot's surname) had flown on their current 49 Squadron tour before meeting its demise. This figure is only a guide and should be treated with a certain amount of tolerance. Several factors could effect the make up of each crew on an individual operation. For example, winter colds would often ground a crew member, and his place would be taken by a 'spare bod', he would therefore lag behind his crew on the amount of ops completed towards his tour. Also, some airmen could be on their second tour; the figure shown refers to their current tour only.

For the purists, I have tried to include as many aircraft serial numbers as possible; these are correct to the best of my knowledge. Unfortunately not all aircraft code letters were recorded; those shown were collected from various sources including personal logbooks.

PREFACE

This book is not the official history of 49 Squadron. It would be pretentious of me to make such a claim; that task must be left to those much more qualified than myself. What I have attempted to achieve in compiling this study is hopefully to provide a 'bridge' between those who served on the squadron, and succeeding generations.

As the years slip by and World War II recedes into history, it becomes even more imperative that we retain links with our Nation's past. Not one of those lives lost defending our freedom should have been in vain... nor their sacrifice go unrecorded or forgotten.

49 Squadron was just one of many bomber squadrons that carried the war to a relentless and ruthless enemy. It must be remembered that each member of an aircrew had to be a volunteer. They were nearly all in their teens or early twenties, some were still at school when war was declared in 1939. Most had just been starting out on the path of life when Hitler interrupted. They came from various backgrounds, occupations and countries. None of them wanted to be at war with Germany, but when duty called, it fell upon their generation to come forward, to do their bit... and to pay the price.

Night after night, in some windswept corner of a desolate Lincolnshire field, youthfully they clambered aboard their dormant weapons of war. Each man extremely conscious that he faced the possibility of a horrific death. Not for them a military band or bugle charge, just a lonely vigil in a hostile black sky, where their all too brief lives could be violently terminated in the stark bright flash of a sudden explosion, or with inert limbs... but able minds, transfixed to the walls of a rapidly spinning, doomed bomber... how long does it take to spiral down from 20,000 feet? Then there are the unforgiving clutches of the North Sea... just minutes to live in the middle of winter... days in the summer.

Recognition of the role played by the ground staff could never be overstated. Without exception, every former 49er aircrew member that I interviewed, at some stage requested of me 'don't forget the ground lads and WAAFs - without them we could never have carried out our tasks'. For many, work on a bomber station was extremely hard and exacting, but they never faltered in their given duties. Ground staff also suffered their share of casualties; during the war no less than 1,479 and 91 W.A.A.F.s died whilst serving with Bomber Command. A further 52 male ground staff became prisoners of war.

If you are of the post war generation and after reading this book, you, and perhaps your children, have a better understanding of what came to pass during the war years, if the next time you hear the name Scampton mentioned on your television or read the name Fulbeck on a signpost that flashes by, or you happen to travel the road between Reepham and Fiskerton and stop at the simple stone that bears testimony to the location of the old airfield... and if you happen to say; *"Oh yes, this is where 49 Squadron flew from...and died from... I REMEMBER, I read about them in a book!"*

Then, and only then....... will I have perhaps repaid a little of the enormous debt we all owe to those who once proudly served with 49 SQUADRON, ROYAL AIR FORCE, BOMBER COMMAND.

ACKNOWLEDGEMENTS

During the research for this book I have had the pleasure of meeting so many wonderful people and as a result numerous lifelong friendships have been established. To all those who so kindly took the time to help and contribute, I offer my sincere and grateful thanks.

49 Squadron veterans:

Leslie 'Uncle Will' Hay - for his tireless work at the Public Records Office, and all his generous support. **Tom Gatfield** - the engine and the driver! and 49 Squadron's greatest ambassador. **Ted Cachart** - the quality of these printed pages bear testimony to his expertise in converting my basic word processed text into this illustrated publication... and his endless patience with me. **Jack Shearing** - his diary gave enormous inspiration.

John Aldridge	Norman Alty	Jim Bain	Tom Bennett
David Boughton	Len Bradfield	Jack Branch	Bernard Browning
Johnny Chaloner	Juan Christian	H. Church	Eric Clarke
Bert Cole	V. Collins	Wes Coluhoun	Gordon Cooper
Lou Crabbe	Don Deeley	Jack Dolman	Bob Drinnan
Jim Edwards	Ron Eeles	Jim Flint	Don Foster
Harold Fricker	Jack Gadsby	Ken Gibson	Les Hammond
Des Harris	Jack Harvison	Tom Hawkins	Dennis Hiscock
Vin Howard	Eric Jones	Stuart Keay	Chaz Kind
Fred Lowe	Allan (Spud) Mahony	Len Mellor	Alan Morgan
Johnny Moss	Eric Newton	Harold Olerenshaw	Tom Page
John Peaker	Larry Pederson	Bob Petty	Eric Reed
Deryck Richmond	Clive Roantree	Peter Roberts	D. Saxton
Jack Shearing	John Simpson	Trevor Simpson	Norman Smith
Dot Everitt (nee Smith)	Bob Souter	Zoe Stocks	Tom Taylor
Doug Tritton	Pat Walters	Jack Wattam	Bert Weatherley
Ernie Webb	Maurice White	J. Wilkinson	Peter Williams
Jack Winter	Vi Winters	Charlie Wright	

Friends, relatives and acquaintances

Bill Ansell	Peggy Barlow	Colin Blower	Dave Boril
Keith Coldron	Eddy Coward	Ernst Guse	Mr J.G.J. de Haan
Joan Kirwan	Allan Mitchell	Harry Moyle	Brian Nichols
E. Nightingale	Don Palmer	Fred Panton	Harold Panton
John Rose	Joy Stopani	Jeff Stuffins	Freda Styles
Bob Walkinton	Arthur Whitlock		

A special thanks to my dear wife Diane, whose help and encouragement saw me through the difficult times, and not forgetting my 'crew' of seven children, Jodie, Lindsay, John, Thomas, Kimberley, Rosanna and Tamara who kept well out of the way whenever the word processor was switched on.

"Take these men then, as your examples. Like them, remember that prosperity can be only for the free, that freedom is the pure possession of those alone who have the courage to defend it."

(Pericles)

IN THE BEGINNING

In the beginning; No 49 Squadron, RFC, was formed at Dover, Kent, on 15 April, 1916 under the command of Major A.S. Barratt. The first eighteen months were spent as an aircrew training unit equipped with B.E.2c's and R.E.7's.

In November, 1917 the squadron re-equipped with D.H.4's and moved to La Bellevue aerodrome in France. Here the squadron was employed in the day-bomber role as part of the 3rd (Army) Wing. The first bombing raid was made on 26 November, 1917 when 8 D.H.4's were despatched to bomb Rieux; 4 aircraft bombed the primary target, 3 bombed Sailly instead and 1 completely aborted. No opposition was encountered on this occasion, but three days later the squadron ran into the Richthofen Circus and during the fight one squadron aircraft was lost.

Counter-battery photography started in January 1918, when formations of about seven machines were sent over the enemy lines; 3 carried cameras and the others acted as escorts. During the German advance the squadron did a good deal of low bombing to check the breakthrough of the enemy.

At the end of March, No 49 Squadron moved up to the Dunkirk area, where they re-equipped with D.H.9 aircraft. Raids were made on Thourout, Ostend, Zeebrugge and Bruges. Eventually the squadron moved south again and in June, from Fourneuil, near Beauvais, it was engaged in intensive low-flying attacks on ground targets as well as long-distance bombing raids. In one week, from 10 to 17 June, the squadron shot down seventeen enemy aircraft.

In July a move was made to the French front, but the squadron was soon returned to the British front in August in anticipation of a counter-offensive on the Somme, and once more was detailed for low-level bombing. This work so depleted the squadron that Nos. 49 and 27 Squadrons had to join forces and go over the lines in one formation. Until the Armistice the squadron was therefore engaged in high-altitude day bombing in the face of intensive opposition. Many successful raids were made on important objectives, and many enemy aircraft were destroyed.

The squadron's last operational mission in World War One was 10 November, 1918 (pm) when 7 D.H.9's bombed Charleroi junction. During its eleven months or so of active service, No.49 Squadron dropped 120 tons of bombs, destroyed 56 enemy aircraft and drove down another 63 out of control; its pilots and observers won the following decorations - 10 DFC's, 4 Croix de Guerre, 1 DFM and 1 Meritorious Service Medal.

In May, 1919, the squadron was posted to Bickendorf, Germany as part of the Army of Occupation. Post-war disarmament led to its disbandment on 18 July, 1919.

IN THE BEGINNING

HONOURS AND AWARDS - 1917

Capt G. Fox-Rule	D.F.C.	Capt H.I. Rough	D.F.C.
Capt C. Bowman	D.F.C.	Lt V. Dreshfield	D.F.C.
Lt E.H. Tredcroft	D.F.C.		
Major B.S. Benning	Croix de Guerre		
Capt G. Fox-Rule	Croix de Guerre		

HONOURS AND AWARDS - 1918

2/Lt P.T. Holligan	D.F.C.	2/Lt W.A. Owens	D.F.C.
Lt A.R. Spurling	D.F.C.	2/Lt E.A. Simpson	D.F.C.
Sgt F.W. Bell	D.F.M.	Lt L.A. Keating (USAS)	D.F.C.
Sgt F.L. Roberts	Croix de Guerre		
Capt F.W. Lowen	Croix de Guerre		

When Tom Gatfield (Secretary of 49 Squadron Association) was on holiday in Italy, he and his wife Marion visited the site of the 'Tragic Poet' at Pompei.

Set in the path just inside the entrance gate was a mosaic of the dog shown left. You can just see the words Cave Canem by it's front paws.

As this was reputedly created in the 6th century BC it must be the earliest recorded version of 49 squadron's now famous motto.

It is believed that this is the base from which the squadron crest was designed although the dog is very different to the Beagle (some say Greyhound or Whippet) currently used.

CAVE CANEM

`At first sight, the badge seems inappropriate for a Bomber Squadron, but it is indicative of the performance of the Hawker Hind when compared with its contempories, hence the greyhound.'

10 February, 1936: No 49 Squadron re-formed at Bircham Newton, Norfolk, from a nucleus provided by 'C' Flight of No 18 Squadron. It was equipped with Hawker Hind light bombers and initially commanded by F/Lt J.C. Cunningham. In August, 1936 it moved to Worthy Down where at a Station Parade on 14 June 1937, Air Commodore Goble CBE, Air Officer Commanding No.2 (Bomber) Group presented the squadron with its official badge, depicting a racing greyhound surmounting the motto: "Cave Canem" (**Beware of the Dog**).

Concluding his speech the Air Commodore stated :

"This, I think, is the first occasion on which an officer of the Dominion Forces has ever presented a badge to a squadron of the Royal Air Force... or any other Air Force and it gives me particular pleasure to hand the badge to your Squadron Commander, S/Ldr W.E. Dipple, for when I commanded a squadron some twenty years earlier, he was one of my good flying officers."

IN THE BEGINNING

14 March, 1938: Under the command of S/Ldr P.McGregor-Watt, the squadron moved to Scampton in Lincolnshire. At this time the RAF eagerly awaited delivery of the new generation of bombers, namely the Handley Page Hampden and Vickers Wellington. In the meantime, the squadron continued training with their Hawker Hinds.

Hawker Hinds known to have served with the squadron carried the following serials:

K5384, K5385, K5402, K5412, K5442, K5443, K5455, K6616, K6641, K6642, K6643, K6644, K6645, K6646, K6647, K6713, K6806, K6839 L7194

Cpl Edwards (left) standing by the wheel of a Hawker Hind at Scampton in 1938 (J. Wilkinson)

Hawker Hind K5443 displays 49 Squadron's number forward of the fuselage roundel. The Squadron's 'greyhound courant' badge set in grenade frame is just discernible on the aircraft's fin. (49 Squadron collection)

IN THE BEGINNING

A snatched photograph of the very first Hampden to join an RAF Bomber Squadron. L4034 is seen here outside the hangers at Scampton in September 1938.
(J Wilkinson)

20 September, 1938: Entry into front-line service by the Hampden and Wellington was almost simultaneous, with the Hampden making it a few weeks ahead of the Wellington, when Hampden L4034 arrived on 49 Squadron; 20 September, 1938.

AN AIRMAN REMEMBERS

Posted to 49 Squadron in January 1938 as an Armourer, Mr J. Wilkinson, remembers this period of the squadron's history:

"The squadron was still at Worthy Down near Winchester when I joined them. We shared Worthy Down with two other squadrons:, one flying Handley Page Heyfords and the other Westland Wellesleys and of course 49 with their Hawker Hinds. The Royal Navy took the station over in March, and 49 moved to RAF Scampton in Lincolnshire.

Scampton was a new station and not quite finished when we arrived so for the first two months we lived in wooden huts, until the barrack blocks were ready. The hangars and servicing facilities were much better than we had been used to and the grass airfield was large and flat (no runways in those days).

About the beginning of August 1938, we got news that 49 Squadron was to be the first unit to get the new Handley Page Hampdens and very shortly the first one arrived.

At the time of the September 1938 Crisis, the squadron had half Hinds and half Hampdens, but within a month or so we were fully equipped with Hampdens. The next few months saw the squadron personnel almost double in numbers and a lot of training on the new aeroplanes for aircrew and groundcrew was carried out.

In April 1939, the squadron went to RAF Evanton near Invergordon in Scotland for the first practice camp with Hampdens. It was a new experience using the new automatic bomb sight but everything went well apart from the odd practice bomb being dropped before reaching the range. The stay at Evanton was enjoyed by everyone.

When the war started in 1939 it was hard work for the Armourers, who spent a lot of time bombing up, then taking them off and bombing up again with a different load of bombs."

IN THE BEGINNING

By November, 49 Squadron, now a part of No.5 (Bomber) Group, could boast a full complement of 12 Hampdens; the **first squadron to receive the Hampden** and the **first all-Hampden unit in the Royal Air Force.**

No 83 Squadron was also resident at Scampton and received its first Hampden on 31 October, 1938, being fully equipped by 9 January, 1939.

The bulk of the bomber crews were junior officers, on short-term service engagements. A minority of airmen were 'regulars' from such RAF backgrounds as Halton's Apprentice School. Most squadrons had a small number of pilots and observers from the countries of the Empire, who had come to England to join the Royal Air Force.

As the war clouds once again gathered over Europe, both Scampton squadrons were destined to go to war in Hampdens. The last peacetime air exercises were held only two weeks prior to the outbreak of war with Germany... very few of the young aircrew had ever fired a shot 'in anger'.

HAMPDEN CRASH

Just one month before the war started, F/Lt George Lerwill overshot Scampton in L4039 during night training. Fortunately the crew were all unharmed.

This `morning after' photograph shows XU-D straddling the road on 2 August 1939. Note the squadron's pre-war codes `XU'. (J, Wilkinson)

Officially the first Hampden to join 49 Squadron; L4039 at Scampton, September 1938. (RAF Scampton)

SHEFFIELD'S "OWN" BOMBER SQUADRON MAY VISIT CITY IN NEAR FUTURE

'The above small headline appeared in the Sheffield Telegraph on 5 May 1939'. The item carried on to say:

'A visit to Sheffield may shortly be paid by the city's "own" Royal Air Force Unit, No 49 Bomber Squadron, which is stationed at Scampton, six miles north of Lincoln. The Commanding Officer of the Squadron; in a letter of greeting to the Lord Mayor of Sheffield (Alderman W.J. Hunter), says he would like to come over and see the Lord Mayor, and if possible arrange a visit to the squadron'.

'Wing Commander J.S. Chick, the C.O., said yesterday that as Sheffield had no aerodrome they would have to land at Doncaster or Finningley RAF station. The scheme of affiliation for RAF Squadrons to the principal cities and towns in the country came into operation on Monday, the 21st anniversary of the formation of the RAF.'

"If the squadron visits the town to which it is affiliated, the public will be able to view the aircraft on the ground, if there is an aerodrome nearby."

**"COME THE THREE CORNERS OF THE WORLD IN ARMS,
AND WE SHALL SHOCK THEM. NOUGHT SHALL MAKE US RUE,
IF ENGLAND TO ITSELF DO REST BUT TRUE."
(SHAKESPEARE, KING JOHN)**

IN THE BEGINNING

1 SEPTEMBER, 1939

W/Cmdr J.S. Chick MC AFC, now commanded 49 Squadron. On the first day of September 1939, the unit strength consisted of:

Officers:	24	
Airmen:	214	
Initial Equipment:	16	Hampdens
Immediate Reserve:	5	Hampdens
Other:	4	Avro Ansons for Training

The Royal Air Force had six Hampden squadrons operational; all were in 5 Group and stationed in Lincolnshire. Nos. 44 and 50 Squadrons resided at Waddington, 61 and 144 at Hemswell, 49 and 83 at Scampton.

As a precaution against attack by the Luftwaffe on aerodromes, all squadrons made use of dispersal airfields further inland. Scampton had been allocated Newton near Nottingham and Ringway, Manchester.

On Friday 1 September, 49 Squadron had 6 Hampdens dispersed at Newton, which left 6 serviceable and 7 unserviceable Hampdens at Scampton; a further 2 Hampdens were at the Handley Page works, Radlett, undergoing repair. The following morning all aircraft returned from Newton to Scampton. All day long at Scampton, as on every other bomber station, there was tremendous activity. Around the perimeter sand-bagged gun emplacements were being constructed and Gas officers ran around placing yellow detectors in all appropriate places.

MT vehicles were deployed throughout the camp and tractors pulled Hampdens along cinder tracks way out into the haze of the Lincolnshire countryside to distant dispersals away from enemy eyes.

Deep below Station Headquarters was the operations room, where in the gloom of blue lighting, the Station Commander and his staff busied themselves with maps and photographs. In the huge hangars, riggers and fitters toiled to make yet another aircraft serviceable and available. But for the aircrew who were officially 'standing by', this was a time of idle waiting... lying on the grass in the sunshine, much of their flying clothing discarded.

That evening, with everyone confined to camp, some pretty heavy drinking took place. As usual on these occasions, the squadron's only real enemy was their station rivals... 83 Squadron. After the ensuing 'battle' the boys were content to sleep off their hangovers next day.

THE DAY WAR BROKE OUT!

3rd SEPTEMBER, 1939: This Sunday morning found the aircrew, as usual, down at flights sipping their morning tea, waiting for the NCO in charge of Maintenance to give them clearance to test fly the kites. As 11.00hrs approached, radios were being switched on around the station, and indeed around the world. In silence a nation listened to Chamberlain's solemn words telling the world that 'a state of war now exists between Britain and Germany'. It was on!... the proverbial 'balloon had gone up'.

Never before had Hampdens been air tested with such diligence; everyone aboard keenly aware that the next time they took to the air it could well be against the enemy. A snatched lunch in the Mess was interrupted by the Tannoy:

'All crews to the lecture room immediately - that is all'.

In the lecture room, crews were addressed by the Station Commander, Group Captain Emmett. The big South African said only a few words... that we were now in the war, that he expected the full support of all officers and men on the station to back him up and to back Bomber Command up in whatever operations we had to carry out. He said the German Air Force was not very good, and will have suffered losses in Poland. Detailed operational orders for the Hampdens of 5 Group had been drawn up long before the outbreak of war. Within six hours of the declaration, Operational Order B2 had been implemented. At briefing, with the crews all gathered round a table, the Station Commander thus began:

"You are going to attack the German pocket battleships which are lying in the Schillig Roads at the entrance to the Kiel Canal. If by any chance there are no warships there, you may bomb the ammunition depot at Marienhof... but on no account must you bomb civilian establishments! The weather will be bad and you will have to attack very low. Return if you think an attack cannot be carried out according to plan."

Two formations of nine aircraft would take part in this daylight attack, three from 49 Squadron plus six from 83 Squadron at Scampton, and nine from 44 Squadron at Waddington; take-off was set for 18.00hrs. 49 Squadron crews detailed were as follows:

L4040	F/L G.F. Lerwill.	L3046	F/O R.A.B. Learoyd.	L4093	SGT T.P. Pratt
	P/O D.E. Pinchbeck		P/O J.K. Bennett.		SGT R.J. Jennings.
	P/O A.S. Mirylees.		SGT J. Law.		SGT A.R. Cadman.
	AC2 R.L.J. Dutton.		AC1 S. Taylor.		AC1 F. Talbot.

At Scampton the Hampdens ran up their engines and taxied out. No 49 Squadron's three aircraft were the first to go, led by F/Lt George Lerwill (L4040) - **The Very First** aircraft in 5 Group to take-off against the Germans. Thankfully everyone managed to become airborne as the formation began to gather over Lincoln Cathedral before proceeding as ordered to Horns Reef Light Ship 55 32N 07 15E.

THE DAY WAR BROKE OUT!

Time passed slowly as the enemy coast came ever closer. The Hampdens were flying at 1,000ft when they spotted a German flying boat pass 500ft below them. It was a Dornier 18 and was last seen heading south as fast as it could go. Forty-minutes before interception of the German fleet, the cloud suddenly descended to 300ft. After a further twenty minutes, due to the worsening weather, it was obvious that a successful attack could not be made. The formation very reluctantly turned for home.

The Hampdens re-crossed the coast near Boston, during the hours of darkness. By 22.30hrs all Scampton's aircraft had safely returned. It was a very disappointed group of airmen that descended from their machines. They had faced the dangers of operational flying, experienced all the tension and emotions, yet were prevented at the very last moment from pressing home their attack.

So the first day of the war drew to an end... it had been an abortive show perhaps, but in the momentous years ahead, the men of No 49 Squadron would have ample opportunity to play their part in the defeat of Hitler's Germany.

THE CALL TO ARMS

The nation once again prepared itself for a war, and as in the First World War, young men were not slow in answering the call. One such man was Deryck Richmond; after leaving school Deryck entered the jewellery trade but just twelve months later, during the first week of the war he had enlisted as an Instrument Repairer II. Deryck recalls:

"I was accepted on the strength of a visible 'trade test', a bit of trigonometry and questions on setting up a 'Boley lathe'. They posted me to Cranwell where I tagged on to the end of a nearly concluded Boy Apprentices course."

By November 1939, Deryck found himself posted to 49 at Scampton, a 'front-line' Bomber Squadron. He continues;

"I was the very first wartime non-regular to join the unit. When I arrived at the Instrument section all it consisted of was an Instrument Repairer II who was awaiting posting and whom I never saw, plus LAC Strange from 'M Flt'. We were attached to 'A Flt' under F/Sgt Buckingham. I knew nothing... I walked around my first Hampden three times trying to find the way in, when suddenly the canopy was pushed back and the head of an airframe rigger appeared; he shouted 'I've kicked the blind-flying panel and nothing's fallen out!'... he then gave me a thumbs-up and disappeared from whence he came. The learning process started with many days (and nights) spent in an empty hangar. I was later joined by John 'Blondie' Derrek on 'A Flt' and Vic Collins and Paddy O'Neale on 'B Flt'; together we worked on all flight duties."

THE CALL - TO - ARMS

Deryck still holds dear many memories of his wartime service, the sad days and the not so sad:

"We used to stand on the aircraft wheels to prime the engines... 'petrol on, switches off, sucking in', and if we had over-primed the result was a dousing of petrol on your head! I well remember standing by the landing beacon deciding which way to run if the pilot got it wrong - setting out the goose-neck flares and if there was an air-raid warning, kicking them over and stamping them out... after the first few our boots were well paraffined and burning nicely."

Deryck served on the squadron throughout the war rising to the rank of F/Sgt. He was destined for the Far East with the 'Tiger Force', but the Atom Bomb changed all that.

From the outbreak of war, reconnaissance aircraft had regularly sighted enemy warships in the vicinity of the Heligoland Bight, but by the time their sighting reports were received, it was too late to despatch the bombers. It was therefore decided to send squadrons of bombers out on patrol, and if a warship was sighted, an attack could commence at once. No 5 Group's poorly armed Hampdens were committed to these operations, and began daylight patrols over the North Sea in search of the enemy.

During one such operation on 29 September, 144 Squadron from Hemswell suffered five Hampdens shot down after being intercepted by Bf 109 fighters of 1/ZG26. This unfortunate flight was led by the former 49 Squadron O/C, W/Cmdr J.C. Cunningham who was reported 'missing'.

No 49 Squadron had not yet been called upon to contribute aircraft to these patrols but operational training programmes continued. It was during training that the squadron sustained its first wartime casualties.

4th October, 1939: At 11.15hrs, one of 49 Squadron's Avro Ansons crashed on fire in the grounds of a Mental Hospital at Radcliffe, killing the pilot, P/O Brian Harker and the W/Op. The aircraft had been carrying out W/T practice at the time. Both crew members are buried in Newport Cemetery, Lincoln.

Crashed 5096	P/O B.L.G. Harker	Pilot	(Killed)
	AC2 F.L. McGurk.	W/OP	(Killed)

BLIND APPROACH DISASTER

23 November, 1939: At noon, on a very foggy winter's day, S/Ldr McGregor-Watt was practicing a new blind approach system at Waddington. Visibility was down to 50 yards as Hampden L4034 made a normal approach at very low level. The aircraft flew across the aerodrome without shutting off its engines, when suddenly it struck a hangar at the far side of the landing ground.

Three members of the crew; AC1 S. Taylor, AC1 F.D. Talbot and AC2 W.O. Kelly were killed instantly. The remainder of the crew; S/Ldr P. McGregor-Watt, Cpl T.A. Keating and AC1 D. McGarvie all died within a few hours.

The next day, S/Ldr Allen was posted in to Scampton from 44 Squadron to replace the unfortunate S/Ldr McGregor-Watt. At the same time S/Ldr W.C. Rae, RAAF., was posted to Hemswell and F/Lt Lowe was granted the acting rank of Squadron Leader.

Crashed L4034	S/L P. McGregor-Watt	Pilot	(Killed)
	AC2 F.L. Talbot		(Killed)
	AC1 L. McGarvie		(Killed)
	LAC W.G. Kelly		(Killed)
	AC1 S. Taylor		(Killed)
	CPL T.A. Keating		(Killed)

THE FARMHOUSE

It was during this period that the Air Ministry decided to expand the flying field at Scampton, and the farmhouse on the northern boundary of the drome was in the way of the proposed expansion. Aisthorpe House, as it was called, had to be knocked down. W/Cmdr Johnnie Chick suggested that the job could be done by using 500lb bombs!... it would provide low-level bombing practice, and the results of the bombs being dropped at low altitude could be assessed.

A competition between the two squadrons (49 and 83) was quickly organised and everyone waited for the big day. The reputation of the squadron was at stake, not to mention various 'unofficial' wagers. At the last moment the Air Ministry stepped in and decreed that only dummy bombs fitted with a live smoke charge could be used.

One by one the Hampdens ran in at about 100 feet and although they tried extremely hard, the results were rather poor. Both squadrons were learning that low-level bombing is harder than it first appears. In the end 49 Squadron won the day, when ironically the instigator of the event, W/Cmdr Chick, swept the field by placing his bomb through one of the bedroom windows.

The following poem was found in the records and may refer to the Farmhouse Incident

CONGRATULATIONS TO FORTY NINE
THE ACES OF THE BASE,
WE REGARD YOUR EFFORTS - ALL VERY FINE
AS A SHARP KICK IN THE FACE.

WE LOOK TO YOU FOR ADVICE AND TIPS
ANYTHING YOU CAN SPARE
WE TOO WOULD LIKE SOME DIRECT HITS
OR A FIX THAT'S REALLY THERE.

YOUR TRAINING, SKILL AND NATURAL FLAIR
FOR BOMBING IS UNSURPASSED,
WE GROVEL AND BEG FOR A TINY SHARE
OF THE KNOWLEDGE THAT LEAVES US AGHAST

PLEASE HELP US BEFORE YOU GO AWAY
(OUR EGOS ARE ALL DOWN),
SO WE PERHAPS CAN WIN ONE DAY
AND THEN REGAIN OUR CROWN.

PLEASE DON'T THINK WE ARE JEALOUS
OR HAVE AN ULTERIOR PLAN,
WE APPRECIATE HOW GOOD YOU ARE,
- IT'S ALL A FLASH IN THE PAN.

(AUTHORS NOT KNOWN BUT POSSIBLY 83 SQDN)

NORTH SEA SWEEP

2 December, 1939: For only the second time since war was declared, the squadron was called into action. At 07.30hrs the squadron was ordered to 'stand up' six aircraft from each flight. At 11.45hrs three aircraft from 'B Flt' under the command of F/O B.A. Mitchell, carried out a sweep over the North Sea. They carried 4x500lb SAP bombs with orders to attack fleet targets. Nothing was seen worth bombing, so bomb loads were jettisoned and the dejected crews returned to base at 17.07hrs.

During the day, S/Ldr acting W/Cmdr W.C. Sheen had been posted in from 106 Squadron, Finningley to take Command of the squadron from W/Cmdr Chick, who was posted out a few days later to 40 (M) Group.

THE CALL - TO - ARMS

THE 'DEUTSCHLAND'

December, 1939: At 21.00hrs on 20 December the squadron received instructions to bomb the pocket battleship 'Deutschland', which had been reported in the vicinity of the Norwegian coast. They were then required to return to the Scottish base of Leuchars.

The following day, the 21st, twelve Hampdens took-off from their Scampton base. Over Lincoln they met up with twelve Hampdens of 44 Squadron from Waddington and under the command of W/Cmdr Sheen, the formation headed towards the North Sea, passing over Skegness.

On reaching the Norwegian coast, they turned northwards and spread out in line abreast as they hunted for the 'Deutschland'. But the search was in vain, and at the limit of their range the Hampdens turned and headed for Scotland.

Sleet and rain showers reduced visibility on the return flight and the two squadrons became separated. The Scampton flight made landfall in Northumberland where it was intercepted and recognised as friendly by twelve fighters of 43 Squadron. By 15.47hrs most of the formation were landing at nearby Acklington. Meanwhile, 44 Squadron had crossed the coast south of Dunbar. Hurricanes of 72 Squadron intercepted them and informed control that they were Hampdens. No 602 Squadron Spitfires from Drem (the same base as the Hurricanes) were also scrambled, and without at first recognising the aircraft, proceeded to shoot down two of the Hampdens.

At Acklington, one of 49 Squadron's aircraft short of fuel was having problems. Piloted by Sgt Marshall it crashed into a Chapel at Broomhill on the edge of the aerodrome. As a result, the pilot was seriously injured and sadly two members of the crew were killed. Also injured in the crash was the 2nd pilot/navigator, P/O J.M.D. Irvine.

Crashed: L4072	AC1 E. Humphrey	(Killed)
	Sgt S.Potts.	(Killed)

THE FIRST WARTIME CHRISTMAS

Christmas Day, 1939: As in previous years, an age old RAF tradition was re-enacted. All officers served the airmen with their Christmas fare, and during this time the airmen could refer to the officers in whatever terms they wished. As can be imagined numerous rude and foul remarks filled the air.

Naturally the beer flowed freely and soon the old squadron rivalries surfaced... a yell of
'Up the Dogs'
immediately received the retort
'it's not 81, it's not 82; it's .... 83',
and with this the Corporals' and Airmens mess turned into pandemonium.

When plates started to fly, the officers made a tactical withdrawal as the risk of serious injury became a distinct possibility.

Christmas Dinner Menu in the Corporals and Airmens Mess.
Scampton 1939. J, Wilkinson)

Whilst the 'erks' enjoyed their party it was a similar picture in the Sgts' Mess. The officers could not begin their festivities until they had fulfilled their traditional duties.

Then it was high spirits all round, for these young men knew all too well that for many of their generation, this might be their last Christmas

JANUARY 1940

If November and December are remembered for the rain and fog, then January 1940 would be remembered for the snow. But before the extreme winter weather closed down all the English bomber stations, the squadron was able to despatch its first night time sorties.

18 January, 1940; LEAFLETS: During the early evening of the 18th, three 49 Squadron aircraft were detailed to drop 'Nickels' (leaflets), over three German towns; each aircraft would drop 300,000 leaflets. Those crews detailed were as follows:

L4092	P1177	P1174
W/Cmdr Sheen;	S/Ldr G. Lowe;	S/Ldr R.S. Allen;
P/O D.B. Drakes;	P/O K.H. Beauchamp;	P/O E. Parker;
Sgt C.F. Fennell;	Sgt R. Nixon;	Sgt Burnhill;
Sgt Appleton.	LAC W.R. Williams.	LAC Dutton.
Target: - **Hannover**	Target: - **Bremen**	Target: - **Brunswick**

S/Ldr Bob Allen (Brunswick) described the difficulties he and his crew encountered:

"We took-off at 17.15hrs and crossed the English coast north of Skegness. At 6,000 feet the cloud cover was 10/10ths. Shortly after, the communication in the aircraft became unserviceable, and it was necessary to call upon the observer to act as runner between the wireless operator and navigator. In this respect it was difficult to attract his attention when required. We were flying at 17,000 feet with the temperature at - 33° when the observer bawling into the intercom, managed to inform me that the W/op was unconscious, that he had fallen off his seat and was jamming the rear bulkhead door thus preventing the observer from getting out to render aid.

The navigator then made his way aft with great difficulty through having no oxygen, and managed to bring the W/op round after 15 minutes. It was presumed that the W/op was overcome with cold as the heating system was u/s from take-off.

The navigator reported that it was not possible to work comfortably in the front cockpit whilst the bags of 'Nickels' were stowed there. The 'Nickel' chute worked satisfactorily but the task of emptying four bags was very exhausting. The observer found it impossible to empty more than one bag as the bundles of leaflets jammed in the chute and blew back into the aircraft. The task was very tiring. We returned to base, landing at 22.25hrs."

KINLOSS

During January, a rumour had been circulating that both Scampton's squadrons (49 and 83) were about to move station. The rumours became fact when on the 25th January, a 'rail party' departed for Kinloss. The next day the advance 'air party' took-off for the same location. Meanwhile 83 Squadron were also on the move north to Lossiemouth.

From their respective bases both squadrons were to engage in the hunt for submarines and to stand-by in case of a chance to attack German warships.

FEBRUARY / MARCH 1940

For the first five days of the month the squadron was on 'stand down'. On 19th February, the squadron said goodbye to F/Lt Lerwill who left to go to 106 Squadron. Then for the next two days both ground and air parties made the long trip up to Kinloss and attachment to 18 Group. During their stay at Kinloss, Lt Collett, Royal Navy, was attached to the unit for liaison duties.

26 February, 1940: The first exercise order came an hour before lunch; W/Cmdr Sheen led seven aircraft on a navigation and recognition flight. Each Hampden carried 2x500lb bombs as they flew out over the North Sea via Kinnards Head. They carried out a 'square search' within a radius of 20 miles to observe surface vessels. Orders had been given that only submarines were to be attacked. The crews landed back at Kinloss in time for tea without locating any targets. S/Ldr Allen (P1174) took as navigator Lt Collett, along with F/O Butler and AC1 Gadsby.

Two days later, six aircraft under the command of F/Lt Mitchell carried out a similar task, with the same negative result.

MARCH 1940

The squadron was to carry out one more operation from their temporary Scottish home;

2 March, 1940: Six Hampdens were dispatched to carry out a 'square search' over the North Sea. Each aircraft carried 2x500lb bombs, but all returned with their loads intact and 'nothing of interest' to report.

4 March, 1940: During the afternoon, two sections under the command of S/Ldr Allen practiced intercepting flying boats out at sea. All five aircraft were home in time for tea.

Whilst at Kinloss the squadron used one of its Avro Ansons for communication flights. After departing Scampton to head north, the pilot in Anson (N5094) was forced to make an emergency crash landing near Acklington. The crew were reported safe but the Anson was beyond repair.

19 March, 1940: On this day the squadron received orders to return to Scampton and rejoin 5 Group. The move was carried out over a period of three days at the end of which Lt Collett ceased to be attached to the unit.

28 March, 1940: Back at Scampton the aircrews continued night flying training, and it was whilst landing at night that Hampden P1177 overshot and crash landed. Luckily the crew members were unhurt, the aircraft was repaired and went on to serve at an OTU.

49 SQUADRON RAF KINLOSS 1940

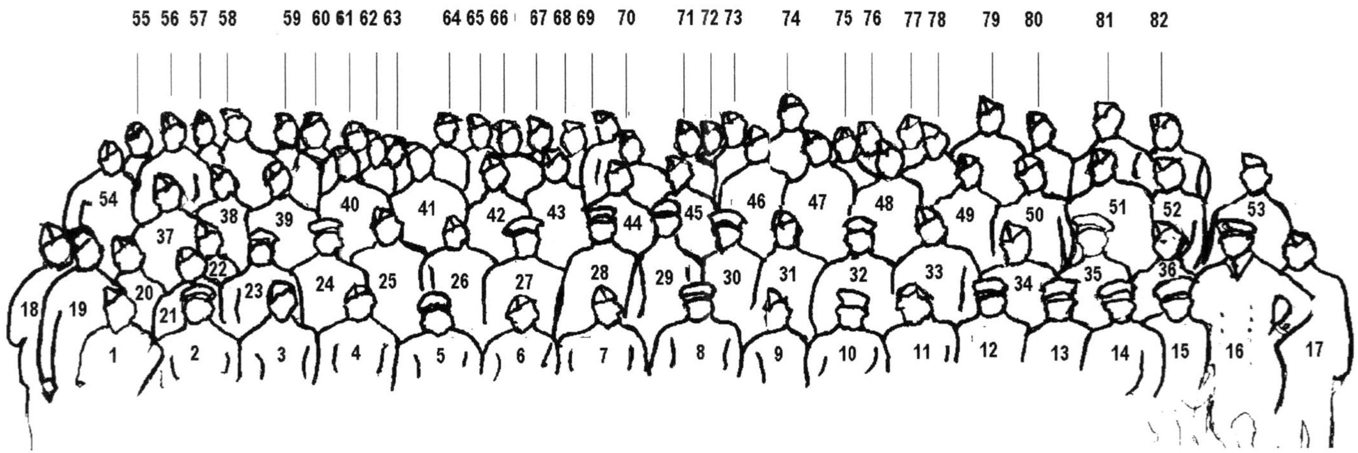

1. Sgt 'Arsey' Ayres (GS)
2. P/O Derek Pinchbeck
3. F/O Laurence C Deane
4. F/O Peter S Butler
5. F/O Roderick A B Learoyd
6. F/Lt Basil A Mitchell
7. S/Ldr Geoffrey Lowe ('Drain')
8. W/Cdr Walter C Sheen
9. F/Lt Nelles W Timmerman
10. F/Lt E W Briggs (Adjutant)
11. F/O Derrick P W Rowan-Robinson
12. P/O K H P Beauchamp ('Penny')
13. F/O Douglas S Forsyth ('Skin')
14. F/O Peter Ward-Hunt
15. F/Lt Scott (Intelligence Officer)
16. Lt Collett (Royal Navy Liaison)
22. A/C Ron Hodkinson
23. P/O David B Drakes
24. P/O J Lewis
25. P/O L Reavell-Carter
26. P/O D A J McClure
27. P/O John K Bennett
28. P/O W C A Lodge
29. F/O Tiddy (Intelligence Officer)
30. P/O H V Matthews
31. P/O Courtenay A Weeks
32. P/O Thos Murray
33. P/O Alfred P B Horden (Probably)
34. P/O E Donald Parker
35. Anthony Bryan-Smith
36. P/O T R Fox
37. Cpl George E Appleton
38. A/C William A Watson
39. A/C Don Foster
40. Sgt A W T Hills (Bill)
41. Sgt Ninian L Jones (Probably)
48. Sgt R Cooke
53. A/C Frank R Hibbert
54. LAC Thomas W Bell
55. A/C C Robinson
56. A/C Ronald L J Dutton
57. LAC George R J Parsons
60. LAC W Ellis (Which one?)
63. A/C J W Gibson
71. LAC Norman Hornsby
81. A/C John D Gadsby

–

A collection of signatures from the back of the Kinloss group photograph

APRIL 1940

The month started with 'Security Patrols'. HE 115 minelaying German seaplanes were becoming an increasing problem, so the German seaplane bases in the Sylt, Norderney and Borkum areas were given attention in an attempt to restrict activity. An indication of the nature of these patrols can be gauged from this vivid account given by Don Foster; at the time, Don was flying as W/Ag in F/Lt Nells Timmerman's crew:

"We took off from Scampton at 19.00hrs in Hampden L4038 to carry out a 'Security Patrol' over the Sylt area. Our task was to look out for flarepaths on the water and to see if we could catch German flying boats in the act of landing or taking off. It was a clear moonlit night and the moon's reflection laid a golden path on the water. It was very warm and pleasant as we flew along at about 6,000ft. Suddenly, in the path of the moon we spotted a Flakship (Flakkreuzer). At the time the Germans had carried out many dive-bombing attacks in Belgium and Holland which had interested many in our squadron.

F/Lt Timmerman turned until we were in striking distance and then he dived... down down down we went. As W/op I was also the rear gunner and my view was the sky over the tail. Light flak started coming up and I had a long look at these colourful objects shooting past like a string of bright coloured onions. Down we went to nought feet, two bombs were released and then the big pull on the elevator... we swooped over the ship at mast height. I had a fleeting glimpse of the guns with sailors grouped around them. Up we climbed at a very steep angle. This time I had a full view and was looking straight down the barrels of many guns! A strange sight as slowly, slowly these bright onions climbed towards me, red, green, blue, all colours. As they closed in they seemed to suddenly swerve away and disappear from sight and were gone... none fortunately connected.

Back at 6,000ft and 30 minutes later after flying perhaps 70 miles, there in the sea below was a flarepath. We hung around for some time when lo and behold a second Flakship. To cut a long story short the attack was a repetition of the first, flaming onions and all."

'DOWNWIND'

8 April, 1940: S/Ldr J.W. Gillan AFC was posted in from the Air Ministry. He was granted the acting rank of W/Cmdr, and took command of 49 Squadron in lieu of W/Cmdr Sheen, who in turn was posted to 5 Group HQ. In 1938, S/Ldr Gillan flew a Hurricane (which has a top speed of 335mph) down from Scotland at an average speed of 408mph... this earned him the eternal name of 'Downwind Gillan'.

9 April, 1940: As the squadron made welcome their new CO, they were saying goodbye to an old friend... Hawker Hind K5402, the last aircraft of the squadron's previous equipment had been allotted to 24 MU. F/O White had the honour of delivering the 'old girl' to Ternhill.

MINELAYING

At the Air Ministry, the Admiralty together with Bomber and Coastal Commands, discussed plans and methods of laying mines from the air. AVM A.T. Harris, by now Air OC 5 Group, suggested that his Hampdens would be most capable of carrying out this task and that the North Sea and Baltic areas involved were well known to his crews.

As a result, the six Hampden squadrons of 5 Group along with Coastal Command Beauforts were given the task. Scampton's 49 and 83 Squadrons were allotted the areas of Neustadt/ Travemünde and Swinemünde.

Minelaying operations were given the code name 'Gardening'... the mines were called after 'vegetables'... and these would be 'planted'.

11/12 April, 1940: RECCE: Six 49 Squadron aircraft carried out a night recce of Frederica, Denmark. The Hampdens took-off after 22.00hrs at ten minute intervals. No bombs were carried and machine-gun fire against land targets or inland water transport was forbidden. Leaflets were dropped in populated areas, and each aircraft had to ensure that they were not East of 4° E after dawn. The sorties were carried out satisfactorily.

13 April, 1940; MINELAYING: Three aircraft were ordered to stand-by for minelaying operations that night. Each Hampden carried 'Water melons', and the task of planting them had to be completed by 22.30hrs. The crews detailed were:

L4045	Forsyth	L4092	Mitchell	P1318	Allen
	Murray		Mathews		Parker
	Ellis		Fennell		Reavell-Carter
	Hibbert		Dutton		Williams

The sorties were carried out according to plan and it is interesting to note that F/Lt Mitchell recorded:

"Mines laid - trip took 7 1/4 hours and petrol consumption worked out at 70 Gallons per hour."

14/15 April, 1940; MINELAYING: F/O Haskins, P/O Drakes and A/C Foster were posted out to Finningley on an operational crew training course. Meanwhile three aircraft were 'stood up' for gardening. Take-off was 19.00hrs at 5 minute intervals. F/O Forsyth and F/Lt Mitchell were 'on' again, and were joined by S/Ldr Lowe. Bad weather intervened and prevented the mines being planted. Both Mitchell and Forsyth returned to base safely, but S/Ldr Lowe (L4043) and crew were experiencing severe difficulties. S/Ldr Lowe reported the following:

"We did not lay our mines due to bad weather which rapidly deteriorated on the way home. I was having trouble with all my flying instruments but the compass and turn and bank indicators were still working. Eventually we managed to make contact with Hemswell and they gave us a bearing which proved to be inaccurate. Shortly after crossing the coast an aerodrome was sighted flashing a red 'D'. We were unable to get a response so decided to send an 'SOS' on the Aldis lamp... again nothing happened... we then fired a red Very light and this time searchlights came on to the north of us."

S/Ldr Lowe made for the searchlights with the intention of being 'brought in' by them.

One engine then packed up but they managed to maintain height on one. When this engine started to spit and cough the captain offered his crew the option to bale out... none wished to jump. The aircraft was rapidly becoming uncontrollable and the captain decided to force land on the coastline; the pilot continues:

"I instructed the crew to collect in the compartment behind the pilot's seat. I held off as long as possible but the aircraft swung violently towards the cliffs and rocks below. I managed to correct this slightly, but not enough to clear a line of rocks running out into the sea. When I was holding off and practically stalling, I pulled the nose up and landed on a tail slide with very little speed."

P/O Anthony Bryan-Smith was attempting to join the other two members of the crew amidships when the aircraft landed. He was only half-way through the rear door and was killed instantaneously. The navigator, P/O Beauchamp received slight cuts on the hand, the W/Op, AC1 Appleton bumped his head and was slightly concussed and the pilot escaped with a cut lip. The Hampden crashed at about 04.00hrs near Ryhope, south of Sunderland.

Crashed: L4043	S/L Lowe	Pilot	(Injured)
	P/O Beachamp	Nav	(Injured)
	Cpl Appleton	W/Op	(Injured)
	P/O Bryan-Smith		(Killed)

17/18 April, 1940; MINELAYING/RECCE: On the two previous evenings aircraft had been detailed for gardening sorties only to have them cancelled at the last minute. However, on the 17th, 4 aircraft dropped mines in the 'Carrot' area and 2 were sent on a recce...' no bombs to be carried and no land targets to be attacked whatever'. One of the squadron's Hampdens was lent to Waddington to enable them to complete their own sorties. W/Cmdr Gillan flew on this operation, his first with 49. His crew consisted of; P/O Campbell, Sgt O'Brian and LAC Bell. They took-off in Hampden P1175 at 20.05hrs and returned to Scampton at 02.15hrs after a successful sortie.

21/22 April, 1940; MINELAYING - BALTIC: Again bad weather delayed operations but on the 21st, 8 aircraft managed to get away on gardening sorties in the West Baltic. All aircraft returned to base with positive results although not without incidents; F/O Robinson (L4045) and crew became coned in searchlights over Sylt. Heavy anti-aircraft fire was turned on them, but through the skill of the pilot, they managed to evade the lights and escape into cloud. F/O White (P1175) overshot whilst landing back at Scampton; he and his crew, consisting of Sgt Jones, LAC Hornsby and Sgt Hurst escaped unhurt.

S/Ldr Allen (P1318) with his crew of P/O Parker, P/O Reavell-Carter and AC Williams took off from Scampton's flarepath spot on 19.00hrs; he later reported:

"We planted our vegetables and then decided to go on a recce. During the flight 10 enemy ships were spotted at anchor in the River Elbe.

From the river we flew on towards Schleswig... near the town an aerodrome came into view with flarepath and hangar lights on! One aircraft could be seen doing a circuit and another was just taking off."

With typical squadron spirit and true to his own character, S/Ldr Allen cheekily took advantage of the situation... he went on to describe what happened next:

"We joined in the circuit with the German aircraft and flew around the aerodrome four times... nobody took any notice of us and after taking notes of buildings and runway headings etc, we set course for home, landing at 02.10hrs."

23/24 April, 1940; MINELAYING - BALTIC: 5 of the squadron's aircraft were sent gardening; all completed their tasks with success, but on return they were diverted to other airfields; landings were made at Feltwell, Marham, Martlesham Heath and Bircham Newton. Diversions were seldom a straight forward affair as Don Foster recalls:

"I was working on QDM's from base when I got the message that Scampton was fog bound and that we were advised to land elsewhere. So we stooged off fed up and tired. It was 03.00hrs and my oxygen had given out. Try as I would, I was unable to raise the H/F D/F station to which we were heading. We were over cloud and had seen nothing for hours... lost to buggery and petrol getting low after 8 hours in the air, the navigator did not know if we were over land or sea and nobody answered on the radio. Then at 10,000 feet, starved of oxygen, knackered, cold and hungry I suddenly had a bright idea... if I could get a fix from Bircham Newton, a M/F D/F station which had an aerodrome attached (unlike Hull, Heston and Newcastle etc) then all our problems would be solved... so I thought.

So after changing the coils, I blasted out the callsign for Bircham and sure enough back they came loud and clear, bless them! Then in my best 24 words per minute morse, I requested a course to steer to reach them. Snag... at the time the Air Ministry was wary of German aircraft intruding and homing in on our bases with QDM's purporting to be one of us, and then bombing the airfield. Therefore the Air controllers invented a system whereby we could identify ourselves as friendly. We were given secret printed sheets, and if challenged by the ground station, the friendly aircraft was obliged to give from the sheet, three numbers for the hour in question G.M.T. Bircham demanded the numbers for '5'... a frantic search on my copy and I tapped back '254'. Long pause, then damn it, '9 imi' he sent - another desperate search and I sent back '296', another long pause. By now Timmerman and the Navigator were thinking about a wheels-up landing and whether the dinghy was working O.K.

Birchams reply came at last, '4 imi' they sent. The air was blue... I shouted, kicked and threw things... Bircham Newton was a s---house! and it was manned by s---houses of the first water. I calmed down and tried again. Had I got the wrong time? the numbers changed every hour. Sod it! I tapped out the numbers shown. '376', to which I added a signal 'D' to indicate emergency. At last, at last, at last, 'send out your continuous signal' came back. They were going to give me a Q.D.M. a very unusual request to that type of station. Steering the course they gave, we eventually flew over their flarepath which soon disappeared into fog. Round we went, wheels down as F/Lt Timmerman felt his way round... down we came, no time for another circuit... bump, bump we were down.

As we taxied off the grass runway lined with gooseneck flares, we had no need to cut the engines, they cut themselves, we were out of juice!"

It is of note that during their 'planting', W/Cmdr Gillan instructed his rear gunner to open fire on a 250 ton vessel!... 'to distract the crew from seeing where we had planted'. The vessel replied with tracer which burst well to the left and below; W/Cmdr Gillan landed back at Martlesham.

25/26 April, 1940; MINELAYING - BALTIC: This would prove to be the squadron's most costly and saddest nights of the war so far; 8 Hampdens fought their way through terrible weather to the now familiar gardening areas in Kiel Bay. Only one aircraft dropped vegetables successfully, the remainder failed due to the bad conditions. Returning home the squadron was diverted to Montrose where 4 aircraft landed and a fifth landed at Leuchars. 3 aircraft and crews were missing. The reason why two of the aircraft failed to return will never be known, but the third gained the unenviable distinction of being the **first** bomber to be shot down by a German night fighter:

Hampden P1319, flown by P/O Arthur Benson fell victim to Fw Förster, a member of IV[N]/JG.2, the very first German night fighter unit. This unit operated Messerschmitt Bf 109D's which had the cockpit hoods removed. The Hampden came down in the North Sea off Sylt. The body of Sgt Robert Mackenzie was washed ashore on 30 May near Rantum, and now rests in the Kiel War Cemetery; the rest of the crew were never recovered.

Hampden L4040 piloted by F/O David White and crew came down at Hornum in Germany; all four crew members are buried in Hamburg Cemetery.

Hampden L4092 flown by F/O Derrick Rowan-Robinson and crew came down in the North Sea; the body of Sgt Arthur James was the only one recovered, and he is now in Becklingen War Cemetery. His fellow crew members are remembered on the Runnymede memorial.

FTR: P1319	P/O A.H. Benson	(Missing)
	P/O A.P.B. Hordern	(Missing)
	LAC J.D. Openshaw	(Missing)
	Sgt R.I.L. MacKenzie	(Killed)
FTR: L4040	F/O D. White	(Killed)
	Sgt N.L. Jones	(Killed)
	LAC N. Hornsby	(Killed)
	Sgt P.J. Hurst	(Killed)
FTR L4092	F/O D.P.W. Rowan-Robinson	(Missing)
	P/O C.A. Weeks	(Missing)
	Sgt A.F. James	(Killed)
	LAC T. Hogarth	(Missing)

MAY 1940

May began with the squadron continuing minelaying operations, then during the dawn of the 10 May, 1940, the long-anticipated German offensive in the west commenced.

The German armies, including Airborne troops, smashed their way into the neutral countries of Holland and Belgium. From this point on the British and French troops were steadily pushed back towards the Channel around the port of Dunkirk. Preventative raids west of the Rhine had been restricted by politics, but now this was to change when on the 15 May, 1940, the War Cabinet authorised Bomber Command to strike across the Rhine into the German heartland.

Pre-war plans were now implemented and the true bombing offensive against Germany could begin.

1/2 May, 1940; MINELAYING: At 15.00hrs on the first day of the month, 8 of the squadron's aircraft were requested for minelaying. 6 aircraft were dispatched to the Nasturtium area... 1 failed to take-off, 4 planted correctly and 1 planted in the wrong place.

Earlier, W/Cmdr Gillan and F/Lt Timmerman had taken-off for the Eglantine area. It was in that area that F/Lt Timmerman and crew, consisting of Lewis, Batho and Powell in Hampden L4068, engaged and shot down a small German seaplane; they believed the twin-floated plane to have been an Arado 196.

All aircraft returned safely with Lowe and Learoyd landing at Montrose.

4/5 May, 1940; MINELAYING: Just two aircraft were called for operations, one from 'A Flight' the other 'B Flight'. F/O Forsyth (L4045) took-off first, with his crew comprising Murray, Ellis and Hibbert. They encountered numerous searchlights and were engaged by heavy anti-aircraft fire in the target area.

F/Lt Learoyd (P1318) and crew of Stretton, Law and Bell completed their gardening in the 'Onion' area. Both crews landed back at Kinloss as instructed at briefing.

On this day it was announced that F/Lt N.Timmerman had been awarded the Distinguished Flying Cross.

5 May, 1940: F/O Butler, P/O Bennett, LAC Parsons and LAC Titley were posted to Finningley for crew training. They therefore avoided the large squadron parade on the tarmac in front of 49's hangars. The occasion was the visit to the Station by The Under Secretary of State for Air, Captain H. Balfour. All crews were paraded and congratulated on their efforts and continuing hard work.

6/7 May, 1940; MINELAYING: Six of the Squadron's Hampdens attempted to lay mines in the 'Hollyhocks' area but were prevented from doing so by adverse weather conditions. All returned safely. Next day the squadron was stood down due to the bad weather.

11/12 May, 1940; MÜNCHEN GLADBACH - GERMANY AT LAST!
This was a significant date in the operational history of the squadron. On this day, 6 of the unit's aircraft, along with 13 other Hampdens and 18 Whitleys raided a German town for the very first time. The purpose of the raid was to attack road and rail communications.

Each aircraft carried 4x1000lb instantaneous bombs. All 49 Squadron crews returned home safely except for one; P/O Drakes (L4068) and crew had made a successful attack on the target, but during their return, trouble struck. The starboard engine had failed and as they flew across France they were unable to maintain height. The skipper realised that a Channel crossing was not feasible, so a suitable landing site was paramount.

At 03.50hrs, P/O Drakes crash-landed on the French coast near Ault, 3 miles north of Le Treport. The pilot and crew, consisting of P/O Fox, Sgt Fennell and A/C Watson were uninjured in the incident and managed to return to operational duties on the squadron.

FTR: L4068	P/O Drakes	P/O Fox
	A/C Watson	Sgt Fennell

14/15 May, 1940; BOMBING: Just one aircraft from the squadron joined 11 other Hampdens from other units in attacking road and rail targets in Holland. The aircraft came home safely.

15/16 May, 1940; DORTMUND/BOHWINKEL: Ninety-nine aircraft from Bomber Command attacked 16 different targets in the Ruhr. 49 Squadron contributed 9 to Dortmund and 3 to Bohwinkel. Order of Battle for the evening was as follows:

P1347	Gillian,	Michie,	Harrison,	Bell.
P1318	Allen,	Carker,	Williams.	Reavell-Carter,
L4095	Timmerman,	Lewis,	Batho,	Powell.
L4038	Burnett,	Gower,	Bunting,	Hodgkinson.
P4305	Mitchell,	Matthews,	Matthews,	Dutton.
P4321	Forsyth,	Murray,	Ellis,	Hibbert.
L4036	Hills,	McClure,	Lowe,	Reynolds.
L4060	Ward-Hunt,	Cooke,	Nixon,	Gibson.
P2063	Campbell,	Haskell,	Baum,	Gadsby.
P4304	Lowe,	Beauchamp,	Halls.	Appleton
P1333	Pinchbeck,	Jennings,	Reid,	Foster.
L4045	Pratt,	Cadman,	Harris,	Howden.

2 aircraft failed to drop their bombs on 'a target' both due to bombing mechanism failure.

MAY 1940

THOROUGHBRED!

Sgt Pratt (L4045) and crew on return from Germany, missed England! and landed 'Queenie' on Curragh racecourse near Dublin in Southern Ireland. The Irish gave them 200 gallons of fuel and said 'clear off' before you are interned. They then flew up to Aldergrove and from there back to Scampton, much to the amusement of their colleagues.

17/18 May, 1940; HAMBURG: Ten of the squadron's Hampdens took-off from Scampton at 5 minute intervals. Their target was the oil refinery at Hamburg. With the exception of one aircraft, all made successful attacks. S/Ldr Lowe, with P/O Beauchamp as 2nd pilot dropped the first salvo on the refinery setting it ablaze. This allowed the remaining aircraft to locate and bomb the target more easily.

All aircraft returned safely, but with several diversions.

19/20 May, 1940; BOMBING: Twelve of the unit's Hampdens joined 66 other aircraft in attacking German troop communications. The squadron's targets were railway and industrial buildings in Germany. F/Lt Timmerman was unable to locate the target, but on the return journey, he and his crew attacked 4 destroyers and one other ship! F/O Ward-Hunt in Hampden P1176 was hit in one of the outboard tanks which punctured. He and his crew managed to make a safe landing at Feltwell. All 49's aircraft returned safely.

21/22 May, 1940; KREFELD/AACHEN: At 15.00hrs orders came through requesting 8 aircraft to stand-by for bombing. The first of these left Scampton at 21.00hrs followed at 5 minute intervals by the other 7. Each Hampden carried 4x250lb General Purpose bombs plus incendiary containers. All crews delivered successful attacks, with Sgt Pratt (P4321) and crew consisting of Harris, Mathews and Walker claiming a direct hit on a train. All 49's aircraft returned safely.

23/24 May, 1940; KREFELD/AACHEN: This was a repeat of the operation carried out two nights earlier, with the squadron managing to put up 12 aircraft. The weather was very poor with heavy rain and thunderstorms but despite the adverse conditions, 10 of the unit's Hampdens made good their attacks.

Not for the first time S/Ldr Lowe and crew were having their share of excitement. As they returned home after dropping their load, a convoy opened fire on them about 40 miles east of Skegness. No damage was sustained and they returned back furious but safely with the rest of the squadron.

25/26 May, 1940; KREFELD/AACHEN: At 06.00hrs, 12 aircraft were ordered to stand-by at one hours notice... by 13.30hrs this was cancelled. Then at 16.00hrs it was 'on' again... 10 aircraft required for bombing, the first getting away just after 21.00hrs. The Hampden flown by F/O Butler and crew failed to return from this operation and it is thought they were victims of flak over the target area; none of the crew survived. P/O John Bennett and LAC George Parsons are buried in the Adegem Canadian War Cemetery in Belgium; F/O Peter Butler and Sgt John Harrison are remembered on the Runnymede Memorial.

FTR: P1318	P/O J.K. Bennett	Pilot	(Killed)
	LAC G.R.J. Parsons	W/OP	(Killed)
	Sgt J. Harrison		(Missing)
	F/O P.S. Butler		(Missing)

26 May, 1940: At 15.20hrs, H.M. King George V1 honoured the station with a visit. He inspected and spoke to the Officers and Men of 49 Squadron. The King was pleased to honour F/Lt Timmerman with the award of the DFC, and congratulated S/Ldr Lowe and Sgt Hills on winning the DFC and DFM respectively. (These were received the previous day).

27/28 May, 1940; LEAVES/COLOGNE: Orders came through late, at 16.00hrs; 12 aircraft were required to attack communications behind the battle front. By 22.50hrs all 12 Hampdens were armed and away.

Crews claimed hits on a variety of targets, but 3 aircraft were unsuccessful in their attempts, P/O Mathews did not drop his bombs as the wrong plugs had been inserted and Sgt Haskins was unable to locate the target; he also reported that the searchlights over the east coast of Britain had been very troublesome. F/O Learoyd and crew were unsuccessful owing to the poor visibility caused by smoke from various fires. The pilot therefore proceeded to fly around the Ruhr Valley giving his gunners, Sgt Law and LAC Ellis instructions to fire at will. The crews intention was to cause as much disturbance as possible, and in doing so they expended 1,100 rounds.

F/O Forsyth's de-brief report was both terse and poignant...

"Dunkirk burning furiously".

HONOURS AND AWARDS - MAY 1940

F/Lt N.W. Timmerman	D.F.C.
S/Ldr G. Lowe	D.F.C.
Sgt A.W.T. Hills	D.F.M.

F/lt Timmerman receives the D.F.C. from H.M. King George VI at Scampton on 26th May 1940, Standing on the left is Sir Cyril Newall and G/Cpt Warmesly. W.O. Jones can be seen on the extreme right of the photograph (Mr Collins)

From the left:
S/Ldr Lowe D.F.C.,
Sgt Hills D.F.M., and
F/Lt Timmerman D.F.C.
The other three aircrew are members of 83 Squadron
(Mr Collins)

H.M. King George V1 congratulates S/Ldr 'Tubby' Lowe on his award of the D.F.C. and Sgt Hills for his D.F.M.
(Mr Collins)

JUNE 1940

By 4 June, 1940: the evacuation of Dunkirk was completed. The fall of France now left German forces manning the coast of Europe, from the border of France with Spain, up to Norway in the north.

Britain, led by her new Prime Minister, Winston Churchill, was not prepared to talk of peace. The nation braced itself and awaited Hitler's invasion armies. The Royal Navy was still powerful, but first the Germans had to overcome the RAF and soon the Battle of Britain would be fought in the skies over southern England. Fighter Command bore the brunt of these air battles, but it was the men and machines of the RAF bomber forces who carried the fight into the German's homeland.

1/2 June, 1940; GERMANY: Whilst the evacuation of Dunkirk was still in progress, sorties were dispatched in an attempt to disrupt enemy troop and aircraft movements behind their lines.

A contrived photograph, but never-the-less a very pleasing shot of P1333 F-Freddie, along with other 49 Squadron Hampdens being 'bombed up' in the fields to the south of Scampton's hangars, during the high summer of 1940. It was this aircraft that Sgt Stretton and crew were forced to crash land in Holland; all survived to become PoW's.
(RAF Scampton)

Twelve 49 Squadron Hampdens departed Scampton (in pairs at 5 minute intervals) bound for Germany, but only two aircraft were successful in attacking their targets; Sgt Haskins (L4036) and crew of Apps, Wood, Cartwright later reported:

"We attacked an aerodrome believed to be Spickerroog, 4 bomb bursts were observed on the landing ground away from the hangars."

F/O Mitchell (P4305), Sgt Spickett, Reid, LAC Dutton stated:

"We attacked Spickerroog which was surrounded by a ring of light flak."

All aircraft returned safely home.

3/4 June, 1940; GERMANY: During the evening, 6 of the squadron's aircraft joined a 142 strong force attacking various targets from Hamburg to Frankfurt. All 49's Hampdens were successful and all returned home unscathed.

4/5 June, 1940; GERMANY: Again, various targets were attacked in Germany. The squadron put up 11 aircraft but F/O Peter Ward-Hunt had to return early with engine trouble. The remainder of the squadron made good their attacks on Frankfurt. No aircraft were lost from Scampton.

6/7 June, 1940; HAMBURG/RIVER ELBE: Group requested 6 aircraft to bomb Hamburg plus another 6 for minelaying in the River Elbe. Take-off commenced at 21.05hrs with the Hampdens going off in pairs.

The squadron had mixed fortunes... of the 6 bombers, 4 were successful, 1 bombed an alternative target and the sixth aircraft was unable to locate the target owing to darkness. The 'gardeners' fared less well... of the 5 crews that managed to get away, only one placed its mines; P/O Drakes (L4195) with P/O Fox, Sgt Boyd, LAC Watson, successfully planted in the `Eglantine' area.

8/9 June, 1940; AMIENS: Twelve Hampdens took-off from Scampton in pairs at 10 minute intervals, their objective being the railway system in the area around Amiens.

P/O E.D. PARKER G.C.

The last pair of aircraft to roll down Scampton's grass runway were those piloted by P/O Pinchbeck and P/O Parker. As the latter's Hampden neared the end of the take-off run it developed severe engine trouble. The aircraft managed to become airborne but a few moments later L4044 came crashing back down to earth. After extricating himself from the downed bomber, the pilot, with the help of two local farmers, managed to rescue the wireless operator from the wreckage. P/O Don Parker's crew, consisting of P/O Lockhead, Sgt Lloyd and Sgt Robinson were all injured but thankfully survived.

The Hampden had come to rest at the top of Carlton Hill on the SW boundary of Scampton aerodrome; the crash timed at 23.05hrs.

For his actions on this day, P/O E.D. Parker was awarded 'The medal of the Military Division of the Most Excellent Order of the British Empire for Gallantry', which in September 1940 was renamed the George Cross.

Note: During the winter of 1940/41, F/O Don Parker GC joined 29 Squadron, a night fighter unit stationed at Wellingore south of Lincoln. Flying Beaufighters, he completed a successful tour in the company of another bomber type, F/Lt Guy Gibson; both pilots were destined to return to Bomber Command where they would eventually meet a gallant death.
The remainder of the squadron, with the exception of one, made successful sorties, the last one arriving home at 04.30hrs.

10/11 June, 1940; RAILWAYS: Once again, communication targets were attacked by a mixed force of Wellingtons, Whitleys and Hampdens. No 49's contribution of 12 aircraft made successful attacks and returned home safely.

11/12 June, 1940; GVIET: Just one aircraft from the squadron was required to carry out a collaboration attack with another of 83 Squadron, on the River Gviet. Sgt Pratt (P4321) and crew later reported seeing their bombs burst on the east side of the river. Both crews returned home safely to Scampton.

12/13 June, 1940; MINELAYING/FRANCE: Twelve 49 Squadron aircraft departed Scampton; 6 on gardening sorties, the remaining 6 were to seek military targets to bomb in France. Of the gardeners; F/O Haskins was forced to return early with engine trouble and the Pinchbeck crew could not locate their objective, but the remaining 4 aircraft all planted correctly. Only one of the bombers failed to find a target to bomb, that of P/O Beauchamp and crew.

NIGHT FIGHTER ACES?

On the night of 12/13, S/Ldr Bob Allen (P1333) and crew experienced a most extraordinary evening of events. Whilst on route to their target they suddenly found themselves in the company of a Heinkel 111, which with the nerve and skill of night fighter aces, they soon dispatched in flames.

Buoyed on by this success, they continued towards their objective when once again another enemy aircraft was encountered. This time it was a JU 86 and it too fell victim to the Hampden's guns. The victorious crew then 'pressed on' to make a successful bombing attack on a cross-roads near Laon, arriving back at Scampton at 04.00hrs.

The remainder of 49's aircraft returned home safely. It came as no surprise to the squadron, when on the 26 June, 1940, S/Ldr R.S. Allen and Sgt Williams were awarded the DFC and DFM respectively. The other two members of the crew were Sgt A.R. Cadman and LAC Stretton.

13/14 June, 1940; RAILWAYS: Twelve Hampdens were sent to bomb the railway sidings at Fargniers in France, where it was believed that the wagons were being used to store petrol. 10 aircraft attacked the primary target, whilst F/Lt Timmerman DFC dropped his bombs on Chaulay Station - F/O Forsyth and crew brought their bombs home. All of the squadron's aircraft returned home safely.

17/18 June, 1940; GERMANY: A total of 139 aircraft attacked numerous targets in the Ruhr and Northern Germany. 49 Squadron contributed 10 Hampdens of which all made successful bombing attacks on various targets.

Once again a 49 Squadron aircraft turned 'night fighter' when F/Lt Timmerman DFC with fellow crew members P/Os Lewis, Stevens and LAC Bell in L4093, spotted an enemy plane about to land at Schipol aerodrome in Holland. Adopting the guise of an 'Intruder', the Hampden crew dived upon their prey, machine-gunning him into the ground. After this success they turned their attention to the then aroused aerodrome, dropping four bombs, hitting buildings on the NE side of the drome. P/O Campbell and crew added their weight of bombs to the bombing of Schipol. F/O Mitchell was the last 49er back to Scampton, landing at 04.35hrs.

18/19 June, 1940; GERMAN RAILWAYS: One 49 aircraft in collaboration with another from 83 Squadron attacked railway communications in NW Germany. P/O Mathews and crew of Sgt Fennells, P/O Fawcett and LAC Gadsby bombed the railway junction at Munchen Gladbach.

19/20 June, 1940; AERODROMES: Seven aircraft were detailed to attack enemy airfields in collaboration with 144 Squadron from Hemswell. All aircraft attacked with good results and returned home.

20/21 June, 1940; AERODROMES: Again enemy airfields were the objective of 6 of the squadron's aircraft. W/Cmdr Gillan, P/O Drakes and F/O Ward-Hunt dropped their bombs on the aerodrome, whilst F/O Burnett and P/O Pinchbeck bombed factory buildings. P/O Matthews failed to locate a target due to cloud cover.

21/22 June, 1940; RAIL TARGETS: Three Hampdens left Scampton shortly after 22.00hrs bound for a railway communication target. P/O McClure, operating for the first time as a 1st Pilot, had to return early with engine trouble. P/O Matthews had another frustrating trip with one of his engines continually cutting out. Eventually he and his crew turned for home jettisoning their bombs in the sea.

The night was not a total washout for the squadron; Sgt Stretton and crew in P1347, made a spirited attempt to bomb a train at a junction near Bohmte and Diepholz... the train escaped destruction, but the line sustained damage.

23/24 June, 1940; GERMANY: The squadron was up in strength, dispatching 14 Hampdens, on a night when the weather was the main enemy. The outcome of the sorties varied, with some returning with their bombs, and others attacking targets of opportunity.

Only F/O Learoyd managed to bomb the primary. The de-brief of S/Ldr Lowe DFC and crew gives an example of the troubles encountered:

"Bombs jettisoned at Flensburg to maintain height due to a severe thunderstorm."

26/27 June, 1940; MINELAYING/COMMUNICATIONS: The momentous events in the skies over Kent marked 26th June 1940 as the day that the 'Battle of Britain' began.

Many of the bomber crews up in the north eastern counties, were unaware of happenings in the south, or its significance, for them it was 'ops again tonight' as usual.

Orders came through from Group by 15.00hrs; 8 aircraft required for bombing and a further 7 for minelaying. The bombers' targets consisted of Marshalling yards, trains, aerodromes and canal barges. Take-off began at 21.00hrs with 2 aircraft departing every 5 minutes.

The minelayers were to operate in the Kiel area, and it was over the Kaiser Wilhelm Canal that F/Lt Mitchell's P4305, sustained flak damage, which brought the Hampden down.
F/Lt Mitchell and air gunner, P/O Reavall-Carter survived to become POW's. The remaining two crew members, Sgt's Bill Spickett and Ron Dutton, were sadly both killed; they are buried in Kiel War Cemetery.

P/O Reavall-Carter took part in the famous 'Great Escape' from Stalag Luft III at Sagan. He was actually caught at the exit from the tunnel and put back inside the camp. Perhaps this helped save his life, for had he been re-taken at large, he would most probably have been one of the fifty who were murdered by the Germans after being recaptured.

Post-war, P/O Reavall-Carter remained in the RAF eventually becoming a S/Ldr. In 1948, he represented England at the Olympic Games where he threw the 'discus'.

FTR P4305	F/L B.A. Mitchell	Pilot	(P.o.W.)
	P/O L. Reavell-Carter		(P.o.W.)
	Sgt R.L.J. Dutton	W/OP	(Killed)
	Sgt W.A. Spickett		(Killed)

JUNE 1940

28/29 June, 1940; AERODROMES: Twelve aircraft were ordered to attack enemy airfields, taking off just after 21.30hrs, at 5 minute intervals. P/O Lewis, operating for the first time as 1st pilot had to return early with engine trouble. The rest of the squadron completed their sorties and returned safely.

29/30 June, 1940; DORTMUND-EMS CANAL: Just two Hampdens were dispatched against lock gates on what was to become a notorious target for Bomber Command. For one of the crews operating this night, the target would hold even more significance in the weeks ahead. P/O Drakes lifted from Scampton at 22.00hrs followed 10 minutes later by F/O 'Babe' Learoyd and crew.

On reaching the target, Drake's crew was only able to drop one of their delayed action bombs due to the accumulator being low on juice. F/O Learoyd attacked and bombed the gates, but his interrogation report gives no indication of the results. Both crews were home by 04.00hrs.

30 June/1 July, 1940; GERMANY: Twelve aircraft attacked various targets in Germany. Only one Hampden failed to find a target. All returned safely.

HONOURS AND AWARDS - JUNE 1940

S/Ldr R.S. Allen	D.F.C.
Sgt W.R. Williams	D.F.M.

Illustration by John Ward

JULY 1940

On the first day of July 1940, the squadron strength stood at 33 Officers and 308 Airmen. Initial Equipment consisted of 19 Hampdens plus one Miles Magister which was used for training purposes!!

2/3 July, 1940; MINELAYING: Six of the squadron's aircraft were detailed for gardening; take-off time was set at 21.30hrs with the Hampdens leaving in pairs every 5 minutes. Just one crew failed to find their target, but P/O's Lewis and Drakes both added to their successful planting of mines by also bombing an airfield each. All aircraft returned safely.

3/4 July, 1940; GERMANY/HOLLAND: Three experienced crews were dispatched on bombing sorties. With 10/10ths cloud cover S/Ldr Lowe DFC was unable to locate the target and jettisoned his bombs on the way home - P/O Matthews suffered severe icing and jettisoned his bombs south of München, whilst S/Ldr Allen DFC and crew bombed a target of opportunity; all 3 came back safely.

4/5 July, 1940; GERMAN PORTS: Bomber Command dispatched 73 aircraft to attack naval targets in Northern Germany. Just one Hampden was detailed from 49 Squadron, that of P/O Pinchbeck and crew, who completed their task successfully. One Hampden from Hemswell failed to return from operations.

5/6 July, 1940; KIEL/MINELAYING: Twelve aircraft detailed by the squadron - 10 sorties were successful, all returned safely.

8/9 July, 1940; MINELAYING: Twelve detailed for gardening - 12 airborne - 8 successful. All aircraft returned safely.

9 July, 1940: F/O's D.S. Forsyth and K.H. Beauchamp were awarded D.F.C.s and Sgt D.E. Edwards a D.F.M.

9/10 July, 1940; GERMANY/HOLLAND: P/O Beauchamp DFC, did not have a chance to celebrate his award in the mess that night; his was one of 6 crews detailed for operations. W/Cmdr Gillan and crew were the first away from Scampton in P4350; he later reported:

"We dropped our bombs in the basin where the 'Von Tirpitz' was lying, regrettably the results could not be seen."

Sgt Jennings with his crew consisting of Baume, Bingham and Foster attacked and bombed the airfield at Borkum; Sgt Pratt with Harris, Pope and Walker bombed the very 'hot' docks at Wilhelmshaven. The remaining 3 aircraft completed their tasks and all 6 returned home safely.

JULY 1940

13/14 July, 1940; GERMANY/HOLLAND: Thirteen aircraft made various bombing attacks - 11 were successful and all returned safely.

15/16 July, 1940; GERMANY: Just 2 Hampdens were dispatched by the squadron; P4350, crewed by Apps, Bunting, Ball and Brooke, reported attacking an airfield. F/O Ward-Hunt (P4384) with Reid, Gibson and Morrison bombed a railway junction at Goch; on return they landed at Worthy Down.

18/19 July, 1940; GERMANY: Fifteen squadron aircraft were requested by Group, with 14 eventually becoming airborne. All but one bombed; Sgt Roberts and crew returned with their bombs, unable to locate a target. All aircraft returned safely.

20/21 July, 1940; MINELAYING: Twelve aircraft were dispatched, and all 12 planted their mines correctly in the Baltic Sound. Not content with their gardening sortie, Sgt Stretton and crew of O'Brien, Jelley and Davison, released 2 bombs on a ship just south of Copenhagen which resulted in near misses.

The 12 Hampdens returned home to base with the exception P/O Michie (L4077) and crew. At 04.35hrs and seriously low on fuel, the pilot made a successful forced-landing at Bircham Newton. Thankfully the crew all walked away from the wreck.

Crashed L4077	P/O Michie	Pilot	(Injured)
	Sgt Lowe		(Injured)
	A/C Bellamy		(Injured)
	Sgt Corbett		(Injured)

23/24 July, 1940; GERMANY/HOLLAND: Seven aircraft dispatched - 7 sorties successful with all aircraft returning safely home.

On the 24 July, the squadron said goodbye to one of its most popular Officers; Canadian, F/Lt Nells Timmerman DFC who had flown with 49 from the onset of hostilities. By his example of determination and daring airmanship, he had helped promote 49 Squadron into one of Bomber Commands premier units.

F/Lt Timmerman, was now being 'rested' and was posted to 14 OTU at Cottesmore, but he would later return to ops, becoming CO of 408 RCAF Squadron at Syerston, where he would complete his second tour on Hampdens. At the time of writing, Nells is still alive and well, and living in Canada.

25/26 July, 1940; GERMANY: Nine aircraft requested, and 9 airborne. Various targets were bombed, with just one aircraft failing to identify its objective. All 9 returned safely.

26/27 July, 1940; ST NAZAIRE: Again 9 aircraft requested, this time to attack oil installations in France. 49 Squadron was the only unit operating over the target. F/O Burnett with Gower, Bingham and Hodgkinson as crew, gave a good example of the night's results at their post operational de-brief: *"We dropped our bombs across the western part of the oil installations causing a small explosion and starting a fire."* All 9 aircraft returned safely.

29/30 July, 1940; GERMANY: Fifteen aircraft in conjunction with 144 Squadron (Hemswell) attacked various targets in Northern Germany. All the aircraft from both squadrons returned safely.

HONOURS AND AWARDS - JULY 1940

F/O D.S. Forsyth	D.F.C.
P/O K.H.P. Beauchamp	D.F.C.
Sgt G.E. Appleton	D.F.M.
W/Cdr J.W. Gillan A.F.C.	D.F.C.
P/O T.C. Murray	D.F.C.
Sgt W. Ellis	D.F.M.
Sgt F.R. Hibbert	D.F.M.

Illustration by John Ward

AUGUST 1940

3/4 August, 1940; KIEL: Fourteen of the unit's Hampdens set out to attack the docks at Kiel where the German ships, Gneisenau and Scharnhorst lay; P/O Gower (P1347) and Sgt Stretton (L4060) both put in attacks on the Scharnhorst with Sgt Stretton reporting:

"One of our bombs started a small fire on the quay alongside the ship."

Sgt Roberts (P1333), P/O Pinchbeck (P4350) and Sgt Hills (L4129) bombed the Gneisenau; Sgt Hills reported:

"Results could not be seen owing to heavy and accurate flak."

The remaining aircraft attacked other targets including dock installations.

P/O Fox (P2112) with Paramore, Watt and Chamberlain as crew, bombed Nord Holz aerodrome as a last resort target. On return to England they encountered bad weather which caused them to make a forced-landing at Harlaxton near Grantham. Fortunately, none of the crew was injured; landing timed at 04.15hrs.

Sgt Unsworth (P4351) and crew also found themselves in difficulties; low on fuel, the pilot was forced to ditch in the sea 10 miles off Skegness but close to the SS Sheraton. The crew, consisting of Sgt Pilot Unsworth, Sgt's Imber and McDonald plus LAC Allwood were in the water for just one hour before being rescued; ditching timed at 06.40hrs. The remainder of the squadron returned unscathed.

FTR P4351	Sgt J. Unsworth	(Rescued)
(Ditched)	Sgt Imber	(Rescued)
	Sgt McDonald	(Rescued)
	LAC Allwood	(Rescued)

6/7 August, 1940; MINELAYING: Twelve aircraft were detailed for gardening and for the first time they took-off in 'threes' at 3 minute intervals.

Of these, 7 crews planted their mines with success in the Friedrichshafen area. Unfortunately the squadron suffered the loss of one aircraft, when Sgt Bob Jennings DFM and crew failed to return.

FTR P4377	Sgt R.J. Jennings DFM	Pilot	(Missing)
(EA-K)	Sgt R.F. Batho	NAV	(Missing)
	Sgt J.F. Lindsay	W/OP	(Missing)
	Sgt J. Jones	A/G	(Missing)

AUGUST 1940

8/9 August, 1940; GERMANY: Six aircraft were dispatched to attack enemy aerodromes - 5 crews claiming successful attacks.

11/12 August, 1940; RUHR - "RAZZLE": Recent intelligence reports suggested that Germany's armament reserves were being stored in numerous areas within the Black Forest. British scientists soon came up with an unusual weapon with which to counter these 'scattered' objectives.

Given the curious name of 'Razzle', it consisted of two square sheets of celluloid about six inches long, and in the middle, surrounded by damp cotton-wool, was placed a piece of phosphorus. The idea was for the 'razzle' to be dropped into the forest and once the cotton-wool dried, the phosphorus would smoulder and set light to the celluloid which burnt with a fierce flame for about 10 seconds.
Pilots were requested to plan routes to their primary targets so that they passed over areas of the Black Forest.

So it was on the night of the 11th August, that the squadron received the unusual order; '9 to stand-by for 'Razzle' and to destroy the oil refinery at A 108'.

Eight aircraft claimed successful attacks, with F/O Haskin's de-brief report stating:

"Razzle done, then bombed factory sheds about 1 mile east of target."

Sgt Stretton (P1323) and crew had sustained heavy flak damage over Germany; their aircraft's hydraulics had been shot through and as they attempted to land at Scampton, a crash-landing resulted. Fortunately, both the crew and the Hampden lived to fight another day.

Sadly, P/O Richard Gower and crew in R-Robert, were shot down by flak over Dortmund. All the crew were killed and are now buried in the Reichswald Forest War Cemetery.

FTR: L4036	P/O R.F. Gower	Pilot	(Killed)
(EA-R)	P/O E.A. Harris	NAV	(Killed)
	Sgt A.J. Baum	W/OP	(Killed)
	Sgt P.W.N. Jelley	A/G	(Killed)

12/13 August, 1940; DORTMUND-EMS CANAL: With the war now almost one year-old, the people of Lincolnshire had become accustomed to the nocturnal endeavours of Bomber Command. So when, during recent weeks, several Hampdens made repeated low passes along certain canals in the area, most locals paid little attention. Maybe in the days to come, when reading their newspapers about the much publicised daring raid on the Dortmund-Ems Canal, then perhaps for some 'the penny may have dropped'.

AUGUST 1940

After many hours of practice flying and poring over plasticine models, the 'op' was at last on. During Monday evening 12 August, 11 Hampdens lifted from their Scampton home around 21.00hrs, 5 were from 83 Squadron and 6 from 49 Squadron. Of the attacking force, 2 failed to locate the target whilst 4 carried out diversionary attacks, leaving the remaining 5 to make the main attack.

Under intense enemy fire, F/Lt Pitcairn-Hill and crew of 83 Squadron went in first and although very badly shot up, they managed to put their bombs in the right spot. The second and third attacks were made by 83 Squadron crews; both were shot out of the sky, crashing near the target. The fourth attacker was P/O Matthews and crew of 49 Squadron; they ploughed their way through the light flak being hit repeatedly. With one engine out of action, a successful attack was made. P/O Matthews and crew now had the task of nursing their battered aeroplane back to Scampton on the one remaining good engine.

F/Lt Learoyd and crew of 49 Squadron, having seen the previous attacks, now confronted the full force of the German defences head-on. With searchlights almost blinding him, the pilot brought his Hampden down to 150ft above the canal. Ignoring the ferocity of the deadly cannon shells, both pilot and bomb aimer concentrated intensely on the task at hand. The bombs were placed spot on target and their mission was accomplished with complete success! But now they too, like the Mathews crew, faced the return journey with a badly damaged aircraft. Both engines were still going strong, but there was a problem with the hydraulic system.

Not wishing to endanger his crew any further, F/Lt Learoyd circled Scampton until it became daylight before bringing M-Mother in for a trouble free perfect landing. The Mathews crew had also made it safely home.

This was one of the first times during the war, that a special attack had been made by specially trained crews. It turned out to be a completely successful attack, carried out by the men who had actually planned it. This was not to be the last time that such a high-profile operation would be flown from RAF Scampton.

Air Ministry Orders No 256/1940: It was announced today, that in recognition of most conspicuous bravery, during the Dortmund-Ems raid, A/F/Lt R.A.B. Learoyd has been awarded the Victoria Cross. This was indeed a most popular award; 'Babe' Learoyd was extremely well liked and a much respected member of the squadron. All ranks shared with pride, the honour of his award. F/Lt Learoyd's mother was asked for her comments by a 'Daily Mail' reporter, Mrs R.B. Learoyd replied:

"We are still waiting for Roderick to ring up and say something about his award. It is just like him to keep quiet about it - he hates fuss. We feel very proud - the V.C. calls for a celebration but we can do nothing until Roderick gets in touch with us."

Other aircrew members who took part in the raid also received awards: P/O Matthews, for gallantry in operations against the enemy received the DFC, whilst two leading aircraftmen, LAC W.R. Rich and LAC Robert S. Allwood had the distinction of being the first LACs to receive the DFM. LAC Rich was the gunner in the aircraft of F/Lt Learoyd VC; LAC Allwood had flown with P/O Matthews DFC.

49 Squadron's Flt Learoyd received the first Victoria Cross awarded to a member of Bomber Command in WWII.

On the 15 August, shortly before the announcement of his VC, F/Lt Learoyd was posted to the Air Ministry as personal assistant to Sir Rupert Brooke Popham.

No 49 Squadron's 'Order of Battle' for the Dortmund-Ems Operation, with post-operational interrogation reports:

P4304 S/Ldr Lowe DFC; Sgt Unsworth; P/O Halls; Sgt Appleton:

"Target not identified, so bombed Texel Island."

P4403 F/Lt Learoyd; P/O Lewis; AC Rich; Sgt Ellis:

"Attacked target, aircraft severely damaged."

L4195 F/O Drakes; Sgt Boyd; LAC Farnell; Sgt Watson:

"Diversion attack successfully carried out."

P1347 F/O Riley; Sgt Roberts; Sgt Simpson; LAC Wright:

"Diversion attack successfully carried out."

L4060 Sgt Haskell; Sgt Butcher; Sgt Boyns; AC Briggs:

"Diversion attack successfully carried out."

P4404 P/O Matthews; Sgt Fennell; Sgt Gadsby; AC Allwood.

"Successfully bombed, aircraft suffered severe damage from enemy action."

14/15 August, 1940; PAUILLAC: Ten aircraft carried out attacks on an oil refinery in the Bordeaux area, with P/O Pinchbeck and crew scoring direct hits on three tanks. All aircraft returned unharmed, but Sgt Cooke made a crash-landing at base in P2111; the crew was uninjured and the Hampden proved repairable.

15/16 August, 1940; GERMANY: Nine aircraft dispatched for bombing - 6 were successful.

AUGUST 1940

16/17 August, 1940; MERSEBURG: Eight of the unit's Hampdens attempted to bomb the oil target of Merseburg. One aircraft brought its bombs back; only P/O Pinchbeck claimed to have attacked the primary.

Sgt Stretton (P1333) and crew failed to return from this operation. It was confirmed later that they had in fact crash landed near Breda in Holland and that all 4 crew members had been taken prisoner.

FTR: P1333	Sgt M.G.P. Stretton	Pilot	(P.o.W.)
(EA-F)	Sgt C.H. Butcher	NAV/Pilot	(P.o.W.)
	Sgt K.N. Farrow	W/OP	(P.o.W.)
	AC1 Lindsay	A/G	(P.o.W.)

17/18 August, 1940; MINELAYING/BOMBING: Eight aircraft were detailed for operations; 2 bombers and 4 of the gardeners successful.

18 August; Sgt W.R. Evans Pilot; Sgts Hitchings Pilot; A. Salter W/AG; R. Turnbull W/AG; posted in from Finningley.

21/22 August, 1940; BOMBING: Five aircraft were dispatched, but bad weather prevented successful sorties. F/Sgt Campbell (L4060) dropped his bombs on 'some' lock gates and Sgt Unsworth bombed a concentrated anti-aircraft battery near Emden; 3 aircraft did not bomb.

22/23 August, 1940; MINELAYING: Twelve aircraft were dispatched for gardening operations; 10 were successful. F/O Burnett (P1347) and crew also bombed an aerodrome near Norlaix and F/O Haskins and crew after planting their mines, attempted to bomb a large armed trawler, but unfortunately the bombs did not hit. All aircraft returned safely.

23/24 August, 1940; MINELAYING: Seven aircraft were dispatched for gardening operations, 5 of which were successful; all returned safely.

25 August; F/O Hodges Pilot; Sgt J. Leslie; posted in from 106 Sqdn.

25/26 August, 1940; BERLIN: The attack by German bombers on London and other English cities the previous evening, signalled Bomber Command's long awaited attack on Berlin. Crews who had previously been given the night-off, now pleaded to be put on the Battle Order; almost everyone wanted to be amongst the first crews to bomb the German capital. W/Cmdr 'Downwind' Gillan felt compelled to 'pull rank' in order to procure an aeroplane from one of his junior pilots so as to be one of the first over Berlin.

Bomber Command sent 46 Hampdens together with several Wellingtons; 49 Squadron contributed 12 aircraft, and all made attacks in the target area.

Bad weather and thick cloud prevented accurate bombing, and then, as the bombers turned for home they had to contend with a very strong head wind. The Hampdens were already flying at the limit of their endurance and as such 3 were lost and 3 more ditched in the sea on their return flight. Sadly, one of the ditched aircraft was P4416 L-London from 49 Squadron. It was piloted by P/O Nicoll Fawcett (P4416); he and his crew are still officially reported as missing and are remembered on the Runnymede Memorial.

FTR P4416	P/O N.B. Fawcett	Pilot	(Missing)
(EA-L)	Sgt J.C. Clarke	NAV	(Missing)
	Sgt J. Baker	W/OP	(Missing)
	AC1 G. Reay	A/G	(Missing)

27/28 August, 1940; MINELAYING/BOMBING: Three aircraft were detailed for gardening of which 2 were successful; a further 9 aircraft were detailed for bombing sorties of which 4 made good their attacks. P/O Mathews DFC (L4129) attempted 'target photography' for the first time, but it proved unsuccessful. All of the squadron's aircraft returned safely.

28/29 August, 1940; GERMANY: Five aircraft were detailed to make bombing attacks, of which 4 were successful; all 5 returned safely to base.

30/31 August, 1940; GERMAN AIRFIELDS: Twelve aircraft were dispatched and all except one bombed a variety of targets. P/O Fox and crew were the last of the 12 to land back at Scampton, touching down just before 05.30hrs.

31 August/1 September, 1940; GERMAN AIRFIELDS: Only 5 aircraft were required for the night's operations. Of these, 3 bombed separate German airfields - one bombed a blast furnace 10 miles south east of Celle and the remaining aircraft failed to find a target.

SATELLITE DISPERSALS

It had become practice at Scampton that if an aircraft was not required for that evening's operation, it would be flown over to the satellite airfield for dispersal (in case of attacks by enemy intruders). Scampton's satellite was at Dunholme Lodge, just 2 miles to the East. Once at Dunholme the aircraft were dispersed in such a way as to try and blend in with the countryside. One way of achieving this was to remove a section of hedge line, the Hampden would then be towed into position so that its wings were parallel with the line of the remaining hedge.

During the afternoon of 31 August, Sgt Roberts was detailed to fly P2135 the short distance to Dunholme; this Hampden and pilot were not scheduled for that evening's operation. As the aircraft climbed out from base, P2135 stalled in the turn and came crashing to earth in a field adjacent to the drome, tragically killing all on board.

SEPTEMBER 1940

Crashed: P2135	Sgt R.F. Roberts	Pilot	(Killed)
16.15hrs	AC1 T. Robinson		(Killed)
	AC1 G.W. Snowden		(Killed)
	AC2 S. Hall		(Killed)

2/3 September, 1940; LORIENT: Six aircraft from the squadron attacked the submarine base at Lorient; 5 were successful, the sixth was unsuccessful due to 'an error of judgment'.

3/4 September, 1940; VARIOUS TARGETS: Four aircraft left Scampton just after 20.20hrs. P/O Mathews (P4404) bombed Lastrop aerodrome; P/O Pinchbeck (P2145) and crew had no success and returned with their bombs. Sgt Haskell (P2143) attacked Celle aerodrome and McClure (P2134) bombed a railway near Hanover.

4/5 September, 1940; STETTIN - OIL TARGET: Five aircraft from 49 Squadron operated from Mildenhall this night. Four were successful in bombing the primary target, whilst the crew captained by F/O Hodges (P1347) failed to return.

GREAT BRITTANY!

In the cold grey light of dawn, F/O Bob Hodges and crew sighted the coastline of what they presumed to be Cornwall. Having been airborne for over 9 hours, shortage of fuel made landing imperative. As they entered the circuit of what they thought to be St.Eval, much to their consternation, they were greeted by light flak. Beating a hasty retreat the pilot gradually climbed to a safe height, and with his engines showing the first signs of fuel starvation, he ordered his crew to bale out.

After holding his aircraft steady whilst his crew escaped, the pilot then elected to crash land the aircraft (there being insufficient height for his own safe escape). A successful crash landing was made, and much to the surprise of the pilot, Sgt Wyatt was still aboard; intercom problems prevented him from receiving the order to jump. The broken wreck of Hampden D-Donald had come to rest in a field near St Brieuc... in Brittany! The crew became prisoners or war, but while in a camp at Toulouse in southern France, F/O Hodges and Sgt Wyatt managed to escape and returned to England via Gibraltar. Over a year later, Bob Hodges, by now a Wing Commander, joined 161 Special Duties Squadron at Tempsford where he participated in many clandestine operations. Happily he survived the war, receiving a Knighthood for his deeds as a mark of gratitude from a thankful nation.

FTR: P1347	F/O L.M. Hodges	Pilot	(Escaped)
(EA-D)	Sgt S.J. Hitchings		(P.o.W.)
	Sgt J.H. Wyatt		(Escaped)
	Sgt L.C. Turnbull		(P.o.W.)

SEPTEMBER 1940

5/6 September, 1940; STETTIN: Again, the squadron operated from a base in East Anglia; this night it was Marham in Norfolk. The seven Hampdens detailed, were all airborne by 19.45hrs. Five aircraft completed their attacks on Stettin, whilst Sgt Haskell (L4093) and crew attacked the airfield at Rodbyhaun. P/O Drakes (X2900) and crew were in the last aircraft to return, landing at 05.40hrs. This left one aircraft outstanding; later that Friday morning, back at Scampton, it was confirmed F/Lt Haskins and crew were officially missing.

F/Lt Haskins had actually ditched in the Channel, short of fuel, in a desperate bid to reach the English coast. The pilot displayed great skill in bringing the aircraft down without injury to his crew... but had the misfortune of being nearer the enemy's side of the water than ours. They were rescued from their dinghy by the Germans off Calais, to become POW's.

FTR: **P4350**	F/L J.D. Haskins	Pilot	(P.o.W.)
(EA-L)	Sgt W.L. Evans	Pilot	(P.o.W.)
	Sgt R. Cartwright	W/OP	(P.o.W.)
	P/O J.V. Silverston		(P.o.W.)

A snapshot of L4060 (EA-H) flying over a misty Lincolnshire countryside in the company of an unidentified (EA-J). L4060 first operated with 49 Sqdn in December 1939. On the evening of 7-10-40, the aircraft was severely damaged in a crash landing following a training exercise. Fortunately, the crew were uninjured but the Hampden never flew with the squadron again.

SEPTEMBER 1940

6/7 September, 1940; GLADBACH/EMMERICH: The squadron had 4 aircraft airborne, but bad weather prevented two from making successful attacks, although one of these, P/O Pinchbeck (P2068) did manage some 'razzling'.

P/O Murray (L4045) and crew could not locate the primary, but bombed a blast furnace in the vicinity of Gladbach.

Whilst landing back at Waddington, after dropping their bombs on the marshalling yards at Emmerich, P/O Beauchamp (P4304) and crew were 'machine gunned' by an enemy 'intruder'. Fortunately this attack was, as stated in the report; *"without effect"*.

INVASION ALERT

At 21.50hrs on the evening of Saturday 7th September, Scampton SHQ received Invasion Alert No.1, and as of 00.01hrs 8th September, the following actions were to be implemented:

Para 1. All aircraft in operational squadrons which are not detailed for operational missions during the next 12 hours, are to be bombed up and brought to stand-by. Crews to remain on stations. Bombs; 6x250lb G.P. fused, also 2x250lb A.S. on wings fused instantaneous.

Para 2. Stations to inform Group how many aircraft they are prepared to receive from Flying Training Command and 22 Group under the Banquet scheme.

Para 3. Station defence personnel, both ground and A.A. to be kept ready for immediate action by day and night.

7/8 September, 1940; PORTS/BARGES: Bomber Command dispatched 92 aircraft against the Channel ports where German invasion barges were being assembled.

The Squadron had 5 aircraft airborne by 20.15hrs, and each carried 2x250lb bombs under each wing in addition to the normal bomb load. All aircraft carried out their sorties and returned unscathed, although P/O Lewis (P4403) and crew 'hit something near Boston and the machine became almost out of control'. P/O Riley (P2145) and crew were the last home, touching down at 00.30hrs.

8/9 September, 1940; HAMBURG: The squadron dispatched 8 aircraft to attack the dockyards at Hamburg. Seven aircraft bombed the primary target, whilst F/O Ward-Hunt (P1176) and crew attacked the secondary target, being the ship concentrations in Delfeil harbour.

Of the 133 bombers dispatched on operations this night, 8 failed to return; 1 Hampden was lost bombing Hamburg, but all 49's aircraft returned safely.

SEPTEMBER 1940

10/11 September, 1940; OSTEND: The concentration of barges in the Channel ports were again attacked by Bomber Command, with 106 aircraft being dispatched. 49 Squadron launched 7 aircraft against the port of Ostend, of which 4 made good their attacks; the others being forced to return with bombs intact, due to the bad weather.

Bomber Command lost 2 Hampden and 2 Whitley crews from the night's work.

13/14 September, 1940; OSTEND: The relentless bombing of the invasion barges continued, with the squadron contributing 10 Hampdens to the force of 92 aircraft. All the aircraft attacked with success, although P/O McClure (P4321) had five bombs fail to release due to a technical failure. P/O Riley (P2145) and crew also attacked the railway station.

15/16 September, 1940; ANTWERP: Eleven aircraft from 49 Squadron joined in the attack on the concentration of shipping and barges at Antwerp. Bomber Command had 155 aircraft attacking varied targets on the continent, but the biggest effort was against the Channel ports.

It was on this evening that 18 year old Sgt John Hannah, a wireless operator in an 83 Squadron (Scampton) Hampden earned Bomber Command its second Victoria Cross. After his aircraft was hit by flak, Sgt Hannah elected to stay in the Hampden instead of baling out; he received severe burns when putting the fire out. The Hampden returned safely to base; there were no losses from the night's other efforts.

17/18 September, 1940; ANTWERP/FLUSHING: The squadron had 15 aircraft airborne by 19.45hrs bound for the Channel ports. All aircraft carried out successful attacks with S/Ldr Allen (P2095) and crew also making four machine gun attacks on a large water power station, 4 miles south of the target.
Of the 194 aircraft dispatched by Bomber Command, 2 failed to return; all 49's were safe.

18 September, 1940; Motor Cycle Tragedy: At 23.59hrs on the night of Wednesday 18th September, P/O Clifford Lockhead (aged 20) was killed in a motor cycle accident. The young officer is buried in St. John's Churchyard, Scampton.

19/20 September, 1940; DORTMUND-EMS/OSTEND: Again, the squadron managed to launch 15 aircraft; 10 for aqueduct and embankment attacks on the Dortmund Ems Canal and 5 for barges and shipping at Ostend.

When crossing the enemy coast near Ostend, P/O Fox (P2134) and crew attacked a German aircraft using their front guns; the engagement proved inconclusive.

The squadron had poor results this night, with only 6 aircraft able to complete their bombing sorties, 4 of which were on the Dortmund Ems Canal. Fortunately there were no losses.

21/22 September, 1940; OSTEND: Just 4 of the unit's aircraft participated in the night's attack against the Channel ports; all 4 were successful and returned safely without incident.

22/23 September; 1940; LE HAVRE: Eleven of the unit's aircraft were detailed for an attack on the port at Le Havre, each armed with 6x250lb bombs plus two additional 250lb bombs on wing racks. Take-off started at 00.30hrs, each taking off at 3 minute intervals.

Of the attackers, 10 succeeded in bombing the Le Havre area. P/O Fox (L4195) and crew were unable to reach the target due to engine trouble, but elected to attack barges at Dunkirk instead.

All aircraft returned to base safely, P/O Murray (P4404) and crew the last to land at 06.20hrs.

23/24 September; BERLIN: The squadron dispatched 4 aircraft to attack targets in the Berlin area, but only P/O McClure (L4195) and crew managed to achieve an attack on the primary target.

F/O Ward-Hunt (P1176) and crew were 20 miles east of Celle when one engine failed, forcing them to jettison their bomb load. F/O Burnett (X2962) and crew experienced severe icing and could not hope to reach Berlin; they elected instead to bomb the docks at Bremen.

P/O Lewis (L4093) and crew also suffered from icing problems and also bombed an alternative target. They selected a railway bridge over the Vaser/Elbe Canal near Hanover for their 4x500lb bombs. All 4 aircraft returned back to base safely by 03.50hrs.

24/25 September, 1940; LE HAVRE: The 4 aircraft dispatched by 49 Squadron made successful attacks on shipping and barges in the port on Le Havre, and returned safely to base.

25/26 September, 1940; BERLIN: Take-off commenced at 18.45hrs, with the unit's Hampdens lifting off at 5 minute intervals until 9 aircraft had become airborne; their destination was a power station in the Berlin area. 5 aircraft managed to attack the primary target; the crews of Sgt Hills (L4129) and Sgt Cooke (P4404) bombed the marshalling yards at Hanover, whilst P/O Drakes (L4195) and crew disturbed Templehof aerodrome. P/O Riley (X2959) attacked another alternative target.

All aircraft returned to base safely, F/Lt Learoyd VC (P4403) and crew being the last to land at 04.45hrs

SEPTEMBER 1940

26 September, 1940; The following personnel were posted out to 14 OTU Cottesmore after completing their tours:

F/Lt Burnett; F/O Murray DFC; P/O Pinchbeck; P/O Lewis; P/O Parker; Sgt Foster; Sgt Bunting; Sgt Haines; Sgt Gibson; Sgt Ellis/580668; Sgt Ellis/537328

28/29 September, 1940; LE HAVRE/DORTMUND-EMS: The unit was requested to send 6 aircraft to the Dortmund-Ems Canal, with a further 5 aircraft helping to keep the pressure on the invasion fleet in Le Havre.

Because of the weather, the Canal force was unable to locate their target. Three of the Le Havre attackers managed to press home their attacks on the port area.

Sgt Unsworth (L4129) and crew bombed Texel aerodrome, P/O Hopkins (P2068) and crew dropped their load on the marshalling yards at Münster, whilst S/Ldr Lowe (P4304) and crew attacked another drome 4 miles SE of the Dortmund-Ems.

All aircraft returned to base by 07.00hrs.

29 September, 1940: The month ended in tragedy when at 23.30hrs on this Sunday night, one of the unit's Hampdens on a training flight, flew into high ground at Haigh near Wakefield in Yorkshire, whilst in a turn at 1,000ft. Sadly all three members of the crew were killed. Sgt pilot Fred Catley (aged 21) and W/Ag Sgt Bert Hastie (aged 21) are buried in St. John's Churchyard, Scampton. Sgt Bill Nichol (aged 26) also pilot, is buried in Ayr Cemetery Scotland.

Crashed	**P2134**	Sgt F.N.C. Catley	Pilot	(Killed)
		Sgt B.V. Hastie	W/AG	(Killed)
		Sgt W. Nichol	Pilot	(Killed)

OCTOBER 1940

On Tuesday 1 October 1940: The strength of the Unit on this date stood at:

27	Officers	18	Hampdens
338	Airmen	1	Magister (Used for training!)

1/2 October, 1940; COLOGNE: At 15.00hrs, orders came through from Group detailing 10 aircraft for an attack on a synthetic oil plant near Cologne.

49's Hampdens began taking off around 19.00hrs at 5 minute intervals. Five made successful attacks on the primary target, the remaining 5 attacked aerodromes.

7/8 October, 1940; MINELAYING/BOMBING: At 18.00hrs, 12 aircraft from the unit started taking off at 10 minute intervals. Of those dispatched, 6 were successful in their 'gardening' with 5 going on to bomb the docks at Lorient.

Of the 6 bombers; 5 completed their sorties with P/O Drakes (L4195) and crew dive-bombing flak concentrations on the return journey. All of the 49 Squadron aircraft operating, returned safely to Scampton. Whilst the squadron was away on operations, Hampden (L4060) crash landed at Scampton following night flying training; the crew escaped uninjured.

10/11 October, 1940; KIEL: S/Ldr Allen DFC was posted out to HQ 7 Group, following S/Ldr Jefferson's posting in from 106 Squadron a few days earlier.

During the afternoon of the 11th, 49 Squadron received orders detailing 11 aircraft for an attack on Kiel. Ten of the aircraft dispatched located and successfully bombed the docks. The remaining aircraft, Sgt Apps (P2143) and crew, were unable to reach the primary due to excessive engine vibration and elected to bomb the seaplane base at Norderney.

All aircraft returned safely to Scampton.

12/13 October, 1940; GERMANY: The 11 aircraft from the squadron that had been dispatched against various targets in Germany, started to arrive back over Scampton in the first hours of Sunday 12 October.

Shortly before 01.15hrs, Sgt Richman (P2095) made his landing approach too fast. His attempt to overshoot the flarepath failed and the Hampden came to rest through a hedge on the airfield boundary. Fortunately both crew and aircraft escaped serious injury. The remaining 49 Squadron aircraft all returned after completing successful sorties.

14/15 October, 1940; BERLIN: Of the 6 aircraft dispatched by the squadron, only the crews piloted by P/O Drakes (L4195) and P/O Shaw (P4404) managed to bomb the primary target; the remainder found alternatives. All returned safely to Scampton, Sgt Ball (X2959) and crew being the last to land at 05.45hrs.

OCTOBER 1940

16/17 October, 1940; BORDEAUX: At 16.00hrs on the afternoon of Wednesday 16th, orders were received detailing 12 aircraft for bombing and gardening; the main target being the submarines at Bordeaux. Take-off began at 19.00hrs at 5 minute intervals until all 12 were airborne. Bad weather was to play a significant part in the night's proceedings, especially when the aircraft returned.

Four crews managed to complete successful sorties, despite some considerable resistance; Sgt Ball (X3001) and crew laid their 'vegetables' in the basin, but in doing so had the top of one rudder shot away, a shell passed through the wing, and the tailplane was riddled with machine gun fire; the crew was able to land safely at Marham.

The Hopkins' (P4404) crew whilst dropping their mines received shrapnel damage to the tail boom.

Sgt Bates (X2900) and crew were unsuccessful and returned early in severe weather. The pilot attempted to land at Abingdon; he aborted one landing run, but while trying to overshoot, S-Sugar crash landed. Fortunately the crew were all uninjured.

Sadly this was not the case in Kent, where P/O Evans (4195) made a forced landing at Lenham. In the crash, the rear gunner, LAC Glover was thrown clear and the navigator Sgt Molineux received a broken leg. The wireless set caught fire where, tragically. the W/op Sgt Robert Potter (aged 20) was trapped; he unfortunately perished in the wreck. The accident happened at about 04.15hrs.

Another tragedy occurred near Andover in Hampshire, where desperately short of fuel, F/O Charles Pitman (aged 30) and crew, F/O R.C. Parker, Sgt J. Brown and Sgt P. Flanagan in Hampden P2143 crashed and were sadly all killed.

By mid morning, 11 of the squadron's aircraft had been accounted for, which left one outstanding. Sgt pilot Dennis Imber (aged 21) and crew had failed to return from the night's operations. It is now known that their aircraft was shot down by flak and they were all killed. The crew are buried together in Ambares-et-Lagrave Cemetery near Bordeaux.

FTR: L4129	Sgt D.S. Imber	Pilot	(Killed)
(EA-)	Sgt R.F. Rose	Pilot	(Killed)
	Sgt F. Corbett	W/AG	(Killed)
	Sgt K.C. Friend	W/AG	(Killed)
Crashed P2143	F/O C.D. Pitman	Pilot	(Killed)
(EA-)	F/O R.C. Parker	Pilot	(Killed)
	Sgt J. Brown	W/OP	(Killed)
	Sgt P. Flanagan	W/AG	(Killed)

OCTOBER 1940

Crashed L4195 (EA-H)	P/O Evans	Pilot	(Uninjured)
	Sgt Molineux	NAV	(Injured)
	Sgt R. Potter	W/AG	(Killed)
	Lac Glover	A/G	(Uninjured)

19/20 October, 1940; BERLIN: Of the 6 aircraft detailed for operations, only one managed to get airborne. S/Ldr Jefferson (P2145) and crew took off from Scampton at 16.20hrs but were unable to locate the primary target. They did however locate and bomb an aerodrome.

20/21 October, 1940; BERLIN: Of the 8 aircraft dispatched by the unit, one managed to bomb the primary target, the remainder bombed targets of opportunity in the area. On return, the aircraft flown by Sgt Shaw (P4404) and crew was damaged on landing at Waddington.

P/O Green (X2962) and crew became lost in the bad weather and very low on fuel. They eventually crash landed in a field at Veryan near Truro in Cornwall. P/O Green and Sgt Hirst were unhurt, but P/O Bingham and Sgt Coutts received injuries; Green and Hirst flew on the squadron's next operation on the 24th to Hannover.

24/25 October, 1940; HANNOVER: Taking off just after midnight, the squadron eventually had 8 aircraft airborne. Of these, 2 bombed Hannover and 4 attacked alternative or last resort targets. All aircraft returned safely.

25/26 October, 1940; KIEL: Of the 4 aircraft dispatched, 3 bombed the primary target, whilst S/Ldr Jefferson (X3027) and crew attacked a factory near Schleswig; all 4 returned without incident.

27/28 October, 1940; HAMBURG: Again the squadron was successful with 6 out of the 8 aircraft dispatched hitting the primary target of Hamburg; the remaining 2 bombed alternative targets.

The squadron's troubles only really began when they arrived back over England. German intruder aircraft were abroad, and the area around Lincoln was always a favourite hunting ground for them. Sgt Green (X3001) and crew were attacked whilst orbiting the 'Q' site; the damage sustained by the Hampden included all 3 tyres burst and the accumulators shot out. Fortunately the pilot was able to make a successful emergency landing without injury to himself or crew.

Far more serious was the plight of F/O Bufton (X3027) and crew whose aircraft had been shot down by Lt Volker of 1/NJG2. The pilot managed courageously to force land his doomed Hampden in the sea, within a mile of the Skegness coast.

Despite the proximity of the ditching to the foreshore (it is said that the men's call for help could be heard from Skegness seafront) the rescue services were unable to reach the crew in time and tragically all perished; the body of P/O Ballas-Anderson was never recovered.

Note: In 1994, a propeller blade from this aircraft (recently recovered) was on display in the Skegness Lifeboat Station.

Crashed X3027	F/O J.R. Bufton	Pilot	(Killed)
(EA-A)	P/O K. Ballas-Anderson	Pilot	(Missing)
	Sgt F.J.W. Bichard	W/AG	(Killed)
	Sgt R.F. Robertson	W/AG	(Killed)

28 October, 1940: It was officially announced that LAC Rich and LAC Allwood had both received the Distinguished Flying Medal.

29/30 October, 1940; BERLIN: Yet another night of bad flying weather saw the unit putting up only 2 aircraft for a raid on Berlin. In the conditions, both were unable to reach the primary target. Sgt Richman (X2985) and crew jettisoned when the oil pressure dropped drastically, and the Scoltock crew (X3050) bombed the docks at Wilhelmshaven. Both crews were safely back at Scampton by 00.55hrs.

HONOURS AND AWARDS - OCTOBER 1940

F/O W.J. Burnett	D.F.C.
Sgt A.R. Cadman	D.F.M.
LAC J.E.G. Allwood	D.F.M.
LAC W.R. Rich	D.F.M.

Handley Page, creator of the Hampden presents portraits to Sgt Hannah (83 Squadron) and far right, W/Cdr Learoyd (49 Squadron) who both won V.C.s flying out of Scampton.

NOVEMBER 1940

1/2 November, 1940; MINELAYING/BREST/RECCE: At 15.00hrs, orders were received detailing 5 aircraft for gardening in the 'Jellyfish' area. Crews were told to ensure that their take-off times ensured a daylight return. This was so that a 'special' reconnaissance could be carried out. All crews were to report any shipping seen on their route to and from the area. Of the 5 aircraft dispatched, 4 were successful in laying their mines; all returned safely.

3/4 November, 1940; KIEL: The unit detailed 6 aircraft for operations on a wet and windy Sunday night. It was well past 01.00hrs of Monday morning before the squadron's aircraft began to grasp for height over their Scampton base. Sgt Richman (X3029) and crew staggered into the air during a torrential rainstorm, causing their Hampden to 'swing'. The pilot fought a desperate battle to stay airborne, but eventually gravity won and D-Donald came back earth 4 miles west of Scampton. Fortunately, all the crew were safe; the crash was timed at 01.44hrs. Of the five remaining aircraft sent to attack the docks at Kiel; one aircraft managed to locate the primary, the remaining 4 attacked alternative targets. On their return, all 5 were diverted to Leuchars.

Crashed X3029	Sgt Richman	Pilot	(Unhurt)
(EA-D)	Sgt Davies		(Unhurt)
	LAC Upton		(Unhurt)
	Sgt Reid		(Unhurt)

5/6 November, 1940; MAGDEBURG: Just 3 aircraft set out for Germany, with take-off again after midnight. The Wright crew (X3028) abandoned their attack on the primary due to weather and dropped their bombs on flak guns and searchlights near Cloppenburg. Sgt Shaw (X3021) and crew had to jettison their bombs due to icing; they landed back at Waddington; Sgt Bates (P4321) suffered the same problems, landing at Hemswell.

6/7 November, 1940; VARIOUS: Of the 8 aircraft detailed by the squadron, 7 eventually took-off, and all managed to find targets to attack before returning safely.

8/9 November, 1940; MUNICH: The squadron had 8 aircraft airborne, take-offs starting at 17.30hrs. Of these 7 were successful on the primary, Sgt Price (X3028) and crew having been forced to return early with engine trouble. All aircraft returned safely to base.

THE NISSEN HUT TRAGEDY

10 November, 1940: Shortly after 01.30hrs on Tuesday 10th, No 83 Squadron Hampdens were becoming airborne for a minelaying operation. During their take-off run, the aircraft of Sgt Garwell (X2964) and crew smashed into a nissen hut.

Tragically, three men inside the hut, 19 year old AC1 Ronald King (a member of 49 Sqdn) AC2 William Fraser and AC2 Robert Rennie (believed to be airfield defence personnel) were killed in this ghastly accident. The aircrew survived the accident unharmed.

NOVEMBER 1940

10/11 November, 1940; DANZIG/MANNHEIM: At 15.00hrs, orders came through requesting 6 aircraft for operations as follows: One to be equipped with long range tanks to attack any identified military objectives in Danzig - Nickels to be dropped on Danzig, the remaining 5 aircraft to bomb the primary - all aircraft to return to base during daylight.

Three aircraft were to attack 15 minutes before the main raid to set fire to the target and assist the following aircraft (49 the first Pathfinders?) these were to carry incendiaries only.

Of the five aircraft sent to attack the primary; one returned early with engine trouble, P/O Green and crew were successful, 1 bombed the inland port of Mannheim, 1 returned early with engine failure!

The fifth aircraft failed to return from operations. F/O Alan Bulmer (aged 21) and crew (X2985) were last heard of 30 miles from the Norfolk coast attempting to reach home; tragically they never made it. The crew is remembered on the Runnymede Memorial.

The aircraft fitted with long range tanks (X3028), was flown by Sgt Price and crew, consisting of P/O Reid plus Sgts Young and Chamberlain. Their flight to Danzig was carried out under very bad flying conditions; icing was severe and snow made navigation extremely difficult. They located and dropped bombs on a railway target and also dropped leaflets over Danzig.

For their actions this night, Sgt Gordon Price received the Distinguished Flying Medal and the navigator, P/O Reid was awarded the Distinguished Flying Cross.

FTR X2985	F/O A. Bulmer	Pilot	(Missing)
(EA-W)	P/O D.W. Wakeford		(Missing)
	Sgt D.W. Watt		(Missing)
	Sgt G. Herdman	W/OP	(Missing)

OPERATIONAL FATIGUE

11 November, 1940: Having landed at a neighbouring base at 05.35hrs following their successful bombing of Mannheim, Sgt Ball (P2068) and crew flew back to Scampton later that morning. Whilst making his landing, the pilot failed to lower the undercarriage and the aircraft crash landed, fortunately without harm to the crew.

This accident, caused by an error of judgement by the pilot was put down to operational fatigue, causing him to forget.

Crashed P2068	Sgt P.A. Ball	Pilot	(Uninjured)
	Sgt Pinney		(Uninjured)
	Sgt S.G. Pickard		(Uninjured)
	Sgt S.W. Bentley		(Uninjured)

NOVEMBER 1940

12/13 November, 1940; BOCHUM: All 5 of the squadron's aircraft returned to base after making successful sorties into Germany. They all returned to Scampton around breakfast time on Wednesday 13th.

Shortly before 09.00hrs, P/O Green (X3001) and crew informed the watch office that they thought there was a problem with their undercarriage. The pilot decided to give his crew, consisting of Sgt's Hirst, Hugget and McIver, the opportunity of baling out over the satellite airfield at Dunholme Lodge - which they did. P/O John Green then proceeded to make a normal landing at Scampton, touching down at 09.09hrs. Both crew and aircraft were reported as OK.

13/14 November, 1940; GERMANY: Four of the unit's aircraft made unsuccessful sorties into Germany, but bad icing and engine problems forced all four to abandon their attempts and return home. The Barlow crew (X3050) did however manage to unload their bombs on an AA battery north of Hamburg.

14/15 November, 1940; GERMANY: Six aircraft from the squadron made successful sorties into Germany and returned safely to base.

15/16 November, 1940; HAMBURG/KIEL: Five aircraft were detailed for operations, but S/Ldr Jefferson (X3057) and crew did not take-off when their wireless went u/s. The four aircraft dispatched by 49 Squadron went on to complete successful trips: Gordon Price (X3021) and crew bombed the docks area of Kiel, whilst 3 aircraft attacked a small gas works in the middle of a populated area of Hamburg; all returned safely, the Cooper crew (X3054) landing at Bircham Newton whilst P/O Green (X3001) and crew put down at Finningley.

16/17 November, 1940; HAMBURG: This operation was carried out in exceptionally bad weather, with Bomber Command dispatching 130 aircraft against targets in the Hamburg area. None of 49's six Hampdens found the primary target; 4 bombed alternative targets and the other 2 abandoned their sorties.

The Bowden crew (P4321) suffered engine problems shortly after take-off and within the hour had returned to base, emplaned in the reserve aircraft and eventually dropped their bombs on a flak battery near Neuromünster! All aircraft returned safely from their sorties.

19/20 November, 1940; LÜTZKENDORF: The squadron detailed 5 aircraft to attack the oil refinery at Lützkendorf. The Ball (X3054) and Bowden (P1176) crews both made attacks on the primary, the latter crew landing back at North Coates - a third aircraft bombed an alternative target; a fourth crew returned with their bombs (both of these a/c returned to Hemswell). The fifth aircraft failed to return; it is presumed that the crew, piloted by 21 year old Basil Fulton (X3024) ditched somewhere in the North Sea. All four crew members remain listed as 'missing', and their names are recorded on the Runnymede Memorial.

FTR X3024	Sgt B.T.M. Fulton	Pilot	(Missing)
(EA-H)	Sgt T.H. Mellon		(Missing)
	Sgt L. Ball		(Missing)
	Sgt D.G.B. Steell		(Missing)

22/23 November, 1940; VARIOUS/THE RUHR: Just after 16.45hrs on Friday 22, the squadron launched 8 aircraft; 2 against a Ruhr target, and 6 on the aircraft factory at Bordeaux. One bombed AA positions near Oberhausen; another bombed lights 'resembling' marshalling yards at Duisberg. Of the 6 Bordeaux bombers; each effected successful attacks, with bombs seen to fall amongst buildings. All 49's aircraft returned from operations.

NEVER VOLUNTEER FOR ANYTHING !

24/25 November, 1940; HAMBURG: Three of the squadron's aircraft bombed AA concentrations in Hamburg, whilst a fourth bombed Rensberg and Sylt.

A fifth aircraft failed to return from the Hamburg raid: The fate of this aircraft is recounted by crewmember Des Dunphy, in Harry Moyle's excellent book 'The Hampden File'. From the book, we learn that Aircraftman Second Class Hoskins was in fact a member of the Scampton airfield defence guard. On the very morning of the fateful raid, he had enquired of the Flight Commander about going on an Air Gunners course... the Commander, short of gunners for the night foray needed no further prompting. AC2 Hoskins on his very first flight was destined to become a prisoner for the rest of the war.

His aircraft, X3052, had the misfortune of still being over enemy territory as dawn was breaking. Three Bf109s from III/JG54 pounced and Lt Wubke was credited with shooting the Hampden down. Des Dunphy gives great credit to his pilot Sgt Philips for making a successful crash landing of their blazing Hampden:

"The fact that we were not all killed is due entirely to the skill and coolness under fire of Sgt Philips, to whom we all owe our lives. The Hampden was completely burned out; the only fatal casualties were our pigeons."

Their aircraft had come down near Den Helder in Holland.

FTR X3052	Sgt F. Philips	Pilot	(P.o.W.)
(EA-C)	Sgt D.C. Dunphy	P/NAV	(P.o.W.)
	AC2 S.R. Hoskins	A/G	(P.o.W.)
	Sgt E. Terpey	W/OP	(P.o.W.)

NOVEMBER 1940

27/28 November, 1940; COLOGNE: Of the five aircraft from the unit that departed Scampton, none were successful in finding the primary; 1 jettisoned off the Dutch coast; 1 attacked a railway at Düren; another attacked a light railway near Arnsberg; a fourth attacked flak concentrations believed to be in the Cologne area.
The fifth aircraft, flown by P/O Evans (P4321) and crew had instrument problems in the target area; they eventually made it back to England, where the pilot successfully force-landed at Christchurch aerodrome. The crew members were all uninjured. The squadron's remaining four aircraft made it safely back to base.

Forced landed	**P4321**	P/O Evans	Pilot	(Uninjured)
		Sgt Parrish		(Uninjured)
		P/O Halls		(Uninjured)
		Sgt Davies		(Uninjured)

HONOURS AND AWARDS - NOVEMBER 1940

P/O J. Lewis	D.F.C.
P/O E.D. Parker G.C.	D.F.C.
Sgt W. Ellis D.F.M.	Bar to D.F.M.
Sgt G.F. Fennell	D.F.M.
Sgt G.E. Price	D.F.M.
F/O G.F. Reid	D.F.C.

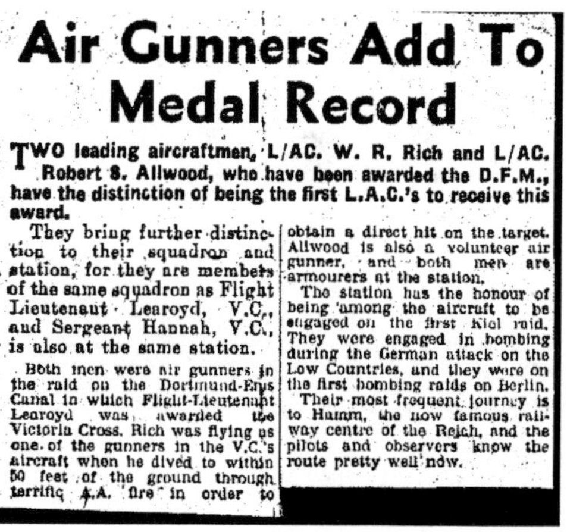

Air Gunners Add To Medal Record

TWO leading aircraftmen, L/AC. W. R. Rich and L/AC. Robert S. Allwood, who have been awarded the D.F.M., have the distinction of being the first L.A.C.'s to receive this award.

They bring further distinction to their squadron and station, for they are members of the same squadron as Flight Lieutenant Learoyd, V.C., and Sergeant Hannah, V.C., is also at the same station.

Both men were air gunners in the raid on the Dortmund-Ems Canal in which Flight-Lieutenant Learoyd was awarded the Victoria Cross. Rich was flying as one of the gunners in the V.C.'s aircraft when he dived to within 50 feet of the ground through terrific A.A. fire in order to obtain a direct hit on the target. Allwood is also a volunteer air gunner, and both men are armourers at the station.

The station has the honour of being among the aircraft to be engaged on the first Kiel raid. They were engaged in bombing during the German attack on the Low Countries, and they were on the first bombing raids on Berlin.

Their most frequent journey is to Hamm, the now famous railway centre of the Reich, and the pilots and observers know the route pretty well now.

A unique photograph of Cpl W R Rich D.F.M. who, as an L.A.C. along with L.A.C. R S Allwood had the distinction of being the first L.A.C's to receive this award. Both were armourers on 49 Squadron who had volunteered for flying duties as Air Gunners.

DECEMBER 1940

1/2 December, 1940; WILHELMSHAVEN: A small force of 10 Hampdens was dispatched against Wilhelmshaven, 5 of which were from 49 Squadron. Take-off was set for the early hours of Monday 2nd, so that a daylight return could be made. 10/10ths cloud over Germany rendered the primary target attack a failure, but the unit's aircraft did manage to unload their bombs on flak concentrations on the Frisian Islands. All 10 aircraft returned safely.

On this day, 49 Squadron received orders of a very different nature from those operations usually detailed.

NIGHT FIGHTERS!

2nd Executive Order for operations night 1/2 December, 1940.

> 'No 49 Squadron to provide 4 aircraft to take-off in an experiment to be carried out as to the possibility of their intercepting and destroying enemy bomber aircraft over their target by concentrating 20 Hampden aircraft in a stepped up patrol over the area being attacked. A patrol would operate if large scale enemy formations attacked either Coventry, Birmingham, Derby, Manchester, Sheffield , Bristol, Liverpool or Wolverhampton.
>
> 'Timing:-The initial time at which aircraft are to be in the area will be known as 'zero hour' and will be signalled to the Executive "GO" and the patrol area will be given at the same time - 1½ hours before 'zero hour'. The period of patrol is to be 4 hours. It is essential that aircraft do not arrive in the patrol area before zero hour or remain there after zero hour plus 4 hours, since the guns, together with the searchlights, will be operating in the period outside 'zero, to zero plus 4 hours'. Each aircraft is to be allotted a sky layer of 500ft. Layers allotted to Scampton 16,000 to 20,000ft. Aircraft to carry maximum ammunition supplies and additional air gunner to man the midship's guns'.

The fighter patrol (4 aircraft) stood by from 18.00hrs, on the night of December 1st - it did not operate. On the following three nights the patrol stood by but was not called.

On the night of 5th, the squadron was detailed to attack a synthetic oil plant in Germany, but this too was cancelled.

6/7 December, 1940; NIGHT PATROL/AERODROMES: After four nights of waiting, 5 of the squadron's night patrol aircraft took off to 'destroy enemy aircraft', (those attacking Bristol) in conjunction with 15 Hampdens from other squadrons.

One aircraft reported seeing bomb bursts and fires in the patrol area but did not sight enemy aircraft; a similar report was given by a second crew. The Wright crew (X3057) landed at Harwell due to icing and W/T failure. The same problems were encountered by another aircraft from the squadron, causing the crew to land at Boscombe Down. The fifth aircraft reported seeing 2 fires south-east of the city but inadequate heating and oxygen trouble forced them to return.

The second operation of the night involved 10 aircraft from the unit joining 45 other Blenheims, Whitleys and Hampdens in an attack against Luftwaffe bomber airfields in the Occupied Countries. All aircraft encountered severe icing and static conditions; 2 returned with their bombs, 2 returned after jettisoning in the sea. Sgt Ball (P2145) and crew bombed flak positions at Le Touquet and the Fisher crew (X3021) attacked the flarepath at Vannes drome before returning to land at Honnington. One aircraft landed back at Boscombe Down with engine trouble.

F/O Ken Michie (X3028) and crew had returned from France, when the aircraft suddenly went out of control whilst in the Scampton circuit. There was insufficient height for the pilot to recover and S-Sugar fell to ground near Welton village just 1 mile east of the drome. Miraculously, one member of the crew survived; the nav/pilot Sgt Barrier. Sadly his fellow 3 crew members perished in the wreck. The crash was timed at 00.10hrs.

More tragedy was to befall the squadron this night when it was later established that 2 aircraft had failed to return from operations: Sgt pilot Stuart Greeves (X3050) and crew came down in the North Sea, to the west of Ostend due to flak damage. All four members of the crew are still officially classified as missing.

SGT JOHN SHAW

The second aircraft that failed to return was piloted by Sgt John Shaw (P4404). This crew's story is extensively covered in Harry Moyle's 'Hampden File'. Briefly, whilst attacking a German airfield (in France) the Hampden received extensive flak damage, which resulted in the aircraft crash landing in trees and heavy snow some 50 miles south of Paris. All 4 crew members survived but with some needing hospital treatment, so the crew asked a helpful French family to inform the Germans.

It was from Stalag Luft that John Shaw attempted to escape by using the 'invisible man' act, which involved crawling across the snow to the wire covered in a white sheet. Spotted by one of the guards, John stood up and raised his hands in surrender and turned to face the German guard who then shot and killed the 23 year old pilot.

The Germans did hold an inquiry into the incident, but its conclusions are not recorded. John Shaw was buried with full military honours.

Sgt David Young, who had been the crew's W/Ag on the night they crashed, was witness at the funeral. To quote David Young:

"John was a good pilot and a very brave man. He died a hero's death, doing his duty for his country. I hope his family has heard the circumstances of his death."

A third member of the Shaw crew was F/Lt Brian Evans pilot/nav; he was one of those murdered in cold-blood by the Germans after what has become known as 'The Great Escape'.

FTR P4404	Sgt J.C. Shaw	Pilot	(Murdered)
(EA-R)	F/L B.H. Evans	P/Nav	(Murdered)
	Sgt D. Young	W/AG	(P.o.W.)
	Sgt W.K. O'Leary	W/AG	(P.o.W.)
FTR X3050	Sgt S.G. Greeves	Pilot	(Missing)
(EA-N)	Sgt M.H. Davies	W/OP	(Missing)
	Sgt E.F. Parish	W/OP	(Missing)
	Sgt L. Young	A/OB	(Missing)
Crashed X3028	F/O K.W. Michie	Pilot	(Killed)
(EA-S)	Sgt G.V. Davenport-Jones	W/OP	(Killed)
	Sgt Barrier	NAV	(Survived)
	Sgt T. Goldie	W/AG	(Killed)

8/9 December, 1940; NIGHT FIGHTER PATROLS: Eight aircraft were detailed for patrols, taking off between 18.55hrs and 19.24hrs - weather was clear with good visibility. Those crews detailed were as follows:

X3134 Howell;	X3057 Tench;	X3135 Donaldson;	P2145 Morphett
X3060 Smith;	L4045 Baird;	X3063 Bowden;	X3021 Bates

No aircraft encountered the enemy; 1 crew reported a Wellington passing over within 30 feet, easily visible against the sky. Another crew saw a Hampden 500ft above, again easily visible. One aircraft was picked up by 2 searchlights which went out after the colour of the day was flashed. In another incident, inaccurate flak near Bicester was encountered by one crew and the colours of the day were shown without effect.

16/17 December, 1940; MANNHEIM: Bomber Command launched approximately 100 aircraft against Mannheim on a cloud free moonlit Monday night. 49 Squadron contributed 10 aircraft of which 5 bombed the primary target; 1 attacked a railway station and another bombed railway lines.

Returning home, the Morphett crew (P2145) crash landed at Tangmere; both crew and aircraft lived to fight another day.

One 49 Squadron aircraft failed to return; the unfortunate crew piloted by F/Lt Tony Scoltock (X3063) is believed to have crashed in the sea off the Isle of Wight. The crew was all posted as missing; their names are recorded at Runnymede.

The raid itself was not a success; the cost had been 3 aircraft lost with a further 4 crashing in England.

FTR X3063	F/L A.T.N. Scoltock	Pilot	(Missing)
(EA-)	Sgt E.S. Rimes	W/OP	(Missing)
	Sgt J.H. Tiedeman	A/OB	(Missing)
	Sgt A.M. Wood	W/OP	(Missing)

20/21 December, 1940; BERLIN/COLOGNE: The squadron detailed 11 aircraft for operations; 3 (fitted with long range fuel tanks) were to attack Berlin; the remainder to bomb Cologne. All were instructed to land back in daylight. Of the Berlin raiders, two completed their sorties, whilst P/O Green (X3059) and crew had to return early with engine trouble.

All 8 aircraft sent to Cologne completed their sorties. The success of this operation was ensured by the bright moon and cloudless sky; all 49's aircraft returned safely.

22/23 December, 1940: FRANKFURT: The squadron dispatched 11 aircraft against targets in the Frankfurt-On-Main area. The exact location of the targets on this night was made difficult due to heavy snow and ground mist. All 49's aircraft returned safely.

CHRISTMAS 1940

The second Christmas of the war gets brief mention in 49 Squadron's Operational Record Book. With 'no operations' ordered between the 23rd to the 28th December, the book merely records: 'No ops carried out by any a/c nor by the enemy during the Christmas period'.

28/29 December, 1940; LORIENT/MINELAYING: Back to work as usual on the night of Saturday 28th, with 8 aircraft requested by Group; 5 were to attack the submarine base at Lorient whilst the remaining 3 were to go gardening off Kiel.

Of the bombers, 1 did not operate due to engine failure. The target was cloud covered forcing one crew to jettison their bombs and return, another crew bombed the target whilst the remaining 2 crews attacked alternatives.

The gardeners were instructed to set out as early as possible (17.25hrs) in view of the possible deterioration of weather. They flew across the North Sea after leaving the Lincolnshire coast 6 miles north of Mablethorpe. In the target area, 2 were successful in placing their mines, the third jettisoned. All 49's aircraft returned safely to base.

DECEMBER 1940

On the night of the 29th, submarines were again planned as the target, but a bad weather front moving through the eastern counties soon put paid to any attempts by Bomber Command to operate.

HONOURS AND AWARDS - DECEMBER 1940

S/Ldr R.S. Allen D.F.C.	Bar to D.F.C.
F/O D.E.I. Pinchbeck	D.F.C.
Sgt E. Powell	D.F.M.
Sgt R.J. Reynolds	D.F.M.

Illustration by John Ward

JANUARY 1941

A New Year, and a new Commanding Officer - Wing Commander Gillan said farewell to 49 Squadron and headed off to a fresh career in the Air Ministry. His position was taken up by recently promoted Wing Commander Jefferson, a former S/Ldr with the squadron. The 'new boss' took charge of a unit that could boast 18 fully operational Hampden Mk 1's, and one old Magister for training purposes. The establishment of personnel stood at 27 Officers and 399 Airmen.

1/2 January, 1941; BREMEN: Barely had the effects of the New Years Eve 'Bash' worn off before Group orders were rattling down the line; a maximum effort was requested for operations against Bremen. 49 Squadron could provide 10 aircraft, and these were detailed to attack an oil refinery on the outskirts of Bremen town. Snow was already beginning to fall heavily as all 10 aircraft became airborne by 16.56hrs.

P/O Newhouse (L4045) and crew returned early with airscrew problems, but were prevented from taking off in the reserve aircraft due to the worsening snow storm. Sgt Bates (AD719) was forced to land at Bircham Newton on the outward leg, with engine trouble.

Of the 8 remaining sorties, 2 found the target - the other 6 attacked objectives in and around Bremen. Over Bremen, the Tench crew (X3135) had a close call when a burst of heavy flak struck the right side of the navigator's perspex hitting him in the shoulder, fortunately without serious injury.

Bomber Command dispatched 141 aircraft this night, of which all returned, but 4 crashed in England. 49's aircraft all landed away from base; 2 landed at Alconbury; 1 at Wyton; 2 at Brackley; 1 at Abingdon and 1 at Stanton Harcourt - all were safely accounted for by midnight.

5/6 January, 1941; MINELAYING: Ten of the unit's aircraft were dispatched on minelaying sorties, 5 being successful. Sgt Bowden (X2072) and crew had engine trouble and returned early, landing at Boscombe Down. On return, the remaining aircraft were diverted to St Eval, but tragically P4322 piloted by Gordon Price DFM, failed to land. The Hampden is believed to have crashed into the sea 20 miles off the South coast; all four crew members were reported missing.

FTR P4322	P/O G.E. Price DFM	Pilot	(Missing)
(EA-N)	Sgt T.H. Chamberlain		(Missing)
	Sgt C.A. Small (Rep of Ire)	W/OP	(Missing)
	Sgt W.B.C. Winning	2nd Pilot	(Missing)

JANUARY 1941

11/12 January, 1941; WILHELMSHAVEN/TIRPITZ: Weather at Scampton, on the afternoon of Wednesday 11, was good with a thin layer of cloud around 15,000ft. Shortly after midnight, the squadron prepared to take-off; by 01.45hrs eight of the unit's Hampdens were airborne for Wilhelmshaven in search of the Battleship Tirpitz. By the time the target area was reached, the cloud had thickened to such an extent that only 2 aircraft succeeded in finding the target - the others bombed the dock areas.

Flying home across the North Sea in the early morning, F/O Fisher (AD719) and crew were fired upon by an enemy aircraft when within 30 miles of the English coast, fortunately without receiving damage. The squadron's Hampdens started to arrive in the vicinity of Scampton just after 07.00hrs. It was some time later that news came through to base that a 49 Squadron aircraft had come to grief near the Lincolnshire village of Northorpe, not far from Kirton Lindsey airfield - no survivors were reported. It was later discovered that the aircraft had crashed without bombs on board, so it was assumed that P/O Hugh Newhouse (L4045) and crew had completed their sortie and were attempting to regain Scampton when the fatal crash occurred.

No reasons for the crash (timed at 07.30hrs) were ever established. The remaining aircraft landed safely at base, Mervyn-Jones and crew (P1176) were the last to touch down at 09.00hrs.

The crashed aircraft, L4045, was known to the squadron as "The Queen". She had achieved an amazing total of 786hrs 10mins of operational flying time before the crash

Crashed L4045	P/O H.F.P. Newhouse	Pilot	(Killed)
	Sgt P.C. Prosser	W/OP	(Killed)
	Sgt H. Irving	NAV	(Killed)
	Sgt L. Jackson	A/G	(Killed)

HONOURS AND AWARDS - JANUARY 1941

F/O P. Ward-Hunt	D.F.C.
P/O J.J. Campbell	D.F.C.
P/O J.H. Green	D.F.C.
Sgt J. Unsworth	D.F.M.

FEBUARY 1941

4/5 February, 1941; DÜSSELDORF: After two earlier false starts, the unit dispatched 6 aircraft in conjunction with 12 from 83 Squadron to attack Düsseldorf. One 49 aircraft was detailed to carry a camera for 'special reconnaissance'; the crew was instructed to photograph the target and any other suitable objectives.

Five of 49's aircraft managed to bomb the target, although 8/10ths cloud covered the area. The aircraft from both squadrons all returned with the exception of Sgt Baird (P4299) and crew of 49 Squadron; fortunately all four of the crew survived to become P.o.W.'s

FTR P4299	Sgt W.J. Baird	Pilot	(P.o.W.)
(EA-)	Sgt R.I. Eastwood	2nd Pilot	(P.o.W.)
	Sgt T.R.H. Hawkes		(P.o.W.)
	Sgt L.W. Homard	W/OP	(P.o.W.)

7/8 February, 1941; DUNKIRK: Shipping and barges at Dunkirk were the targets for 27 Hampdens of 5 Group. The unit's contribution was 12 aircraft of which 8 bombed successfully. Again, one of 49 Squadron's aircraft carried out a photo reconnaissance; all aircraft returned to their bases.

10/11 February, 1941; HANNOVER: Bomber Command dispatched 222 aircraft against industrial targets in Hannover. 49 Squadron had 12 aircraft airborne, following a briefing in which the Scampton Intelligence Officer had exhorted crews to cause 'maximum destruction' of their specified target.

Whilst over Holland, Canadian pilot F/Lt John Green DFC (X3001) and crew fell victim to a German night fighter piloted by Lt Leopold Fellerer of II/NJG.2. The doomed aircraft crashed near Zuidscharwoude in Holland. Three members of the crew survived and were taken prisoner; sadly Sgt David Cruickshank, who had also baled out, was already dead when his parachute came to earth at Broek op Langendijk. He had sustained a head wound and it is presumed that he struck the tail plane when jumping; Sgt Cruickshank is buried in Alkmaar Cemetery, Holland.

INTRUDER

Another night fighter was yet to add to 49's misery this night, but this time it was much nearer to home. A German intruder aircraft being flown by Oberleutnant Kurt Herrman and crew, was 'prospecting' in the Scampton area as Sgt Bates (AD719) and crew awaited permission to land. A burst of fire soon set their Hampden alight; Sgt's Bates and Blower managed to escape by parachute before the aircraft crashed to the ground near Langworth. Unfortunately, the two remaining members of the crew both perished.

FEBUARY 1941

FTR X3001	F/L J.H. Green DFC	Pilot	(P.o.W.)
(EA-H)	Sgt D.A. Cruickshank	A/OB	(Killed)
	W/O A.L. Bryceson	W/AG	(P.o.W.)
	W/O H.E. Fisher	W/AG	(P.o.W.)
Crashed AD719	Sgt G.M. Bates	Pilot	(Survived)
(EA-)	Sgt J. Butterworth	A/OB	(Killed)
	Sgt D.A. Caldwell	W/AG	(Killed)
	Sgt Blower		(Survived)

14/15 February, 1941; HOMBERG: The squadron sent a force of 11 aircraft to attack a synthetic oil plant near Homberg. Due to bad weather, only one aircraft was successful in bombing the primary target, with three others attacking alternatives. All aircraft returned safely, although 7 were diverted to other airfields.

21/22 February, 1941; MINELAYING: Just two aircraft from the unit joined 10 from 83 Squadron on gardening operations. Sgt Richman (AD744) and crew were forced to return early, landing at Upper Heyford with their W/T out of action. The Lowe (X3135) crew carried on to plant their vegetables successfully; the pilot later reported that his aircraft had flown on auto controls for at least 3 hours without any problems.

25/26 February, 1941; DUSSELDORF: Of the 11 aircraft dispatched against Düsseldorf, 2 returned early with technical problems. The remainder flew on but were unable to locate the target due to cloud; 8 bombed flak and searchlight concentrations.

28 February/1 March, 1941; WILHELMSHAVEN: A mixed force of 114 Blenheims, Hampdens, Whitleys and Wellingtons were sent to attack the Battleship Tirpitz at Wilhelmshaven naval base. The squadron had 12 aircraft airborne; only 4 aircraft located and bombed the main target, the remainder, hampered by cloud, bombed targets of opportunity. All 49's aircraft returned safely - one Blenhiem failed to return.

HONOURS AND AWARDS - FEBRUARY 1941

F/O L.O. Halls	D.F.C.
Sgt E.R. Simpson	D.F.M.

MARCH 1941

3/4 March, 1941; COLOGNE: At 19.05hrs, twelve 49 Squadron Hampdens began taking off bound for Cologne. Of these, 7 managed to make successful attacks with one aircraft carrying out photographic reconnaissance. Two further aircraft attacked Duisberg; another bombed an aerodrome in Holland and one bombed flak concentrations. P/O Henderson (AD739) and crew encountered a concentration of searchlights 50 miles in from the Dutch coast, and were held in the cone for several minutes. After breaking free unharmed, they proceeded to Cologne where they bombed through a gap in the cloud cover; all 49's aircraft returned safely.

12/13 March, 1941; HAMBURG/BERLIN: The squadron dispatched 11 aircraft to join other Bomber Command aircraft in attacks on Hamburg's shipyards and Berlin. All completed successful sorties without loss to the squadron, although P/O Mervyn-Jones (P2126) and crew were very low on fuel as they returned to England; they managed to scrape in for a safe landing at Donna Nook airfield on the Lincolnshire coast.

13/14 March, 1941; HAMBURG: The success of German U-boats operating in the North Atlantic during this period was causing grave concern. British, Allied and neutral ships carrying much needed supplies to Britain were being sunk at an alarming rate.
Whilst the Royal Navy, short of escort vessels, tried to stem the losses, Bomber Command was given the task of attacking the German Navy at source.

Of the 5 aircraft detailed by 49 Squadron for an attack on the Blohm & Voss dockyards in Hamburg, only 4 managed to become airborne. They joined a force of 139 bombers (including 5 of the new Avro Manchesters) in a successful attack. The force suffered the loss of 6 aircraft, but all 49's returned to base. The Barlow (X3151) crew spotted an Me109 but it had disappeared before the gunners could take action. Sgt Morphett (X3136) and crew received flak damage to the rear gunners door and suffered hydraulic systems failure but they continued on to bomb the target.

17/18 March, 1941; BREMEN: Ten aircraft (one carrying camera) detailed by the squadron were airborne from Scampton by 01.20hrs of the 18th. They joined in a small but successful attack on Bremen's shipbuilding yards without loss to the unit. Most crews experienced flak in varying degrees of intensity and nearly all reported fires in the target area.

21/22 March, 1941; LORIENT/MINELAYING: The squadron prepared 8 aircraft for operations; in the end just 6 took off between 18.23hrs and 22.28hrs. Of these, 2 bombed the submarine pens at Lorient and 2 were successful in dropping mines. F/O Fisher (X3060) and crew dropped their wing bombs on an aerodrome and then went on to shoot down an enemy aircraft!

Tragedy was to befall the crew piloted by P/O Robert Wilson (X3054). Returning to England from the French coast, their aircraft struck high ground on Dartmoor killing the 25 year- old pilot and his three fellow crew members.

MARCH 1941

Crashed X3054	P/O R.D. Wilson	Pilot	(Killed)
(EA-)	Sgt R. Brames	W/AG	(Killed)
	Sgt R.L.A. Ellis	2nd Pilot	(Killed)
	Sgt C.J. Lyon	A/G	(Killed)

A stone on Hameldown Tor, Dartmoor, marks the crash site.

23/24 March, 1941; KIEL: Whilst Wellingtons and Whitleys went to Berlin, 31 Hampdens including 6 from the squadron, made a very scattered attack on Kiel. Of 49's aircraft; four were successful in attacking the primary, the remaining two dropped their bombs on Bremen.

All aircraft returned safely to base.

27 March, 1941: Whilst attached to 14 OTU at Cottesmore, Sgt Pilot D. Barclay was sadly killed in a flying accident. The Hampden in which he was flying (P4313) crashed into high ground near the village of Laxey on the Isle of Man. Three members of the crew were killed; a fourth member survived though injured.

27/28 March, 1941; DUSSELDORF: The squadron launched 8 aircraft to attack Düsseldorf, all were successful. Sgt Morphett (AD739) and crew later reported:

"We bombed with throttles open to avoid defences which were very heavy - IFF used to check activity of searchlights."

All of the squadron returned safely, the Bowden crew (AD729) landing at Horsham St. Faith.

30/31 March, 1941; BREST/MINELAYING: Bomber Command went after the 'Scharnhorst' and 'Gneisenau' in Brest harbour with 109 aircraft. 49 Squadron provided 9 aircraft for the battleship attacks with a further 3 going gardening. At de-brief, the Pinney (X3134) crew reported:

"Dived from 14,000 feet to 11,000ft to release stick. Both ships firing heavy and light flak - about 50 searchlights active."

All aircraft dispatched on operations this night returned safely - the gardeners laid their vegetables, but the bombers were not successful in hitting the ships.

HONOURS AND AWARDS - MARCH 1941

F/Lt S.W.R. Howell	D.F.C.
Sgt G.H. Bates	D.F.M.

APRIL 1941

1 April, 1941: With the battle cruisers Scharnhorst and Gneisenau at Brest, Hampdens of 49 and 83 Squadrons were moved to the forward base of St Eval. Maintenance personnel had already travelled down and were shortly joined by the 'striking force' commanded by W/Cmdr Jefferson, 49 Squadron.

Reconnaissance sorties were planned for Tuesday 1st April but these had to be cancelled.

3/4 April, 1941; BREST: The unit dispatched four aircraft from St Eval starting at 18.30hrs. Whilst three carried out minelaying sorties, the Becket crew (X3136) dive bombed one of the battle cruisers, attacking from 9,000ft, releasing their bombs at 6,000ft. Returning from their minelaying trip, Sgt Ball (P4403) and crew overshot on landing at St Eval and crashed through a hedge - fortunately all the crew were unharmed.

Crashed (P4403)	Sgt Ball	Pilot	(Unhurt)
(EA-M)	Sgt Batchelor		(Unhurt)
	Sgt Bentley		(Unhurt)
	Sgt Calvert		(Unhurt)

6/7 April, 1941; MINELAYING: Twelve aircraft from the unit carried out successful minelaying sorties; P/O Mervyn-Jones (AD739) and crew were the last to return to base after expending 170 rounds attacking a flak ship.

7/8 April, 1941; KIEL: At 20.05hrs, the unit dispatched 12 aircraft to attack Kiel. All were successful except for two; P/O Fisher (P4304) who returned early with starboard engine trouble and the Henderson (X3060) crew with defective heating in the navigator's position. Most of the aircraft used the 'glide attack' approach over the target. All aircraft were safely home by 04.20hrs.

9/10 April, 1941; BERLIN/MINELAYING: At 20.25hrs the squadron started launching 11 Hampdens against Berlin, whilst a further aircraft set out on a solo minelaying sortie. The 11 bombers carried out successful sorties although Merrall's (AD805) crew bombed a railway station at Schonburg as an alternative.

Attacking from between 9,000 and 6,000ft, several aircraft had great difficulty in escaping the flak owing to the 'excellent' searchlights. On the return leg, the Lamb (P2068) crew of Neill, Smith-Gander and Calvert, encountered a German night fighter; the gunners believe that during the encounter the enemy aircraft was fatally damaged. Over the target, F/O Smith (X3060) and crew received numerous flak hits. Shrapnel damaged the undercarriage and flaps, necessitating the use of the emergency landing gear before a safe touch-down was made at Scampton. All of the unit's Hampdens returned safely.

APRIL 1941

12/13 April, 1941; BREST/MINELAYING: Shortly after midnight on the 13th, twelve 49 Squadron Hampdens set out to bomb and lay mines in the Brest area. The attack was hampered by 10/10ths cloud which caused 4 aircraft to abandon their sorties; the remaining 8 claimed to have bombed successfully. All aircraft returned safely.

14/15 April, 1941; BREST: A mixed force of 94 aircraft including 46 Wellingtons, 20 Whitleys, 3 Stirlings and 25 Hampdens attempted to bomb the battle cruisers in Brest harbour; 10 of the Hampdens were from 49 Squadron. Again cloud cover foiled any accurate bombing, but fortunately Bomber Command did not suffer any losses.

16/17 April, 1941; BREMEN/MINELAYING: Of the 12 squadron aircraft that took-off from Scampton between 22.49hrs and 23.45hrs, 11 were detailed to bomb Bremen, the other was to lay mines.

Cloud and mist in the Bremen area forced 6 of 49's aircraft to seek alternative targets; the Kerrridge (AD744) crew returned home without bombing. P/O Mervyn-Jones (P2126) and crew, after bombing Wilhelmshaven, managed to evade a tailing JU88 by slipping into cloud. One Whitley and one Wellington failed to return from the 107 strong force; all 49's aircraft returned safely.

17/18 April, 1941; BERLIN: By 20.40hrs, the last of 10 aircraft detailed by the squadron, was airborne bound for the German capital. Six aircraft failed to bomb the main target of which 5 attacked alternative targets. The Eshelby (X3151) crew reported seeing German fighters co-operating with the searchlights. All 49's aircraft returned safely, but Bomber Command lost 8 aircraft from the 118 dispatched.

24/25 April, 1941; KIEL: The squadron contributed 10 aircraft to a scattered attack on Kiel. One aircraft failed to bomb the primary and attacked Flensburg instead; the remainder bombed Kiel. All of the unit's aircraft returned unharmed; 1 Whitley failed to return from the operation. A further 49 Squadron aircraft, that of Sgt Huggett (AD733) and crew, successfully planted mines in the 'Nectarine' area.

26/27 April, 1941; HAMBURG: A force consisting of 28 Hampdens and 22 Wellingtons was sent to attack Hamburg. Cloud in the target area plus the heavy defences made accurate bombing very difficult. 49 Squadron dispatched 9 aircraft, of which 7 were successful. One Hampden crew failed to return from the operation, but they were not from 49 Squadron.

HONOURS AND AWARDS - APRIL 1941

Sgt F.J. Gardiner	D.F.M.
Sgt W. Milne	D.F.M.

SERGEANTS' MESS

The following verbatim account is given by 49 Association member Mr F. Lowe, who was then a twenty one years old Sergeant pilot in the R.A.F.(VR)

"The years take their toll of the memory as well as of the body, so it comes as no surprise to realise that I am not sure whether it was Spring or Summer when it happened. Neither am I sure whether the target was Bremen or Emden. I do know that it was 1941 and that I have been swept along through 51 years before attempting to write an account of what was at the time a harrowing experience. Now, with the advantage of hindsight and in safety, the experience had its humorous side.

I was captain of a Hampden bomber with 49 Squadron based at Scampton. Having been told that we would be 'on ops' that night, we had air-tested our Hampden in the morning and attended the briefing session in the afternoon. An early dinner was provided in the Sergeants' Mess, the usual soup, main course and sweet. After an hour or so of rest we proceeded to the 'flights' to don our flying gear before being taken out to the aircraft in dispersal. On arrival at the aircraft, it was normal practice for the captain and three crew members to spend a last penny (pee now or forever hold your pee!) before getting aboard. However, we noted that our under-gunner had moved further away from our usual gathering point (the tail) and was spending considerably more than a penny. This non-standard practice should have alerted us, but we boarded our aircraft, blissfully unaware of the unpleasant ordeal we were to experience in addition to the unwelcome attentions of the enemy.

We carried out our initial checks and taxied out to the take-off point before completing final checks and being given the green light for take-off. As I recall, the North Sea crossing was uneventful. Unless there was plenty of cloud cover, the journey was potentially hazardous for the aircraft would be clearly silhouetted against the light of the Northern sky, risking attack from enemy night fighters approaching from the southern darkness. The feeling of vulnerability had on occasions produced spasms of anal sphincters but it soon became obvious that all four of us were experiencing the symptoms of incipient diarrhoea before we had even reached the enemy coast. Personal disaster was only averted by the use of extreme muscle control! Our confidence was further shattered on discovering that cloud base over our target was only about 4,000ft. We made our bombing run at 3,500ft, narrowly avoiding being coned by the searchlights and surviving a number of near misses by both light and heavy flak.

The discomfort we had previously experienced with diarrhoea became almost unbearable as we made our way home and we gave serious consideration to landing in a field in Holland in order to relieve ourselves! As this may well have resulted in even greater catastrophe, we kept going, increasing our air speed to 150mph instead of the usual 130mph for a lightly loaded Hampden. On safe arrival at Scampton, I taxied as quickly as possible to dispersal. The whole crew leapt from the plane and headed towards the latrines before the propellers had stopped turning. Discarding flying gear as I ran, I all but made the cubicle. The last few yards necessitated an uncomfortable waddle. My under-gunner who had kept pace with me was heading for an adjacent cubicle when disaster struck. Trousers at half-mast, the inevitable happened. The other two crew members, slightly slower off the mark, paid the penalty before even reaching the loos.

We heard later that the pilot of another crew, upon suffering the symptoms on the outward trip had made a brave and imaginative effort to overcome the problem. Engaging 'George' he told his under-gunner to come behind the pilot's seat with the paper bag which contained the rations - chocolate etc. The Hampden was a narrow aeroplane, no room to sit side by side and the back of the pilot's seat hinged, so that in an emergency, it was possible to change pilots in flight, albeit, with some difficulty. He quickly undid his Sutton harness, dropped his seat back and removed his parachute. Easing his body out of his Sidcot flying suit, he pushed down his trousers and pants, enabling the gunner to hold the ration bag beneath his backside. Having relieved himself, he had to go through the rigmarole of re-dressing. Only a few minutes after completing this marathon exercise, an uncontrollable spasm made a mockery of all his efforts. Meanwhile, the rear gunner had sealed the ration bag and its unsavoury contents which indue course were dropped with precision over the target area.

In more ways than one, quite a stink was raised over this episode. A new issue of clothing was necessary and an enquiry by the MO placed the blame firmly upon the soup which had been served in the sergeants' mess. None of the commissioned crews had suffered the same fate. The cook responsible for the potent soup was quietly transferred to another station. We wished him a fond farewell!"

P4403 (EA-M) was flown by F/Lt Learoyd when he won his Victoria Cross on the Dortmund - Ems Canal operation. The aircraft overshot whilst landing at St Eval on return from Brest. Sgt Ball and crew were fortunately unharmed.

(49 Squadron Collection).

MAY 1941

1 May, 1941. The Unit strength stood at 27 Officers and 453 Airman. Aircraft on charge: 21 Hampdens and 1 Magister.

2/3 May, 1941; HAMBURG/MINELAYING: On the night of Friday 2nd May, a mixed force of 95 bombers made a successful attack on Hamburg. 49 Squadron sent 11 aircraft of which 9 found their targets and the other 2 bombed in the vicinity. The squadron record book states: 'The large bombs caused, in most cases terrific explosions and debris was seen hurled into the air. One or two very large fires were caused; estimated to be in one case 400sq yds in area. Weather in general good and no difficulty from flak concentrations. Several 49 crews reported using the 'glide approach' method of attack dropping their bombs from 10,000ft.

All of 49's aircraft (including a further 2 dispatched on minelaying sorties) returned without harm, although one report shows that the Howell crew (AD759) suffered an undercarriage failure when landing back at Dunholme Lodge. Bomber Command suffered the loss of 3 aircraft from the raid.

4/5 May, 1941; BREST: Bomber Command sent 97 aircraft after the Scharnhorst and Gneisenau again, with 49 Squadron sending 12 Hampdens. The weather was good and in the moonlight most crews reported seeing the cruisers - direct hits were observed; no aircraft were lost.

5 May, 1941: F/Lt E.I. Davis was posted to the unit for medical duties.

6/7 May, 1941; HAMBURG/MINELAYING: The unit detailed 11 Hampdens to take part in an attack on Hamburg, with an additional 2 aircraft for gardening sorties. The two minelayers were very successful, enjoying good weather!

For the force of 115 aircraft sent to bomb Hamburg, conditions were very different with poor visibility being encountered. Only 4 of 49's bombers claimed success - no aircraft were lost from the raid.

8/9 May, 1941; HAMBURG/MINELAYING: Between 22.08hrs and 23.00hrs, the unit managed to get 16 aircraft airborne from Scampton for operations - 13 headed for the shipbuilding yards at Hamburg whilst 3 set out to lay mines in the Nectarine area. Bomber Command had a total of 188 aircraft bound for Hamburg. Bright moonlight and good weather enabled the target to be found easily and many bursts and numerous fires were observed. Command suffered the loss of 4 aircraft, but all 49's aircraft returned home safely.

After laying their mines, Sgt pilot Hind (AD805) and crew consisting of Tree, Hurst and Jowett, were fired upon by flak ships at 2,000ft - they descended to 100ft and heavily machine gunned the convoy, then radioed its position to No 5 Group. Sgt Hind had only been posted in to 49 Squadron the previous day.

MAY 1941

10/11 May, 1941; HAMBURG: Again good visibility over Hamburg resulted in the bombers completing successful sorties. 49 Squadron had 15 aircraft airborne, their target being the electricity power station at Altona. A force of 119 aircraft carried out various attacks in the Hamburg area from which 4 failed to return.

Most of 49's crews reported night fighter activity and two encountered flak ships. The Lamb (AD896) crew escaped by taking evasive action when attacked by an Me110; the Hannan (X3057) crew reported seeing 2 aircraft being held in searchlights before being shot down; P/O Lowe (P2068) and crew had combat with a night fighter eventually diving down to 500ft. they believe the fighter was hit. This crew also reported seeing an aircraft fall in flames when 90 miles from Mablethorpe.

Sgt Woolston (AD845) and crew returned with their port engine out of action. At 05.30hrs, the pilot made a successful forced-landing in a field at Bedfield, near Martlesham in Suffolk. The crew was unhurt, but the aircraft was beyond repair. The remainder of 49's aircraft had returned safely to base by 06.10hrs.

12/13 May, 1941; MANNHEIM/MINELAYING: Fifteen aircraft were detailed for an attack on a chemical factory at Mannheim and one further aircraft was to lay mines in the Nectarine area. All the aircraft took-off between 22.00hrs and 22.40hrs. Though cloud was encountered over the Dutch coast, all 12, including the gardening aircraft were successful, reporting fires being started in the target area. The remaining aircraft bombed alternative targets, particularly Cologne. No aircraft were lost from the raid.

INTRUDER SHOT DOWN

Whilst the squadron's aircraft were still over enemy territory, German intruders were making scattered raids over eastern England. In bright moonlight, a Ju88 attempted to attack Scampton aerodrome. The alert airfield defence gunners (including Cpl Walter Billingham) were successful in shooting down the Junkers, the doomed aircraft falling into fields just north of the drome. The aircraft exploded on impact, with wreckage being scattered over a wide area. The crew was buried two days later in the graveyard at St. John the Baptist Church in Scampton village; they received full military honours

16/17 May, 1941; COLOGNE: Twelve aircraft were detailed to cause 'maximum damage' to Cologne. All aircraft took-off at 5 minute intervals between 22.10hrs and 22.55hrs. A new route was followed via Aldeburg which was successful in evading much searchlight and flak activity. In the target area, ground mist and hazy cloud made pinpoint bombing impossible, but normal reconnaissance photography was carried out. 5 of the unit's aircraft (including one that suffered an engine failure on the outward journey) bombed alternative targets. All aircraft returned safely to Scampton by 06.10hrs. Command suffered the loss of one Whitley from the total force of 93 aircraft.

25/26 May, 1941; MINELAYING: No 5 Group dispatched 48 Hampdens on minelaying operations off Brest and St Nazaire - 49's contribution consisted of 14 aircraft. The weather was exceptionally bad, and all aircraft encountered severe rainstorms and static in almost 10/10ths cloud. Only 7 of the squadron's aircraft were successful in planting their mines. Two aircraft had engine problems; P/O Pratt (X3060) lost his starboard engine through lack of oil, and the Kerridge (AD744) crew also had one engine fail. In both cases, the crews completed their sorties.

Sgt Pinney (X3134) and crew went into a spin and lost the starboard slot, but the pilot recovered and managed to make a safe landing at Middle Wallop. All of the unit's aircraft were diverted on return; 10 landed at Boscombe Down, 1 at Abingdon, 1 at Netheravon, 1 at Cottesmore and 1 at Middle Wallop. All of 5 Group's aircraft returned safely.

27/28 May, 1941; MINELAYING: At 22.00hrs, 9 aircraft from the squadron began taking off on minelaying sorties. One aircraft returned early with engine trouble and 2 aircraft were unsuccessful in finding their target due to the cloudy conditions.

For the first time since 21 March, the squadron suffered an operational loss; sadly S/Ldr David Smith (AD729) and crew were reported missing; it is feared that they came down in the sea. The crew names are remembered on the Runnymede Memorial.

FTR AD729	S/Ldr D.A. Smith	Pilot	(Missing)
(EA-N)	F/Sgt J.G. Leslie		(Missing)
'B'Flt	Sgt J.R. Butler		(Missing)
	Sgt G.A. Hadaway		(Missing)

49 Squadron M.T. Section (D. Smith)

JUNE 1941

10/11 June, 1941; BREST: Three operations were planned only to be scrubbed before the squadron managed to get airborne for Brest.

Ground haze and smoke screens made results difficult to observe as 104 aircraft attacked German warships in Brest harbour. 49 Squadron contributed 13 bombing aircraft to the attack whilst 3 more laid mines in Quiberon Bay. Over Brest, flak from the cruisers was of a 'light nature'; no aircraft were reported missing.

12/13 June, 1941; SOEST: This was an all Hampden attack, with 91 aircraft dispatched against the railway yards at Soest. 49 Squadron detailed 17 aircraft for the trip, but by 23.10hrs only 13 had managed to become airborne. Haze and cloud made accurate bombing difficult with only 42 aircraft claiming to have bombed the primary target; only 4 aircraft from the unit were successful on Soest - the remainder bombed Hamm, Dortmund and Münster.

The Green (AD976) crew were unable to locate Soest so they bombed a flak concentration that had bracketed them; 15 minutes later they were attacked by another heavy gun battery and shrapnel penetrated the cockpit striking the W/Op Sgt Denovan and injuring his left foot. Sgt Denovan continued to obtain fixes until an emergency landing was made at Harwell.

Whilst over Hamm, the Cooke (AD856) crew managed to avoid the attentions of an Me109 which attacked them from the starboard side. Another Me109 was seen some distance away, but it did not spot the Hampden.

Two Hampdens failed to return, but all 49's were safe.

13/14 June, 1941; BREST: Again Brest was the target for 110 aircraft but weather and smoke screens ruined any concentrated bombing. The squadron had 14 aircraft airborne and all reported attacks on the docks and cruisers; all aircraft returned safely.

16/17 June, 1941; COLOGNE: Bomber Command sent a mixed force of Hampdens, Whitleys, Wellingtons and Halifaxes totalling 105 aircraft to attack Cologne. In fine but hazy weather the first of 15 Hampdens from 49 Squadron started to take-off at 22.30hrs.

Over Germany, 12 of these managed to find Cologne by using the Rhine and flak concentrations as pin points. Two crews bombed Ostend whilst another returned with their bombs due to an oil leak in the port engine. The attack on Cologne was not successful; 2 Whitleys and 1 Wellington failed to return.

JUNE 1941

18/19 June, 1941; BREMEN: Fourteen of the unit's aircraft were part of a 100 strong force that encountered low cloud in the target area. 12 Hampdens from 49 Squadron reported attacking the primary target - 3 Wellingtons and 3 Whitleys failed to return; all 49's aircraft returned safely to base.

22/23 June, BREMEN: Another attempt to bomb Bremen was again thwarted by ground haze and the 70 aircraft dispatched made only a scattered attack. 1 Wellington and 1 Hampden failed to return. The squadron had 13 aircraft airborne, of which 10 claimed to have attacked the primary target.

Whilst over the Frisian Islands, the Hirons (X3060) crew were picked up by searchlights during which time they saw an enemy aircraft below. They dropped their bombs on the island and then descended to attack the aircraft. After firing 200 rounds the enemy plane broke up and fell in flames. All 49's aircraft returned safely.

25/26 June, 1941; KIEL: On a night of fine weather and local ground haze, 30 Hampdens and 17 Wellingtons caused light damage to Kiel.

The squadron had 14 aircraft airborne of which one, the Falconer (X3060) crew, were bound for the Frisian Islands to lay mines.

The Villiers (X3151) crew narrowly escaped being hit by a fighter which flew immediately overhead and was only avoided by the pilot pushing the Hampden's nose down. Sgt Huggett (AD896) and crew were hit by flak over Kiel, but returned safely to base. P/O Falconer (X3060) and crew were prevented from placing their mines due to thunder and lightning storms west of Terschelling; they returned with their vegetables. One account shows that this aircraft overshot whilst landing back at Scampton at 04.40hrs; it went through a hedge and cartwheeled into a field. The pilot, and crew consisting of Sgt Stuart, Sgt Knowling and Sgt Drinkell were all unhurt.

FLIGHT SERGEANT HIND D.F.M.

Whilst in their post operational interrogation back at Scampton, Sgt pilot Green (X3134) and crew reported seeing an aircraft being shot down and exploding in mid-air. Just one Hampden failed to return from the raid; that Hampden was (AD788) piloted by Sgt Hind of 49 Squadron:

In Harry Moyle's 'Hampden File', there are extracts from a letter (held in the PRO) written home to his parents by Sgt Hind, whilst in Stalag VIIIB. Written after six months of captivity, it begins by saying how pleased he was to receive promotion to Flight Sergeant and to hear he had been awarded the DFM. He then goes on to explain what happened to him and his crew:

"It was a terrible time with the fires, but I stuck trying to help Hancock and Co (his crew) until I was exhausted. Then God stepped in, and with the tail gone it was hopeless ... but it was duty."

Later in the letter and almost apologising for being a nuisance, he writes:

"So sorry about the details of my injury. You have heard all now, apart from slight head burns. Left leg and hand are well scarred too. My trousers were burnt right off me and I was a sorry mess when I reached earth."

Sgt Hind was obviously most distressed that his fellow crew members had not survived; all three are buried in the Kiel War Cemetery.

FTR AD788	F/S S.N. Hind DFM	Pilot	(P.o.W.)
(EA-V)	Sgt C.W. Hancock	W/Ag	(Killed)
'B'Flt	Sgt C.L. Ray	2nd Pilot	(Killed)
	Sgt P.E. Whiting	A/g	(Killed)

28/29 June, 1941; MINELAYING: The unit sent 13 Hampdens to lay mines in area 'Rosemary'. 10/10ths cloud sometimes down to 500ft did not prevent 11 aircraft from planting their vegetables in the Elbe and Heligoland areas. The remaining two aircraft returned with their mines - all returned safely.

30 June/ 1 July, 1941; Four aircraft from 49 Squadron were detailed to attack Düsseldorf, taking off from Scampton between 23.10hrs and 23.20hrs. Very accurate flak and intense searchlights created many problems; 3 of the aircraft were unable to pin point the target but did bomb in the estimated area.

JUNE 1941

DITCHING ORDEAL

The fourth aircraft failed to return from the operation; Engine trouble on the flight to Düsseldorf eventually forced Sgt pilot Woolston (X3134) and crew to ditch in the sea at 02.30hrs. They successfully evacuated the Hampden and climbed aboard the automatically released dinghy.

The crew now embarked upon an ordeal that was to last for nearly nine days. They survived on just a few ounces of chocolate, 36 Horlicks tablets, some boiled sweets and 1½ pints of water. Several RAF aircraft were seen during this time, but it was not until 10.43hrs on the morning of the ninth day that a Hampden (from Hemswell) passing within a quarter of a mile at 2,000ft spotted the mirror flashes from the downed airmen.

The Hampden dropped a dinghy close by and the Woolston crew were able to recover it with its much needed water supply and provisions. Eventually they were picked up by an RAF Launch. The four men were in remarkably good shape and after plenty of water and hot tea, they were able to go up on deck; the airmen were taken to SHQ No.16 R.C. Great Yarmouth. But for the good sense shown by the crew whilst in the dinghy and the diligence displayed by the Hampden crew that spotted them, the end to this happy saga could have been so very tragic.

FTR X3134	Sgt B. Woolston	Pilot	(Rescued)
(EA-C)	Sgt P. McKay		(Rescued)
'A'Flt	Sgt E.B. Chandler		(Rescued)
(Ditched)	Sgt G. Wood		(Rescued)

HONOURS AND AWARDS - JUNE 1941

F/O T.P.E. Barlow	D.F.C.
P/O F.H. Bowden	D.F.C.
P/O C.F.M. Jones	D.F.C.
Sgt P.A. Ball	D.F.M.
Sgt R.E. Richman	D.F.M.

JULY 1941

1 July, 1941: The squadron was increased by an extra flight (to be known as 'C' Flight) with relative increases in personnel and equipment. Posted strength of the squadron:
32 Officers and 554 Airmen. Initial Equipment - 24 Hampdens plus 3 Reserves; Training aircraft - 1 Tiger Moth.

3/4 July, 1941; BREMEN: Fourteen Hampdens were successfully dispatched against Bremen's shipyards with Bremerhaven or Wilhelmshaven as the alternatives. 10 aircraft were unable to claim attacks on the main target due to haze and low cloud and bombs were either jettisoned or returned - 2 aircraft bombed Bremerhaven town and the remaining two bombed flak positions.

The Tench crew (AD759) later reported:

"We cruised round the area for five minutes followed by a twin - engined night fighter. Unable to see the target the wing bombs were jettisoned on searchlights before returning home."

Of the 68 aircraft sent by Bomber Command to Bremen, 2 Wellingtons and 1 Hampden failed to return; all 49's were safe.

5 July, 1941: W/O Walter Doe was involved in a accident when his motorcycle collided with a car on the Ermine Street, near Lincoln. W/O Doe was taken to Bracebridge Military Hospital where sadly, he later died from his injuries.

5/6 July, 1941; OSNABRUCK/MINELAYING: No 5 Group dispatched 39 Hampdens to attack Osnabruck; 49 Squadron contributed 11 aircraft, with a further 3 aircraft detailed to lay mines off the Frisian Islands. Bombing results were reported as good, but 2 Hampdens failed to return; one was from 61 Squadron at Hemswell, the other came from 49 Squadron.

SGT JAMES FLINT RAF (VR)

The aircraft that failed to return to base, was piloted by Sgt James Flint (AD856). He and his crew had departed Scampton at 22.30hrs on the night of Saturday 5 July. Shortly after crossing the Dutch coast, they were intercepted by night fighters, receiving some damage before eventually shaking their attackers off. The crew continued on to make a successful bombing attack before returning back across the North Sea.

Just 50 miles from the English coast, cannon shells from two German Me110 intruders ripped into the Hampden, mortally wounding the W/op, Sgt Fitch. Very cartridges were ignited inside the Hampden and on another attack the port engine was put out of action. Within sight of the English coast, the Germans eventually broke off their attack and turned tail. Jim Flint fought valiantly to keep his stricken aircraft airborne but was eventually forced to ditch AD856 just off the Norfolk coast near Cromer.

The pilot managed to escape through the hatch above his seat, but soon realised the navigator had not followed. Re-entering the quickly submerging bomber, Jim found the navigator badly wounded on the aircraft floor. At considerable personal risk and with superhuman strength, he managed to pull the inert body from the wreck, before P-Peter slipped below the waves. Within 50yds of the shore, a soldier came to the airmens help. Sadly, the navigator later died of his wounds at 11.00hrs the following morning, police recovered the body of Sgt Fitch from the beach near Cromer.

For his display of exceptional heroism under continuous attack, Sgt James Flint was awarded the Distinguished Flying Medal.... then for his bravery in trying to save the life of his navigator, Sgt James Flint was also awarded the George Medal - an extremely exceptional occasion with two gallantry awards being granted for the same action.

Sgt Atkinson (W/Ag), recovered from his wounds and returned to operations with 49 Squadron, but sadly he and his new crew (AD419) failed to return from Hüls on the night of 28/29 December 1941; they are remembered on the Runnymede Memorial.

FTR AD856	Sgt J. Flint	Pilot	(Injured)
(EA-)	Sgt A.S. Benningfield		(Killed)
'A'Flt	Sgt J.D. Fitch		(Killed)
	Sgt E.C. Atkinson		(Injured)

With the planned closure of RAF Scampton in October 1995, many veterans gathered to pay their final tribute to the men and women who had served at this historic station.

Seen here alongside his portrait in the mess, is 82 year old Jim Flint

After completion of his tour with 49 Squadron, Jim went on to command 50 Squadron at Skellingthorpe.
(James Flint)

JULY 1941

6/7 July, 1941; BREST: Although the night was clear and cloudless, smoke-screens in the target area prevented accurate bombing of the German warships, as 88 Hampdens and 21 Wellingtons passed over Brest.

The squadron had dispatched 10 aircraft from Scampton, but one soon returned with mechanical problems. The remaining aircraft went on to complete successful sorties although the Walker (AD976) crew were caught in a light flak barrage, and received hits in the tail; they returned safely to base.

Sgt Ken Letford (AE132) gave the following de-brief report:

"Made a glide attack from East to West on the dry docks from 9,500ft. On approach, the searchlights were placed horizontally in the direction of aircraft and an Me110 attacked us from the rear, but avoiding action caused it to be lost from view."

3 aircraft failed to return, 2 Hampdens and 1 Wellington. Unfortunately, one of the Hampdens was AD739 from 49.

P/O Henderson and crew are believed to have crashed in the sea, the victims of flak.

FTR AD739	P/O A.J. Henderson	Pilot	(Missing)
(EA-A)	F/S I.M. Fisher		(Missing)
'A'Flt	Sgt H. Aldridge		(Missing)
	F/S K. Coney		(Missing)

8 July, 1941: S/Ldr Acting Wing Commander Stubbs DFC was posted to 49 Squadron from 97 Squadron, Coningsby.

8/9 July, 1941; HAMM: The squadron had 13 aircraft airborne, bound for the marshalling yards in Hamm. AE132 returned early due to failure of the boost gauge - AD971 suffered compass swing and AE145 had W/T failure; 8 of the remaining aircraft claimed to have made successful bombing attacks. Sgt Hugget (AD896) and crew, consisting of Hiles, Cameron and Pointer, were intercepted by an Me110 fifteen minutes before the target. The engagement lasted for 20 minutes during which time six attacks were made by the night fighter. The enemy was dodged by a series of steep climbing turns with the Hampden's gunners each expending 150 rounds. The crew claimed that the Me110 was probably shot down.

Of the 73 aircraft detailed to attack Hamm, 4 Whitleys and 3 Hampdens failed to return - all 49's aircraft returned safely.

9 July, 1941: At 12.10hrs, Scampton SHQ received the news that Sgt Woolston and crew (see 30 June/1 July) were recovered safe and sound, after their dinghy had been spotted by a Hampden from Hemswell.

JULY 1941

10/11 July, 1941; COLOGNE: A force of 130 Wellingtons and Hampdens was prevented by bad weather from making an accurate attack on Cologne. 49 Squadron sent 14 aircraft, with only six claiming definite success. Of the others, 1 bombed Calais docks, 1 Coblenz and another Dinen. Several crews spent a long time in the target area because of the difficulty with ground haze; 2 aircraft jettisoned their bombs and a third brought its bombs back. Photographs were taken by two crews.

The Fisher (AD979) crew spent 30 minutes searching for the target. They attracted the attention of an Me109 and dived into a cloud to escape. They then set course for Calais where they bombed the docks from 10,000ft. Over 50 searchlights coned the Hampden and flak damage was received as the pilot dived to 6,000ft. All 49's aircraft returned home, but 2 Wellingtons were lost from the operation.

12/13 July, 1941; WILHELMSHAVEN/BREMEN: The unit sent 12 aircraft to attack the railway station at Wilhelmshaven. Only seven aircraft attacked the main target; two were unsuccessful due to navigational problems with several crews experiencing severe electrical storms.

After bombing the railway line near Wilhelmshaven station, the Hannan (AD976) crew, consisting of Jackson, Cheetham and Rogers, were attacked by an Me110 as they passed over Wangeroog. The fighter made 5 attacks as the Hampden made a series of steep diving turns. The gunners believe they shot the enemy aircraft down having fired over 150 rounds each.
Sgt Batchelor (AD910) and crew could not pin point Bremen nor Wilhelmshaven due to heavy flak and searchlights. They located Cuxhaven and bombed from 12,000ft; 2 bursts were seen in the docks area. On return, they encountered navigational problems and with petrol desperately low, the pilot made a forced landing 5 miles N/E of Pocklington. Fortunately the crew survived unhurt but the aircraft was wrecked; the crash occurred at 07.45hrs. All other 49 Squadron aircraft returned safely.

Crashed AD910	Sgt Batchelor	Pilot	(Unhurt)
(EA-Y)	Sgt Williams		(Unhurt)
'C'Flt	Sgt Calvert		(Unhurt)
(Written off)	Sgt Sgt Betts		(Unhurt)

14/15 July, 1941; MINELAYING: Just after 23.15hrs four of the unit's aircraft were airborne for the Nectarine and Eglantine areas (Frisian and Elbe). Each Hampden laid its mines and returned safely.

16/17 July, 1941; HAMBURG: Of the 11 aircraft sent by the squadron to Hamburg, just four were successful in bombing the main target; 5 other aircraft bombed alternative targets. Of the two unsuccessful aircraft, one suffered a drop in oil pressure and the other returned with its bombs after the crew found the target(s) cloud covered.

The Latey (AE126) crew was trailed by an enemy fighter which made 3 unsuccessful attacks before the Hampden found sanctuary in cloud. Of the 107 aircraft detailed by Bomber Command, 3 Wellingtons and 1 Hampden failed to return from the Hamburg operation; all 49's were safe.

17 July, 1941: Wing Commander Jefferson was posted out to 25 OTU at Finningley and Acting Wing Commander Stubbs DFC became 49 Squadron's new Commanding Officer.

20/21 July, 1941; COLOGNE: Sixteen Hampdens from the squadron, including W/Cmdr Stubbs (AE126) helped make up a mixed force of 113 Wellingtons, Hampdens, Whitleys and Stirlings sent to attack a cloud-covered Cologne. A scattered raid was made on Cologne's railway system without loss.

23/24 July, 1941; FRANKFURT: In poor visibility, 33 Hampdens attacked Frankfurt. The force included 18 aircraft from 49 Squadron, of which 15 made successful attacks. The Tree (X3136) crew gave the following post operational interrogation report:

"We searched for 45 minutes and caught glimpses of the river through Frankfurt - Dropped a stick of bombs on the town - Accidentally performed a loop!!! but the crew was uninjured."

One aircraft (50 Sqdn) was lost from the operation.

25/26 July, 1941; HANNOVER: Of the 14 squadron aircraft sent to Hannover, one returned early with W/T failure, 10 successfully bombed the main target and the remainder attacked Hamburg and alternatives. From the force of 55 aircraft dispatched, 4 Whitleys and 1 Hampden (83 Sqdn) failed to return.

P/O Cooke (X3151) and crew, returning from Hannover, ran out of fuel 2 miles South of Scampton. At 05.14hrs, the pilot made a successful crash landing in fields just North of Lincoln, when the Hampden's engines finally failed. The crew escaped without injury.

Crashed X3151	P/O Cooke	Pilot	(Unhurt)
(EA-T)	Sgt Evans		Unhurt)
	P/O King		(Unhurt)
Written off	Sgt Newall		(Unhurt)

27 July, 1941; F/Sgt George Appleton DFM, was killed this day when the Hampden (P1162) in which he was Wop/Ag stalled on take-off. At the time, F/Sgt Appleton was on a training detachment at the Central Gunnery School, Castle Kennedy. The 20 year-old is buried in West Road Cemetery, Newcastle- upon-Tyne.

JULY 1941

28/29 July, 1941; MINELAYING: The last operation of the month involved 18 of the unit's aircraft laying mines in the Kiel area. It is to the squadron's credit that despite intense cloud and driving rain, 12 Hampdens accurately placed their mines.
Of the remainder, one jettisoned and the rest returned with their loads. Several aircraft took the opportunity to attack various targets with their wing bombs; these included an aerodrome, a train and a jetty.

The widespread mist and fog meant that most of the Hampdens were diverted away from Lincolnshire on their return; 1 landed at Manby, 4 at Linton, 1 at Driffield, 2 at North Luffenham, 1 at Thornaby, 1 at Wittering, 1 at Acklington, 1 at Benson and 2 at Catfoss - 4 did manage to scrape in at base. Of the 42 Hampdens sent on this 5 Group operation, 1 failed to return, and 1 crashed landed near Swinderby; both were from 50 Squadron.

HONOURS AND AWARDS - JULY 1941

P/O A. Paterson	D.F.C.
Sgt J.F. Becket	D.F.M.
Sgt J.H. Bentley	D.F.M.
Sgt W. Hirst	D.F.M.
Sgt P.E. Merralls	D.F.M.

Scampton, summer 1941. Hampden AE236 (EA-P) Popeye I It failed to return from Keil 7/8 September '41. Sadly P/O John Bromham and crew were all killed
(49 Sqdn Association)

AUGUST 1941

When Group Captain R.H.S. Speight assumed command of Scampton in August 1941, the base had an establishment of 2,300 personnel and both squadrons (49&83) could boast 27 Hampdens per unit. The station was capable of launching 30 operational sorties on average per night.

2/3 August, 1941; KIEL: The unit dispatched 16 bombers and 3 minelayers for operations in the Kiel area. In poor weather, the bombing aircraft completed their attacks, whilst one of the minelayers failed to find the target area due to cloud.
All aircraft returned safely, although 4 landed away, 1 each at Langham, Leconfield, Crail and Dunholme Lodge.

5/6 August, 1941; KARLSRUHE: Bomber Command sent 97 aircraft to destroy workshops at Karlsruhe on the River Rhine. Of the 50 Hampdens dispatched, 17 were from 49 Squadron. In bright moonlight, crews had little difficulty in finding the target; one of the squadron's crews received a recall signal, which could not be challenged and they returned home.

The squadron also sent 2 aircraft to lay mines off the east coast of Denmark; one crew was successful whilst the other was forced to break off its attack due to intense flak. All 49's aircraft returned safely, but 3 aircraft failed to return from the operation.

6/7 August, 1941; CALAIS: No 49 Squadron selected 5 of its 'beginners' to go on the night's raid against Calais. In terrible weather with 10/10ths cloud and severe icing conditions, 2 of the unit's aircraft were successful in finding and bombing the target whilst a third bombed a flarepath at the target's estimated position. Of the 38 aircraft dispatched by Bomber Command, only 14 found the target. Two aircraft failed to return, both were Hampdens (44 & 144 Sqdns) but all 49's were safe.

7/8 August, 1941; ESSEN: The Krupps works received an attack by over 100 aircraft, including 12 Hampdens from the unit. Of these, 9 made attacks on the main target, the remaining 3 bombed the alternatives at Oberhausen, Wesel and Krefeld.
Two Hampdens and 1 Stirling failed to return; all 49's returned safely, although Sgt Green (AD896) and crew did receive some flak damage.

11/12 August, 1941; ROTTERDAM: In cloudy conditions, only onc of thc squadron's 6 aircraft managed to find the target with success; all returned safely.

12/13 August, 1941; MAGDEBURG/HANNOVER: In wet weather with low mist and poor visibility 13 of the squadron's aircraft set out for Germany, but 5 were recalled soon after crossing the coast. Of the remaining 7 aircraft, one attacked Osnabruk, another Bremen and a third Wilhelmshaven - the rest bombed the main targets.

Four Wellingtons failed to return from the Hannover raid, but all aircraft returned from Magdeburg; all 49's were safe.

AUGUST 1941

14/15 August, 1941; BRUNSWICK: Eighty-one Hampdens went after railway targets in the Brunswick region. The squadron launched 24 aircraft of which 2 returned immediately; the remainder continued, with 11 aircraft able to locate and bomb the primary objective despite low cloud and haze. All the others attacked alternative targets at Arnhem, Bremen, Saldstedt, Hannover, Minden and Lehrte.

At 03.20hrs, in poor visibility, the Owens crew (AE262) overshot on landing back at Scampton. Fortunately the crew comprising Owens, Donald, Kettlewell and Drinkell all survived unhurt. Squadron records make reference to a further two aircraft overshooting on this night but do not identify the crews.

17/18 August, 1941; BREMEN/MINELAYING: The two 'gardeners' took off from Scampton at 21.00hrs and flew on to complete successful sorties, one landing back at Coningsby on return. The squadron's 10 bombers started taking off at 22.30hrs bound for the Focke-Wolf factory, situated in the south western part of Bremen. Due to unfavourable weather and cumulus cloud only 4 aircraft claimed definite successes. Of the 59 aircraft dispatched by Bomber Command, 2 Hampdens failed to return; all 49's came home safely.

18/19 August, 1941; COLOGNE: Starting at 21.00hrs, 17 of the unit's Hampdens began taking off at short intervals, but they soon encountered exceptionally bad weather conditions with severe icing, static and thunder. Two aircraft were on minelaying sorties and of these only one completed its task, the other returned with vegetables intact. Only 3 of the bombers claimed successes, 5 other aircraft returned with their loads or jettisoned the same, the remainder bombed flak defences along the Danish coast as alternative targets. Of the 62 aircraft dispatched, 4 Whitleys and 1 Wellington failed to return; 1 Hampden (106 Sqdn) crashed on return. All 49's aircraft returned safely.

23 August, 1941: It was announced that S/Ldr G.R. Tench has been awarded the Distinguished Flying Cross and that Sgt's A. Denovan and P.J.N. Lamb have been awarded Distinguished Flying Medals.

24/25 August, 1941; DUSSELDORF/INTRUDER PATROL: Of the 8 aircraft dispatched by the squadron, 6 were sent to bomb Dusseldorf and 2 were to attack searchlight concentrations.

COLLISION TRAGEDY

Hampdens began returning to Scampton shortly after 02.00hrs on Monday 25 August. Because of recent intruder activity around Hampden bases by German night fighters, our aircraft had elected not to use navigation lights whilst in the airfield circuit. It is not certain if this was the case on this particular morning, but whilst 49 and 83 Squadron aircraft were awaiting permission to land, H-Harry from 49 Squadron and F-Freddy of 83 Squadron hit each other over the village of Hackthorn to the north east of Scampton airfield.

The wreckage from both aircraft fell to the ground around Whale Jaw Farm, tragically there were no survivors. The accident was timed at 02.50hrs. Sgt Owen McMahon (pilot of the 49 Squadron aircraft) is buried in Scampton Churchyard, whilst his three fellow crew members were each returned to their respective home towns for burial.

Scampton's night of anguish was sadly not yet over, for at 04.00hrs as AE223 of 83 Squadron returned to dispersal from operations, the aircraft suddenly exploded killing all the crew and four ground crew members. It is thought that a wing bomb which had failed to release over the target, became dislodged when the aircraft landed and taxied back to its point. All 49's remaining aircraft returned safely.

Crashed AD967	Sgt O.B. McMahon	Pilot	(Killed)
(EA-H)	Sgt E. Welbourne	W/Ag	(Killed)
	Sgt I.D. MacKinnon	A/G	(Killed)
	Sgt G.F. Upton	2nd Pilot	(Killed)

26/27 August, 1941; COLOGNE/MINELAYERS/INTRUDERS: Nearly 100 bombers found Cologne in clear conditions, and good bombing results were claimed. The squadron had 14 aircraft airborne, a mixed force of bombers, minelayers and intruders. 11 aircraft claimed successes, including 2 'gardeners' and the intruders (attacking searchlights 10 miles west of Cologne) flying at low level, forced many searchlights to be extinguished - 1 Wellington and 1 Whitley failed to return from the operation; all 49's aircraft came home safely.

28/29 August; DUISBERG: The eight aircraft sent from 49 Squadron encountered haze and flak at the target. Sgt Cook in AD744 received injuries to the hand and the under gunner's door was taken off.

It soon became clear that 2 of the squadron's aircraft had failed to return. P/O Bernard Fournier (AD971) and crew became victims of a night fighter. At 03.30hrs their aircraft fell in flames into the Waddenzee just south of the Isle of Ameland; there were no survivors. The 21 years old pilot and his crew are buried in Nes Cemetery, Ameland, Holland.

It is believed that P/O Thomas Pratt (AE126) and crew also fell to the cannons of a night fighter. They also came down into Waddenzee and again, sadly, there were no survivors.

The body of Sgt Charles Hodkinson came ashore near Richel on the 8th September; the following day the body of 25 years old P/O Pratt was found. Sgt Arthur Willis was washed ashore on the 10 September and on 12th, P/O Harry Tonge was found near Vliehors.

AUGUST 1941

FTR AD971 (EA-O)	P/O B.M. Fournier	Pilot	(Killed)
	Sgt D.H. Barrett	Nav	(Killed)
	F/S E.R. Palmer	W/Ag	(Killed)
	Sgt D. Watson	W/Ag	(Killed)
FTR AE126 (EA-N)	P/O T.P. Pratt	Pilot	(Killed)
	P/O H.C. Tonge	Nav	(Killed)
	Sgt A.C. Willis	W/Ag	(Killed)
	Sgt C. Hodkinson	W/Ag	(Killed)

29/30 August, 1941; FRANKFURT: Bad weather thwarted an attack by over 140 bombers on the railway and harbour installations of Frankfurt. 49 Squadron had 10 aircraft airborne on this night of poor flying conditions with 10/10ths cloud and severe icing conditions. The Broomfield crew (X3057) limped back across the sea with their aircraft's starboard engine repeatedly cutting out. After sending out an SOS, the pilot eventually made a successful landing at Manston shortly after 02.45hrs.

The remainder of the squadron began landing back at Scampton between 05.00 and 06.00hrs.

31 August/1 September, 1941; COLOGNE/INTRUDER PATROLS: By 20.30hrs, the squadron had 14 aircraft airborne bound for Cologne. Five of the aircraft were to carry out intruder sorties against searchlights, whilst 9 were to bomb Cologne. Again bad weather with 10/10ths cloud prevented the total force of 103 aircraft from making good their attacks. Only five of 49's aircraft claimed definite successes, and the intruders had to drop to very low levels in order to extinguish the searchlight belts. The Gillies crew (AE194) of Rushton, Baker and Thomas reported at de-brief:

"Dived on searchlight at Cologne and put it out - they appeared to be expecting intruders and fired on us with tracer - bombs and all ball ammunition expended on searchlights from 1,500ft."

From this operation, 3 Hampdens, 1 Manchester and 1 Wellington failed to return; all 49's aircraft returned safely.

HONOURS AND AWARDS - AUGUST 1941

S/Ldr G.R. Trench	D.F.C.
Sgt A. Denovan	D.F.M.
Sgt P.J.N. Lamb	D.F.M.
Sgt J. Flint	D.F.M.

SEPTEMBER 1941

2/3 September, 1941; BERLIN: Take-off began at 19.30hrs when 12 aircraft set out to attack Berlin; a further 2 aircraft were detailed to lay mines in the Schiermonnikoog. Over Berlin difficulties were encountered with the Anti-Aircraft Fire but 9 of the unit's aircraft managed to make successful attacks on the main target; the remainder found alternative targets. One of the gardening crews brought its mines back, unable to locate the correct area due to cloud down to 300ft. The Bow (AD805) crew successfully mined from 800ft in 9/10ths cloud after locating and making a run from Ameland.

Two Halifaxes, 2 Hampdens and 1 Manchester failed to return from Berlin and a further 2 Hampdens were reported missing from the minelaying sorties. For those tired crews that eventually reached home shores, they found Lincolnshire covered with intense fog. Most of the unit's aircraft landed away at other dromes and 2 were forced to make crash landings due to fuel shortage. In both these incidents none of the crew members was hurt:

Sgt Samuel (X3136) and crew consisting of Sgts West, Watchorn and Tilley forced-landed K-King at Thornham Ling common in Norfolk at 05.50hrs.

Sgt Flint (AE203) and crew, consisting of F/Sgt Gadsby, Sgt Jardine and Sgt Combes brought F-Freddy down at Stradbroke in Suffolk short of petrol.

6/7 September, 1941; MINELAYING: At 13.00hrs during the afternoon of Saturday 6th, six aircraft and one reserve were detailed to fly to Kinloss for operations; at 15.00hrs the 7 aircraft were airborne for Kinloss.

Together with 18 Hampdens from sister squadrons, the 6 aircraft from 49 Squadron were detailed to lay mines in the approaches to Oslo Fiord where the battle cruiser 'Von Scheer' was situated. The force took off at 20.30hrs in clear weather. En route the aerodromes at Ebjemoen and Tronsberg were bombed as well as a flak ship. No opposition was encountered and with excellent visibility all aircraft were successful in carrying out their duties.

The 49 Squadron force consisted of:

AD896	Jenkins	McGuffie	Woodroffe	Sauders
X3057	Broomfield	Block	Chandler	Kehoe
AD980	Scorer	Huntly-Wood	Tansley	Hunter
AD744	Robinson	Sanderson	Price	Mossop
AE224	Drakes	Beany	Cheetham	Watson
AD733	Falconer	Darwin	Knowling	Woolgar

One Hampden from the total force failed to return; AE319 from 83 Squadron was shot down by flak and fell into the Fiord. The returning aircraft began landing back in Scotland shortly after 05.00hrs on the 7th.

Running short of fuel, the Hampden being flown by Sgt Robinson (AD744) and crew forced-landed 8 miles south west of Banff. The crew received injuries, including one member who fractured a leg and arm. Later the same day, the crew was returned to Scampton sick bay.

Crashed AD744	Sgt R. Robinson	Pilot	(Injured)
	Sgt J.C. Price	W/Ag	(Injured)
	Sgt H. Sanderson	2nd/P	(Injured)
	Sgt W. Mossop	W/Ag	(Injured)

7/8 September, 1941; BERLIN/KIEL: A force of nearly 200 aircraft was sent to Berlin, with good results being reported by crews. The squadron contributed 5 aircraft of which 4 were successful, the fifth bombed Kiel as an alternative. 15 aircraft failed to return from this operation, but all 49's were safe although 3 were diverted to other aerodromes.

Three aircraft from the unit were detailed to attack Kiel, 2 completed their sorties and returned safely. Of the 51 aircraft dispatched against Kiel, 3 failed to return and one of these came from 49 Squadron. Tragically 22 year-old P/O John Bromham (AE236) and crew all perished and are buried together in Kiel War Cemetery.

FTR AE236	P/O J.W.T. Bromham	Pilot	(Killed)
	Sgt P.J. Duffy	W/Ag	(Killed)
	Sgt E.V. Durham	2nd Pilot	(Killed)
	Sgt A. Kettlewell	W/Ag	(Killed)

8/9 September, 1941; KASSEL: The unit had 8 aircraft airborne by 20.32hrs, five were detailed to attack Kassel and 3 were to lay mines off the Danish coast. The weather over Kassel was clear and all the bombers made successful attacks. In two cases, Me109's were encountered but fortunately avoided; the Andrews crew (AE355) later reported:

"Located target without trouble in moonlight - no bombing results seen owing to intense activity - light flak up to 10,000ft - followed by an Me109 which turned away when we flew into flak!"

One of the gardeners returned 90 minutes after take-off with the W/Op violently sick; the other 2 completed their sorties. Fortunately no losses were incurred on this night.

P/O Jones (AD805) and crew consisting of Sgts Thorndyke, Taylor and Kassel ran short of fuel only a few miles from their home base at Scampton. At 06.32hrs the pilot forced-landed R-Robert in fields near Lenn Farm, North Carlton; as in all good forced-landings, the crew walked away unharmed.

SEPTEMBER 1941

12/13 September, 1941; FRANKFURT: Eleven aircraft were detailed for the marshalling yards at Frankfurt and a further 3 to lay mines in the Baltic. Only 13 aircraft became airborne, one having a taxiing accident just before take-off. One gardener returned to base, unable to make an accurate fix due to thick cloud; the remaining 2 aircraft were successful in planting their vegetables.

Of the bombers, 7 attacked the primary target and 3 attacked alternatives. Bomber Command dispatched 130 aircraft on the raid, of which 2 Wellingtons failed to return. The Hampdens of 49 Squadron all returned safely with 2 aircraft landing away.

14 September, 1941: F/Lt P.M. De Mestre DFC was posted to this unit from 44 Squadron at Waddington.

15/16 September, 1941; HAMBURG/LE HAVRE/MINELAYING: Between 19.15hrs and 22.30 hours, the squadron launched 16 aircraft; 10 to attack the shipyards at Hamburg, 1 'freshmen' to bomb the docks and shipping at Le Havre and 5 to lay mines in the Baltic. Of the gardeners, 4 were successful, the fifth failed to locate the target area due to cloud. Of the bombers, 6 successfully bombed the main objective. Sylt, Wilhelmshaven, Bremerhaven and Bremen were alternatives attacked by the remaining aircraft. The 'freshmen' crew, piloted by Sgt Davis (AE227), saw their bombs burst in the area of No. 1 dock in Le Havre.

Hamburg received a visit from 169 aircraft of which 8 failed to return. Of the 45 'freshmen' crews on the Le Havre trip, one Wellington was reported missing. No minelaying aircraft were lost; all 49's aircraft returned without trouble.

28/29 September, 1941; FRANKFURT: With a gap of nearly two weeks since the previous operation, 49 Squadron was asked to provide 14 Hampdens for a small scale attack on Frankfurt. 4 aircraft were scrubbed from the trip, and just before take-off a fifth suffered tail wheel collapse at the taxiing point.

At 22.50hrs the squadron started to launch the first of 9 aircraft. For one unfortunate crew disaster struck early; 11 minutes after take-off, Sgt Walker and crew (AE376) struck the ground whilst in a shallow dive; tragically all the crew were killed. Their Hampden, E-Echo, came down in Burton Park just north of Lincoln at 6 minutes past midnight.

Of the aircraft that reached the target area, 4 bombed successfully and 2 had to abort their attempts. Of the 30 Hampdens and 14 Wellingtons dispatched on the raid, 1 Wellington and 1 Hampden failed to return; the missing Hampden was that piloted by F/Lt Mundy DFC (AD733) from 49 Squadron. The cause of this loss has not been established, but happy to say the crew survived to become POW's.

Crashed AE376	Sgt A.C. Walker	Pilot	(Killed)
(EA-E)	Sgt A. Raine	W/Ag	(Killed)
	Sgt R.E. Greenhalgh	A/G	(Killed)
	Sgt T.H. Smith	O/Bs	(Killed)
FTR AD733	F/L J.D. Mundy DFC	Pilot	(P.o.W.)
(EA-B)	Sgt P.C. Darwin	Pilot	(P.o.W.)
	Sgt A. Winton	W/AG	(P.o.W.)
	F/S F. Hibbert DFM	W/AG	(P.o.W.)

Bad weather on return to England caused 5 of the unit's aircraft to divert to other aerodromes.

29/30 September, 1941; HAMBURG: Seven aircraft were detailed for operations, of which 6 were to attack dock installations, whilst the Jenkins (AD896) crew were to bomb the Battle Cruiser 'Admiral Von Sheer'.

The Alfry (AE145) crew returned early with oil pressure problems in their port engine. Of the remainder, 3 went on to bomb the primary target and another bombed Cuxhaven. S/Ldr Bennett (AD980) and crew had to jettison their bombs after flak knocked out the starboard motor; they were then chased by an enemy fighter which they managed to evade.

Of the 93 aircraft dispatched, 2 Wellingtons failed to return. All 49's aircraft returned to base.

30 September/1 October, 1941; HAMBURG/CHERBOURG: On the last night of the month, Hamburg was again the target. 82 aircraft were dispatched by Bomber Command of which 7 were contributed by 49 Squadron. Weather conditions prevented clear identification of the target and accurate bombing did not occur. Most crews experienced severe icing; the Jacobs (AD909) crew reported:

"Pitot head iced up and had to jettison wing bombs to maintain height."

The Jones (AE227) crew suffered heavy icing 60 miles from Cuxhaven and were unable to maintain their height:

"We could not jettison as bomb doors would not open so turned back - wing bombs jettisoned later."

All 49's aircraft returned safely to base, including the two 'freshmen' crews that had attacked Cherbourg; 1 Wellington failed to return from Hamburg.

SEPTEMBER 1941

HONOURS AND AWARDS - SEPTEMBER 1941

F/S R. Woolston	D.F.M.
Sgt W.L. Donley	D.F.M.
Sgt F. Lowe	D.F.M.
Sgt G. Wood	D.F.M.

Harvest time 1941 as a trio of 49 Squadron Hampdens sail serenely southwards passing over the RAF fighter airfield of Wellingore some 10 miles south of Lincoln. Four Spitfire/Hurricanes are just visible at the bottom of the photograph.

Of the Hampdens nearest is AD980 (EA-V); it later passed to 408 RCAF Sqdn eventually crashing at Balderton.

Leading the vic is AE354 (EA-S); she met her fate on the evening of 18-12-41 crash landing heavily at Scampton following an attempted overshoot.

AE240 (EA-P) at the top of the photo survived until 12-2-42 when flak brought her down off the Dutch coast during the 'Channel Dash'; there were no survivors from Sgt Holt's crew. (RAF Scampton)

OCTOBER 1941

1/2 October, 1941; KARLSRUHE: At 18.03hrs, 6 Hampdens from the unit began taking off at short intervals, all bound for Karlsruhe. As the attacking force of 44 Hampdens and 1 Wellington approached the target they began to receive 'recall' signals. Group was extremely concerned that the fog forecast for eastern England could prove disastrous for the returning bombers.

Most aircraft found targets of opportunity on which to unload their bombs before turning for home. Of 49's returning aircraft, 3 landed at base, 1 at Barkston Heath, 1 at North Luffenham and the sixth found sanctuary at Dishforth.

The single Wellington on the raid was reported missing.

3 October, 1941: At 15.00hrs the 10 aircraft that had been alerted for operations were stood down. 4 aircraft were detailed to undertake practice low flying attacks against Ferry Bridge power station.

12/13 October, 1941; HÜLS/BREMEN: The 4 bombers detailed for Bremen became airborne shortly after 19.00hrs whilst a larger force of 12 Hampdens set out for the chemical factory at Hüls just after midnight.

Flying as an air gunner in Sgt Robinson's crew (AD976) this night was Sgt Eric Clarke; he was commencing a tour that would take over one year to complete and include 3 different types of aircraft. Eric recalls:

"I joined 49 Squadron from 16 OTU Upper Heyford, on 18th September, 1941 (as a Wop/AG) and quickly realised that I was sadly under trained. I didn't do any flying with the squadron until my very first op, when I flew as an air gunner to Hüls.

Maybe the squadron had suffered some losses because morale was very low. The CO, W/Cmdr Stubbs DFC, called all aircrew to the briefing room one day and slated us in no uncertain terms. He told us that the only reason we were Sergeants, was to keep us out of the German salt mines if taken prisoner...from then on he was referred to as 'Salt mine Stubbs'. I actually liked him, and flew with him on several Manchester test flights."

Both targets were totally cloud covered and as a result bombing was scattered. Of the 99 aircraft sent to Bremen, 2 Wellingtons and 1 Hampden failed to return. The Hüls raid was made up of 79 Hampdens and 11 Manchesters of which one of each type failed to return; all 49's aircraft returned.

OCTOBER 1941

13/14 October, 1941; COLOGNE: No 5 Group sent 30 Hampdens and 9 Manchesters to Cologne, the force becoming airborne in the first hours of the 14th.

49 Squadron had planned to send 9 aircraft, but another taxiing accident prevented one taking off. During the whole operation the raiders were plagued by severe icing conditions. It was due to icing that Sgt Hiles (AE241) and crew spiralled down in a terrifying right hand spin from 14,000ft reaching 6,000ft before the pilot managed to regain control; on pulling out, all aileron control was broken. The crew, consisting of Lock, Spilsbury and Warren, then set course for base where a successful forced-landing was made.

Sgt Latty (AD979) and crew of Combes, Mossop and Hunter reported clearly seeing the target which was practically flak free. Just after leaving the target, icing caused the starboard engine to cut out. The pilot managed to fly the Hampden back on one engine, landing at Martlesham Heath aerodrome just after 06.30hrs.

The Ratcliffe crew (AE397) reported being attacked by two fighters, but the combats were inconclusive, and the Hampden escaped without injury. No aircraft were reported missing from the raid.

16/17 October, 1941; DUISBURG/INTRUDER: The squadron dispatched 7 bombers to attack Duisburg; yet again a taxiing accident prevented an eighth aircraft from taking off. A further 3 aircraft were detailed to carry out searchlight suppression sorties. Because of 10/10ths cloud, none of the bombers were able to pinpoint the primary target and only estimated positions were bombed.

The intruders were successful in breaking up the searchlights. From the 87 strong force, 1 Wellington failed to return.

20/21 October, 1941; BREMEN/MINELAYERS: At 18.00hrs, 16 of the squadron's Hampdens began taking off from Scampton. Of these, 6 were bombers, 10 were 'fire raisers' and 2 were minelayers.

Both minelayers successfully planted their mines off the Frisian Islands. The force sent to Bremen had difficulty in locating the target due to ground haze and darkness; only 5 aircraft found the primary. 2 aircraft returned with their bombs, and the remaining bombers found alternative targets.

All 49's aircraft returned safely, but 5 aircraft failed to return from the 153 strong force.

OCTOBER 1941

22/23 October, 1941; MANNHEIM: Weather over the target plus severe icing and static prevented a force of 123 making a concentrated attack on Mannheim; only 58 aircraft managed to bomb the primary target.

49 Squadron contributed 16 aircraft of which only 6 claimed definite successes. All of the unit's aircraft returned safely despite various icing problems. They were all diverted to Horsham St. Faith where the Newmarch crew (X3057) suffered an undercarriage collapse, but escaped unhurt.

One Hampden (408 Sqdn) failed to return from the raid.

31 October/1 November, 1941; MINELAYING: During the last week of October, two large operations were planned, but cancelled at the last minute. On the last evening of the month 2 crews were detailed for minelaying in the 'Nectarine' (Frisian Islands) area.
Sgt Downes (AE419) and crew of Black, Hardy and Wisdom later reported:

"Attacked at 800ft - good visibility - splash seen as vegetable entered water - rear gunner fired 100 rounds at 2 large ships which had opened up."

Sgt Cook (AE240) and crew consisting of Manders, Thomas and Hallam also placed their mine in the primary place. Both crews were back at Scampton before midnight.

HONOURS AND AWARDS - OCTOBER 1941

F/O R.J. Hannan	D.F.C.
Sgt W.A. Bunn	D.F.M.
Sgt J. Leslie	D.F.M.

AD960 (EA-L)
Attacked and damaged by an Me110 returning from Berlin on 2/3 Sep 1941. The Jenkins crew survived unhurt from a crash landing near Waddington

NOVEMBER 1941

1/2 November, 1941; ANTI-SHIPPING/MINELAYING: Just before 22.00hrs, 4 of the unit's Hampdens set course from Scampton via Mablethorpe for northern Germany. In bright moonlight, 2 of these aircraft went on to successfully plant mines in Kiel Bay, whilst the remaining 2 sought shipping targets off the Frisians. In heavy rain with visibility down to 1,500yds, F/Lt De Mestre (AD980) and crew attacked shipping from 1,000ft - a near miss was made on one ship, but the remainder overshot. During the attack, the Hampden was hit by flak and the rear gunner, P/O Holmes was wounded. The crew returned to Scampton safely, landing at 00.19hrs where P/O Holmes was admitted to the SSQ.

The second aircraft detailed for anti-shipping patrol was piloted by S/Ldr Drakes (AE224) - nothing was heard from this crew after take-off, and they were reported as missing. It is now thought that a night fighter shot them down into the North Sea - their bodies were never recovered. S/Ldr David Baron Drakes and crew are remembered on the Runnymede Memorial.

FTR AE224	S/L D.B. Drakes	Pilot	(Missing)
(EA-Z)	P/O V.D. Beaney	2nd Pilot	(Missing)
	P/O W.H. Cheetham	A/Ob	(Missing)
	F/S W.A. Watson	W/AG	(Missing)

3/4 November, 1941; ANTI-SHIPPING PATROL: Three aircraft were detailed for operations, 2 for minelaying and one for anti-shipping. At 16.00hrs the 'gardeners' were cancelled but at 17.51hrs, Sgt Robinson (AD976) and crew of Hewitt, Mossop and Price, departed Scampton bound for Terschelling.

In poor visibility and low cloud they attacked a flak ship with their 2x250lb wing bombs from 800ft. After spending 2½ hours in the target area, no other targets were found, so the crew returned with their 4x500lb bomb load landing at Scampton shortly after midnight.

5/6 November, 1941; MINELAYING/CHERBOURG: At 00.40hrs the squadron dispatched 10 aircraft to lay mines in the 'Forget-me-not' (Kiel Bay) area - all were successful and returned safely.

At 03.30hrs a further 5 aircraft were sent to attack Cherbourg - 4 successfully bombed the port area and the fifth attacked flak concentrations. All aircraft returned safely.

7/8 November, 1941; COLOGNE/OSTEND: The squadron detailed 17 aircraft to attack Cologne railway station and 2 to the power station at Knapsack; a further Hampden was sent to Ostend. Sgt Stewart (AE357) and crew failed to take-off owing to a taxiing accident.

Only 3 aircraft made successful attacks on Cologne, and the Knapsack attack also failed, but most aircraft bombed alternative targets. Sgt Hamer (X3135) and crew found the haze over Ostend so thick that there was a danger of hitting the town, so they returned home with their bomb load.

All aircraft returned to base, but P/O Cook (AE240) came back from Cologne nursing a broken shoulder, flak having smashed into their aircraft over the target, hitting the pilot, breaking his clavicle. The rear gunner also received concussion.

8/9 November, 1941; ESSEN/INTRUDER: At 10.00hrs, 5 of the squadron's aircraft were detailed for operations against Essen; 3 on bombing sorties and 2 for searchlight-suppression and intruder attacks. The two intruders took off just after 17.14hrs, followed by just one bomber, piloted by Sgt Freeman (L4125) and crew.

Bomber Command had dispatched 54 aircraft on the bombing raid assisted by 8 Hampden intruders. Large fires were started in the target area but the cost was high with 3 Wellingtons, 2 Whitleys and 1 Hampden reported missing.

One Hampden failed to return from the intruder operations and it unfortunately came from 49 Squadron: W/O Christopher Saunders DFM (P1206) and crew were shot down by a German night fighter flown by Ofw Ney of II/NJG 2. The aircraft was hit over the Dutch coast and set on fire; it was seen to circle before crashing at Berkhout, south west of Hoorn in Holland. The wreckage sank deep into the marshy ground and the bodies of Sgt John Kehoe (of Eire) and Sgt Stanley Mullenger have never been recovered. The pilot and navigator, Sgt James D'arcy are both buried in Bergen General Cemetery.

FTR P1206	W/O C.A. Saunders DFM	Pilot	(Killed)
(EA-Z)	Sgt J.M. D'arcy	NAV	(Killed)
	Sgt J.E. Kehoe	W/AG	(Missing)
	Sgt S.G. Mullenger	W/AG	(Missing)

9/10 November, 1941; HAMBURG: Over 70 aircraft set out for Hamburg of which 17 were from 49 Squadron. Their target was the Blomm & Voss works or alternatively, the town itself. Eight of the unit's aircraft attacked the primary objective in conditions of good visibility, the remaining aircraft, owing to less favourable conditions of cloud, bombed alternative targets.

One Wellington failed to return from the operation; all 49's aircraft landed back at Scampton shortly after midnight, with the exception of 2, one landing at Acklington, the other at Topcliffe.

NOVEMBER 1941

HACKTHORN HALL TRAGEDY

11 November, 1941: In the late afternoon of Tuesday 11th November, Sgt Pilot Keith Bryant was detailed to ferry X3135 over to Dunholme Lodge. The pilot took along 2 members of the ground crew, LAC Andrew Wilson and AC2 Walter Fulcher. The Hampden was seen to make a steep left hand turn before crashing into the ground at Hackthorn Hall, north east of Scampton aerodrome; tragically all onboard were killed.

Crashed	**X3135**	Sgt K. Bryant	Pilot	(Killed)
		LAC A.G. Wilson		(Killed)
		AC2 W.H. Fulcher		(Killed)

23/24 November, 1941; LORIENT: Eighteen aircraft from the squadron helped make up the force of 51 Hampdens and 2 Manchesters sent to bomb the docks at Lorient. Of the unit's Hampdens, 13 were successful in bombing the primary target. All aircraft returned safely from the operation.

SCAMBLESBY ACCIDENT

25 November, 1941: Just two weeks after the fatal flying accident involving Hampden X3135, another of the squadron's Hampdens crashed whilst on a training flight; 20 year-old Sgt Pilot Ron Hough and Sgt George Edward Smith were both killed instantly when their aircraft, AD759 spun into the ground at Scamblesby up on the Lincolnshire Wolds, during low flying. At 14.55hrs during the afternoon of Tuesday 25th, Hampden AD759 was seen making a very low approach towards the village of Scamblesby where Sgt Smith's family lived. Tragically the Hampden's wing struck the ground and the aircraft crashed through fields just on the edge of the village. Sgt Smith, whose relatives still live in the village, is buried in St. Martin's Churchyard, Scamblesby whilst Sgt Hough rests in Clayton-le-Moors cemetery in Lancashire.

Crashed	**AD759**	Sgt R.R. Hough	Pilot	(Killed)
		Sgt G.E. Smith	W/AG	(Killed)

26/27 November, 1941; EMDEN: Total cloud cover caused the failure of this operation, on which 14 of the unit's Hampdens set out. None of the participating aircraft found the main objective; 9 attacked alternative targets and 5 returned to base with their bomb loads, unable to see the target area.

Of the 100 strong force dispatched by Command, only 55 claimed to have bombed Emden. 2 Wellingtons and 1 Hampden (106 Sqdn) were reported missing. All 49's aircraft were safely back at Scampton before midnight of the 26th.

NOVEMBER 1941

30 November/1 December, 1941; HAMBURG: On this night, visibility in the bright moonlight was excellent as 18 of the squadron's aircraft joined in an attack on the shipyards at Hamburg. Eleven of the unit's Hampdens found the primary target, 5 bombed the alternatives of Cuxhaven, Wilhelmshaven and Hamburg town; 2 further aircraft failed to bomb due to mechanical problems.

Bomber Command had over 180 aircraft airborne for the Hamburg operation and of these, 13 were reported missing. All 49's aircraft landed safely back at base.

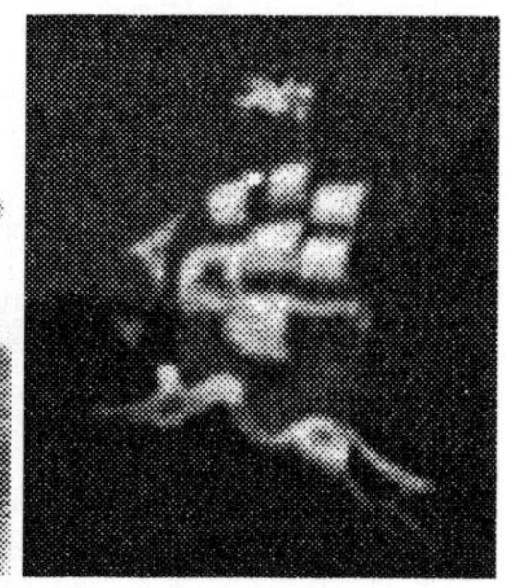

AE224 (EA-Z)

'The Golden Hind' as flown by S/Ldr Drakes and crew pictured left. (l - r) P/O W H Cheetham A/Ob, P/O V D Beaney 2nd Pilot, S/Ldr W H Drakes Pilot, F/S W A Watson W/AG. Aircraft and crew failed to return on 1/2nd Nov 1941. (Dr John Allin)

HONOURS AND AWARDS - NOVEMBER 1941

Sgt J. Flint	D.F.M./ G.C.
S/Ldr A.W.Hiron	D.F.C.
F/Lt H.W.H. Fisher	D.F.C.
P/O D.B. Falconer	D.F.C.
Sgt A.G. Smith	D.F.M.
Sgt B.G. Tree	D.F.M.

DECEMBER 1941

7/8 December, 1941; AACHEN: Weather had prevented any chance of operations during the first week of December, but on Sunday 7th, the unit was detailed to contribute 6 aircraft for an attack on the Nazi Headquarters in the town of Aachen. The aircraft all became airborne in good weather conditions during the first hours of Monday morning, but 10/10ths cloud over the target prevented the target being located. 3 of the unit's aircraft did not bomb, the remaining 3 found alternative targets.

Little damage was suffered by Aachen, for the loss of 1 Halifax, and 2 Hampdens, from a total force of 130 aircraft.

All 49's Hampdens landed safely back at Scampton in daylight, around 08.00hrs.

KILLED ON ACTIVE SERVICE

8 December, 1941; The squadron suffered its sixth flying accident casualty within a month, when Sgt Thomas Hardisty was reported 'killed on active service'.

On Monday 8 December, Sgt Hardisty was the wireless operator on Hampden AE227, taking part in a practice flight around the local area of Scampton. For some unexplained reason, Sgt Hardisty fell to his death from the aircraft. The Welton Police reported, an airman subsequently identified as Sgt T.H. Hardisty was killed after baling out over Sudbrooke. There is no further information as to the cause of this tragedy; 21 years old Thomas Hardisty is buried in St. John the Baptist Churchyard, Scampton.

10 December, 1941; AURICH/WILHELMSHAVEN (DAYLIGHT): At midday on Wednesday 10th, two of the squadron's Hampdens set out on a daylight attack against a Dutch and German coastal target.

The Jenkins crew (AE368) of Close, Woodroffe and Tilley, were briefed to attack Aurich. Weather prevented the primary from being attacked, but the railway sidings at Wittmund were bombed as an alternative. Hits were seen on the sheds on the south side of the station and over 2,000 rounds were fired with many hits seen on trains, buildings and the station.

The Walker crew (AE132) of West, Campbell and Andrews, were to attack Wilhelmshaven. Again 10/10ths cloud prevented the main objective being found, so the crew elected to bomb a railway target in north west Germany. Direct hits were seen when a stick of bombs fell across the railway line, station and factory. Both crews had returned to base by 17.57hrs.

12 December, 1941; BREMERHAVEN/CUXHAVEN (DAYLIGHT): Shortly after 10.00hrs, the unit dispatched 2 aircraft for daylight sorties against targets in Germany.
The Hodges crew (AT124) of Cadman, Fry and Ellis were unable to attack the barracks at Bremerhaven due to lack of cloud cover in the Frisian Islands area. The crew returned safely with its bomb load.

The Robinson crew (AD979) of Black, Price and Mossop were also detailed to bomb barracks, this time at Cuxhaven. These could not be located, so the crew then went on to bomb and strafe the local aerodrome.

Facing intense ground fire Sgt Pilot Robinson took his aircraft down to 100ft to carry out the attack. During the assault, one hangar was seen to blow up and 2 aircraft were set on fire on the ground; the town was also machine gunned. Inevitably the Hamden sustained numerous flak hits and was severely shot up. Sadly, F/Sgt Stuart Black RNZAF, was struck by fragments from a cannon shell and killed.

The pilot now had to get the battered aircraft back to England. Making landfall over the Norfolk coast, the aircraft made for Bircham Newton, where without the use of hydraulics (rendered useless by cannon shells) he managed a successful crash-landing; timed at 16.35hrs. F/Sgt Black is buried in Great Bircham Churchyard in Norfolk.

Crashed AD979	Sgt R.J. Robinson	Pilot	(Unhurt)
	F/S S.C. Black RNZAF	Nav/Pilot	(Killed)
	Sgt J. Price	W/AG	(Unhurt)
	Sgt W. Mossop	W/AG	(Unhurt)

16/17 December, 1941; WILHELMSHAVEN/MINELAYING: The unit put 19 aircraft up, 5 for minelaying in the Brest area and 14 to bomb the railway station at Wilhelmshaven. Of these, 4 'gardeners' successfully laid their mines, the other returned with its mine unable to locate the target. The force of 83 bombers sent against Wilhelmshaven achieved little damage, but fortunately no aircraft were lost from the raid.

21 December, 1941; INTRUDER OPERATIONS (DAYLIGHT): No 5 Group attempted daring daylight intruder operations using 12 Hampdens of which 6 were from 49 Squadron. Each crew was briefed to attack separate targets.

The aircraft took off just after midday but all returned to base after a short period (3 hours) as per instructions at briefing. H.Q. 5 Group had given specific orders that if there was insufficient cloud cover the sorties must be abandoned, and this is what occurred.

23/24 December, 1941; RENNES: Two aircraft were detailed to lay mines in the Rennes area and then go on to drop leaflets from 10,000ft. In bright moonlight and cloudless conditions, both aircraft carried out their sorties and returned safely to Scampton.

24 December, 1941; INTRUDER OPERATIONS (DAYLIGHT): During the late afternoon of Christmas Eve, 1941, six of the squadron's crews set out on intruder sorties. But once again, after 3 hours, they all received the recall signal due to an absence of cloud cover over north west Germany.

The following day, Christmas Day, there were 'no' operations, but at 10.00hrs on Boxing Day 18 crews were ordered to stand-by to attack targets in northern Germany.

Not until 16.00hrs did they receive a 'stand down' signal.

28/29 December, 1941; HÜLS: At 09.30hrs on the morning of Sunday 28th, Group orders rattled in requesting 20 of the squadron's Hampdens for an attack on the synthetic rubber plant at Hüls. Take-off began at 17.30hrs with all aircraft becoming airborne without any problems. The attack was carried out by 81 Hampdens of 5 Group and the bombing results were reported as good. Group lost 4 Hampden crews from the raid; 2 from 144 Sqdn, 1 from 408 Sqdn, and the fourth was AE419 flown by Sgt Archie Watt and crew. The bodies of this crew have never been recovered and it is believed that the aircraft came down in the sea. Sgt Watt and his crew are remembered on the Runnymede Memorial. It was a very sad note on which to finish the troubled year of 1941.

FTR AE419	Sgt A.C. Watt	Pilot	(Missing)
(EA-T)	Sgt E.G. Sawdy	Nav/Pilot	(Missing)
	F/S E.C. Atkinson	W/AG	(Missing)
	Sgt H.W. Wisdom	W/OP	(Missing)

HONOURS AND AWARDS - DECEMBER 1941

F/O G.R. Scorer	D.F.C.
Sgt D.J.P. Broomfield	D.F.M.
Sgt W.C. Samual	D.F.M.

Illustration by John Ward

JANUARY 1942

On New Years Day, 1942 the squadron strength stood at; 35 Officers and 650 Airmen. The Initial Equipment held; 26 Hampdens and 1 Tiger Moth.

2 January, 1942; INTRUDER PATROLS (DAYLIGHT): Four of the squadron's Hampdens again attempted daylight 'roving patrols' over northern Germany. 3 aircraft returned with their bombs after finding the cloud cover insufficient.

The Hamer crew (AE368) of Haddock, Watchorn and Minchin attacked Leeuwarden aerodrome from 50ft!.. they saw the bombs enter the runway, but no bursts were seen. The crew returned the friendly waves from bargees on the Dutch canal. All four had returned safely back to Scampton by 15.53hrs.

2/3 January, 1942; RENNES/MINELAYING: Whilst 4 of the unit's aircraft practiced dusk circuit and landings, 2 other aircraft slipped out on operational sorties. The McGuffie crew was sent to lay mines off the Frisians, but at 600ft they were still unable to identify land from sea; after 30 minutes searching, they returned with their vegetables. The Burton crew went on a leaflet sortie to the Rennes area; on return they diverted to Exeter aerodrome.

4 January, 1942; INTRUDER PATROLS (DAYLIGHT): During mid-morning, 6 of the unit's aircraft took off, bound for various targets in northern Germany. 5 aircraft made successful bombing attacks as the following interrogation reports reveal:

AE241 Jenkins, Clough, Woodroffe, Steel:

"Attacked factory and built up area unidentified from 100 feet - 10/10ths cloud. Direct hits seen on 2 factories and 1 train between Bremerhaven and Cuxhaven - 6,000 rounds fired."

AD909 Bond, Kirby, Potter, Collins:

"Bombed unidentified built up area - poor visibility - clearly saw target at 50 feet."

AD865 Freeman, Bush, Smith J, Higgins:

"Bombed unidentified area 20 miles N.E. of Bremerhaven from 50ft. Cloud 2/300ft and haze over target. 1 stick across power station, another in centre of built up area. All ammunition used in strafing various objects - 8 bursts seen but no fires."

AE396 Rawstone, Mansbridge, Gadsby, Smith K.I:

"Attacked unidentified built up area in neighbourhood at Basbeck at 100ft. Hit by flak - no material damage."

AD962	Jones,	Thorndyke,	Taylor H.	Taylor S:

"Owing to poor light and visibility, attacked unidentified built up area from 500ft - presumed Cuxhaven - no bursts seen. Flak hit a/c and injured gunner. Landed Driffield on return."

AE148	Alfrey,	James,	White,	Jones:

"No target attacked. Circled 15 minutes near Elbe estuary, flak shell hit mainplane damaging aileron. Load jettisoned and returned to base."

5/6 January, 1942; BREST/MINELAYING: The 'Scharnhorst' and 'Gneisenau' plus the naval docks were subjected to an attack by 154 aircraft. During the early hours of Tuesday 6th, the squadron dispatched 10 aircraft for the Brest attack, and 4 for minelaying in Quiberon Bay. As a fifth minelayer aircraft made its take-off run, the port engine cut out and a crash landing was made on the airfield.

Fortunately the Burton crew (AE372) of Black, Hardy and Barret were uninjured in the incident. The aircraft was repaired and later returned to operations.

All 49's aircraft returned safely, despite F/O Jenkins (AE241) and crew exchanging shots with a couple of Me109's! No other aircraft were lost from the operation.

CRASH AT SOUTH CARLTON

6 January, 1942: At 07.00hrs on the morning of Tuesday 6th, Hampden AD896 M-Mother, approached Scampton to land after night training. As the aircraft passed over the small hamlet of South Carlton, one of the engines suddenly cut out. The aircraft stalled then fell into Middle Street Killing two of the crew including the pilot, Sgt Geoffrey West. Also killed in this tragic accident was wireless operator, Sgt George Atkins. Fortunately there were no civilian casualties in the village. It cannot be established if these were the only two airmen aboard the aircraft that fatal morning.

Crashed AD896	Sgt G.L. West	Pilot	(Killed)
(EA-M)	Sgt G.T. Atkins	W/OP	(Killed)

9/10 January, 1942; BREST/MINELAYING: Around midnight, Scampton once again reverberated to the sound of Hampdens taking off for operations. 49 Squadron were sending 9 aircraft after the battle cruisers in Brest harbour, whilst 5 more aircraft were to plant mines in the Brest area.

Only one of the bombers managed to make a bombing attack; the Massey crew (AD980) dropped their bombs on gun emplacements in the dock area. The remaining 8 aircraft returned to base with their bombs.

Of the minelayers, 3 were successful in planting their mines, 1 was unable to find the target area and the fifth was sadly reported missing: P/O Thomas Jacobs (AD909) and crew are presumed to have come down into the sea and their bodies have never been recovered. The crew is remembered on the Runnymede Memorial.

FTR AD909	P/O T.F. Jacobs	Pilot	(Missing)
(EA-H)	P/O P.T. Close	A/OB	(Missing)
	Sgt W.B. Robertson	W/AG	(Missing)
	Sgt J. Warren	W/AG	(Missing)

14/15 January, 1942; HAMBURG/MINELAYING/EMDEN: Shortly before 17.00hrs, the squadron prepared to launch 17 aircraft for operations, but three aircraft failed to become airborne after one of them crashed on take-off. Of the bombers that did become airborne, 3 failed to find their target (Blohm & Voss yards), 3 out of the 5 minelayers were unsuccessful, but the 2 'freshmen' crews did make attacks on Emden. Of the 95 aircraft sent to Hamburg, 2 Wellingtons and 2 Hampdens failed to return. All 49's aircraft returned safely, although they were all diverted to bases throughout eastern England.

17/18 January, 1942; BREMEN/EMDEN/MINELAYING: At 09.30hrs the squadron was ordered to ‘stand up’ 18 aircraft for operations; 12 to bomb the main railway station at Bremen, 5 to lay mines off Heligoland and 1 ‘freshman’ crew to attack Emden docks. Take-off commenced at 17.00hrs, all becoming airborne at 2 minute intervals. 10 aircraft (including the ‘freshman’) failed to attack any target - 6 bombers attacked targets including searchlight and flak concentrations. The gardeners laid their mines in the area of Wangerooge and Schiermonnikoog. Three Wellingtons were lost from the Bremen raid; all 49's aircraft returned safely to base.

20/21 January, 1942; EMDEN: The squadron sent 5 Hampdens to attack Emden; 2 aircraft failed to attack any target owing to icing and failure of heating and 2 aircraft bombed the primary target. Of the fifth aircraft, no signals were received and the aircraft was reported missing. F/O Alex Harvey (AT148) and crew were shot down over Groningen by Obfw Paul Gildner of II/NJG.2. Sadly, all the crew perished when S-Sugar fell to earth near the farm of Mr Ritsema at Roodehaan, Noorddijk in Holland. The crew rest together in Noorddijk General Cemetery.

FTR AT148	F/O A.M. Harvey	Pilot	(Killed)
(EA-S)	Sgt W.A. Gray	A/OB	(Killed)
	Sgt J.W. Hallam	W/AG	(Killed)
	Sgt R.M. Knapman	A/G	(Killed)

21/22 January, 1942; EMDEN: The ‘freshman’ crew of Sgt Williams (AT126) were sent to attack Emden, but their intercom went u/s forcing them to return without bombing.

JANUARY 1942

22/23 January, 1942; MINELAYING: The Williams crew (AT126) set out to lay mines off the Frisians. In good visibility with a slight haze and no cloud, the crew completed their sortie successfully, seeing the parachutes open before entering the water.

25/26 January, 1942; BREST: At 16.50hrs, with snow and ice on the ground, the squadron began to dispatch 17 Hampdens, all briefed to attack the German warships in Brest harbour. At 17.12hrs, immediately after take-off, Hampden O-Orange piloted by Sgt Charles Stewart (AT129) crashed to earth near the small hamlet of Bransby between Sturton and Saxilby; there were no survivors. It is thought the aircraft may have been brought down by ice collecting on its flying surfaces.

THE BRANSBY MEMORIAL

Exactly 50 years after the crew of Hampden AT129 sadly perished, a special memorial service was held near the crash site. The aircraft actually came down in fields which now form part of the Bransby Home of Rest for Horses. Mr Peter Hunt, secretary of the home, helped plan the event which was conducted by Padre Andy McMullan from RAF Scampton.

Attending were relatives of the crew; Mrs Eileen Morris, sister of Albert Hibbitt and Mrs Jean Lawbuary, sister of Leonard Jardine together with Eric Clarke (ex-49er) who actually flew on the Brest raid with S/Ldr Bennett. Tom Page (ex-49er) and the author were also privileged to be in attendance. A small plaque in memory of crew members, Charles Stewart, Ken Northrop, Albert Hibbet and Len Jardine was unveiled.

Each Remembrance Day, Eric Clarke and Tom Page lay a wreath the Bransby memorial, and the service is attended by Mrs D Smith (Nee Everitt - ex WAAF) who drove the unlucky crew to their aircraft that night.

Of those aircraft that continued on towards Brest, one returned early to base with mechanical problems, 8 aircraft failed to attack any target owing to the effect of 10/10ths cloud making fixes impossible. The remainder attacked alternative targets within the dock area. There were no further losses from the operation.

Crashed AT129	Sgt C.D.S. Stewart	Pilot	(Killed)
(EA-O)	Sgt A. Hibbitt	W/AG	(Killed)
	Sgt K.E. Northrop	W/AG	(Killed)
	Sgt L.A. Jardine	W/AG	(Killed)

27/28 January, 1942; BREST: The squadron dispatched 17 aircraft just after midnight, once again bound for the 'Scharnhorst' and 'Prince Eugen' at Brest. Seven aircraft failed to attack any targets due to heating failures and inability to find the target (4 due to navigational errors), 6 aircraft bombed the primary target. All aircraft returned safely to base.

JANUARY 1942

28/29 January, 1942; BOULOGNE: At 19.00hrs, 3 aircraft were dispatched to attack harbour installations and drop 'nickels'. 2 crews saw their bombs enter the target; they then went on to drop leaflets in the area. The third crew returned their bombs to base, being unable to pinpoint the target until too late to bomb. All 3 aircraft were back at Scampton by 23.31hrs.

During the same night, Munster had received an attack by 55 Wellingtons and 29 Hampdens - 1 Wellington and 4 Hampdens failed to return, all four Hampdens coming from 106 Squadron, Finningley. At 05.30hrs on the 29th, 49 Squadron sent 2 aircraft out for a search of the North Sea for any of the missing aircraft. After 6 hours the aircraft returned, their long and diligent search unsuccessful.

31 January/1 February, 1942; BREST: Bomber Command sent 72 aircraft to bomb this port once again. The squadron contributed 18 Hampdens; of these 8 failed to attack any targets due to technical problems, 1 bombed the battle cruisers and the rest attacked the docks.
The defences around Brest were getting increasingly 'stiff', and as a result 3 Manchesters and 2 Hampdens were reported missing; all 49's aircraft returned safely.

HONOURS AND AWARDS - JANUARY 1942

P/O R.J. Robinson D.F.C.

The memorial plaque at Bransby erected in honour of the crew of Hampden AT129 which crashed after take-off. Sgt pilot Charles D S Stewart, Sgt Kenneth E Northrop, Sgt Albert Hibbitt and Sgt Leonard A Jardine.

FEBRUARY 1942

1 February, 1942: The squadron was highly delighted to receive notification that P/O's G.R. Scorer and R.J Robinson had both been awarded the Distinguished Flying Cross and that Sgt Pilot W.C Samuel and F/Sgt Broomfield had been honoured with the Distinguished Flying Medal. All four recipients were serving pilots on 49 Squadron.

6 February, 1942; MINELAYING (DAYLIGHT): Ten aircraft were detailed to lay mines off the Frisians in an attempt to destroy the 'Scharnhorst' and 'Gneisenau'. All aircraft became airborne during mid-morning and carried out their sorties in daylight. Nine aircraft laid mines in the primary positions and one in a channel in the ice near Texel.
Of the total force of 46 minelayers sent by Group, one Hampden failed to return; all 49's aircraft returned safely.

7 February, 1942; MINELAYING (DAYLIGHT): No 5 Group sent 32 Hampdens to lay mines off the Frisians, again in daylight. The squadron put up 5 aircraft, all taking off around 11.00hrs; 2 aircraft planted vegetables in the primary positions, 1 laid mines in an alternative position, the remaining 2 aircraft did not drop their loads as there was insufficient cloud cover in the area.
The force was intercepted by German fighters with the result that 3 Hampdens were shot down. Fortunately, 49's aircraft were not amongst the victims, in fact one 49 Squadron aircraft helped even up the score:

P/O Alfry (AE261) and crew of Wright, White and Jones were themselves attacked by two ME 109's. In the ensuing battle, the Hampden's gunners were successful in shooting down one of their adversaries, and forced the second aircraft to break off its attack; the Hampden returned safely to base.

Sgt Hill (AT111) and crew of Lowson, McGrenery and Ralph, were hit by flak whilst in cloud over Wangerooge; the starboard engine was hit and the heating system rendered u/s. Skilfully, the pilot made a safe return to base. All 49's aircraft were back at Scampton by 16.30hrs.

8 February, 1942: It was announced that Sgt J.C. Price and Sgt J. Mossop had both been awarded the DFM.

10/11 February, 1942; BREMEN: Several aircraft were delayed at take-off time as some Hampdens became stuck in the heavy snow, but eventually the squadron got 12 airborne by 01.46hrs. En route to Bremen, most aircraft suffered various problems, including ASI's icing up, heating system failures and engine problems.

A force of 55 aircraft was sent to attack the railway station at Bremen. In the event, 5 of 49's Hampdens were unsuccessful in attacking any target, 1 bombed the primary target and the remainder attacked alternative targets. There were no losses reported from the operation.

THE CHANNEL DASH

12 February, 1942: In recent months, Bomber Command had dropped over 3,000 tons of bombs on the battle cruisers 'Scharnhorst' and 'Gneisenau' and the light cruiser 'Prinz Eugen' as they resided in the French port of Brest. The two larger ships had both been badly damaged, and the threat of further damage had prevented the ships from sailing out into the Atlantic on another raid against allied shipping.

In a daring and well-executed operation, the Germans sailed their 3 ships straight up through the English Channel to bring them back to the greater protection of a German port. What followed on the part of the British Command has since been labelled as a catalogue of catastrophes, needless to say that the German warships achieved their destination unharmed.

Heavily armed and protected by the Luftwaffe, the Germans exacted a heavy toll during the gallant British attempts to stop their breakout; Fighter Command lost 16 aircraft and the Fleet Air Arm had 6 Swordfish destroyed. Bomber Command's part in the action involved 244 aircraft of which 15 were lost in action, and a further 2 crashing on return. Only 5 Group had been on a 4 hour 'stand by', as bomber Squadrons made frantic efforts to prepare their aircraft. Eventually, 5 Group contributed 64 Hampdens and 15 Manchesters to attack the German warships; 9 Hampdens were reported missing and one crashed on return.

49 Squadron's participation was prompted by a signal from Group received at 10.00hrs requesting 20 aircraft to attack the 'Scharnhorst' and 'Gneisenau' at sea! Cpl Trevor Simpson recalls the urgency with which the preparations were carried out, and he is almost certain that this was the occasion when the Hampdens were taxied into a hangar, bombed up and then taxied out! P/O Jeffreys and crew were the first away at 13.27hrs, as AT180 climbed away into the murky weather conditions. The remaining aircraft took off at intervals, the last off being Sgt Hamer (AD968) and crew at 15.03hrs.

In low cloud and rain with extremely poor visibility, only 3 of the squadron's aircraft found the primary target:

AE261 De Mestre, Wright, Bell, Thorn:

"Cruisers attacked at 3/4,000ft in 5/10ths cloud and heavy rain. Bombs overshot. 4 bursts seen near rear of the three."

AE368 Newmarch, Brown, Andrews, Thighe:

"Attacked from 2,500ft in patches of cloud. Clearly saw 3 Large ships at correct time and position. Target in sights but did not see bursts. Consider that bombs fell close to warships. Violent avoiding action necessary."

AD931 Alfry, Lowson, White, Jones:

"Attacked primary target from 2,000ft in 10/10ths cloud. 2 large warships and 3 small vessels seen in line. Bombs seen to undershoot, though 2 bursts were seen."

During the operation, F/O Jenkins (P1153) and crew reported being attacked by a Wellington bomber off The Hague - this aircraft had no squadron markings.

The Alfry crew were the last to touch down back at Scampton at 19.18hrs leaving 4 of the squadron's aircraft overdue. Later that Thursday evening, after failing to receive any communications, these four crews were reported as missing.

It is now believed that two of the aircraft were shot down by German fighters, AE132 piloted by F/Sgt Charles Pollitt and AE396 flown by Sgt Edward Phillips. What we do know for certain is that these two crews plus that of Sgt Mervyn Holt (AE249) disappeared into the dark waters of the North Sea without trace; they are all remembered at Runnymede.

The fourth aircraft, P5324 piloted by Sgt Thomas Downes also came down in the sea, though the cause cannot be determined. What has been established is that the bodies of 3 of the unfortunate crew were recovered from a Dutch beach in the days that followed. The tragic loss of these brave young airmen was compounded by the fact that the warships arrived at their destination without harm. At Scampton the following day, life went on as usual. No ops were ordered, which gave ground crews a chance to catch up on their work. On the other side of the airfield, 83 Squadron continued to struggle manfully with their new charges of Avro Manchesters. One of 49's aircraft practiced beam approaches, whilst a further 3 aircraft were readied for circuits and landings as soon as it became dark. Meanwhile the orderly room staff had prepared and sent 16 telegrams.

FTR P5324	Sgt T.K. Downes	Pilot	(Killed)
(EA-T)	Sgt D.G.F. Poxon	A/G	(Killed)
	Sgt B. Hunter	W/AG	(Killed)
	Sgt T.H.F. Wood	Pilot	(Missing)
FTR AE132	F/S D.C. Pollitt	Pilot	(Missing)
(EA-U)	Sgt R.J. Cridge	W/OP	(Missing)
	Sgt I.S. Greenstreet	A/OB	(Missing)
	Sgt W. Smith	A/G	(Missing)
FTR AE396	Sgt E.W. Phillips	Pilot	(Missing)
(EA-W)	Sgt A. Jackson	W/OP	(Missing)
	Sgt K.W. Heard	Pilot	(Missing)
	Sgt L.C. Toghill	A/G	(Missing)
FTR AE240	Sgt M.H. Holt	Pilot	(Missing)
(EA-P)	P/O S.W.A. Way	W/AG	(Missing)
	Sgt E.G. Green	Pilot	(Missing)
	Sgt C.L. Lee	A/OB	(Missing)

FEBRUARY 1942

14 February, 1942: On this day the following new directive was sent by the Air Ministry to Bomber Command heralding the onset of 'area bombing':

"IT HAS BEEN DECIDED THAT THE PRIMARY OBJECTIVE OF YOUR OPERATIONS SHOULD NOW BE FOCUSED ON THE MORALE OF THE ENEMY CIVIL POPULATION AND IN PARTICULAR OF THE INDUSTRIAL WORKERS"

14/15 February, 1942; MANNHEIM: The squadron had 12 aircraft airborne around 16.00hrs bound for the railway station at Mannheim. In the event, the target only received slight damage from the 98 strong force.

One Whitley and 1 Hampden failed to return from the operation; the Hampden was G-George from 49 Squadron. It was subsequently located in the English Channel. After bombing searchlights and flak batteries in Mannheim, P/O Ralf Allsebrook and crew were returning across the sea on one engine. Within sight of the English coast, the other motor cut out and the Hampden was ditched at 02.30hrs west of the Needles on the Isle of Wight. The crew took to their dinghy, but were soon suffering from cold in the bitter conditions.

P/O Allsebrook and crew owe their lives to a Beaufighter returning from patrol, whose crew spotted the lights in the sea. The emergency services were alerted and the very grateful crew was rescued by a Naval Coastguard launch, with 3 of the crew suffering from frost-bite. Ralf Allsebrook went on to fly Lancasters with 49 Squadron, and eventually transferred to 617 Squadron, where, on 15/16 September 1943 he and his crew were shot down and killed whilst attacking the Dortmund-Ems Canal.

After bombing Mannheim, Sgt Hamer (AT112) and crew managed to regain England after over 9 hours flying. They were desperately low on fuel which eventually gave out forcing the pilot to make a forced-landing. M-Mother came to earth at Glossmore Farm on the Ponders Bridge to March road near Upwood. Despite a heavy landing in which the Hampden was destroyed, all the crew escaped safely.

FTR AE397	P/O R.A.P. Allsebrook	Pilot	(Rescued)
(EA-G	Sgt Stanbridge	A/OB	(Rescued)
(Ditched)	Sgt Wilkinson	W/AG	(Rescued)
	Sgt Woolgar	W/AG	(Rescued)
Crashed AT112	Sgt R.N. Hamer	Pilot	(Unhurt)
(EA-M)	Sgt Haddock		(Unhurt)
	Sgt Minchin		(Unhurt)
	Sgt Watchorn		(Unhurt)

FEBRUARY 1942

A snapshot of Denis Saxton (on right) taken in front of what is believed to be P/O Allsebrook's Hampden. The nose emblem is a Teddy bear character. (D. Saxton)

16/17 February, 1942; MINELAYING/LEAFLETS: No 5 Group dispatched 37 Hampdens and 12 Manchesters to plant mines off the Frisians. The 14 aircraft dispatched by 49 Squadron carried out their duties with mixed success. A further aircraft flown by the Hooper crew (AT126) successfully dropped Nickels (leaflets) from 1,000ft over Paris and returned safely.

From the minelaying force, 1 Hampden and 1 Manchester failed to return; the Hampden was C-Charlie from 49 Squadron.

It is presumed that F/O Gordon Jenkins (AT124) and crew came down in the North Sea. The bodies of this unfortunate crew have never been recovered; they are remembered on the Runnymede Memorial.

FTR AT124	F/O G.R. Jenkins	Pilot	(Missing)
(EA-C)	P/O J.T.B. Clough	NAV	(Missing)
	Sgt J.A. Steele	W/AG	(Missing)
	Sgt J.A. Woodroffe	W/AG	(Missing)

18/19 February, 1942; MINELAYING: Twenty-five Hampdens, including 12 from 49 Squadron, were detailed to plant mines off Wilhelmshaven and Heligoland. 8 of the unit's aircraft mined in the correct position, 3 planted mines in alternative positions and 1 failed to locate the target area due to poor visibility. 1 Hampden from 420 Squadron failed to return.

FEBRUARY 1942

22 February, 1942: Air Marshall A.T. Harris succeeded Sir Richard Peirse as C - in - C., Bomber Command. He inherited a force which was made up of the following aircraft:

Night Bombers		Day Bombers	
Wellingtons	221	Blenheims	56
Hampdens	112	Bostons	22
Whitleys	54		
Stirlings	29		
Halifaxes	29		
Manchesters	20		
Lancasters	4		
Total	**469**	**Total**	**78**

22/23 February, 1942; WILHELMSHAVEN/EMDEN: A force of 50 Wellingtons and Hampdens were sent to bomb the floating dock at Wilhelmshaven, with which the Germans may have been planning to repair the 'Scharnhorst' or 'Gneisenau'. The target was cloud-covered and most bombers dropped on an estimated position.

The squadron sent 12 Hampdens; 6 failed to attack any target, 5 bombed flak in the target area and 1 bombed the docks at Wilhelmshaven. The Carter crew (P1153) was detailed to attack Emden, but an overheating port engine forced them to return without attacking; all aircraft returned safely.

AT112 (EA-M) Bob Hamer and crew survived unhurt after crash landing short of fuel. They came down near Upwood on return from Mannheim 14/15 Feb 1942. (49 Squadron Collection)

FEBRUARY 1942

24/25 February, 1942; MINELAYING: The squadron dispatched 15 aircraft on minelaying sorties; 14 to lay mines off Heligoland Bight and 1 off Terschelling.
In low cloud and icing conditions, 5 Hampdens mined the primary area, 7 mined last resort targets and 3 returned to base with their mines. Of the 51 aircraft operating this night, 2 Hampdens (144 Sqdn) were lost.

26/27 February, 1942; KIEL/MINELAYING: Bomber Command sent 33 Wellingtons, 10 Hampdens and 6 Halifaxes to attack the floating dock at Kiel where the 'Gneisenau' was being repaired. The warship was hit on the bows by a high-explosive bomb, killing over 100 of her crew. Later the ship's guns were removed and she was taken to Gdynia never again to be a fighting force.

The squadron detailed 4 Hampdens to bomb the cruiser; 2 were unsuccessful due to severe icing problems, whilst 2 bombed the primary target. At the post operational interrogation, the Hodges crew (AT156) reported:

"Bombed in bright moonlight - Identified mainly from map but Kiel stood out in outline against snow. Bombs went on target and 1 fire started - wing bombs ditched on the way out to lessen petrol consumption. Front perspex holed by light flak over Kiel canal."

The unit also sent 8 gardeners to plant mines off Heligoland; of these 6 were successful, 1 returned early with engine failure and 1 failed to pin-point the target area.

Two Wellingtons and 1 Halifax were lost from the Kiel operation, whilst all the minelayers returned safely.

D Saxton and fellow ground crew members near 49 Squadron's hangars, Scampton in the early 1940's.
(D Saxton)

MARCH 1942

3/4 March, 1942; BILLANCOURT: Bomber Command sent 235 bombers to attack the Renault Factory at Boulogne-Billancourt, just west of the centre of Paris; a factory which produced lorries for the German forces. The force attacked in 3 waves (most experienced crews first) flying at very low level and using numerous flares. All possible precautions were taken to avoid French civilian casualties.

49 Squadron's Operational Record Book states: '*9 aircraft detailed - 17.30hrs all airborne, reached and thoroughly bombed the primary target. All crews saw bursts and fires resulting. Conditions were perfect. The moon and excellent visibility making identification easy - absence of flak - a most successful operation in all respects'*. A report from HQ Bomber Command stated: 'Results appear colossal. Have to be seen to be believed - hardly a roof standing. Area around gasometer flattened. Tank repair shop shattered.' Over 300 bombs had fallen on the factory, destroying 40 per cent of the buildings and stopping production (estimated 2,300 vehicles) for 4 weeks.

Tragically, over 350 French civilians were killed in the attack, few having taken to the shelter before the bombing thinking the bombers were passing over bound for Germany. The raiding force suffered the loss of 1 Wellington.

49 SQUADRON ORDER OF BATTLE - 3/4 MARCH 1942

AT156	Hodges	Rushton	Ellis	Ash
AT227	Newmarch	Brown	Andrews	Clarke
AT179	Rawstorne	Mansbridge	Maloney	Short
AT180	Massey	Rand	Smith	Webley
P1310	De Mestre	Petersen	Bell	Whitfield
AT174	Andrews	Dunne	Gauld	Drew
P1314	Hill	Haddock	McGrenery	Jones
AE227	Davis	Manders	Griffiths	Smith
AE261	Alfrey	Black	Horne	Jones

8/9 March, 1942; ESSEN: The squadron detailed 14 Hampdens for the planned heavy attack on Essen Old Town. 1 aircraft cancelled and another suffered under-carriage collapse prior to take-off. Of the remaining 12 aircraft, 10 successfully bombed the primary target, 1 returned with intercom failure, landing at Waddington and another bombed an alternative target.

On a clear night, and despite the leading aircraft being fitted with 'Gee', the 211 bombers were prevented from making accurate attacks due to industrial ground haze. 8 aircraft failed to return; all 49's returned safely.

MARCH 1942

10/11 March, 1942; ESSEN: The squadron contributed 11 Hampdens for an attack on 'Point B' in Essen Old Town. It proved to be an evening of very mixed fortunes for the crews of 49 Squadron, as they took off to join a force of 126 Bombers. P/O Cook (AD980) and crew returned early with oil system trouble in both engines. Sgt Slingo (L4086) and crew failed to get their undercarriage to lock in the retracted position; unable to climb and maintain a satisfactory airspeed, they were forced to return to base. Intercom failure caused the early return of P/O Jeffreys (AT172) and crew, and a further aircraft returned after only 40 minutes due to the pilot being sick.

Only 5 of the unit's aircraft made bombing attacks, and these were on alternative targets. The Alfrey crew (L4086), whilst bombing fires in an estimated position of Essen, received numerous shrapnel holes in the fuselage, tail plane, flaps and both starboard and port wings, but a safe landing was made back at Scampton.

At 03.35hrs after returning from Essen, Sgt Freeman (AE241) and crew made a forced landing in a Kent field near Manston after becoming lost and low on fuel. Sgt Gaunt, the wireless operator/air gunner was slightly hurt in the incident. Four aircraft failed to return from the raid, and 1 of these came from 49 squadron; P/O Bill Andrews (AT174) and crew were sadly all killed when E-Echo was brought down over Germany. The crew are buried along side each other in the Reichswald Forest War Cemetery, near Kleve.

FTR AT174	P/O W.H.T. Andrews	Pilot	(Killed)
(EA-E)	Sgt S.T. Drew	W/AG	(Killed)
	P/O J.B. Dunne	A/OB	(Killed)
	Sgt A.A. Gauld	W/AG	(Killed)

12/13 March, 1942; MINELAYING/NICKELS: Nine aircraft were dispatched to lay mines in the Heligoland area and 1 to drop leaflets in the Lille district. P/O Kay (AE368) and crew successfully completed their leaflet sortie over Lille, whilst 7 of the gardeners planted in the right place. All aircraft returned safely to base.

17 March, 1942: P/O Derek Cook and P/O Bob Manders were both sadly killed when their Hampden flew into a hill in fog. The accident happened 11.25hrs at Derry Farm near Branscombe in Devon. The crew (including F/Sgt Jack Gadsby and Sgt Eric Clarke) had been detailed to ferry P1226 back to Scampton after it had been repaired. On the morning of the 17th, P/O's Cooke and Manders had taken the Hampden up for a brief test flight alone, when the accident happened. News got back to Scampton that Gadsby and Clarke had also been killed, but this was incorrect.

23 March, 1942: The squadron records state that F/O H.M. McGuffie was killed on this date, whilst on active service near Dunholme Lodge, Lincolnshire, on `Blind Approach Training'.

MARCH 1942

24/25 March, 1942; MINELAYING: Bomber Command dispatched 35 aircraft to lay mines off Lorient. The squadron sent 6 aircraft, all becoming airborne by 18.33hrs; all 6 were successful in placing their mines, and all returned safely, 1 to Upper Heyford and the others to Exeter aerodrome. Two aircraft from the force failed to return; one of these was a Lancaster from 44 Sqdn at Waddington; the first of this type to be lost during the war.

25/26 March, 1942; MINELAYING/NICKELS: The squadron sent 1 aircraft on a nickel sortie to Lille, and the crew returned to base safely. 6 further aircraft were detailed to lay mines off Bordeaux and all returned without any problems to Exeter.

26/27 March, 1942; MINELAYING: Five of the unit's Hampdens successfully placed mines off Bordeaux before returning safely to Chivenor.

28/29 March, 1942; LUBECK: In bright moonlight, 234 Bomber Command aircraft set out to attack the distant German target of Lubeck. A considerable percentage of the force made good their attacks which resulted in the target receiving very heavy damage. It proved to be the first major success for Bomber Command against a German target. The squadron contributed 10 aircraft for the assault, but 2 were soon forced to return early.

Sgt Burton (AT179) and crew had reached a point 5 miles east of Mablethorpe before engine trouble made them turn for home. The Alcock crew (AT196) also failed to reach the target area due to engine and heating trouble.

Around midnight, the squadron's remaining aircraft arrived over a clear target and most attacked between 9 to 10,000ft.

F/O Jeffreys (AT180) and crew were the last aircraft to land back at Scampton, touching down at 04.59hrs. All 49's aircraft had returned safely, but 7 Wellingtons, 3 Stirlings, 1 Hampden and 1 Manchester were reported missing.

31 March, 1942; Mole Operations: The squadron attempted 6 daylight bombing sorties into northern Germany, but all aircraft returned after 4 hours due to insufficient cloud cover.

HONOURS AND AWARDS - MARCH 1942

F/O Walker	D.F.C.
F/O Wood	D.F.C.

APRIL 1942

1/2 April, 1942; HANAU/LOHR: Thirty-five Wellingtons and 14 Hampdens were detailed to attack railway targets at low-level. The squadron sent 3 Hampdens all airborne by 20.10hrs. This experimental operation proved very costly, with 12 Wellingtons and 1 Hampden (144 Sqdn) failing to return.

Of 49's aircraft, 2 attacked alternative targets; the Alcock crew (AD870) bombed shipping off the Frisians, whilst Sgt Williams (AD931) and crew attacked lock gates, a small town and a crossroads. Both returned safely.

Meanwhile, the Burton crew (AT217) attacked a railway line near Langeoog. During the bombing run, they were heavily engaged by flak, and during violent evasive action the bombs fell into the sea. The aircraft received some structural damage from flak, but the crew were able to regain base.

Sgt Davis (AT196) and crew departed Scampton just after midnight, bound for Paris. They successfully dropped nickels over the target having made a good fix on the River Seine; they arrived safely back at Scampton at 06.25hrs.

5/6 April, 1942; COLOGNE/LEAFLETS: A mixed force of 263 bombers was sent to bomb Cologne on a night of poor visibility and thick cloud. 49 Squadron started taking off from Scampton during the first hour of Monday 6th, 11 Hampdens becoming airborne by 00.38hrs.

The attack on Cologne was scattered and stretched right across the city. As well as dropping bombs, aircraft also dropped leaflets within the target area. Five aircraft failed to return from the raid, 4 Wellingtons, and one 49 Squadron Hampden. A night fighter shot P/O Kay DFM (AT156) and crew down over Philippeville, Belgium. The pilot and Sgt Ainger were able to escape from the stricken aircraft to become POW's, but Sgt's Bob Brown and Jim Waddell were sadly killed; they rest side by side in Charleroi Cemetery, Belgium.

The squadron also dispatched 4 successful nickel sorties to a moonlit Lille. All aircraft returned safely to base where the Worthy crew (AD964) reported seeing 6 enemy aircraft on various headings, with no interceptions being made.

FTR AT156	P/O D. Kay DFM	Pilot	(P.o.W.)
(EA-C)	Sgt R.W.B. Brown	A/OB	(Killed)
	Sgt J. Waddell	W/AG	(Killed)
	Sgt S. Ainger		(P.o.W.)

APRIL 1942

6/7 April, 1942; ESSEN: This was a night of severe electrical storms and icing, as over 150 main force bombers attempted to continue the bombing campaign against Essen. Cloud over the target prevented most of the force finding the primary, with Essen reporting only light damage. 49 Squadron had provided 5 aircraft, of which the Ratcliffe crew (AD190) bombed the primary on an estimated ETA, 3 abandoned their attacks due to icing, and the fifth was reported missing. F/Sgt Leslie Davis (AT126) and crew are believed to have come down in the North Sea; the crew is remembered on the Runnymede Memorial. 4 other aircraft were reported missing from the operation.

FTR AT126	F/S L. Davis	Pilot	(Missing)
(EA-Z)	Sgt M. Griffiths	W/Ag	(Missing)
	Sgt C.A.V. Hartley RAAF	W/Ag	(Missing)
	Sgt D.P. Warmsley	A/OB	(Missing)

8/9 April, 1942; HAMBURG/NICKELS: Again electric storms and icing hampered a record number of 272 main force aircraft as they laboured towards Hamburg. The attack eventually turned out to be a failure. The squadron had sent 11 bombers, but due to the thick cloud and icing, just 6 aircraft bombed alternative targets, with the remainder being prevented from carrying out bombing sorties. All 49's Hampdens returned to base safely, whilst 4 Wellingtons and 1 Manchester were reported missing.

49 Squadron also dispatched 5 nickel sorties to Paris of which 3 were successful; 2 abandoned their tasks due to communication problems. All returned safely to Scampton.

10/11 April, 1942; ESSEN/NICKELS: Despite forecasts of clear weather conditions over the target, a main force consisting of over 250 bombers, found Essen covered in cloud. 49 Squadron had 13 Hampdens airborne of which 8 attacked the primary target but were unable to see the results.

The squadron also dispatched a single nickel sortie; the Gould crew (AD799) delivered their 'paper work' to Paris before returning safely to Scampton.

Bomber Command suffered the loss of 14 aircraft on the Essen raid, mainly due to the heavy flak defences in the Ruhr. Of the 5 Hampdens reported missing, 2 were from 49 Squadron: F/Lt Marshall (AT190) and Sgt Webster managed to escape from their downed bomber, but two fellow crew members perished when the aircraft came down in Germany; Sgt Bill Collins and Sgt Stuart Woodhead are both buried in the Reichswald Forest Cemetery.

F/O Reg Worthy (AE421) and crew were shot down by a night fighter flown by Reinhold Knacke of 2/NJG.1. The combat took place over Holland, with the doomed Hampden falling into the Ijsselmeer.

The body of F/O Worthy was recovered from the water's edge on 22nd May and that of Sgt Anthony Considine, at Laaxum four days later; his watch had stopped at 02.16hrs.

Sgt John Wilkinson is buried in Stavanger, Norway whilst the body of the fourth crew member, Sgt Tom McGrenery was never found; he is remembered at Runnymede.

FTR AT190	F/L C. Marshall	Pilot	(P.o.W.)
(EA-A)	Sgt W.A. Collins	W/Ag	(Killed)
	Sgt S. Woodhead	A/OB	(Killed)
	Sgt F. Webster	W/Ag	(P.o.W.)

FTR AE421	F/O R.P. Worthy	Pilot	(Killed)
(EA-P)	Sgt A.T.P. Considine	A/OB	(Killed)
	Sgt J.W. Wilkinson	A/G	(Killed)
	Sgt T.H. McGrenery	W/Ag	(Missing)

12/13 April, 1942; ESSEN/MINELAYING: This was another disappointing raid on Essen, in which 251 bombers were dispatched with only 173 claiming to have bombed the primary target.

The squadron sent 12 aircraft on operational sorties this night; 11 to bomb Essen whilst the Gould crew (AT191) carried out a successful gardening trip in the Le Havre area.

In poor visibility and with icing problems, only 2 aircraft claimed to have attacked the primary target. Five aircraft suffered engine trouble forcing the abandonment of their sorties. The Cumming crew (AT228), struggling to keep height on a faulty engine, jettisoned their bombs 'safe' over France. They were then intercepted by an enemy night fighter, and in the ensuing battle, the Hampden received structural damage to the port main plane and centre section. The crew valiantly fought off their attacker and eventually escaped, returning to Scampton just after midnight

After successfully bombing Essen from 14,000ft, Sgt pilot James (AT196) and crew arrived back over England in the early hours of Monday 13th, desperately short of fuel. Flying at 5,300ft the engines suddenly cut out - the pilot gave the order to bale out before leaving the aircraft himself. Tragically the remainder of the crew failed to get out in time and all three were killed in the crash. The Hampden dived into the ground at Chamberlain Charity Farm, Fitling near Aldbrough in Yorkshire. The remainder of the 49 Squadron returned safely, but 10 aircraft were reported missing from the Essen raid.

Crashed AT196	Sgt James	Pilot	(Safe)
(EA-)	Sgt H. Taylor	W/Ag	(Killed)
	Sgt J.T. Smith	A/G	(Killed)
	Sgt W.J. Marshall	A/OB	(Killed)

APRIL 1942

14/15 April, 1942; DORTMUND: The squadron contributed 7 aircraft to the main force attack on Dortmund. Of these, 3 returned early with engine failure, 3 attacked alternative targets and 1 aircraft failed to return. The raid itself was very scattered with bombs falling over a wide area of the Ruhr. Bomber Command suffered the loss of 5 Wellingtons and 4 Hampdens.

The missing 49 Squadron Hampden was piloted by P/O Williams. It is thought that he and his crew were caught by a night fighter, which brought their aircraft down in Germany. The pilot and Sgt Ralph, an air gunner, survived to become POW's. Sadly Sgt Horace Brown and Sgt Leslie Webbe were killed; they rest along side each other in the Reichswald Forest Cemetery at Kleve in Germany.

FTR AD931	P/O H.G. Williams	Pilot	(P.o.W.)
(EA-X)	Sgt H.S. Brown	W/Ag	(Killed)
	Sgt L.W. Webbe	A/OB	(Killed)
	Sgt W. Ralph	A/G	(P.o.W.)

15/16 April, 1942; DORTMUND/NICKELS: The squadron detailed 5 aircraft for bombing Dortmund and 1 for a nickel sortie to Lille. The Read crew (AD965) successfully carried out the nickel operation dropping their leaflets from 11,000ft over the primary.

In conditions of thick cloud and icing, only the Floyd crew (AD799) found and bombed Dortmund. Of the others, 3 located and attacked alternative targets. Sgt Slingo and crew (AT217) found it impossible to identify the target due to the thick cloud; they returned with their 2,000lb bomb to Scampton.

Of the 152 aircraft dispatched, 3 Wellingtons and 1 Stirling failed to return.

16/17 April, 1942; MINELAYING: Two crews were dispatched from Scampton to lay mines in the Lorient area. The light and visibility were extremely poor, and the Read crew (AD980) were unable to fix their position so returned home with their load. The James crew (AT180) managed to get a fix on Belle Island and were able to place their mine in the alternative area from 700 feet at 00.42hrs. They returned safely to Scampton touching down at 04.25hrs.

Friday 17th April, 1942: A notable day for 49 Squadron, for on this day the unit received its first 3 Avro Manchesters. Since January, 49 had witnessed 83 Squadron's trials and tribulations with this notorious type, knowing all too well that their time was soon to come. As if to rub salt into the wound, whilst 49 Squadron began working up on the Manchester, they were forced to watch enviously as 83 re-equipped with the mighty Lancaster.

APRIL 1942

MANCHESTERS

It was not intended for the squadron to operate the Avro Manchester, merely to 'work up' on the type in preparation for the Lancaster. Consequently the unit received mainly early Mk I Manchesters; several of which were not fitted with mid-upper turrets.

49 Squadron was destined to have a brief but tragic operational association with the Manchester and would achieve the dubious distinction of suffering the highest percentage loss rate of any other Manchester unit.

17/18 April, 1942; HAMBURG: The squadron began to run down the number of Hampdens available for operations, as crews began preparing for operations on the Avro Manchester. When orders were received for an attack on Hamburg, the unit offered just 5 aircraft.

Joining a force of 170 plus aircraft, these 5 crews experienced industrial haze in the target area. 3 of the unit's Hampdens released their bombs on alternative targets whilst the other 2 attacked last resort targets. All 49's aircraft returned to base, but the main force suffered the loss of 7 Wellingtons and 1 Manchester.

19/20 April, 1942; MINELAYING: On the evening of Sunday 19th April, the squadron dispatched 3 aircraft to lay mines in the Terschelling area. All 3 Hampdens were airborne from Scampton by 20.46hrs, crossing the Lincolnshire coast near Mablethorpe heading for Ameland.

Two of the aircraft carried out their sorties in very difficult conditions. In extreme darkness and haze, both crews were forced to carry out time and distance runs to plant their vegetables, before returning to base. The third aircraft was reported 'missing without trace'; Sgt Frank Slingo (AT217) and crew are believed to have come down in the North Sea off the Frisian Islands. On 13 July, the body of F/Sgt Ernie Jackson was washed ashore on the island of Rottumeroog. The pilot is buried in Sage War Cemetery near Oldenburg, Germany. The bodies of Sgt Ian McLaren and Sgt Ray Webley were never found, and they are remembered on the Runnymede Memorial.

They were the final Hampden crew to be lost by 49 Squadron during the Second World War.

FTR AT217	Sgt F.W. Slingo	Pilot	(Killed)
(EA-S)	F/S E.W. Jackson	W/Ag	(Killed)
	Sgt I. McLaren	A/OB	(Missing)
	Sgt R.J. Webley	W/Ag	(Missing)

22/23 April, 1942; MINELAYING: The squadron sent 3 Hampdens to place mines in the Kiel Fjord. The Read crew (AT180) returned early when their starboard engine failed.
The remaining two aircraft placed their mines in the alternative target area.

This treasured snapshot shows Don Deeley (second from left) and colleagues in front of AT217 S-Sugar, only days before the Hampden failed to return from ops 19/20-4-42. Don was the artist responsible for the 'Eagle' emblem painted on Sugar's nose. (D. Deeley)

23/24 April, 1942; ROSTOCK: Whilst the majority of the 160 plus main force made an incendiary attack on this distant Baltic port, a small force of 5 Group aircraft went after the Heinkel aircraft factory just outside the town.

49 Squadron briefed 3 crews for the Heinkel attack, with take-off set at 21.45hrs. Bob Hamer (AT227) lifted the last of the 3 Hampdens detailed off Scampton's grass runway at 21.47hrs. The Hamer crew had the honour of being the last 49 Squadron Hampden crew to take-off on an operational sortie.

ORDER OF BATTLE 23/24-4-42

AT178	Read	Kirby	Andrews	Cane
AT191	Bond	Valentine	Potter	Grain
AT227	Hamer	Laidlow	Minchin	Welch

Bombing conditions were good and all three Captains reported seeing their bombs burst in the target area. All 3 aircraft returned safely to Scampton, the last one landing at 06.31hrs.

APRIL 1942

26 April, 1942: 49 Sqdn received a large influx of additional aircrew personnel, all posted in from No 25 Operational Training Unit at Finningley. It was at this former unit that the new intake had been trained on the Avro Manchester.

FAREWELL TO THE HAMPDEN

The Rostock raid marked the end of 49 Squadron's operational association with the Handley Page Hampden; an aircraft type which they had introduced into R.A.F. service and carried out the first operational Hampden sorties of the war. On Monday 27 April, 49 Squadron said their final farewell to the Hampden when all the remaining aircraft were allotted away to 144 Squadron. The unit now looked forward with trepidation to ops on Manchesters, they also reflected on the final month of Hampden ops which showed a loss of no less than 7 aircraft... and their gallant crews.

HONOURS AND AWARDS - APRIL 1942

F/O R.A.P. Allsebrook	D.F.C.
F/S T.W. Bell	D.F.M.

49 Squadron carried out more Hampden sorties than any other squadron in 5 Group Bomber Command.

Avro Manchester MK 1. Illustration by John Ward

MAY 1942

THE MANCHESTER ERA - A DANGEROUS LIAISON

1 May, 1942; On the morning of Friday 1 May, the posted strength of 49 Squadron stood at 29 Officers and 655 Airmen.

Aircraft held on charge: 11 Avro Manchesters, which represented the operational equipment, with a further 7 Manchesters awaited. The squadron also held 1 Puss Moth and 1 Tiger Moth for training purposes.

2/3 May, 1942; RENNES-NICKELS: At 10.30hrs the squadron received orders from Group detailing 5 Manchesters to drop leaflets in the Rennes area. The Order of Battle for this, the squadron's first Manchester operation was as follows:

L7469	L7386	L7287	R5771	L7484
P/O Farrington	P/O Jeffreys	P/O Perry	P/O Shackleton	F/S Carter
P/O Catty	P/O Ransome	P/O Watts	Sgt Lowson	Sgt Haynes
Sgt Gould	F/S Lewis	Sgt Haines	Sgt Minchin	F/S James
Sgt Hogg	Sgt Maloney	Sgt Clyde	Sgt Patey	Sgt Yeates
Sgt Astbury	Sgt Middleton	Sgt Rudge	Sgt Shannon	Sgt Halliday
Sgt Millett	Sgt Clarke	Sgt Steer	Sgt Miles	Sgt Probert
Sgt White	Sgt Harrison	Sgt Gibbs		F/S Whitehill

All 5 aircraft were airborne from Scampton by 21.00hrs, with an estimated time over the target area at around midnight. Four aircraft successfully carried out their sorties over Rennes; F/Sgt Carter (L7484) reported flak and searchlights in the vicinity but they were not troublesome.

The fifth aircraft, that piloted by P/O Jeffreys (L7386) had an unserviceable DR compass and the crew were forced to drop their nickels over a last resort target. All aircraft were safely back at Scampton by 03.15hrs.

4/5 May, 1942; AMIENS-NICKELS: Two Manchester crews were sent to drop leaflets in the area of Amiens. Sgt Burton (L7287) and crew approached the target at 11,000ft shortly before 23.30hrs. Ground haze prevented positive identification, so a time and distance run was made upwind dropping the leaflets on ETA. P/O Floyd (L7398) and crew arrived 30 minutes later, dropping their leaflets from 10,000ft. Both aircraft returned safely to base.

7/8 May, 1942; HELIGOLAND-MINELAYING: Bomber Command dispatched 81 aircraft on minelaying operations. 49 Squadron contributed 4 Manchesters, on what proved to be an unsuccessful night for the squadron. Take-off was at intervals starting shortly after midnight. P/O Shackleton and crew had to transfer to the reserve aircraft (L7421) which made them late taking off, with insufficient time in which to reach the primary target and return to base before dawn, the Shackleton crew reluctantly abandoned their sortie and returned to Scampton.

P/O Farrington (R5771) and crew were within 40 minutes of the target area when their port engine started giving trouble. The mine was dropped safe from 1,000ft and the crew returned safely to Scampton, despite being fired at by a British naval convoy off Spurn Head.

F/Sgt Carter (L7484) and crew found the weather conditions unfavourable and the crew returned their mine to base.

P/O Jeffreys (L7386) and crew carried out their sortie in ideal weather conditions, the mine being seen to enter the water; they landed back at Scampton at 06.03hrs.

9/10 May, 1942; HELIGOLAND-MINELAYING: The unit returned again to lay mines north of Heligoland, when two crews, piloted by F/Sgt Carter (L7287) and P/O Floyd (R5771) successfully carried out their sorties in ideal conditions. Both aircraft were back at Scampton by 05.30hrs.

Scampton Station Sick Quarters Staff circa May 1942.(Mrs D. Smith)

MAY 1942

WING COMMANDER LEONARD CAIN SLEE

13 May, 1942: On Wednesday 13 May, the squadron welcomed W/Cmdr Leonard Slee to the unit; he arrived for duty at Scampton, having formerly been at Coningsby. On the 14th, W/Cmdr Slee commenced an illustrious association with the unit, when he officially assumed command of 49 Squadron from W/Cmdr Stubbs DFC, who was posted to H.Q. No 92 Group at Winslow.

49 SQUADRON'S CONVERSION FLIGHT

18 May, 1942: The squadron received authority to form a third flight to be known as the Conversion unit. S/Ldr Peter Ward-Hunt (formerly of 207 Sqdn) was appointed to command the unit which initially held on strength 2 Lancasters and 2 Manchesters.

Provisional personnel posted this new unit included the following:

8	Flight mechanics (airframes)	12	Flight mechanics (engines)
1	Equipment assistant	4	Instrument repairers
1	Wireless operator	1	Equipment Assistant
3	Armourers		

This was the first positive indication to aircrew, that the much awaited re-equipment to Lancasters was on the horizon.

19 May, 1942: The 6 aircraft detailed for minelaying sorties, were stood down at 16.00hrs, when the operation was cancelled. That evening, 4 of the unit's aircraft did take-off for a searchlight co-operation exercise over London.

Whilst over Grantham, F/Sgt Freeman and crew (L7287) were in collision with a Lancaster of 83 Squadron. Cpl Trevor Simpson has cause to remember the occasion well as he recalls:

"83 only had to change a wing tip, we had to change a mainplane. Whilst we were changing the mainplane (which took a long time waiting for a new one to come through) the Manchester was cannibalised for other items. I'm pleased to say someone else had the task of making the kite serviceable again for the Cologne raid. Fortunately, as parts had been removed, they were replaced by the duff item with a label stating that it was deficient."

MAY 1942

GROUND LOOP!

During this period, Trevor Simpsom remembers an incident involving the unit's Tiger Moth:

"One of our Manchesters was being run up outside the hangar at Scampton just as the Group Captain and Wingco taxied across the rear of it in the Tiger Moth... and whoops!... over it flipped, ending up-side down with the two exalted gentlemen hanging from their straps, not wishing to let go in case they dropped on their heads and breaking their necks in the process."

One is left to wonder if those at the controls of the Manchester were aware of the Tiger Moth (and its occupants) as it passed behind them!

24 May, 1942: F/Sgt D.H. Rowlands, Pilot, (formerly of 97 Sqdn) was posted to the squadron and immediately attached to the Conversion Flight. Records show that during the Conversion Flight's existence, at least 3 Lancasters were used for training; R5850 and R5855 were both ex-83 Squadron (but had not operated with that squadron). A third aircraft, W4258 was also used. It was R5850 in which F/Sgt Rowlands flew 49 Squadron's first operational Lancaster sortie. All 3 Lancasters were eventually transferred to 1661 Conversion Unit when that unit was formed later in the year.

25 MAY, 1942: JACK GADSBY DFM

A short line in Eric Clarke's diary reads; 'F/Sgt Jack Gadsby DFM (67 Ops on Hampdens) posted - I am appointed i/c 'B' Flt Wireless Ops.' A/C2 John Gadsby started his remarkable operational association with the Hampden with F/Lt Lerwill and crew, against the "Deutchland" in December 1939, and it concluded on 19/20 April, 1942 with his final trip to Terschelling with the Burton crew (AT180). By then, Jack had completed an astounding 67 operational flights in Hampdens, including the famous Dortmund-Ems attack in which Learoyd earned his Victoria Cross.

Very few men can claim such a proud record and justly, Jack Gadsby DFM is held in extremely high esteem by his fellow 49er survivors.

30/31 May, 1942; COLOGNE (THE FIRST 1,000 BOMBER RAID)

The Squadron was able to detail 13 aircraft, but 1 became unserviceable and had to be withdrawn. The maximum effort required resulted in 83 Squadron borrowing 3 Manchesters from 49's Conversion Flight.

With a full moon beginning to rise, 49's Manchesters (along with 13 Lancasters from 83 Squadron) started taking off from Scampton at 22.50hrs. A record 1,047 aircraft were dispatched, of which sadly, a record 41 failed to return.

MAY 1942

The Cologne attack was a dramatic success for Bomber Command and a great boost to the morale of the country. This 1,000 bomber raid, and the two that followed, would be a turning point in the history of Bomber Command. The publicity confirmed Bomber Command as one of the main forces taking the war to the enemy, and its commander 'Bomber' Harris would forever remain in the public eye.

The following, is a brief account of 49 Squadron's performance on the night of 30/31 May, taken from the post operational intelligence reports.

L7287 F/Lt Paramore - Take-off 22.50hrs - Landed 04.10hrs.
"Bombs dropped on target. Fired on by unidentified aircraft but not damaged".

L7290 P/O Floyd - Take-off 22.55hrs. - *"Aircraft FAILED TO RETURN from operation".*

L7389 Sgt Burton - Take-off 22.58hrs.
"Dropped bombs on target. Engine and airframe trouble plus intercom failure".

L7429 F/Sgt Carter - Take-off 23.00hrs - *"Aircraft FAILED TO RETURN from operation".*

R5775 P/O Jeffreys - Take-off 23.03hrs - Landed 04.42.
"Load dropped on target and bursts seen. Successful in every respect".

L7524 P/O Perry - Take-off 23.05hrs - Landed 23.50hrs.
"Aircraft started to vibrate and lost height. Landed at Docking after 45 minutes flying".

R5794 P/O Shackleton - Take-off 23.08hrs - Landed 03.40hrs - *"All bombs dropped on target".*

L7479 P/O Farrington - Take-off 23.10hrs - Landed 05.17hrs.
"Target easily located and bombs dropped".

L7526 S/Ldr Bennett - Take-off 23.11hrs - Landed 03.37hrs
"Bombs dropped in city west of river. Target was visible over 100 miles away".

L7421 F/Sgt Lewis - Take-off 23.13hrs - Landed 04.23hrs.
"All bombs dropped on target. Bursts not seen owing to evasive action being taken".

L7493 S/Ldr Ward-Hunt (with W/Cmdr Slee) - Take-off 23.20hrs - Landed 04.07hrs.
"Bombs dropped from 10,000ft at 01.16hrs. Excellent conditions in every respect".

L7398 F/Sgt Rowlands - Take-off - Landed 03.47hrs.
"Bombs dropped in target area. Followed by JU 88 which approached twice but broke away on evasive action being taken".

MAY 1942

The squadron suffered its first Manchester casualties when 2 aircraft failed to return from Cologne:

P/O Philip Floyd (L7290) held his flak shattered aircraft steady whilst his grateful crew jumped to safety. Before the pilot could escape, the aircraft plunged into the ground instantly killing P/O Floyd and front gunner, Sgt John Smith. Those crew members who escaped by parachute landing in the Mulheim-Oberhausen area. The 2nd pilot, Sgt Randall RAAF, was posted missing, but the remaining 4 crew members survived to become POW's.

P/O John Carter (L7429) and crew came down in the North Sea. The crew remain officially 'missing without trace'; they are remembered on the Runnymede Memorial.

FTR L7290	P/O P.N. Floyd	Pilot	(Killed)
(EA-)	Sgt D.E. Randall RAAF	2nd Pilot	(P.o.W.)
	Sgt J.R. Valentine	NAV	(P.o.W.)
	Sgt F.E. Woodrow RNZAF	W/AG	(P.o.W.)
	Sgt J. Smith	A/G	(Killed)
	Sgt E. Probert	A/G	(P.o.W.)
	Sgt J.F. Wight	A/G	(P.o.W.)

FTR L7429	P/O J.P. Carter	Pilot	(Missing)
(EA-)	F/S D. Block	2nd Pilot	(Missing)
	Sgt G.C. Haynes	NAV	(Missing)
	Sgt L.J. Yeates	W/AG	(Missing)
	Sgt M.S. Ash	A/G	(Missing)
	Sgt A.G. Welch RAAF	A/G	(Missing)
	Sgt J.C. Ramsey	A/G	(Missing)

HONOURS AND AWARDS - MAY 1942

S/Ldr P.M. de Mestre D.F.C.	D.S.O.
S/Ldr P.D.S. Bennett D.F.C.	Bar to D.F.C.
F/Lt L.P. Massey A.F.C.	D.F.C.
S/Ldr I.D. Hodges	D.F.C.
F/Lt L.F. Ratcliff	D.F.C.

JUNE 1942

1/2 June, 1942; ESSEN: On Monday 1 June, Bomber Command carried out a 2nd planned 1,000 bomber raid, this time to Essen. The actual force dispatched, amounted to 956 aircraft, the majority being Wellingtons. It was some Wellington crews from 3 Group that provided 'raid leaders', who were tasked to drop flares in the target area.

By the beginning of June, 49 Squadron could boast 15 Manchesters on unit strength, of which 8 were detailed for the Essen raid. A ninth aircraft, a Lancaster from 49's Conversion Flight was also put on the Battle Order. The bombing of Essen proved to be very scattered, mainly due to the ground haze and layers of low cloud.

The following are brief extracts from the intelligence reports and those given by returning 49 Squadron crews:

Lancaster R5850 F/Sgt Rowlands - 49's first Lancaster sortie.
"Attacked primary from 16,000ft at 01.06hrs".

Manchester L7389 S/Ldr De Mestre - Take-off 00.56 (70 mins late) owing to engine trouble.
"Unable to reach Dutch coast on time. Trip unsuccessful".

Manchester L7493 Sgt Burton -
"Attacked from 9,500ft at 01.29hrs. Slight damage by heavy flak".

Manchester L7398 P/O Perry -
"Attacked from 11,000ft at 02.00hrs in moonlight. Large fires seen. Shrapnel hit rear turret".

Manchester L7526 P/O Jeffreys -
"Primary attacked from 9,000ft at 02.02hrs. Bomb bursts seen in target area, large fires started".

Manchester L7479 P/O Farrington - Late start (00.50hrs)
"Aircraft returned to base as there was insufficient time to reach the target".

Manchester R5775 F/Lt Paramore -
"Attacked primary target from 9,000ft at 01.50hrs. Line of bursts seen. Weather good".

Manchester L7421 F/Sgt Lewis -
"Attacked primary from 9,000ft at 02.15hrs. Bombs dropped in large concentration of fires".

Manchester R5794 P/O Shackleton - *"Aircraft failed to return".*

A total of 31 bombers failed to return from the Essen raid; 15 wellingtons, 8 Halifaxes, 4 Lancasters, 1 Hampden, 1 Stirling, 1 Whitley and 1 Manchester... the Manchester being from 49 Squadron:

An SOS distress signal was received from P/O Bill Shackleton (R5794) and crew at 02.19hrs saying that the starboard engine was unserviceable and a fix given... sadly nothing further was received. The Manchester came to earth near Arendonk in Belgium, killing 5 members of the crew. Although specific information is currently not available, it is confirmed that Sgt's Shannon and Nolan survived to become POW's.

FTR R5794	P/O W.C. Shackleton	Pilot	(Killed)
	F/S R.H.H. Garratt	2nd Pilot	(Killed)
	Sgt G.J.A. Miles	A/G	(Killed)
	Sgt E.A. Patey	A/G	(Killed)
	Sgt F.W.M. Wilson	A/OB	(Killed)
	Sgt R.C. Shannon	W/AG	(P.o.W.)
	Sgt C.D. Nolan	W/AG	(P.o.W.)

3/4 June, 1942; LILLE - NICKELS: In bright moonlight, 2 Manchesters from the squadron departed Scampton during the early hours of June 4th. Their task was to drop leaflets in the Lille area of France.
Despite the ground being covered in a heavy haze, the crews of Sgt Webster (L7325) and P/O Elliot (L7287) both carried out their sorties successfully and returned to base, landing shortly after 05.00hrs.

5/6 June, 1942; RENNES - NICKELS: W/Cmdr Slee (L7469) and crew carried out a single leaflet dropping sortie to Rennes. The trip was successful, but not without incident as the crew's terse de-brief indicates: 'Photoflash went off before reaching target - all W/T services u/s - IFF eventually made to work.' One notable aspect of the sortie is that the pilot managed to coax his mount up to 15,000ft over the target area.

6/7 June, 1942; EMDEN: In good weather conditions, a main force of 233 aircraft set out to attack the German town of Emden. With only a slight ground haze over the target, successful bombing results were achieved by the crews. 49 Squadron detailed 7 aircraft for the operation, but only 5 managed to become airborne from Scampton by 23.30hrs. During their approach to the target, P/O Farrington (L7479) and crew struggled to reach a safe operational bombing height. They attempted to jettison some of the load in order to reduce weight, but unfortunately all the load fell away.

F/Sgt Lewis (L7524) and crew bombed the centre of the town at 01.30hrs from 10,000ft, then 15 minutes later Sgt Webster (L7526) and crew crossed the town at 14,000ft to drop their load on the eastern side of the target.

The price of success was paid for in the loss of 9 crews out of the total force - 3 Manchesters, 3 Wellingtons, 2 Stirlings and 1 Halifax failed to return.

Tragically, two extremely experienced aircraft captains and their crews from 49 Squadron were amongst those reported missing: Five crew members of the aircraft piloted by S/Ldr Peter De Mestre DSO DFC (L7469) were killed and the captain plus two others were reported missing.

A second crew, that piloted by F/Lt Roger Paramore DFC (L7287) came down in the sea; they have never been recovered. In the space of just one week, the Manchester's heinous reputation had been proven within 49 Squadron, after the grievous loss of 5 aircraft and 35 airmen.

FTR L7469	S/L P.M. De Mestre DSO DFC	Pilot	(Missing)
	Sgt A.F. Buttel RAAF	2nd Pilot	(Killed)
	P/O R.H.J. Thorndyke	A/OB	(Missing)
	F/S M.E. Whitehill RAAF	A/G	(Killed)
	Sgt G.C. Whitfield	W/AG	(Killed)
	Sgt L.J. Jones	W/AG	(Missing)
	Sgt D.S. Halliday	W/AG	(Killed)
FTR L7287	F/L R.E.R. Paramore DFC	Pilot	(Missing)
	Sgt H. Whittemore	2nd Pilot	(Missing)
	P/O H.J. Vincent	A/OB	(Missing)
	Sgt H.C. Hood	W/AG	(Missing)
	Sgt A. Logie	W/AG	(Missing)
	Sgt R.H. Seaton	A/G	(Missing)
	Sgt J.H. Pollock	A/G	(Missing)

Whilst the main force continued with bombing operations, the squadron's Manchesters were not called upon to take part. The usual practice training flights were still carried out.

20 June, 1942: At 11.30hrs, on the morning of Saturday 20th June, the squadron was asked to provide 4 Manchesters for a sea search. The previous evening, Bomber Command had attacked Emden and 9 aircraft had failed to return - a sea search was made in case any of these aircraft had ditched.

It was an ironic tragedy, when a 49 Squadron crew, that piloted by Sgt John O'Brien RAAF and Sgt Charles Goldring (L7387) crashed into the sea themselves. Only two bodies were ever recovered, that of Sgt Terence McKenna RAAF and Sgt Price RAAF. Their fellow crew members are remembered on the Runnymede Memorial.

FTR L7387	Sgt J.O. O'Brien RAAF	Pilot	(Missing)
	Sgt C.E. Goldring	Pilot	(Missing)
	Sgt T.F.B. McKenna RAAF	A/OB	(Killed)
	Sgt H.W. Price RAAF	W/AG	(Killed)
	Sgt K. Allen RAAF		(Missing)
	Sgt N.J. Rogers		(Missing)
	Sgt A. Garos		(Missing)

25/26 June, 1942; BREMEN: Every type of aircraft available in Bomber Command was assembled for the third 'Thousand Force' attack, this time to attack the town of Bremen: 472 Wellingtons; 124 Halifaxes; 96 Lancasters; 69 Stirlings 51 Blenheims; 50 Hampdens; 50 Whitleys; 24 Bostons; 20 Manchesters; 4 Mosquitoes:

With Coastal Command and the Army Co-Operation Command providing a further 107 Wellingtons and Hudsons, the total force amounted to 1,067 aircraft... greater than the first 'thousand' raid on Cologne.

This was the last time Bomber Command would employ the Avro Manchester on operations. 49 Squadron, one of the last Manchester units, detailed 6 Manchesters and 1 Lancaster for the Bremen raid. When take-off time came, just 4 aircraft from the squadron (along with aircraft from 83 Squadron) actually became airborne; 3 Manchesters (49 Sqdn) departed Scampton just before 23.30hrs, followed shortly after midnight by W/Cmdr Slee (R5850) and crew in one of the Conversion unit's Lancasters. Just 36 minutes after departure, the W/Cmdr and crew were back at Scampton, the hydraulics on their Lanc having failed. The unit's 3 Manchesters went on to complete successful bombing attacks as follows:

L7453 (EA-T)	Take-off 23.22hrs	Landed 04.06hrs	
Sgt Heard	Sgt Lewis	Sgt Hartley	Sgt Short
Sgt Gibbs	Sgt Reynolds	Sgt Franklin	

'Alternative target - town of Bremen attacked from 8,000ft at 01.40hrs. Cloud 9/10ths. Visibility above cloud good. Bombs dropped in Bremen area but results not seen."

R5788	Take-off 23.23hrs	Landed 05.12hrs	
Sgt Webster	Sgt Copestake	Sgt Osborne	Sgt Delatorre
Sgt Cowan	Sgt Evison	Sgt Arnold	

'Attacked alternative - town of Bremen at 01.40hrs from 12,500ft from the north. Cloud 10/10ths. Bombed what was taken to be the target from reflections of fires on cloud."

R5772	Take-off 23.24hrs	Landed 05.29hrs	
P/O Elliot	Sgt Laidlaw	Sgt Clarke	Sgt Cullen
Sgt Ross	Sgt Bolton	Sgt Cumberland	

'Attacked alternative target - the town of Bremen. 10/10ths cloud with occasional breaks. Results of bombing not seen. Considerable number of fires in target area."

(The last 49 Sqdn Manchester to land from operations).

The Bremen raid, whilst not as destructive as the Cologne attack, was much more successful than the Essen 'Thousand' raid. Strong winds during the bombing, fanned fires which spread throughout the town. A total of 53 aircraft failed to return from the operation. This proved to be 49's final operation using the Avro Manchester.

A very well known, but a classic contemporary photograph showing two 49 Squadron Manchesters, (EA-T) and (EA-K), lining up with Lancasters of 83 Squadron prior to take off from Scampton's grass, bound for Bremen. Sgt Heard and crew are at the controls of Manchester L7453 (EA-T). It is interesting to note that this photograph was taken after 23.00hrs, but it is daylight (Double British summertime). On the original print, a Manchester can be seen flying from right to left centre of picture, and what appears to be an Oxford is approaching from the left (under the Lancaster's Merlin). (RAF Scampton)

JULY 1942

July was a month of intensive training, as the squadron 'worked up' on the Avro Lancaster. Using newly delivered Lancasters as well as the Manchesters, both the 'old lags' and those airmen freshly posted in from OTU's trained hard together. Training consisted of local flying both day and night, practice bombing and air firing practice, cross country exercises, fighter affiliation and searchlight co-operation flights. Team work between the ground staff and the flyers, all under the leadership of S/Ldr Slee, forged 49 Squadron into a highly motivated front-line Lancaster unit, which emerged ready for operations by the end of July 1942.

49 SQUADRON'S FIRST ALL LANCASTER OPERATION

31 July/1 August, 1942; DÜSSELDORF: Orders for an operation were received on 30 July detailing 11 aircraft, but just 2 hours before take-off the trip was cancelled. It appeared that July would now slip by without an operation being mounted by the squadron, the first time since the war began. Then at 10.00hrs on the morning of Friday 31st, the teleprinter rattled out orders for an attack on Düsseldorf.

Eleven aircraft were prepared, and at 00.33hrs (technically August) S/Ldr Barnard (R5890) and crew lifted the first of 49's eleven Lancasters away from Scampton. The Battle Order consisted of the following aircraft:

R5890	S/Ldr Barnard	R5744	S/Ldr Couch	R5762	F/O Bonnett
R5751	F/O Wright	R5658	P/O Elliot	R5896	F/Sgt Lewis
R5892	P/O Farrington	R5889	P/O Green	R5752	W/Cmdr Slee
R5757	F/Sgt Webster	No Number	F/O Ransome.		

Of these aircraft - 9 attacked Düsseldorf, F/Sgt Lewis (R5896) and crew bombed Texel aerodrome and P/O Farrington's (R5892) aircraft suffered a failure in the fuel system forcing the crew to abandon their task and return home.

All 49's aircraft returned safely, S/Ldr Couch and crew being the last to land at 06.52hrs. On a night when Bomber Command operated 630 aircraft - 16 Wellingtons, 5 Hampdens, 4 Halifaxes, 2 Lancasters and 2 Whitleys failed to return.

49 Squadron suffered the highest percentage Manchester loss rate in Bomber Command

AUGUST 1942

On Saturday 1 August, 1942, the posted strength of 49 Squadron stood at: 39 Officers and 534 Airmen. Aircraft held amounted to 17 Lancasters - with 1 Lancaster still outstanding.

Languishing out on 49's dispersals were 12 redundant Manchester aircraft all awaiting disposal.

In the corner of one hangar resided the Tiger Moth and Puss Moth.

11/12 August, 1942; NICKELS-VICHY: Just 3 of the unit's aircraft were detailed for individual leaflet dropping sorties over Vichy; all completed successfullyand returned to base.

12/13 August, 1942; NICKELS-AMIENS: P/O John Lowrie (L7567) and crew successfully carried out a leaflet sortie over France, and returned safely to Scampton just after midnight.

GOODBYE TO 83 SQUADRON

15 August, 1942: It had been decided at Bomber Command HQ., that 83 Squadron would be the first Lancaster unit in the newly formed Pathfinder Force. Saturday morning of 15 August, saw 83 Squadron depart Scampton, which had been their home for the last three years. With much friendly ribaldry mixed with a large amount of emotion, 49 personnel said farewell to their sister squadron. Both units had come through very tough times together, but despite their sometimes open rivalry they always shared a common bond; now, as 83 departed for its new home at RAF Wyton, that special link would be forever broken.

15/16 August, 1942; DÜSSELDORF/MINELAYING: On a very dark and hazy night, 131 bombers were sent to attack Düsseldorf. In poor visibility the bombing was scattered and little damage was inflicted. 49 Squadron detailed 11 Lancasters for the bombing operation, whilst 2 further aircraft went minelaying off the Frisians. Of the bombers, 9 attacked the primary target.

W/Cmdr Slee (R5752) and crew were unable to identify the primary so attacked a built up area in the Ruhr.

F/Lt Cooke (W4107) took off 33 minutes late due to compass and IFF failures; unable to reach the target in time, the crew elected to bomb Rotterdam docks as an alternative.

P/O McDonald (R5757) and crew dropped their mines in the allocated position.

P/O Lowrie and crew's efforts were thwarted by low cloud and rain; they returned to base with a full load.

All 49's aircraft returned safely from operations, although 2 Lancasters, 1 Wellington and 1 Hampden were lost on the Düsseldorf raid whilst 1 Stirling failed to return from minelaying.

AUGUST 1942

Scampton circa August 1942: 49 Squadron Gunnery Section under the command of F/Lt Rogers. Photograph was taken outside of No 2 Hangar. (Jack Dolman)

17/18 August, 1942; OSNABRUCK: The squadron contributed 12 aircraft for an attack on Osnabruk. Conditions over the target were reported as fair, with 6/10ths cloud. 9 of the unit's aircraft claimed to have attacked the primary. A further 2 bombed what they believed to be Osnabruk and 1 crew could not identify anything on the ground so made their attack on two small fires.

Of 139 aircraft dispatched by Command, 5 were reported missing; all 49's returned safely.

18/19 August, 1942; FLENSBURG: This was the first time that the recently formed Pathfinder Force was employed; they contributed 31 of the 118 aircraft dispatched. Winds were encountered over the target which had not been forecast. Although half the Pathfinders claimed to have marked the target... and with the majority of the main force reporting that they had bombed the right place, Flensburg was not actually hit.

49 Squadron had 11 Lancasters airborne, all detailed to attack the submarine building yard at Flensburg; 8 claimed success on the primary, 1 bombed Flensburg Fjord and 1 attacked a built up area in Flensburg.

P/O Perry (R5896) and crew failed to complete their sortie due to their engines overheating. S/Ldr Barnard (R5890) and crew had the pleasure of taking G/Cpt Whitworth (Scampton Station Commander) along on this trip.

All 49's aircraft returned safely, but the force lost 4 aircraft including one Pathfinder Halifax.

AUGUST 1942

20/21 August, 1942; MINELAYING: The squadron detailed 9 aircraft for minelaying operations, in 3 separate locations. Four aircraft successfully planted their mines in the Bornholm area, off Swinemunde, 1 aircraft planted in the primary area, 1 in the alternative, and the third in the last resort position. Of the 2 aircraft sent to Arkona, 1 planted successfully, but the other Lancaster, piloted by P/O McIntyre (R5896) ran into strong ground defences on the Danish coast; after taking violent evasive action, the Dr and gyro compasses were unserviceable. They were forced to return to Scampton with their mines.
All aircraft detailed returned safely to base.

24/25 August, 1942; FRANKFURT-ON-MAIN: The squadron detailed 16 aircraft for operations against Frankfurt, but by take-off time, 10 had been cancelled, and just 6 aircraft became airborne from Scampton by 21.33hrs.

They joined a mixed force of 226 bombers led for only the second time by the Pathfinder Force. Cloud over the target area made it extremely difficult for the marker crews and as a result the bombing was not concentrated. All 6 aircraft from Scampton, including that of W/Cmdr Slee (R5752) completed their tasks before returning to base.
A total 16 aircraft failed to return from the operation.

27/28 August, 1942; KASSEL/NICKELS: Shortly after the Mant crew (R5890) had set off for Rheims on a leaflet sortie, 12 further aircraft from the unit departed Scampton bound for Kassel. In bright moonlight, the Pathfinder illuminators carried out their task well, and the German town received severe damage from over 300 bombers.
But on return, the bombing force was heavily mauled by German night fighters, who were mainly responsible for the losses incurred; 31 aircraft failed to return. All 49's aircraft returned safely to base by 03.00hrs.

28/29 August, 1942; NUREMBERG: On Friday night, 28 August, the squadron had 10 Lancasters airborne by 21.30hrs all destined for Nuremberg in southern Germany. Over Nuremberg, Pathfinders used 'target indicators' for the first time, to mark the aiming point. Approaching from the south, the squadron's crews were able to make fixes from the river, canal and autobahn which were clearly visible in the bright moonlight.

The town received only moderate damage despite the accuracy of the markers. Again, the force suffered heavy losses with the Wellington Squadrons bearing the brunt of the casualties.
From the 159 aircraft dispatched, 23 were reported missing - 14 Wellingtons, 4 Lancasters, 3 Stirlings and 2 Halifaxes.

Two of the missing Lancasters were from 49 Squadron:

F/Sgt Ed Burton (R5897) and crew were all killed when their aircraft was brought down over Germany. All the crew are buried in the Durnbach War Cemetery.

AUGUST 1942

F/O John Lowrie RNZAF (L7567) and crew were caught by a night fighter over Holland and were shot down at 00.10hrs. The aircraft crashed at Maasbracht, 6 miles from Roermond; sadly, five of the crew were killed and are buried in a collective grave in Mook War Cemetery, whilst Sgt's Allen and Gordon were initially reported as missing, but later confirmed as being P.o.W.'s.

These two aircraft were the first Lancasters to be lost by 49 Squadron. The remainder of the squadron returned safely; 7 to Scampton, whilst P/O Neil Green (R5889) and crew landed at Tangmere.

FTR R5897	F/S E.G. Burton	Pilot	(Killed)
(EA-)	Sgt K. Newberry RAAF	2nd Pilot	(Killed)
	Sgt G.A. Swan RAAF	Nav/Ab	(Killed)
	Sgt J. Breivis RCAF	A/G	(Killed)
	F/S L.J. Capton RCAF	A/G	(Killed)
	Sgt E.C. Ibbotson	W/Ag	(Killed)
	Sgt J.D. Osbaldeston	A/G	(Killed)
FTR L7567	F/O J. Lowrie RNZAF	Pilot	(Killed)
(EA-)	Sgt J. Allen	F/E	(P.o.W.)
	Sgt G.H. Gordon	Nav/Ab	(P.o.W.)
	Sgt R.P. Dobson RAAF	Nav/Ab	(Killed)
	F/S N.R. Mitchell RCAF	W/Ag	(Killed)
	Sgt E.A. Berrett	W/Op	(Killed)
	Sgt W.D. Pierce RAAF	W/Ag	(Killed)

Illustration by John Ward

SEPTEMBER 1942

The vacancy left at Scampton due to the departure of 83 Squadron was to be filled by 57 Squadron, whose personnel started to arrive at their new base during the first week of September. 57 Squadron was being transferred from 3 Group based at Methwold, where the unit left behind their ageing Wellingtons in anticipation of receiving new Lancasters.

1/2 September, 1942; SAARBRUCKEN: At 12.10hrs, orders came through from Group requiring 8 aircraft for operations; at 14.50hrs the target was given as Stuttgart, then at 18.15hrs it was changed to Saarbrucken with take off set for midnight.

The squadron joined a Main Force stream comprised of 231 bombers, all bound for Germany. The Pathfinders marked what they thought to be the aiming point and a heavy attack then took place. Reconnaissance photographs later showed that the flares had actually gone down over Saarlouis some 13 miles from Saarbrucken (both towns were on a similar bend on the River Saar). All 49's aircraft completed their sorties before returning safely to base; 4 aircraft failed to return from the operation.

2/3 September, 1942; KARLSRUHE: This time the Pathfinders got it spot on, and the town of Karlsruhe received a heavy attack from 200 bombers. The squadron contributed 9 aircraft to the attack, 8 of which returned safely to Scampton having completed their tasks successfully. Unfortunately the ninth aircraft failed to return. Lancaster R5763, flown by 21 year-old P/O Ron Lewis and crew, crashed in Belgium; records show that one member of the crew survived and successfully evaded, three members were killed and are buried in Heverlee War Cemetery, whilst their three colleagues became prisoners of war.

FTR R5763	P/O R.G. Lewis	Pilot	(Killed)
(EA-)	Sgt T.W. Hayes	F/E	(P.o.W.)
	Sgt J.H. Pearson RAAF	Nav/Ab	(P.o.W.)
	Sgt R.G. Reynolds	W/Ag	(Killed)
	Sgt W.D. Cane	W/Ag	(P.o.W.)
	Sgt W.S. Collins	A/G	(Killed)
	Sgt E. Bradshaw	A/G	(P.o.W. Died in captivity)

4/5 September, 1942; BREMEN: On this night, the Pathfinders introduced a new technique which involved 'illuminators' who lit the area with white flares followed by 'visual markers' who dropped coloured flares after first identifying the aiming point. 'Backers-up' would then drop incendiary loads onto the coloured markers.

Bomber Command launched 251 bombers in clear weather conditions, and they found Bremen accurately marked with coloured flares and fires, which resulted in Bremen receiving heavy damage. 12 aircraft failed to return.

49 Squadron launched 8 aircraft - 4 were detailed to bomb Bremen town centre, the remaining 4 were to attack the Focke Wulf works in the town.

En route, P/O Perry (R5894) and crew were attacked by a German night fighter which raked the aircraft with cannon fire. After the combat, one of the gunners, Sgt Steer baled out; it is not known if the gunner was wounded. The bomb load was jettisoned over enemy territory and the aircraft returned early to base. The remainder of the squadron completed their sorties successfully before returning to Scampton.

6/7 September, 1942; DUISBURG - NICKELS/RHEIMS: Sgt Thom (R5744), flying as captain for the first time, successfully completed a leaflet sortie in the Rheims area of France. Meanwhile, the Main Force, comprising 207 bombers attacked Duisburg.
The squadron dispatched 9 aircraft, all of which attacked the target successfully.

Whilst on their bomb run P/O Jeffreys (R5752) and crew received three direct hits from flak, during which time the 2nd pilot, Sgt Gregory-Coleman RAAF and Sgt Maloney were wounded. The aircraft Captain managed to nurse his Lancaster back to England where over Orfordness he ordered four crew members to parachute to safety. P/O Jeffreys remained at the controls in order to attempt a safe landing with his wounded comrades onboard. A belly landing was made at Martlesham Heath airfield, but sadly too late for Sgt Gregory-Coleman who had succumbed to his injuries; he is buried in Ipswich Cemetery. Sgt Maloney recovered from his injuries, whilst P/O Jeffreys (injured in the landing) soon returned to duty.

The remainder of the squadron returned safely to Scampton; 8 main force aircraft were reported missing.

Crashed R5752	P/O G.S. Jeffreys	Pilot	(Injured)
	Sgt W.P.J. Gregory-Coleman RAAF	2nd Pilot	(Killed)
	Sgt J. Harrison		(Safe)
	Sgt O.D. Blaha	W/AG	(Safe)
	Sgt W.L. Van Der Dasson RCAF		(Safe)
	Sgt J.C. Morgan		(Safe)
	Sgt P. Maloney	W/AG	(Injured)

8/9 September, 1942; FRANKFURT: Shortly before 20.30hrs, the squadron started dispatching 8 aircraft, all briefed to attack Frankfurt city centre. Just 10 minutes after take-off, magneto failure on the starboard outer engine of W4113 forced F/Sgt Heard and crew to jettison their load 20 miles east of Mablethorpe before returning early to Scampton.

Over the target, Pathfinders failed to locate the aiming point, with the result that most of the bombs fell outside of Frankfurt. Of the 249 sent, 7 were reported missing.

The squadron's effort resulted in 6 aircraft bombing the primary, with F/O Bonnett (R5889) and crew bombing Weisbaden as the alternative. All returned safely to base.

SEPTEMBER 1942

9/10 September, 1942; MINELAYING/KATTEGAT: Two 'freshmen' crews piloted by Sgts Eyre (R5751) and Mant (R5890) carried out successful mining sorties in good weather conditions. Bomber Command had 34 aircraft tasked for minelaying sorties of which 1 Lancaster failed to return. Both of 49's aircraft returned safely to base.

10/11 September, 1942; DÜSSELDORF: The squadron detailed 12 crews to attack the industrial centre of Düsseldorf. All aircraft became airborne from Scampton by 20.58hrs and joined a main stream force totalling 479 aircraft, which included some OTU, aircraft.

The Pathfinders used 'Pink Pansies' to successfully mark the target and a devastating raid developed. All 12 Lancasters from 49 Squadron carried out their tasks and safely returned to base. 33 aircraft failed to return, with the Wellington Squadrons again bearing the brunt of the losses.

13/14 September, 1942; BREMEN: Training aircraft from the OTU's were used again to help make up a combined force of 446 bombers destined for Bremen.

Again, a heavy attack resulted, this time for the loss of 21 bombers. The squadron supplied 13 aircraft, 8 of which attacked the primary target with 5 bombing alternatives; all returned safely to base, the Gould crew (R5812) being the last to touch down at 04.24hrs.

14/15 September, 1942; WILHELMSHAVEN: The squadron put 12 aircraft up for the Wilhelmshaven trip, but P/O McIntyre (R5896) and crew were forced to return 3 hours after take-off with their starboard outer engine u/s.

On a night which saw the last bombing operation to be flown by Hampdens, the centre of Wilhelmshaven received heavy damage by over 200 bombers. Losses were light, with 2 Wellingtons reported as missing. All 49's aircraft were back at Scampton by 00.16hrs, having completed successful sorties.

16/17 September, 1942; ESSEN: The squadron detailed 13 aircraft for an attack on the Krupps works in Essen, but 2 had to be scrubbed having returned from Swinderby too late to be bombed up. Of the 11 that got away by 20.43hrs, P/O Fawke (R5898) and crew were soon back with engine trouble; the constant speed unit and immersion pump for the starboard centre tank having become unserviceable.

Essen received a scattered but damaging raid from over 360 bombers, but RAF losses were high, losing 39 aircraft. One of the 9 Lancaster crews lost, came from 49 Squadron and was captained by one of the unit's Squadron Leaders: Henry Barnard (R5890) and crew were sadly all killed when their aircraft came down in the target area. The crew are now all buried in the Reichswald Forest War Cemetery, after initially being interred at Nord Friedhof, Düsseldorf.

The remainder of the squadron landed back at Scampton by 01.50hrs, W/Cmdr Slee and crew being the last to land after spending over 20 minutes in the Essen area, searching in vain for the target; they landed back at base with bombs onboard.

FTR R5890	S/L H.W. Barnard	Pilot	(Killed)
(EA-)	Sgt K.A. Bouffler	F/E	(Killed)
	F/O O.D. Thomas	2nd Pilot	(Killed)
	F/S A.B. Brooks DFM	W/AG	(Killed)
	Sgt A.L. Caron RCAF	A/G	(Killed)
	Sgt W.J. Hoban RAAF	W/AG	(Killed)
	P/O D.B. Moody	W/AG	(Killed)

18/19 September, 1942; MINELAYING: Between 19.30hrs and 20.04hrs, the squadron dispatched 10 Lancasters on minelaying sorties in the Pillau, Swinemunde and Kattegat areas. All 10 crews completed their tasks before returning safely to base. Of the 115 aircraft detailed by Bomber Command for gardening operations this night, 2 Lancasters, 2 Stirlings and 1 Wellington failed to return.

19/20 September, 1942; MUNICH: Whilst a medium sized raid was carried out on Saarbrucken, Bomber Command also sent 68 Lancasters and 21 Stirlings to attack Munich. 49 Squadron detailed 10 Lancasters for the latter raid, and all carried out successful sorties in clear weather conditions. The unit's Lancasters had all returned safely to Scampton by 04.41hrs, but the force had suffered the loss of 3 Stirlings and 3 Lancasters.

A nicely composed photograph showing Cpl Mary Pratt and F/Lt Evans in Scampton's Intelligence Section. (Zoe Stocks)

SEPTEMBER 1942

23/24 September, 1942; WISMAR: At 10.40hrs the squadron received a 'stand down', but at 12.20hrs this was withdrawn as 10 aircraft were required for an effort on Wismar. Take-off began at 21.11hrs with 6 aircraft detailed to attack Wismar town whilst 4 bombed the nearby Dornier factory.

The raid was carried out by 5 Group Lancasters only, with 83 aircraft taking part. Thick cloud was encountered over the target and most crews attacked at low level. Of the 4 aircraft detailed to attack the Dornier works, 2 bombed the factory, 1 bombed a flak position and 1 returned bombs to base. Only 1 aircraft bombed Wismar town, whilst 2 found alternatives and 3 returned their loads to base.

24/25 September, 1942; MINELAYING: During the evening of the 24th, the squadron dispatched 5 aircraft on minelaying sorties - 1 aircraft mined off Pillau, 2 off Bornholme, 1 off Polwysep Hel and the fifth off Warnemünde.

All aircraft completed their allotted tasks with success. The Cooke crew (W4107) after attacking their primary (Warnemünde) at 23.18hrs carried on to bomb Praesto aerodrome with 2x250 pounders and then flying at 400ft, machine-gunned a 1 1/2 miles-long German army convoy. This crew landed back at Scampton, whilst the remaining 4 aircraft received diversion orders to land at Marston Moor.

This proved to be the last operation of the month.

Lancaster W4113 seen here in the markings of 1661 H.C.U. Winthorpe. In her former life W4113 operated with 49 squadron during late 1942 from Scampton. It was in this aircraft that Sgt Gould and crew flew the dramatic Le Creusot daylight raid.
(49 Sqdn Collection)

OCTOBER 1942

1/2 October, 1942; WISMAR: The squadron took part in the 5 Group attack on Wismar detailing 12 aircraft for the operation. They took-off from Scampton just before 18.30hrs; 8 were detailed to bomb the town and 4 to bomb the Dornier factory on the outskirts.

In bad weather conditions with poor visibility, 8 of the unit's aircraft attacked the primary target whilst 3 bombed alternatives. Unable to locate the primary, the Miller crew (R5658) had to jettison their load due to fuel shortage before heading home. The inclement weather persisted and prevented crews from regaining base; 10 landed away at Acklington, 1 at Charter Hall and 1 at Brunton.

DIXON EXERCISE

4 October, 1942: At 15.22hrs, F/Sgt Heard briskly lifted the unit's Tiger Moth into the air on this early autumn afternoon bound for Woodford. Thundering down the grass runway shortly afterwards came 7 of the squadron's Lancasters. They were 49's contribution towards 'Dixon Exercise', a 5 Group practice flight which involved over 90 aircraft. The exercise involved flying at extremely low levels over both land and sea in loose formation, culminating in a simulated bombing attack on Wainfleet Sands. The purpose of this practice flight and the subsequent 'Dixon Operations' was not revealed to the crews, but they were all well aware that a daylight penetration was being planned.

5/6 October, 1942; AACHEN: This was a night of electric storms and thunderheads as Bomber Command fought their way into Germany. 257 heavy bombers arrived in the Aachen area only to find that the Pathfinders had been unable to mark the target sufficiently; the inevitable result was an extremely scattered attack.

Of the 10 Lancasters supplied by the squadron, 8 bombed the primary using either time and distance runs or an estimated time of arrival (ETA) over the aiming point. The remaining 2 aircraft bombed alternative targets. The attacking force lost 10 aircraft with a further 6 crashing in England on return; all 49's aircraft returned safely to base.

6/7 October, 1942; OSNABRUCK: At 09.50hrs, Group requested 11 aircraft for operations, and at 12.10hrs Osnabruck was given as the target. During the night-flying tests, 3 aircraft were scrubbed due to engine faults. One aircraft showed low oil level on one motor, and traces of lead-bronze was found in the filters; a suspected big end failure was diagnosed.

Eventually 8 of the unit's aircraft became airborne shortly before 19.30hrs. The Gould crew (R5912) was forced to return early with a port engine u/s. Like many of the 237 strong force the squadron used the Pathfinder illuminated Dummer See (a large lake north-east of the town) to get a fix, before flying on to bomb on time and distance runs. The attack was concentrated in the town centre where considerable damage was inflicted.

The cost was 2 Lancasters, 2 Halifaxes and 2 Stirlings. All 49's aircraft were safely back at Scampton before midnight.

OCTOBER 1942

7 October, 1942: 7 aircraft for 'Dixon Exercise'-cancelled
8 October, 1942: 7 aircraft airborne on 'Dixon Exercise'.
9 October, 1942: 9 aircraft airborne on 'Dixon Exercise'.
10 October, 1942: 10 aircraft airborne on 'Dixon Exercise'.
11 October, 1942: 9 aircraft airborne on 'Dixon Exercise'.

12/13 October, 1942; WISMAR: The scheduled 'Dixon Exercise' automatically cancelled, when Group came on the 'blower' requesting 10 aircraft for an attack on Wismar town and the Dornier factory.

Take-off for 49 Squadron began at 17.47hrs when P/O Fawke opened the taps on R5912. The squadron climbed away from Scampton to join other 5 Group Lancasters en route for Wismar. Despite the very dark night and bad visibility this moderate force started several fires within the target area. Two crews failed to return, and one was the unfortunate 49 Squadron crew piloted by 21 year-old F/O Richard Elliott (W4116). Their Lancaster came down in the sea, and sadly the crews bodies were never recovered; they are remembered on the Runnymede Memorial.

FTR W4116	F/O R.F. Elliott	Pilot	(Missing)
(EA-)	Sgt A.R. Hendrie RNZAF	F/E	(Missing)
	P/O G.L. Laidlaw RAAF	NAV	(Missing)
	F/S W.C.H. Ross RAAF	W/OP	(Missing)
	Sgt G. Hodge	A/G	(Missing)
	F/S J.K. Cullen RAAF	A/B	(Missing)
	F/O J.W.B. Horne	A/G	(Missing)

This operation was the first to be mounted by 57 Squadron from Scampton, after its conversion from Wellingtons to the Lancaster.

F/O Gerry Fawke (R5898) and crew exercise M-Mother over the North Sea in the company of other 5 Group Lancasters; all practicing for the forthcoming Le Creusot daylight operation.
(T. Bennett)

OCTOBER 1942

ODE TO 57'S ARMOURERS

During one of 57 Squadron's early operations with Lancasters, several of their aircraft had not been fully 'bombed up' in time for take-off. The Armourers from 49 Squadron were called upon to accomplish the task for them. In order to remind 57 Armourers of this event (on every possible occasion), a poem was composed by a 49 Armourer... and it went like this:

'Now 57 Armourers, we know that you are duff!
You had to call on 49 to help you do your stuff.
On arrival at dispersal, we found to our dismay,
The kites were ready for take-off and the bombs around you lay.

The W.O. and all his men were stood there very still,
When out jumped Armourers '49' and went in to the kill.
We knew that ops would shake you and you were in a spin,
We think it was a ruddy shame you had to call us in.

So remember 57, whenever you 'shoot the line',
The boys who came to help you out....
WERE GOOD OLD 49!' Cpl/Amr J. Wattam

13/14 October, 1942; KIEL: The squadron sent 8 Lancasters to Kiel where the Germans had prepared decoy fires. As the 288 strong Main Force approached the target, shortly after 21.00hrs, they also had to contend with ground haze and a smoke screen. The strategy employed by the ground defences succeeded in deflecting at least half of the bombers away from their primary target.

All 49's aircraft returned safely, and all claimed to have found and bombed the primary, although the McIntyre crew (R5896) had a 1x4000lb HC hang up over the markers (they managed to get rid of it out at sea on return). Bomber Command lost 8 aircraft - 5 Wellingtons, 1 Lancaster, 1 Stirling and 1 Halifax.

15/16 October, 1942; COLOGNE: With the first-take-off timed at 18.47hrs, the squadron managed to launch 9 Lancasters against Cologne by 19.15hrs. They joined a Main Force numbering nearly 300 aircraft. Again the Germans employed a decoy fire site, but despite being hindered by wrong wind forecasts, the Pathfinders managed to lay enough markers to attract sufficient bombers.

But losses were high with 18 aircraft failing to return. All 49's aircraft returned without harm, all claiming to have attacked the primary target.

Most crews reported seeing the river which was illuminated by Pathfinder flares. F/Sgt Heard and crew (W4113) spent 32 minutes in the target area before bombing; the Mant crew orbited for 20 minutes before finding the aiming point. The Perry crew (W4245) reported seeing 1 aircraft being shot down over the target and another over Holland.

16 October, 1942: 7 aircraft airborne on 'Dixon Exercise'.

OCTOBER 1942

OPERATION ROBINSON (LE CREUSOT)

17 October, 1942; LE CREUSOT (DAYLIGHT): The weather forecast for this day was favourable, so in the early hours, the codename 'Operation Robinson' was signalled to the 8 Lancaster Squadrons of 5 Group.

During briefing at Scampton, the crews of 49 and 57 Squadrons learned for the first time, what their low-flying practice flights had been for. They were to take part in a set piece daylight attack on the large Schneider factory at Le Creusot, 300 miles into France. Aircrew of 49 Squadron were also informed that the operation was to be led by their CO, W/Cmdr Slee, and that the squadron would be in the vanguard of the attack. The force detailed to attack Le Creusot comprised of the following Squadrons:

49 Squadron (Scampton)	10 Lancasters W/C Slee,
57 Squadron (Scampton)	10 Lancasters W/C Hopcroft, DFC
44 Squadron (Waddington)	9 Lancasters W/C Burnett, DFC
9 Squadron (Waddington)	8 Lancasters W/C Southwell
106 Squadron (Syerston)	10 Lancasters W/C Gibson, DFC
61 Squadron (Syerston)	5 Lancasters W/C Coad, DFC
50 Squadron (Skellingthorpe)	12 Lancasters W/C Russell
207 Squadron (Langar)	15 Lancasters W/C Jeffs, AFC

ORDER OF BATTLE - 49 SQUADRON

W4181	Sgt Mant	R5898	P/O Fawke	W4113 Sgt Gould
R5757	P/O McDonald	W4235	F/O Green	W4196 W/Cmdr Slee
W4773	P/O Armstrong	W4761	P/O McItyre	W4306 F/O Bonnett
R5744	S/Ldr Couch			

At Scampton, take-off was set for midday and a large gathering of station personnel assembled in front of the Hangars for this 'special send off'. They were not too disappointed; Leonard Slee, took point at the head of a vic formation, then at 12.09hrs all 10 aircraft surged forward in unison.

They charged across Scampton's grass field heading south west as they skimmed across Tillbridge Lane still keeping low as the Lincoln Edge fell away to the Trent Vale.

The three towers of Lincoln Cathedral passed to port as the flight, closely pursued by 57 Squadron, set course for the Group rendezvous at Upper Heyford in Oxfordshire. The 94 Lancasters left England at Lands End flying south west still well below 1,000ft. Skirting the Brest peninsula, they crossed the French coast between St Nazaire and La Rochelle at less than 300ft.

An extremely rare, almost unique photograph, shows 49 Squadron Lancasters as they thunder away from the runway at Scampton bound for Le Creusot.

It was taken secretively from the wing of a non-operational Manchester by Cpl Trevor Simpson, near 49's hangars and the firing range.
(T.N. Simpson)

Without fighter escort, the Lancasters flew 300 miles across France at tree-top height. Crossing the Loire, the gaggle reached their final turning-point near Nevers. With just over 40 miles to their objective, they fanned out as the various Squadrons positioned themselves for their allotted section of the target, as practised over Wainfleet. Then there below in the gathering dusk, sprawled the 287 acre Schneider steel works. W/Cmdr Slee's navigator, P/O Grant (assisted by F/O Jim Catty; map reading from the bomb aimers position) was spot-on... and the attack commenced.

W/Cmdr Gibson broke away with a small force of 6 Lancasters to attack the Henri Paul transformer station at Montchanin.

The remaining 88 bombers attacked from between 4,000 and 7,000ft - the official time of the first bombs to hit the target is 18.09hrs; W/Cmdr Slee (W4196), F/O Green (W4235) and P/O McDonald (R5757) all released their loads at this time. But 49's Operational Record Book shows that F/O Dick Bonnett and crew (W4306) had in fact been first to bomb at 18.08hrs. With scarcely any opposition, the next seven minutes saw 200 tons of high explosive and incendiary bombs rain down on the works. The 1,000 pounders were fused to explode at any time within the next 90 minutes; whilst the hapless fire crews would probably be busy coping with the many incendiary fires.

As darkness fell, the Lancasters pulled away to make their way back home independently.

At Group HQ and the bases, their return was waited with considerable apprehension. As the estimated time of return passed, 23 aircraft were still overdue. Eventually, the spaces on the ops board's slowly filled until just one (at Syerston) remained blank:

S/Ldr W.D. Corr and crew (W4774) of 61 Squadron failed to return from the transformer attack. Another victim was flight engineer, Sgt R.S. Wilson, who was killed when his 207 Squadron Lancaster was attacked by three Arado seaplanes, 2 of which were destroyed; the Lancaster returned safely. These were to be the only casualties from this extremely dramatic display of air-power.

OCTOBER 1942

The race to get back to Scampton appears to have been won by the McDonald crew, who touched down at 21.17hrs. One hour later, as F/O Neil Green's Lancaster was marshalled into dispersal, the groundcrew's torches picked out the smashed front and mid-upper turrets, damaged as the result of a bird strike over France. S/Ldr Couch and crew joined the circuit on 3 engines, just after 22.20hrs; the port inner had to be closed down with serious coolant problems just after crossing the English coast coming home.

At interrogation, 49's exhilarated crews all reported excellent bombing results. Only later did recce photographs show that some of the 88 aircraft involved, had bombed short of the target. For their actions during the operation, both W/Cmdr Slee and P/O Grant were deservedly awarded the DSO.

It is a damp autumnal morning at Scampton. A watery sun does its best to break through as a quartet of 49 Sqdn Lancasters await the attention of their caring ground crews. (RAF Scampton)

22/23 October, 1942; GENOA: The squadrons of 5 Group were 'stood down' until the evening of Thursday 22nd, when Bomber Command recommenced the campaign against Italy to coincide with the opening of the Eighth Army offensive at El Alamein.

In ideal conditions with clear moonlight, 112 Lancasters guided by the Pathfinders, carried out a successful attack on the old town of Genoa. Departing Scampton just after 17.20hrs 49 Squadron provided 10 aircraft for the operation; all completed successful sorties. On return, 5 aircraft landed away - 4 at Oakington and 1 at Cottesmore. At de-brief, P/O Neil Green and crew (W4235) gave the following descriptive report:

'Attacked Genoa at 21.25hrs. Bright moon, no cloud, visibility excellent. I identified headland in harbour, east side also docks and town. Industrial buildings could be seen. Bombs seen to burst on east side of harbour near aiming point. Bursts seen to be starting fires. Biggish fire north of town. We could still see the glow 20-30 miles after leaving."

No aircraft were lost from the raid.

OCTOBER 1942

24 October, 1942; MILAN (DAYLIGHT): At 06.30hrs, on the morning of Saturday 24 October, orders came in on the teleprinter giving details for a daylight attack on the Italian town of Milan. In this hazardous operation, the 88 Lancasters of 5 Group were to fly independently across France, using the cloud as cover, before arriving at Lake Annecy, the Group's rendezvous.

By 12.24hrs, the squadron had despatched 9 aircraft, but S/Ldr Cracknell and crew were forced to return early in W4314 when the port outer engine failed.

The bombers arrived over a surprised Milan around 17.00hrs. They descended below the cloud base of 4,500 feet, in order to deliver 135 tons of bombs during the next 18 minutes.

Three Lancasters failed to return; 1 came down near Milan and 2 over Northern France. P/O Green and crew (W4235) were attacked by a Fiat CR 42 fighter; the Lancaster received slight damage, but the Lanc's gunners, Adamson and Denovan, hit the fighter which dived away damaged.

PUT ASIDE TO DIE

A 49 Squadron Lancaster, W4306, crashed in England on return from Milan. The following account includes parts of a transcript for an Australian film called 'Wings of the Storm'. They are the words of a W/O Westmore Arthur Coluhoun, a crew member aboard that fateful Lancaster:

Wes Coluhoun was born at Drouin, Victoria, on 20 August, 1920. After attending the local primary school and Warragul High School, he joined his father's business as a butcher and baker in the main street. At the age of 19, he enlisted in the RAAF and was called up for service on New Years Day 1941. After Initial Training at Bradfield Park, he went to Canada for training at No 3 Wireless Training School at Winnipeg and gunnery school at Jervis. Sailing from Halifax, his draft took 13 days in convoy to reach Liverpool, finally arriving in Bournemouth in October 1941. After a number of wireless training schools, he was posted to OTU at Cottesmore on Hampdens... Wes continues:

"I was posted to 49 Squadron, Scampton, on Avro Manchesters. There I was crewed up with a chap called Burton (who was later killed on ops). Our first op was the 1,000 bomber raid on Cologne; a few days later we went to Essen. Coming in for the first time it looked terrible - a wall of flak in front of you. But once we got through, it wasn't so bad.

After two ops they sent me off to do a special gunnery course. They were going to play hell with a big stick at that time; they were going to fly the Lancasters in daylight, and we were going to have control of the flight pattern, and tell them how to formate so that the formation could defend themselves. It wouldn't have worked ... half of them wouldn't have known what you were talking about, and the radio we used, the TR9, was so unreliable as to be useless for talking between aircraft; air to ground was OK. The course was scrubbed when they realised they couldn't achieve what they wanted.

I went back to Scampton, and Glory be! the four engines came in. Dick Bonnett was getting his crew together and asked me to go with him so I said yeah. It was illegal... he already had a wireless operator so I joined him as top gunner, and then we used to swap over to give the wireless operator a break while he went to sit up in the turret. Dick Bonnett was an Englishman, late 20's - he had been a captain or something in the army so he came straight in as a flight lieutenant. There was Bill Myers, he'd be about 26; he was the bomb aimer. Australian Dick Dangerfield was the navigator - first class, spot on, he used to get sick when we were shot at but he'd carry straight on. Then there was Ray Lawrence, the wireless operator, also Australian. Eric Brooks was the rear gunner, he was English, and the flight engineer was called Bob Wallace.

The pilot got the DFC and the navigator and bomb aimer each got the DFM because we got something like 13 shots in a row on the aiming point. It got quite embarrassing at one stage because when we were at briefing and they asked the Bonnett crew to stand up as an example.

I've been in quite a few associations and organisations but I can't remember any bonds that were as close as those we had in the crew. We did everything together... on leave I used to want to see my father's relatives up in Scotland. We used to work six weeks and then have a week off... just completely get away for a week. I went to get a ticket for Scotland, but the skipper said you're not going to Scotland, that's all there is to it, you're coming down to London... we're going to have real beano... and we did! The whole lot of us went with him. He was a good sort. You know, he was a bit stand-offish for a while, but we broke through those barriers very quickly. We were a very good crew... having confidence in the other fellow and knowing what he is going to do.

The daylight raid to Milan... at briefing we were told the target was the railway marshalling yards because there was a lot of stuff there going through to the Middle East to supply Rommel. We had to bomb the Railway Station, get it burning; we carried a 4,000 pounder and incendiaries.

We went through the clouds, bombed the station and then they got stuck into us. They knocked our hydraulics out, we couldn't close the bomb doors, no undercart, we didn't think we could get back to England. We dropped straight on to the deck, and I've never seen anything so funny in my life. There was this ack-ack battery down the road, with all its barrels pointing at us, and they ran away from it because they saw us coming down the road, bomb doors open, one engine on fire, and this juggernaut coming down the street at rooftop height. So they abandoned it and ran, our gunners having a go at them.

The engine was still burning, so we pressed the extinguishers and thought it had gone out, but it was still burning inside the wing. We wondered how to get home; we managed to get to 6 or 7,000ft and I remember we were going down through one valley in the Alps and Dick Bonnett said 'I hope to Christ this valley hasn't got an end to it!' We were pretty calm - it's hard to explain, but you get to the stage where anything that's going to happen is going to happen, and you've done your best and there's nothing more to do about it.

Anyway, we got through the Alps, then over France a German fighter had a go at us but we hopped into a cloud; this was about 10 miles north of Le Havre, or so we thought. When we came out of the cloud we were right over the town and Jeez did they give us the lot. She was shuddering and shaking as we copped more flak... we didn't think we'd get out of France again. We realised the motor was still burning when the empty fuel tank blew up in the starboard wing when we were over the Channel.

She still held together, and we had the wireless on - we turned the Identification Friend or Foe on - we turned it on stubb 3, the emergency stubb, we didn't want to break radio silence, but just wanted to send an SOS on the IFF... just red. Anyway they brought us in through the Ford searchlights - just kept waving us in. It was dark now, about eight or nine o'clock. I don't think we had much fuel left... we couldn't get high enough to bale out... no climbing power. I can remember seeing the spire of Chichester Cathedral go past. We followed these searchlights and they took us to Ford - 30 or 40 searchlights came up in a cone so it was as bright as day.

They did everything they could to give us a hand. So we started to make an approach, and we rightly got in a crash position; we had to get the rear gunner out because he was in bit of a daze from when the flak had hit us... he wasn't in too good a shape. As we reduced speed, the starboard wing just dropped over and she went straight in. The fuselage broke in half just behind me... she was burning... I turned around but my legs weren't working too good... I grabbed one chap, he was the rear gunner. I could hear someone moaning but couldn't see who it was... grabbed him by the harness and started back out again, then someone grabbed my arm and stuck a needle in it. And thats the last I can remember."

Wes's ribs had impacted into his lungs, he was so badly injured that he was put aside to die... Eric Brookes, who Wes had pulled to safety, died a few days later from his injuries... Wes was the sole survivor. He spent 18 months in hospital, where his courage and the skills of the medical teams pulled him through from his horrific injuries. Wes returned to Australia, resuming service as a radio instructor at Point Cook, where he remained until the war ended.

After demobilization he returned to Drouin to run the family business until 1970, despite a background of pain and ill health. In 1947, he married Essie, and together they brought up 3 children. He was a respected member of the local community, making his contribution to numerous organisations. In later years Wes's health deteriorated and he had frequent visits to hospital. He was to have told his story in Howard Griffith's epic 'Wings of the Storm', but was too ill at the time of filming. he died on 16 October, 1988.

F/Lt Dorian Dick Bonnett DFC and his crew are buried in Littlehampton Cemetery, Sussex, except for rear gunner, Sgt Brookes, who is at rest in Wandsworth Cemetery.

OCTOBER 1942

On a happier note; at about 21.30hrs on the evening of 24 October, after Sgt Jimmy Thom had trundled W4761 back into her Scampton dispersal, out jumped Eric Clarke Wop/Ag, to celebrate the completion of his operational tour. It began over a year earlier, and included ops on three different types of aircraft. Starting on Hampdens (12/13-10-41) with Sgts Robinson and Bow, then into 1942 with P/O Donald, S/Ldr Bennett DFC, Sgts Slingo and Downs, before converting to Manchesters and flying four ops with P/O Jeffreys and crew. Lancasters soon arrived, and nine trips were flown with F/Lt Cooke DFC, before his final three being flown with Sgt Thom... 26 ops, and none of them easy.

Eric was posted to 23 OTU at Atherstone, where as a F/Lt, he became Chief Signals Instructor. It was while at Atherstone that Eric was reunited with 'Cookie' his old skipper; Flt Cooke DFC said that to his knowledge, Eric had twice been recommended for a DFM - in 1943 he was Mentioned in Despatches. Today, in his Yorkshire home, Eric laments...

"I was one of the very lucky ones."

Crashed W4306	F/L D.D. Bonnett DFC	Pilot	(Killed)
	Sgt R.J. Wallis	F/E	(Killed)
	F/S R.D. Dangerfield RAAF DFM	NAV	(Killed)
	F/S R.G. Lawrence RAAF	W/OP	(Killed)
	Sgt W.A. Colquhoun	A/G	(Injured)
	P/O W.H.I. Myers RAAF DFM	B/A	(Killed)
	Sgt E. Brookes	A/G	(Killed)

HONOURS AND AWARDS - OCTOBER 1942

P/O G.S. Jefferys	D.F.C.
F/O D.D. Bonnett	D.F.C.
Sgt R.D. Dangerfield	D.F.M.
Sgt W.H.I. Myers	D.F.M.

Scampton late 1942. Sgt Fred Blocksidge, Flight Engineer on P/O Neil Green's crew. Illustration by John Ward

NOVEMBER 1942

6 November, 1942; OSNABRUCK: On the morning of Friday 6th, the squadron detailed 3 aircraft for Moleing (using low cloud as cover) sorties against Osnabruck. W/Cmdr Slee and crew (W4196) were first away at 11.15hrs shortly followed by S/Ldr Cracknell (W4314) and Sgt Mant RAAF (W4761).

In solid cloud, the Cracknell crew could not identify the target and dropped their bombs on the estimated time of arrival (ETA). Sgt Mant encountered the same problems but elected to return with bombs onboard.

W/Cmdr Slee's crew comprised; Sgt Gumbley RNZAF (second Dickie), P/O Grant RAAF, DSO, Sgt Pass, F/Lt Bain DFM, P/O Astbury RAAF and Sgt Mills. They were trailed at one time by two Me 109s before escaping into cloud. The evasive action upset the navigation, so the pilot descended to 100 feet in order to gain a fix. Flying in rain and drizzle, just north of the town of Osnabruck, they sighted a railway line coming from the east. As a railway station came into view, they pulled up 700ft in order to release their bombs.

All 3 aircraft had returned safely to base by 15.30hrs. They arrived back as the station were preparing aircraft for an attack on Genoa, that evening.

SHOOTING FIGHTERS!

One interesting aircraft modification that was carried out during this period is recalled by Cpl Trevor Simpson:

"Whilst at Scampton, we had to do a modification on W/Cmdr Slee's Lancaster, so that a newsreel photographer could take shots during daylight raids (like those flown to Creusot and Milan). The newsreel cameraman was called 'Skeets' Kelly (killed in a helicopter crash post war) who was very famous in his field. I had to work with him; he produced the hand-held camera to be used, and I had to fit a removable windscreen to the top hatch forward of the mid-upper turret.

I also had to cut a hole in the hatch where a mid-under turret had been proposed. Again, a streamlined faring was fitted, so that the camera could protrude underneath. I went up on the air test with him and W/Cmdr Slee to try these positions out. I remember Skeets standing there saying 'cor this is marvellous... I shall be able to get the fighters coming in a treat from here!' He didn't seem to have any concern for his own safety if fighters were coming in... only that he would get wonderful shots!"

6/7 November, 1942; GENOA: Genoa was one of Rommel's main supply bases for North Africa. In clear conditions, the Pathfinders dropped flares over the town which enabled the bombers to easily pick out ground details. The successful attack was carried out by 72 Pathfinder and 5 Group Lancasters of which 2 failed to return. 49 Squadron's 5 aircraft carried out successful sorties before returning to Scampton, the Webster crew (R5757) being the last to land at 07.41hrs.

NOVEMBER 1942

7 November, 1942: A new squadron came into being this day at Scampton; No 467 Squadron RAAF formed up with Lancasters, and recruited several of 49 Squadron's Australian personnel. The first to leave were Sgt pilot Mant RAAF and crew, four of which were Australians.

7/8 November, 1942; GENOA: At 09.15hrs, Group relayed orders asking for a Maximum Effort for another attack on Genoa. This time Bomber Command was also including Halifaxes, Wellingtons and Stirlings on the raid. The squadron offered 12 aircraft, but during NFT's one aircraft suffered an engine failure and was cancelled.

Eventually, at 17.21hrs the squadron launched the first of 11 Lancasters, 6 to attack the port and 5 to bomb the dock installations. Within a few hours, two aircraft had returned; the McIntyre crew (W4761) suffered a port outer engine failure and a u/s rear turret. The Perry crew (W4107) returned early with engine trouble on the starboard inner and port outer.

S/Ldr Couch and crew (R5744) gave a fairly comprehensive de-brief report after returning from the successful attack: *'Climbed from base to 10,000ft and reached the French coast at 13,000ft. Much searchlight activity. Light and visibility good. Identified docks and bay to west of target which was illuminated by flares and seen in sights. Numerous fires."* Returned 02.08hrs.

All 49's aircraft returned safely to Scampton, but 4 Halifaxes, 1 Lancaster and 1 Wellington out of the 175 strong force failed to return from the operation.

9/10 November, 1942; HAMBURG: On Monday night the Main Force returned to Germany, with 213 aircraft attacking the centre of Hamburg. Reverting to a northerly target (as opposed to Italy) brought the inevitable battle with the weather. As such, the force encountered high winds, icing and 10/10ths cloud up to 6,000 feet thick. The result was a very scattered raid with many bombs falling in the River Elbe and open country.

The squadron contributed 8 Lancasters, all of which experienced extreme problems in finding the target, dropping their bombs on estimated positions. The Perry crew (W4245) descended to 11,000ft but quickly iced up; their aircraft received 12 flak holes. The Miller crew (R5757) was shadowed by 2 enemy aircraft in the Kiel area, but after violent evasive action, the fighters ceased to follow.

Altogether 15 bombers failed to return; all 49's Lancasters were safely back at base shortly after midnight.

10/11 November, 1942; MINELAYING: During the late morning, Group asked for volunteers to make up a mining effort in the Gironde River area. The squadron sent the 'freshman crew' captained by Sgt pilot Mapp (R5912).

This crew managed to drop their mines from 700ft, in the primary position, despite the dark night and low cloud; they returned to Scampton at 23.53hrs.

12 November, 1942: Scampton was honoured with a visit from His Majesty King George VI. The King arrived at approximately 11.00hrs, and was introduced to several members of 49 Squadron outside one of the unit's hangars. The other resident Squadrons (57 & 467) were also visited.

Royal visit - 12 November, 1942: The crew of the Squadron Commander were presented to His Majesty; they are (from left to right), Sgt Mills; Sgt Pass; F/O Eyre; H.M. The King; W/Cmdr Slee DSO; P/O Astbury RAAF; F/O Grant RAAF, DSO; F/Lt Bain DFM. (J. Bain)

13/14 November, 1942; GENOA: Back to Italy, and just after 18.00hrs, 67 Lancasters (from 5 Group) led by Pathfinder Stirlings set out to cross the Alps to attack Genoa. 49 Squadron sent just 3 crews, and all were operating for the first time. They were captained by the following pilots: Sgt Gumbley RNZAF (R5757); Sgt Johnstone RCAF (W4181) and Sgt McDonald RNZAF (W4245).

The unit's aircraft passed over Genoa at 8,000ft in a clear, cloudless night. The harbour, docks and rail junction were easily identified. A successful bombing raid was carried out by the moderate force, without any losses.

NOVEMBER 1942

15/16 November, 1942; GENOA: In bright moonlight, 78 Lancasters, Halifaxes and Stirlings revisited Genoa. The clear conditions enabled many crews to obtain good fixes over Savona before flying on to Rapelles from where target flares could easily be seen. Again, good, accurate bombing developed.

Returning high above the Alps, two members in the McIntyre crew (W4235) suffered badly from lack of oxygen; Sgt's Fowler and Holder were using the old type of oxygen mask. Of the 8 aircraft detailed by the squadron, 6 landed back at Scampton, 1 at Wyton and 1 at Thorney Island. For the second night, no aircraft were lost from the operation.

20/21 November, 1942; TURIN (FIAT WORKS): Orders detailing a raid on the Fiat factory were received at 10.00hrs, and the squadron could offer 11 crews for the operation. Take-off began at 18.08hrs led by W/Cmdr Slee DSO (W4196) and crew. Weather was reported as good, with 8/10ths cloud at 3,000ft - visibility was 2 1/2 miles, with a 5 mph north-westerly wind.

The squadron passed over Turin around 22.20hrs at 6,000ft, in good visibility. All of the unit's bomb aimers managed to achieve the aiming point in their sights, despite haze, and the smoke which rapidly developed. Sgt Gumbley RNZAF and crew (R5762) made several runs due to the poor lateral visibility, before bomb aimer, Sgt Hyde, confidently released their load.

One new crew was operating with the squadron; Sgt Singleton (W4181) and crew encountered a fighter 20 miles south-east of Le Havre. But an accurate and aggressive burst of fire from Sgt Halsall in the rear turret, forced the enemy aircraft to break off its attack. The crew flew on to land safely at Bradwell Bay. The remainder of the squadron landed back at Scampton. Defences over the target had been meagre, with no losses being suffered by the 77 strong force.

22/23 November, 1942; STUTTGART: Ground haze and thin cloud over Stuttgart prevented the Pathfinders from locating the centre of the city. With the help of a bright moon, the 7 Lancasters from 49 Squadron, did manage to pick up the river from the north and were able to gain good fixes. The Main Force arrived over Stuttgart just after 22.00hrs, and for the next hour over 200 bombers dropped their loads mainly in the south of the city. W/Cmdr Slee and crew (W4196) made several dummy runs before bombing, from just 5,000ft.

At Scampton, 5 of the unit's Lancasters had returned safely; Sgt Mapp and crew (R5912) telephoned base, to say that they had landed unharmed at North Luffenham. Eventually, it became apparent that Sgt Singleton and crew (W4181) had failed to return.

Some fifty years later, Eric Singleton recalls the reason why his Lancaster was prevented from returning to base:

"After dropping our bombs, unfortunately before getting clear, the aircraft was shot at, and received several direct hits. The starboard inner engine was on fire and there was fire in the fuselage... I thought we were going to have an explosion."

After a deterioration of the situation, four members of the crew baled out, but Sgt Singleton decided to see just how far he could continue to fly the damaged aircraft. The two remaining crew, mid upper gunner Eddie Pope and rear gunner Les Saunders, with great effort succeeded in extinguishing the fuselage fire, and miraculously, a short time later, the engine fire went out. Eric continues:

"We crossed the coast, and I thought we were North of the Cherbourg Peninsula en route for England. After a short time, seeing apparently 'friendly' land below us, I decided to bring the Lancaster down."

After a rather bumpy descent, skirting one field, shooting through a hedge before eventually coming to rest in a second field, Sgt Singleton and his intrepid gunners clambered out of the aircraft to find a reception party waiting. Eric later proclaimed:

"I thought it was the Home Guard, but as they asked us to put up our hands, we realised they were Germans!"

The Lancaster crew had erroneously landed on the Channel Island of Sark which was occupied by Germany during the Second World War, and as a result, Sgt Singleton and crew (including those who had baled out earlier) were to spend the rest of the war in POW camp.

This 49 Squadron Lancaster was the only plane to land on the Island during the war, and the place in which it came down is still affectionately known by the islanders as 'Aeroplane Field'.

Half a century later, Seigneur Beaumont, the Governor, invited Eric, and his wife Gwendolyn back to the island under much less hostile conditions. After a tour of the island by the traditional transport of horse and cart, the party visited the place where W4181 had 'landed'. But there was one more surprise to come... as they stood in the field, a lone Lancaster bomber (BBMF Flight) flew over... it was an extremely emotive moment.

Parts of the aircraft still remain in the field, and former Sgt Pilot Singleton was presented with a small piece, as a memento of both of his visits!

5 Lancasters, 3 Wellingtons and 2 Halifaxes were reported missing from the operation.

NOVEMBER 1942

FTR W4107	Sgt E.J. Singleton	Pilot	(P.o.W.)
(EA-)	Sgt R. Wood	F/E	(P.o.W.)
	Sgt K.C. Corry	NAV/B	(P.o.W.)
	Sgt A.G. McInnes	W/AG	(P.o.W.)
	Sgt E. Pope	A/G	(P.o.W.)
Crew on their	Sgt D.J. Hills	B/A	(P.o.W.)
2nd operation	Sgt L.W. Saunders	A/G	(P.o.W.)

27/28 November, 1942; STETTIN (CANCELLED): The squadron detailed 5 'inexperienced' crews for ops against Stettin, but just 5 minutes after take-off (17.10hrs) the trip was scrubbed, and the aircraft returned to base.

28/29 November, 1942; TURIN: The final operation of the month was a Main Force attack on Turin by a total of 228 aircraft. 49 Squadron managed to get 10 aircraft airborne by 18.53hrs, F/Sgt Bill Townsend and crew (W4113) being the last away. At 21.09hrs, F/O Eyre and crew (W4196) were back early over Scampton, their port outer feathered, therefore rendering the rear turret u/s.

The Webster crew (R5757) arrived over the target at 22.29hrs flying at 6,500ft; they later reported: *"Light, no cloud, slight haze. Saw and identified river - target in sights - bombs seen to explode in centre of town, about 18 fires seen in town. Trip well planned. Target easily identified by flares."*

It was after this operation that a Stirling pilot, F/Sgt R.H. Middleton RAAF of 149 Squadron, was awarded a posthumous Victoria Cross. It was also the first time 8,000lb bombs had been dropped on Italy (2 aircraft from 106 Sqdn).

49 Squadron's 9 aircraft had all returned safely to Scampton by 03.21hrs, F/O McDonald (R5751) and crew being the last to touch down. During the Squadron's absence, one of the unit's aircraft that had been detailed to carry out a cross-country flight, crash landed. The rear gunner, Sgt Lowden, was taken to the SHQ suffering from shock and lacerations of the forehead and face.

HONOURS AND AWARDS - NOVEMBER 1942

W/Cdr L.C. Slee	D.S.O.
F/O A.S. Grant	D.S.O.
F/S J.D. Gadsby	D.F.M.
F/Lt N.C. Green	D.F.C.
P/O G.E. Fawke	D.F.C.
P/O J.R. McDonald	D.F.C.

DECEMBER 1942

During the final month of 1942, bad weather seriously restricted operations. At the beginning of December, raids were planned for four nights in succession, only to be cancelled later the same day. At 09.45hrs on the fifth night, the squadron was prepared for ops against Mannheim... this time Bomber Command sallied forth in strength.

6/7 December, 1942 MANNHEIM: A Main Force of 270 plus arrived over a cloud-covered Mannheim where Pathfinders were having difficulties in marking the target. Most crews were forced to bomb on dead-reckoning or ETA's. The squadron's 6 Lancasters passed over the town shortly after 20.15hrs at heights from between 13,000 down to 8,000ft. All bombed successfully; 4 claimed to have bombed the Mannheim area and 2 the town itself... the cloud cover had rescued Mannheim from serious damage.

The force suffered the loss of 10 aircraft over the continent, but continued severe weather conditions over England, caused 4 more of the returning bombers to crash. The squadron's aircraft all returned safely, and were all diverted; 5 landed at Marham and 1 at Warboys.

7/8 December, 1942; MINELAYING (BAYONNE): On the morning of Monday 7th, Group asked if the squadron had any experienced 'gardeners' available... "we offered one." Mid-morning the squadron also detailed 6 aircraft for low flying and practice bombing over Wainfleet.

At 16.31hrs, F/O Perry and crew (W4761) lifted away from Scampton bound for the Bayonne to lay mines. The crew managed to gain a good fix north of the Adour river, having seen the furnaces of a factory along its banks. At 21.57hrs, in clear visibility, the Perry crew planted their vegetables in the primary area from 1,000ft. In the small hours of Tuesday, W4761 slipped in over Scampton's boundary hedge and touched down safely at 02.40hrs.

8/9 December, 1942; TURIN: Group requested 12 aircraft for the night's effort on Turin; the squadron could only offer 11, one of which was withdrawn at 16.00hrs due to a faulty starboard engine. Take-off began at 17.30hrs, but a further aircraft failed to become airborne when a starter motor burnt out. Eventually 9 of the unit's aircraft climbed away to join the other 124 Lancasters, Halifaxes, Stirlings and Wellingtons, all setting out to cross the Alps before descending into Italy.

As the force approached, they could clearly see that the Pathfinders had done a good job in illuminating the target. The squadron's aircraft began attacking shortly after 21.00hrs. Sgt Johnstone RCAF and crew carried out their bombing run at 21.04hrs. After a safe return to Scampton, this crew gave the following de-brief report, which is typical of others operating this night:

"Attacked primary at 7,500 feet. Quite light, no cloud. Visibility fairly good. Identified bend of river NE of town, Built up area in sights. Incendiaries seen near aiming point. Fires started. One hole in bomb doors due to flak."

9/10 December, 1942; TURIN: Bomber Command was back over Turin on the evening of Wednesday 9th. A mixed force of 227 bombers (including 7 from 49 Squadron) found fires still burning from the previous night's raid; the smoke and ground haze made the Pathfinder's task extremely difficult.

The squadron had managed to get 8 aircraft airborne from Scampton, but F/O McDonald and crew jettisoned their bombs and returned early; R5757 had developed an hydraulic leak which covered the floor with oil. The remaining crews all carried out successful attacks on the town of Turin, but all 7 reported aiming problems due to the haze. The squadron's aircraft all returned safely to Scampton, the Gumbley crew (ED348) being the last home, touching down at 02.06hrs. Bomber Command lost 3 aircraft from the operation.

Scampton briefing 1942 style being conducted by S/Ldr Townsend. (Zoe Stocks)

DECEMBER 1942

20/21 December, 1942; DUISBURG: After the frustration of no less than 8 scrubbed operations (all due to bad weather), the squadron eventually contributed 11 aircraft to the Main Force attack on Duisburg. Scampton's Lancasters began marshalling for take-off shortly before 18.00hrs, F/O Jeffreys and crew (ED318) being the first away. As the take-offs continued the sky to the south of Lincoln suddenly erupted with a blinding flash. Personnel at Scampton and on the other bomber stations that surrounded the city knew instantly what had happened.

They had all been reluctant witnesses of a collision between two Lancasters. Both aircraft (W4182/9 Sqdn & W4259/44 Sqdn) had been gaining height over their Waddington base when the disaster happened. Full of fuel, incendiaries and 'cookies', death must have been instantaneous for the 14 crew members. The remains of men and bombers fell to earth near the top of Canwick Hill and towards Bracebridge Heath.

Over 230 bombers were sent to attack the town and dock areas. Several of 49's crews navigated to the target by following the River Rhine. They arrived over a well marked target, where an excellent raid soon developed.

49 Squadron's effort can be best summed up by the de-brief given by F/Lt Neil Green and crew (ED310): *"Attacked primary at 19.57hrs from 11,000 feet. No cloud underneath, thin layer 8/10ths at about 14/15,000 feet. Bends of Rhine and docks clearly visible on run up. A large fire was burning in centre of town and against this, a largish factory with tower and chimney. This target was so clear as to be irresistible although it was actually on the edge of the target area. Bombs seen to explode on and near the factory alongside dock area - landed 22.21hrs."* A total of 12 aircraft failed to return; 6 Lancasters, 4 Wellingtons and 2 Halifaxes.

By 23.00hrs, nine of the unit's aircraft had landed back at base; then at 23.15hrs, F/O Armstrong (W5773) called up, asking for permission to land. Just one overdue... the time continued to slip agonisingly by, until reluctantly a corporal chalked the words 'missing without trace' against the names of Sgt Edward Johnston RCAF and crew. Unknown at the time, the unfortunate 21 year old pilot and his crew, had been hit by flak as they made their way home across Holland. The mortally damaged Lancaster smashed onto the Dutch coastline, just south of Ijmuiden... there were no survivors.

FTR R5762	Sgt E.I. Johnston	Pilot	(Killed)
(EA-)	Sgt F.W. Morris	F/E	(Killed)
	Sgt G.A. Wainwright	NAV/B	(Killed)
	Sgt A. Howison	W/AG	(Killed)
	Sgt S.J. Wick	A/G	(Killed)
Crew on their	Sgt M. MacClellan	B/A	(Killed)
4th operation	Sgt R.A. Bignell	A/G	(Killed)

DECEMBER 1942

21/22 December, 1942; MUNICH: This attack on Munich, by 137 aircraft of 1 and 5 Groups and the Pathfinders, would prove to be 49 Squadron's final operation of the war, to be flown from RAF Scampton .

The posted 'Order of Battle' for Munich was as follows:

W4196	W/Cmdr Slee	W4314	S/Ldr Cracknell	ED318	F/O Jeffreys
W4181	F/O Eyre	W4773	F/O Armstrong	ED348	Sgt Gumbley
R5744	F/L Green	R5898	F/O Fawke	W4245	Sgt Cole
W4235	F/O McDonald	W4761	Sgt Thom		

All 11 aircraft were airborne from Scampton by 18.46hrs, but Jimmy Thom and crew (W4761) were soon having problems. Their starboard inner engine failed immediately after take-off at 1,000ft. The aircraft would not climb on 3 engines, so the pilot flew out to sea, where after struggling to 2,000ft the bombs were jettisoned, and an early return was made.

As the stream made its way to Southern Germany, F/O Eyre and crew (W4181) were intercepted and attacked by a night fighter. The pilot took violent evasive action, and with skill, they escaped the fighter's attention. But the combat had taken its toll on the Lancaster as one of the starboard motors suddenly seized solid. The pilot could not maintain height, and the crew were forced to jettison their bombs live over Reutlingen, before returning home safely.

Munich was covered by a thin layer of stratus cloud and ground fog. Crews were compelled to make dead reckoning runs, before bombing on ETA's. The attack proved to be a failure, with most of the Main Force bombs falling in open country. It is possible that the Germans may have also employed decoy fires. The percentage loss suffered by the attacking force had been high, with 8 Lancasters, 3 Stirlings and 1 Wellington being reported missing.

On return to Lincolnshire, most of Scampton's aircraft were diverted to other airfields; although 3 put down at base, 1 landed at Linton, 3 at Rufforth, 1 at Wigsley and 1 at Scorton... all had returned safely.

Following what was no doubt a very 'Wet' Christmas 49 Squadron then prepared themselves for the move to the newly built airfield at Fiskerton just east of Lincoln.

HONOURS AND AWARDS - DECEMBER 1942

Sgt P. Maloney	D.F.M.

JANUARY 1943

FISKERTON AIRFIELD

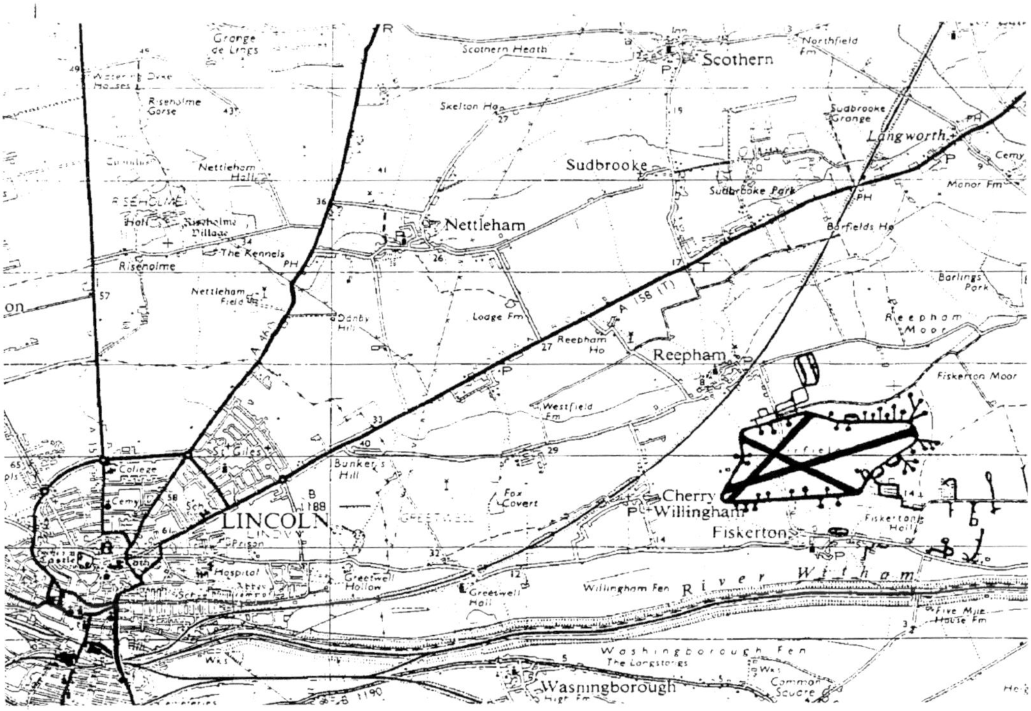

This map shows the location of Fiskerton airfield just 5 miles east of Lincoln and alongside the River Witham.

49 SQUADRON'S NEW HOME

49 Squadron moved from Scampton to Fiskerton and became operational in the three weeks following Christmas '42. Only the basic 'essential' buildings were available, but extra buildings were gradually added over the next two years.

The origins of the airfield at Fiskerton (which is located 5 miles E of Lincoln) can be traced back to the early part of the war. An area of farmland just north of the village was surveyed and found suitable, requisitioned by the Air Ministry and construction commenced. Various contractors were employed to build a Class 'A' type airfield, with the work being completed by November 1942. With an elevation of 50 feet above sea level, and no natural obstructions, the nearest permanent landmark was Reepham Church one mile to the north-west.

Fiskerton airfield conformed to the standard heavy bomber base pattern. Its three intersecting concrete runways were linked by an encircling perimeter track, around which 36 aircraft hard standings were dispersed.

FISKERTON AIRFIELD

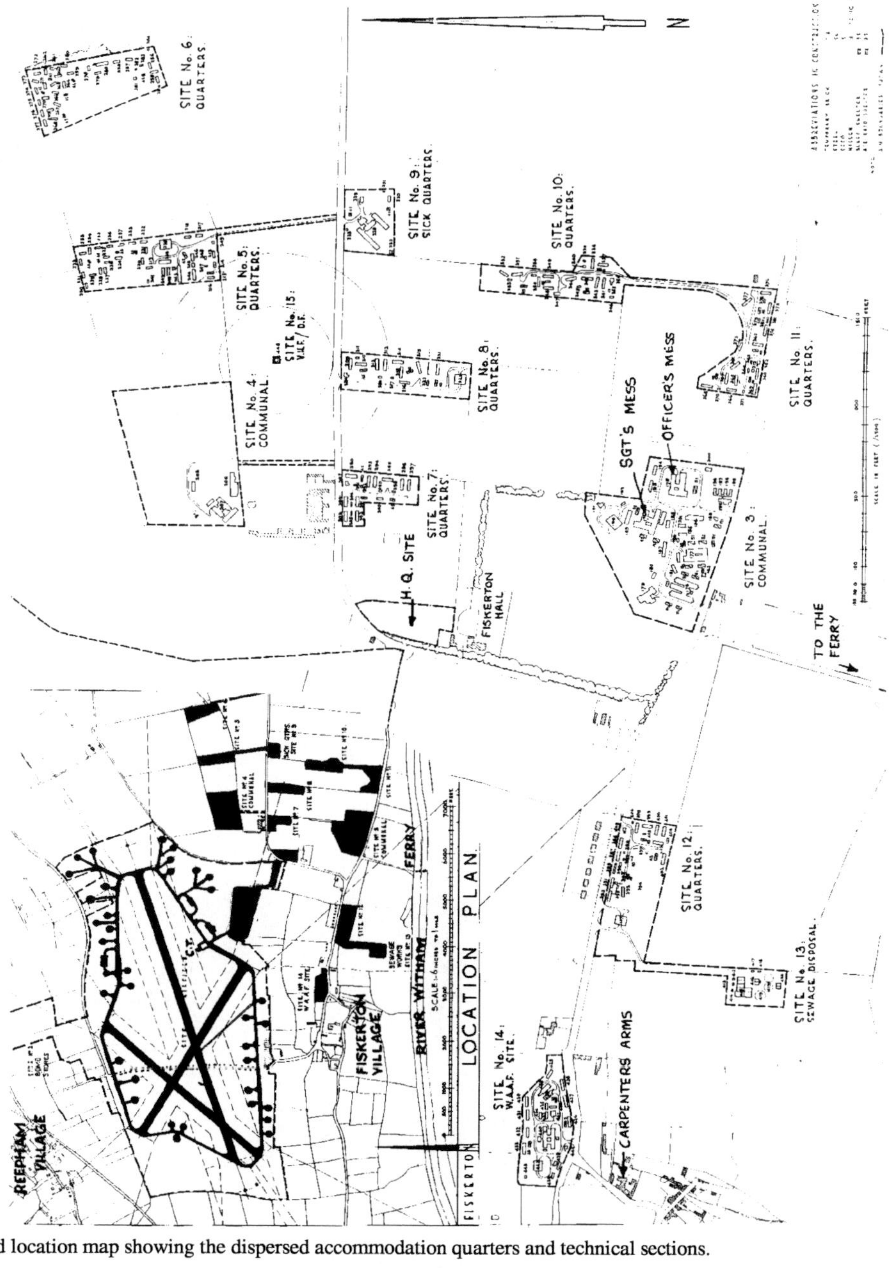

Enlarged location map showing the dispersed accommodation quarters and technical sections.

All three runways cut across the Fiskerton/Reepham road which was duly closed for the duration of the war (and for several years after). The main east-west runway which was 2,000 yards long and lying at an angle of 71 degrees, happened to be in direct line with Lincoln Cathedral. The other two intersecting runways were both 1,400 yards in length, all three being 50 yards wide.

The technical site was situated in the south-east corner. To support and accommodate a bomber squadron, Fiskerton was eventually provided with three hangars; a T2 and B1 on the technical site itself and a further T2 on the opposite side of the airfield, adjacent to the bomb dumps. The hangars were reserved mainly for major maintenance, general servicing being carried out on the dispersal points. During most of 49 Squadron's period at Fiskerton, only the two T2 hangars were in situ.

The Bomb Stores lay to the north, close to the village of Reepham, and had capacity for the storage of 800 tons of various types of bombs. In addition, there were facilities to store 1,000,000 rounds of small arm ammunition.

The aviation fuel storage tanks (capacity 24,000 gallons) were situated off the southern perimeter track, just across the road from the Old Rectory. Petrol and oil were located near the MT pool on the technical site.

Living accommodation was for a 'Scale 1 Bomber Squadron' being located on the south and south eastern side of the airfield, in and around the village. There were sites at: The Crescent, Ferryside, Woodlands and Longwood on or near the Bardney Road and Hallfields, Fenlands, Moorlands and Birchill flanking the quiet lane towards Barlings.

Accommodation and demand on catering fluctuated when diverted crews landed (especially when FIDO was operational), the additional personnel being housed in buildings near the Gymnasium on Moor Lane.

St Clements Church, Fiskerton, which contains 49 Squadron's Roll of Honour and is the site of a memorial to 49 and 576 Squadron personnel who died in the course of their duties. (Ted Cachart)

JANUARY 1943

FISKERTON GOES TO WAR

16/17 January, 1943: BERLIN: Saturday dawned grey and cold. In the small village of Fiskerton, nestling on the edge of the River Witham valley, men sipped a last cup of hot tea before setting out into the bitter winter's morning on their journeys to work. Snug and warm in bed, school children enjoyed their Saturday morning lie-in, perhaps anticipating their weekly trip into town to visit the pictures, whilst mum did her shopping round Lincoln market. When entering Lincoln and travelling along Monks Road, they may have caught a glimpse of some of the damaged houses wrecked by a lone German bomber the previous evening.

A normal wartime Saturday for Fiskerton's civilian population perhaps, but not for the personnel of RAF Fiskerton. After two weeks of intensive preparation following its move from Scampton, 49 Squadron was once again on operational status. On scores of other airfields throughout Lincolnshire and the eastern counties the scene was very similar; groundstaff, both men and women, toiled hard in their efforts to prepare aircraft in readiness for that evening's foray. Meanwhile, in distant, chilled billet huts, 49 Squadron aircrew were just awakening. They dressed hurriedly, standing on beds to keep blanket-warmed feet away from the freezing cold floors. After the briefest of visits to the ablutions, overcoats were donned for a brisk walk along Ferry Road to the Mess, where the welcoming warmth of a cooked breakfast awaited. Tension within the Mess was high as rumours circulated that ops were on that night. Up on the airfield main site, aircrew gathered at the flight offices. As the flying programme was posted, men craned their necks to read the names; when a crew confirmed that they were indeed 'on', then that strange feeling in the pit of the stomach returned.

W/Cmdr Slee had decided to field his strongest side; 16 crews were detailed all flying brand new Mk III Lancasters, probably the first squadron in Bomber Command to dispatch a full squadron of Mk III's.

Wing Commander Leonard Cain Slee DSO.
(later Group Captain DSO,DFC) (49 Sqdn collection)

The Lancaster Mk III had American produced Packard Merlin engines fitted (the engines being the only difference between a Mk I and III).

Performance was almost identical, though the American carburation system did give the aircraft a more economical cruising rate. This initial batch of Mk III Lancasters operated by 49 Squadron was fitted with 'needle blade' propellers; the Hamilton (broad blade) propellers, usually associated with the Packard Merlin were slowly introduced later in the year.

JANUARY 1943

ORDER OF BATTLE - 16 JANUARY 1943:

ED441
W/C L.C. Slee
F/O R.A. Jackson
P/O C.W. Hammond
Sgt K Bolton
Maj W.P. Mullock (Army)
P/O C.K. Astbury
Sgt H.W. Mills

ED450
S/L D.A. Cracknell
Sgt W.T. Beesley
F/O M.D. Deloford
F/S N.G. Ball
Sgt A.M. McDairmid
Sgt W.C. White
Sgt H. Frost

ED444
F/O R.G. Armstrong
Sgt C.L. Howard
Sgt H. Wilkinson
Sgt J. Bremner Major
Sgt W. Halsall
F/S A.A. McKenzie
Sgt R.M. Elliot

ED467
F/O J.R. McDonald
Sgt K.F. Stauffer
F/S G.G. Bellamy
Sgt W.K. Gibbs
F/S G.C. Blair
F/S R.W. Wright
F/S J.D. Routledge

ED452
F/S T.V. Webster
Sgt F.S. Clarkson
F/S F.J. Copestake
Sgt N.H. Arnold
Sgt E.R. Morris
Sgt E.H. Monture
Sgt M.J. Ball

ED445
F/O M.A. Eyre
Sgt J.D. Dwyer
F/O J.N. Catty
F/S R.S. Hogg
Sgt H.W.C. Kerr
Sgt N.L Vander Dasson
Sgt M.J. Campbell

ED448
F/L R.A. Allsebrook
Sgt I. Moore
W/O N.A. Botting
P/O A.S. Grant
Sgt I.G. Jones
Sgt R.B.S. Lulham
Sgt S. Hitchin

ED416
F/O G.S. Jeffreys
P/O W. Watts
F/O D.J. Robertson
Sgt R.S. Fermor
F/S N.E. Mortimer
Sgt H. Cowan
Sgt J.G. Harrison

ED438
Sgt B.A. Gumbley
Sgt J. Campbell
P/O R.G. McCracken
Sgt J.W. Turner
Sgt C.W. Morley
Sgt R. Hyde
Sgt P.R. Davies

ED440
S/L E.G. Couch
Sgt S.J. Maples
P/O P.K. Hopkin
F/S Denovan
Sgt J.A. Fowler
Sgt C.E. Boswell
Sgt C.N. Holden

ED431
F/O G.E. Fawke
Sgt E.L. Cole
P/O T. Bennett
F/S J.P.R Fortin
Sgt D.S. Bratt
Sgt G.G. Osler
Sgt H.E. Walters

ED427
Sgt J.N. Thom
Sgt E.B. Ayres
Sgt J.H. Prior
F/O E.J.F. Dunand
Sgt A.J. Clover
Sgt A.E. Horne
Sgt J.W. Coulson

ED428
Sgt E.L. Cole
Sgt W. Bramley
F/O F. Ridley
Sgt L. Grey
Sgt E. Phillips
Sgt J. Browne
Sgt J. Wood

ED435
Sgt B.F. Gilmore
Sgt A.G. Stretch
Sgt J.W. Hudson
Sgt S.D. Fish
Sgt J.P. Logan
Sgt G.D. Reed
Sgt E.R. Darrell

ED432
Sgt J. McDonald
Sgt D. Twist
P/O H. Schofield
P/O A. Sutherland
Sgt W. Tennant
Sgt J. Gibbon
Sgt J.W. Coulson

ED434
W/O I.P. Mapp
Sgt T.A. Bayliss
F/S R. Dixon
Sgt B.G. Abraham
Sgt K. Ovenden
Sgt J.T. Erratt
Sgt R.T. Sherratt

Later that morning, aircrew made ready to go out to their allotted Lancasters. On operational days aircraft would be taken up on a Night Flying Test (NFTs) to check for any snags etc. This usually lasted about 30 minutes and consisted of mainly local flying.

ED441 (EA-D). Delivered to the squadron on 29-12-42, D-Donald flew it's first operation to Berlin 16/17-1-43, piloted by W/Cmdr Slee. It eventually failed to return from Pilsen 16/17-4-43 when flown by Sgt Penry and crew; only the rear gunner survived.
(49 Sqdn collection)

On 16 January, the main briefing was timed for just after lunch, which suggested an early take-off time. In the large Nissen hutted briefing room, each crew sat in rows awaiting the arrival of the C.O. and his entourage. Conversation focused on what the 'target for tonight' would be. At one end of the room a heavy curtain concealed a large wall map of Europe on which lay the answer to much speculation. Everyone rose to their feet as W/Cmdr Slee entered, slicing his way through the charged atmosphere aiming straight for the small raised area behind the closed curtain. In his wake were his two Flt Commanders, S/Ldr Couch and S/Ldr Cracknell plus the Station Commander and the various station specialists. The crews were soon invited to be reseated. W/Cmdr Slee wasted little time...

"Tonight gentlemen... you will visit BERLIN".

The curtain was thrown back and the route revealed; probing eyes followed the tape that stretched across the map from Fiskerton to the German capital. It had been over 14 months since Bomber Command last struck at Berlin and for most men operating that night it would be their first opportunity to write 'Berlin' in their Log Books. One by one the specialists delivered their talks; heads and minds buzzed with so much condensed information but clarity returned when crews were eventually requested to synchronise watches. After final words of encouragement from the C.O. and the Station Commander, crews stepped out into the dull light of a January afternoon.

Take-off time was set for 16.30hrs, so there wasn't much time for a meal and any last minute jobs. Soon the Locker Room bustled with men struggling into their flying gear, whilst outside others waited for the WAAF drivers to bring round the crew buses that would ferry them out to far-flung dispersals. At the dispersals squatted battle readied Lancasters, and in attendance were their diligent ground crews who had been labouring feverishly throughout the day.

The aircrew travelled out to the aircraft often in boisterous humour, cracking well worn jokes with Dot or Vi and the other patient WAAF drivers... such antics helped relieve the tension. In the villages of Fiskerton and Reepham, locals prepared to settle down for the evening by the fireside listening to their radios. But the increasing rumble of 64 Packard Merlin engines brought the realisation that the first operation to be flown out of RAF Fiskerton was about to commence.

Young children ran excitedly out into the gathering gloom, to vantage points on the perimeter fence in order to get a better view. They watched spellbound as each Lancaster passed by, the rhythmic threshing of their propellers disturbing the dusk.

At the end of the main runway a large number of station personnel had gathered to wave the boys off. Dusk was rapidly turning into night as S/Ldr Cracknell (ED450) turned the first aircraft onto the main runway.

The Lancaster's menacing nose pointed directly towards Lincoln Cathedral some 5 miles to the west; the time was 16.36hrs when S/Ldr Cracknel released the brakes on A-Apple sending her surging down the concrete strip. Older villagers turned their eyes skywards as the Lancasters laboured into the air, thundering out over the small hamlet of Cherry Willingham... and more than a few quietly said a prayer for the safe return of all 'their' brave young aviators.

Eventually all 16 Lancasters became airborne, Sgt McDonald (ED432) and crew being the last away, their Lancaster's red, green and white navigation lights gradually disappearing into the blackness; it was now 17.00hrs... and suddenly... there was silence.

THE BIG CITY

The 16 Fiskerton aircraft joined a force of 201 other heavies all bound for Berlin. Mechanical difficulties soon hampered 49 Squadron's new machines with four being forced to return early, something every crew hated.

Sgt Jimmy Thom (ED427) was first to 'boomerang' in O-Orange, landing back at 18.47hrs on three engines.

Sgt Bernard Gumbley RNZAF (ED438) in R-Robert requested permission to land at 19.50hrs.

S/Ldr Cracknell (ED450) in A-Apple pressed on with his port outer u/s, but unable to maintain height and retain fuel, he reluctantly turned for home, landing at 21.10hrs.

F/O Jeffreys (ED416) in J-Johnny, was suffering excessive petrol consumption and could not continue; he landed at 22.46hrs.

Those crews who made Berlin found the target covered by haze. They also found the defences poor with the result that only one Lancaster was lost from the entire force. Bombing damage was considered to be disappointing.

Note: The missing Lancaster was piloted by F/Lt Don Parker GC who had been awarded the George Cross for rescuing his crew from their crashed 49 Squadron Hampden (see June 1940). After completing a tour on Hampdens followed by a second tour on night fighters, he returned for a third tour as a Flight Commander on 61 Squadron at Syerston; he and his crew were sadly all killed.

Fiskerton village was awakened just after midnight when the first Lancaster to return from Berlin entered Fiskerton's circuit. It would be 01.20hrs before the last aircraft touched down... all 49's Lancasters had come home safely.

MAY I PANCAKE PLEASE?

One amusing episode during the landing is recalled by P/O Tom Bennett, navigator in Gerry Fawke's (ED431) M-Mother:

"We were next to land behind S/Ldr Eric Couch... his voice could be heard informing the WAAF in the Watch Office that he was now in the 'funnels' and then 'finals'. Moments later he announced that he had cleared the runway. With that, Gerry, our pilot turned to us and said 'well I didn't bloody well see him land!' We continued with our own approach and landed. At de-brief we soon learned that whilst S/Ldr Couch may have been talking to Fiskerton control, at the time he was actually landing at RAF Wickenby, several miles to the north east of Fiskerton."

The unfortunate S/Ldr and his navigator, P/O Hopkin, were to be the recipients of much mischievous humour in the mess for several days after.

17/18th January, 1943; BERLIN: Over 180 bombers followed the same route back to Berlin as the previous night. F/Lt Allsebrook (ED438) flying P-Peter, returned to base after crossing the coast due to oxygen failure. The ground of northern Europe was snow covered, but above the clouds in the moonlit sky, vapour condensation trails marked the bombers passage. Despite good visibility over the city, the Pathfinders were unable to accurately mark and most bombs fell-away to the south of the city.

German night fighters attacked the bomber stream with good effect with 22 bombers failing to return home. Amongst those missing were F/O Gordon Jeffreys DFC, and crew of 49 Squadron, whose Lancaster had taken off from Fiskerton at 17.04hrs, along with 8 other 49 Squadron aircraft. This unfortunate crew were the first to be lost on operations flying from RAF Fiskerton; three members of the crew were killed and are buried in Kiel War Cemetery.

On return to England, fog caused the squadron to be diverted to Coltishall, except for Sgt Cole (ED428) in Q-Queenie, who had to put down at Waddington due to fuel shortage.

FTR ED444	F/O G.S. Jeffreys	Pilot	(Killed)
(EA-C)	Sgt R.S. Fermor	F/E	(P.o.W.)
A' Flt	F/O D.J. Robertson	NAV	(P.o.W.)
	F/S N.E. Mortimer	W/OP	(P.o.W.)
	Sgt H. Cowan	A/G	(Killed)
	F/O C.A. Watts	B/A	(Killed)
	Sgt J.G. Harrison	A/G	(P.o.W.)

21/22 January, 1943; ESSEN: Seventy-nine Lancasters, including 7 from 49 Squadron, led by 3 Pathfinder Mosquitoes were dispatched to Essen. Over the target they encountered 10/10ths cloud cover and had to drop their bombs blind on estimated positions. All 49's aircraft returned safely to base; 4 Lancasters were lost on the raid.

JANUARY 1943

23/24 January, 1943; DÜSSELDORF: Whilst Halifaxes and Stirlings attacked Lorient, a force of 80 Lancasters was sent to the Ruhr town of Düsseldorf. As on the previous night's raid to Essen, the target was obscured by cloud. Eight Lancasters had departed Fiskerton by 17.56hrs. Within three hours, Sgt McDonald (ED438) returned to Scampton, unable to carry on due to the rear guns not firing. Sgt Gumbley's crew (ED416) experienced similar problems with front and rear turrets, so they too returned early to base.

Before midnight the remaining 6 aircraft were back over England, their sorties completed. Moans and groans were uttered by the crews as they received diversion orders; 4 landed at Tangmere, whilst F/Lt Allsebrook (ED450) put S-Sugar down on the grass airfield at Bodney in Norfolk; W/O Mapp (ED434) landed T-Tommy at Waterbeach.

27/28 January, 1943; DÜSSELDORF: The thin layer of cloud over the target did not prevent the 'Oboe Mossies' from using ground marking for the first time. The 162 heavies attacking this night included 9 from 49 Squadron. A tenth aircraft, piloted by Sgt Gilmore (ED428) had taken-off, but whilst the rear gunner was rotating his turret it severed the oxygen tube forcing an early return.

The bombing was well concentrated in the south of the town, and all 49's aircraft carried out their duties successfully. S/Ldr Couch (ED440) and crew dropped their 4,000lb 'cookie' on the third attempt. Six of the raiding force failed to return; all 49's were safe.

30/31 January, 1943; HAMBURG: The last raid of the month was to the U-boat base and industrial city of Hamburg. Situated on the River Elbe and close to the coastline of north west Germany, this target proved ideal for the first ever use of H2S. Pathfinder Halifaxes and Stirlings used this new device to mark the target for the 148 strong attacking force. Eleven Lancasters lifted from Fiskerton around midnight into a clear, cold, starlit night, with a promise of good weather on their return. F/Sgt G.B.S. Miller (ED450) and crew were setting out on their first operation together.

Hamburg received a scattered attack with many of the bombs falling in the river or surrounding wetlands. Sgt Gumbley (ED416) piloting J-Johnny, had a bomb door buckled by the 4000lb 'cookie' as it was released. Five Lancasters were lost on the raid, but all of 49's aircraft headed for home across the North Sea. About an hour out from base, the returning aircraft were informed that the cloud base over Fiskerton was down to 600 feet and that in the driving rain, visibility was 600 yards.

The WAAF controller strongly advised crews to land away. Four aircraft heeded this advice; one went over to Wigsley, whilst Sgt Thom put down on the grass runway at Scampton. Sgt Gilmore found refuge at Pocklington up in Yorkshire and S/Ldr Couch landed at Swinderby; but 6 of the squadron's Lancs did manage to scrape into Fiskerton by 06.55hrs.

This left just one aircraft outstanding... aloft in the gloom of this miserable Sunday morning were the tired young men in F/Sgt Elliot Cole's crew. In their flak damaged Lancaster, the crew groped around in the murky sky over Fiskerton airfield, searching desperately for a clear gap that would give them a glimpse of the flarepath, home and safety.

The 23 year old Australian pilot made his approach from the north west, heading for one of the shorter runways. The Lancaster had just passed low over Hawthorn Road, close to the village of Reepham when Q-Queenie suddenly thumped into the ground (possibly after hitting a tree); the time was 07.15hrs.

For those listening on the ground the crash came with a sickening jolt. Crash crews, already in their vehicles sheltering from the rain, sped off in the direction of the sound. 'Queenie' had in fact come down on the opposite side of the main Grimsby to Lincoln railway line, making access very difficult for the rescuers.

Miraculously, the mid/upper gunner, Sgt E. Phillips had survived, but sadly the other six members of the crew had all perished; it was a very tragic end to a dreadful morning.

Crashed ED428	F/S E.L. Cole, RAAF	Pilot	(Killed)
(EA-Q)	Sgt F.S.T.S. Pittard,	F/E	(Killed)
'B'Flt	F/O F. Ridley,	NAV	(Killed)
	Sgt J.A.G. Browne RAAF	W/AG	(Killed)
	Sgt E. Phillips	A/G	(Injured)
	F/S L. Grey RAAF	B/A	(Killed)
	Sgt W.C. Wood	R/G	(Killed)

Note: Five of the crew are buried at St. John the Baptist Church, Scampton; the sixth man, Sgt Wood, is buried in East Ham, Essex.

OPERATIONAL SUMMARY - JANUARY 1943

Date	Target	Desp	E/R	FTR	Remarks
16/17	BERLIN	16	4	-	
17/18	BERLIN	9	2	1	F/O Jefferys FTR
21/22	ESSEN	7	2	-	
23/24	DÜSSELDORF	8	2	-	
27/28	DÜSSELDORF	10	1	-	
30/31	HAMBURG	11	-	1c	F/S Cole crashed at base
Total of sorties flown		61			
Failed to return		1 + 1c			

FEBRUARY 1943

1 February, 1943: Aircraft on charge consisted of: 1 Lancaster Mk 1 awaiting disposal, 17 Lancaster Mk 111's representing initial equipment plus 1 Tiger Moth and 1 Puss Moth... held for training purposes!

2/3 February, 1943; COLOGNE: On the night of Tuesday 2 February, 7 Lancasters climbed out of Fiskerton through layers of thick cloud. Over the North Sea they were still in cloud at 21,000ft with temperatures down to -40 degrees.

A force of 161 four-engined bombers converged over a cloud-covered Cologne where Pathfinders had dropped markers by using both Oboe and H2S. Damage reports show that the city sustained bombing over a wide area, but with no serious concentration. Bomber Command lost 5 aircraft in total; 3 Lancasters, 1 Halifax and 1 H2S equipped Pathfinder Stirling. The Stirling, along with its secret H2S set had literally 'fallen' into the Germans hands. Eventually the Germans were able to develop a device which enabled their night fighters to home in on a bomber using H2S.

The squadron suffered the loss of a crew this night; F/Lt Bob Jackson (ED440) and crew had taken-off at 18.51hrs flying their first operation from Fiskerton. Their aircraft was shot down by a night fighter and crashed between Kessel and Helden in Holland. Six of the crew are buried in Nijmegen Cemetery. Lancaster Mk III, ED440 was flying its 4th operation.

FTR ED440	F/L R.A Jackson	Pilot	(Killed)
(EA-L)	F/S H.M. Magder RCAF	NAV	(Killed)
	F/O E.J.F Dunand RCAF	W/AG	(Killed)
	Sgt A.J. Clover	A/G	(Killed)
	P/O A.W. Lane	B/A	(Killed)
	Sgt A.R. McMahon	F/E	(P.o.W.)
	Sgt L.G. Alexander	A/G	(Killed)

* F/Sgt Magder has the Star of David on his headstone.

3/4 February, 1943: HAMBURG: Bad weather with severe icing was the main concern of the bomber crews as they clawed their way out of base. Over the North Sea they were soon confronted by a tremendous cold front which prevented 3 of the squadron's aircraft from proceeding. Gerry Fawke (ED427) O-Orange, with his starboard-inner engine u/s could not hope to climb over the front; F/O Armstrong (ED497) had trouble with one of C-Charlie's super-chargers and F/Sgt Miller also experienced engine problems; all three jettisoned their bombs and returned to base.

They were not alone; of the 263 aircraft provided by all Groups, only 153 managed the scattered attack on Hamburg. Just 2 of the squadron's aircraft reached the target. Ralph Allsebrook (ED448) and crew along with Sgt McDonald and crew; the latter struggled to open R-Robert's bomb-doors but finally managed to get their load away.

Despite the bad weather, German night fighters were still extremely effective with 16 bombers failing to return.

F/O Gerry Fawke and crew most probably photographed at Fiskerton during Jan/Feb 1943, shortly before they completed their tour.
(left to right):

F/Sgt Fortin (W/Op);
Sgt Cole (F/Eng);
P/O Bennett DFM (NAV);
F/O Fawke DFC (Pilot);
Sgt Osler DFM (B/A);
Sgt Bratt (M/U);
Sgt Walters (R/G).

*Sgt Douglas Stuart Bratt was KIA 5/6-3-43.
(T. Bennett)

4/5 February, 1943: TURIN/LORIENT: In a brief respite from German targets, Command dispatched 188 aircraft against Turin, whilst 128 aircraft made an incendiary attack on Lorient. Both attacks caused serious damage for the loss of 4 aircraft. 49 Squadron provided 6 aircraft, 3 for each target with all crews achieving successful results.

S/Ldr Cracknell (ED469), Sgt Gilmore (ED438) and Sgt Miller (ED467) and crews visited Turin, whilst F/O Armstrong and crew plus two new crews, piloted by Sgt Duncan (ED416) and Sgt Hogg (ED497) flew to Lorient.

11/12 February, 1943: WILHELMSHAVEN: At 17.23hrs the first of 49 Squadron's 6 Lancasters rolled down the runway. Bill Townsend (ED435) and crew in K-King were the last away, as the Duty staff in the Watch Office remained on call should any aircraft 'boomerang'. Their wait was not in vain... shortly after 20.00hrs K-King called the tower for landing instructions -just before crossing the enemy coast the Townsend crew decided to turn back when their rear turret went out of action.

The town of Wilhelmshaven and its naval dockyards were cloud-covered when the Pathfinders arrived. As the 177 strong Main Force approached they found the target had been marked with very accurate parachute flares (sky-markers) by the use of H2S. Wilhelmshaven received a devastating blind-bombing attack for the cost of 3 Lancasters. Fiskerton's 5 Lancasters were all safely home before midnight.

13/14 February, 1943: LORIENT: On a clear moonlit night 466 heavies set out once again to pound Lorient's U-boat base on the Biscay coast of France.

The squadron supplied 10 aircraft for the raid. In all, Bomber Command lost 7 aircraft including 2 Lancasters - one came from 103 Squadron at Elsham Wolds, the other was from 49 Squadron. F/Sgt Gifford Miller and crew had reached the south coast near Plymouth on return from Lorient, when tragedy struck. In the darkness over the Sound, their aircraft sliced into the unseen steel cable of a barrage balloon. The Lancaster came down on the western end of the breakwater, disintegrating as it fell into the sea. The crews final moments have never been established for sadly they all perished in the crash and their bodies were never recovered.

FTR ED450	F/Sgt G.B.C. Miller	Pilot	(Missing)
(EA-G)	F/O R. Allin	NAV	(Missing)
'A'flt	Sgt K. Hands	W/AG	(Missing)
	Sgt W. Noble	B/A	(Missing)
	Sgt S. Young	F/E	(Missing)
	Sgt W. Halsall	A/G	(Missing)
	Sgt F.H. Allen	A/G	(Missing)

Note: The remains of ED450 are still there today, though the wreckage is now well broken up and scattered by the tides. The site is frequently visited by the local diving club... a sad memorial to a brave crew. The Captain of the Royal Naval Diving School at Bovisand, took Dr John Allin, the son of the navigator, to the scene; then, after dinner, presented him with a fire extinguisher, polished to perfection, from the wreck. Needless to say, John was lost for words.

14/15 February, 1943: MILAN: A force of 142 Lancasters carried out a concentrated attack on this weakly-defended Italian target. F/O Eyre (ED445) had to return early with rear turret trouble, but 7 of the squadron's Lancasters navigated their way through the majestic splendour of snow covered Alpine peaks to reach the target.

All 49's aircraft returned safely after an eight and a half hour flight. Two Lancasters (from other units) were lost.

16/17 February, 1943: LORIENT: A force of 377 aircraft attacked Lorient, with the majority dropping mainly incendiary loads. The visibility was clear and all 7 Lancasters from Fiskerton made successful attacks and completed their sorties. The squadron had put up one new crew, that of Sgt W.M. Stables (ED437).

18/19 February, 1943: WILHELMSHAVEN: Although the Pathfinders claimed to have marked well, bombing photos showed that most of the 195 strong Main Force attack fell in open country. Ironically all of the 8 aircraft from 49 Squadron reported having the target indicators in their sights. Four Lancasters were lost on this operation, but all 49's returned safely; 2 landing at base, the remaining 6 at Scampton.

FEBRUARY 1943

19/20 February, 1943: WILHELMSHAVEN: Bomber Command sent 338 aircraft to Wilhelmshaven again, to make amends for the previous nights poor show. But yet again the raid was a failure and this time for the loss of 12 aircraft. 49 could only manage to put up 3 aircraft, each of which claimed to have bombed the markers before returning unharmed.

21/22 February, 1943: BREMEN: A medium force of 129 heavies bombed a cloud covered Bremen. The squadron contributed 7 aircraft but Sgt Townsend (ED437) and crew soon returned with W/T failure; the remainder reported bombing both sky and ground markers.
On return, the squadron was diverted to bases in Yorkshire, with S/Ldr Couch (ED584) U-Uncle, landing at Linton and the remaining 5 at Leeming.

22 February, 1943. At 11.20hrs, 5 Group squadrons were stood down from operations. On this day F/O Armstong and crew were posted out 'tour expired', having been with the squadron since June 1942. Each member was posted to a training unit where they could pass on their invaluable combat experience; F/O Armstrong went to 1485 Bombing and Gunnery Flight at Fulbeck.

25/26 February, 1943: NUREMBURG: Eight Lancasters set out from Fiskerton to join 329 four-engined bombers on the long trip to Nuremburg. Sgt Stables had to return early with his port-outer and starboard-inner engines giving problems. The remaining 7 aircraft reported concentrated attacks around the markers, but later recce photos showed the bombing to have fallen on the northern edges of the town. Command lost 9 aircraft; none were from 49 Squadron.

26/27 February, 1943: COLOGNE: At 10.35hrs Group came on the 'blower' requesting 9 aircraft for a raid on Hamburg or Bremen... but by 11.10hrs this had been altered to Cologne. Sgt Price (ED431) and crew were the last away, leaving Fiskerton at 19.25hrs. Over 400 aircraft dropped their loads in the south-west area of the city. Sgt Gumbley (ED445) and crew approached the target at 18,000ft just after 21.20hrs; he described the scene:

"The visibility was hazy with no cloud -we could see the green Pathfinder markers in the centre of the concentration and held this in our sights; bombs were seen exploding in a triangle of 3 markers and lots of incendiaries were seen strewn around the outside of the town; we saw several aircraft fall, probably due to collision or fighters!"

The flak came a little too close to Sgt Stables (ED426) and crew in P-Peter. Sgt Stables reported: *"We had bombed from 17,000ft in good visibility. P/O Ken Gibson, our bomb aimer, held the green T.I.'s in the sights -11 minutes after leaving the target the port-inner engine failed due to flak damage sustained over the target, but we managed to return to base on the remaining 3 engines."*

All nine of the squadron's Lancasters were home by midnight, but throughout the Command 10 aircraft had failed to return.

27/28 February, 1943: FRISIAN ISLANDS (MINELAYING): At 10.00hrs Group requested one aircraft for a gardening sortie off the Frisian Islands. A new crew piloted by Sgt Ed Tickler (ED434) was given the task and took-off from Fiskerton at 18.59hrs on this, their first operation. Sgt Tickler had flown in this same aircraft to Cologne the previous evening, as 2nd dickie to S/Ldr Couch.

On arriving in the target area, Sgt Tickler's aircraft, now flying at low level, was engaged by gunfire from a flak-ship. The Lancaster's gunners returned fire in an attempt to silence the ship's guns, but during this exchange the aircraft rear turret was slightly damaged .

The crew pressed-on in poor visibility but ran into searchlights and more light-flak; this time the Lancaster received numerous hits in the cockpit, port wing and again in the rear turret. In the encounter the flight engineer, Sgt Downing received severe head injuries which were to prove fatal. The pilot had been hit in the shoulder and his left side and momentarily lost control of the aircraft. Fortunately control was soon regained with the assistance of the navigator, Sgt Matthews. Despite this damage the crew managed to carry out their duties and dropped the mines in the correct place. It was only after carrying out the task that Sgt Tickler informed the crew of his injuries.

Whilst Sgt Lowens, the bomb aimer, helped fly the aircraft, Sgt Webb, the wireless operator, gave the pilot first-aid and tried to help the dying flight engineer. After crossing the Lincolnshire coast near North Coates, the crew spotted the small grass airfield at RAF Donna Nook. With the assistance of his crew, Sgt Tickler made a good landing, but then collapsed with exhaustion over the controls. The Lancaster swung off the grass runway and struck a military vehicle that had come to the aid of the stricken aircraft. The unfortunate flight engineer, Sgt D. Downing, sadly died from the injuries he received.

For their actions this night Sgt Edward Wells Tickler received the Conspicuous Gallantry Medal; Sgt's J.L. Mathews RCAF, G.J. Lowans RCAF and G.B. Silvester the DFM and Sgt's M.G. Webb RCAF and W.A. Davies were Mentioned in Despatches. Sgt Tickler later received his commission. The Lancaster involved, ED434, was repaired and rejoined the squadron.

After a period of convalescence, Sgt Tickler was posted to Swinderby where he finally managed to get back on flying. In early 1944 he formed a new crew and they were posted to 57 Squadron at East Kirkby. Their 13th trip together was the infamous Nuremberg raid; F/Lt Tickler's Lancaster was brought down by an ME 110 night fighter; three members survived including Ed Tickler, who became a POW in Stalag Luft 1 at Barth.

28 February/ 1 March, 1943; ST NAZAIRE: The weather all the way through February had been unpredictable, and the last day of the month was no exception. The morning started fine, but high gusting winds soon developed bringing with it rain squalls.

FEBRUARY 1943

Weather-beaten crews gathered at briefing to learn that the evening's target was St Nazaire; the second U-boat base to be selected for demolition. A large force consisting of 437 aircraft was dispatched. Fiskerton's contribution (8 aircraft) was a mixture of experienced crews and novices. Both W/Cmdr Slee (ED441) and Sgt Townsend (ED432) were flying their 21st operations, whilst Sgt Pilots Tolchard (ED590) and Penry (ED497) were taking their respective crews on ops for the first time.

The other 4 crews detailed were piloted by Sgt Stables, Sgt Gilmore, F/Lt Allsebrook (soon to complete his second tour) and Sgt Duncan.
The raid caused widespread damage to the port and the town, with 49 Squadron crews reporting good results and 'very extensive fires'.

Bomber Command lost 5 aircraft; 2 Wellingtons, 1 Stirling and 2 Lancasters. Sadly, one of the Lancasters came from Fiskerton. The aircraft, flown by 26 year old Canadian pilot W/O Fred Duncan and crew, came down in the target area; sadly all onboard perished. Some rest in a joint grave at Loire-Atlantique in France, with crew members of an 83 Squadron Lancaster brought down on the same night.

FTR ED467	Sgt F.C. Duncan RCAF	Pilot	(Killed)
(EA-E)	Sgt R. Brookes	F/E	(Killed)
'A'Flt	F/O R.G. McCracken	NAV	(Killed)
	Sgt H. Kay	W/AG	(Killed)
	Sgt D.W. Belsham	A/G	(Killed)
Crew on their	F/S A.M. Dickie RCAF	A/B	(Killed)
9th operation	Sgt J.A. Kelly	A/G	(Killed)

Ralf Allsebrook, third from left, at Fiskerton in early 1943 with his crew at the rear of Lancaster ED597 (EA-B).

By the time Ralf was killed in action with 617 Sqdn on 16th Sept 1943, he was a F/Lt with a D.S.O. and D.F.C.

In his Hampden days he had a lucky escape after hitting a balloon cable over Sheffield on 14th/15th Feb 1942, he and his crew were rescued from the sea after ditching in AE397 of 49 Sqdn.
(Harry Moyle)

FEBRUARY 1943

OPERATIONAL SUMMARY - FEBRUARY 1943

Date	Target	Desp	E/R	FTR	Remarks
2/3	COLOGNE	7	-	1	F/O Jackson FTR
3/2	HAMBURG	5	3	-	
4/5	TURIN	3	-	-	
7/8	LORIENT	3	-	-	
11/12	WILHELMSHAVEN	6	1	-	
13/14	LORIENT	10	-	1	F/S Miller FTR
14/15	MILAN	8	1	-	
16/17	LORIENT	7	-	-	
18/19	WILHELMSHAVEN	8	-	-	
19/20	WILHELMSHAVEN	3	-	-	
21/22	BREMEN	7	1	-	All diverted
25/26	NUREMBURG	8	1	-	
26/27	COLOGNE	9	-	-	
27/28	MINELAYING	1	-	1c	Sgt Tickler c/l
28/29	ST NAZAIRE	8	-	1	Sgt Duncan FTR
Total of sorties flown		93			
Failed to return		3 + 1c			

HONOURS AND AWARDS - FEBRUARY 1943

S/Ldr E.G. Couch M.B.E.	D.F.C.
F/Lt G. Hewitt	D.F.C.
F/O J.S. Holme	D.F.C.
F/S T.V. Webster	D.F.M.
F/S R.W. Wright	D.F.M.
Sgt Bennett	D.F.M.
Sgt D.D. Blaha	D.F.M.
Sgt N.B. Lewis	D.F.M.
Sgt E.E. Osler	D.F.M.

MARCH 1943

1/2 March, 1943; BERLIN: A force of 302 Lancasters, Halifaxs and Stirlings caused much damage to the south-west of Berlin.

W/Cdr Slee (ED441) and crew were the first away from Fiskerton at 18.47 hrs; they were followed by a further 8 Lancasters. 11 aircraft had been detailed but Sgt Stables (ED584) withdrew after becoming sick and Sgt Gumbley RNZAF (ED416) suffered magneto drop on J-Johnny.

All crews attacked and later reported many fires. The Eyre crew (ED438) were hit by flak after being coned in searchlights whilst F/Sgt Gilmore (ED 435) and crew were hit in the nose section over Osnabruck, All 49's Lancasters returned safely to base, whilst Bomber Command lost a total of 17 aircraft.

3/4 March, 1943; HAMBURG: Although the night was clear the H2S equipped Pathfinder crews slipped up and marked Wedel, a small town several miles downstream from Hamburg.

Fiskerton contributed 8 Lancasters to a total force of 417 bombers. Returning crews reported seeing numerous fires. Despite PFF's mistake the Hamburg area received some heavy damage.

10 aircraft failed to return; 4 Lancasters, 2 Halifaxes, 2 Stirlings and 2 Wellingtons. All 49's aircraft returned safely although the Price crew (ED435) had been damaged in combat. They had been attacked by night fighters in the target area and were forced to jettison their bombs at 21.50 hrs at 20,000 ft. Several hits were sustained and the starboard inner engine was put out of action as the Lancaster lost 3000 ft.

Experiencing heavy vibration throughout, the crew landed N-Nuts back at base at 00.46 hrs.

THE BATTLE OF THE RUHR

New tactics and advanced devices, such as 'Oboe', had been developed throughout the recent winter. These combined with the steady build up in aircraft strength, convinced 'Bomber' Harris that his squadrons and crews would be able to carry out a major effort against Germany.

By early March 1943, Bomber Command was ready to start a 'spring offensive'. During the next four months, forty-three major raids would be carried out, two-thirds of which would be against targets in the Ruhr. The remaining attacks would be wide ranging, thus preventing the enemy concentrating his night-fighter and flak defences around the Ruhr cities. Harris later called this campaign 'The Battle of the Ruhr', and the opening round would be 5/6 March, 1943.

5/6 March, 1943; ESSEN: A mixed force of 442 Lancasters, Halifaxes, Stirlings, Wellingtons and Oboe Mosquitoes was despatched to Essen, of which 56 returned early before reaching the target.

49 Squadron crews detailed for operations:

ED487	Sgt Penry;	ED497	F/L Allsebrook;	ED584	F/S Gilmore
ED432	Sgt Townsend;	ED438	Sgt McDonald;	ED445	F/O Eyre;
ED416	Sgt Gumbley;	ED431	Sgt Thom:		

At exactly 19.13hrs, the first 49 Squadron Lancaster lifted from Fiskerton's twinkling flarepath and by 19.31hrs the last of the 8 aircraft detailed, had climbed away into the dark, moonless night. High above home base navigators gave their pilots a course that headed them towards Mablethorpe, and from there to Egmong on the Dutch coast. From Egmong they flew to a point 15 miles north of Essen, where Pathfinders had placed yellow ground markers. From here the bombers began their run-up to the target.

The attack was in three overlapping waves, Halifaxes first followed by Wellington/Stirlings and then the high flying Lancasters. At the rate of 11 aircraft a minute, the main force passed over Essen within forty minutes. Shortly before midnight 49 Squadron's Lancasters started to land back at Fiskerton. The tired but eager crews clambered aboard the crew buses which ferried them to de-brief where most gave optimistic reports of a 'good show'.

Meanwhile, back at the darkened airfield, to the ground-crew of M-Mother came the sad realisation that their charge would not be coming home. Their worst fears were later confirmed... Jimmy Thom DFM, the popular Scots pilot and his young crew had all perished during the operation. It is believed that they were shot down by Ltn Denzel, west of Texel and crashed into the sea.

Later that morning, reconnaissance photographs showed that the returning crews' optimism was not unfounded. 160 acres of the target had been destroyed with the main area of damage being between the Krupps works and the city centre. But a price had to be paid; Bomber Command lost 14 aircraft and crews.

Sgt Pilot James Myles Thom DFM, RAF(VR), A photo in civilian clothes often carried by aircrew as an escape aid.

FTR:ED431	Sgt J.M. Thom DFM	Pilot	(Missing)
(EA-M)	Sgt D.G. Fairlie	F/E	(Missing)
'B'Flt	F/S J.H. Prior	NAV	(Missing)
	F/S K. Bolton	W/AG	(Missing)
	Sgt D.S. Bratt	A/G	(Missing)
Crew on their	W/O A.M. Horne (DFM RCAF)	B/A	(Missing)
18th operation	Sgt F.H.L. Vines	A/G	(Missing)

8/9 March, 1943; NUREMBURG: The second large operation of 'the battle' was against a distant target. Nuremburg lay beyond the range of Oboe and therefore it had to be marked with a combination of H2S and visual means. This resulted in the bombing being spread over a large area, but although the attack was not concentrated,

49 Squadron put up 8 Lancasters;

ED597	F/L Allsebrook	ED438	Sgt McDonald	ED441	Sgt Hogg
ED416	Sgt Gumbley	ED427	F/S Gilmore	ED497	Sgt Penry
ED590	F/L Green	ED445	F/O Eyre		

All the crews completed their sorties successfully except Sgt Penry (ED497) and crew:

"We were unable to fix our position over the Channel, and realised we could not make up the lost time".

Sgt Penry landed C-Charlie back at Scampton. Bomber Command lost 8 aircraft from the 335 despatched.

9/10 March, 1943; MUNICH: 49 Squadron again contributed 8 Lancasters to the 264 aircraft despatched against Munich.

ED584	Sgt Stables	ED426	Sgt McDonald	ED441	Sgt Hogg
ED469	F/L Green	ED597	F/L Allsebrook	ED448	F/O Eyre
ED416	Sgt Gumbley	ED427	F/S Gilmore		

F/Lt Green (ED469) and crew found their intercom had become u/s, so having no alternative they brought A-Apple home.

Over the target, wind caused the bombing to spread into the western part of the city rather than the centre. Despite this, much damage was caused. By 0430hrs all Fiskerton's brood were safely gathered in, but throughout the Command, 8 crews failed to return.

11/12 March, 1943; STUTTGART: Of the 314 aircraft sent to Stuttgart, 10 were from 49 Squadron.

ED590	F/L Green	ED597	F/L Allsebrook	ED448	F/S Gilmore
ED441	Sgt Hogg	ED429	Sgt McDonald	ED445	F/O Eyre
ED453	Sgt Penry	ED432	Sgt Towsend	ED431	Sgt Stables
ED...	Sgt Gumbley				

This raid was not a success... for the first time the Germans used dummy target indicators. The cost was 11 aircraft missing, but this figure did not include any from the squadron... all 49's Lancasters landed back at Fiskerton except Sgt Hogg (ED441) and crew... they landed at Scampton 'as orders stated'.

12/13 March, 1943; ESSEN: A large force of 457 bombers approached a well marked Essen, the Oboe Mossies had done their work well. Of the 10 crews from 49 Squadron, 6 had been to Stuttgart the previous night. For Sgt Cyril Anderson (ED416) and crew this was their first trip together... on leaving the target the port inner engine cut out, forcing them to return on 3 engines.

Just 11 days later, they, along with another 49 Squadron crew (Sgt Townsend) would be selected by W/Cmdr Guy Gibson for the new 617 Squadron; but below them on this night was the giant Krupps works which was in the centre of wide scale destruction.

The defences were stronger than the previous visit and resulted in 23 planes failing to return; 49's were all safe.

This photograph of S/Ldr Cracknell (extreme right) and crew was taken at Fiskerton on 24-3-43 at the end of their tour. Included are;

F/Lt M.D. Deloford (Nav);
Sgt W.T. Beesly (F/Eng);
Sgt W.C. White (B/A);
Sgt A.M. McDairmid (A/G);
Sgt H. Frost (A/G);
F/Sgt N.G. Ball (W/Op);
plus two 'A' Flt ground crew members.

Lancaster ED469 (EA-A) failed to return just six-nights later from Berlin 29/30-3-43 when flown by F/O Mabee RCAF and crew on their first operation; only the bomb aimer survived. (49 Sqdn collection)

22/23 March, 1943; ST-NAZAIRE: It had been ten days since the last operation... the English weather had been its temperamental self. The days were fine with the early spring sunshine becoming pleasantly warm... but each evening low-lying mist crept over the Lincolnshire countryside. On the evening of Monday 22nd the waiting was over... St Nazaire, an easy one! Harris was keeping his pledge in the war against the U-boats. Over 280 heavies made a concentrated attack on the port area of this German submarine base.

W/Cmdr Slee (ED702) in his favoured Lancaster, D-Dog, led the 14 strong contingent from 49 Squadron. As the Wingco arrived over the target he found that a smoke screen was in operation; four times he and his crew were coned in searchlights, and on one occasion the mid upper gunner was hit by shrapnel in the eye. Still unable to make a positive identification, W/Cmdr Slee decided to jettison the bomb load on their 5th run over the target.

A new crew were 'cutting their teeth' this night... F/O Southern (ED721) and crew flew in the new T-Tommy. This kite replaced ED434, damaged a few weeks earlier at Donna Nook.

F/Lt Neil Green (ED719) and crew were hit by a 'rocket propelled incendiary shell' about 2 miles west of the target... it severed the rudder controls and put out the pilot's and bomb aimers intercom. Their own incendiary load was jettisoned and a safe return was made, landing at Cranfield.

Bad weather on the return to England caused 8 of 49's aircraft to land away at various other airfields, but by early morning all crews had been accounted for.

SQUADRON "X"

25 March, 1943: Strange things were happening over at Scampton; a new squadron was in the process of being formed from 'selected' crews. Its commander was a W/Cmdr Guy Gibson, the former C.O. of 106 Squadron, Syerston, who had just completed his third operational tour. Two crews were posted out from 49 Squadron to the fledgling Squadron 'X'. The two crews selected were totally different in operational experience:

Sgt Bill Townsend's crew was nearing the end of a tour, which would bring the 22 year old pilot a well earned DFM. On the other hand, Sgt Cyril Anderson's crew was just beginning a tour, having freshly arrived from 1654 HCU on 23 Feb.

In the event, although the Anderson crew received their posting to 617 on the 24 March, they didn't actually go to the new unit until early April, deciding to 'get some in' (5 ops) with 49 Squadron first.

Both crews survived the actual 'Dams' operation. Cyril Anderson and crew returned to Fiskerton and 49 Squadron in June, but their luck ran out in September when they failed to return from Mannheim; all were killed.

26/27 March, 1943; DUISBURG: The MT driver from 1661 HCU, Winthorpe, turned into the gates of RAF Fiskerton with another load of fresh young airmen destined for operational flying. Sgt Jock Morrison and crew clambered down from the lorry onto an airfield bristling with activity... the squadron was 'on' that night, and 10 Lancaster's were being prepared for a trip to Duisburg.

All 10 aircraft were away by 19.17hrs, but over the next three hours, 3 returned with faults; Sgt Price (ED426) had port-outer engine trouble, Sgt Stables (ED584) had the same problem and Sgt Millar RCAF (ED441) and crew attempting their second operation, returned when the artificial horizon went u/s. The remaining 7 made successful sorties, all landing back at base shortly before midnight.

27 March, 1943. Arriving this day, from 1660 HCU at Swinderby was the crew of the incoming new C.O., W/Cmdr Peter Warren Johnson AFC, who was to follow them in a few days time.

MARCH 1943

27/28 March, 1943; BERLIN: By 10.30hrs, orders were through requiring 10 aircraft for Hamburg or Berlin... at 15.00hrs the target was confirmed as Berlin. W/Cmdr Slee (ED702), flying his 24th operation with the squadron, led 9 aircraft away from Fiskerton by 20.49hrs. The tenth Lancaster was scrubbed when Sgt pilot Stables reported unfit to fly.

All the remaining 9 crews completed their sorties, with both W/Cmdr Slee and Sgt Price (ED721) sustaining flak damage to the underside of their respective Lancasters. 6 aircraft landed back at base and 3 landed at Scampton.

29/30 March, 1943; BERLIN: The last operation of the month was a return trip to the 'Big City'. Twelve Lancasters were offered and a take-off time was set for 18.30hrs. The take-off time was altered twice before the squadron departed to join the other 317 heavies heading for the German capital. Weather conditions were severe, with icing problems and badly predicted winds. Three of the squadron's aircraft were forced to return early; Sgt Gumbley (ED416) and crew in J-Johnny, decided to head for Wittering's long grass runway, with their air speed indicator u/s. Sgt Millar (ED584) and crew in U-Uncle struggled with 'temporary failure' of flying controls and engines due to icing; they managed to put down at Docking. Sgt Price (ED426) P-Peter, returned with Sgt Potts his navigator feeling seriously ill.

Three crews were operating for the first time - they were piloted by; P/O Taylor (ED721) in T-Tommy, Sgt Fyffe (ED435), and Canadian F/O Mabee (ED487) who had visited Berlin two nights earlier, as second dickey flying with W/Cmdr Slee.

The bulk of the bombing fell in open countryside to the south east of Berlin. Aircraft losses included 11 Lancasters, 7 Halifaxes and 3 Stirlings... 2 of the Lancasters were from 49 Squadron. Of the three fresh crews operating this night, two were missing.

After being damaged by flak over the target, Sgt Fyffe and crew struggling for home were eventually shot down by a German night fighter flown by Hauptmann Herbert Lütje of 111./NJG1. Their Lancaster crashed between Heeten and Raalte in Holland; three of the crew perished and are buried in Raalte.

F/O George Mabee RCAF and crew were shot down by a night fighter, crashing near Neustadt at 03.26hrs. Six of the crew were killed; the rear gunner, Sgt Jones (who was seriously injured), survived to become a PoW. The remainder of the crew are buried together in Hannover.

It is perhaps interesting to reflect that the other 'new' crew flying this night (P/O Taylor's) went on to complete a distinguished tour with the pilot being awarded the DFC.

Sgt Tolchard (ED44) and crew nearly became the third victim of the night, when flak splinters entered the windscreen just above the pilot's head and also went through the perspex in Sgt Doe's mid-upper turret.

MARCH 1943

FTR ED435	Sgt D.W. Fyffe	Pilot	(P.o.W.)
(EA-N)	Sgt E.R. McCracken	F/E	(P.o.W.)
'B'Flt	Sgt T. Fazakerley	A/G	(Killed)
	Sgt R.C. Link	NAV	(P.o.W.)
	P/O A.T.L. Cullum RCAF	B/A	(P.o.W.)
Crew on their	W/O F.A. McNutt RCAF	W/AG	(Killed)
1st operation	Sgt J. Robertson	A/G	(Killed)
FTR ED469	F/O G.F. Mabee RCAF	Pilot	(Killed)
(EA-A)	Sgt J.A. Cross	F/E	(Killed)
'A'Flt	Sgt W. Carr	NAV	(Killed)
	Sgt A.S. McLaren	W/AG	(Killed)
	Sgt R.W. Brown	A/B	(Killed)
Crew on their	Sgt G.A. Jones	A/G	(P.o.W.)
1st operation	Sgt J.G. Jewell	A/G	(Killed)

OPERATIONAL SUMMARY - MARCH 1943

Date	**Target**	**Desp**	**E/R**	**FTR**	**Remarks**
1/2	BERLIN	9			
3/4	HAMBURG	8	-	-	
5/6	ESSEN	8	-	1	Sgt Thom FTR
8/9	NUREMBURG	8	1	-	
9/10	MUNICH	8	2	-	
11/12	STUTTGART	10	-	-	
12/13	ESSEN	10	-	-	
22/23	ST NAZAIRE	14	-	-	8 diverted
26/27	DUISBURG	10	3	-	
27/28	BERLIN	9	-	-	
29/30	BERLIN	12	3	2	P/O Mabee FTR Sgt Fyffe FTR

Total of sorties flown	106
Failed to return	3

HONOURS AND AWARDS - MARCH 1943

W/Cdr L.C. Slee D.S.O.	D.F.C.
F/O M.D. Deloford	D.F.C.
F/O A.S. Grant D.S.O.	D.F.C.

APRIL 1943

On April fools day, 1943, the squadron's establishment of aircraft was at full strength; 16 Lancaster Mk 111's represented the initial equipment and there were 4 Mk 111's in reserve plus 2 further Lancs surplus.

By 10.05hrs a complete 'stand down' was received from Group, and maximum training was ordered. During the evening 3 of the newly arrived crews were dispatched on an infra-red bombing sortie over Northampton; the crews of Sgt's Tomlin, Nixon and Morrison completed the exercise successfully. The next day was also a stand down with maximum training; 9 aircraft carried out bombing and formation flying practice.

3/4 April, 1943; ESSEN: Ten of the squadron's Lancasters were part of a 348 strong force of heavies sent to attack Essen. All 49's crews reported good results in the concentrated attack that developed over Essen. Briefed to bomb at 20,000ft, Sgt Penry (ED441) and crew were unable to maintain height due to power loss in their starboard engine. Forced down to 12,500ft over the target, the crew successfully carried out their task. They later reported that the fires were visible from 100 miles away.

Bomber Command sustained the loss of 21 bombers over the continent, with an additional 2 Halifaxes crashing in England. Sgt Tolchard (ED448) and crew nearly became an addition to these losses when their own Lancaster was fired upon by another Lancaster, fortunately without causing serious damage. All Fiskerton's aircraft returned safely to base.

4/5 April, 1943; KIEL: This was the largest bombing force dispatched so far in the war (excluding the 1000 raids). A mixed force of 577 bombers including 9 Lancasters from Fiskerton, found a cloud-covered target poorly marked by the PFF.

As F/O Southern (ED590) pointed out at de-brief: *"If arrangements had been made for alternative 'Wanganui' instead of 'Paramatta', the bombing would have been successful."*

Four of the new pilots to the squadron flew as 'second-dickies' this night... they were F/O Bone and Sgts Morrison, Tomlin and Nixon. 12 aircraft failed to return, but all 49's were safe.

P/O Tom Taylor recorded; *"There was quite a large amount of flak, but the biggest danger was that of collision with our own aircraft."*

5 April, 1943. Command required offers for gardening, but the squadron declined the invitation.

W/Cmdr W.P. Johnson AFC., the new C.O., arrived from the Conversion Unit at Swinderby... his crew had proceeded him by a few days.

During the afternoon, 4 aircraft, flown by F/O Bone and Sgts Morrison, Tomlin and Nixon carried out practice bombing on the Wainfleet range.

8/9 April, 1943; DUISBURG: Four aircraft flew up to Kirton Lindsey during the morning, (including W/Cmdr Johnson) for a spot of fighter affiliation whilst F/Sgt Gilmore went over to Wainfleet for air firing.

The effort for the night was 7 for Duisburg, taking off shortly after 21.00hrs. Once again thick cloud had prevented accurate marking by the PFF. The attacking force of 392 made a scattered attack causing only moderate damage.

Heavy flak was encountered in the target area; Sgt Hogg RNZAF (ED441), with the new Winco on board, had 3 pieces of flak smash into their starboard wing root only just missing a fuel tank. Sgt Tolchard's (ED448) mid-upper gunner, Sgt Doe, had a near-miss when unbeknown to him at the time, a piece of flak penetrated the port side just below his turret.

By 02.50hrs, 6 of the squadron's Lancasters were back home, but the seventh, F/O Derek Southern and crew, flying their 4th operation with 49, failed to return; their Lancaster came down near Hubbelrath in Germany at 23.45hrs. The 22 year-old pilot, (holder of the DFM) is buried along with his crew in the Reichswald Forest War Cemetery. They were one of 19 aircraft missing from the raid.

Missing ED590	F/O D.J.N. Southern DFM	Pilot	(Killed)
(EA-L)	Sgt C.J. Tiley	F/E	(Killed)
	F/O J.B. Lapping	NAV	(Killed)
	F/O A.L. Munro	W/AG	(Killed)
	P/O J.L. Rollins RAAF	A/G	(Killed)
Crew on their	Sgt G.S. Pring	B/A	(Killed)
4th operation	Sgt H. Chatterton	A/G	(Killed)

9/10 April, 1943; DUISBURG: A return trip to Duisburg was the target for tonight, but this time the force was much smaller, with just 104 Lancasters being led by 5 PFF Mosquitoes. The squadron put 5 aircraft up and of these Sgt Penry (ED452) soon returned with his starboard inner engine shut down. Cloud again foiled the markers and the bombing was scattered. Of the small force, 9 failed to return but 49's returned safe and sound.

10/11 April, 1943; FRANKFURT: Just 4 aircraft left Fiskerton to join 488 other bombers on yet another weather ruined attack on the Ruhr. W/Cmdr Johnson (ED702) flew as captain for the first time with the squadron flying D-Donald. All 4 crews reported bombing the 'red glow under the clouds.

APRIL 1943

13/14 April, 1943; LA SPEZIA: The dock area of La Spezia received the attention of 211 heavy bombers causing heavy damage. 49 Squadron's effort for the night consisted of 9 aircraft for bombing whilst 2 more laid mines in Spezia Bay. Four new crews operated on the bombing raid and each crew had a different story to tell:

F/O Bone (ED438) and crew suffered an engine fire in the starboard-inner and returned early to Fiskerton making a safe emergency landing.

AFRICA OR BUST

During briefing, crews had been advised that should they have difficulties then recently captured airfields in North Africa were now available. Three Bomber Command aircraft took advantage of these new Allied airfields including the 'freshmen' crew of Sgt Nixon's (ED453) from 49 Squadron. They landed at Maison Blanche 'in distress' just after 05.10hrs. This young crew were very good pals with their 'A Flt' ground crew, and one ground crew member, Sgt Trevor Simpson, remembers this occasion very well:

"After G-George had failed to return from the Italian trip, we were soon informed that the crew had diverted to North Africa due to fuel shortage. There was a strong feeling among us that Nixon's crew had done it just for the hell of it! Sgt Nixon returned from Africa via St Eval where, on landing they had to 'pull the bottle'(use the emergency air) to lock down the undercarriage. I had to go down and service this equipment before flying back with them the following day, dumping leaflets that should have been dropped over the target, off the North Devon coast. We landed at Chivenor en route to drop off a Stirling pilot who had hitched a lift."

The third crew in this quartet of newboys, was piloted by Sgt Tomlin (ED584) ... they had a straightforward and successful trip, landing back at Fiskerton in the daylight. The final 'sprog' crew was that of Sgt Morrison's (ED435); at the post-operational interrogation, Jock Morrison reported the following;

"The trip started OK and we were on track across France, but inability to fix on the Italian coast confused the navigator. We discovered that the DR compass was out and we were more or less lost".

Some years later, Tom Page, F/E on the crew put down on paper his recollections of this, his first operation:

It was the last day of March 1943 when we arrived at 49 Squadron. The crew were all Sgts ... Jock Morrison, Pilot; Hughie Annett, bomb aimer; Jimmy Dorian, navigator; Ralph Green, wireless operator; Taffy Evans, rear gunner; Ernie Green, mid upper gunner and myself, Tom Page, the flight engineer. We had completed 53 hours as a crew on Manchesters and Lancasters, flying out of Winthorpe with 1661 HCU.

On 13 April, after twelve short local sorties we were dispatched on our first operational bombing sortie. The pilot Jock, had already flown on two operations under instruction as a second pilot with experienced crews. The target was the docks at LaSpezia in the North West of Italy. Our route took us out over the South coast of England and across Southern France. All went well and I remember the Navigator saying on the intercom, 'target in 30 minutes'. Thirty minutes passed and, although it was a fairly clear night, there was no sign of any raid in progress and we were over the Mediterranean Sea. We flew on for a while, still over the sea and nothing sighted, until we realised we were lost! Conscious of the fuel supply and the return flight, I told the Skipper of my worries, already half of the fuel tanks load of 2,154 gallons had gone. So we decided to jettison the bomb load over the sea.

A new course was set for home after seeing land, believed to be Corsica or Sardinia. Everything was done to achieve range, high boost and low revs on all engines. An ETA was given for the south coast of France... this came and went and still no coast line. It wasn't until thirty minutes after this that the bomb aimer shouted 'Coast line' and identified it as Montpelier. A fresh course was given by the Navigator and we flew on, a lone Lancaster crossing France and expecting opposition any moment. A new ETA for crossing the French coastline was given, and once again the same thing happened, no coastline when the time arrived. We flew on and on until some time later a new course to port was given.

By this time daylight was not far away so down went the aircraft's nose as we increased speed, expecting to see enemy fighters at any moment. At last we crossed the coastline, travelling fast at 3,000ft with light ack-ack fire coming up from the sand dunes. In moments we were out to sea and comparative safety, but fuel was getting very low. Numbers 2 and 3 tanks on both sides were empty and the flying time left was short.

Another coastline appeared and the Pilot, Nav and Bomb Aimer discussed the situation... was it England or somewhere up in the low countries? As it grew closer, great sighs of relief as it proved to be England, but then we could not get a reply to our calls to 'Darkie'. We decided to fly westwards just off the coast, not only to identify ourselves, but to locate our position and find a suitable airfield upon which to land. In the early morning mist, we eventually landed ay Dunsfold airfield in Surrey. Our fuel tanks read zero and we expected the engines to cut at any time. On inspection afterwards, we found about 30 gallons of fuel left between the four engines. With the aircraft tail down the No 1 tanks showed a dry bottom through the filler caps. We had used 2124 gallons of fuel in 10hrs 50minutes of flying time. I cannot remember the air mileage flown, but it would have given us well over the figure of 'one air mile per gallon' the amount we always aimed at.

Post mortem of the flight after returning to Fiskerton later that day, (to find we had been posted 'missing') revealed that the P4 gyro compass carried in the aircraft, had gone wrong putting us well off track every time. By back tracking on the navigation, not only had we missed the target and flown a long way South into the Med, but had flown almost due North back over France on the return."

Note: The crew went on to complete a successful tour, though not without a few more scrapes. Tom Page continued in the RAF post-war retiring as a Squadron Leader. The remaining crews from 49, returned from the operation without incident.

F/Sgt (Later F/O) Tom Page, flight engineer on W/O Jock Morrison's crew.
Photograph taken at Fiskerton.
(T.J. Page)

14/15 April, 1943; STUTTGART: Group asked for 8 aircraft and the squadron offered 7, but just before the take-off time of 21.18hrs gremlins struck again forcing Sgt Price to pull out at the last minute. Of the 6 that got away Sgt Millar (ED445) and crew, had all four engines surge at 15,000ft; losing height they found it necessary to return, landing at Tangmere at 00.30hrs.

Sgt Tolchard (ED497) had taken-off 11 minutes late and by the time the final turning point had been reached they were over 20 minutes behind time. Crossing the south coast just west of Folkestone, coastal defences suddenly opened fire on them. Further into the sortie the crew decided that they were too far behind to carry on and returned early to Fiskerton.

The remaining 4 squadron aircraft participated in a heavy attack on Stuttgart in which the main feature was the notable 'creepback' by both the main force and the PFF backers-up.
49 Squadron aircraft were not among the 23 aircraft listed missing from the raid. F/O Bone (ED432) and crew managed to complete their first operational sortie.

16/17 April, 1943; PILZEN: In the light of a full moon, 327 heavy bombers went after the Skoda armaments works. Aircraft from the squadron pressed home their attacks with great determination; W/Cmdr Johnson (ED702) and crew made two runs over the smoke covered target before releasing their load. S/Ldr Gilpin (ED805) and crew reported:

"On our third run we thought we saw factory sheds ahead and green T.Is., and many 4,000lb bombs seen exploding."

Ralph Allsebrook (ED597) and crew with S/Ldr Storey as 2nd Pilot, went down to 6,000ft in an effort to locate the target. Unfortunately the bombing photos brought back, showed the raid to have been a failure, with a large asylum building several miles away being mistaken for the factory.

To make matters worse, the cost had been very high; 18 Halifaxes and 18 Lancaster crews failed to return. Four of the 7 aircraft dispatched by 49 were home by 06.09hrs and 20 minutes later Scampton control reported F/Lt Allsebrook had slipped in there for breakfast.

But sadly, back over at Fiskerton in the bright light of an early spring morning two dispersal points lay empty: Sgt Dave Penry and crew had failed to return on this their 12th operation; their Lancaster crashed in the Amiens area, only the air gunner Sgt Kerr survived, becoming a POW; the rest of his crew are buried in France. F/O Alex Bone and crew on just their 2nd trip had also tragically perished in the night; they are presumed to have come down in the sea.

Missing ED441	Sgt D.T. Penry	Pilot	(Killed)
(EA-D)	Sgt C.G. Bamford	F/E	(Killed)
'A Flt'	F/S A.N. Dixon	NAV	(Killed)
	Sgt T.C. Robertson	WAG	(Killed)
	Sgt J.F. Fletcher	A/G	(Killed)
Crew on their	Sgt C.L. James	B/A	(Killed)
12th operation	Sgt H.W.G. Kerr	A/G	(P.o.W.)
Missing ED427	F/O A.V. Bone	Pilot	(Missing)
(EA-O)	Sgt R.N.P. Foster	F/E	(Missing)
'B Flt'	Sgt C.W. Yelland	NAV	(Missing)
	Sgt R.C. White	WAG	(Missing)
	Sgt R. Cope	A/G	(Missing)
Crew on their	Sgt R.J. Rooney	B/A	(Missing)
2nd operation	P/O B.E. Watt RCAF	A/G	(Missing)

18/19 April, 1943; LA SPEZIA/GARDENING: Six aircraft from the squadron were on tonight, 4 required for bombing the dock area and 2 for minelaying in Spezia Bay.
Two of the Spezia crews were operating with 49 for the first time; S/Ldr Storey's (ED459) and Sgt Anderson's (ED435).

All crews landed safely after successful sorties, with 5 putting down at base and S/Ldr Storey landing at Langar.

20/21 April, 1943; STETTIN: W/Cmdr Johnson led 9 aircraft away from Fiskerton forming part of a mixed force of 339 Bombers. In perfect visibility and with good PFF marking, a tremendous hammer-blow was delivered to the town of Stettin. 100 acres of the centre were destroyed for the loss of 13 Lancasters, 7 Halifaxes and 1 Stirling.

F/Lt Scorer (ED813) flying the first op of his second tour received a return 'baptism of fire'; attacking the target at the briefed height of 10,000ft, flak shattered the perspex in the rear turret. Despite this handicap, the occupant, Sgt J.A. Fowler managed to drive-off a determined attack by a German night-fighter.

Sgt Jack Price (ED426) and crew flew onto a concentration of markers, but just as the bomb aimer, Sgt Glover, held the green TI's in the sights, they were violently rocked by heavy flak causing the load to be dropped NW of the markers. Pulling hard out of the target area into the moonlit night, one of the gunners suddenly yelled a cork-screw order to his captain. During the frantic gyrations, both gunners, Sgts King and Hefferon returned fire, claiming hits on a JU 88.

Sgt Millar (ED445) and crew had delivered a good attack on Stettin, and were flying home with a full moon for company. They re-crossed the enemy coast near Vordingsburg where Sgt Millar takes up the story:

"At 02.12hrs, we saw a trawler opening fire on another aircraft, so we dropped to sea level enabling the rear gunner, Sgt Foster, to give the trawler three short bursts with the mid upper gunner, Sgt Earnshaw adding another. The deck of the trawler was sprayed so effectively that it ceased fire."

By 06.15hrs all of the squadron's Lancasters had returned, with the exception of Sgt Adam Anderson and crew, who on only their 2nd operation were reported missing; the 20 year-old Lancaster pilot and crew had in fact been shot down over Denmark. Light flak had set fire to the incendiaries and the aircraft began to burn furiously. At 23.35hrs, the pilot crash landed his Lancaster (with the bombs still on board) 12 kilometers NNW of Ringkobing. Three crew members were killed in the crash and Sgt Anderson died later in hospital; the remaining three crew members survived to become PoW's. Their comrades rest in Lemvig Cemetery.

A rather scratched, but significant photograph of ED620 (EA-K) - seen on a dispersal to the rear of the main hangar at Fiskerton, during the afternoon of Tuesday 20 April 1943.

Standing in front of her are (from l to r), Cpl Bob Best, Fitter; Cpl Willaims; Andy McGowan, rigger; LAC Smith; LAC Jones; Cpl Ken Brailey. That night Sgt Anderson and crew flying ED620 failed to return from Stettin; their 2nd operation, the aircraft's first. (T.N. Simpson)

FTR ED620	Sgt A. Anderson	Pilot	(Killed)
(EA-K)	Sgt A. Telfer	F/E	(Killed)
'A Flt'	Sgt G. Boulton	N/AB	(P.o.W.)
	Sgt G.J. Evans	WAG	(Killed)
	Sgt G. Barclay	A/G	(P.o.W.)
Crew on their	Sgt W.A. Cook	A/B	(Killed)
2nd operation	Sgt W.P. Hayworth	A/G	(P.o.W.)

Sgt 'Nicky' Nixon running up ED453 G-George at dispersal on 22-4-43.

Just visible in the trees behind the groundcrew figure is the 'Old Vicarage' at the top of the hill into Fiskerton village.

The Nixon crew failed to return from the Oberhausen raid on 14/15-6-43 in this aircraft.

Note the 'Mandrel' aerial clearly visible on the nose. (T.N. Simpson)

26/27 April, 1943; DUISBURG: A large force of 561 bombers made a not too successful raid on Duisburg. The 7 aircraft dispatched from 49 Squadron all reported scattered bombing. F/Sgt Gilmore (ED434) took Sgt Cole along as second pilot and F/Sgt Hogg (ED497) carried S/Ldr Storey. All of the squadron's crews reported successful sorties and all returned safely. Bomber Command lost 17 aircraft.

27/28 April, 1943; MINELAYING (FRISIAN ISLANDS): At first, the effort for the night was to be 9 Lancasters on Dortmund, but this was cancelled, and instead 4 of the unit's aircraft were briefed for minelaying off the Frisian Islands.

Bad visibility played havoc; the two new crews of Sgts Cole (ED721) and Robinson (ED427), despite several attempts, could not carry out their duties. Sgt Morrison returned with six mines still onboard whilst Sgt Nixon, flying in misty conditions, made a timed run and dropped the mines. At de-brief, Sgt Nixon (ED453) recorded: *" 'Mandrel' used"*.

Bomber Command had dispatched 160 aircraft on this, the biggest gardening operation so far in the war.

The effort resulted in the loss of 1 Lancaster; all 49's were safe.

APRIL 1943

Fiskerton, summer 1943: ED445 H-Harry (photographed from EA-F) taxies back to dispersal after an air test; on inboards only.

Side entrance from Fiskerton village comes in just off to the left of the photo - now near the (Ex) ROC building.
(T.N. Simpson)

30 April/ 1 May, 1943; ESSEN: As the last hours of April faded into the dawn of May, a moderate mainforce dropped their loads on 'Oboe'-assisted sky-markers through 10/10ths cloud. Although the resulting attack was not concentrated new damage occurred within the city. Twelve aircraft were lost from the 305 dispatched. 49 had contributed 6 Lancasters; F/Sgts Hogg and Gilmore once again carried 'second dickies'; Sgt Moss flew with Hogg and Sgt Robinson with Gilmore. All the squadron's aircraft returned safely to base, although F/Sgt Hogg (ED497) and crew sustained flak hits over the target. P/O Taylor (ED721) commented on the bad routing out of the target with the danger of collision with incoming aircraft.

OPERATIONAL SUMMARY - APRIL 1943

Date	Target	Desp	E/R	FTR	Remarks
3/4	ESSEN	10	-	-	
4/5	KIEL	9	-	-	
8/9	DUISBURG	7	-	1	F/O Southern FTR
9/10	DUISBURG	5	1	-	
13/14	SPEZIA	11	1	-	1 a/c landed in N. Africa
14/15	STUTTGART	6	2	-	
16/17	PILZEN	7	-	2	Sgt Penry FTR F/O Bone FTR
18/19	SPEZIA	6	-	-	
20/21	STETTIN	9	-	1	Sgt Anderson FTR
26/27	DUISBURG	7	-	-	
27/28	GARDENING	4	-	-	
30/1	ESSEN	6	-	-	
Total of sorties flown -		87			
Failed to return		4			

HONOURS AND AWARDS - APRIL 1943

Sgt E.W. Tickler	C.G.M.
F/S J.L. Matthews	D.F.M.
F/S E.J. Lowans	D.F.M.
Sgt G.B. Silvester	D.F.M.

A cheerful photo taken of some 49 Squadron ground staff at Fiskerton in early 1943. Many well remembered faces but only half remembered names. Fortunately, of the MT WAAFs, only a few have escaped identification:

(back row l to r)

Unknown; Olive Binns; Anne Horan; Joan Fitchette; Unknown; Hilda Woodgette; Unknown.

(front row l to r)

Joan ?; Lilian Yule; Dorothy Everette; Joan Pinette; Eva Barrack; Dot Cory; Peggy Whitelaw; Anne Vigors.

(Mrs D.Smith)

MAY 1943

On Wednesday 19 May, 1943, No. 52 Base was established with RAF Scampton designated as the Base Station; this was a new form of streamlining aimed at utilising man-power and resources more efficiently.

A Base Station was usually one of the pre-war aerodromes and it would have one or posibly two sub-stations. The sub-stations were the wartime-built airfields, where facilities were often very basic. The Base Station would take full charge of administration etc of the squadrons at each sub-station, and would also provide a central maintenance pool. With this new type of organisation, sub-station personnel consisted of only those directly involved in putting Lancasters into the air and keeping them there.

No. 52 Base, Scampton had No 57 Squadron in residence plus the newly formed No 617 Squadron. Now it was to have two sub-stations; Fiskerton, with 49 Squadron, and by the end of May, Dunholme Lodge. Dunholme, like Fiskerton, was an airfield built 'for the duration' and had the standard pattern three concrete runways. The pre-war aerodromes were built without concrete runways and with bomb-loads increasing, these pre-war grass airfields soon had to close for runway laying. Waddington's disgruntled residents, No 44 (Rhodesia) Squadron, were moved over to Dunholme Lodge with its dispersed living accommodation... and mud! Scampton would close for runway laying in August, but would still remain the Base HQ.

4/5 May, 1943; DORTMUND: May started with three operations cancelled on successive nights, but on Tuesday the 4th, twelve aircraft managed to get away, joining 596 bombers setting out on what was to be the first major attack on Dortmund. All 49 Squadron crews claimed good results and considered the target 'well bombed'. Severe damage was indeed inflicted on the town despite the use of decoy fires by the Germans. One new crew had been dispatched by the squadron, that captained by Sgt Moss (ED597), and again F/Sgt Hogg (ED452) acted as 'taxi driver' when he took along another fresh pilot, fellow New Zealander F/Lt Munro, whilst S/Ldr Gilpin (ED805) took Sgt Tozer as 2nd pilot.

SEVEN MEN

The months and years of blood, sweat and tears that go into aircrew training culminate in the moment that bonded crews complete their first operation. So it was in the early hours of Wednesday 5th May, that Sgt Johnny Moss (ED597) flew B-Baker and his tired but happy crew back in over the Lincolnshire coast. Navigating was Dave Jones with Ernie Roden as flight engineer; down in the nose was bomb aimer Len Bradfield. Sammy Small listened out on the radio whilst in the top turret sat Terry Wood and bringing up the rear was tail gunner Ronnie Musson.

The tension of the last few traumatic hours had slowly begun to give way to an overwhelming feeling of at last 'we've got one in!'

After calling 'Bonfire' Control (callsign for Fiskerton) Johnny Moss was given a place in the stack, flying around the airfield circuit. Eventually B-Baker's turn came to land. Slowly they let down, the remains of the ancient Barlings Abbey slipping under the port wing... lower now, passing over Barlings House and rushing past Birchill Farm with eyes fixed on the welcoming flarepath of lights... just a few seconds more and the huge tyres would kiss the threshold of home and safety. A screech of rubber and they were down.

Suddenly, without warning, the controls were wrenched from the pilot's grasp as the huge bomber careered off to the left, out of control. Unbeknown to the crew, flak over Dortmund had riddled and punctured their port tyre. On landing, the tyre deflated causing the wheel to dig-in, forcing the undercarriage to collapse. As the giant propellers churned up the ground the outboard motor was torn away. The helpless crew was transfixed until their stricken Lancaster ceased its act of self-destruction. Then within moments, those taxing hours of training become second nature as a perfect emergency exit was executed with each member of the crew escaping... shaken but unharmed.

The crash crews soon arrived on the scene, spraying foam to quench any hint of fire, whilst the MO made his rounds and checked everyone out OK. Seven men, survivors of an incident that happened all too frequently on wartime bomber airfields, and not always with the same fortunate ending. Seven men, resting together on dew moistened grass, smoking and laughing, their adrenalin enhanced senses filling nostrils with a pervading smell of freshly turned soil... the soil which their Lancaster had just ploughed.

To the east, the first rays of sunlight announced the dawn of another warm summer's day. Transport arrived, driven by an ever-cheerful WAAF... de-brief, breakfast and then bed, for it's back to work again tonight ... there's a war on! Seven men; ahead of them lay more operations, more warm summer days, more dangers... and sadly, towards the end of those warm summer days, of these seven men just two would still be alive.

12/13 May, 1943; DUISBURG: This was the fourth raid on Duisburg during the Battle of the Ruhr. It received a well concentrated attack by 572 bombers. The PFF marking was spot-on and severe damage was caused to this, the largest inland port in Germany.

The squadron had put up 7 aircraft; F/Lt Munro captained his crew for the first time, taking a brand-new Lancaster, ED625 'EA-B'. F/Sgt Hogg (ED497) took Sgt Watson as 2nd pilot and F/Sgt Gilmore (ED432) carried F/O Millar as 2nd pilot. It is of note that F/Lt Munro, F/Sgt Hogg and F/Sgt Gilmore were all members of the RNZAF.

All of the squadron's crews completed successful sorties. The only incident happened to P/O Tom Taylor's (ED721) crew; when over the target a piece of heavy flak smashed through the bomb aimer's blister missing Bob Seddon by inches.

MAY 1943

13/14 May, 1943; PILZEN: A force of 168 aircraft (nearly all Lancasters from 5 Group) made another attempt to hit the Skoda armaments factory. Once again the target proved too hard to find and mark for the PFF, with the result that most of the bombing fell in open country. W/Cmdr Johnson's (ED426) own de-brief remarks help to confirm the problems:

"The attack was seen to be in progress a long way from our position on ETA at target - we turned into the target and arrived 16 minutes late - I believe we attacked the target but as we were the only aircraft there and no longer any T.Is, we cannot be sure."

Flying with the W/Cmdr was Pat Kelly, one of the finest navigators in 5 Group.

The squadron had made a big effort for this raid, putting 14 Lancasters up by 21.54hrs, including the new crew of Sgt Kirton. (ED719).

49 Squadron Armoury Football Team April/May 1943; winners of the Squadron Cup. The match took place on Fiskerton's village pitch near the Church (although this photo is taken back on camp) - unfortunately the score and opponents have not been recorded.

(Back row l to r)

'Tich' Walmsley (in uniform); Bob Pearson; George Longhurst; Tony Murrel, goalkeeper and also licensee of the Adam and Eve pub, Lincoln; Alan Shepherd; Reg Jarrett; Jack 'Shag' Wattam; Ned Few (in uniform).

(Front row l to r)

LAC Lovejoy; Jack Dolman; Ernie Thirtle; Fred Berry; Paddy Connor. (J.Dolman)

THE FOUR MINUTE MILE

At 01.03hrs, shortly after setting off for Pilzen, Sgt Jock Morrison (ED452) and crew arrived back early over Fiskerton flying on three engines, having jettisoned their 4,000lb 'cookie' at sea. The pilot requested permission to land from Flying Control, whilst informing them that he still had 6 x 500lb bombs on board. The Control Tower in turn gave permission to land but insisted that they use one of the short runways, not wanting to risk making a mess of the main runway, thus forcing the returning squadron to be diverted.

Sgt Morrison, assisted by his flight engineer Tom Page, brought F-Freddie in over the bomb-dump from the Barlings direction on the Reepham side of the airfield. The short runway they were approaching pointed SSW, and had a slight incline just after the threshold. As they descended a sudden gust of sidewind floated the aircraft, which eventually settled down further up the runway... too far up the runway! With a heavy load and concrete quickly running out, the pilot realised the inevitable and yelled a warning to the crew. 'Freddie' plunged off the end of the runway losing her undercarriage in the process. Before she had stopped sliding, escape hatches had been jettisoned and the crew, although encumbered by flying gear, had dismounted from the wreck and were attempting to achieve the '4 minute mile' across farmland... at night! With lungs fit to burst and hearts pounding against their Mae Wests, an exhausted but intact crew of seven, watched as the crash crews arrived. They dowsed the aircraft to prevent the chance of fire or explosion - Fiskerton had witnessed two crash landings in as many weeks and yet again 'The Reaper' had been denied.

Over the target, the remainder of the squadron dropped their loads on the markers, believing a well concentrated attack had been achieved.

P/O Taylor (ED721) and crew lost their intercom 10 minutes before the target, but completed the sortie successfully.
F/Lt Munro (ED625) and crew, on only their 2nd operation, were attacked no less than five times by fighters; combining excellent flying skills with very good co-operation between the gunners, P/O Fernie and Sgt Dreaver RNZAF, the crew of B-Baker survived, claiming one fighter as 'probable'.
Sgt Robinson (ED663) and crew on their 3rd operation, were badly shot up by flak over the target. They sustained considerable damage but with determination the crew made it home. At interrogation, Sgt Robinson praised the skills of his navigator, P/O Duckam.

Thirteen aircraft (2 battle-damaged) returned safely, to land on Fiskerton's 'unscathed' main runway.

Crashed ED452	Sgt J. Morrison	Pilot	(uninjured)
(EA-F)	Sgt T.J. Page	F/E	(uninjured)
'A'Flt	Sgt J. Dorian	Nav/B	(uninjured)
	Sgt R.I. Green	W/AG	(injured)
	Sgt H.J. Maggs	A/G	(uninjured)
	Sgt H.C. Annett	B/A	(uninjured)
	Sgt G. Green	A/G	(uninjured)

17 May, 1943: SGT JOHN MINCHIN - DAMBUSTER: On the morning of Monday 17 May, the world learnt of the dramatic attack by 617 Squadron on the Ruhr dams the previous evening. Whilst not wishing to describe in detail the exploits of 617 in a book concerning 49 Squadron, mention must be made of Sgt John William Minchin.

John was posted to 49 Squadron at Scampton during October 1941; as a wireless operator on the squadron, he completed a full tour in Hampdens and Manchesters. He participated in 49's last Hampden sortie as a member of Bob Hamer's (AT227) crew and also took part in 49's first Manchester operation in P/O Shakleton's R5771. After a spell at 26 OTU, he returned to Scampton in April 1943 as a member of the new 617 Squadron.

As a wireless operator on F/Lt John Hopgood's crew during the night of the dams raid, Minchin was badly wounded in the leg when M-Mother was hit by flak en-route to the Möhne Dam. Sgt Minchin sat for almost an hour at his radio set nursing this terrible injury before the target was reached. M-Mother, the second aircraft to attack, was severely hit by ack-ack on the run-in and set on fire. The bomb was released but hit the parapet wall and exploded. F/Lt Hopgood struggled valiantly to keep his blazing aircraft airborne in order for the crew to bale out. Tony Burcher evacuated his rear turret and made for the crew door. There he was confronted by the pained face of John Minchin, who had dragged himself the length of the fuselage, his leg almost severed. All Burcher could do to help his comrade was to clip on Minchin's parachute and push him out into the darkness, pulling his D-ring in the process.

The Lancaster crashed 3 miles to the north-west of the dam and exploded in flames. Just two members of the crew survived; bomb aimer P/O Fraser RCAF and the gallant F/O Anthony Burcher RAAF. Sadly, John Minchin along with four of his fellow crew members did not survive... a very tragic end for a very brave band of men.

THE CAR DRIVER WHO ACCIDENTLY KILLED NIGGER

Author: During the early 1960's, as a young lad, I earned extra pocket money by cleaning customer's cars at my father's garage in Cherry Willingham. One of my regular 'clients' was Mr Jim Howe who lived in Church Lane. Knowing of my interest in wartime aviation, Mr Howe disclosed to me that it was in fact he who had knocked down and killed Guy Gibson's dog Nigger.

The accident happened as shown in the film, except it occurred on the day before the raid, and not on the actual day as shown in the movie. There is one other important aspect of the film that I wish to correct in this 'exclusive revelation'; Mr Howe did actually stop his car following the accident and he helped carry Nigger back to Scampton's Guard Room, before leaving his sincere condolences to the owner.

23/24 May, 1943; DORTMUND: On this Sunday night, a tremendous force of 826 bombers was launched against Dortmund. In clear weather conditions, the PFF marked accurately and a devastating attack was the result. Large areas of the town were destroyed and nearly 2,000 buildings flattened and for the first time Bomber Command had dropped over 2,000 tons of bombs and incendiaries in one night. RAF losses amounted to 38 aircraft.

49 Squadron had dispatched 13 aircraft into the fray, with two new crews being blooded; those of F/Os Millar (ED726) and Thomas (ED813). Authorised bombing height was 20,000ft, but due to the failure of one engine, P/O Tom Taylor (ED721) and crew found themselves approaching the target at considerably less height than that; after having to weave through searchlights and run the gauntlet of flak, they eventually released their load at 14,000ft!

Things were not much safer at 19,500ft where F/Lt Munro (ED625) and crew were once again having their share of excitement; shortly before 'bomb release', a cluster of 30lb incendiary bombs rained past them striking their starboard wing. Despite the damage, they continued the bombing run and lucky B-Baker brought them safely home once again.

The returning squadron crews brought back graphic descriptions of the burning town. It soon became clear after de-brief that once again 49 had yet another 'new crew' missing; sadly F/O Thomas's aircraft had been brought down near Essen.

Missing ED813	F/O I.W. Thomas	Pilot	(P.o.W.)
(EA-W)	P/O J. Grant	F/E	(P.o.W.)
'B Flt'	F/O Duthie	NAV	(P.o.W.)
	P/O R. Christy	WOP	(Killed)
	Sgt G.R. Evans	A/G	(Killed)
Crew on	P/O T.G.H. Lewis	B/A	(Killed)
1st operation	Sgt R.H. Ancell	A/G	(Killed)

25/26 May, 1943; DÜSSELDORF: Twelve Lancasters taxied round to the end of Fiskerton's main runway, preparing to join over 700 other bombers bound for Germany. Trundling along from the north side of the airfield, Sgt Hogg in EA-L experienced brake pressure failure and had to pull out; the remaining 11 aircraft were all airborne by 23.40hrs.

Sgt Tomlin (ED584) was forced to return early in U-Uncle with the rear turret u/s. The remaining squadron aircraft pressed on and participated in a raid that proved to be a failure. Cloud had prevented accurate marking and the Germans used the tactic of decoy markers. Tragically 27 bombers failed to return; all Fiskerton's were safe. The only incident ocurred when flak holed the perspex in Sgt Nixon's (ED453) cockpit.

27/28 May, 1943; ESSEN: Sky-markers descended onto a cloudy Essen as over 500 bombers approached to make their attack. Unfortunately the bombing was scattered and 'creepback' also developed with the result that Essen received limited damage.

49 Squadron had dispatched 12 Lancasters with Sgt Watson (ED497) and crew operating for the first time. All of the squadron's aircraft returned safely, although Sgts Nixon (ED453) and Morrison (ED719) were both caught in searchlights over the target. Sgt Morrison and crew were held for over half a minute, but by vigorous flying they managed to find the sanctuary of dark sky.

29/30 May, 1943; WUPPERTAL: At 10.35hrs, 12 of the unit's aircraft were requested for ops. During the morning the crews flew the usual NFT's, but during the afternoon an unusual break in the proceedings occurred:

WINGS OVER SHEFFIELD

The City of Sheffield, which had 'adopted' the squadron earlier in the war, had recently presented a Silver Rose Bowl to the Officers Mess at Fiskerton. To mark 'Wings for Victory' a flight of 49 Squadron Lancasters flew in formation over Sheffield during the afternoon of Saturday 29 May. Onc pcrson who has very good grounds to remember this flight was LAC Peter Hammett, an engine fitter on 'A' Flight He recalls that eventful day:

"I wanted to go on the formation flight to Sheffield, and whenever possible Sgt Nixon and crew would take me on NFT's and other local training flights. On this occasion 'Nicky' was on leave so I asked Jock Morrison but he said he was taking SHQ staff officers and VIP's - he suggested I try the pilot of H-Harry who had just arrived on squadron.

The pilot's name was Watson and he said if it was O.K. with the unit, then he had space. He asked if I had a chute, to which I replied that I didn't, and never had on previous flights... OK he said, if anything goes wrong we will have to crash land.

Eventually we took off and formed up in a Vic formation, H-Harry being part of W/Cmdr Johnson's 'V' on his port side. This worked well for a while but due to air pockets etc, H-Harry slewed in very close to the Wingco's tail. I was standing behind the engineer and our starboard engines nearly gave the poor rear gunner a hair cut. This manoeuvre received a torrent of abuse and 'advice' from the W/Cmdr, not surprisingly, but it was enough to completely un-nerve the young pilot who probably had only a limited amount of hours on Lancs.

The rest of the flight was uneventful, until we arrived back at Fiskerton... from experience I knew our approach was wrong. We made a series of jerky corrections to our flight path but the approach was too steep and panic was setting in. Eventually we hit the runway nose down and burst a tyre; we shot back into the air with an almighty bounce coming down on the grass and removing what was left of the undercarriage.

The nose and all four engines were smashed but we probably owe our lives to the fact that the Lancaster was such a good aircraft. The crew was taken to the sick bay for check-ups and then, soon after, put in another aircraft to do circuit and bumps to regain their confidence. The silly part was that the M.O. (Sgt Nixon's brother) who arrived with the ambulance and fire tenders, told me to get out of the way - it always surprised me that it never ocurred to him that I had come out of the aircraft as well! after all I was licking a badly cut hand.

Nicky (Sgt pilot Nixon) arrived back from leave the next day and on hearing the tale, said I was going on an NFT with them - I started to say I would give it a miss when the crew lifted me into the aircraft and shut the door. Landing was always nerve-wracking after that, but I still carried on flying whenever possible."

F/O Desmond Harris, navigator in F/Lt Munro's crew recorded the following in his Log Book: *"Take-off 14.30, Squadron formation - Sheffield and bombing - duration 1hr 50mins."* Today when recalling the event Des reflects:

"We most probably frightened the towns-people to death - Sheffield had seen its fair share of bombers during the war."

His Log Book also records that he and his crew were airborne again that same day, when at 21.50hrs they departed Fiskerton bound for Wuppertal in the Ruhr, on their 7th operation.

What Peter Hammett and Des Harris (and all those who flew on the Wings flypast) may not have known at the time is that, below in the town centre, thousands of Sheffielders had gathered for the parade. The main focus of their attention was the first public appearance (following the Dams Raid) of W/Cmdr Guy Gibson. Outside the town hall, Gibbo was mobbed by an ecstatic crowd wishing to shake his hand, possibly gain his autograph, or merely to just try and touch him. From the town hall balcony, W/Cmdr Gibson took pride of place beside Mrs Churchill who was to take the salute from the large parade, as overhead thundered the Lancasters of 49 Squadron.

Of the 12 aircraft put up by the squadron this night, three returned early; Sgt Tolchard (ED448) had his port outer engine fail; Sgt Moss (ED416) had compass trouble and a rear turret u/s, whilst Sgt Robinson (ED805) had intercom failure.

Nine of the squadron's aircraft flew on to take part in the most successful raid of the 'Battle of the Ruhr'. Accurate marking and bombing started huge fires which destroyed over 1,000 acres of built-up area. This was without doubt, the severest raid suffered by any German town so-far in the war.

Of the 719 Lancasters, Halifaxes, Stirlings, Wellingtons and Mosquitoes, 33 aircraft failed to return. All nine aircraft came home safely to Fiskerton.

MAY 1943

OPERATIONAL SUMMARY - MAY 1943

Date	Target	Desp	E/R	FTR	Remarks
4/5	DORTMUND	12	-	1c	Sgt Moss c/l
12/13	DUISBURG	7	-	-	
13/14	PILZEN	14	1	1c	Sgt Morrison c/l
23/24	DORTMUND	13	-	1	F/O Thomas FTR
25/26	DÜSSELDORF	11	1	-	
27/28	ESSEN	12	-	-	
29/30	WUPPERTAL	12	3	-	Sgt Watson c/l (non-operational)
Total of sorties flown		81			
Failed to return		1 + 3c			

HONOURS AND AWARDS - MAY 1943

S/Ldr D.A. Cracknell	D.F.C
F/O R.G. Armstrong	D.F.C.
F/O C.K. Astbury	D.F.C.
F/S R.S. Hogg	C.G.M.
F/S J.N.P. Martin	D.F.M.
Sgt J.H. McDonald	D.F.M.

Fiskerton, May/June 1943: Cpl Bob Best walks back to the point as his charge ED416 J-Johnny departs for an air test. 'Johnny' is being taxied in the direction of Cherry Willingham (west) along the southern perimeter track. F/Sgt Kirton and crew took ED416 to Mannheim 5/6-9-43 and failed to return. (T.N. Simpson)

JUNE 1943

As with the previous month, June began with several operations in succession being 'scrubbed', many right at the last moment. Whilst this exerted extreme mental pressure and physical stress on the aircrew, it did give the hard pressed groundcrews valuable time in which to prepare the squadron's unserviceable Lancasters. As a result at 10.00hrs on Friday 11 June, when orders for ops that night came through, 49 Squadron could offer 17 aircraft.

11/12 June; DÜSSELDORF: The 'maximum effort' put up by the squadron consisted of no less than five new crews: Sgt Hutchinson (ED584); Sgt Frost (ED434); Sgt Powell (ED448); Sgt Kirton (ED416); F/Lt Dunnett (ED497). Within two months, 4 of these crews would be posted missing and the fifth crew broken up.

Two early returners were Sgts Kirton and Morrison; the former had the ASI go u/s, and the latter had intercom trouble. Over 700 bombers delivered a heavy attack on Düsseldorf, despite a PFF Mossie inadvertently dropping a load of T.I's 14 miles to the NE of the target, which drew some of the attacker's attention.

All 49's remaining aircraft returned to base safely, but Bomber Command lost a total of 38 bombers.

'A' Flt dispersal at Fiskerton circa June 1943: Lancaster ED416 J-Johnny about to be refuelled from the bowser. Just discernible are the legs of an instrument 'basher' who is standing on the tyre of the undercarriage putting fresh silica gel (drying agent) in the instrument circuit - there is a tin of gel standing on the wheel. (T.N. Simpson)

12/13 June; BOCHUM: Fifteen aircraft were detailed for Bochum, but whilst coming around the peri-track, F/O Thomas slipped O-Orange off the concrete and became bogged down. The other 14 managed to become airborne only to have 2 return early again; F/Lt Dunnett (ED497) had the rear turret go u/s in C-Charlie; then shortly after midnight, M-Mother came back with the pilot, Sgt Powell (ED448) suffering with stomach trouble (he never flew with the squadron again).

Two more new crews were starting their tours; they were piloted by Sgt Oglesby (LM306) and Sgt Petty (ED426). Both took part in this well-executed raid in which good Oboe sky-marking led to heavy bombing in the town centre.

Fourteen Lancasters and 10 Halifaxes were lost from the raid. Unfortunately one of the Lancasters reported missing was from Fiskerton; P/O John Hutchinson (ED584) and crew's Lancaster came down on farmland belonging to Mr J. Duteweert near Marienheem in Holland. The pilot's body and that of his 19 year old mid upper gunner, Sgt Edward Pearson were never found. The rest of the crew are buried in Raalte Cemetery.

FTR ED584	P/O J. Hutchinson	Pilot	(Missing)
(EA-U)	Sgt C.W. Dudley	F/E	(Killed)
'B Flt'	P/O C.S. Olson	NAV	(Killed)
	Sgt B.R. Cripps	W/AG	(Killed)
	Sgt E.H. Pearson RCAF	A/G	(Missing)
Crew on their	Sgt E.W.H. Johnson	B/A	(Killed)
2nd operation	F/S L.E. Workman RNZAF	A/G	(Killed)

14/15 June, 1943: OBERHAUSEN: An all Lancaster force of 197, guided by 6 Oboe Mossies made an successful attack on Oberhausen. Despite the target being cloud-covered, accurate sky-marking enabled the bombers to do considerable damage.

Twelve Lancasters lifted from Fiskerton's runway, the last one away by 22.32hrs. F/O Millar (ED726) returned early in V- Victor due to errors in the compass. The remaining 11 crews found themselves engaged in a savage battle from both flak and fighters which resulted in Bomber Command losing 17 aircraft. De-briefs back at Fiskerton told the story;

Sgt Robinson (ED663): *"Searchlights and flak over the target were well concentrated; returning over Holland we were attacked by two JU 88's"* - they returned unharmed. F/Lt Dunnett (ED497) returned with 2 incendiary cases hung up.

F/O Thomas (ED438): *"During our run into the target, the starboard side of the cockpit was hit by heavy flak seriously wounding the flight engineer, Sgt J. Dryne."* With their sortie completed the crew returned safely to base with the wounded crew member.

Sgt Kirton (ED416): *"There was quite a lot of heavy flak at 22,000ft."*

Sgt Hales (DV166) and crew departed the target area with one incendiary container hung up. On the return leg, they were attacked by an ME 110 which caused damage to the Lancaster's rear turret and starboard-inner engine cowling. The gunners, Sgts Amos and Frazer put up a tremendous fight in this life and death struggle; their matter-of-fact interrogation report clinically gives the outcome:

"We successfully engaged the enemy and saw his port engine burst into flames; he side -slipped and disappeared into the clouds below."

The bomb aimer, Sgt Patterson, was slightly injured in the encounter, but soon returned to duty. It was now daylight outside Fiskerton's Intelligence room, as Sgt Robinson and crew, the last to be interrogated, wearily made their way over to the locker-rooms... it had been a long night. W/Cmdr Johnson took one last look at the operations board before 'turning in' to catch a few hours sleep... 3 crews were well overdue and later that morning were posted as 'missing without trace'; twenty-three next-of- kin letters would have to be written.

Of those missing: Sgt Frost (ED434) and crew had been shot down by a German night fighter flown by Hauptmann Hans-Dieter Frank I./NJG1. The aircraft fell to the ground 2 kilometers East of Dodewaard, Holland at 01.13hrs. The pilot and flight engineer survived to become POW's in Stalag 357, Kopernikus; the remainder of the crew are buried in Uden War Cemetery.

Sgt George Cole (ED432) and crew were also caught by a night fighter and their aeroplane fell at Castle Doorwerth, west of Arnhem in Holland. Two of the crew survived; Sgt Arnold sustained shrapnel wounds to his legs and was thrown clear; both became POW's.

It has recently come to light, that the graves of the crew members who perished have been constantly tended by Geertruida Oosterhaar and was awarded the MBE in 1974. A schoolgirl at the time of the crash, Geertruida well remembers the night the Lancaster came down near her home. The crew lies at rest in Oosterbeek Cemetery near the many graves of the Airborne soldiers who died in the Battle for Arnhem.

At the 1993 Squadron reunion held at Woodhall Spa, Geertruida Oosterhaar was a very special 'guest of honour'; the squadron veterans took this opportunity to show Geertruida their deeply felt appreciation for the devotion she has shown over the years to some of their fallen comrades.

W/O Norman Nixon (ED435), whose brother happened to be the Medical Officer at Fiskerton, was killed along with his crew over Germany, their Lancaster crashing near Lembeck; the crew are buried together in the Reichwald Forest Cemetery.

FTR ED434	Sgt R. Frost	Pilot	(P.o.W.)
(EA-)	Sgt N.C. Hitchcock	F/E	(P.o.W.)
	F/O A.E. Whittaker	Nav	(Killed)
	Sgt J.R. Coulsey	W/AG	(Killed)
	F/S W.L. Chatfield RCAF	A/G	(Killed)
Crew on their	Sgt V. Horsley	A/B	(Killed)
3rd operation	Sgt P.A. Toms	A/G	(Killed)

FTR ED432	Sgt G.S. Cole	Pilot	(Killed)
(EA-N)	Sgt J.P. Harper	F/E	(Killed)
'B Flt'	Sgt C.A. Barnett	Nav	(Killed)
	Sgt J.R. Arnold	W/AG	(P.o.W.)
	Sgt J.H. Bryan	A/G	(P.o.W.)
	Sgt J.W. Deacon	B/A	(Killed)
Crew on their	Sgt H.R. Rhodes	A/G	(Killed)
8th operation	Sgt H. Biggin	Extra Nav	(Killed)

Missing ED453	W/O N. Nixon	Pilot	(Killed)
(EA-G)	Sgt C. Wilde	F/E	(Killed)
'A Flt'	F/S S.D. Bird RCAF	Nav	(Killed)
	Sgt R.T. Moore	W/AG	(Killed)
	Sgt R.K.B. Muir	A/G	(Killed)
	Sgt N.W. Fyfe	B/A	(Killed)
Crew on their	Sgt F.R. Fowler	A/G	(Killed)
10th operation	Sgt E. Dangerfield	Extra W/AG	(Killed)

16/17 June, 1943; COLOGNE: The squadron contributed 9 aircraft to the total force of 202 bombers sent to attack Cologne. The Pathfinders used H2S to place sky markers over a cloud covered target. Only half the Main Force managed to bomb with the remainder being turned back due to the adverse weather. The cost to Bomber Command was 14 Lancasters... and their crews. Those aircraft that did get through caused widespread damage to the housing areas of the city.

Seven Lancasters landed safely back at Fiskerton, each crew having completed successful trips; but as W/Cmdr Peter Johnson, still in his flying gear, scanned the operations board he realised that 2 more of the squadron's aircraft had failed to come home.

S/Ldr George Storey's Lancaster (ED785) had come down in the Scheldt Estuary near Flushing, Holland; the body of the Squadron Leader (on his second tour) was recovered from the sea near Westkapelle on 21 June. He is buried along with five of his fellow crew members in Flushing Cemetery; Sgt Bill Waring's body has never been found; Sgt Webb, the Candian W/AG, managed to bale out and became a PoW (Camp 357).

F/Lt Charles Dunnet (ED497) and crew also failed to return, shot down by a night fighter (Hptm Manfred Meurer I./NJG1). The Lancaster crashed near Helmond in Holand. They are all buried in Eindhoven (Woensel) Cemetery.

Missing ED785	S/L G.G. Storey	Pilot	(Killed)
(EA-)	Sgt G.S Underlin	F/E	(Killed)
	F/O R.C Blythe	NAV	(Killed)
	Sgt M.G. Webb RCAF	W/AG	(P.o.W.)
	Sgt H. Buttrey	A/G	(Killed)
	Sgt W.H. Waring	B/A	(Missing)
Crew on	Sgt M.E. Bunn RCAF	A/G	(Killed)
7th operation	Sgt Burnside	2nd Pilot	(Killed)

Missing ED497	F/L C.W. Dunnet	Pilot	(Killed)
(EA-)	Sgt R.F. Middlebrook	F/E	(Killed)
	Sgt R.G. Smith	NAV	(Killed)
	Sgt M.F. Haley	W/AG	(Killed)
	P/O C.A. Edwards	A/G	(Killed)
Crew on	Sgt W.A. Dutton	B/A	(Killed)
3rd operation	Sgt R.M.W.Selby-Lowndes	A/G	(Killed)

THE SHUTTLE RAIDS

With the Allied advances made in North Africa, the airfields of Blida and Maison Blanche came within range of aircraft based in England. Lancasters were to be the first to exploit the possibilities of attacking industrial targets deep into Southern Germany, before flying on to land in North Africa. Equipment for receiving the type (Lancasters) was shipped out to North Africa with orders that it should be installed by the full-moon period in mid-June. The former Zeppelin sheds at Friedrichshaven on the north shore of Lake Constance were being used to manufacture radar and radio equipment, including the Wurzburg radar sets which assisted the German night fighter to intercept British bombers. Under the codename 'Operation Bellicose', these old Zeppelin works were selected for an attack. With the short summer nights, the Germans assumed that Bomber Command could only attack shallow penetration targets such as the Ruhr. With most of their night fighters based around Northern Europe, Germany soon learned that her southern targets would never again be safe from Allied bombing, summer or winter.

20/21 June, 1943; FRIEDRICHSHAVEN (OPERATION BELLICOSE): Orders were received just four days before the operation. 49 Squadron was given the honour of leading the attack, and the unit's former C.O., G/Cpt Leonard Cain Slee DSO, DFC was to be the 'Master Bomber'. Following the successful use of VHF by Guy Gibson on the Dams raid, G/Cpt Slee intended to use this new tactical innovation by giving instructions using radio, over the target.

On the beautiful summer's evening of Sunday 20 June, 56 Lancasters from 5 Group lifted from their airfields around Lincoln on the very first 'shuttle raid'.

Leonard Slee (ED702) took his faithful D-Donald, the aircraft he had previously flown in as C.O. of 49 Squadron. For this special operation he had gathered together a crew of tour-expired and seasoned veteran 49ers, including Gerry Fawke as pilot, Major Johnnie Mullock (5 Gp flak liaison officer) and the notorious Australian bomb aimer, Keith Astbury.

The remaining 5 aircraft from 49, were all flown by experienced senior crews.

ED625 'B' F/Lt Munro RNZAF; ED416 'J' Sgt Millar RCAF;
ED721 'T' F/Lt Taylor; ED426 'P' P/O Price RCAF; EE134 'Y' S/Ldr Gilpin:

Note: Records show that on the 16 June, Jack Price and crew had received their postings to 83 Squadron PFF (for which they had volunteered). It would appear that this pleasant Californian serving in the RCAF, had been requested to delay his crew's departure until after the African trip. Unfortunately the Price crew did not survive their tour on PFF, going down whilst stationed at Coningsby.

Fiskerton, June 1943: Shadows begin to lengthen as P/O Jack Price and crew are snapped with their ground crew just before take-off (possibly for Friedrichshaven). The photograph is taken on the Reepham side of the airfield near the bomb dumps. Jack Price is standing below the large letter 'E'. (Chas Kind)

Near Cologne, G/Cpt Slee's aircraft lost one engine due to flak, and he was forced to hand over control to his deputy, W/Cmdr Cosme Gomm, C.O. of 467 RAAF Squadron. The force had been preceded by 4 Pathfinder Lancasters from 8 Group which had been unable to mark the target accurately. With the defences now fully alerted and putting up much heavy flak, Gomm ordered the bombers to go in at 11,000ft in the bright moonlight. The bombing was in two separate parts, the first bombs were aimed at the TI's, whilst the second phase was 5 Group's new technique of 'time and distance' bombing runs. W/Cmdr Gomm managed to broadcast corrections during the bombing, resulting in several crews putting their loads (4000lb Cookie, 7x1000lb) within a quarter of a mile of the intended aiming point, causing a considerable amount of damage to the target. The attacking force then flew on southwards towards North Africa, thereby denying the German night-fighters in France and Belgium any chance of intercepting them.

JUNE 1943

All the squadron's aircraft made the trip to the friendly African shores without any mishaps; F/O Des Harris, navigator in Bob Munro's (ED625) crew recorded in his log book a flying time of 10hrs 10mins, whilst F/Lt Tommy Taylor's log shows 9hrs 55mins, very long hours, but very successful sorties.

F/Lt Tommy Taylor recalls this unique operation:

"Those aircraft fitted with the new gyro bomb-sights were to bomb independently and those with the old sights were to make a 'time and distance' run. This method would enable the target to be hit even if obscured by smoke.

"We had been briefed to switch on our radio at exactly midnight on the Master Bomber frequency as we had rehearsed the raid at Wainfleet bombing range. However on the night of the actual trip, I couldn't wait and switched on a minute or two early to hear the closing bars of 'Deutschland Uber Alles', so we were using one of their frequencies!

The plan was to fly in a circle round the target until called in by the Master Bomber, then the aircraft fitted with the gyro bomb-sights would turn in and bomb and the remainder would turn over a pre-arranged prominent landmark onto a predetermined heading for a calculated time and then drop. Unfortunately I had just passed the turn-in when the time and distance aircraft were called in to bomb, so I had to make a complete circuit before attacking. Thus we were the last to bomb and so had the maximum attention from the light flak when heading out. Bob Seddon, our bomb aimer, said there was a lot of flak coming up and both the gunners reported flak being hosepiped towards us. It was the first time I had seen tracer above and below the cockpit at the same time.

As we flew across the Mediterranean to land in North Africa the sun came up over the sea. The sky was blue, the sea was blue and all the crew were fast asleep. When the coast of Africa appeared on the horizon ahead, I kicked Eric Stanley, the flight engineer into life and he woke the rest of the crew. Jock Stopani, the wireless operator, soon had a bearing on Maison Blanche beacon and in a short time we were in the circuit.

Within minutes all the aircraft, some short of fuel, were calling for permission to land... the American Air Traffic Controller eventually gave up in disgust yelling 'Get in the pattern and land when you can'. Everyone did after being airborne for nearly 10 hours."

North Africa 'Operation Bellicose' June 1943: Taking in the sun; (from l to r) Tom Taylor; Joe Taylor (Gilpin crew); Davies (Millar crew); Bob Munro RNZAF; Jimmy Bain (Gilpin crew). (T.D. Taylor)

21/22 June, 1943; KREFELD: A mixed force of over 700 bombers set out in moonlight to bomb this German city. Clear conditions enabled the Pathfinders to drop their ground-markers perfectly, the resulting bombing destroyed almost 50 per cent of the built-up area in the city centre.

However, there was a price to be paid... the clear moonlit conditions also assisted the night fighters and 44 of the raiders were shot down. The 7 aircraft from Fiskerton (including the new crew of F/O Randall's (LM308)) all made it safely home, but not without the odd moments of excitement.

F/O Thomas (ED438) and crew had their mid-upper turret go u/s shortly after crossing the Dutch coast, but the crew decided to 'press on'. When just 8 minutes from the target the starboard engine suddenly cut out. Unable to maintain height, they reached Krefeld at 15,000ft, several thousand feet below the Main Force. Once again the crew elected to uphold tradition, and pressed on to the target. Back at Fiskerton, eager ears listened out for the Thomas crew, who eventually returned safely, one hour overdue.

P/O Moss (ED719) and crew received damage on their bomb run when flak punched a hole through the starboard main plane, flap and aileron, but a perfect landing was achieved back at Fiskerton.

22/23 June, 1943; MULHEIM: Six Lancasters departed Fiskerton's runway to become part of the 557 bombers dispatched against Mulheim. Sgt Robinson (ED663) and crew returned early when their aircraft lost the use of its port-outer engine. The raid on Mulheim was successful and 49's five remaining crews completed their sorties, Command lost a further 35 bombers. P/O Tomlin (ED448) and crew, had the starboard tyre deflate on landing; no serious damage resulted, but on further inspection more flak holes were found in the aircraft's fuselage. Two crews happened to report seeing Krefeld still burning from the previous night's attack.

23/24 June, 1943; LA SPEZIA (From Maison Blanche): No 5 Group still had 50 plus aircraft away in North Africa. On the return leg of the 'Shuttle Raid' crews were briefed to bomb La Spezia's oil depot and armaments store, then fly home to England.

Four aircraft from 49 Squadron left Maison Blanche carrying 1x4000lb 'Cookie' and 5x500lb GP bombs. Shortly after take-off S/Ldr George Gilpin and crew had to return to North Africa with engine trouble. F/Lt Munro (ED625), Sgt Millar (ED416) and F/Lt Taylor (ED721) continued on and joined a small force of 52 Lancasters in a successful bombing attack on the Italian target of La Spezia from 9,000ft. All bombers then made the return journey to their home bases in England. Sgt Millar and F/Lt Munro arrived back at Fiskerton by 04.43hrs without any problems. Meanwhile F/O Taylor and crew were having all sorts of fun! Tom Taylor takes up the story:

"On the Friedrichshaven raid, Slee lost a 'donkey' and commandeered Jack Price's aircraft for his own return trip (W/Cmdr Slee came home on 27 June, via Gibraltar). We split Jack's crew between the remaining 49 crews and I had the navigator and flight engineer, Sgts Potts and Greavison. Briefing had been held in the old airport lounge at Maison Blanche. The navigators, after having tried to draw lines with their maps on wicker lounge tables decided that it would be easier to lay their maps on the floor. With the navigators on their knees and other crew members helping hold the maps flat, it was quite a sight. Mercator never dreamed of these 'projections'.

With nine up, T-Tommy took off for the target. After bombing we changed fuel tanks prior to climbing over the Alps. As soon as the flight engineer changed tanks the two starboard engines stopped, 'change back!' I yelled, which he did and they started up again. We now involved our passengers and by experimenting, we decided that the centre tank was blocked. My navigator, John Costello, having been assured by the flight engineer(s) that they could cross-feed the starboard engines from the port tanks and thus use all the fuel except that trapped, estimated that we could either go back to Maison Blanche or fly to the South coast of England, but we did not have enough to make Fiskerton. The two 'odd' crew members said they were due to go on leave as soon as they returned (pre-posting to PFF), so I had no choice.

We pressed on back to England without any further problems and landed at Tangmere in Sussex, the famous Fighter Command station.. duration 8hrs.50mins. The Duty Officer was hauled out of bed to be greeted by chaps dressed in khaki shorts and wearing pith helmets! Whilst I was on the phone to Scampton to tell them I was safely down and that Gilpin had returned to Africa, the Duty Officer arranged meals and accommodation and chided me for being so long on the phone. He said my crew was tired and needed sleep... Me too, I told him."

Note: Whilst in Africa the Taylor crews 'pigeon' laid an egg. (Homing pigeons were frequently carried enabling position messages to be sent if one crashed or ditched - the practice ceased around this period).

P/O Jack Price RCAF (middle back row holding mascot) and crew photographed with 'B' Flt ground crews at Fiskerton, possibly at the time of their departure for 83 PFF Sqdn at Wyton having volunteered for Pathfinders; sadly they did not survive their PFF tour. (Mrs D. Smith)

JUNE 1943

24/25 June, 1943; WUPPERTAL: A force of 630 bombers, including 7 from 49 Squadron made a successful attack, after the PFF had accurately placed their markers. Sgt Pilots Jupp and Bull operated for the first time with their crews. None of the 34 aircraft lost were from Fiskerton, although Sgt Watson (JA691) and crew did survive two combats with an enemy aircraft... hits were observed striking the night-fighter, but results could not be confirmed. Seven Lancasters had landed safely back at Fiskerton by 04.29hrs with the Watson kite sporting perforations in her port wing.

25/26 June, 1943; GELSENKIRCHEN: This was the first attack on this Ruhr 'oil target' since 1941. Oboe Mosquitoes found the target cloud-covered and were unable to place their markers with accuracy; as a result the raid was not a success. Sgt Eyles (ED438) and crew on their first operation, coolly orbited the target; later Sgt Eyles reported: *"We waited for fresh flares to be dropped, but as flak was bursting close, I decided to bomb the red glow in the clouds."* Of the 473 aircraft taking part, 30 failed to return.

All 49's Lancasters returned safely, although F/O Randall's crew (JA691) almost became victims, after an extremely close encounter with an enemy night-fighter. The Randall crew was flying the same kite in which Sgt Watson and crew had had their combats the previous night. At interrogation F/O Randall reported the following: *"We were on our way to Gelsenkirchen when a JU 88 made an attack; after evasive action, we completed an orbit to resume our course to the target. The JU 88 then came in again, this time from the starboard beam; the gunners, Sgts Slaughter and Buchanan opened fire at 400 yards. He flew over the my cockpit and collided with the port wing, tearing off the port aileron and damaging the flaps and outer fuel tank."*

This incident happened at 01.25hrs, about 15 minutes before ETA at the target. Unfortunately the destruction of the enemy aircraft could not be confirmed. The crew jettisoned the bomb load and limped back to Fiskerton landing at 03.55hrs.

28/29 June, 1943; COLOGNE: Bomber Command sent 608 bombers to attack Cologne, on a night when weather forecasts were not promising. The Oboe Mossies had to use the less reliable sky-markers over the cloud-covered city, and marking was 10 minutes late. Despite all these set-backs, Cologne received its most devastating attack of the Battle of the Ruhr.

The Main Force lost a total of 25 aircraft.

The squadron had provided 9 Lancasters for this operation; F/Lt Taylor took along newly arrived S/Ldr Graham Day, as second pilot. P/O Moss (ED625) and crew were forced to return early, after attempts by the gunners and flight engineer to mend a broken oil pipe in the rear turret failed; the bomb doors were only partly open when the load was jettisoned, and once again B-Baker came back with bumps and bruises.

JUNE 1943

A notable feat of airmanship was displayed by W/Cmdr Peter Johnson (ED702) and his flight engineer, Sgt Gottwaltz, on this operation. As they approached Cologne at 19,000ft above 10/10ths cloud... the red TI's were seen cascading down. Suddenly their aircraft was hammered by heavy flak which damaged 3 of the engines. The pilot ordered 1x500lb HE and some IB's to be jettisoned to lighten the aircraft. The starboard engine was now on fire and the port-inner had lost all pressure, whilst the outer engine began to surge. Peter Johnson continued on the bombing run, and the bomb aimer released their load with the TI's in his sights.

The struggle to regain England was achieved, with the pilot and Sgt Gottwaltz coaxing every mile out of the labouring Lancaster. W/Cmdr Johnson later put in his report:

"This was an exceptional performance by the flight engineer over the target when engaged by heavy flak - it was he who was responsible for the safe return of the aircraft."

OPERATIONAL SUMMARY - JUNE 1943

Date	Target	Desp	E/R	FTR	Remarks
11/12	DÜSSELDORF	17	2	-	
12/16	BOCHUM	14	2	1	Sgt Hutchinson FTR
14/15	OBERHAUSEN	12	1	3	Sgt Cole FTR Sgt Frost FTR W/O Nixon FTR
16/17	COLOGNE	9	-	2	F/L Dunnett FTR S/L Storey FTR
20/21	FRIEDRICKSHAVEN	6	-	-	Landed N Africa
21/22	KREFELD	7	-	-	
22/23	MULHEIM	6	1	-	
23/24	LA SPEZIA	4	1	-	From N Africa
24/25	WUPPERTAL	7	-	-	
25/26	GELSENKIRCHEN	7	-	-	
28/29	COLOGNE	9	1	-	

Total of sorties flown	98
Failed to return	6

JULY 1943

Fiskerton, June/July 1943: Canadian pilot 'Dusty' Millar and crew alongside ED445 H-Harry. On 3 July (after 14 ops on 49) the crew was posted out to 83 PFF Sqdn after volunteering to become pathfinders. They would survive until the night of 26/27 November 1943 when they failed to return from Berlin:
(l to r) Unknown;
Sgt King B/A (KIA);
Sgt Pennells Nav (KIA);
Sgt Millar RCAF, Pilot (KIA);
Sgt Birks F/E (KIA);
F/Sgt Foster A/G;
Unknown;
Sgt Harsley W/Ag (KIA):

Jimmy Harsley spent much time at 'A' Flt dispersal with the ground crew. Sgt Trevor Simpson remembers; *"Jimmy used to come to work with us, he was dead keen to see what made a Lanc tick - he was a great guy."*
Lancaster ED445 passed to 50 Sqdn Skellingthorpe and it too failed to survive the Battle of Berlin. (T.N. Simpson)

3/4 July, 1943; COLOGNE: Good ground marking by the Oboe Mossies led to Cologne receiving a severe blow from over 600 heavy bombers. 49 Squadron put up 13 Lancasters including a 'freshman' crew piloted by Sgt Coxill (ED721). The night saw the first deployment of a new German unit, Jagdgeschwader 300. Equipped with single-engined fighters, it operated in and around the target area, the German pilots using the illumination from the target fires to spot their victims. The code name for this technique was Wilde Sau (Wild Boar). Bomber crews were unused to being attacked over the target and on this night several crews reported being shot at by other bombers. In reality these would have most likely have been 'Wild Boar' attacks.

Thirty aircraft failed to return from the raid; 12 were brought down in the target area, and both flak gunners and Wild Boar pilots claimed these as their victories. But it was flak that caused the only damage to two of 49's aircraft:

Sgt Eyles (ED438) reported: *"The leading edge inboard of the port outer engine was holed by flak, causing the rear turret to become u/s."* Sgt Jupp's (ED416) aircraft also received minor flak damage. All of the squadron's aircraft returned safely to base except for one which put down at Dunholme.

THE HUNGRY PILOT OFFICER

It was during this period that 617 Squadron would often ask to borrow kites from 49 Squadron, as their 'specials' had gone into storage. In fact 617 actually flew some operations with some EA coded Lancasters. This was also the time that a young Sgt pilot named Johnny Moss had received notification of his promotion to Pilot Officer. One morning whilst on his rounds, W/Cmdr Johnson spotted Johnny still wearing his Sgts uniform, and immediately dispatched the fledgling Officer off into Lincoln to be fitted out in his new uniform.

A few days later the Moss crew was detailed to ferry ED999 over to 617 Sqdn at Scampton, where transport would pick them up after lunch and return them to Fiskerton. Landing at Scampton just in time for lunch, the six NCO members of the crew shot off to the Sgts' Mess leaving their lonely pilot to find his way to the Officers' Mess.

With trepidation, P/O Moss in his brand-new uniform entered the hallowed halls of Scampton's Officers' Mess ... the first time he had been in any Officers' Mess. Taking one deep breath Johnny stepped into the bar, from where most of the noise was coming. There he was confronted by some of the most highly decorated Bomber Command types in the Royal Air Force, including Guy Gibson, Mick Martin, Dave Shannon, Bill Townsend etc., a host of DFM'S, DFC's, DSO's and Bars not to mention a CGM and a VC. Johnny departed the scene as smartly as he had entered. It was a very hungry young Pilot Officer who made the road journey back to RAF Fiskerton ... too late for lunch.

8/9 July, 1943; COLOGNE: After 5 frustrating days, in which 3 operations had been planned, only to be scrubbed at the last minute, 280 plus Lancasters eventually took off to pay another visit to Cologne. Fiskerton put up 14 aircraft, including two new crews piloted by S/Ldr Day (ED999) and Sgt Edy (DV178).

Accurately-dropped Oboe sky-markers led to a successful raid causing heavy damage to the western parts of the city. 49's crews reported good sorties although several suffered 'hang ups' caused by icing.

Cyril Anderson (ED416) and crew had returned to 49 Squadron to complete their tour, after taking part in the famous 'Dams raid'. On this trip, the rear gunner had a close call when a piece of flak whipped through the perspex of his turret, missing him by inches.

Sadly, one of the 7 Lancasters lost this night was from 49 Squadron; Sgt pilot, Stan Eyles (who was only 20 years old) and his crew all perished when they were shot down by a night fighter. Oblt Heinz-Wolfgang Schnaufer (II./NJG1) sent them crashing into the banks of the Albert Canal near Antwerp; at 02.53hrs. The crew are buried together in Antwerp Cemetery.

FTR ED663	Sgt S.C. Eyles	Pilot	(Killed)
	Sgt D.W. Neale	F/E	(Killed)
(EA-)	Sgt D.R. Fullager	NAV	(Killed)
	Sgt G.G. Shepherd	W/AG	(Killed)
	Sgt M. Barrett RCAF	A/G	(Killed)
Crew on their	Sgt W.S. Ashworth	B/A	(Killed)
4th operation	Sgt R.E. LaBrie RCAF	A/G	(Killed)

9/10 July, 1943; GELSENKIRCHEN: Over 400 bombers attempted to attack Gelsenkirchen through 10/10ths cloud cover. Of the 6 Oboe Mosquitoes, 5 had equipment failure, and the sixth dropped his sky-markers in error several miles away. Eleven aircraft were detailed from the squadron, of which one had to return early; Sgt Coxill's aircraft experienced trouble with the rear turret.

At de-brief, the crews knew nothing of the Pathfinder's difficulties, and reported seeing markers and explosions in their sights. Three crews reported flak damage; Sgt Anderson for the second night running, had flak penetrate the perspex, this time through bomb aimer's Gilbert Green's blister. F/O Millar (ED726) received heavy flak damage to the bomb bay, with a piece of shrapnel hitting the mid-upper gunner's parachute harness without causing him injury. F/Sgt Oglesby and crew brought ED426 back with flak holes in the port mainplane, the fuselage and the starboard-outer engine.

Twelve aircraft failed to return, but all 49's came home safely.

12/13 July, 1943; TURIN: The allies war against the Italians was going very well. With extra pressure brought to bear by Bomber Command, it was hoped that Germany's ally would soon capitulate. Turin was selected for an attack by 295 Lancasters. The route took them well out into the Bay of Biscay and across Southern France thus avoiding heavily defended areas. Many crews reported heavy icing over France, and encountering thunder-clouds over the Alps. S/Ldr Gilpin was forced to return early with the rear turret u/s.

These long haul trips to Italy were not considered easy by crews and to prove the point 13 Lancasters failed to return. Among those missing was F/O John Millar and crew from 49 Squadron. Perhaps the raid three nights earlier had been an omen... ED726 with the Millar crew had been blasted by flak over Gelsenkirchen. It had been repaired just in time for them to take part in the Turin trip, the crew's fateful 13th operation. The crew have no Known graves, but are remembered on the Runnymede Memorial.

After slipping out over the Brest coast at 1,000ft on the return leg, the Moss crew spotted three other Lancasters heading for home but flying at least 15 degrees off track to the west. Contact was attempted using the Aldis lamp but without success. Doubts crept into the Moss crew as to the correctness of their own course... but these were soon dispelled when their predicted landfall was made.

Severely low on fuel, four of the squadron's aircraft made for southern airfields. P/O Tomlin landed at Christchurch, P/O Anderson at Upper Heyford and W/O Morrison at Exeter. P/O Moss (ED999) and crew (having been in A-Apple for over 10hrs) landed at the very small fighter airfield of Bolt Head, and in doing so 'scuffed it up a little', much to the displeasure of the Station Commander.

Returning to Fiskerton next day, the Moss crew learnt of the loss of W/Cmdr Nettleton VC and crew (C.O. of 44 Sqdn Dunholme Lodge) somewhere off the Brest Peninsula.
To this day, bomb aimer Len Bradfield feels sure that Nettleton's aircraft was one of the three they had sighted in the early morning light off the French coast.

FTR ED726	F/O J.G. Millar AFM	Pilot	(Killed)
(EA-V)	Sgt P. Goodyear	F/E	(Killed)
'B' Flt	F/S J.W. Gillin RCAF	NAV	(Killed)
	Sgt H.J. Read	W/AG	(Killed)
	Sgt D.W. Bettinson	A/G	(Killed)
Crew on their	F/O G. Lockie	B/A	(Killed)
13th operation	Sgt R. Burnett	A/G	(Killed)

16/17 July, 1943; NORTHERN ITALIAN TRANSFORMER STATIONS: The intention of this operation was to destroy electricity supplies to the railways carrying German troop reinforcements to the battle front in Sicily. A force of 24 Lancasters from 5 Group had tried and failed the previous night, before flying on to North African bases.

On this, their second Shuttle raid, 49 provided three crews; S/Ldr Gilpin (ED946); F/Lt Munro (ED625); P/O Tomlin (JA851):

Take-off was from Scampton just after 22.00hrs, the force being led by 57 Squadron's C.O., W/Cmdr Hopcroft, with S/Ldr Gilpin as his second in command; 44 Squadron from Dunholme Lodge also provided crews.

Seven aircraft successfully bombed the Cislago station. S/Ldr George Gilpin (ED946) attacked the primary target from 1,000ft and then went on to attack the secondary from 1,500ft. By the light of a full moon, F/Lt Munro (ED625) and P/O Tomlin (JA851) bombed Reggio Nel Amelia from 2,500ft. All aircraft then flew on to Blida airfield in North Africa, landing around 08.45hrs. One Lancaster (from another sqdn) was lost on the raid.

24/25 July, 1943 LEGHORN (FROM BLIDA): Bad weather delayed the 5 Group Lancasters return from Africa to England until the 24th when they bombed Leghorn docks and installations on the return leg. The bombing, from the force of 33 Lancasters was reported as scattered, but P/O Tomlin (JA851), attacking from 15,500ft records: *"The oil refinery to the north east of the town was seen to explode and catch fire - our own bombs were seen to burst in the centre of the iron foundry."* All aircraft returned safely to England.

24/25 July, 1943 HAMBURG: On the same night as shuttle raiders were returning from Africa, 'Bomber Harris' decided to launch his follow up to the Battle of the Ruhr... an all-out attack on the Reich's second largest town, Hamburg. What was to become known as the Battle of Hamburg consisted of 4 major raids in which it was intended to drop 10,000 tons of bombs.

For the first raid, conditions were clear... H2S marking was used as the distance was too great for Oboe. A mixed force of 791 bombers was dispatched of which 728 aircraft dropped 2,284 tons of bombs in 50 minutes.

WINDOW

A new and major tactical innovation was introduced during the Battle of Hamburg. For some time scientists had been devising a way of jamming German ground radar. They came up with a very simple and relatively inexpensive method which was given the code name 'Window'. Window was in fact strips of black paper 27 centimetres long and 2 centimetres wide, with aluminium foil stuck to one side. Dropped in bundles of 2,000 strips held together with elastic bands, it formed a huge cloud of aluminium strips. The German Wurzburg radar sets which controlled the night-fighter interceptions and radar-predicted flak guns plus the smaller airborne Lichtenstein radar sets, were all rendered useless when swamped by so many false echoes.

Window had been perfected by April 1942, but Bomber Command was prevented from using it until British radar had been made immune from its use... since the Germans would soon realise its potential and use it themselves. Little did the British realise that the Germans had also developed this type of jamming method in parallel, and they also had not introduced it first for the very same reason. During this intervening period, Bomber Command had lost 2,200 aircraft. Needless to say, when they learned of this delay, the aircrews were furious and the word ‘murder’, was heard in many a flight office throughout eastern England during July 1943.

Leading aircraft from the 791 strong Main Force started releasing bundles of Window shortly after passing over Heligoland; the effect was immediate as the German defences were thrown into total confusion. F/Sgt Kirton (ED416) and crew, who flew over the target with their starboard inner engine u/s, reported: *"One bundle of Window carried away the Marconi aerial - Searchlights weaving about hopelessly."*

The method of releasing Window by most crews was via the aircraft's window, which resulted in several aerials being lost. P/O Cyril Anderson (JA892) and W/O Jock Morrison LM306), had the disconcerting dilemma of having the mid upper turret blacked out by these metal strips. The only other incident occurred when F/Lt Taylor's (ED721) mid-upper gunner, Sgt Stopani, succeeded in scaring away a night-fighter with one short burst, just after leaving the target.

All of 49's crews returned safely, leaving behind them a target well alight. 12 aircraft failed to return; 1.5 per cent of the force.

EA-R seen through EA-J's undercarriage.
Jock Esson, rigger on J with hand on hat.
Photo taken in June 1943.
(49 Sqdn Collection)

25/26 July, 1943; ESSEN: The following evening, with the concept of Window still fresh, 705 bombers were sent to Essen; 49 squadron dispatched 14 aircraft and took the opportunity to blood three new crews; they were piloted by W/O McCabe RNZAF (ED448), F/O Coates (JA892) and F/O Cottingham (LM306). Three other crews were forced to return early with mechanical problems.

The raid was successful with the Krupps works being heavily damaged; Bomber Command lost 26 aircraft. All 49's Lancasters returned to base, including Sgt Petty (JA894) and crew who had a lucky escape when they were hit by incendiaries from an aircraft above; one bomb actually passed through the spinner of the starboard outer engine and penetrated the cowling fortunately without catching fire.

27/28 July, 1943; HAMBURG: This was the night of the notorious firestorm, when 729 aircraft dropped 2,326 tons of bombs on Hamburg. The squadron contributed 16 Lancasters to the attack, again with three new crews, those of; Sgt Gospel (ED721), P/O Hidderley (ED416) and Sgt Greig (EE134).

Window was used, and it would appear with great success, P/O Tomlin (ED805) reports: *"Defences seemed hopelessly confused, searchlights probably numbering 100 were directed aimlessly."* Losses were lighter than usual with 17 aircraft failing to return.

Bob Petty (JA894) and crew were once again involved in trouble, this time with a night fighter. The 'Monica' system had been successful in warning them of the approach of a JU 88.. the enemy fighter turned in to attack from the starboard quarter and Eddie Smith the rear gunner opened fire. The fighter then broke away to try his luck from the port quarter; both Eddie and the mid upper gunner 'Shorty' Roberts were waiting... they opened fire together causing the night fighter to burst into flames and they reported seeing it hit the ground.

All 49's aircraft were safely home by 04.19hrs.

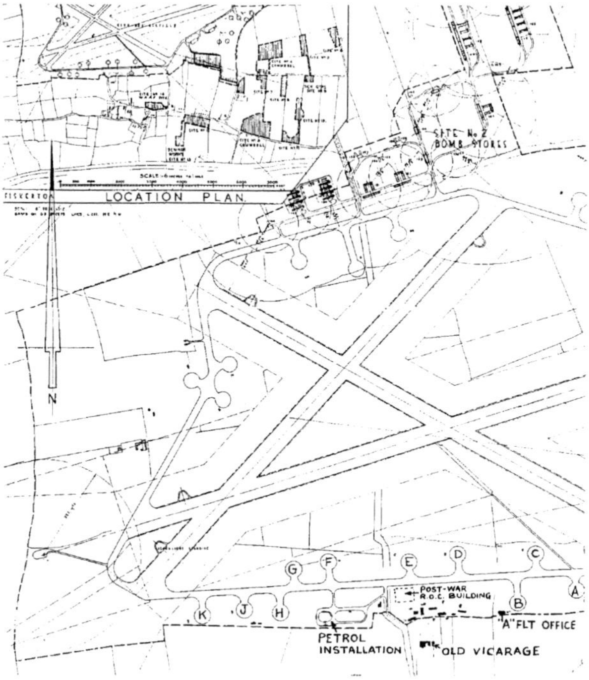

Plan of the western side of Fiskerton airfield.

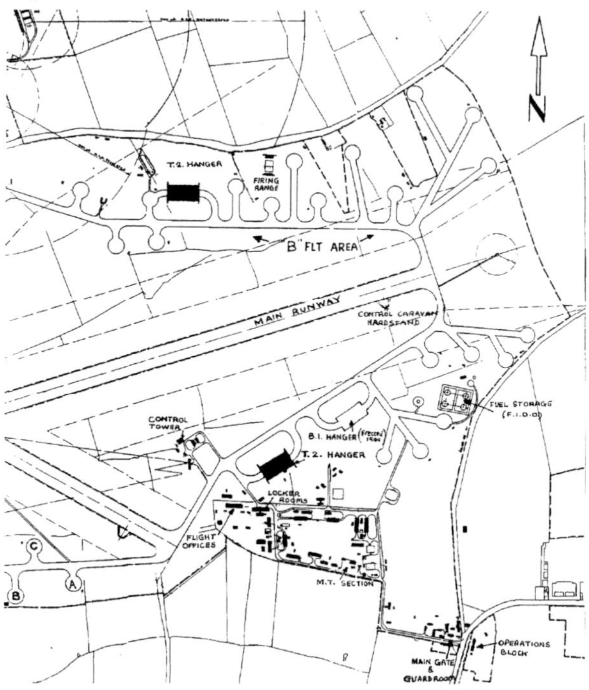

Plan of the eastern side of Fiskerton airfield

29/30 July, 1943; HAMBURG: After a night's rest for the crews, Bomber Command returned to Hamburg. Over 700 aircraft attempted to bomb the northern parts of the town that had escaped the firestorm. Fiskerton sent 16 Lancasters into the battle but had Sgt Greig (EE134) return early with the rear turret u/s.

The loss rate was starting to creep up again slightly, with 28 bombers being brought down. Evidence of searchlights co-operating with fighters was reported at de-brief. Sgt Hales stated: *"We arrived early at the target and made 3 orbits, cones appeared to be working with fighters - 2 aircraft were seen being shot down."* All 49's aircraft returned safely.

30/31 July, 1943; REMSCHEID: A small Main Force of 273 bombers led by Oboe Mosquitoes attacked this previously unbombed target. The squadron sent only 4 aircraft, and all 4 completed successful sorties. The force lost 15 aircraft, a high percentage loss of 5.5 per cent. Again this was probably due to the 'Wild Boar' fighters with searchlight co-operation. P/O Tomlin confirmed this at interrogation: *"Many enemy fighters in target area working effectively with searchlights".* S/Ldr Day (ED999) added: *"Flak practically nil - searchlights indicated position by circling our aircraft."*

F/Lt Taylor (ED721) took along Sgt Ernie Webb as second pilot; shortly after leaving the target they were hit by flak near the rear turret. Fortunately the only damage incurred was to the elsan, which disgorged its contents liberally.

The attack on this small town was devastating, with over 80 per cent of the target being destroyed. The following night, ops were cancelled at 22.30hrs at the very last moment; too late for crews to make a trip into Lincoln with its beckoning pubs and cinemas.

OPERATIONAL SUMMARY - JULY 1943

Date	Target	Desp	E/R	FTR	Remarks
3/4	COLOGNE	13	-	-	
8/7	COLOGNE	14	-	1	Sgt Eyles FTR
9/10	GELSENKIRCHEN	11	1	-	
12/13	TURIN	12	-	1	F/O Millar FTR
16/17	NORTH ITALY	3	-	-	Landed N. Africa
24/25	LEGHORN	3	-	-	From N. Africa
24/25	HAMBURG	12	-	-	
25/26	ESSEN	14	3	-	
27/28	HAMBURG	16	-	-	
29/30	HAMBURG	16	1	-	
30/31	REMSCHEID	4	-	-	
Total of sorties flown		118			
Failed to return		2			

AUGUST 1943

At the beginning of August the unit strength stood at:-40 Officers and 601 Other Ranks. Aircraft on Charge - 16 Lancaster Mk 111 with 2 in reserve and a further 3 surplus.

2/3 August, 1943; HAMBURG: Bomber Command pressed on with its fourth and final attack during the battle against Hamburg when 740 bombers were dispatched in severe weather conditions.

Of the 15 aircraft sent by the squadron, all encountered thunderstorms and lightning which gave icing problems. Five crews turned back unable to climb above the thunderheads; F/O Smeaton (ED416) and crew flying J-Johnny, managed to complete a successful first sortie. Pathfinders were unable to mark accurately and as a result the bombing was scattered; 30 aircraft failed to return but all 49's made it back to base.

Fiskerton, July/Aug 1943: F/Lt Munro and crew photographed alongside ED625 'EA-B'.
(l to r)
B. Dreaver RNZAF, R/Gunner *
J. Reddish, F/Engineer;
B.L. Schauenberg RCAF W/op
R.C. Munro RNZAF, Pilot;
J.A. Fernie, M/U Gunner
J.D. Harris, Navigator.

Lancaster ED625 (EA-B) failed to return from Nuremburg 10/11-8-43 with P/O Moss and crew.
(J.D. Harris)

* Sgt B Dreaver was killed 13-8-43. Believed to be in a Wellington that crashed whilst on gunnery exercise. Buried St Johns Churchyard, Beck Row, Suffolk.

9/10 August, 1943; MANNHEIM: Three planned operations had been cancelled but on the 9th, 457 bombers managed to set out for Mannheim. The squadron, now back to full strength was able to put up 17 Lancasters. Two new crews were operating; Sgt Webb (ED721) and Sgt Stanton (JA851). The latter's aircraft port-outer engine failed forcing the crew to return to base early after jettisoning their bomb load.

Despite being a medium-sized raid, considerable damage was done to the town, with all returning 49 crews reporting successful sorties. Sgt Edy (DV178) and crew were attacked by a single-engined fighter near the target, but the combined skills of the Australian mid-upper gunner Sgt Mason and Canadian rear-gunner Sgt McDonald sent the fighter spinning down in flames.

All 49's aircraft returned safely, with one exception: Sgt Watson (ED719) and crew flying K-King were well into France when trouble first struck The port-outer engine started to overheat and had to be shut down. Bert Cole the crew's bomb aimer continues the story:

"A discussion broke out amongst the crew as to whether we should carry on or not... with a tail wind of 70 knots and the security of the bomber stream we opted to head into Germany, so Cliff Green our Welsh navigator gave our skipper the course. Incendiaries were shed to lighten the load, but as we progressed the port inner engine suffered the same symptoms as the outer. Since we had come so far, we once again decided to 'press on' arriving over the target much later than the Main Force. We crabbed our way over Mannheim on the two good engines all by ourselves and totally unopposed. Away went the 'cookie', but as we departed the target flak and searchlights started up again... they must have feared a second wave of attacks.

Not long after leaving the target the Lancaster was becoming too difficult to fly and 'Lol' Watson our skipper could not keep her straight any longer. In his usual laconic Yorkshire accent Lol instructed us to put on our parachutes. I said that mine had been on for the last hour! so he then told me to open the nose escape hatch... I did that half an hour ago! came my reply."

All the crew parachuted down safely to become PoW's for the rest of the war.

Next morning back at Fiskerton, Len Bradfield learned of the loss of his very close friend Bert Cole. He and Bert had come through air bomber training together, they went to the same OTU and HCU, and fate determined that both their crews be posted to 49 Squadron. Now that Bert was missing, no more visits to The Crown or The Falcon in Lincoln... but on that following evening of the 10th August, fate would have another trick to play!

Bomber Command lost 6 Halifaxes and 3 Lancasters.

FTR ED719	F/S L.E. Watson	Pilot	(P.o.W.)
(EA-K)	Sgt E.C. Lynch	F/E	(P.o.W.)
'A' Flt	F/S C.T. Green	Nav	(P.o.W.)
	Sgt J. Goodall	W/AG	(P.o.W.)
	Sgt J.W. Turner	A/G	(P.o.W.)
crew on their	Sgt H. Cole	B/A	(P.o.W.)
11th operation	Sgt M.E. Scarfe RCAF	A/G	(P.o.W.)

10/11th August, 1943; NUREMBURG: Over 650 heavy bombers made a successful attack on the centre and southern areas of the city. 49 Squadron sent 12 aircraft on the raid... 11 made good their attacks, but the twelfth never made the target: ED625 B-Baker being flown by P/O Johnny Moss and crew was on course for Nuremburg when disaster struck; Sgt Len Bradfield, bomb aimer, recalls the Lancaster's final moments:

"We were on time and flying at 21,000 feet when attacked by two JU 88s. The first came in from 4 o'clock high hitting and setting fire to the port outer engine; the second came from astern, 6 o'clock level. He raked the fuselage and during this action, the cannon fire may have killed both our gunners, Terry Wood in the mid upper turret and Ronnie Musson in the rear. The bomb bay was set on fire and Johnny immediately ordered the crew to bale out. At the time, Sammy Small our wireless/op had gone back to see if he could help the gunners. I went out through the nose hatch as the remainder made their way into the nose behind me."

As Len left the stricken bomber he could see enemy tracer still striking the Lancaster... then suddenly, the bomb load exploded in a blinding flash. Seconds later, the pilot found himself floating to earth on an open parachute. His last recollections were of holding the aircraft steady as the navigator and flight engineer climbed down into the nose to bale out; at that moment the aircraft must have exploded. Sadly just two members of the crew, Len Bradfield and Johnny Moss survived the ordeal with their lives.

Fate once again intervened in Len's parallel career with his old friend Bert Cole, for he was now, like Bert, a PoW (Luft 6). Pilot, Johnny Moss also became a prisoner (Luft 3) but managed to make his escape later in the war, joining up with American Infantry troops... but that's another story. Len also made his bid for freedom during that infamous POW forced march during the winter of 1944/45. Hiding amongst frozen sugar beat, Len soon developed frost-bite in his feet and toes with the inevitable consequences.

The circumstances in which W/op Sammy Small, the navigator Dave Jones and flight engineer Ernie Roden died have never been established, but it is thought that they were unable to escape the aircraft before it disintegrated. They are buried together with the two gunners at Rheinberg in Germany.

The remaining squadron aircraft all returned safely, but Bomber Command had lost 16 aircraft.

FTR ED625	P/O J.H. Moss	Pilot	(P.o.W.)
(EA-B)	Sgt E.H. Roden	F/E	(Killed)
'A' Flt	Sgt D.G. Jones	Nav	(Killed)
	Sgt R.J. Small	W/AG	(Killed)
crew on their	Sgt T.A. Wood	A/G	(Killed)
16th operation	Sgt L.F. Bradfield	B/A	(P.o.W.)
	Sgt C.R. Musson	A/G	(Killed)

12/13 August, 1943; MILAN: A medium sized force of 504 bombers made a successful attack on Milan for the loss of just one Lancaster. The squadron contributed 13 aircraft with all returning safely after completing their sorties. The only moment of danger came when F/O Cottingham (ED702) and crew were fired upon twice by an enemy aircraft as they approached the Alps; fortunately no damage was sustained by their Lancaster.

AUGUST 1943

14/15 August, 1943; MILAN: A small force of 140 Lancasters added further damage to Milan, again losing just one aircraft. Fiskerton sent 6 Lancasters, but F/Sgt Coxill (LM337) had to return early with the rear turret u/s. S/Ldr Todd-White's (ED805) crew had their starboard engine catch fire. The problem was soon handled by the crew and the sortie carried out, but duty staff in the Watch Office had an anxious wait as the station's newest Squadron Leader landed an hour overdue, on this the crew's first operation of a second tour.

15/16 August, 1943; MILAN: A force of 199 Lancasters made a concentrated attack on a now exhausted Milan, but this time as the crews returned across France the German fighters were waiting. Seven Lancasters failed to return home. 49 Squadron had dispatched 8 aircraft of which one failed to return: It is believed that P/O Leslie Gospel and crew were hit by flak on their homeward leg. The Lancaster crashed near Rugles in France, at 02.45hrs. Two of the crew survived, and both managed to escape back to England. Tragically one of them, Sgt Philo, was later killed on ops (3-4-45).
The remainder are buried at Cheronvilliers, France.

FTR LM337	P/O L.W. Gospel	Pilot	(Killed)
(EA-V)	Sgt R. James	F/E	(Killed)
'B Flt'	Sgt C. Witheridge RCAF	NAV	(Evader)
	Sgt H. Hedge	W/AG	(Killed)
	F/S C.W. Taylor RAAF	A/G	(Killed)
crew on their	Sgt S.J. Philo	B/A	(Evader)
4th operation	Sgt A.E. Huntingford	A/G	(Killed)

17/18 August, 1943; PEENEMUNDE: This was a 'special' raid in which Bomber Command was tasked to attempt a night time precision raid on the German research establishment at Peenemunde, on the Baltic coast. It was here that the V-2 rockets were built and tested.

It was essential that a decisive blow be struck against this target, and crews were made well aware at briefing that they would have to return the following evening if sufficient damage was not incurred. Such was the importance of this raid, that most of the squadrons operating, were led by their Wing Commanders.

A force of 596 bombers started leaving their home airfields on a pleasantly warm summer's evening. Twelve Lancasters had been detailed from the squadron; at 21.35 W/Cmdr Peter Johnson released the brakes of ED702 sending the first aircraft and crew speeding down Fiskerton's runway. Five miles beyond the runway's end lay the city of Lincoln with its majestic Cathedral silhouetted against the setting sun.

The bombers followed behind a small force of 8 Mosquitoes from 139 Squadron PFF. The Mossies were led by none-other than G/Cpt Cain Slee, 49's former C.O. Their task was to overfly Peenemunde an hour before the attack, then go on to bomb Berlin, dropping 'Window' in their wake. It is estimated that this ploy diverted at least two Groups of enemy fighters away from the main target.

The attack took place in bright moonlight (to assist accurate bombing), and was conducted by a 'Master of Ceremonies', W/Cmdr John Searby of 83 Squadron. PFF had carried out a dress rehearsal for this role on 7th August over Turin. Bombing was in three waves, with 5 Group (including 49 Squadron) being in the third wave. Most of 49 Squadron's aircraft bombed from about 7,000ft. By this time, the German controllers had realised the real target and had re-directed the night fighters. In conjunction with strong flak defences, the fighters took a heavy toll of bombers, especially the 3rd and final wave.

For the first time the German fighters were using a new weapon, codenamed 'Schrage-Music'. It consisted of two 30mm cannon mounted to point upwards from the fuselage. So equipped the pilot slipped underneath an unsuspecting bomber and aimed shells up into the wing fuel tanks. Once perfected, an experienced crew could bring a bomber down using very few rounds. Forty aircraft fell, with 5 Group losing 17 - Fiskerton had 4 Lancasters shot down, one-third of those dispatched by 49 Squadron: Sgt Charles Robinson and crew were attacked and shot down after bombing. The fighter attacked from the rear... rear gunner F/Sgt Jack Wallner RCAF managed to shout a warning to the pilot before both he and the enemy opened fire. Five of the crew managed to make their desperate escape but unfortunately both gunners perished.

S/Ldr Richard Todd-White and crew were flying on only their second trip of a second tour. All the crew died when S-Sugar was brought down; five members were never found (possibly parachuted into the Baltic). The pilot is buried in Sweden and his 19 year-old gunner, Sgt George Humble is buried in Poland. The crew had only been on the squadron a week.

P/O Tom Tomlin DFC from Plymouth, was shot down by Lt Hans Meissner; flying an ME 110... the radar operator had guided the pilot onto his target, then from a range of fifty metres below and behind, Meissner pumped a short burst into the bomber's starboard inner engine; the Lancaster fell away in flames. All on board the Lancaster were killed, including F/Sgt George Silvester DFM, former member of Ted Tickler's crew when Ted earned his CGM. Only the pilot's body was recovered and he is buried at Aabenraa, Denmark. (It would appear that the pilot stayed at the controls of his aircraft whilst his crew parachuted).

Moments later Lt Meissner picked up F/O Harry Randall's aircraft and in seconds shot them down using the same method... this aircraft crashed in Denmark with no survivors; they too are buried at Aabenraa. The crew's flight engineer was Sgt Les Henley. Formerly in the Army, he had joined the RAF in 1940 and managed to get on ops at the age of 43, which was well above the average.

Returning crews brought back good reports of a target well bombed, knowing that a second attack would not be needed.

New Zealand pilot, W/O McCabe and crew almost became the squadron's fifth victim of the night, when they were engaged by a fighter 11 minutes after leaving the target. But the crews gunners, Sgts Falk and Ford managed to destroy their attacker before it destroyed them.

It has been estimated that this raid put back the V-2 programme by at least two months, which in turn reduced the eventual scale of the rocket attacks in late 1944. Such knowledge was not readily available to a squadron coming to terms with the loss of 28 men and 4 aircraft.

FTR JA851	P/O T.E. Tomlin DFC	Pilot	(Killed)
	Sgt K.E. Watson	F/E	(Killed)
(EA-)	P/O W.J. Rooke RAAF	Nav	(Killed)
	Sgt C. Stancliffe	W/AG	(Killed)
crew on their	P/O T. Tonkin DFM	A/G	(Killed)
23rd operation	F/S W.A. Davies	B/A	(Killed)
	F/S G.B. Silvester DFM	A/G	(Killed)
FTR ED805	S/L R.N. Todd-White	Pilot	(Killed)
(EA-S)	Sgt A. Purrington	F/E	(Killed)
'B' Flt	F/O H.O. Batchelor	Nav	(Killed)
	F/O B. James	W/AG	(Killed)
	Sgt G. Humble	A/G	(Killed)
crew on 2nd	F/O F. Plant	B/A	(Killed)
op 2nd tour	Sgt T. Brocklehurst	A/G	(Killed)
FTR JA892	Sgt C Robinson	Pilot	(P.o.W.)
(EA-)	Sgt W. Boyd	F/E	(P.o.W.)
	F/O P.F. Duckham	Nav	(P.o.W.)
	Sgt A.E. Anderson	W/AG	(P.o.W.)
	Sgt D. Parkin	A/G	(Killed)
crew on their	F/O W.J. Lowe	B/A	(P.o.W.)
13th operation	F/S J. Wallner RCAF	A/G	(Killed)
FTR JA691	F/O H.J. Randall	Pilot	(Killed)
(EA-L)	Sgt L.J. Henley	F/E	(Killed)
	Sgt L.F. Freeman	Nav	(Killed)
	Sgt R. Fowlston	W/AG	(Killed)
	Sgt N.W. Buchanan RAAF	A/G	(Killed)
crew on their	Sgt W.J. Stiles	B/A	(Killed)
8th operation	Sgt R.W. Slaughter	A/G	(Killed)

AUGUST 1943

22/23 August, 1943; LEVERKUSEN: Over 460 bombers (including 9 from Fiskerton) made an unsuccessful attack on Leverkusen. Five aircraft were lost from the force but all 49's returned safely, including Sgt Blackmore (ED721) and crew flying their first operation.

23/24 August, 1943; BERLIN: Bomber Command now began a short series of raids to test the German defences around Berlin in preparation for the forthcoming winter campaign. Over 725 bombers were dispatched with 9 being sent by the squadron and 9 safely returning. This raid resulted in Bomber Command suffering the greatest loss so far in one night, when 56 aircraft failed to return. 49 Squadron crews reported numerous cones of searchlights working in co-operation with night fighters.

F/O Tom Taylor and crew (with 'B'Flt ground staff) proudly gathered in front of their faithful ED721 'T for Tommy'.F/O Taylor (later F/Lt, DFC) is fifth from left on the front row wearing the cap. (Mrs J. Stopani)

27/28 August, 1943; NUREMBURG: Of the 12 aircraft sent by the squadron on the long haul to Nuremburg, four were flown by new crews: F/Sgt Brunt (ED999); Sgt Jones (JA690); F/Sgt Barnes RAAF (ED448) and Sgt Hodgkinson (ED426). All the squadron's crews including the 'freshmen', had successful sorties and safe returns.

Bombing by 674 aircraft suffered from creepback despite repeated requests from the Master Bomber. 33 Main Force aircraft failed to return.

AUGUST 1943

This was F/O Smeaton (ED416) and crew's seventh and last operation with 49 Squadron before being posted to 83 Squadron PFF. Note: They failed to return from Berlin in November 43.

30/31 August, 1943; MÖNCHEN GLADBACH: Fifteen Lancasters climbed away from Fiskerton forming part of a stream containing 660 bombers heading for Germany. The force made a double attack on Mönchen/Rheydt, causing severe damage. Flying in the stream were two more new crews from the squadron; F/Sgt George RAAF (ED416) and F/Lt Pike (LM306).

All of the squadron's aircraft returned to Fiskerton, with the only combat reported by Sgt Greig, whose mid/upper gunner scared off a fighter with a two-second burst of fire. Twenty five aircraft failed to return home.

31 August/1 September, 1943; BERLIN: On the last night of August 1943, the squadron dispatched 16 Lancasters to Berlin, but Sgt Blackmore was soon forced to return when JB139 developed intercom problems.

Strong German defences plus difficulties encountered by the H2S equipped Pathfinders combined to make this raid a failure. Once again the force of 622 raiders suffered heavily, with 47 of their number going down.

All 49's aircraft came home unscathed, although F/O Thomas (ED438) and crew in R-Robert, tangled with a night fighter over the target. Both gunners, Sgts Minns and Boxer managed to drive their attacker off.

Fiskerton, circa summer 1943.

Chas Kind (left) and 2 fellow 'B Flt' ground crew (L. Church Fitter & S Gibbs Rigger) enjoying the sun leaning on a 4000lb Cookie.

The photograph was taken on the Reepham side of the airfield adjacent to the bomb dumps.
(Chas Kind)

AUGUST 1943

OPERATIONAL SUMMARY - AUGUST 1943

Date	Target	Desp	E/R	FTR	Remarks
2/3	HAMBURG	15	-	-	
9/10	MANNHEIM	17	-	1	FTR F/S Watson
10/11	NUREMBURG	12	-	1	FTR P/O Moss
12/13	MILAN	13	-	-	
14/15	MILAN	6	1	-	
15/16	MILAN	8	-	1	FTR P/O Gospel
17/18	PEENEMUNDE	12	-	4	FTR P/O Tomlin FTR S/L Todd-White FTR F/O Randall FTR Sgt Robinson
22/23	LEVERKUSEN	9	-	-	
23/24	BERLIN	9	-	-	
27/28	NUREMBURG	12	-	-	
30/31	MÖNCHEN G.	15	-	-	
31/1	BERLIN	16	1	-	
Total of sorties flown -		144			
Failed to return		7			

ED805 (EA-S) `B' Flight Ran off the concrete coming out of dispersal on the night of 10/11th August bound for Nuremberg. `Sugar' also prevented another aircraft (just visible under the port wing) from taking off. S/Ldr Richard Todd-White and crew failed to return from Peenemunde on 17/18th August in ED805.
(J.A. Edwards)

SEPTEMBER 1943

A frequently published but excellent study of a 49 Squadron Lancaster. For the first time we can reveal the identity of the pretty Waaf driver who is confidently manoeuvring O-Oboe into dispersal circa Aug/Sep 43 - she is in fact LACW Lilian Yule. It was in this aircraft that Sgt Ernie Webb and crew survived a fighter attack over Mannheim. The rear turret was shattered by cannon-fire, with gunner Percy Horten receiving serious wounds. DV238 was repaired and returned to ops with 44 Squadron at Dunholm Lodge (49 Squadron collection)

2/3 September, 1943; MINELAYING (FRISIAN ISLANDS): September's operations started with two new crews making their first trips; laying mines. Despite a cloudy evening, the crews of Sgt Kerr (ED426) and Sgt Tavener (ED721) completed their sorties without any problems.

3/4 September,1943; BERLIN: Because of recent heavy losses suffered by Halifaxes and Stirlings when attacking Berlin, only Lancasters were sent on this raid. Some damage was caused by the 316 Lancasters but most bombs fell short of their target. Again losses were heavy with 22 Lancasters going down.

The squadron put up 13 aircraft, but F/Sgt Barnes (DV238), returned early with the rear turret u/s. Many fighters were evident as F/Sgt Kirton (ED416) confirms:

"An ME 110 made 3 attacks on us just after 'bombs gone' at 23.35hrs. The gunners returned fire and the fighter's port engine was seen to catch fire and he disappeared from view. Another enemy aircraft made a single attack, but we did not open fire on this."

SEPTEMBER 1943

DIVERSION TO DISASTER

On return from Berlin, the Lancasters were diverted to bases in Northern England. This was the last thing F/O Harold Coates and crew needed after nursing their badly damaged Lancaster back from Berlin, where JB126 had been hit by flak 10 seconds after bombs away!

When 15 miles from Blyth, off Tynemouth, in heavy mist, the struggling pilot was forced to ditch his crippled plane. Such were the sea conditions that the aircraft broke up on impact. Sadly Sgt's Pawson, Kendrew and Jack, died before the Rescue launch arrived. The unfortunate flight engineer, Sgt Sacre, was seen in the water but was subsequently lost. The pilot was last seen in his cockpit under the water. Sgt Underwood the bomb aimer and Sgt Nelson RAAF air gunner, were both taken to hospital with slight injuries and shock. The ditching occurred at 03.57hrs. Of the remaining squadron aircraft, six landed at Middleton St George, one at Croft, one at Wyton and three at base.

FTR JB126	F/O H.K. Coates	Pilot	(Killed)
(EA-)	Sgt J.G. Sacre	F/E	(Killed)
	Sgt H. Jack	NAV	(Killed)
Ditched off	Sgt C. Kendrew	W/AG	(Killed)
Tynemouth	Sgt R.C Nelson RAAF	A/G	(Injured)
Crew on their	Sgt Underwood	B/A	(Injured)
11th operation	Sgt G.S. Pawson	A/G	(Killed)

5/6 September, 1943; MANNHEIM: Twelve Lancasters from Fiskerton took part in this double attack by 605 bombers on Mannheim/Ludwigshaven, which caused severe damage to both targets.

Thirty-four of the raiders were brought down on a night when fighters were very active... it was a fighter that raked the underneath of J-Johnny flown by F/Sgt Kirton (ED416) and crew of 49 Squadron, shortly after 'bombs away'. The gunners, Don Burdett and Nick Batty, who together had successfully fought and downed an ME 110 two nights previously, had little chance this night. Don Burdett did manage to shout a warning but terminal damage was sustained in the first attack... the bomb bay was ablaze and the port wing was burning furiously. Bomb aimer 'Pop' Mathison was having trouble opening the nose hatch so Sgt Wilby the flight engineer went down to help. Wireless operator Jim Davies informed his skipper that he was ready to bale out and went to the rear door. 'Bunny' Perry, navigator, was standing beside the pilot when the aircraft suddenly lurched and he was thrown to the floor... the next thing he remembered was floating down by parachute.

Next day, 'Bunny' Perry was re-united with his skipper in a German hospital where F/Sgt Kirton was being treated for a knee wound... the pilot remembered preparing to leave his seat when the aircraft exploded and he too found himself parachuting down.

An unopened parachute, belonging to Jim Davies the Wop/Ag, was shown to F/Sgt Kirton whilst in hospital. It is assumed that this unfortunate crew member struck the tail plane on exit, which either killed him outright or rendered him unconscious and therefore unable to pull the 'D' ring. F/Sgt Kirton went to Stalag 357 and F/O Perry to Luft 3.

The four remaining crew members were all reported killed but the cause is not clear... the pilot was under the impression that his crew had baled out over the target. There is some speculation that after parachuting into a populated area they may have been summarily executed by civilians. German records have not yet revealed if the bodies were found in the aircraft wreckage.

Authors Note: Mr Rod Price, cousin to one the victims, Sgt W.A. Batty, is at the moment of writing, researching this incident. The wreckage of J-Johnny fell in Rheinhau Forest, just South of Mannheim. All the squadron's remaining aircraft returned safely.

Missing ED416	F/S B.Kirton	Pilot	(P.o.W.)
(EA-J)	Sgt F. Wilby	F/E	(Killed)
'A' Flt	F/O B. Perry	Nav	(P.o.W.)
	Sgt J.O. Davies	W/AG	(Killed)
	Sgt W.T. Batty	A/G	(Killed)
crew on their	P/O W.J. Mathison	B/A	(Killed)
14th operation	Sgt D. Burdett	A/G	(Killed)

6/7 September,1943; MUNICH: Over 400 Lancasters and Halifaxes found a cloud over the target which spoiled the marking. Only half of 49's ten aircraft managed to bomb the T.I's, the remaining 5 used a timed run.

Once again the absence of heavy flak meant fighters were abroad... F/O Reg Hales (DV166) later reported: *"A great number of fighters seen over and around the target."* F/Sgt Hodgkinson (ED448) and crew can readily confirm this: "*We were caught in searchlights over the target, just after 'bombs away' a fighter attacked us*" - the crew's combined efforts saved the day, and M-Mother came home unscathed with the 9 other Lancasters from Fiskerton. Bomber Command lost a total of 29 bombers.

RAF DUNHOLME 'LODGERS'

Despite having been open for just nine months, Fiskerton's concrete had begun to show signs of deterioration. The problem became so acute that by September the main runway had become unsafe for operations. On 10th September it was decided to fly all further operations from No. 52 Base's other satellite airfield, Dunholme Lodge, in conjunction with No 44 Squadron, the resident unit. Dunholme, whilst able to house 49's Lancasters on the airfield, could not provide accommodation and messing for the aircrews. The problem was solved in a quite unique way... operational aircrew would continue their pre-op routine at Fiskerton, but once they had been briefed and had dressed for battle, instead of being ferried to waiting Lancasters at their home airfield they were taken several miles by crewbus to Dunholme Lodge.

As well as posing a security headache, this also re-exposed crews (who had mentally prepared themselves for that night's rigours) to the 'ordinary' world outside. As they passed through the outskirts of Lincoln, a bemused public, by now well used to military convoys, had seldom seen so many flying-clothed airmen at one time. In the early hours of the morning, a return journey would be made following the operation, when tired and exhausted crews were taken back to Fiskerton for de-brief, a meal and finally bed! It was whilst being ferried over to Dunholme that ED448 M-Mother was wrecked due to hydraulic failure. F/Sgt Oglesby and crew were all safe but the Lancaster was a write off. The crash landing was at 20.58 hrs.

Gordon Cooper, wireless operator in Eric Hidderley's crew, well remembers this period of operations:

"It was a strange feeling leaving the environs of an operational airfield and to see the world outside continuing as normal, and to think that in just a few short hours we would be flying through German skies filled with flak and fighters."

Doug Tritton, a flight engineer also recalls:

"Drivers were not allowed to let us out until we reached our destination. One morning on our return, we hadn't a cigarette between us... our driver insisted we each have one of his. We were doubly grateful as cigarettes were scarce then."

For several crews during this period, these 'excursions to Dunholme' were the last bus trips they would ever make in their all too brief lives.

Fiskerton's repairs were completed by 24th October, and operations re-commenced from there in November.

THE FERRY DROWNINGS

Talk to any veteran who served at Fiskerton during the war, and they will all remember the chain ferry across the River Witham at Five Mile House. It was situated at the end of the lane that ran down from near the domestic sites on Ferry Road. Again many veterans remember that there was a terrible drowning accident involving the ferry, but not many can remember who or when. Now, after research by 'Uncle Will' the names of the unfortunate airmen have been established:

On the evening of Tuesday 7 September, a group of 49 Squadron armourers were returning from Lincoln on the train having had a 'session' in their local, possibly the "Adam and Eve" at the top of Lindum Hill (the licensee of this hostelry happened to be a 49 Squadron Armourer). Using the ferry to cross over to the Fiskerton side, the short journey became a boisterous one, and some members fell into the Witham and became trapped under the ferry. Tragically two airmen perished in the water before they could be rescued. Both victims came from the London area; AC.1 George Archie Bown was 32 and is buried in the City of London Cemetery, Manor Park, East Ham, and 22 year-old LAC John Desmond Cousins is in Hampstead Cemetery.

22/23 September, 1943; HANNOVER: This was the first time in 2 years that Hannover would receive a major raid. Over 700 aircraft were to carry out this, the first in a series of four raids... on this night 26 aircraft would fail to return.

During the morning those 49 Squadron crews on the 'Battle Order' flew their kites out of Fiskerton on Night Flying Tests. They then landed them at Dunholme where ground crews loaded the bombs and fuel etc ready for the evening's operation. In the meantime the aircrew were ferried back to Fiskerton by motor transport.

Note; although Fiskerton's main runway was under repair, the two short runways were still active. This situation was often taken advantage of by 'senior' crews returning from ops... instead of landing back at Dunholme, they slipped into 'Fisky', thus saving themselves the extra bus journey.

49 Squadron managed to get 11 Lancasters airborne from Dunholme by 19.24hrs. All reported successful sorties with 4 landing back at Fiskerton shortly after midnight, the remainder at Dunholme by 00.48hrs.

23/24 September, 1943; MANNHEIM: The northern part of Mannheim suffered bombing from 628 aircraft. It cost Bomber Command 18 Lancasters, 7 Halifaxes and 7 Wellingtons.

After their mid-afternoon bus trip from Fiskerton, 13 crews had climbed away from Dunholme Lodge by 18.56hrs. Once over the target, fighters were again much in evidence. The use of searchlights in co-ordination with fighters accounted for many of the losses.

CONED OVER MANNHEIM

Pilot Ernie Webb's Lancaster became coned with searchlights over the target and he and the crew knew what to expect next!.. the fighter came in from the rear hitting and causing damage to the aft portion of the Lancaster. Percy Horten in the rear turret returned fire, driving off their attacker, whilst evasive action was taken by the pilot. The pilot managed to find dark sky and relative safety. It wasn't until much later that Percy revealed that he had in fact been hit by cannon fire.

On return to base, Ernie was given a priority landing with his gunner needing urgent attention. The aircraft, DV238 O-Oboe, was taken to No. 52 Base pool for repair and later returned to ops with 44 Sqdn. Percy was taken to RAF Hospital Rauceby for repair, then he too returned to ops with his old... and welcoming crew.

Sadly, the luck of two other 49 Squadron crews did not hold out. Cyril Anderson and his 'Dambuster' crew flying in the Wingco's aircraft, D-Donald, failed to return and were all later reported killed... this would have been their 21st operation. The crew are buried at Rheinburg in Germany. F/Sgt Dave Stanton and crew, on only their third trip were also missing and they too were all later reported killed; their graves are in the Durnbach Cemetery, Germany.

Fiskerton, circa Aug/Sept 1943: F/Sgt Webb and crew, who successfully carried out their tour between August 1943 and January 1944. (Back row l to r), Harold Hayes, flight engineer; Fred Woodhouse, mid/upper gunner; Harold Olorenshaw, bomb aimer; Percy Horton, tail gunner (WIA 23/24-9-43); (Front row l to r), Eric Lovick, wireless operator; Ernie Webb, pilot; Johnny Chaloner, navigator.
(H. Olerenshaw)

SEPTEMBER 1943

In the cool, damp early hours of the 24th, eleven battle weary crews travelled back to Fiskerton by road through an English countryside still cloaked in darkness. Past Nettleham to Lincoln then via Greetwell and Cherry Willingham, the whining axles of this small convoy slowly snaked its way amongst a still sleeping nation, it's valiant cargo desperate for their own beds.

> "Just turn over and try to sleep
> Lie in the dark and let them go
> Theirs is a world you'll never know
> Lie in the dark and listen." Noel Coward

This happened to be the final operation with 49 Squadron, of W/O Bull and crew; they were transferring to 617 Squadron. Whilst with 617, they along with 3 other crews, were sent to Tempsford the 'Special Duties' station. On the night of 10th December 1943 four Lancasters went to drop supplies to the Resistance, near Doullens in France. 'Chuffy' Bull and crew were shot down; five crew members survived but sadly the W/OP and rear gunner were killed. The aircraft in which they were flying happened to be ED886 'O', the very same aircraft in which ex-49ers Bill Townsend and crew flew their epic 'Dams' sortie.

FTR JB301	F/S D. Stanton	Pilot	(Killed)
(EA-)	Sgt J. Tunley	F/E	(Killed)
	Sgt C.F. Walton	NAV	(Killed)
	Sgt E.W. Howell	W/AG	(Killed)
	Sgt N. Fleming	A/G	(Killed)
crew on their	Sgt J. Spiers	B/A	(Killed)
3rd operation	Sgt G.A. Bicknell	A/G	(Killed)

FTR ED702	P/O T. Anderson	Pilot	(Killed)
(EA-D)	Sgt R.C. Patterson	F/E	(Killed)
'A' Flt	Sgt J.P. Nugent	NAV	(Killed)
	Sgt W.D. Bickle	W/AG	(Killed)
	Sgt A.W. Buck	A/G	(Killed)
crew on their	Sgt G.J. Green	B/A	(Killed)
21st operation	Sgt E. Ewan	A/G	(Killed)

27/28 September, 1943; HANNOVER: Faulty wind forecasts used by the Pathfinders, resulted in 678 bombers making a concentrated attack, but several miles away from the centre of Hannover. Again losses were severe, with 38 aircraft going down.

Twelve of the squadron's aircraft took-off from Dunholme led by the new C.O., W/Cmdr Alex Adams. (W/Cmdr Johnson had been posted out to Woodhall Spa on the 15th of the month).

FRIEND OR FOE

It came as one hell of a shock to W/O Jupp (JB299) and crew, when the shadowy shape of a Lancaster flying close by suddenly opened fire on them.

They were flying at 21,000ft just short of Hannover when tracer bullets ripped into S-Sugar. The pilot's intercom went u/s and thinking his skipper had been hit, Sgt Darnton jettisoned the bombs. Sgt Allwood in the rear turret was wounded by the tracer and one of the engines was also hit. W/O Jupp later reported: *"Quick thinking by the flight engineer, Sgt Taylor in feathering the engine was instrumental in enabling the aircraft to be brought back."*

The Jupp crew were not the only ones to have problems with friendly fire during this trip; Jock Morrison and his crew in JB295 were just finishing off their coffee when 'all hell broke loose'. Nearing home, a British convoy, just off the Wash had opened fire on the returning bomber, injuring W/OP Sgt Green. Reg Hales (JB235) and crew also encountered the same convoy and they too were 'shot up!'.

F/Sgt Brunt (JB231) and crew had been hit by flak over the target which set fire to the starboard outer engine. The fire was soon extinguished, but they were forced to return on three engines.

Despite these difficulties, all 49's aircraft returned safely although they were widely dispersed - 3 landed at Feltwell, 1 at Waterbeach, 1 at Wickenby, 1 at Docking, 1 at Fiskerton and the remainder at Dunholme.

29/30 September, 1943; BOCHUM: The last operation of the month involved 8 of the squadron's aircraft flying out of Dunholme. One Lancaster, flown by the Coxill crew went mining in the 'Privet' area, whilst 7 Lancs went to bomb the German town of Bochum.
All landed safely after successful sorties; 4 at Fiskerton, 3 at Dunholme and one at Croft.

OPERATIONAL SUMMARY - SEPTEMBER 1943

Date	Target	Desp	E/R	FTR	Remarks
2/3	MINELAYING	2	-	-	
3/4	BERLIN	14	-	1	F/O Coates FTR
5/6	MANNHEIM	12	-	1	F/S Kirton FTR
6/7	MUNICH	10	-	-	
22/23	HANNOVER	11	-	-	From Dunholme
23/24	MANNHEIM	13	-	2	F/S Stanton FTR P/O Anderson FTR From Dunholme
27/28	HANNOVER	12	-	-	From Dunholme
29/30	BOCHUM	7	-	-	From Dunholme
	MINELAYING	1	-	-	From Dunholme
Total of sorties flown		82			
Failed to return		4			

Fiskerton's 'Five Mile House' Chain and Windlass Ferry over the river Witham to the Railway Station
Illustration by John Ward

POSTINGS - 49 SQUADRON FISKERTON OCTOBER 1943

5th	F/Sgt Roantree RAAF and crew posted in from 1660 HCU Swinderby	TE
6th	F/Lt Carfoot and crew posted in from 1654 HCU Wigsley	FTR
7th	P/O Wares and crew posted Missing Without Trace	FTR
8th	S/Ldr Miller RNZAF and crew posted in from 44 Squadron	TE
12th	F/O Palmer and crew posted in from 1654 HCU	FTR
	F/Lt Tancred and crew posted in from 1654 HCU	FTR
13th	P/O Young RCAF, P/O Scott RCAF, P/O Orchard, Sgt Vidow, Sgt Cachart, Sgt Crossman, Sgt Sykes posted in from 1660 HCU	FTR
22nd	F/Sgt Hodgkinson and crew posted Missing Without Trace	FTR
	P/O Tavener and crew posted Missing Without Trace	FTR
	P/O Ratcliffe and crew posted in from 1654 HCU	FTR
	P/O Teager and crew posted in from 1654 HCU. P/O Teager as '2nd dickie' FTR	P.o.W.
24th	P/O Simpson and crew posted in from 1654 HCU	TE
26th	F/Lt Pike and crew posted out to 207 Squadron where they failed to return	FTR
29th	F/O Bailey and crew posted in from 1660 HCU. F/O Bailey as '2nd dickie' FTR	KIA
	F/O Bacon and crew posted in from 1660 HCU	FTR

Key: FTR - Failed To Return. TE - Tour Expired (completed). KIA - Killed In Action.

OCTOBER 1943

1/2 October, 1943; HAGEN: The fine weather of early October 1943, enabled operations to be carried out on four consecutive nights. During the evening of the 1st, eleven of the squadron's aircraft joined an all Lancaster force in pulverizing the industrial areas of Hagen. Just one aircraft, that of Sgt Webb (EE186) had to abandon the trip early, when the rear turret went u/s.

From a total of 243 Lancasters, 2 failed to return; all 49's came home safely.

At interrogation, a furious W/Cmdr Adams (JB305), who had flown E-Easy during the raid, insisted that both he and his navigator should 'not' be credited with this sortie; on a night of total cloud cover, he and his crew had bombed Cologne on an estimated position.

The W/Cmdr reprimanded himself as Captain for not having a 'drill' for checking the compass, and his navigator for sheer complacency!

2/3 October, 1943; MUNICH: Over 290 Lancasters plus 2 Fortresses (from the American 8th Air Force) made a poor attack on Munich. 5 Group, which made up over half the force, made a 'time and distance' run independent of the Pathfinders. Many crews were unable to pick up the Wurmsee lake and scattered bombing resulted.

Again, 11 Lancasters from the squadron left Dunholme's runway, but F/Lt Thomas (ED438) soon returned with the rear turret u/s. 8 aircraft failed to return from the raid, but 49's all returned unharmed.

3/4 October, 1943; KASSEL: Unfortunately, the H2S equipped 'blind marker' Pathfinder aircraft overshot the aiming point. Ground haze prevented the 'visual markers' from making corrections with the result that the loads from over 540 bombers fell on the Kassel's western suburbs and villages; 24 aircraft failed to return.

The squadron had dispatched 7 Lancasters from Dunholme. F/Sgt Brunt (JB362) and crew despite having their mid upper turret go u/s on the way out, decided to continue with their sortie. All 49's aircraft returned without loss.

4/5 October, 1943; FRANKFURT: Clear weather and accurate Pathfinding led to Frankfurt receiving its heaviest blow of the war so far. Over 400 bombers, including 8 from 49 Ssquadron, caused heavy damage to the eastern parts of the city and inland docks. All of 49's kites came home safely, including the new crew of P/O Reynolds in W5010.

Note: This 'older' kite had come to the squadron via the Bombing Development Unit, but it was soon pushed over to 9 Squadron at Bardney where it would survive until February 1944.

OCTOBER 1943

7/8 October, 1943; STUTTGART: Lancasters from 101 Squadron, Ludford Magna, operated for the first time with A.B.C. (night-fighter communications jamming equipment) on board. Over 340 Lancasters, including 11 from 49 Squadron bombed a cloud-covered target marked by H2S. Two crews from 49 were making their maiden sorties; P/O Ewens (ED999) A-Able, and the unfortunate crew captained by P/O Don Wares in P-Peter:

Towards midnight a night fighter attacked ED426 as P/O Wares and crew returned home across France. Two engines were put out of action and as the aircraft lost altitude the pilot ordered the crew to jettison everything that was not needed. P-Peter was now at tree top height as they flew over the forest of Commercy. At 02.00hrs trees ripped away the wings as the Lancaster smashed into the hill of Bezimont. Of the seven crew members, four survived the crash. The pilot, and wireless operator, Raymond Barlow, who had only recently married Peggy Angus 25-9-43, succeeded in reaching Switzerland on foot and eventually returned to England.

The two gunners, one of whom was slightly injured, walked to America Farm where they were cared for by local people and given civilian clothes. They were captured two days later by the Germans, and after two months in Fresnes prison, they were transferred to PoW camp in Poland. Ray Barlow and Gilbert Attwood, one of the gunners, revisited the site of the crash in September 1993; it is hoped that a small plaque is to be erected on site, in memory of their three comrades who were killed and who are buried in Choley-Merillot War Cemetery.

This is the only known photograph of a 49 Squadron Lanc carrying any form of nose adornment, in this case a bomb tally. LAC Church smiles down from the pilot's seat of ED426 (EA-P) on her 'B' Flt dispersal at Fiskerton.

W/Cmdr Slee frowned upon nose embellishments and early attempts to break this code resulted in that aircraft being lost. The practice quickly became considered unlucky in a squadron, where, some crews were becoming increasingly superstitious of even having their photographs taken before an op.

It wasn't until Jan 1944, that aircraft appeared with even a code letter on the nose (usually under the small nose window and on the port side only). For a period at Fiskerton the code letter 'L' was considered 'taboo' and completely discarded. So what can we conclude from this rare photograph of the exceptional ED426 displaying 44 bomb symbols; firstly, Californian pilot Jack Price flew most of his ops in this Kite, and Americans were well known for their liking for bomb tallies. Although his crew always carried a small knitted lucky mascot, perhaps Jack was not superstitious and, thumbing his nose at fate, decided to start the trend. We shall never know as sadly Jack and his crew were later killed on PFF.

Author's Note: Unfortunately 49's operational records can be inconsistent, and an exact tally of sorties flown by ED426 cannot be confirmed, but I am certain she never made the 50 mark. On my first attempt to verify her total, I was shocked when it showed she went down on her 45th trip - the very next operation after having her nose embellishment photographed! I can state that ED426 met her demise in her middle to late forties on the night 7/8-10-43. The unfortunate crew, piloted by P/O Don Wares, were on their 1st operation.

Four other Bomber Command crews failed to return from this operation; the remaining 49 Squadron aircraft all returned safely, but were diverted to airfields in East Anglia.

Five members of P/O Wares' crew who failed to return from Stuttgart 7/8-10-43.

They are (from l to r),
Ray Barlow, W/Op, evader;
Tim O'Leary, Nav, Killed;
Archie Brownlie
(note pilot's wings), Killed;
Elmer Hepburn RCAF, B/A killed;
F/Sgt Fitzgerald RAAF, (PoW).

(Mrs Peggy Barlow)

OCTOBER 1943

FTR ED426	P/O D. Wares	Pilot	(Evader)
(EA-P)	Sgt A.H. Brownlie	F/E	(Killed)
'B Flt'	Sgt T.T. O'Leary	NAV	(Killed)
	Sgt J.R. Barlow	W/AG	(Evader)
	Sgt G. Attwood	A/G	(P.o.W.)
Crew on their	F/O E.J. Hepburn RCAF	B/A	(Killed)
1st operation	F/S W. Fitzgerald RAAF	A/G	(P.o.W.)

8/9 October, 1943; HANNOVER: The unit welcomed a new Squadron Leader on 8 October when S/Ldr D. Miller RNZAF and crew transferred over to 49 from 44 Squadron. S/Ldr 'Dusty' Miller became a very popular character on the squadron and with 'B' Flt in particular. Ops were on again that night, and 49 offered 10 aircraft (not including S/Ldr Miller). As on the previous evening, two new crews were being tested, F/Sgt White (LM306) and P/O Tavener (ED438).

Clear conditions over the target led to a concentrated attack. Of the 504 aircraft dispatched, 24 failed to return. All of the squadron's Lancasters came home safely.

REVERSE GEAR!

Whilst the squadron was operating from Dunholme, a maintenance flight remained at Fiskerton, servicing and mending the lame ducks. SNCO Fitter, Trevor Simpson, recalls the following dramatic spectacle, which occurred on 18 October, 1943:

"We had worked on a new aircraft lettered 'L'. After finishing the checks, one of our pilots was to ferry it over to Dunholme. I saw it start its take-off run, and was just going into the flight office when my corporal shouted 'Look, look!!' I was just in time to see the aircraft swing on take-off. To our amazement, it continued its swing and went right through 180 degrees and continued down the runway backwards at about 90 knots. Even so, it might have got away with relatively little damage, but there was a drainage ditch along side the runway, and the tail wheel dropped into this and was sheared off.

After that, the undercart collapsed and it became a write off; I don't suppose its flying hours had reached double figures. Fortunately, no one was hurt."

The Lancaster in question was JB411, which had only been delivered to the squadron on 5 October 1943 and the crew involved was piloted by F/Sgt Ron Brunt.

Top:
Dodge Crew bus (RAF 16423) at Dunholme Lodge Sep/Oct 1943.

2 of the MT drivers who drove us to Dunholme and brought us back - no matter what time of day or night.

Dot Smith (Nee Everett) (Left) and Vi Veness (NeeWinters) (Right) as they were then. (1943)

They are just as happy and cheerful today (1997)

(49 Sqdn Collection)

OCTOBER 1943

8/19 October, 1943; HANNOVER: Nine days had elapsed before the squadron operated again. W/Cmdr Adams led 14 of the unit's Lancs away from Dunholme, bound for Hannover. S/Ldr Miller (JB314) flew with the squadron for the first time, as did the crew piloted by F/Sgt Foster RAAF (ED438).

Cloud cover prevented the Pathfinders from marking successfully and as a result most of the bombs from 360 Lancasters fell in open country. 49's Lancasters bombed without any hitches, and all returned safely; unfortunately 18 aircraft from other squadrons were not so fortunate.

20/21 October, 1943; LEIPZIG: In appalling weather conditions, 358 aircraft from Bomber Command set out to bomb the distant target of Leipzig. Of the 15 Lancasters from 49 Squadron that departed Dunholme, two returned early with technical problems; Eric Jones (JB421) had fuel pump failure in the port centre tank and Sgt Blackmore (JB314) had compass problems. Two new crews participated in the night's events, those of F/O Palmer and F/Lt Carfoot. Several crews reported having to orbit the target for several minutes before the markers went down.

All crews reported severe icing conditions during the trip; Reg Hales took JB235 up to 26,500ft and still found himself in solid icing cloud. Despite the adverse weather and the long distance flown, all 49's Lancs made it safely back, whilst 16 aircraft from other units failed to return.

22/23 October, 1943; KASSEL: Eight Pathfinder 'visual markers' found the centre of Kassel after the H2S 'blind' marker overshot the target. The consequences proved to be horrendous for this German city.

The bombing, by nearly 570 was so concentrated that a firestorm was created, but not on the scale of the Hamburg storm in July. The squadron had dispatched 11 Lancasters, including the new crew piloted by F/Lt Tancred (JB231).

Returning crews found bad weather conditions over Base and were widely diverted throughout Lincolnshire; 3 managed to land at Fiskerton, 2 at Dunholme, 1 at Ludford Magna, 1 at Faldingworth and 1 at Blyton. The Blackmore crew was the last 49 Squadron Lancaster to land, scraping in at Bardney by 00.19hrs. At de-brief, F/Sgt Foster (ED438) and crew reported being attacked by a fighter shortly after leaving the target but managed to shake it off without sustaining damage.

Bomber Command paid heavily for their success with 24 Halifaxes and 18 Lancasters failing to return. Sadly two of the missing Lancasters were from 49 Squadron... the crew piloted by 21 year old F/Sgt Alan Hodgkinson was all killed over Germany and are buried together in Hannover; their 23 year-old rear gunner Frank Ricketts had only been married a few weeks.

Joan Kirwan from Royston was a bridesmaid when her cousin Winnie Gaskin married Frank on 2 October, 1943, at St. Johns Church, Leytonstone, London E11.

Fifty years later she has never forgotten Frank or that day, Joan recalls;

"I was one of the bridesmaids and received a gold cross which I still have, I remember hearing from my mother that Frank was worried about going back after his leave; the odds were so much against them finishing their tour with such heavy losses. He was a lovely kind of young man and we were all very fond of him, especially my uncle and aunts."

The other missing aircraft was JB413; it crashed near Wunsdorf, with five members of the crew surviving. Sadly their pilot, P/O Philip Taverner and the 20 year old Australian rear gunner, F/Sgt Edwin Parker, were both killed; they too have their graves in Hannover War Cemetery.

Sgt Richard Frank Ricketts (KIA 22/23-10-43) came from a village with the delightful name of Chewton Mendip, and was the youngest son of a farming family.

A stained glass window was put in the local church as a memorial to him.
(Mrs J. Kirwan)

An illustration by John Ward of JB231 EA-N (Nancy Pants) as flown by F/O Johnny Young (RCAF) & Crew.

OCTOBER 1943

Missing JB416	F/S A. Hodgkinson	Pilot	(Killed)
(EA-)	Sgt R.E. Harnett	F/E	(Killed)
'B Flt'	Sgt A.G. Fisher	Nav	(Killed)
	F/S J. Foley	W/AG	(Killed)
	Sgt D. Durrell RCAF	A/G	(Killed)
Crew on their	Sgt R.A. Ford	B/A	(Killed)
11th operation	Sgt R.F. Ricketts	A/G	(Killed)
Missing JB413	P/O P.A. Taverner	Pilot	(Killed)
(EA-)	Sgt W. Kemp	F/E	(P.o.W.)
'B Flt'	Sgt I. Spence	NAV	(P.o.W.)
	Sgt R.H. Norman	W/AG	(P.o.W.)
	Sgt N.C. Dunbabin	A/G	(P.o.W.)
Crew on their	Sgt R.K. Drinnan RCAF	B/A	(P.o.W.)
3rd operation	F/S E.E. Parker RAAF	A/G	(Killed)

The month ended with a series of 'stand downs'; on the 30th October, 18 aircraft were detailed for ops, but this was cancelled at 16.15hrs giving crews just enough time to get off camp and into Lincoln for the evening.

On the 28th, the Pike crew were posted out to 207 Squadron at Spilsby where F/Lt Pike became a Squadron Leader... sadly they failed to return from ops whilst with that squadron.

P/O Taverner and crew, who failed to return from Kassel 22/23-10-43.
(l to r)
N. Dunbabin, M/U gunner; Ivan Spence, Nav; (P.o.W.); Phil Taverner, pilot (KIA); Bob Drinnan RCAF, B/A; Ron Norman, W/AG; Earle Parker RAAF, R/G (KIA)
(R. Drinnan)

OCTOBER 1943

OPERATIONAL SUMMARY - OCTOBER 1943

Date	Target	Desp	E/R	FTR	Remarks
1/2	HAGEN	11	1	-	From Dunholme
2/3	MUNICH	11	1	-	From Dunholme
3/4	KASSEL	7	-	-	From Dunholme
4/5	FRANKFURT	8	-	-	From Dunholme
7/8	STUTTGART	11	-	1	P/O Wares FTR
					From Dunholme
8/9	HANNOVER	10	-	-	From Dunholme
18/19	HANNOVER	14	-	-	From Dunholme
20/21	LEIPZIG	15	-	-	From Dunholme
22/23	KASSEL	11	-	2	F/S HodgkinsonFTR
					P/O Taverner FTR
					From Dunholme

Total of sorties flown	98
Failed to return	3

Dot Everett and unknown ground crew sitting on a 'Cookie' near N'Nan in 'B; flight dispersal. (Ted Cachart)

NOVEMBER 1943

As the long winter nights approached, they brought along adverse weather. Crews, exhausted after hours of flying in severe icing conditions, battling through flak, searchlights and night fighters would often return over England to yet another enemy, equally as dangerous but this time a natural one... fog!

FIDO

The 'boffins' came up with an answer to this problem which was given the title Fog Investigation Dispersal Operation, or FIDO for short. The system involved pumping petroleum (mixed with alcohol) along a continuous line of pipes installed on both sides of the main runway. When ignited, huge flames shot into the sky where the resultant heat created a thermal effect, which in turn lifted the fog away from the runway. Only fifteen airfields would receive this expensive but life saving system and Fiskerton was one of those selected.

The contract for installation at Fiskerton was given to Messrs Austin Monk and the on-site assembly was to be carried out by Strong-Arc Welding Co., of Lincoln. Fortunately 49 Squadron was operating from Dunholme Lodge during the latter part of the work. Fiskerton's first trials took place in late October and early November and gave several of the squadron's crews a welcome opportunity to practice landings in the turbulent effects created by such tremendous heat.

FIDO was lit on 21 November, this time for night landing trials. Unfortunately, neither the residents of Fiskerton village nor the Lincoln Fire Brigade had been informed of this first full-scale trial. Thinking a terrible accident had taken place, one of the villagers soon phoned the emergency services. After speeding their way from the Monks Road Station, the Brigade arrived at the airfield to be confronted by a six foot high wall of flame stretching for over a mile! Trepidation soon gave way to both astonishment and relief when the fire suddenly went out! All these happenings were much to the amusement of the station personnel who had turned out in large numbers to watch the spectacle. Plied with drinks and hospitality in the Mess afterwards, the firemen soon came round to appreciating the funnier side of the affair.

Fiskerton, November 1943. FIDO being tested during a late November afternoon, giving 49 Squadron crews the opportunity to practice landing by this dramatic system.
(49 Squadron collection)

NOVEMBER 1943

3/4 November, 1943; DÜSSELDORF: It wasn't until 3rd November that Bomber Command was able to send a large force out again, when almost 600 bombers were sent against the German city of Düsseldorf. The 'rest' period had enabled most squadrons to replenish their establishment of aircraft and 49 was no exception. Now re-settled back at Fiskerton (from Dunholme Lodge), the unit was able to provide 18 aircraft for the evening's operation.

F/Sgt White (DV166) was forced to return early in F-Fox when the starboard inner engine cut out completely. Two crews were flying their first operations and both had Dominion pilots; F/Sgt Clive Roantree RAAF (JB235) and crew in C-Charlie plus P/O Johnny Young RCAF (JB473) and crew in Q-Queenie. The raid was successful with many fires reported but Command did lose 18 aircraft and crews.

For the second raid in succession 49 Squadron lost two aircraft: The experienced crew skippered by F/Lt Cecil Thomas were on their 20th op, and carrying a 'second dickie' pilot, P/O Teager. A night fighter got them, with only three crew members able to escape before the aircraft exploded near Cologne. The second aircraft reported missing, was that piloted by F/Lt Carfoot (JB305) and crew on only their second trip:

HE JUST WAVED

F/Lt Norman Carfoot had previously served in Coastal Command (having flown over 2,000hrs) before volunteering for Bomber Command... in search of more excitement! Over Düsseldorf, his Lancaster became coned in searchlights and almost instantly suffered hits from heavy flak. Sgt Church, the crew's navigator, recalls the final moments aboard the aircraft:

"Flak set the port wing on fire and the next moment tracer shells from an attacking JU88 passed inches in front of my chest (Sgt Wood, the W/Op, was killed instantly during this attack). The pilot ordered us all to bale out, but first he asked me to check if the rear gunner was OK; just then, over the intercom, the Aussie voice of F/Sgt Steve List confirmed that he had in fact heard the bale out order. I then put my chute on and followed the flight engineer, Sgt Mason down the steps into the nose ready to jump; the bomb aimer, Sgt Putnam RCAF went first. I turned to take one last look at my skipper, Norman Carfoot, silhouetted by the flames from the blazing wing as he held our doomed Lanc as steady as a rock... he just waved ... I think we both knew then that he wasn't going to make it."

Just those three crew members who jumped from the nose hatch survived; Sgt Church believes that the Lancaster must have exploded shortly after he left the aircraft.

FTR ED438	F/L C.G. Thomas	Pilot	(Killed)
(EA-R)	P/O J.E. Teager	2ndPilot	(P.o.W.)
'B Flt'	Sgt N.D. Panter	F/E	(P.o.W.)
	F/S W.G. Clutterbuck	NAV	(Killed)
	Sgt W.A. Payne	W/AG	(P.o.W.)
	Sgt H. Minns	A/G	(Killed)
Crew on their	F/O C.P. Ross	B/A	(Killed)
20th operation	Sgt G.E. Boxer	A/G	(Killed)
FTR JB305	F/L N.H. Carfoot	Pilot	(Killed)
	Sgt J.S. Mason	F/E	(P.o.W.)
(EA-E)	Sgt H.D. Church	NAV	(P.o.W.)
'A Flt'	Sgt H.L. Wood	W/AG	(Killed)
	Sgt W.H. Marson	A/G	(Killed)
Crew on their	F/S S.G. Putnam RCAF	B/A	(P.o.W.)
2nd operation	F/S S.M. List RAAF	A/G	(Killed)

10/11 November. 1943; MODANE: A buzz went round the briefing room when the target was revealed; Modane, Southern France, an easy one for a change, if any in the winter of 43 could be called easy! Over 300 Lancs, all from 5 Group along with 8 Group PFF were being dispatched in an attempt to damage the railway system on the main line into Italy.

Sixteen Lancasters edged their way around Fiskerton's darkened peri-track towards the main runway. Sgt Coxill (JB178) was first away spot-on 20.20hrs. He was followed by four further Lancs then shortly before 20.36hrs W/O Ernie Webb turned P-Peter onto the threshold... the green light flashed from the control caravan sending the Webb crew speeding along the long necklace of runway lights.

THE KEY TO A CRASH

With a wry smile and a gentleness of manner, Ernie Webb, a softly spoken Yorkshireman clearly recalls those terrifying moments some 49 years earlier, when the bomb and fuel laden Lancaster which he was piloting suddenly went out of control:

"As we collected speed, I suddenly became aware of the starboard wing looming large in the cabin window, then without warning the port undercarriage gave way and the aircraft veered off the runway seemingly in search of the Watch Office, which fortunately flashed past on the port side without impact.

The aircraft slowly ground-looped coming to rest pointing in the direction we had just travelled... within seconds flames were flickering around the engines and wings. I dived out of the small sliding window next to the pilot's seat.

Running around the wing I could see by the light of the flames that the fuselage had broken in two. Cries of help were coming from the rear of the aircraft... dashing round I found the rear turret had been wrenched away and the rear gunner had been thrown out but his flying boot was caught within the turret. In fear of being burnt alive, he was frantically trying to get free... with a simple twist I loosened his boot and we both scrambled for safety together.

By now the station emergency teams had arrived as flames started to engulf the wreckage. I quickly reported to the Medical Officer who immediately enquired as to how many of the crew were unaccounted for, to which I replied two. 'OK' he said 'let's take a look'... and without thinking, I accompanied him back into the burning wreck via the break in the fuselage. By now the ammunition rounds were 'cooking off' and bullets were whizzing all around, but my thoughts were of the bombs just inches below our feet. No trace of the two missing crew members could be found in the front or rear sections so we smartly withdrew to a point of safety."

The scene was quickly becoming an inferno and the firemen decided their task was becoming hopeless, so a tactical withdrawal was made. Some time later the missing crewmen returned to explain that when the crashing aircraft had come to a halt, they both jumped out and ran like mad into the pitch black, fearing an almighty explosion... that explosion finally came some hours later, scattering fragments of Lancaster everywhere. But there is one piece of JB533 P-Peter still remaining; the Yale key and key ring (which opens the Lancaster's main entrance door), which Ernie has kept to this day as a reminder of his crew's very lucky escape.

The following morning, W/Cmdr Adams, who had watched the attempted take-off from the control van stated that he clearly saw sparks coming from the aircraft's port wheel, and felt sure that the tyre had punctured thus causing the crash.

The 49 Squadron crews returning from this successful raid were diverted to dear old Dunholme Lodge. All of the aircraft dispatched by Bomber Command returned safely.

18/19 November, 1943; BERLIN: Now, with the longer dark nights, Harris could mount a series of concentrated attacks against the 'Big City'. This onslaught which would consist of 16 major raids over four months, would later become known as the Battle of Berlin. The plan for this first attack required 440 Lancasters to bomb Berlin over a sixteen minute period starting at 20.56hrs. Meantime a similar sized force of mainly Halifaxes and Stirlings, would be making an attack on Mannheim/ Ludwigshafen.

Despite favourable weather predictions before take-off, crews found themselves hauling their heavily laden Lancasters up through thousands of feet of thick cloud. 49 Squadron put up 19 aircraft led by W/Cmdr Adams in O-Oboe. All of 49's Lancasters managed to reach the cloud-covered target, and the following selected reports give some idea of the squadron's performance during this operation: W/Cmdr Adams overshot the target and orbited, bombing red and green T.Is. on the second run. Landed at Warboys on return.

S/Ldr Day (JB466) overshot by 9 minutes and bombed the fires that were glowing through the clouds as all the T.Is. had been extinguished. Landed at Tangmere on return.

P/O Simpson (LM306) and crew flying their first operation, received a baptism of fire when flak smashed the wind-screen of E-Easy and also damaged the starboard wing tip. The outer engine used a great deal of fuel causing a shortage. They landed at Manston on return.

F/O Cottingham (JB368) and crew in G-George made two orbits whilst waiting for a concentration of T.Is; they too ran short of fuel and landed at Dunsfold.

P/O Don Bacon's (JB371) crew in J-Jig was another on its first op, and they also received the attention of the flak gunners when shell splinters damaged the bomb aimer's perspex and the pilot's cabin. They landed back at Woodhall Spa.

W/O Jupp (JB360) in M-Mother received slight flak damage over the Ruhr and also lost 2 navigator's logs en-route, which were believed lost when dropping 'window'!

W/O Webb (JB473) in U-Uncle, found handling the aircraft hard due to icing conditions. Marking and bombing reported as considerably scattered - H2S and Gee u/s - They had to call 'Darky' on return to England and were directed to Gransden Lodge.

F/O Reynolds (DV166) and crew in F-Fox overshot the target due to wrong wind forecast. They then proceeded to attack against the stream (410 Lancasters) in order to bomb on time.

F/Lt Tancred (JB178) received five flak holes in V-Victor, but casually summed up their trip by reporting "*The weather rather spoilt the effort.*"

BETWEEN ROUTINE CHECKS

Sadly P/O Reg Hales (JB235) landed C-Charlie back at Fiskerton with the squadron's only casualty of the night. During the flight, W/O Hugh Frazer, their tall and pleasant Canadian rear-gunner had been air-sick. Unknown to him, a particle of food had lodged in the oxygen valve of his mask. The atmospheric valve still worked OK but gave only thin air. The 22 year old gunner's life slowly slipped away between the Skipper,s routine checks around the crew stations.

All 49's aircraft returned from the operation, with 8 landing away from base. Nine Lancasters were lost on the Berlin raid, and 23 aircraft failed to return from the Mannheim/ Ludwigshafen trip.

Fiskerton: Back from Berlin 18/19-11-43; F/Sgt Clive Roantree RAAF (JB362) trundles Bandlaw (Aircraft call-sign) D-Dog back into dispersal after bombing Berlin from 20,000ft with a frosted-over windscreen!

Fiskerton: Back from Berlin 18/19-11-43; Operations room Sergeant Zoe Haine chats with pilots (l to r) F/O Reynolds (DV166).and P/O George (JB469) (Mrs Z. Stocks)

One dark night at Dunholme Lodge, Zoe was struck by a crewbus and suffered a fractured skull. Thankfully she made a full recovery in Rauceby Hospital and returned to 49 Squadron.

THE SEVENTH ROUND

Soon after completing their first operation, P/O Jock Simpson and crew took the first available opportunity to visit the hostelries of Lincoln to celebrate becoming operational. A round of drinks was bought at a different pub each time. When it came to the seventh member of the crew to put his hand in his pocket, lo and behold it was the crew's Scots skipper. If the truth were told, after six pints, Jock Simpson remembered very little of paying for his round.

It was quite some time before the crew had another chance to get into town for a drink, but when they did, their first call was at "The Crown" opposite the Theatre Royal. This just happened to be the pub in which Jock Simpson had bought the seventh round during their previous session, only this time it was Jock's turn to buy first. At the bar, the publican recognised Jock from his previous visit: *"The last time you were in Sir, you forgot your change"*, and he produced a pile of coins from the shelf. Jock Simpson, a dyed-in-the-wool Scot was taken aback by this deed and being so delighted, he declared there and then that whenever he and his crew visited Lincoln to drink, "The Crown" would be their only port of call!

22/23 November, 1943; BERLIN: Berlin had enjoyed only a few nights of peace before receiving its heaviest raid of the war so far. Over 760 bombers set out for the German capital - the majority were Lancasters but 50 Stirlings were making what was to be the type's last raid into Germany.

With German night-fighters hampered by poor weather conditions on the ground, the bomber force made a virtual straight in and out attack. But despite this tenuous advantage given to the bombers, 26 of their number were still brought down. The total cloud cover did not prevent Berlin receiving an accurate attack which caused vast areas of destruction.

Fiskerton: Back from Berlin 22/23-11-43.

The time is 23.30hrs on the night of 22 November.

Pilot, Ron Brunt (extreme right bending) and crew are glad to be back on terra firma after a seven hour trip to Berlin.

Tragically, just four nights later (in the same aircraft JB362 D-Dog) they failed to return from Berlin; only the bomb aimer, Sgt Burrows, survived. (49 Sqdn collection)

Fiskerton: Back from Berlin 22/23-11-43. It is now after midnight and W/O Ron Brunt (second from left next to Waaf Officer) and crew are being interrogated about their sortie to Berlin;
"4th wave, over target 20.12hrs at 21,500ft, 10/10ths cloud up to 15,000ft. Flak light over target - no fighters. Doubtful whether TI's were over target according to H2S."
(49 Sqdn collection)

The squadron had detailed 17 aircraft for the operation, but P/O Hales (JB235) had to be pulled out at the last minute. By 16.58hrs, 16 Lancasters were airborne. The Webb crew (JB473) was forced to return early with their rear-turret u/s. Two new crews were 'on' for the first time; F/O Turner and crew reported bombing a cluster of markers, but received severe flak damage to the starboard bomb door in the process: Sgt Keeling (JB231) and crew in N-Nan bombed the centre of 3 red flares with the pilot reporting; *"excellent navigation by Sgt Chapman."*

The squadron suffered the loss of yet another experienced crew, that of Canadian pilot F/O Cyril Cottingham. He and his crew are remembered on the Runnymede Memorial along with F/Lt George Bailey, the 2nd pilot; F/Lt Bailey was an American from Connecticut who had volunteered for the RCAF. F/Lt Bailey's own devastated crew were all returned to Swinderby HCU on the 25th November, where they would have to re-learn the ropes with a new skipper.

Missing JB368	F/O C.M. Cottingham RCAF	Pilot	(Missing)
(EA-G)	Sgt A.J. Mathieson	F/E	(Missing)
'A Flt'	F/O R.B. Richard RCAF	NAV	(Missing)
'	Sgt G. Tabenor	W/AG	(Missing)
	Sgt G.F.A.E.J. Falk	A/G	(Missing)
	F/O M.W. Wright	B/A	(Missing)
Crew on their	F/S C.E. Byers RCAF	A/G	(Missing)
17th operation	F/L G.C. Bailey (USA)RCAF	2nd Pilot	(Missing)

Fiskerton: Back from Berlin 22/23-11-43; shortly after midnight
(l to r) F/O Tebbenham, the station meteorological officer chats with F/O F. Wittmer, navigator, an Australian from Melbourne who has just completed his tour of 30 operations, including five to Berlin. His pilot this night, F/O Eric Hidderley (JB399 'H'), listens with G/Cpt G.J. Grindell RNZAF, DFC, AFC, Commanding Officer of Fiskerton.
(C. Roantree)

23/24 November, 1943; BERLIN: Encouraged by the results of the previous night's raid, Harris decided to send his Lancaster force back again to Berlin. Weary crews could not believe the 'battle orders' when they saw their names down for ops again, and when the target was revealed at briefing a large groan was audible throughout Lincolnshire.

Sixteen Lancs from Fiskerton were detailed for the trip, but overworked ground crews out on freezing dispersals were hard pressed to meet the deadline and 2 aircraft had to be cancelled during the afternoon. Most of the 14 Lancasters that did get away were crewed by men who had flown the previous night. Once again C-Charlie let Reg Hales (JB235) and crew down when the gun turrets started icing up and becoming sluggish - they returned early to base.

The remaining 13 crews carried out their sorties with success and were all home around midnight with the exception of F/O Turner's S-Sugar:

NOVEMBER 1943

SEASIDE SORTIE

F/O Don Turner (JB229) and crew were returning over the North Sea on track, with 1,000ft showing on the altimeter. The conditions were misty, so the pilot decided to let down a little in order to determine landfall. Just as he did the Lancaster suddenly struck the sea and then moments later it was careering up a beach towards sand dunes. A startled but intact crew clambered out into waist high freezing sea water! S-Sugar had in fact come ashore at Chapel-St-Leonards on the Lincolnshire coast 5 miles north of Skegness. The freezing cold crew found' much to their displeasure, that the Lincolnshire seaside, whilst perhaps popular with pre-war summertime holiday makers, was not so alluring in the middle of November 1943. The crew spent the next few days recovering in Scampton sick bay.

The squadron was stood down over the next two days, and during this period P/O Foster RAAF and crew were posted out to the newly formed No 463 Squadron RAAF at Waddington where they continued with their tour.

26/27 November, 1943; BERLIN: On the previous trips Berlin had always been cloud covered, but on this occasion, as 440 Lancasters flew over the target the visibility was clear. Flak defences over Berlin, and fighters on the return leg accounted for 28 bombers and their crews.

The squadron had launched 14 aircraft, but a new skipper, P/O Ratcliffe (JB545) and crew had to return early, landing at Spilsby. Another crew operating for the first time was piloted by Australian Sgt Roy Richardson (JB235). Sgt 'Spud' Mahoney RAAF was the crew's mid-upper gunner and he recalls his fellow crew members on this, their first operation:

"Harry Lowe the bomb aimer, was an American in the RCAF; he was married and had recently become a father (a pair of baby 'bootees' was hung in the cockpit); we always referred to Harry as 'Mum' and so the skipper then became 'Dad'. Sgt Carr was the navigator and we called him 'Junior'. Flight engineer was Jeff Boswell who hailed from Liverpool; he had a twin brother. The W/AG was Sgt Cartwright, and on this trip we had a 'spare bod' in the rear turret called Winterborn.

Shortly after leaving the target we were attacked by an ME 110; both of us gunners opened fire at 100yds, the rear turret soon jammed, but I continued firing and saw my tracer hit the fighter, which then broke away, I think he probably went down."

F/Sgt Edy (JB231) and crew in N-Nan also encountered a night fighter. Their rear turret had been u/s since crossing the enemy coast, but the skill of mid-upper gunner, F/Sgt S.W. Mason, another Australian, soon sent the Do 217 spinning down in flames.

As the bombers returned home, fog covered much of eastern England with many squadrons being diverted. As midnight approached, conditions at Fiskerton were quite severe. Radiation fog was 1;200ft deep and visibility down to 450yds. At 00.15hrs it was decided to light FIDO for 49 Squadron's returning crews. This was the first instance during the war, that FIDO was used operationally to bring down one complete squadron of bombers (Graveley had used its system the previous week to land four Halifaxes).

The boys arrived back over Fiskerton's 'glowing' runway just before 01.00hrs. The honour of being the first to land back from ops at Fiskerton using FIDO, fell to F/O Eric Hidderley (JB399) and crew in their faithful H-Harry; next to land was F/Sgt Edy (JB231) followed by Coxill (JB360), W/O Eric Jones (JB421), P/O George (JB469), Barnes (JB314), W/O Petty (JB371) and P/O Ewens (DV166).

SO CLOSE TO HOME

At 01.02hrs, Sgt Roy Richardson RAAF (JB235) flying 'Bandlaw C-Charlie' entered the 'funnel'. Next in the stack behind C-Charlie was 'Bandlaw A-Able' flown by fellow Australian, F/Sgt Clive Roantree (JB466). The following extract is from Clive's own book, "To Fly Lancasters", and is reproduced here with his kind permission, Clive writes:

"We positioned ourselves to land immediately after C-Charlie. He would turn into the funnel, whilst we were on the down-wind leg and should be clear of the runway as we touched down.

The two parallel bars of fire, one on either side of the runway could be clearly seen with bars of flame at each end to stop the fog rolling into the cleared area. On our practice (November 3rd), we had found that after we turned into the funnel at 600 feet and lined up with the runway, as we approached, the fire on the cross bar reflected on the perspex windshield so that it was impossible for the pilot to see out. To offset the problem my flight engineer called height and airspeed as soon as we lined up on the runway at 600ft. For the inexperienced pilot it could be a frightening experience as it is not until the aircraft crossed the bar of flame at less than 100 feet that it was possible to see clearly and then make a visual landing. Subsequently a shield was placed in front of the bar of flame to prevent windscreen reflection.

On this night, with wheels down, pitch in fully fine with 20 degrees of flap, we were at the end of the down-wind leg ready to make our turn across wind before entering the funnel, when there was a dull flash on the ground right at the beginning of the funnel. I knew that an aircraft had crashed and to my horror realised that it must be Richardson in C-Charlie. I continued the landing procedure turning across wind and there, right below us was an aircraft on fire!

Giving the crew the order that we were going to overshoot, I called flying control, 'Hello Passout, Bandlaw Able over shooting - an aircraft has crashed and is on fire in the funnel - I say again an aircraft has crashed and is on fire in the funnel'.

There was a short pause before we were called again from flying control to repeat the message. Because of the flames from FIDO and the position of the control tower, they could not see the burning aircraft.

After completing our overshoot procedure we continued around the circuit and this time as we were completing the downwind leg, there was a flash of flame on the ground as C-Charlie's fuel tanks exploded. Nerves and senses were now tuned to the dangers as we carefully made our approach in copy book style. There was a slight lift as we crossed the heat rising from the bar at the beginning of the runway and A-Able set down smoothly in a three-point-landing.

It was bad enough when crews were missing over enemy territory, but there was an awful accentuation of loss when a crew had completed its mission and disaster struck so close to home and safety."

Tragically, the Lancaster burning in the funnel was that of the Richardson crew, returning from their first operation. Sgt Allan 'Spud' Mahony, the Lancaster's top turret gunner described what happened on that fateful night, during an interview with the author in 1991.

"We descended into fog as we approached the glare of Fiskerton's FIDO runway. Suddenly, without warning, I felt the Lancaster's undercarriage touch down... we were still a good way out from the runway so we must have landed on farmland. Seconds later there was an almighty impact and I banged my forehead hard... clambering down from the turret in a dazed state, I at first made for the door, then I realised the kite had broken apart so I exited through the break.

I staggered round to the rear turret and banged on the perspex, but could get no response; returning to the front section, I was confronted by flames which were everywhere."

Author's note: The Lancaster had in fact hit a drainage ditch with its main wheels and the impact had broken the fuselage just aft of the trailing edge. Spud's only thoughts were to help the rest of his crew and without hesitation, this tough Aussie gunner re-entered the fiercely burning aircraft. Allan continues with his painful memories:

"The cockpit was a sheet of flame, but I could just make out the skipper still in his seat... I went forward and could see his clothing was on fire... grabbing him by his parachute harness I pulled like hell, but the harness had been burnt part through and it gave way sending me tumbling back into the radio compartment. Regaining my feet, I went back into the heat again to try to get Roy out, but a stronger force seemed to be pulling me back; I then became aware of two figures holding me and one was shouting 'it's too late mate, it's too late... nothing can be done now'. The next thing I remember was being taken to the sick bay."

Sgt Mahony had in fact been restrained and then rescued from his heroic deeds by the station's firemen.

The crash crews also recovered the unconscious rear gunner, Colin Winterborn; he had only been on the squadron a few days having been posted in with the 'freshmen' Simpson crew, with whom he went on to survive a successful tour. Sadly the remaining five crew members all perished in the crash.

This gloomy evening's tragedies had not yet come to an end; W/O Ron Brunt (JB362) had failed to return from Berlin; the 21 year old pilot and his crew, flying in D-Dog, were brought down over Berlin and only the bomb aimer, Sgt Burrows managed to escape with his life; their navigator, Sgt Fred Ashman was only 19 years of age. Around the same time as the Richardson crash, and unbeknown to Fiskerton control, the crew of a severely damaged Lanacaster Mk II from 408 RCAF Squadron, also returning from Berlin, was making a desperate attempt to find Fiskerton's FIDO sanctuary. But their struggle ended abruptly when the pilot was forced to land in open country. With extreme skill born out of a desperation to survive, the pilot brought the aircraft down in fields near the sewage works alongside the Lincoln to Washingborough road. Miraculously, on this dark, fog-bound night, all of the crew walked away unharmed.

Bomber Command lost 28 Lancasters on the raid, with a further 14 crashing in England! 83 PFF Squadron lost two aircraft, and both were crewed by ex-49ers; they were captained by F/O A.B. Smeaton and P/O K.R.G. Millar - sadly all of the crew members were killed.

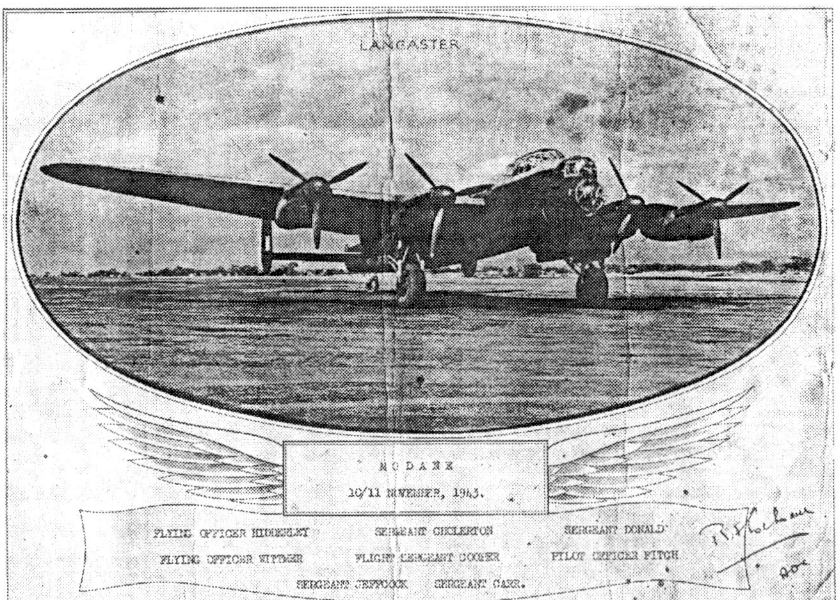

An Aiming Point Certificate awarded to F/O E Hidderley and crew for the Modane Operation Nov 10/11 1943 (Reg Jeffcock)

Note: 49 Squadron Lancaster JB235, involved in the tragic FIDO crash at Fiskerton, was the same aircraft in which W/O Frazer lost his life eight nights earlier, and the same aircraft in which P/O Hales was forced to return early on the two intervening operations.

FTR JB362	W/O R. Brunt	Pilot	(Killed)
(EA-D)	Sgt H. Bronsky	F/E	(Killed)
'A Flt'	Sgt F.E. Ashman	NAV	(Killed)
	Sgt R.W. Norley DFM	W/AG	(Killed)
Crew on their	F/S R.P. O'Dea	A/G	(Killed)
13th operation	Sgt J.G. Burrows	B/A	(P.o.W.)
	Sgt E.D. Wilson	A/G	(Killed)

Crashed JB235	Sgt R.J. Richardson RAAF	Pilot	(Killed)
(EA-C)	Sgt H.G. Boswell	F/E	(Killed)
'A Flt'	Sgt H. Carr	NAV/B	(Killed)
	Sgt L.H. Cartwright	W/AG	(Killed)
	Sgt M.O. Mahony RAAF	A/G	(Injured)
Crew on their	P/O H. Lowe (USA)RCAF	B/A	(Killed)
1st operation	Sgt Winterborn	A/G	(Injured)

On the 27th, P/O Hales and crew were declared 'tour expired'. The OC had decided they had done more than their share and had earned a well deserved rest; Reg Hales was posted over to 1654 HCU at Wigsley as an instructor. The following day, P/O Reynolds and crew received their posting to 97 Sqdn PFF.

Left: 2 Canadians, P/O Johnny Young (on right) with a friend P/O 'Stu' (Radar specialist) enjoying a spot of leave at the home of Ted Cachart in Pinner. October 1943.
(Ted Cachart)

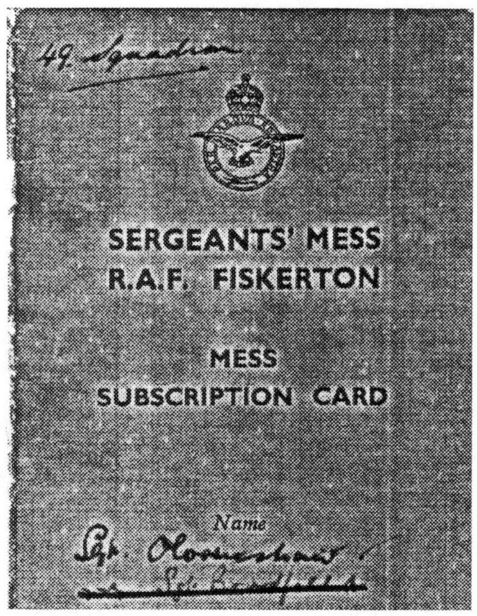

Right: Nothing was ever wasted in wartime - fortunately, Sgt Bradfield survived, becoming a POW and Sgt Olerenshaw went on to complete his tour with the Webb crew.

NOVEMBER 1943

This sorry month came to a close when a planned operation for the night of the 30th was scrubbed during the afternoon.

OPERATIONAL SUMMARY - NOVEMBER 1943

Date	Target	Desp	E/R	FTR	Remarks
3/4	DÜSSELDORF	18	1	2	F/L Thomas FTR
					F/L Carfoot FTR
10/11	MODANE	5	-	1c	W/O Webb cr on t/o
18/19	BERLIN	19	-	-	
22/23	BERLIN	16	1	1	F/O Cottingham FTR
23/24	BERLIN	14	1	1c	F/O Turner c/l
26/27	BERLIN	14	1	1	W/O Brunt FTR
				1c	Sgt Richardson c/l

Total of sorties flown	86
Failed to return	4 + 3c

Illustration by John Ward

DECEMBER 1943

2/3 December, 1943; BERLIN: Thursday 2nd December saw a continuation of the bombing attacks on Berlin. Despite high wind forecasts both at base and over Germany, 450 plus bombers set out for the 'Big City and by 16.45hrs, Fiskerton had dispatched 14 Lancasters. Bombing was scattered owing to the incorrect forecasts, but some industrial areas were hit. As well as strong winds, the bomber force also had to contend with numerous fighters. The German controllers had predicted Berlin as the target well in advance of the bomber's arrival and as a result a total of 40 bombers with their crews were lost.

W/O Bob Petty (JB371) and crew from 49 Squadron was one of those posted missing: On their way to Berlin, J-Jig's rear gunner, Ed Smith, reported that his guns were u/s, but the crew still decided to press-on. During the bombing run they were attacked by an Me110. Owen Roberts in the top turret managed to hit the fighter's engine before one of his guns jammed. Continuing the bomb run, Owen spotted another Me 110 just below them but when he tried to fire his guns, they were either jammed or out of ammunition. To add to their troubles, flak then struck the starboard inner engine which burst into flames immediately.

Without hesitation, Bob Petty gave the bale out order. Six members of the crew (including 2nd pilot, Sgt Tucker) survived to become PoW's. Sadly the bomb aimer, Bill Walke was killed along with the rear gunner, Ed Smith, who although seen to bale out, has no known grave.

The remainder of the squadron started to arrive back over a fog-shrouded Fiskerton around midnight. Visibility was down to less than 800yds, with shallow radiation fog no more than 100ft deep. Shortly before 23.00hrs the order was given to ignite the FIDO burners. Two kites had been badly damaged by flak:

F/Lt Andrew Tancred (JB295) and crew received damage to the inner and outer starboard engines, but after feathering the outer engine they managed to bring R-Robert home on three.

P/O 'Jock' Simpson (DV166) and crew had even more of a problem; on lowering the undercarriage, diligent flight engineer Bob Mower (with the aid of a torch) noticed the port tyre had been punctured and flak damage was also evident on the port inner engine. Base advised them to land at Coleby Grange, a grass night fighter airfield just south of Lincoln. Navigator Dennis Hiscock gave his skipper a new heading, and after a short flight, Jock Simpson skillfully brought F-Fox down without incident... although on lowering the port wing, the defective wheel did wipe out most of the Coleby's landing lights down one side!

F/O Eric Hidderley's crew (JB399) had survived a combat with an Me 210 in which the fighter came off much worse than the Lancaster. All 49's remaining aircraft landed without incident. On this night, four Lancasters from neighbouring airfields took advantage of Fiskerton's FIDO sanctuary.

DECEMBER 1943

FTR JB371	W/O R.W. Petty	Pilot	(P.o.W.)
(EA-J)	Sgt A. Tucker	2nd Pilot	(P.o.W.)
'A Flt'	Sgt G. Lumsden	F/E	(P.o.W.)
	Sgt T. Tullock	NAV	(P.o.W.)
	Sgt S.J. Richards	W/AG	(P.o.W.)
	Sgt O. Roberts	A/G	(P.o.W.)
Crew on their	F/S W.A. Walke	B/A	(Killed)
17th operation	Sgt E. Smith	A/G	(Missing)

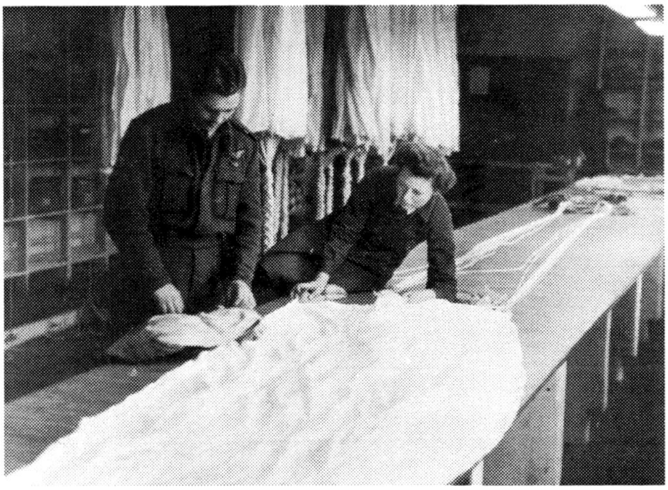

Fiskerton, Dec 1943: F/Sgt Gordon Cooper of Glasgow (Wop/AG in F/O Hidderley's crew and at the time a veteran of 24 operations) poses for an official photograph with parachute packer, LACW Radford. (G.V. Cooper)

3/4 December, 1943; LEIPZIG: Ed Murrow, the famous American broadcaster, flying in a 5 Group Lancaster, witnessed this effective raid made by over 520 bombers. Fiskerton's contribution was 11 aircraft of which all returned safely. Bomber Command had tried to trick the German defences by flying towards Berlin before turning at the last moment towards Leipzig. German night fighters managed to infiltrate the bomber stream before the turn and scored several successes - 24 bombers failed to return.

16/17 December, 1943; BERLIN: Bad weather had prevented the bombers operating for almost two weeks and during this time the usual in and out postings had taken place. Amongst the postings 'out' were P/O Vic Edy and crew who were 'tour expired'. For those crews who still had it to do, Thursday night of 16th saw them back on the road to Berlin once again.

An all Lancaster force of 483 plus PFF Mosquitoes attacked a cloud covered target using sky-markers. 49 Squadron had two new crews operating; Canadian F/O Bill Healey (JB679) and crew flying D-Dog, and P/O Gordon Ratcliffe (JB545) and crew in O-Oboe.

German night fighters had managed to intercept the main force whilst en-route over Holland, and it was here that Oberleutnant Heinz Schnaufer the German night fighter ace shot down the unsuspecting Ratcliffe crew using the dreaded 'Schrage Music'. Their Lancaster came down between Oldetrijne and Sonnega in Holland where recovery of the bodies proved extremely difficult due to the marshy ground. The crew are all buried together in Wolvega Cemetery.

Twenty-five Lancasters had been brought down over enemy territory, but the losses did not end there. Returning over Eastern England, tired crews found low cloud covered many of their bases. A further 32 bombers were lost as a result of crashes or being abandoned when their desperate crews baled-out. No. 1 Group, whose airfields were situated up on the Lincolnshire Wolds suffered the heaviest - fifteen 1 Group Lancasters and their crews perished on what became known as 'Black Thursday'.

NOT EVEN DAMP!

One of 49's Lancasters avoided being added to the 'missing' statistics by the narrowest of margins; only the well trained skills of the crew prevented another loss. Doug Tritton, flight engineer on P/O Russell Ewens' crew gives this account:

"On Thursday 16th December, 1943, we took-off just before tea in a brand new Lancaster bound for Berlin. It was serialed JB714 and coded EA-J for Jig (The previous J-Jig went down on 2/3-12-43). All did not go as well as hoped, for in the split second after our major bomb was released and before the incendiaries fell away we were severely raked by cannon fire from an attacking fighter. Many services were lost and the bomb doors hung open increasing our drag which we discovered later was further increased by a jagged portion of the upper skin of the port mainplane, which was flapping in the airstream.

Carefully watching the fuel gauges, I soon saw that we were losing fuel from one of our larger fuel tanks. This required changing over to run all four engines from the damaged tank to ensure that some use could be made of the fuel before it all leaked away. This was an obvious and recommended course of action. At reduced speed, due to the drag, and reduced power with two superchargers reverting to low gear owing to damage, our fuel consumption was increased tremendously.

Once the damaged tank was exhausted, I could take stock of the fuel remaining and equate that to the distance to go. Keeping a constant check, it seemed that we should make it back, but with very little fuel to spare. We were obviously not expected back as the airfield lights were all out and Lincolnshire was a carpet of blackness. Phil Griffiths our wireless operator, requested a bearing for Fiskerton, then when the navigator said we had overflown the base, this only added to my anxiety. Phil was about to ask for another fix when I cut in and said 'Stop!... we must land immediately' and asked the skipper to put out a distress call. That done the lights of nearby Ingham came on beneath us; I advised that an overshoot was out of the question and we must omit circuit procedure, approach high and be prepared to lose all power at any moment.

Fortunately the undercarriage held as we alighted onto the grass aerodrome. Without brakes, we cut the engines straight away. Unable to taxi, we clambered out of the aircaft to examine the aircraft with torches. The extent of the damage was far greater than expected - the incendiary canisters were totally ruined, torn and riddled with holes. The mainplane and tailplane near the wireless operator and rear gunner's positions were also severely damaged.

The margin by which we escaped death only became apparent two days later when I next saw the F/Sgt in charge of 'A' Flt ground staff. He had gone over to Ingham with a petrol bowser to drain the tanks and found they were dry - he then assumed I had instructed the ground crew at Ingham to carry out this task. I replied that we had agreed on the spot that our own crew would handle the aircraft. 'But the tanks were dry' protested the F/Sgt, 'not merely empty with a drop swilling about in the bottom, not even damp!'.

Not wishing to cause a fuss when back at Fiskerton for de-briefing, we declared 'slight damage' to the Intelligence Officer. Only the squadron's ground staff saw the extent of the damage, hence our modest assessment went into the Operations Record Book. It occurs to me that in fact it was the most badly damaged Lancaster to make a safe landing that I ever saw! Admittedly, I have seen equally tatty specimens since in photographs."

Doug and his crew went on to complete their tour, with most of their remaining trips being flown in the repaired J-Jig.

FTR JB545	P/O G.L. Ratcliffe	Pilot	(Killed)
(EA-O)	Sgt A.E. Marsland	F/E	(Killed)
'B Flt'	Sgt E. Holloway	NAV	(Killed)
	Sgt W.T. Rees	W/AG	(Killed)
	F/S R. Losa RCAF	A/G	(Killed)
Crew on their	Sgt W.R. Day	B/A	(Killed)
1st operation	F/S B.J.V. King RAAF	A/G	(Killed)

20/21 December, 1943; FRANKFURT: Of the 15 aircraft from Fiskerton that set out for Frankfurt, two were new crews piloted by; Sgt Meggison (JB727) in S-Sugar and Sgt Lett (JB399) in H-Harry. German controllers quickly plotted the force of 650 aircraft and night fighters began to take a heavy toll before the bombers were able to reach their target. A total of 41 aircraft failed to return - 6.3 per cent of those dispatched.

Over the target, the Pathfinders had not expected the thick cloud cover which now thwarted their pre-planned ground-marking. Added to this, the Germans lit a decoy fire and were using dummy target indicators. Despite all these setbacks, the RAF were able to inflict a good deal of damage to Frankfurt and its outlying townships.

P/O Alf Blackmore (JB467), a 21 year old pilot and holder of the DFC, along with his crew, failed to return to Fiskerton and were reported missing, their aircraft crashed near Hanau. The crew lie at rest together in the Durnbach War Cemetery in Germany.

DECEMBER 1943

FTR JB467	P/O A.H Blackmore DFC	Pilot	(Killed)
(EA-T)	Sgt T.S. Daniel	F/E	(Killed)
'B Flt'	P/O B.J. Saville	NAV	(Killed)
	Sgt S.V. Domleo	W/OP	(Killed)
	Sgt G.S. Lawn	A/G	(Killed)
Crew on their	F/S H.T. Evans	A/B	(Killed)
15th operation	Sgt P.W. Booth	A/G	(Killed)

23/24 December, 1943; BERLIN: Fourteen Lancasters had been detailed for ops but F/O Young was forced to pull out at the last minute; the remaining 13 aircraft became airborne during the first hour of Christmas Eve. Berlin was yet again covered by cloud which resulted in the force of 390 bombers making a scattered attack in the south-eastern parts of the city; 15 Lancasters were lost.

All 49 Squadron crews completed their sorties without trouble although S/Ldr 'Dusty' Miller (JB314) had to bomb ten minutes late owing to his port inner engine not giving full power. All the squadron were safely down at Fiskerton by 08.15hrs, and after de-brief and breakfast, their beds beckoned. But just before they retired to their perishing cold billets, news had filtered down from Group that the squadron was being 'stood down' for that evening. Tired they may have been, but it was a high-spirited bunch of young men that prepared for a good 'day's sleep, whilst contemplating celebrating an operational free Christmas Eve.

WHISKY? - ON THE KNEE

Not everyone ventured into town over the Christmas period as Ted Cachart (Wop/Ag in F/O Young's crew) well recalls:

"It seemed as if the whole station had gone into Lincoln, but the rear gunner, Len Crossman and myself decided to stay behind. We knew we would have problems getting anything to drink in Lincoln after about 8pm as the pubs would have all run dry. We went to the Sgt's Mess where we were served by the 2 Corporal bar stewards, after a while we were joined by the Station Warrant Officer and a F/Sgt Fitter. For about 4 hours, we were the only ones in the Mess and I remember Len and I were both drinking double whiskies with orange squash. We amused ourselves by playing snooker and putting records on the radiogram.

We were both quietly 'soused' by 10.30pm when the intoxicated(?) 'mob' returned from town, they spilled into the Mess laughing and shouting and calling us all sorts of names for staying in. Our glasses seemed to refill as if by magic and eventually Len passed out.

Some hours later, I woke up in the middle of a field between the Mess and No. 10 site with no jacket or shirt on and soaking wet. I rolled back into my billet, climbed into bed and slept like a baby. I didn't have a hangover next morning, but my knee was swollen like a football. By using two brooms as crutches, I struggled down to the mess for breakfast.

There, Margaret, one of the cooks, with much friendly tut-tutting handed me my very stiff mud-encrusted jacket which she had put into the kitchen to dry overnight.

I then discovered (from some of the more sober revellers from last night) that when Len passed out I had tried to carry him back to the billet on my shoulder but had tripped over a chair and fell heavily on one knee. I then apparently hobbled out of the back door where I must have passed out, falling into a puddle. Someone carried me back inside the mess, removed my wet jacket and shirt and then took me to the first aid post outside the mess; where Len was lying 'spark out on the floor'. They laid me beside him and poured buckets of water over us. Apparently I got up doing swimming strokes and disappeared into the night...I didn't remember Len passing out, trying to carry him or anything else except waking up in the field.

I went sick next day, being admitted into dock with water (whisky?) on the knee and was laid up for a few days. In the meantime, Johnny and the crew went to Berlin with a spare W/Op in my place. It was either late that night or early next morning that word got back to me that they had failed to return. I had some hours of very confused and disturbed thoughts until they boisterously paid me a visit later that afternoon - I vowed there and then that they would never fly again without me along!"

CHRISTMAS 1943

By 10am on Christmas Day 'stand down' order had come through; for once the weather was on the side of the flyers.

As in years past, the Officers served the OR's their Christmas Fare and later that night much 'letting off steam' was enjoyed by all concerned. Fiskerton was commanded by G/Cpt Grindell RNZAF,DFC,AFC, who was definitely the Station Commander around the base but given the slightest opportunity was inclined to 'live it up' in the Mess, and Christmas, 1943 proved to be one of those opportunities. Several stories abound about the antics of this somewhat 'eccentric' G/Cpt from New Zealand. Often mentioned was the use of his service revolver, which was always by his side and on every occasion would be used to shoot rabbits... often through his office window!

As G/Cpt, he was not allowed to fly ops without special permission from Group, and indeed a study of the Operational Record Book does not reveal his name - but talk to some of the 'old lags', and they will tell of sightings of the 'Groupie' wearing a Sgt's Battle Dress Blouse in the Mess or locker rooms just before an operation.

CHRISTMAS DAY
1943.

MENU

Orange Cocktail
+
Chicken Soup.
+
Fresh Fish
+
Roast Turkey; Bread sauce;
Sausage Meat & Onion Stuffing.

Roast Pork; Apple Sauce.

Sprouts; Peas; Roast Potatoes.
+
Christmas Pudding; Rum Sauce.
+
Biscuits & Cheese; Dessert &
Coffee.

+++

The Christmas 1943 menu (Ken Gibson). (The front being faithfully reproduced with typing whilst the back shows the original signatures reproduced by computer scanning - Ted Cachart)

DOWN UNDER

It may well have been during this period of inclement weather that one of the squadron's pilots who hailed from a land of sunnier climes, found himself in a rather embarrassing state. F/Sgt Clive Roantree RAAF departed his billet on an unusually bright and crisp morning.

As was the norm, he jumped onto his service bicycle and sped off in the direction of the Mess and breakfast. He had only travelled a few wheel turns when it suddenly dawned on him that he, and he alone, was the only bod on a bike; everyone else was on foot.

The error of his ways soon became painfully apparent as Clive attempted unsuccessfully to negotiate the first bend along the concrete roadway - one can only conclude that Adelaide doesn't suffer from much 'black ice' during December!

DECEMBER 1943

29/30 December, 1943; BERLIN: The Christmas celebrations had been but a mere bright interlude in Bomber Command's ever darkening war of attrition... for on the night of Wednesday 29 December, Berlin's flak torn skies once again beckoned.

Over 700 bombers approached Berlin from the south, and it was the south eastern part of the city that received the heaviest bombing. The 15 Lancasters from Fiskerton found the city once again covered in cloud, but all completed their sorties without any hitches and were back at base around midnight. Command lost 20 aircraft.

'JONES... THE PILOT'

Two new crews had operated for the first time with the squadron on 29/30 December to Berlin, and both pilots shared the common surname of Jones; Jones T. (JB421) and Jones J.A. (JB727). Added to the already established pilot, P/O Eric Jones, this now brought the squadron's compliment during this period of 'Jones the pilot' up to three; a nightmare for admin/ops staff then... and for the squadron historian some 50 years later!

OPERATIONAL SUMMARY - DECEMBER 1943

Date	Target	Desp	E/R	FTR	Remarks
2/3	BERLIN	14	-	1	W/O Petty FTR
3/4	LEIPZIG	11	-	-	
16/17	BERLIN	16	-	1	P/O Ratcliffe FTR
20/21	FRANKFURT	15	-	1	P/O Blackmore FTR
23/24	BERLIN	13	-	-	
29/30	BERLIN	15	-	-	
Total of sorties flown		84			
Failed to return		3			

Note: No early returns, for which credit must be given to the ground crews who obtained this 100 per cent record during extreme winter conditions.

A Wop/Ag and Navigator wearing just battle dress (and probably flying boots) in the 'hot seats' of a Lancaster. Heat from the engines entered the cabin on both sides of the Wop's position and was controllable by him.

Invariably, he would turn it down a few notches which usually lead to a cry from 'up front' of "Wireless operator - turn up the b......... heat" (or something like that!).

Fiskerton circa Dec 1943: Awaiting the Base Commanders Informal Inspection, Eric Jones and crew parade in front of F-Fox (possibly DV166). Front rank (l to r) Eric Jones, pilot; Pete Whiteley, rear gunner (KIA); Ron Harris, flight engineer; Ken Blackham, navigator; Jock Brown mid/upper gunner; Steve Stevenson, bomb aimer; Jimmy Dorian (Morrison crew). The second rank are members of 'A' Flt ground crew. (E.L. Jones)

In the foreground (l to r) S/Ldr Graham Day, 'A' Flt Commander chats with W/Cmdr Adams. With back to camera, P/O Russ Ewens introduces his crew to Air Commodore Cook, Base Commander 52 Base. Front rank (l to r) F/O Grainger; Sgt Manger; Sgt P. Griffiths; Sgt Tritton; Sgt Lees; Sgt Laws. Second rank, P/O Dickinson and crew who FTR 26/27-4-44. The Lancaster is a brand-new D-Dog (JB679); it too FTR on 26/27-4-44 in the hands of Bob Montgomery and crew. (D.C. Tritton)

No. 49 Squadron,
Royal Air Force,
Fiskerton,
Lincoln.

21st December, 1943.

Dear Sgt Cachart.

Yesterday the following message was received from the Secretary of State for Air:-

"The Prime Minister who has been receiving complete details of the recent bombing operations has asked me to convey his congratulations to the crews who have taken part in the series of great battles over Berlin and Leipzig, and the associated attacks"

The A.O.C. in C. Bomber Command has replied conveying to the prime Minister our gratitude for his message and our heartfelt wishes for his speedy convalescence and return, and stating that his support, advice and unfailing encouragement through four dark and strenuous years have been the mainspring of our effort.

You will agree with me that it is extremely heartening to find the Prime Minister thinking of us at this time in spite of his grave illness, and I feel I must pass his message on to you in this manner for the part you played as a member of aircrew in the attacks in question.

Yours sincerely,

Wing Commander, Commanding,
No. 49 Squadron.

A sample of the letter , signed by Wing Commander Adams, sent to all members of 49 squadron who took part in the Berlin offensive. (Ted Cachart)

JANUARY 1944

1/2 January, 1944; BERLIN: New Year 1944 was heralded in with Bomber Command's ninth attack in the series on Berlin. An all Lancaster force found Berlin as usual covered by cloud which again disrupted any possible concentration of fires. Fiskerton had dispatched 15 bombers, but although being well into Germany, P/O Jock Simpson (JB466) and crew were forced to return in A-Able without reaching the target, due to a petrol leakage from the port inner engine plus the mid-upper guns becoming u/s.

The Dickinson crew (ND383) on their first 'op' and flying in E-Easy, were attacked by two Me 109's; after only short bursts, both the mid-upper and rear turret guns froze up in the Lancaster. With only vocal instructions from his gunners, the pilot managed to evade the fighters and a successful sortie was completed.

Sgt Meggison (JB710) and crew sustained flak damage whilst fending off the attentions of yet another night fighter -they too managed to complete their sortie and returned safely to Fiskerton's FIDO runway.

Of the 421 Lancasters sent to Berlin, 28 failed to return with the majority falling to the high flying Me 110's; all 49's aircraft returned to base. Snow was falling heavily as tired crews tumbled out onto the Fiskerton dispersals, during the first light of Sunday 2nd January.

There to greet them as usual were their ever faithful ground crews. Few present believed that ops would be 'on the cards' again that evening as the snow soon began to settle. How wrong could they be!.. for later the same day most of these cold and fatigued crews would be called upon to clamber aboard their freezing cold Lancasters, once again Berlin bound. But for now in the stillness of a white-carpeted winter's morning, the tension relieved crews wise-cracked with the WAAF drivers as they negotiated the quickly disappearing peri-track. Two crews were making this hazardous return journey over from 49's 'B' Flt dispersal area for the very last time; for in less than 24 hours one crew would all have been killed, whilst the other crew would survive... but only by a miracle!

2/3 January, 1944; BERLIN: Every available person on the station gave a hand in clearing the snow ready for the evening's operation. Take-offs were able to begin 15 minutes before midnight with Fiskerton managing to get 12 aircraft airborne from the 13 detailed.

Just three hours after departure, P/O Russ Ewens (JB178) piloting 'Bandlaw Victor', called up 'Passout' control for permission to land. The calm, clear voice of WAAF Cpl Brown came back giving landing instructions. The crew had been forced to return early when their navigator became ill; wireless operator Sgt Griffiths had guided the aircraft back over Fiskerton using Gee. With such a short time between this and the previous night's operation, Bomber Command could only put up 383 aircraft. Of these, icing conditions forced many of the main force crews to jettison parts of their loads in order to gain precious height.

Just 311 bombers struggled to reach a cloud-covered Berlin where the bombing was spread, with no concentrated fires developing. The German controllers had realised the bombers target in advance and instructed the night-fighters accordingly; most of the 27 Lancasters lost, fell in the Berlin area.

The reason for the total loss of F/Lt Johnny Palmer (JB727 EA-S) and crew has never been established; the pilot, who had recently celebrated his 21st birthday is remembered along with his crew on the Runnymede Memorial; their mid-upper gunner, Derek Prusher, was just 18 years old.

HEAD-ON COLLISION

Canadian skipper F/O Johnny Young (JB231) and crew in N-Nan were in the last wave and on approaching the final turning point before the target were made well aware of the presence of night fighters by the lanes of flares in the sky. For the first time, the 'Fishpond' radar screen was functioning well and Ted Cachart the Wop/Ag reported a large number of 'blips' reflected from the aircraft below them, a number of these were heading in the direction of the final turning point but with the majority heading towards the target.

Up in the top turret sat Allan 'Spud' Mahony (survivor of the FIDO crash in Nov 43) keeping a watchful eye out for fighters as many combats had already been sighted. He had requested the pilot to gently roll the Lancaster so as to give the gunners some vertical vision.
Allan recalls what happened next:

"We were skimming through hazy cloud... the pilot had just lowered the starboard wing when in a split second I saw another Lancaster heading straight towards us and before I could yell a warning, the on-coming Lanc's cockpit struck our aircraft's starboard wing between the two engines."

Ted Cachart the crew's wireless operator continues:

"We were about 30 miles NNE from Berlin when an almighty impact suddenly shuddered throughout the aircraft tipping me out of my seat. My helmet and oxygen mask were ripped away as I dived for the astrodome, just in time to see a large piece of the starboard wing complete with engine disappear. With no intercom or oxygen I grabbed my chute but became stuck to the main spar by the G-force as Johnny and Allan Vidow our engineer fought to pull 'Nan's' nose up. Eventually I slid over the spar and got down to the tail where both gunners stood waiting with the door open.

The well practiced drill for abandoning the aircraft from the rear was: I would go aft and check the mid-upper gunner was out of his turret and whilst he opened and clipped back the door I would help the rear gunner out of his turret. I would be No. 1 to jump. Unable to communicate without my helmet and with both gunners standing ready by the open door, instinct took over, I remember sitting on the step and rolling out, then hanging in my chute watching the aircraft flying away into clouds and wondering if I was supposed to have jumped or not. It would be two days before I knew the rest of the crew had jumped!"

Left: Four members of the lucky Young crew in 1945 (l to r) Ted Cachart Wop/Ag, Alan Vidow F/Eng, Len Crossman R/Gunner, 'Spud' Mahony Mid-upper Gunner (RAAF) and below Ted and Spud when visiting Fiskerton in 1990

Incredibly, all the crew managed to get out safely, but the skipper who was the last to leave did dislocate his shoulder on landing.

On opening his parachute, Allan Mahony had another shock:

"I looked down and all I could see in the semi-darkness was a large area of black. I thought 'My God' it's the sea and this being January there would be no chance of survival. The wind was blowing a gale and making the parachute oscillate violently but as I neared the ground, I realised the blackness was in fact a forest and moments later I was crashing through branches. My fall was halted as the chute snagged on the tree tops and I remained suspended some thirty feet from the ground. After releasing my harness and in attempting to climb down, I fell and hit the forest floor injuring my back."

In fact the fall had broken Sgt Mahony's back and it was never reset properly resulting in Spud having to wear a support harness for the rest of his life. This modest Australian airman who remarkably survived two horrendous accidents has been left with a terrible legacy of war.

Ted Cachart picks up the story:

"After interrogation at Dulag Luft and a short spell in the transit camp, the three officers were sent to Luft III at Sagan whilst the four NCO's (Spud, Alan Vidow, Len Crossman and myself) were sent to Stalag 4B near Muhlberg. During appel (roll call) one evening just after Easter my name was called out and told to be ready to leave next day. No reason given and much speculation during the night (Commissioned, Batman at Luft III, Repatriation, Shot! were all options discussed) The following morning two Luft Waffe personnel told me that I was to be taken back to Dulag Luft for further interrogation.

We travelled for two days by train, always in the reasonable luxury of second class coaches. On the second night sitting in a darkened carriage, I was lighting a cigarette when I sensed the intense stare of the person next to me, then a broad Northern English voice said 'Where are you from?'.

The voice was that of a Royal Army Medical Corp POW who was accompanying a Serbian Officer back to his camp; this officer had been shot through each hand and tortured into insanity. I don't recall if the Orderly had any guards with him or not but remember him asking me if I needed any cigarettes.

The interrogation at Dulag was all about some new radio jamming equipment they found in the wreckage of our Lanc, this had been installed a few days earlier whilst I was in hospital and all I knew was how to switch it on! After 11 days I was sent to Luft 6 at Heydekrug near the borders of Lithuania and I did not see or hear from the rest of the crew until 1945."

Just before entering his Lancaster on the night of that last op, Ted found that he still had his wallet in his pocket. He gave it to WAAF MT driver Dot Everitt for safe keeping. When Ted didn't return, Dot contacted his parents, and some time later, she and Betty Wilcox (a local Reepham girl whose Mother had adopted the crew) visited his home in Pinner and returned the wallet and spent a few days leave there. Also missing in N-Nan that night was 'Nancy Pants', the `Lucky Mascot' rag doll made for the crew by Dot, together with all the groundcrews' caps; they always put them just inside the aircraft's entrance door as a gesture of faith that the aircraft would return.

Note: It is just possible that F/Lt Palmer's S - Sugar was the Lanc that was in collision with N - NAN as it would have been in the same wave, and if slightly ahead of Nan it would have changed course and be heading back across the track of the oncoming tail-enders.

P/O Jock Simpson (JB399) and crew almost became the squadron's third casualty this night when they were engaged by a very determined JU88; a combat in which the Lancaster's gunners felt certain they had destroyed their adversary. But for the skills of the pilot and the reactions of the two gunners, Sgts Walker and Winterborne, the outcome could easily have been reversed.

The crew set out for home in their damaged Lancaster only to receive a diversion call. Dead reckoning by navigator Dennis Hiscock, brought the aircraft over Stradishall, where H-Harry touched down safely at 07.16hrs.

On return to England, the remainder of the squadron were diverted; only P/O Tudor Jones (ND383) and crew managed to get in at Fiskerton.

FTR JB231	F/O .J.E.M. Young RCAF	Pilot	(P.o.W.)
(EA-N)	Sgt A.W. Vidow	F/E	(P.o.W.)
'B Flt'	F/O J. Scott RCAF	NAV	(P.o.W.) (Died in 1996)
	Sgt E.B. Cachart	W/OP	(P.o.W.)
	Sgt M. Mahony RAAF	A/G	(P.o.W.)
Crew on their	P/O L.M. Orchard	B/A	(P.o.W.)
8th operation	Sgt L. Crossman	A/G	(P.o.W.)

Note: Len Crossman was unfortunately killed in a motor cycle accident in 1945.

JANUARY 1944

Missing JB727	F/L C.J.E. Palmer	Pilot	(Killed)
(EA-S)	Sgt P.O. Camm	F/E	(Killed)
'B Flt'	F/O G.T. Young	NAV	(Killed)
	Sgt H. Conrad	W/OP	(Killed)
	Sgt D.D.R. Dallaway	A/G	(Killed)
Crew on their	F/O R. Stobo	A/B	(Killed)
11th operation	Sgt D.F. Prusher	A/G	(Killed)

5/6 January, 1944; POMERANIAN BAY/STETTIN: Whilst five of the squadron's Lancasters joined 343 other aircraft in the main force attack on Stettin, 6 other Fiskerton Lancs were required to drop mines off Schweinmunde.

Stettin had not been heavily attacked since 1941, and this may have led the Germans into thinking that Berlin was once again the target. Despite most of the night fighters being drawn to Berlin, 16 bomber crews still failed to return. P/O Sanders (JB473) and crew flying U-Uncle were on their first operation; during the bombing run, they were attacked by a German night fighter; the gunners, Sgts Machin and Briars returned fire and damaged their attacker making it break away; the crew returned safely after 9hrs 50mins although very low on fuel. They landed at Ludford Magna after an SOS request.

Sgt Dickinson and crew were once again not having life easy in E-Easy; flak had shot a tip off the starboard outer prop and the engine had to be feathered.

The 6 minelaying aircraft carried out their sorties without problems, although F/O Don Bacon (JB710) and crew drew the attentions of one night fighter; the pilot 'corkscrewed' G-George for several minutes until the danger was averted. All of the squadron's aircraft returned safely.

11 January, 1944; P/O Kerr and crew were posted out to 83 Squadron PFF after completing 10 operations with 49 Squadron.

14/15 January, 1944; BRUNSWICK: Nearly 500 bombers, including 9 from 49 Squadron were monitored by the Germans shortly after leaving the English coast, en-route for Brunswick and its important aircraft component and engineering works. After the trip, P/O Clive Roantree's (JB466) de-brief report stated: *"There was a good deal of fighter activity from the coast to the target and for 30 minutes after."*

P/O Eric Jones (JB421) and crew in their favoured aircraft K-King were attacked twice by night fighters -once over the target and the second time south of Hannover. On the second occasion the enemy aircraft was damaged and seen to crash. Subsequently this experienced crew, flying their 21st operation, were happy to claim their victim as destroyed. The raid itself was not a success with much of the bombing falling in open country.

JANUARY 1944

Two new crews had operated with the squadron; F/O Harford (JB178) and crew in V-Victor and an American of the USAAF, Lt Stevens (JB473) in U-Uncle. Both crews completed their sorties but Lt Stevens reported with consternation that it was still daylight as they crossed the enemy coast going out! One of the squadron's aircraft failed to return from the operation; F/Lt Andrew Tancred (JB295) and crew in R-Robert were brought down over Germany. F/Sgt Branigan the flight engineer and navigator Sgt Jerrard were the only survivors. The other crew members are buried in Hannover War Cemetery.

FTR JB295	F/L A.T.L. Tancred	Pilot	(Killed)
(EA-R)	Sgt H.D. Jerrard	F/E	(P.o.W.)
B Flt'	F/S W.E. Branigan	NAV	(P.o.W.)
	Sgt T.J. Smith	W/AG	(Killed)
	Sgt R. Phipps	A/G	(Killed)
Crew on their	Sgt D.H. Shaw	B/A	(Killed)
9th operation	Sgt E.T.E. Sullivan	A/G	(Killed)

Fiskerton, winter 1943/44: Skipper Eric Jones and crew photographed in front of their faithful kite JB421, Bandlaw K-King. They are from l to r; Pat Peacock (W/op); Eric Jones (Pilot); Steve Stevenson (B/A); Ken Blackham (Nav); Ron Harris (F/Eng); Pete Whiteley (A/G); not in photo is Jock Brown (A/G). Note 'Lupino Lane' mascot on rear turret guns. Sgt Peacock & Sgt Whiteley went to Frankfurt 22/23-3-44 with F/Sgt Greig (ND536) and crew and failed to return. K-King lasted until 7/8-5-44 before failing to return from Salbris. (E.L. Jones)

Fiskerton, Jan 1944: Several 'A' Flt ground crew NCO's gather to the rear of JB469 (EA-B), near the flt office (back row l to r) Sgt Ben Bolt; Sgt Jimmy Nowell; Cpl Jimmy Hodgson; Cpl Dave Annat; Sgt J. Roberts. (front row l to r) Sgt Ron Smith; Sgt Trevor Simpson; Cpl Fred Outwin. (T.N. Simpson)

19 January, 1944; W/O Webb and crew were screened after a tour which had seen them go through the 'Battle of the Ruhr' and several Berlin raids. A very relieved Ernie Webb was posted out to 16 OTU as an instructor.

20/21 January, 1944; BERLIN: With the full moon period over, 750 plus bombers approached Berlin from the north and once again found their target cloud-covered. The 12 Lancasters from Fiskerton with the aid of their H2S sets, were able to confirm the aiming point. F/Sgt White (JB469) and crew took B-Baker on this their first operation, and considered the attack to be a good one.

The Dickinson (JB679) crew flew D-Dog instead of E-Easy, but this didn't alter their luck; flak damaged the port rudder trimmer and punctured the tail wheel. Meanwhile, P/O Barnes (JB314) and crew in 'Queenie' had their own problems; over the target they were hit by incendiaries from above and then shortly after leaving the target a 'Halifax' started shooting at them! F/O Adams, flying as second dickie in this crew, must have rued the day his second tour posting came through.

Ten Lancs were back at Fiskerton around midnight. Of the outstanding two, one landed at Wickenby the other at Aldis. Bomber Command lost 35 aircraft from this operation.

21/22 January, 1944; MAGDEBURG/BERLIN: Thirty-four Lancasters and Mosquitoes carried out a diversionary raid on Berlin whilst the Main Force attacked Magdeburg. The Meggison and Keeling crews flew to Berlin whilst 10 other 49 Squadron aircraft took-off for Magdeburg.

One hour after take-off, F/O Harford (ND474) flying T-Tare suffered an engine failure in the starboard outer and returned early.

In the target area, decoy fires and bombers attacking before the Pathfinders had finished their work led to poor bombing results on Magdeburg. Added to this was the heavy toll taken by the night fighters with 57 aircraft going down, of which 35 were Halifaxes. One Lancaster failed to return from Berlin; none of the losses involved 49 Squadron. This was the 'end of tour' operation for P/O Coxill and crew; the pilot was posted to 1661 HCU at Winthorpe.

27/28 January, 1944; BERLIN: Extensive diversionary operations by Stirlings and Wellingtons preceded yet another attack on the 'Big City'. Fiskerton put 13 aircraft up but two were soon to return; F/O Harford (ND474) experienced trouble with T-Tare when the starboard outer yet again gave trouble... was it coincidence that P/O Jones in sister aircraft ND473 O-Orange also suffered a starboard outer failure?

F/Sgt McKenzie and crew on their first operation found the cluster of 'Wanganui flares OK' and completed a good sortie.

Over 500 Lancasters bombed sky markers in a scattered attack from which 33 bombers failed to return. An Me 109 attacked F/Lt Don Bacon (JB701) and crew in G-George just as they were leaving the target; Canadian, Al Richard in the rear turret gave his skipper the necessary evasive action and they escaped safely.

Unfortunately one Lancaster from 49 Squadron was reported missing; it was Australian P/O Keith Barnes DFC and crew on their 23rd operation. This loss stunned many at Fiskerton, who thought the Barnes crew looked good to complete their tour. Four crew members survived, the other three, including their 20 year old pilot are buried in the Berlin War Cemetery.

Missing JB360	P/O K.O. Barnes RAAF	Pilot	(Killed)
(EA-M)	Sgt G.E. Greenwood	F/E	(Killed)
'B Flt'	F/S J. Atkinson	NAV	(P.o.W.)
	Sgt A. Marshall	W/OP	(P.o.W.)
	W/O J.T. Hill RCAF	A/G	(Killed)
Crew on their	F/S D. Grimley	B/A	(P.o.W.)
23rd operation	F/S D. McPhee RCAF	A/G	(P.o.W.)

28/29 January, 1944; BERLIN: Cloud cover over Berlin on this night was broken, which allowed some ground-marking. Bomber Command claimed this to be the most concentrated attack of the series so far.

A mixed force of 677 Halifaxes and Lancasters were subjected to fighter attacks in the target area where most of those reported missing were shot down; 46 aircraft failed to return and yet again it was the Halifaxes that suffered the higher percentage loss rate.

The squadron had dispatched 11 aircraft on the raid and all completed successful sorties. At interrogation P/O George (JB469) and crew (on their 24th op) reported: *"Fires seen for 150 miles on leaving the target,"* and P/O Eric Jones (JB421) and crew (also on their 24th trip) stated: *"The best Berlin effort yet!"* The only damage sustained was by the Harford crew in JB178 when a flak ship put three holes in V-Victor.

30/31 January, 1944; BERLIN: In full moon conditions, the centre and south-western corner of Berlin received a heavy attack through complete cloud cover by over 500 heavy bombers (mainly Lancasters). Large fires developed in the centre although districts outside of Berlin were subject to some widespread bombing. German fighters were late intercepting the bombers, but they still managed to account for many of the 33 aircraft lost.

Fiskerton had 13 aircraft airborne and several reported that night fighters were very active. F/Sgt Cliff Coward, navigator in G-George wrote in his flight log: *"No contacts, but many other a/c were having combats -7 a/c seen to go down."*

JANUARY 1944

Sgt John Hennessey, flight engineer in the same crew, kept a personal diary -the following is his entry for this Berlin trip: *"Too much moonlight for the 'Big City' and too many fighter flares to make one feel happy!! We watched seven people going down in flames as we went in to bomb and I also noticed a parachute opening and it was drifting towards the flames!! Stan's (Sgt Weedon M/U) turret was u/s and so he could not have fired his guns had we been attacked. We arrived home twenty minutes early and that was how I spent my wedding anniversary!!"*

Jack Lett (ND474) and crew in T-Tare are one crew who did have contact with the enemy; during this trip they were engaged by a JU88 and two FW190's! - no serious damage was sustained and a safe return was made.
The Jupp crew in J-Jig, were approached by one fighter and believed they damaged it during the breakaway. All 13 Lancs were back at Fiskerton safe and sound by 12.30am.

OPERATIONAL SUMMARY - JANUARY 1944

Date	Target	Desp	E/R	FTR	Remarks
1/2	BERLIN	15	1	-	
2/3	BERLIN	12	1	2	F/O Young FTR F/L Palmer FTR
5/6	STETTIN	6	-	-	
	POMERANIAN BAY	5	-	-	
14/15	BRUNSWICK	9	-	1	F/L Tancred FTR
20/21	BERLIN	12	-	-	
21/22	BERLIN	2	-	-	
	MAGDEBURG	10	1	-	
27/28	BERLIN	13	2	1	P/O Barnes FTR
28/29	BERLIN	11	-	-	
30/31	BERLIN	13	-	-	

Total of sorties flown	108
Failed to return	4

Fiskerton Watch Office (Control tower) on the evening of 2/3 January 1944.
It is shortly before midnight and 'Passout' control are busy dispatching 12 Lancasters to Berlin from a snow cleared runway.
At 23.46 hrs F/O Johnny Young RCAF and crew took-off in Bandlaw N-Nan.
At 23.55 hrs F/LT Johnny Palmer and crew departed in Bandlaw S-Sugar. Both crews failed to return.
Standing on the left is F/Lt L Bone; seated is Cpl Brown WAAF and to her right is AC1 K G Clarke.
(49 Sqdn collection)

FEBRUARY 1944

For the first two weeks of February, bad weather and a full moon prevented any operations being flown. The squadron was limited to some local flying and H2S training. Crews were alerted for an operation on the 13th but this was cancelled in the late afternoon. The following day the squadron was stood down, but at 10.00hrs on Tuesday 15th February orders came through detailing 18 aircraft for Berlin.

15/16 February, 1944; BERLIN: As before, this enforced 'rest period' enabled Bomber Command to re-equip its battle-depleted squadrons; the result was the largest number of aircraft ever sent to Berlin. A force of 826 bombers, including the new Mk III Halifaxes, set out on the northern route over Denmark bound for the German capital. W/Cmdr Adams put together a scratch crew and borrowed A-Able to lead the squadron away from Fiskerton. Two new crews were also flying, F/Sgt Greig's (ND536) in F-Fox and P/O Clark's (ND492) in R-Roger. They, like the rest of the attacking force found Berlin as usual blanketed by cloud. A total of 2,642 tons of bombs was dropped mainly in the centre and south-western parts of the city.

The small diversionary attack on Frankfurt failed to draw the fighters away and as a result 26 Lancasters and 17 Halifaxes along with their crews were lost. Fortunately all of 49 Squadron's Lancasters returned to base unscathed. For one lucky crew, this was their final operation of a tour that began back in August 43 and included 10 trips to Berlin: F/Lt Eric Hidderley (JB399) and crew left their faithful H-Harry in the trusted hands of 'A' Flight's groundcrew and said their goodbyes to 49 Squadron. Note: JB399 would soldier on with the squadron until being retired in October 44 having 'survived' a long and distinguished career.

19/20 February, 1944; LEIPZIG: If the previous raid had been relatively quiet for the squadron then the Leipzig trip proved to be quite the opposite. Again Bomber Command put up over 800 aircraft, but this time as they crossed the Dutch coast the German night-fighters were waiting, and a running battle ensued all the way to the target. False wind forecasts had many aircraft reaching the target area too early; W/Cmdr Adams (JB466) had to orbit three times and Lt Stevens (ND474) twice. S/Ldr Miller (JB314) returned early in Q-Queenie with generator problems but on landing gave the following report: *"Sky above the North Sea was filled with a/c flying in all directions - some wiser ones with navigation lights on, most without - three a/c seen to explode in air, probably due to collision."*

GERMAN HITCH-HIKER

F/O Bill Healey RCAF (JB679) and crew, flying D-Dog also returned early with a collision report, but this time it was between his kite and that of a German aircraft! A sudden jar shuddered through D-Dog; looking out along the port main plane, Bill saw the shadowy shape of a Ju88 sitting on his wing tip with the German pilot clearly visible. The time was 02.01hrs and they were flying at 21,000ft. Within moments the Junkers fell away, taking ten feet of Lancaster wing with it.

F/O Healey fought for control as they lost height rapidly in a spiral dive. His crew watched as the German burst into flames as it crashed on the ground.

Struggling back to Fiskerton on 3 engines and a severely shortened wing, the Healey crew touched down at O3.39hrs. A daylight inspection revealed extensive damage with the port outer engine pushed askew and the airscrew bent beyond redemption. For his excellent display of airmanship, F/O Healey RCAF was awarded the DFC.

Meanwhile, over the target, P/O Ewens (JB714) and crew were engaged by another Ju88 during their bombing run. The two gunners, Sgt's Lee and Laws, managed to drive their attacker off and the bombs were successfully dropped *"on the residue of a 'Wanganui' flare."*

W/O Jupp (ND533) and crew in M-Mother dropped their bomb load on a concentration of 20 'Wanganui' flares but on leaving the target they were pounced upon by a night-fighter. Fortunately for the crew, but unfortunately for the German, Sgt Allwood in the rear turret was alert to the danger and the night-fighter was soon dispatched in flames. Sgt Briars, rear gunner in P/O Sander's (JB473) U-Uncle reported his turret u/s but the crew had insisted on continuing to the target and a trouble free trip was completed.

P/O J. Jones (ND473) and crew in O-Oboe reported being chased by *"some queer sort of rocket shells believed to be controlled by radio."*

The losses suffered by Bomber Command on this night were horrendous -78 aircraft and crews, which included 44 Lancasters and 34 Halifaxes; this figure represented 9.5 per cent of the force. The Halifax IIs and Vs would never be asked to operate over Germany again following this raid.

The squadron started arriving back over Fiskerton just before breakfast on Sunday morning. U-Uncle was the last to land at 07.40hrs, and it soon became clear that two aircraft were missing: Of these, P/O McKenzie (ND516), pilot of N-Nan, along with the bomb aimer and navigator survived after being brought down over Germany, but sadly the remainder of the crew perished and are buried together in the Berlin War cemetery. Also reported missing were 21 year-old pilot, F/Sgt Ed White (JB469) and crew who were all killed when B-Baker was shot down; they are buried together in Hannover War Cemetery with the exception of Sgt James Ellis the W/Op, who sadly has no known grave but is remembered at Runnymede.

FTR JB469	F/S E. White	Pilot	(Killed)
(EA-B)	Sgt J.R. Ward	F/E	(Killed)
'A Flt'	SGT W.W. S. Compton	NAV	(Killed)
	Sgt J.E. Ellis	W/OP	(Missing)
	Sgt D.N. Stevens	A/G	(Killed)
Crew on their	Sgt J.T. Loveland	B/A	(Killed)
4th operation	Sgt H. Thomas	A/G	(Killed)

FTR ND516	P/O A.J. McKenzie	Pilot	(P.o.W.)
(EA-N)	Sgt W.S. Purdie	F/E	(Killed)
'B Flt'	Sgt C.T. Critchley	NAV	(P.o.W.)
	F/S G. Hobby	W/AG	(Killed)
	Sgt K.A. Archer	A/G	(Killed)
Crew on their	Sgt T.A. Stevens	B/A	(P.o.W.) Died in captivity 11.5.'44
4th operation	Sgt A.C. Grems	A/G	(Killed)

W/Cmdr Alex Adams (third from left in peaked cap) chats with P/O John 'Jock' Simpson before being introduced to his crew, and the ground crew who service his allotted Lanc ND383 E-Easy. On the far left of the picture is OC 'A' Flt, S/Ldr Jim Evans, who most unusually was a navigator; he succeeded S/Ldr Graham Day. The Simpson crew consisted of: Denis Hiscock, Nav (fourth from left); Frank Wheeler, B/A; Bob Mower, F/Eng; Arthur Highman, W/Op; Colin Winterborn, R/G; Dennis 'Johnny' Walker, M/U. (Denis Hiscock)

Zoe Stocks (nee Haine)

20/21 February, 1944; STUTTGART: Crews returning from Leipzig hadn't even retired for a well earned sleep before Group was requesting 15 Lancs for that night's raid on Stuttgart. Just before midnight that Sunday evening, as sleet showers made conditions miserable and dicey, P/O Tudor Jones (JB701) hauled the first of those 15 Lancaster away from Fiskerton.

WHATS COOKING?

Twelfth aircraft away that wintry night was piloted by P/O Frank Clarke. As ND498 reached flying speed, the aircraft began to 'swing' off the runway. In an effort to regain control the undercarriage collapsed and R-Roger scraped along the runway on her belly in a shower of sparks. In seconds, the crew had evacuated the wreck safely as fire soon took hold. Despite strenuous efforts by the crash crews, the fire could not be brought under control and the area was cleared. Because of the 4,000lb 'cookie' onboard, station personnel and villagers were warned of an imminent explosion. R-Roger's 'cookie' eventually cooked! and the resulting spectacular bang scattered bits of Lancaster and concrete runway as far as Sudbrooke Park, well over a mile away. The remaining 3 Lancasters still on the ground had to abort.

The 11 aircraft of the squadron that had managed to become airborne (including a new crew piloted by P/O Ball (JB680) in P-Peter) climbed through 10/10ths cloud to join 587 other aircraft bound for Germany.

Diversion and support operations managed to draw away the fighters for at least two hours with the result that only 9 aircraft failed to return, although a further 5 crashed back in England. Over Stuttgart, 1st wave aircraft managed to bomb the 'Paramatta' ground markers, but as the raid progressed 'Wanganui' flares had to be added.

ALAN MORGAN, FLIGHT ENGINEER

Flying in K-King, P/O Jack Lett (JB421) and crew made a successful attack dropping their bombs from 23,500ft in the 4th wave. Sgt Alan Morgan, the aircraft's flight engineer gives this account of what happened next:

"Shortly after leaving the target the main entrance door blew open. Sgt Campbell the wireless operator was sent back to try and deal with it. After a while, the skipper instructed me to go back and see if I could help. I found the W/OP had passed out from lack of oxygen but I managed to connect him up to the supply at the rest bed and he soon regained consciousness. The skipper then told me to carry on with the attempt to close the rear door. I also passed out when my emergency oxygen bottle expired. At the time I was close to the open rear door with an outside temperature of minus 42 degrees. My skipper sensed that something had gone wrong and reduced height from 22,000ft down to 10,000ft whilst the bomb aimer Sgt Mackew, came to my assistance.

We made an emergency landing at Ford and from there I was taken to Chichester Hospital for treatment on my badly frost-bitten hands. Jack and the rest of the crew flew back to Fiskerton with the bomb aimer acting as flight engineer. As they circled Fiskerton in the daylight they could see the wreckage of ND498 on the runway.

The other returning Lancs had been diverted to Dunholme Lodge, but Fiskerton gave Jack special permission to land, for on their beds back in the billets were the crews' first 14 day leave passes... mine was not collected. Gangrene soon set in, and I was transferred to East Grinstead where all my fingers were amputated, and over the next 12 months I was under the care of Sir Arcibald McIndoe. (Alan had now become a member of the now famous 'Guinea Pig Club'). After treatment, I was put in front of a special medical board which I passed with flying colours returning to flying duties with the Empire Navigation School at Shawbury in May 1945. There I flew as flight engineer on Mk III Halifaxes taking advanced navigators to Gibraltar and various other stations until I was de-mobbed later that year.

After the war, I made a living as a skilled Jig Borer and tool maker, and have led a full life all thanks to the skill of Sir Archibald."

Alan married his childhood sweetheart and has two sons, one is now a dental surgeon, the other a chartered engineer. He is an active member of the Guinea Pig Club and a proud member of the 49 Squadron Association who in turn are very proud to have such a member.

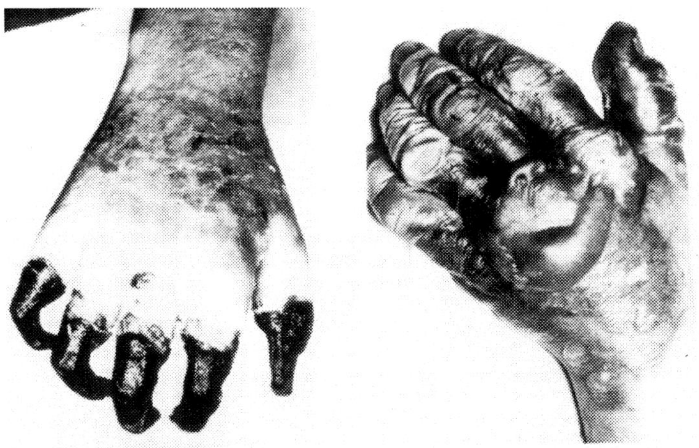

The hands of Alan Morgan, flight engineer, after suffering frost bite on the night of 20/21-2-44 Stuttgart. (A. Morgan)

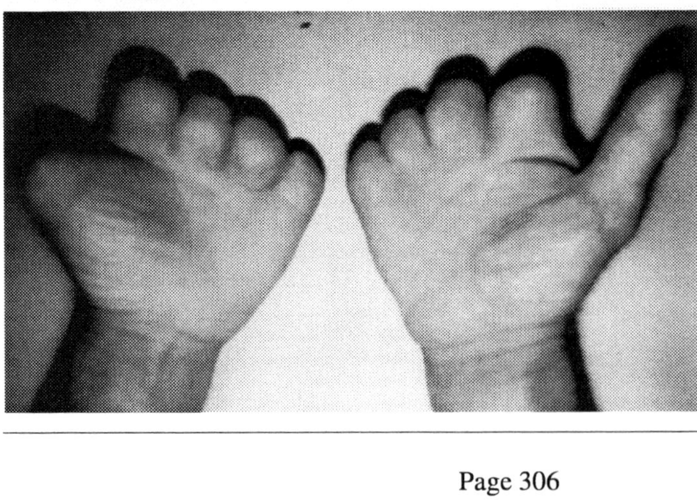

Alan Morgan's hands today. (A. Morgan)

During this period of operations, several crews reported being attacked by 'rocket' type projectiles; probably fired air to air from German night fighters. This splendid contemporary drawing was sketched by wireless operator Arthur Highman (P/O Simpson's crew), at Fiskerton, shortly after his crew's encounter with one of these missiles. (D. Hiscock)

24/25 February, 1944; SCHWEINFURT: For the two days following the Stuttgart raid, Bomber Command was 'stood down'. On Wednesday 23, 16 aircraft had been detailed for ops but were cancelled shortly after lunch. Runway repairs at Fiskerton (caused by P/O Clarke's crash) had not yet been completed, so the squadron's aircraft had remained at Dunholme Lodge where they had landed following the Stuttgart trip.

On Thursday morning orders came through for an attack on Schweinfurt. This was the first time Bomber Command had been ordered to attack Germany's main ball-bearing factories, and it followed a B-17 raid made by the USAAF the previous day. A new tactic was also introduced whereby the main force was split in two, with 2 hours separating each wave. German fighters were drawn up for the first wave, which suffered the loss of 22 aircraft; the second wave lost only 11 aircraft.

Take-off from Dunholme Lodge by 5 'first wave' Lancasters of 49 Squadron started at 18.30hrs. They were led away by F/O Adams and crew who were just beginning their second tour of operations; two hours later a further 11 aircraft from the squadron became airborne. Dunholme was home to No 44 Squadron and they too were flying on this operation. A total force of 734 bombers headed towards southern Germany.

MOSQUITO BITES

W/O Trevor Jupp (ND533) lifted M-Mother away from Dunholme at 20.19hrs, gaining height gradually as they headed south.

The aircraft's navigator was Johnny Chaloner; formerly with the Webb crew. Johnny had a few more trips to do to complete his tour. He had managed to secure a place in the experienced Jupp crew, who were on their 22nd trip, an operation they were destined not to complete, Johnny explains why:

"There was a German air raid going on around London and southern England as we passed over; we were at 14,000 feet and still climbing. About 15 miles north of Brighton we got tangled up in our own searchlights. I had just called the bomb aimer to come up from the nose to help operate the H2S, which he did somewhat reluctantly, when suddenly we were hit with three consecutive bursts of fire; the time was 23.18hrs. The gunners reported it to be a Mosquito, a 'friendly fighter

We soon fired off the colours of the day and the attack discontinued. By now the cabin was full of the smell of cordite; a cannon shell had severed the pilots oxygen tube and shattered the P4 compass alongside him. The elevator controls were hit and there were many other damaging strikes. I think the bomb aimer (Sgt Darnton), must still be congratulating himself to this day that he came up to operate the H2S after he saw the damage around the position he had occupied only minutes before the attack. We were losing height as we staggerd across London (the air raid was still going on) and received the attention from an A.A. barrage as we carried on our way to dump our bombs in the Wash.

We landed on Wittering's long grass runway without brakes or flaps and with bomb doors open at 00.24hrs. The next morning when we went out to inspect our aircraft we found a B-17 parked alongside. Its nose had been blown away, and the cockpit was splashed and dripping with the blood and remains of the unfortunate bomb aimer.

When we got back to base during the afternoon, we found we were on ops that night, Augsburg!"

W/O Jupp received the DFC for his actions this night.

The actual main force bombing of Schweinfurt suffered from undershooting, which lessened the effectiveness of the attack. The two new crews of Sgt Shinn (JB178) and S/Ldr Woodroffe (ND537) both completed successful sorties. P/O Jones (JB701) and crew in G-George had combat with a JU88, which the rear gunner, Sgt Jennings, managed to destroy. F/O Don Bacon (JB680) piloting P-Peter reported seeing many combats en-route to the target; the crew's bomb aimer, P/O Fitch, narrowly missed injury when a piece of flak smashed through his panel. All of the squadron's aircraft returned safely to Fiskerton.

S/Ldr Jimmy Evans commanded 'A' Flt during this period, a very unusual appointment as he was a navigator. He was to fly the rest of his tour with the second tour crew captained by F/O Jack Adams; it was whilst on this crew that S/Ldr Evans earned his DFC.

25/26 February, 1944; AUGSBURG: The squadron had been briefed three times for this 'new' aircraft factory target, but each time bad weather had caused a last minute cancellation. But on Friday evening, 25th February a total force of nearly 600 bombers set out for Augsburg. Once again the main force was split into two waves; Fiskerton's contribution consisted of 9 Lancasters in the first wave and a further 5 in the second wave.

This proved to be a raid of outstanding success, as in the clear night, very accurate Pathfinder ground-markers were easily spotted by the heavies. The centre of Augsburg old town was completely gutted and over 85,000 people were bombed out of their homes. Bomber Command suffered the loss of 21 aircraft and crews. The airmen of 49 Squadron completed their sorties successfully, but not without a certain amount of drama:

FRIEND OR FOE?

P/O John Sanders (JB473) and crew were attacked by an enemy fighter shortly after crossing the enemy coast. The aircraft received numerous hits, but the crew decided to press on. During the approach to the target they were on the receiving end of a burst of fire from what appeared to be, an over-enthusiastic Lancaster gunner! The friendly tracer caused severe damage making large holes in the fuselage, rudder and elevator, setting fire to U-Uncle, just forward of the rear turret. The pilot and flight engineer Tom Nutley, desperately fought for control of the plunging aircraft. In the rear both gunners, Ralph Briars and Roy Machin with the help of the wireless operator Arthur Ward managed to put out the flames as bullets exploded all around them. Despite this damage and with the inter-com rendered u/s, the crew pressed on and bombed the target.

It was a very battered Lancaster that brought the crew safely back to Fiskerton. The skipper commended his crew for their prompt action and 'perfect discipline' under trying circumstances. P/O John Alfred Sanders aged 25, who hailed from Birmingham, received an immediate DFC for his actions; Sgts Briars, Machin and Ward all received immediate DFM's. The crew transferred to 617 Squadron the following month, where they completed a distinguished tour of operations.

FEBRUARY 1944

Guns 'icing up' were a serious problem for F/Lt Woodroffe and crew flying ND537. They received four separate attacks from a night fighter and the frustrated gunners, Sgt's Lewis and Noall, could only put in one short burst of fire. Fortunately the crew survived the encounter and a successful sortie was carried out. All of the unit's aircraft returned safely with F/O Adams (ND516) the last to land at 05.08hrs.

Snow blizzards swept across Lincolnshire on Sunday 27th, and despite a major effort to clear the runways, operations on Monday were finally cancelled.

OPERATIONAL SUMMARY - FEBRUARY 1944

Date	Target	Desp	E/R	FTR	Remarks
15/16	BERLIN	18	-	-	
19/20	LEIPZIG	15	2	2	F/S White FTR P/O Mckenzie FTR
20/21	STUTTGART	11	-	1c	P/O Clarke crashed on take-off, Fiskerton
24/25	SCHWEINFURT	16	1	1c	W/O Jupp cr/landed at Wittering
25/26	AUGSBURG	14	--		Operation flown from Dunholme Lodge
Total of sorties flown		74			
Failed to return		2 + 2c			

Air Sea Rescue

MARCH 1944

When dawn broke on Wednesday 1 March, it revealed the peaceful scene of a snow-covered countryside as far as the eye could see. But by 10.00hrs the teleprinters from Group had been busy, giving details of the evening's planned operation. Everyone on the station was soon put to work clearing the main runway.

1/2 March, 1944; STUTTGART: Shortly after 23.00hrs on a bitterly cold evening, 13 of the squadron's Lancasters including W/Cmdr Adams (JB466), cautiously manoeuvred their way around to the take-off point. Each Lancaster in turn pointed its blunt nose into the freezing 40mph wind before thundering past the smaller than usual knot of well wishers by the control caravan. All became safely airborne, the white landscape still clearly visible despite the hour, as they laboured hard towards thick cloud.

The thick cloud persisted over Stuttgart and spoilt much of the Pathfinders' work, but the bad conditions did help hamper the German fighters' efforts with the result that only 4 of the 557 bombers were lost.

When the squadron returned over Fiskerton it was daylight. The strenuous efforts of the previous day's snow clearing were plain to see with the stark slash of concrete runway standing out in sharp contrast to the white carpet surrounding it. All 13 aircraft were back safely with P/O Ball (ND473) in O-Oboe the last to land at 08.06hrs.

10/11 March, 1944; OSSUN: Bad weather had once again forced a respite in operations, although the squadron did receive briefings on several occasions. During one evening crews even had their engines running before a red flare arched its way into a sleet-laden night sky 'scrubbing' the operation.

On Friday morning 10 March, new operational details came down from Group. Word soon got around the Flight Office that it was a to be a 'special' do. At briefing there was a buzz of anticipation as the target was revealed -Ossun, in the south of France; it was an experimental airfield and factory and 52 Base, (44 Squadron at Dunholme and 49 at Fiskerton) were each to dispatch 12 aircraft to destroy it. The 24 Lancasters were to be led by S/Ldr Miller with F/Lt Adams as his Deputy and F/Lt Don Bacon was to act as support (all three 49ers). Bombing height to be 8,000 feet, and take-off was set for 20.00hrs.

In the misty conditions of last light, W/O Trevor Jupp (ND647) and crew lifted the first Lancaster away from Fiskerton bound for France. The lightly defended target nestled on the edge of the Pyrenees Mountains, which in the moonlight, could be seen covered in snow. At five-minutes to midnight bombs started to fall from the 12 Lancasters of 49 Squadron which made up the first wave. S/Ldr 'Dusty' Miller RNZAF, with W/Cmdr Adams as second pilot, and flying his favourite aircraft 'Q' Queenie JB314, orchestrated the raid using R/T. The attack proved to be a complete success as these short extracts from the interrogation reports clearly show:

ND512 F/Lt Adams - *"Identified target visually and by H2S. Considered good effort, debris rising a considerable height".*

JB466 P/O Roantree - *"Bombed visually, 4 lanes of red glows seen when leaving the target, buildings were on fire".*

JB679 F/O Healey - *"Bomb bursts could be seen right on target, no sign of defences at target".*

ND383 P/O Simpson - *"Raid seemed pretty good".*

JB399 P/O Dickinson - *"Believed to be a good prang".*

JB701 P/O Lett - *"Debris at 4000ft, considered successful effort".*

ND647 W/O Jupp - *"Bomb aimer saw his bombs hit factory".*

ND537 P/O Jones J. - *"Factory buildings well hit, v/g prang".*

JB680 F/Lt Bacon - *"Every evidence of heavy damage being done"*

JB314 S/Ldr Miller - *"A very successful trip".*

ME675 Lt Stevens - *"Good quiet trip with apparently good results".*

ND684 P/O Sanders - *"Several sticks seen on the drome and hits seen of other bombs right on building".*

All aircraft from both squadrons returned safely; F/Lt Don Bacon and crew in P-Peter the last to touch down at 04.26hrs.

15/16 March, 1944 -STUTTGART: A large force of 863 bombers flew across France, almost to the Swiss border before turning north to approach Stuttgart.

SHEFFIELD STARS!

Fiskerton played host to the press for this operation. The 'Sheffield Star' sent a reporter and thankfully a cameraman (49 being Sheffield's own squadron) to cover a 'typical' raid. It resulted in several priceless shots of 49 Squadron preparing to go - and returning from an operation. Most of the press proofs printed here were thankfully rescued by Ken Gibson from a waste bin at Fiskerton! For me personally, their content (despite the variable quality) is both dramatic and moving. In a squadron where photography was especially frowned upon, when Ken first showed me the negatives, they came as a true revelation... a very special moment.

Fiskerton, 15 March 1944: Outside the locker rooms, awaiting the bus for Stuttgart! Amongst these smiling faces are several that would not see the war out. One of the lucky ones is mid/upper gunner Fred Wood (extreme left); Fred now lives happily with his wife in Fiskerton village. By contrast, standing next to Fred and giving the broadest of grins to the cameraman, is rear gunner Al Richards RCAF; less than a month after this photo, his broken body, and those of his fellow crew members (F/Lt Bacon's) lay dead in a Belgium meadow. (Ken Gibson)

Fiskerton, 15 March 1944: Again outside the locker rooms.
Extreme left is diarist John Hennessey, F/E; next to him is Pete Monk, W/Op and then Stan Weedon, M/U gunner.
As members of Don Bacons crew, all three were killed less than a month later 11/12-4-44, victims of 'The Ghost of St Trond'.
(Ken Gibson)

Fiskerton, 15 March 1944: The time is 19.04hrs on a dull Wednesday evening and W/Cmdr A.A.Adams 'Triple A', in the company of 'The Star' reporter, Ernest Taylor waves off the first of 18 Lancs bound for Stuttgart -P/O RoantreeJB466.
(Ken Gibson)

MORE GERMAN NIGHT FIGHTERS UP
SHEFFIELD'S 'OWN' PLANES RAIDED STUTTGART

Sheffield's "own" bombers of the 49th Bomber Squadron. the squadron "adopted" by Sheffield, were among the aircraft which attacked Stuttgart last night.

After watching the bombing up of the machines during the afternoon when I visited their aero-drome with Mr E Gooseman, Editor of "The Star," I saw the cheerful crews take off on their long journey (writes Ernest Taylor).

As each plane passed the airfield controller's cabin, the men returned the "thumbs-up" signal given to them by Wing Commander A A Adams, the squadron commander.

Early today the aircraft began to return after an all round trip of about eight hours. The crew buses were waiting to take them to the crew room for interrogation immediately they landed.

Many of the crews weree glad of the opportunity to stretch their legs after being in the air for so long.

Enjoying their mugs of hot tea- it had been very cold on the trip- they told their stories of what they had seen on the operation.

MORE FIGHTERS UP

Most of them agreed that there had been more German fighters up than on recent trips.

There were stories of several combats with fighters, and the mid-upper gunner and rear gunner of one machine piloted by F/Lt Healey D.F.C., claimed to have shot down a Hu 88.

The German fighter was seen burning on the gorund after it was sent spinning down in flames. The same crew had an encounter with another fighter before they reached the target.

PLENTY OF FIRES

Sergeant Philip Griffiths, who lives in James Street, Rotherham, told me that theirs was one of the first machines over the target.

"We saw plenty of fighter flares but the Germans did not trouble us much," he said. They saw plenty of fires burning as they looked back on their way home.

Griffiths oxygen bottle gave out while on the outward journey, but the rear gunner managed to plug him into another supply just as he was about to pass out.

Sergeant Air Gunner Roy Machin, of the Union Inn, Doncaster Road, Mexborough, described it as "The sort of trip I Like."

They experienced no opposition.

HEAVY FLAK

"Smoke was coming up to a height of between 10,000 and 15,000 feet when we left, and there appeared to be plenty of fires," said Sergeant Navigator Douglas Rolfe, of Fitzalan Road, Handsworth, Sheffield.

Squadron Leader D Miller, D.F.C., a New Zealander who married Miss Marjorie Smith, of Morthennear Thurcroft, just over a year ago, commented on the Germans sending up more fighters than usual.

The flak was also heavy over the target.

With interrogation over, the crews had a breakfast of bacon and eggs before going to their quarters to rest.

FLYING HONOURS FOR CITY MEN

Two Sheffield airmen are included in the latest list of awards for gallantry and devotion to duty in the execution of air operations.

They are; Pilot Officer Denys Taunton, aged 23,who reveives the D.F.C. and Sergeant Reginald Jeffcock, aged 21, who receives the D.F.M.

Pilot Officer Taunton is a former pupil of Firth Park Grammar School, Sheffield. He served in the ranks before being commissioned in 1943.

Sergeant Jeffcock is the son of Mr and Mrs J Jeffcock of 312, Stannington Road, Malin Bridge, Sheffield. He has taken part in many bombing trips over enemy-occupied territory, including raids on Berlin.

CITY HERO WILL NOT TALK

Warrant Officer R Jeffcock, son of Mr an Mrs J Jeffcock, of 312 Stannington Road, Sheffield, recently received the D.F.M. at an investiture at Buckingham Palace. His parents, who also attended the investiture, do not know how their son won the reward. He will not tell them.

49 Squadron was at maximum effort putting up 18 Lancasters including the new crews of F/O Colhoun (ND383), P/O Waugh (ND474) and P/O Montgomery (JB399). High winds over the target caused many problems for the PFF and despite clear conditions the markers and bombing were well scattered, much falling in open countryside.

In the early hours of Thursday morning the first returning squadron Lancaster called up 'Passout' control for permission to land; it was the distinctive Canadian drawl of F/O Bill Healey in 'Bandlaw Dog'; the time was approaching 02.30hrs. During the next hour, villagers throughout Lincolnshire would have their slumber disturbed by scores of Merlin engines, as hundreds of Lancasters returned home.

Fierce combats with night-fighters around the target had accounted for many of the 37 bombers that failed to return, but now, back over the eastern counties with so many aircraft in such limited air-space, another danger was ever present - collision!

It is shortly after 3am on Thursday 16 March 1944 on Fiskerton airfield. A Sheffield newspaper reporter catches Russ Ewens and crew disembarking from JB714 Bandlaw J-Jig back from Stuttgart. They are (from l to r), Sgt Doug Tritton, flight engineer; Sgt Maurice Laws, air gunner; P/O Russ Ewens, pilot; Sgt Joe Pitcher, navigator; Sgt Phil Griffiths, wireless operator, in doorway (from Rotherham); F/O Bob Grainger, bomb aimer. The Ewens crew successfully completed their tour. (D.C. Tritton)

P/O Clive Roantree RAAF (JB466) clearly recalls the events of that early morning:

"The weather was reasonably clear over England and it was easy to see the perimeter lights of neighbouring airfields as we approached base. There were no delays and we took our place, turned in and called our position in the funnel, when ahead of us in the direction of Waddington there was a terrific explosion. It was obvious that two bombers had collided and the flash of the explosion was followed by a fire that seemed to hang in the air... it was devastating!"

The two Lancasters involved were from two different squadrons; E-Easy of 463 Squadron RAAF flown by F/Sgt Graham (ED606) and crew were orbiting their Waddington base when they were struck by (ND637) L-Love of 625 Squadron, making its way back to Kelstern on the Lincolnshire Wolds. Wreckage fell near the villages of Branston and Heighington, south east of Lincoln; there were no survivors.

Back at Fiskerton, the new crew of P/O Thomas Waugh was sadly posted as missing. The 23 year-old pilot and crew are buried in a collective grave at the Durnback War Cemetery.

It is approaching 4am on March 16, and in Fiskerton's Operations room (opposite the main gate), the Roantree crew are being debriefed following the Stuttgart raid.
Pilot, Clive Roantree, is seated centre facing the camera; in a clockwise direction are: standing Jock Lowrie; seated Ken Nelson; Joe Franks; Paddy Paddick; Jack Grimshaw and John Peaker.
(K. Gibson)

FTR ND474	P/O T.W. Waugh	Pilot	(Killed)
(EA-T)	Sgt R. Hoole	F/E	(Killed)
'B Flt'	F/S T.C. McEneaney	NAV	(Killed)
	Sgt W.E. Hardy	WOP	(Killed)
	Sgt D.B. Birbeck	A/G	(Killed)
Crew on their	F/O J.J. Knowles	A/B	(Killed)
1st operation	Sgt J.G. Wise	A/G	(Killed)

18/19 March, 1944; FRANKFURT: Pathfinders marked the target accurately and the bombs from over 800 Lancasters and Halifaxes fell on the eastern, central and western districts of Frankfurt causing heavy damage. Night fighters did manage to infiltrate the bomber stream just before it reached the target; a total of 22 aircraft failed to return.

All of Fiskerton's 16 Lancasters returned unscathed, although F/Lt Woodroffe (ND512) did report an inconclusive combat with a night fighter.

22/23 March, 1944; FRANKFURT: Frankfurt again, and 49 Squadron managed to get 19 airborne but P/O J.Jones (ND473) with P/O Kellow as 2nd pilot had to return early with their port outer engine u/s.

The accurate PFF marking and bombing by over 800 aircraft ensured that Frankfurt suffered yet another heavy blow. At the post-op interrogation W/Cmdr Adams (ME675) reported: *"Congestion fairly severe mainly at 2 turning points next to target. Excellent raid if PFF was on target."*

Diversions had confused the Germans, who at first forecast Hannover as the target, but a few night-fighters did manage to find the bomber stream and 26 Lancasters and 7 Halifaxes failed to return.

Again Fiskerton had suffered losses when two crews were posted missing; F/O Donald Turner (survivor of Chapel-St-Leonards beach crash Nov 43) and crew (except Sgt Velasco A/G who became a PoW) were sadly all killed.

Left: Sgt Linton H. Nightingale, wireless operator/air gunner in F/O Don Turner's crew -KIA 22/23-3-44. (E.J. Nightingale)

Right: F/Sgt Kenneth Anderson, navigator in F/Sgt Ron Greig's crew - KIA 22/23-3-44. (John A. Rose)

F/Sgt Ron Greig and crew also all perished; both crews are buried in the Reichswald Forest Cemetery. Two members of the Greig crew had very nearly completed their tours; F/Sgts Whiteley and Peacock had previously flown with P/O Eric Jones and had only a few more trips left to do.

FTR ND536	F/S R. Greig	Pilot	(Killed)
(EA-U)	Sgt W.F. Edwards	F/E	(Killed)
'B Flt'	F/S K. Anderson	NAV	(Killed)
	F/S C. Peacock	W/AG	(Killed)
	P/O O.R. Rogers RAAF	A/G	(Killed)
Most of crew on	F/S L.J. Phillips	A/B	(Killed)
their 7th op.	F/S H. Whiteley	A/G	(Killed)
FTR ND672	F/O D.G. Turner	Pilot	(Killed)
(EA-F)	Sgt E. Lee	F/E	(Killed)
'A Flt'	F/S S.J. Upton	NAV	(Killed)
	Sgt L.H. Nightingale	W/AG	(Killed)
	Sgt P. Velasco	A/G	(P.o.W.)
Crew on their	F/O W. Pearce	A/B	(Killed)
4th operation	F/S J.N.E. Bennet RCAF	A/G	(Killed)

24/25 March, 1944; BERLIN: After a lapse of five weeks Bomber Command decided that Berlin could do with 'topping up'. Not for the first time incorrect wind forecasts scattered the bomber stream; over the target these strong winds carried the PFF markers out to the south western suburbs of Berlin.

Of the 811 aircraft that set out for Berlin, 17 were from 49 Squadron; P/O Simpson (ND383) was forced to return early in E-Easy with engine trouble and landed at Spilsby.

Over Berlin and on their bombing run, F/O Jack Lett (JB695) and crew in B-Baker were showered with incendiaries from an aircraft above; one went through the port main plane leading edge causing the wing to catch fire. The port-inner engine had to be feathered and the pilot, with great skill and determination put his Lancaster into a steep dive which extinguished the flames.

P/O Bob Montgomery (JB421) and crew were attacked twice by fighters; in one attack the gunners, Sgt Mitchell and F/Sgt Baker claimed a Ju88 as damaged.

On the homeward flight P/O Clark (ND674) and crew were flying near Osnabrück at 21,000ft when suddenly another Lancaster struck them from below; the rear wheel was ripped off and the rear turret severely damaged. Fortunately no injuries were sustained and a successful landing was made at Metheringham at 02.09hrs.

When reaching England there was sufficient fog to justify the use of FIDO. The glow from this could be seen in the sky for several miles. Perhaps this could account for a 101 Squadron Lancaster whilst requesting permission to land at his home base at Ludford Magna (also FIDO equipped), was actually making a wheels up emergency landing at Fiskerton, causing 7 of the squadron's Lancasters to be diverted to Waddington. Of the 811 aircraft dispatched, 72 failed to return plus two crashed in England. This terrible carnage prompted the following de-brief remarks from Bill Healey and crew, who had just completed their 19th operation:

"The hardest trip we have ever done! bombing pretty good but route really hard, many a/c seen being shot up in the Ruhr".

Shortly after the operation F/E John Hennessey (JB680) wrote the following account of the raid in his diary: *"There was mist hanging over the drome when we took-off to visit the 'big city' once more. As we rolled down the runway I could see we were not getting as much power as we could, but skip (F/Lt Don Bacon) just managed to pull her off in time. It was a deadly route for as soon as we crossed the coast of Denmark we ran into a belt of searchlights and saw four kites coned and two were shot down immediately. When we returned to base we found cloud down to the deck and we had to come in on 'FIDO'. The Air Vice Marshall and Air Commodore were at interrogation and we told them in no polite terms what we thought of the route. There was an MC on this raid, his remarks were really funny."*

This was the last major raid by the RAF on Berlin during the war and was eventually defined by historians as the final raid in the 'Battle of Berlin'. In the 16 raids on Berlin, the RAF had lost 441 Lancasters including 60 which crashed in the UK, and 122 Halifaxes including 12 that crashed in the UK; 4 Stirlings were lost in the early raids.

25/26 March, 1944; AULNOYE: Three of the squadron's aircraft were detailed to join a small force sent to attack this French railway yard. In the afternoon N-Nan cancelled, but shortly after 19.00hrs two Lancasters, each containing new crews set out from Fiskerton. Although the weather was clear, the Pathfinders did not mark accurately and most bombs fell wide of the target. Fortunately none of the 192 dispatched were lost, and at interrogation the 49 Squadron crews of P/O Cornish (JB514) and P/O Hodgson (JB399) both reported successful sorties with no opposition.

26/27 March, 1944; ESSEN: Harris surprised the German night fighters when he suddenly switched his attention to the Ruhr. Over 700 bombers set out on this Sunday evening led by 'Oboe' equipped PFF Mossies, which marked the target well. Subsequent reports confirmed that the raid had been successful and the loss of 9 aircraft and crews, represented just 1.3 per cent of the force.

When 49 Squadron crews reported for their post-operational interrogation they painted a different story as the following extracts illustrate;

F/Lt Bacon (ME675): *"Cloud on target prevented T/I's from being seen, impossible to aim bombs accurately."*

F/Lt Woodroffe (ND683): *"Appears to have been a waste of time as there were no markers to aim at when we arrived."*

P/O Ball (ND647): *"Cloud over target made it impossible to obtain accurate bombing."*

P/O Clarke (JB178): *"Cloud made observation impossible, disappointing sortie having to bomb on ETA."*

F/Lt Healey (JB679): *"No T/I's visible due to clouds, a waste of bombs and petrol."*

Of the 17 aircraft sent on this operation 15 made it safely home to Fiskerton although F/Lt Healey and crew were shot at by a fighter over the target, and P/O Dickinson (JB399) and crew had a large hole punched in the leading edge between the fuselage and starboard inner engine. P/O J. Jones (ND473) was slightly injured by a piece of shrapnel which pierced the perspex at the left of his cockpit.

One of the two overdue aircraft, P-Peter, failed to return and was presumed missing; in fact P/O Harold Hodgson age 22, and his crew had all been killed over Germany and are now buried in the Rheinberg War Cemetery. They were flying only their second trip having been to Aulnoye the night before.

The other Lancaster which failed to regain Fiskerton was that of P/O Bert Shinn (ND676) and crew in M-Mother; their story of determination and heroism begins over Essen: At the commencement of their bombing run over the target, they were attacked by an enemy night fighter. The bombs were jettisoned as cannon shells ripped into the rear of the aircraft; rear gunner, Sgt Armstrong battled the fire out after 15 long minutes. The damage sustained included both turrets u/s and the starboard inner and outer engines were practically powerless. During the dive the aircraft had lost 5,000 feet, but as they levelled out, flak or possibly the fighter hit them again; this time the intercom, hydraulics, H2S and Gee were all rendered destroyed. A check on the crew positions revealed that the navigator, Sgt Hague was wounded and the wireless operator, F/Sgt Herd was unconscious with head injuries.

Losing height with just two good engines and the controls very heavy, P/O Shinn somehow struggled back to England. Reaching the Norfolk coast and not knowing if his wireless operator was dead or alive, the pilot ordered his crew to bale out over Swanton Morley; the pilot then went on to make a wheels up crash landing at Coltishall. The pilot's decision to stay with his W/op had been fraught with many dangers. Despite the pilot's valiant effort, when Sgt Mervyn Herd RAAF, was removed from the aircraft, he had already lost his fight for life: It goes without saying that P/O Bert Shinn received an immediate DFC.

Note: Sgt Herd, who was 23 years old, is buried in Cambridge City Cemetery.

FTR JB680	P/O H.S. Hodgson	Pilot	(Killed)
(EA-P)	Sgt R.W. Beresford	F/E	(Killed)
'B Flt'	F/S P.H. Simonson RCAF	NAV	(Killed)
	Sgt C. Bailey	W/OP	(Killed)
	Sgt R. Millns	A/G	(Killed)
Crew on their	P/O G.E. Chute RCAF	A/B	(Killed)
2nd operation	Sgt W.P. Larvin	A/G	(Killed)

30/31 March, 1944; NUREMBERG: Much has already been written regards this operation in which for various reasons, Bomber Command suffered its biggest loss of the war; 31 Halifaxes and 64 Lancasters, 11.9 per cent of the force dispatched failed to return... but 49 Squadron records reveal two very differing stories! The unit's contribution to the night's proceedings involved 16 Lancasters; the first aircraft lifting away from Fiskerton at 21.55hrs.

The Dickinson crew (JB399), were the first to encounter trouble: At twelve minutes after midnight and about one hour before their ETA over the target, H-Harry flying at 21,000ft without warning received cannon strikes from a JU 88. The night fighter's accurate attack hit the No 2 port fuel tank, hydraulics and both turrets. For the next 8 minutes, P/O Dickinson continuously corkscrewed his Lancaster as his three gunners (Sgts Ellenor and Hudson plus an extra mid-upper gunner F/Sgt Edwards) engaged the enemy whilst giving their pilot instructions. Eventually the Lancaster escaped, but the damage received forced the crew to turn for home after first jettisoning their bombs near Bonn. A relieved crew touched down at Fiskerton at 02.42hrs. At interrogation, the pilot gave praise to his gunners; *"their patter throughout the attack was highly commendable."* For their part the gunners claimed the JU88 as damaged during the first burst.

P/O Jones (JB701) received head injuries when his Lancaster received flak damage near Stuttgart. The injured pilot and crew pressed on and completed their sortie without any further combats; the pilot later reported how well his crew behaved throughout.

P/O Cornish (JB473) and crew survived 2 combats with JU88s without sustaining any damage.

F/Lt Woodroffe (ND683) bombed the target at 01.20hrs from 20,000ft (confirmed on H2S); his interrogation remarks gave the first indication of heavy losses:
"Very poor route going so near the Ruhr, tons of Lancs got shot down there!"

These remarks were compounded by F/Lt Don Bacon's report:
"Many combats seen en route - at one time too many a/c going down in flames to log them all!"

Sadly two of those aircraft 'going down' were from the squadron: P/O Leslie Kellow (a Canadian in the RAF(VR) and crew were only on their first operation and were the 36th aircraft to be brought down. Mid-upper gunner, Sgt McAvoy survived from the burning Lancaster; with his face badly burned and crusted, he crawled around for two hours bumping into trees until villagers found him. He was then left in a coal cellar for twelve hours without any attention at all. Cold and in great pain he was placed in a cart with another injured airman; the other airman was in fact the crew's navigator, Sgt David Rowcliffe, who couldn't recognise Sgt McAvoy. At the local hospital, both received devoted nursing attention but sadly David Rowcliffe passed away the next day.

Sgt McAvoy underwent thirty surgical operations for his burns. The remaining five members of the crew had all died in the aircraft, and are buried alongside each other in Hannover War Cemetery.

F/O Bill Colhoun (JB466) from Belfast, piloted A-Able on the crew's 6th operation; a night fighter got them, the 64th to go down. Four members of the crew were killed and included F/O Colhoun and Sgt Leslie Broad who both have no known graves, plus New Zealander, F/Sgt Hector Anderson and Sgt Kenneth Ellam who are buried in Berlin.

The reports by the remaining nine other crews from the squadron surprisingly show this as just another routine trip giving reports such as *"a pretty good route"* and *"nothing of importance was experiened on the way home"* -survival of a bomber crew relied a great deal on experience and skill, but an extra large slice of luck was an important ingredient.

Returning in one of the 14 Lancasters that landed back at Fiskerton was diarist, John Hennessey; the entry in his diary for this his 22nd operation simply says: *"The greatest mistake the RAF has made; for we went to do the attack in moonlight. Fighters intercepted us as soon as we crossed the enemy coast and kites were being shot down all around us... 96 aircraft were missing from the operation -the greatest number yet lost in a single operation."* This is the very last entry in John's diary; next day he went home on leave to see his wife and baby son, returning to the squadron in time to fly the trip to Aachen from which his aircraft failed to return. Just eleven nights after returning from Nuremburg, Sgt John Hennessey F/E, and all his fellow crew members lay dead in a Belgium meadow amongst the wreckage of their shattered Lancaster bomber.

Missing JB314	P/O L.G. Kellow	Pilot	(Killed)
(EA-Q)	Sgt S.G. Silver	F/E	(Killed)
'B Flt'	Sgt D. Rowcliffe	NAV	(Killed)
	Sgt L.E. Walford	W/OP	(Killed)
	Sgt A.J. McAvoy	A/G	(P.o.W.)
Crew on their	Sgt T.C. Baker	B/A	(Killed)
1st operation	P/O J. Latham RCAF	A/G	(Killed)

MARCH 1944

Missing JB466	F/O W.A.L. Colhoun	Pilot	(Missing)
(EA-A)	Sgt A.W. Black	F/E	(P.o.W.)
'A Flt'	Sgt R. Prinn	NAV	(P.o.W.)
	Sgt K. Ellam	W/OP	(Killed)
	Sgt L.H. Broad	A/G	(Missing)
Crew on their	F/S H.W. Anderson RNZAF	B/A	(Killed)
6th operation	Sgt W.A. Simmons	A/G	(Killed)

OPERATIONAL SUMMARY - MARCH 1944

Date	Target	Desp	E/R	FTR	Remarks
1/2	STUTTGART	13	-	-	
10/11	OSSUN	12	-	-	49 Sqdn led operation
15/16	STUTTGART	18	-	1	'T' Sgt Waugh FTR
18/19	FRANKFURT	16	-	-	
22/23	FRANKFURT	19	1	2	'U' F/S Greig FTR 'F' F/O Turner FTR
24/25	BERLIN	17	1	-	Last Berlin operation
25/26	AULNOYE	2	-	-	
26/27	ESSEN	17	-	1 1c	'P' P/O Hodgson FTR 'M' P/O Shinn c/l
30/31	NUREMBURG	16	1	2	'Q' P/O Kellow FTR 'A' F/O Colhoun FTR

Total of sorties flown	130
Failed to return	6 + 1c
Tons of bombs dropped of all types	564.69
Operational hours flown March 1944	817hrs 10mins
Non-operational hours flown March 1944	469hrs 20mins

HONOURS AND AWARDS - MARCH 1944:

W.A. Healey RCAF DFC

APRIL 1944

Preparations for the Normandy invasion by Allied ground forces were continuing with haste, and Bomber Command aircraft would be required to play a very important role in this historic endeavour.

Bomber Command efforts would be directed at railway targets in France and Belgium with a view to isolating the German forces in Normandy, and preventing any reinforcements reaching the front-line by rail. By attacking targets in Normandy and the Pas de Calais area with equal strength, the Allies hoped that the Germans would be deceived into thinking the main landings would be 150 miles further up the coast from Normandy. At the time, aircrews were totally unaware of this massive deception in which they were taking part.

Raids would also take place on other military factories and establishments in France and Belgium in conjunction with the USAAF. Attacks were planned to continue after the invasion in support of the Allied ground forces. 'Bomber' Harris did have reservations about the ability of his bomber crews to hit small targets without injury or death to friendly civilians. In the event, Bomber Command was more accurate when hitting sensitive targets than anyone had ever hoped. Factors contributing to this success included the use of a Master Bomber and 5 Group's new marker force commanded by W/Cmdr Cheshire. But one essential contributing ingredient was the total commitment shown by main force aircrews to their highly demanding tasks. RAF Bomber Command aircrew and ground staff can feel enormously proud of their contributions towards the successful Normandy landings on D-Day, leading to the final liberation of Europe... and rightly so.

5/6 April, 1944; TOULOUSE: The attack on this aircraft repair plant situated near Blagna aerodrome in France, was a 5 Group only affair, using a force of 140 plus aircraft. Marking was carried out by 617 Squadron led by W/Cmdr Cheshire; AVM Cochrane gave permission for Cheshire to use a Mosquito for the first time in the low level marking role. Flying as navigator with W/Cmdr Cheshire was S/Ldr Pat Kelly, a former 49 Squadron navigator, who would later be killed in November 1944 after returning to 49 Squadron.

49...MAIN FORCE LEADERS

At Fiskerton, bad weather prevented 2 of the 12 Lancasters detailed from taking off. The Main Force bombers were headed by 49 Squadron with W/Cmdr Adams, S/Ldrs Adams and Miller acting as leaders. After bombing, S/Ldr Miller orbited the target at 7,500 feet, giving instructions over the R/T to the following 5 Group aircraft. The continuing bad weather over England prevented Fiskerton crews from returning to base; 8 landed at Middle Wallop, 1 at Wing and 1 at Boscombe Down.

S/Ldr Miller's interrogation report gives a conclusive assessment of the raid: *"Bombed 00.19hrs from 7,500ft -No cloud, vis 20 miles. Bombed factory building and green T.I. just off building. Route good -considered a highly successful operation".*

One Lancaster (from another squadron) failed to return.

APRIL 1944

V... FOR VICTORY?

With the combination of warmer spring weather and lighter nights, crews would sometimes spend their last moments on the ground outside their aircraft, prior to starting up for take-off. During this time, G/Cpt Grindell, the Station Commander, would take the opportunity of driving his car around the perimeter track and on passing each dispersal would wave and shout words of encouragement to the 'troops'. His clockwise journey took him firstly through 'A' flt then around onto the northern perimeter and 'B' flt., finally arriving at the main runway threshold, before parking near the control caravan; here he would park up, and wave to each Lancaster crew as they took off.

One evening, as dusk quietly descended upon Fiskerton airfield, Groupie's 'battle wagon' was heard approaching over the rise towards 'A flt's dispersals. Under the nose of their Lancaster, P/O Bob Montgomery and crew waited with baited anticipation. It must be mentioned that the Montgomery crew were not noted for their adherence to military regulations in either discipline or dress. As the G/Cpt's car drew nearer, Bob Montgomery, much to the puzzlement (and amazement) of the watching groundcrew, ordered his crew to line up and then brought them smartly to attention. As G/Cpt Grindell drove past their dispersal giving his cursory salutation, all seven members of the Montgomery crew, in unison bent forward, each giving the Group Captain a 'Churchillian' gesture.

Stunned and somewhat bemused, the G/Cpt's car swerved slightly before proceeding on around the perimeter. After his departure, both air and groundcrew fell about in fits of laughter. Their sounds of mirth mingled with the roar of many Merlins being readied, and the crew were still laughing as they clambered aboard their trusty Lanc... and went off to war. There can be little doubt that G/Cpt Grindell, on later reflection, viewed the whole incident in a jocular vein as was intended.

6 APRIL, 1944: ORDERS OF THE DAY:

'FROM THIS DATE ONWARDS ALL PRIVILEGE LEAVE IS CANCELLED'

Rumours of the impending invasion were rife!

9/10 April, 1944; MINELAYING - DANZIG/KÖNIGSBERG CANAL: Lancasters from 1 and 5 Groups were dispatched for minelaying in the Baltic; of the 103 aircraft sent, 9 were from 49. Using the Danzig force as a feint, 6 Lancasters from 5 Group separated to make a dangerous low-level attack in the Königsberg Canal; three crews were from 106 Squadron, Metheringham, the other three were from 49.

Fiskerton's task force consisted of those crews captained by P/O Roantree (ND792), Lt Stevens USAAF (ME675) and P/O Simpson (ND787).

The canal was known to be well used by U-boats, and a Naval Officer at briefing stressed the importance of this operation. During their trip, P/O Simpson and crew had a torrid time near the target as his de-brief report reveals: *"We were engaged accurately by half a dozen guns which forced us to zero feet, undercover of one of the islands - we were coned again and engaged by accurate flak causing us to abandon the effort."* Lt Stevens and crew made two runs but was unable to locate the canal.

The Roantree crew flew their new 'Bandlaw Able' along the canal at heights below 50 feet to successfully plant mines in the eastern half of the canal.

Meanwhile the Danzig force carried out their sorties with success, but not without a little drama. S/Ldr Miller and crew were attacked by two JU 88's whilst returning over Denmark but they escaped by flying into cloud. P/O Dickinson's crew also encountered fighters but they too managed to evade the enemy.

P/O Ball and crew were the last back to Fiskerton, with ND647 touching down just after 06.45hrs that Monday morning. Altogether 9 Lancasters of the 103 dispatched failed to return; 49's had all come safely home.

Note: 49 Squadron's de-brief report on the Königsberg attack was quite 'matter of fact', whilst the 106 Squadron report was most descriptive - as a result, the three 106 Squadron pilots all received immediate DFC's !

10/11 April, 1944; TOURS: Lancasters from 5 Group delivered an accurate attack on the railway yards at Tours. Fiskerton managed to get 11 aircraft airborne by 20.34hrs including four new crews piloted by;

P/O Green RNZAF	(ND473)	F/O Edwards	(ND537),
F/O Matheson RCAF	(LL899).	P/O Edgar	(JB178),

From the 180 Lancasters detailed, 1 aircraft failed to return; all 49's came back safely.

11/12 April, 1944; AACHEN: This was Aachen's most serious raid of the war and was delivered by 341 Lancasters led by 11 PFF Mosquitoes. The centre and southern parts of the town received heavy bombing and the air-raid services soon lost control.

Just 4 aircraft from 49 Squadron were detailed;

F/Lt Adams	(ND512),	P/O Shinn	(ND647),
F/Lt Bacon	(LL899)	S/Ldr Miller	(ME675).

A total of nine Lancasters were lost on the operation. One of those reported missing came from 49 Squadron. F/Lt Don Bacon and crew were highly experienced; having survived since November 43 including the Battle of Berlin, many on the unit felt sure they would pass the finishing post to complete an excellent tour. But luck always plays a part, and theirs ran out in the night sky over Belgium at the hands of night fighter ace Major Heinz-Wolfgang Schnaufer ('The Ghost of St Trond'); the Bacon crew was his 52nd victim.

'The Ghost of St Trond' - Major Heinz-Wolfgang Schnaufer and crew. Gunner Wilhelm Gansler is on his right and radar operator Fritz Rumpelhardt stands on his left. They were the only complete night fighter crew to be awarded Knight's Crosses.
(Eddy Coward)

In April, 1987 the following item appeared in a local Belgium newspaper:

'Last Monday, a group of English and Canadians paid a visit to Brecht. They were welcomed in the Lord Mayor's House by the Lord Mayor, Mr De Cremer and Alderman Janssens. There was a special reason for their visit, the group were all relatives of the crew members of the British Bomber that crashed during World War 11 in the community of St Lenaarts.

'It was about midnight, when the aircraft crashed in a field next to the farm of Jef Van Riel at Henxbroek, with an enormous explosion. There was a big fire, and all the remaining ammunition was exploding it was impossible to save any of the crew members. The next day at 6am, while letting out his cows, Jef Van Riel found one member of the crew who had jumped out of the aircraft. The body was found some distance from the wreckage and must have died instantly.

'Sometime ago a letter arrived at Brecht from Eddy Coward of Rayleigh in Essex, England. His elder brother Clifford, was the crew's navigator and Eddy was now researching the bomber's last fatal journey. Frans Laps from St Lenaarts went on researching, and asked for some help from Cyriel Verbist from Rijkevorsel, who had already written a book about his village during the war. Eddy Coward had succeeded in tracing the families of each crew member that were killed, which had taken him over 5 years of research.

'After the first contacts, they made plans to visit Belgium and see the place where the aircraft crashed, and also visit the seven graves at Schoonselhof. 'Yesterday, the English/Canadian group -there were two Canadians in the crew- arrived in Brecht and were welcomed by the Lord Mayor, who expressed his gratitude to the families for what their relatives had done for his country.

'Eddy Coward spoke and told the whole story of how the crew had taken off from Fiskerton in England, and after a successful bombing attack on Aachen, they were shot down by a German fighter. The very experienced crew on their 22nd operation consisted of Al Richards and Nick Melnick (Canadians) Peter Monck, Stanley Weedon, John Hennessey, Clifford Coward and Captain Don Bacon (all English). Joe Melnick (aged 75) brother of Nick, told how he and his four brothers all fought during the war, but only three returned; *"But, it was a just cause we fought for, and it was necessary we did it"* said Joe with conviction.

'After a reception at the Town Hall, the group visited the church at St Lenaarts, and later the farm of Jef Van Riel.'

Today, a commemorative plaque (all due to the efforts of brother Eddy) now marks the place where seven young lives were so violently ended. After an interview with the farmer's wife regarding the airman found in the field, researcher Cyriel Verbist recorded her following sentiments:
"He was lying on his back; part of his face was burned... he was very young... a very beautiful boy!"

FTR LL899	F/L D.J. Bacon DFC	Pilot	(Killed)
(EA-P)	Sgt J.P. Hennessey	F/E	(Killed)
'B Flt'	P/O C.W. Coward	NAV	(Killed)
	Sgt P. Monck	W/OP	(Killed)
	Sgt S.W. Weedon	A/G	(Killed)
Crew on their	F/O N. Melnick RCAF	B/A	(Killed)
23rd operation	F/S C.E. Richard RCAF	A/G	(Killed)

18/19 April, 1944; MINING IN POMERANIAN BAY/ JUVISY: On the 14th and 17th bad weather caused the last minute cancellation of operations. Then on the 18th, the squadron detailed 19 aircraft for operations; 10, including W/Cmdr Adams, were sent minelaying in the Pomeranian Bay area, whilst the remaining 9 Lancasters raided Juvisy -both attacks were successful. Three aircraft failed to return from the 168 minelayers, whilst one Lancaster was reported missing from the Juvisy raid. None of the losses were from 49 Squadron, which had operated three new crews on the Juvisy operation.These were captained by:

F/O Armstrong (JB679), F/Sgt Appleyard RAAF (JB421) P/O Rowley (ND533)

With the remainder of the squadron, these 'sprog' crews all completed successful sorties and returned safely to base.

20/21 April, 1944; LA CHAPELLE (PARIS): This was a 5 Group attack employing for the first time the Group's own Pathfinder squadrons. Deploying 247 Lancasters and 22 Mosquitoes (including a few 8 Group Oboe Mossies) an extremely accurate attack was made on this railway target.

The bombing force was divided into two parts; the first wave bombed one half of the target, then an hour later the second force bombed the remaining half. Fiskerton's contribution consisted of 17 Lancasters; all returned safely and at interrogation crews reported good visual accounts of the target being well 'pranged'. A total of 6 Lancasters were lost (all from other squadrons).

This was the final operation by P/O Clive Roantree RAAF and crew; they had come through the Berlin raids unscathed and participated in the daring Königsberg Canal operation. Their first 'nickel' operation from OTU had been to Paris, how fitting they should conclude a tour on the same target.

Fiskerton April 1944: P/O Clive Roantree RAAF and crew on completion of their tour which began 3/4-11-43 Düsseldorf and finished 20/21-4-44 - La Chappelle.
By the entrance door of ND792 'Bandlaw A-Able' they are (from l to r); Jack Grimshaw, F/E; John Peaker,B/A; Clive Roantree RAAF, pilot; Jock Lowrie, W/Op (in doorway); Paddy Paddick,Nav (KIA Feb 45); Ken Nelson RCAF, A/G. (Clive. Roantree)

Fiskerton, April 1944: The 'A' Flt ground crew of 'Bandlaw Able' gratefully remembered by Clive Roantree. (back row l to r); Bamf, engines Cpl; Smudge (Ron Smith), engines; Sgt i/c; Fred (Outwin), Cpl airframes. (front row l to r); Syd, engines; Taffy; engines; Nobby, airframes; Ginge, engines.
(Clive Roantree)

To celebrate finishing their tour, the Roantree crew took the ground crew out for drinks over the river to the Ferry Boat Inn at Washingborough. On the way back to camp, they were ambushed by the local constabulary, which resulted in half of them receiving fines for not having lights on their bikes. *"It was a different world then... war or no war!"* (C. Roantree)

Note: Lancaster ND972 passed to 619 Sqdn in Sept 44 and was destroyed in a crash at Strubby 4 Feb 45.

22/23 April, 1944; BRUNSWICK: For the first time, 5 Group took its low-level marking method to a heavily defended German target. The Mosquitoes placed their markers accurately but a combination of poor visibility and faulty communications between the bomber controllers saved the city from severe damage. Eighteen Lancasters took off from Fiskerton for Brunswick; P/O Simpson and crew being the last away at 23.20hrs. Post-operation reports showed that only a few German fighters contested the 265 strong bomber force, but three crews from the squadron were intercepted. P/O Green RNZAF and crew in ND647 managed to evade an unidentified twin engined fighter, whilst F/O Armstrong's crew encountered a JU88, but fortunately the enemy did not press home its attack.

At 01.23hrs, still on course for the target, the Rowley crew's aircraft was suddenly hit by very accurate cannon fire from an unseen German night-fighter. P/O Rowley put ND533 into a violent corkscrew and managed to evade their attacker, but fire had broken out in the centre of the fuselage and the aircraft soon filled with smoke; both gun turrets had been put out of action in the initial attack. With great determination, the flight engineer, Sgt Hatchett, was able to subdue the flames. A quick assessment of the damage soon established that Sgt Partington, the rear gunner, had tragically been killed at his station. With a defenceless and badly crippled aircraft, the pilot had no alternative but to return to base. They landed back at Fiskerton just before 04.00hrs, where on a very sombre dispersal point, the body of the rear gunner was gently removed; Ralph Partington is buried in his home town of Royton in Lancashire.

One hour later, returning 49 Squadron Lancs started to circle their home base. Another Lancaster touched down with the body of an unfortunate airman on board -P/O Jack Lett landed ND695 at 05.24hrs; over the target, flak had exploded in close proximity to ND695, peppering the fuselage with lethal red hot shell fragments, mortally wounding Gerry Mackew, their 21 year-old bomb aimer; F/Sgt Gerald Victor Mackew now lies at rest in St.Pancras Cemetery, Finchley.

When aircraft fail to return from operations, naturally a sense of sadness is always felt on a station, but on this early spring Thursday morning of 23rd April, as two ambulances slowly wound their way around Fiskerton's peri-track en route to the mortuary, for those on the ground, the human cost of war in the air was brought just a little more into focus. Four Lancasters failed to return from the operation; all 49's returned to base.

23/24 April, 1944; MINELAYING -POMERANIAN BAY: P/O Ewens (JB714) and crew in their faithfull J-Jig were the only aircraft from the unit dispatched on this night. They climbed away from Fiskerton just after 21.00hrs bound for the Baltic. Seven hours and fifteen minutes later they returned having placed their mines in the correct area.

During the operation, 114 aircraft had set out to lay mines in the Baltic; 5 failed to return.

24/25 April, 1944; MUNICH: This was another attack using 5 Group low-level marking by 16 Mosquitoes. A force of 244 Lancasters was dispatched, including 16 from Fiskerton. P/O Green was forced to return early, when JB178 developed a problem in her port-outer engine. The crew captained by F/O Hill and flying in ND647, was operating for the first time.

P/O Simpson (LL912) later reported: *"Searchlights a great difficulty and formed a solid belt of about 300 from target to Augsburg!"* F/O Matheson (LL900) received flak hits over the target which damaged the bombsight and H2S. P/O Ewens (JB714) was also 'hit in places by flak but not detrimentally'. P/O Tudor Jones could not close the bomb doors on JB701 which made it difficult to conserve fuel on the journey home. P/O Montgomery (ND972) reported seeing the glow from many fires for 100 miles after leaving the target.

Perhaps the results of the attack can best be summed up by recalling parts of the interrogation reports given by two 49 Squadron crews; firstly F/Lt Adams (ND512): *"A run was made, bombs dropped and photo taken -whole crew considered raid successful and satisfying."* American pilot, L/t Stevens (ME675), after completing his 21st operation had by now adopted RAF jargon when he proclaimed: *"Considered a first rate prang!"*

Nine Lancasters from the force failed to return; 49 Squadron had 11 return to base, 2 landed at Tangmere and 1 at Hartford Bridge. This left one aircraft unaccounted for. Tragically the lives of P/O Frank Clark and crew had been brought to a sudden and violent end in the night sky over Germany. They are buried together in a Collective Grave in Durnbach War Cemetery.

FTR ND537	P/O F. Clark	Pilot	(Killed)
(EA-)	Sgt F. Shaw	F/E	(Killed)
' Flt'	Sgt D. Rolfe	NAV	(Killed)
	F/S T.R. Connatty	WOP/AG	(Killed)
	Sgt F.J. Castle	A/G	(Killed)
Crew on their	F/S D.G. Adams	A/B	(Killed)
12th operation	F/S F.W. Hubbard	A/G	(Killed)

26/27 April, 1944; SCHWEINFURT: Mosquitoes of 627 Squadron, Woodhall Spa, used 5 Group's low-level marking technique for the first time. The attempt was not accurate and much of the bombing fell outside Schweinfurt.

Meanwhile, German night fighters had managed to penetrate the 215 strong main force taking a heavy toll; 21 Lancasters failed to return. The Fiskerton squadron had 15 aircraft airborne by 21.40hrs. On the way to Schweinfurt, a new crew skippered by P/O Graves-Hook (JB714) was hit by predicted flak over Karlsruhr; it damaged their port outer engine and wing and also smashed into the pilot's cockpit, fortunately without causing harm. The crew 'pressed on' to complete a successful sortie.

The squadron was to suffer the heavy loss of three crews this night: F/Lt Bob Armstrong DFC and crew were all killed and are buried alongside each other in the Durnbach War Cemetery in Germany.

The graves of F/Lt Armstrong's crew in Durnbach War Cemetery. (l eft to right); Robert Armstrong, Pilot, (aged 22), Dennis Cooper, A/G, (19), Douglas Endean, F/E, (23), Raymond Osbourne, NAV, (21).Sidney Foster, W/OP, (21), Leonard Kennedy RCAF, A/B, (25), Thomas Morris, A/G.
"They passed from the darkness of the night into the awaiting arms of God". (Ernst Guse)

P/O John Dickinson and crew also failed to return. After surviving so many close calls in the earlier part of their tour, the 'reaper' finally got them on their 25th operation. Many on the squadron thought that Johnny Dickinson and crew, (who loved flying their Lancaster at very low-level on training flights) had been blessed with that precious bomber crew commodity 'luck', and were sure that they would get through their tour. Seven white headstones in a neat line mark where all seven lie at peace in Ugny-sur-Meuse Cemetery, France.

P/O Robert Montgomery and four fellow members of his crew are buried in Bure Churchyard, Meuse. The two gunners, F/Sgt Baker RAAF (rear gunner) and Sgt Mitchell (mid-upper) managed to parachute to safety. Sgt Richard Mitchell had enlisted in the RAF on 13 December 1939; by February 1941 he was serving with 148 Squadron in the Middle East. September 1943 saw him at 16 OTU followed by 1668 HCU, 51 Base and finally arriving at 49 Squadron on 20th February 1944 as an air gunner in the Montgomery crew.

That was over two months ago; now in the early hours of 27 April 1944 he found himself all alone in the middle of a French field. The events that followed are told in Richard's own words and are taken from his Swiss POW report:

"After walking for 1 1/2 days, I was met by a Frenchman who escorted me to the Police station where I was handed over to the local doctor, After a period of about two weeks, during which time I received treatment for my injuries. I was then sent to another house some 20 kilometeres away where I made contact with the organisation.

They gave me an Identity card, food and a place to sleep for about three weeks. (Sgt Mitchell stayed in the house of Elaine Descharmes called 'Cuves' in Par Clefmont near Chaumont). These people provided a car to the railway station of Chaumont and purchased my ticket to Besancon where I changed trains for Montbeliard and also provided me with an escort. At Montbeliard I was provided with a bicycle and guide, and taken within 6 kilomteres of the Swiss border. From here I was taken to Switzerland by an unknown guide."

Richard Mitchell arrived in Switzerland on 20 June 1944 and by 6 September was back in the UK at the personnel holding flight in Morcambe. Sgt Mitchell was not required to go back to operational flying and after technical training he was posted to No. 2 Flying Instructors School until demob in November 1946. He soon re-enlisted, becoming an Air Traffic Controller; sadly after illness, W/O Mitchell died in 1968.

F/S Baker RAAF became a POW in camp 357, Kopernikus.

Of the 15 Lancasters dispatched by the squadron, 10 aircraft returned to base, 1 landed at Ford, 1 landed at Chipping Warden and 3 failed to return.

FTR JB679	P/O R. Montgomery	Pilot	(Killed)
(EA-D)	Sgt R.J. Boyce	F/E	(Killed)
'A'Flt	F/S S. Smith	NAV	(Killed)
	Sgt T. Parkin	W/AG	(Killed)
	Sgt R.J. Mitchell	A/G	(Evader)
Crew on their	P/O R.F. Cluff RCAF	B/A	(Killed)
19th operation	F/S J. Baker RAAF	A/G	(P.o.W.)
FTR LL908	P/O J.R. Dickinson	Pilot	(Killed)
(EA-)	Sgt R.B. Hainsworth	F/E	(Killed)
'A'Flt	F/S F.W. Wale	NAV	(Killed)
	Sgt C.W.F. Sizer	W/OP	(Killed)
	Sgt J. Ellenor	A/G	(Killed)
Crew on their	W/O N.F. Mackenzie RCAF	B/A	(Killed)
25th operation	Sgt R.H. Hudson DFM	A/G	(Killed)
FTR ND687	F/L R.G. Armstrong DFC	Pilot	(Killed)
(EA-)	Sgt D.E. Endean	F/E	(Killed)
	F/S R.G. Osborne	NAV	(Killed)
	Sgt S.F. Foster	W/OP	(Killed)
	Sgt D.J. Cooper	A/G	(Killed)
Crew on their	W/O L.T. Kennedy RCAF	B/A	(Killed)
5th operation	P/O T.H. Morris RCAF	A/G	(Killed)

APRIL 1944

28/29 April, 1944; OSLO (KJELLER): This was a 5 Group attack by just 51 Lancasters (including 11 from Fiskerton) on an airframe factory near Oslo. Mosquitoes marked the target well and in clear conditions a successful bombing raid was carried out; some of the squadron's crews reported bombing from as low as 5,000 feet. No aircraft were lost.

'VILLAGE INN' TRAGEDY

During the month of April, F/Lt Bill Healey RCAF DFC, and crew were attached to the Bomber Development Unit at Newmarket. Along with a 1 Group crew from 460 RAAF Squadron, Binbrook, they were testing a new radar operated gun turret (A.G.L.T.); the code name for this equipment being 'Village Inn'.

Late Sunday afternoon 30 April, tactical trials using 'Village Inn' were being carried out between an attacking friendly fighter and *Lancaster (ND553), being flown by F/Lt Bill Healey. During the bomber's vigorous evasive actions, the dinghy accidently started to inflate and burst from its stowage hold in the Lancaster's starboard wing. It blew back covering one fin and causing the aircraft to flick onto its back; F/Lt Healey's immediate reaction was to haul back on the control column in an attempt to complete a full loop. With insufficient height, the Lancaster smashed into the ground near Witchford; the time was 16.55hrs. The following 49 Squadron crew members were killed:

Crashed ND553	F/L W.A. Healey DFC RCAF	Pilot	(Killed)
	Sgt F. Boardman	F/E	(Killed)
	Sgt J. Jones	W/AG	(Killed)
	F/O R. Bailes	NAV	(Killed)

Also killed in this tragic accident was Sgt Brian Jagger who had been posted to the BDU in early March 1944; Sgt Jagger was a Dambuster veteran, having flown in the front turret of 617's L-Leather flown by F/Lt Dave Shannon RAAF.

* Lancaster ND553 was a 460 Squadron RAAF aircraft.

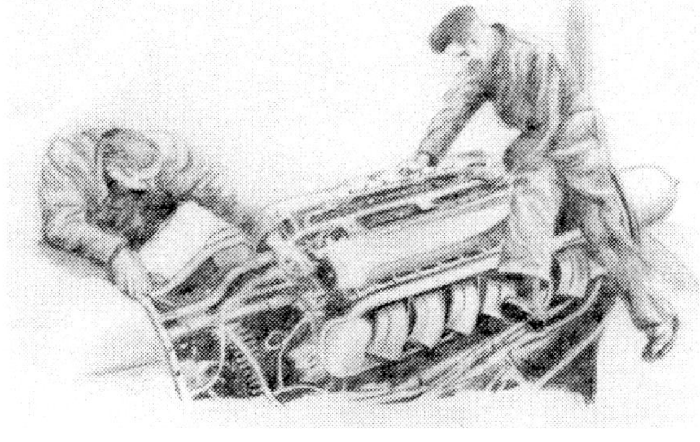

Packard Merlins, built in the USA under licence, powered MKIII Lancasters

APRIL 1944

OPERATIONAL SUMMARY - APRIL 1944

Date	Target	Desp	E/R	FTR	Remarks
5/6	TOULOUSE	10	-	-	Diverted
9/10	DANZIG BAY	9	-	-	
10/11	TOURS	11	-	-	
11/12	AACHEN	4-		1	F/L BaconFTR
18/19	MINING	10	-	-	
	JUVISY	9	-	-	
20/21	LACHAPELLE	17	-	-	
22/23	BRUNSWICK	18	1	-	2 killed
23/24	MINING	1	-	-	
24/25	MUNICH	16	1	1	P/O Clark FTR
26/27	SCHWEINFURT	15	-	3	P/O Montgomery FTR F/L Armstrong FTR P/O Dickinson FTR
28/29	KJELLER	11	-	-	

Total of sorties flown	131
Failed to Return	5
Tons of bombs dropped of all types	498.03
Operational hours flown during April 1944	666hrs 45mins
Non-operational hours flown during April 1944	439hrs

HONOURS AND AWARDS - APRIL 1944

S/Ldr Miller D.F.C.	D.S.O.
P/O A.W. Shinn	D.F.C.
F/Lt J.F.W. Adams	D.F.C.
P/O J.A. Sanders	D.F.C.
SGT R.H. Hudson	D.F.M.

MAY 1944

Unit strength: 55 Officers and 414 Other Ranks. Aircraft on charge: 16 Lancaster Mk I's and III's - plus 2 reserves

The squadron welcomed a new Commanding Officer when Wing Commander Malcolm Crocker DFC and Bar, arrived at Fiskerton from East Kirkby. At his former base, he had been the CO of 630 Squadron since November 1943, following his promotion whilst operating with 57 Squadron. W/Cmdr Crocker believed in leading from the front and within days of his arrival he was flying on operations.

1/2 May, 1944; TOULOUSE: Just after 21.30hrs, on Monday the first day of May, 12 of the unit's Lancasters took off to join 119 other aircraft from 5 Group bound for France. Their targets were the aircraft assembly and explosives factories in Toulouse. Both targets received accurate attacks without the Group losing any aircraft. Three new crews were flying their first operations with the squadron; they were piloted by: P/O Dod (JB473), F/Lt Botting (ND512) and P/O Brady (ND787).
All aircraft and crews were safely back at Fiskerton by 05.55hrs after completing successful sorties.

A photograph of F/Lt Botting and crew taken at OTU. Flying their first operation on 1/2-5-44; 'Buzz' Botting was destined to become CO of 49 Squadron. (Back row l to r), F/Sgt Bishop, wireless operator; F/O Jimmy Edwards, navigator; F/Sgt Wilmot RAAF, bomb aimer. (Front row l to r), Sgt Bennett RCAF, air gunner; F/Lt Botting, pilot; F/Sgt Timms, air gunner. (J.A. Edwards)

3/4 May, 1944; MAILLY-LE-CAMP: The target, a German military camp which housed the 21st Panzer Division, lay close to the northern French village of Mailly. The force consisted of 346 Lancasters from 1 and 5 Groups plus 16 Pathfinder Mosquitoes. W/Cmdr Cheshire led the low-level marking of the target, which went well, but when W/Cmdr Deane the main force Controller ordered the force to come in and bomb, his VHF transmissions were drowned out by a wrongly tuned American forces wireless broadcast. The delay was fatal; it enabled German night fighters to roam at will amongst the orbiting Lancasters, resulting in a dreadful loss of men and machines. Eventually, 42 Lancasters fell in the battle which ensued around the markers and on the bombers' return route.

S/Ldr Sparks, the Deputy Controller (who was shot down himself later in the raid) eventually brought the main force in for an accurate attack in which 1,500 tons of bombs were dropped, causing great damage.

W/Cmdr Crocker (JB421) operated with 49 squadron for the first time, flying K-King; the squadron had 14 aircraft airborne over Mailly this night. Also operating for the first time were P/O Carrington RAAF and crew in LM808. Over the target, P/O Bill Green RNZAF (JB178) and crew were on their bombing run when a Lancaster dead ahead of them suddenly just blew apart. Debris crashed through the perspex nose and windscreen of their aircraft causing the log and charts all to disappear into the breeze. Harassed by fighters after leaving the target, the Green crew gratefully managed to make base with the aid of Gee. Following his crew's return, F/Lt Adams (ND512) submitted this de-brief report:

"As we bombed, there were aircraft within 200yds of us. The congestion over the target was ridiculous to a point of suicide!"

JUMP SON - JUMP!

Two 49 Squadron airmen failed to return from Mailly, but their aircraft and the remainder of the crew did! Rear gunner, Sgt Ron Eeles recalls that fateful night that would eventually, by a twist of fate, save his own life and that of the mid/upper gunner, Sgt Quick. Mailly was the crew's 16th operation together under the leadership of skipper P/O Ted Ball, who on this night was piloting (ND647) N-Nan, Ron recalls:

"The day had been uneventful until we were advised that operations were on that evening. After briefing we, as a crew, were apprehensive of the raid arrangements in view of the planned concentration of aircraft over the target in such a short space of time.

P/O Martin DFM, an air gunner, was to accompany us; I understood his task was to observe anti-aircraft activity. As I recall he was not attached to the squadron.

Our take-off time was 21.57hrs with the usual 'wave off' by station personnel at the end of the runway. I had a sense at this time that something was different as I did not have the same exhilaration when taking off on full power. Due to this feeling of foreboding I thought I would not be coming back and that something was going to happen. What had also struck me as strange was that when I entered my turret at dispersal, for the first time our W/Op had closed my turret doors behind me (they were difficult to close oneself)... I thanked him... the last time I was to speak to any member (except Sgt Quick) of the crew again.

On arrival at Mailly we were directed to proceed to a point 15 miles away and then orbit a yellow marker. After a few minutes we did not like this at all as visibility was clear and from experience, not the time to be hanging around enemy territory. We circled for about 30 minutes, becoming increasingly worried and unable to receive any radio instructions (American music was drowning out all signals).

It was then I became aware that several Lancasters were going down in flames; five aircraft had the fire along the leading edge of the mainplane. I saw some of these planes impact on the ground with the usual dull red glow. My job was to keep my eyes open for enemy aircraft so I did not dwell for more than fleeting seconds on the shot down Lancs.

At this stage I did not see any night fighter activity nor anti-aircraft fire but with regards to the latter we were still orbiting 15 miles from the target. At about 00.30hrs my pilot commenced the run in to the target and I could then see several planes burning on the ground. I do not remember hearing any instructions to the pilot from outside sources, but obviously he would have obtained clearance to proceed.

During the bombing run, there was a sudden bang and a blinding pink red flash along the port side of the aircraft, followed immediately by the pilot saying (not shouting) 'Christ, put on chutes chaps'. Within a second of this the plane was hit again by flak along the fuselage. There was a sizzling sound in the intercom system and then it went dead. The pink red glow on the port side persisted and I assumed we were on fire.

I was disconnecting my electric suit plug and leaving my flying helmet on the seat when I now come to a point that has always mystified me, and to this day I still think of it at times... I had a vision of my Mother's face outside of the turret and she was saying 'Jump son, jump', I was at this stage about to vacate the turret anyway.

My experience of this vision may not be believed and that is why I have never recounted it to anyone before, but I can assure anyone it is perfectly true. Shortly after my arrival as a POW at Stalag Luft 3, I wrote of my turret experience in a log book provided by the Red Cross but deleted it as I was convinced no one would ever believe it... but it happened, believe or disbelieve.

On leaving the turret and attaching my parachute I saw the mid-upper gunner (Sgt 'Speedy' Quick) already opening the door with an axe. As I reached him he jumped; I could see nothing in the fuselage as it was full of smoke and the plane seemed out of control. I rolled out the door in the recommended way although my legs brushed along the underside. Fortunately my flying boots stayed on."

Ron was eventually captured and became a PoW, but that, as he says, is another story. He did meet up again with Sgt Quick after the war but then their paths separated. When Ron joined the 49 Squadron Association in 1992, he was looking for just one name on the nominal roll, and he found it. Now he and 'Speedy' are re-united again and have become close friends once more... just like they had been back in 1944.

Meanwhile, back in the treacherous sky over Mailly, P/O Ball had not in fact abandoned N-Nan, as his post-operational interrogation report reveals:

"We approached the target at 7,200 feet in the first wave. Bombs were jettisoned on the point of bombing as the aircraft was hit by flak and filled with smoke. I gave the orders to put on parachutes, then the intercom went u/s... the gunners baled out, then Eric Wardman, the flight engineer, saw an enemy aircraft on the starboard quarter. I continued violent turns down to zero feet managing to lose the fighter. The starboard-outer engine had to be feathered due to fire and the port-outer was giving only half power - returned safely to base."

For his fine display of airmanship and skill, P/O G.E.Ball was awarded an immediate DFC. Why did the understandable actions of the two gunners ultimately save their lives?... two months later whilst operating against a V1 site, F/Lt Ball DFC and crew were one of two 49 squadron crews who failed to return; there were no survivors from either aircraft.

Despite the carnage that took place in the night skies over northern France this night, all 49's aircraft returned safely to base.

Gunners, Sgt Quick (left of centre) and Sgt Ron Eeles (right of centre) outside the locker rooms at Fiskerton in March 1944. They both failed to return from Mailly 3/4-5-44 but survived to become PoW's. (K. Gibson)

7/8 May, 1944; SALBRIS: An ammunition dump at Salbris was the target for 58 Lancasters and 4 Mosquitoes from 5 Group. The unit had 14 aircraft airborne including two new crews piloted by F/O Simpkin (JB701) and P/O Anderson (JB421). The bombing was accurate causing much damage, but the raid did cost 7 Lancasters, one of which came from 49 Squadron:

P/O Arthur Anderson and crew, flying their first operation with the squadron were sadly all killed and are buried in St. Doulchard Cemetery, Cher, France.

P/O Edgar (ND792) and crew were lucky not to be amongst those reported missing; light flak damaged their starboard main plane just behind the inner-engine and fuselage, but a safe return was accomplished.

P/O Carrington (LM539) reported that whilst in the target area 2 rockets were fired at them from an enemy aircraft... fortunately they missed.

On returning to England, only 3 aircraft managed to land at Fiskerton, with the other 10 being diverted. The diversion was the result of an extremely curious and almost comical accident at Fiskerton. On this night, a recently arrived crew had been detailed to fly a cross-country night exercise. They returned and landed at Fiskerton only minutes before the squadron was due back from Salbris. Coming to a stop at the end of the main runway, the pilot found he had lost all brake pressure. Not wishing to run the risk of slipping off the concrete he remained stationary whilst awaiting assistance. This incident is recalled in the 49 Squadron Association Newsletter, December 1994 as follows:

LOCAL WAAF AND THE LANC PRANG

This story is true, only the names have been changed to protect the innocent - our 'heroine', Waaf Wing-Ding! The year 1944... the squadron, 49 of RAF Fiskerton, Lincs. Blue-eyed, blonde job, Waaf Wing-Ding was an LACW Driver MT, with a Good Conduct Stripe (three years undetected crime). Her duties included ferrying aircrew to their aircraft which inevitably provided a selection of admirers. She also claimed the amorous attention of the Senior N.C.O. fitter of 'B' Flight, Sgt Speedy who did everything at the double, but was a dedicated and respected engineer.

Then a Canadian pilot, P/O Peedy, a 'goof' (lady's man) and a 'snargasher' (Canadian trainee) arrived. New to the station, he spent time with Waaf Wing-Ding riding round the dispersals getting to know the place. This put Chiefy Speedy in a frenzied flap.

One night when landing from a test flight in a nearly new Lancaster, P/O Peedy came to a halt near the end of the runway - to query why, Chiefy Speedy emerged. Seeing his rival in the cockpit put him in a wizard panic. Although the props were still turning, he banged on the fuselage to be admitted by Scruff the mid-upper gunner (later S/Ldr). Speedy was now on full bore and flung himself at the pilot who froze on the stick.

The struggling suitors caused the Lanc to veer off the concrete onto the grass. In the confusion, the under-cart lever was activated and the aircraft pancaked, almost 'hopping the twig' (to crash). Chiefy Speedy was put on a 'fizzer'. He must have been a Gen King, for, not to lose his expertise, his only punishment was 'demoted by one rank'. Reporting back to Waaf Wing-Ding, in injured tones he said, 'I've lost a rank over you'.

Relating this incident 50 years on, a still blonde, wide-eyed Waaf Wing-Ding innocently proclaimed, 'and I wasn't really interested in either Speedy or Peedy!'

Those on the ground who witnessed the incident recalled how the Lancaster seemed to 'pirouette' around the airfield until finally collapsing her own undercarriage. The dawning light of Monday morning, 8 May 1944, revealed the sad sight of a wrecked aircraft. This once elegant 'dancing Lancaster' had had her finest hour; LL912 would never fly again, but her crew would, going on to complete a distinguished tour of operations with 49 Squadron.

Of the 3 returning aircraft that did manage to land back at Fiskerton; all three crews reported at interrogation that the target was well hit with smoke rising to the bombing height of 7,000ft. P/O Edgar summed up his report by stating that; *"the target was truly wiped out!"*

FTR JB421	P/O A.L. Anderson	Pilot	(Killed)
(EA-K)	Sgt R.L. Fowls	F/E	(Killed)
'A'Flt	P/O J.C. Roach RCAF	NAV	(Killed)
	W/O R.W. Long	W/OP	(Killed)
	Sgt B. McLeod	A/G	(Killed)
Crew on their	F/S F.J. Pinch	B/A	(Killed)
1st operation	Sgt E.W. Rushton	A/G	(Killed)

9/10 May, 1944; GENNEVILLIERS: W/Cmdr Crocker piloted one of 13 Lancasters dispatched by 49 Squadron for an attack on two French factories including that of Gnome & Rhone. A total of 56 Lancasters and 8 Mosquitoes from 5 Group hit both targets, but sadly, in doing so, some French civilians were killed and injured. The Group suffered the loss of 5 Lancasters, but all 49's returned safely.

11/12 May, 1944; BOURG-LEOPOLD: Haze over this military camp in Belgium made marking by the Mosquitoes extremely difficult. The Master Bomber reluctantly ordered the raid to be abandoned for fear of hitting nearby housing. Of the 190 orbiting Lancasters, 94 had already bombed before receiving the 'cease bombing' order.

Fourteen Lancasters had been dispatched by 49 Squadron including two new crews piloted by F/O's Pederson RCAF (ND695) and Powell (JB178). F/O Powell was one of 6 crews from the squadron that actually bombed before the abandonment.

Fighters were once again present and 5 Lancasters failed to return. All 49's were safe, although P/O Edgar (ND792) and crew had their share of troubles as their de-brief shows:

"We reached the target and made 2 bombing runs but did not attack as Controller ordered 'cease bombing'. We were then attacked by a fighter, in which our Lancaster sustained damage to the port side of the fuselage, cutting the trimmer wires to the elevators and rudders - the starboard flaps were damaged with mainplane and aileron trimmers also cut; the root of the tail plane was hit rendering the rear turret u/s."

P/O Edgar arrived over the emergency airfield at Woodbridge in Suffolk; once there the crew elected to stay with their skipper as he attempted to land his crippled bomber. Great skill and determination brought the battered aircraft into a safe landing, but the tension within that Lancaster during those final few moments on the approach must have been tremendous, for as instructed, the crew had brought back their bombs! - P/O A.G. Edgar was awarded an immediate DFC.

19/20 May, 1944; AMIENS: During the morning of Friday 19th, as preparations were being made for that evening's attack on a railway target at Amiens, preparations of a very different kind were being made in Germany. In one of the worst atrocities of the war involving PoWs, over a period, the Gestapo shot 50 Allied airmen who had been recaptured after escaping from Stalag Luft III Sagan in March. The killings were carried out on Hitler's orders.

Only 3 PoW's out of 79 made it back to England from what became known as 'The Great Escape'. Twenty men were sent back to Stalag Luft III and they told fellow PoWs of the killings.

The aircrew of 5 Group who climbed away from their Lincolnshire bases bound for Amiens, would learn little of these events in Germany until months later. Their main preoccupation this night was the cloud they found covering the target.

One of 49's aircraft pulled out of the operation just minutes before take-off when a gun turret went u/s; this left 16 Lancasters from Fiskerton to join 84 others on the operation. Because of poor weather conditions, the Master Bomber called for the bombing to cease, but by then 37 aircraft had already released their loads; seven crews from 49 Squadron dropped their bombs, including two new crews piloted by P/O Lacy (ND695) and F/O Arnold (LM572).

One incident occurred when a piece of red hot flak pierced the perspex in Sgt Robert Berry's mid-upper turret, missing him by only a fraction; this was in P/O Carrington's aircraft (LM539). In their absence, fog had developed over 5 Group's Lincolnshire home and as a result Fiskerton operated FIDO to receive her own brood and several other of the Group's Lancasters. All 49's aircraft returned safely to base - one 5 Group Lancaster failed to return from operations.

21/22 May, 1944; DUISBURG - KIEL BAY: A total of 19 aircraft was detailed for operations on the 21st; 7 were required to attack Duisburg and 12 for minelaying in Kiel Bay. The minelayers took-off first and included the new crew of P/O Bell (ME675). The Duisburg force departed 25 minutes later with W/Cmdr Crocker (ND787) and crew in attendance.

Lancasters were joined by Halifaxes in minelaying; of the 107 aircraft dispatched, 3 aircraft failed to return; all 49's aircraft completed successful sorties.

The Main Force attack on Duisburg involved 510 Lancasters and 22 Mosquitoes. Because of the cloud cover, Oboe sky-marking was used and the southern areas of the city did sustain damage, but crews returning to Fiskerton were highly critical of the 'insufficient and disturbing marking'. W/Cmdr Crocker had in fact bombed an 'unidentified Ruhr area'. The cost was high, with 29 Lancasters failing to return - sadly one of the missing Lancasters came from 49 Squadron; P/O Henry Carrington RAAF (from Kalgoorlie, Western Australia) and crew were brought down over Holland.

The only other Australian crew member, F/Sgt Silver, was the sole survivor. P/O Carrington is buried alongside his crew in Roosendaal en Nispen Cemetery, Holland. Sgt Robert Berry of East Ham, the crew's mid-upper gunner, was just 19 years old.

On return from PoW Camp, W/O Silver RAAF applied to become a member of the 'Caterpillar Club'; his application reads as follows:

"Dear Sir, Life is sweet and I'm thankfully disposed towards an Irving Chute; May 44 saw me float earthwards... of course, if the chute had failed to function, a year's PoW life would not have materialised - that can be overlooked. I wish to apply for membership of the Caterpillar Club.
Faithfully yours S.A. Silver AUS 419348 W/O"

FTR LM539	P/O H.J. Carrington RAAF	Pilot	(Killed)
(EA-D)	Sgt R.F. Coleman	F/E	(Killed)
	Sgt J.H.E. Hales	NAV	(Killed)
	Sgt R.C. Hill	W/AG	(Killed)
	Sgt R.W. Berry	A/G	(Killed)
Crew on their	F/S S.A. Silver RAAF	B/A	(P.o.W.)
7th operation	Sgt L. Foulkes	A/G	(Killed)

22/23 May, 1944; BRUNSWICK: Over 220 Lancasters from 1 and 5 Groups plus 10 Mosquitoes made up the force sent to Brunswick; 17 became airborne from Fiskerton, but a new crew piloted by F/Sgt Baker (ND957), was forced to return early with compass and intercom problems.

As the Master Bomber arrived over Brunswick with his 5 Group marker force, they found 10/10ths cloud covering the target; the met forecast had predicted clear weather. With these conditions the 5 Group method of marking could not cope, and the raid became a failure. At interrogation back at Fiskerton, crews reported bombing the concentration of fires, and also 'Wanganui' flares as they disappeared into cloud.

P/O Lacey (ND383) and crew had their H2S blister shot away by accurate flak in the target area. Thirteen Lancasters were lost on the raid, and once again one came from 49 Squadron.

It is not known if the loss of P/O Philip Graves-Hook and crew was the result flak or fighter... there were no survivors. The 24 year-old pilot rests along-side his crew in Becklingen War Cemetery in Soltau, Germany.

Missing NE125	P/O P.R. Graves-Hook	Pilot	(Killed)
(EA-K)	Sgt E.G. Jones	F/E	(Killed)
	F/O W.G. Johnson RCAF	NAV	(Killed)
	Sgt N.M. Goldberg	W/OP	(Killed)
	F/O F.A.N. Clifton	A/G	(Killed)
Crew on their	F/O F.E. Sinden	A/B	(Killed)
7th operation	F/S G.H. Little	A/G	(Killed)

27/28 May, 1944; MORSALINES: Five coastal-battery positions along the French coast were the targets for a force of 272 aircraft; 49's target was the medium-battery at Morsalines.

To help make up 49 Squadron's contribution to 18 aircraft, 2 Lancasters were borrowed from 619 Squadron over at Dunholme Lodge; these were flown by two new crews captained by S/Ldr Bazin (LM378) PG-J and P/O Sullings (EE134) PG-Y. P/O Ross (ND383) and crew also operated for the first time, and later at de-brief reported; *"a very easy trip"* in E for Easy.

All five targets were bombed satisfactorily for the loss of one Lancaster and one Mosquito. All 49's aircraft landed back at Fiskerton safely, with F/Sgt Baker (ND533) being the last home at 02.50hrs.

LYNCH LAW

Germany, 30 May, 1944: From this day on, Allied aircrew shot down over Germany could no longer expect any mercy from the civilian population. Reichsleiter Martin Bormann issued a directive to all district and regional National Socialist leaders to the effect that lynch law was now approved by the Berlin government.

This directive followed a newspaper article by the Reich propaganda minister, Josef Goebbels published on 27 May. Under the headline 'Comments on the Enemy Air Terror', Goebbels concluded that in view of the *"criminal combat methods"* now employed by the Allied air forces, the German people in their own defence, should not be prevented from rewarding murder with murder.

Martin Bormann's directive gave the government seal of approval to Goebbels's incitement to mob justice.

31 May/1 June, 1944; MAISY: Operations the previous evening had been scrubbed shortly after briefing due to weather. This night, 5 Group was requested to send 68 Lancasters to attack the German gun-battery near Maisy, on the French coast. Fiskerton had 14 aircraft airborne shortly after 23.00hrs; all received the W/T message to return without bombing, when the target was found to be covered by 10/10ths cloud.

Whilst landing back at Fiskerton, P/O Ball's (LM541) Lancaster received some structural damage; an investigation later that morning revealed that the tyres had been badly cut, and deflated on touchdown. This incident may have been the reason for 7 of the squadron's aircraft being diverted; 2 went to Silverstone and 5 to Turweston. F/O Edwards just about summed up everyone's feelings about this operation in his interrogation report: *"Poor weather... poor affair!"*

OPERATIONAL SUMMARY - MAY 1944

Date	Target	Desp	E/R	FTR	Remarks
1/2	TOULOUSE	12	-	-	
3/4	MAILLY	14	-	-	
7/8	SALBRIS	14	-	1+1c	P/O Anderson FTR 1 a/c wrecked at base
9/10	GENNEVILLIERS	13	-	-	
11/12	BOURG-LEOPOLD	14	-	-	1 a/c to Woodbridge
19/20	AMIENS	16	-	-	
21/22	DUISBERG	7	-	1	P/O Carrington FTR
	KIEL BAY	12	-	-	
22/23	BRUNSWICK	17	1	1	P/O Graves-Hooke FTR
27/28	MORSALINES	18	-	-	
31/1	MAISY	14	-	-	Bombing aborted

Total of sorties flown	151
Failed to return	3
Tons of bombs dropped of all types	654.54
Operational hours flown during May 1944	850hrs 50mins
Non-operational hours flown during May 1944	556hrs 15mins

HONOURS AND AWARDS - MAY 1944

S/Ldr J. Evans D.F.C.	Bar to D.F.C.
F/O K.N. Gibson	D.F.C.
P/O L.E. Taylor	D.F.C.
P/O A.G. Edgar	D.F.C.
P/O G.E. Ball	D.F.C.

JUNE 1944

After the hectic period of operations during May, the new month began with great expectations of the much anticipated land invasion of France. Bombing attacks had now switched to the coastal gun-batteries, and the first day of June saw the squadron standing-by with 17 Lancasters, bombed-up and ready to attack more coastal defences. The day's terrible weather made this trip a candidate for a 'scrub' and sure enough, just after briefing, all operations were cancelled.

2/3 June, 1944; WIMEREUX: A force of 271 aircraft did attack coastal defences on the Pas de Calais coast. This was all part of a continuing deception, where the Normandy batteries would not be bombed until the last night before the invasion. Seventeen Lancasters from 49 Squadron were part of a force that attacked the guns at Wimereux near Boulogne; W/Cmdr Crocker (ME675) took Major Greenhaugh along as a passenger.

Cloud obscured the target, which spoiled the attack, and eventually the order to 'cease bombing' was given. One Lancaster was reported missing, but all 49's aircraft returned to base with all crews reporting a quiet trip.

5/6 June, 1944; NORMANDY COASTAL BATTERIES: On the previous day, Sunday 4 June, good news had been received from Italy, where it was reported that the US Fifth Army had at last entered Rome. That morning, the squadron was once again detailed for operations but at 18.00hrs, orders came through cancelling the trip.

The weather on Monday 5 June, didn't look too promising either; the day started dull with south westerly winds bringing in frequent rain showers across Lincolnshire. So it came as a big surprise when at 10.00hrs orders rattled through from Group requesting a maximum effort; 20 aircraft, each to be armed with 18x500lb H/C bombs. An air of excitement began to sweep through Fiskerton's intelligence section as more details of the night's planned operation were revealed: Over 1000 bombers were to be dispatched against 10 different batteries along the Normandy coast. It looked almost certain that the long awaited invasion was imminent.

British and American paratroopers and glidertoops were already landing in darkened Normandy fields during the first hours of 6 June, as 20 Lancasters prepared to make their take-off runs from Fiskerton; P/O Ross (ND512) and crew were the last away at 01.37hrs; 49's targets were the defences at La Pernelle. Fortunately this was one of only two targets relatively cloud free and the Pathfinders' markers were clearly visible. Bombing started around 03.30hrs, preceding the invasion from the sea by just a few hours.

Navigators were requested not to switch their H2S sets on during the return leg, but many did, and the screens confirmed their suspicions; the Channel showed a snow storm of blips - the invasion of Europe had started.

There was much excitement at interrogation even though the invasion had not yet been officially announced. All crews completed successful sorties including the new boys of P/O Smiley (ND787) and Sgt Deacon (ND957). Bomber Command lost 3 aircraft from these coastal battery attacks.

6/7 June, 1944; CAEN: Again 20 aircraft were requested for an attack on communications in the Normandy battle area. One Lancaster cancelled at the last minute with brake trouble, but P/O Lacy (JB399) led 19 aircraft away at 00.23hrs, bound for Caen. Bomber Command sent over 1,000 bombers to attack several targets inland from the invasion beaches. 49 Squadron's aircraft all made their attacks, and as one crew put it; *"if the marking was OK, the bombing was OK!"*. There was light flak in the area, and S/Ldr Bazin (ME808) was struck on the side of his head when flak exploded close to D-Dog, but the spirited S/Ldr managed to pilot his crew safely back to Fiskerton. All of the squadron's aircraft returned to base, with Sgt Deacon (LL900) being the last to land at 05.32hrs, having received slight flak damage after leaving the target. Bomber Command lost 11 aircraft with six 5 Group Lancasters going down on the Caen raid.

8/9 June, 1944; PONTAUBAULT: The previous day's weather had been cold and wet, and by 18.45hrs operations were once again scrubbed. Thursday 8 June, saw an improvement with sunny periods; 483 aircraft were dispatched in an attempt to prevent German reinforcements reaching the Normandy beachhead from the south. Fiskerton sent 21 aircraft against the marshalling yards at Pontaubault, but P/O Smiley (JB714) was forced to return early with navigational problems. Weather to and from the target was exceptionally bad, but cleared sufficiently to enable a well concentrated attack to be carried out. A total of 4 aircraft was lost on operations, including 2 Lancasters from the Pontaubault raid; all 49's returned safely. This was the night that 617 Squadron dropped the first 12,000lb 'Tallboy' bombs, in a raid on the Saumur railway tunnel.

Lancaster ND787 Bandlaw F-Fox operated from Fiskerton during the summer of 1944 Regularly flown by the Edwards crew, she was pensioned off to 1668 HCU in Sept 44 when 49 started to re-equip with 'Village Inn' Lancasters.
(J. A. Edwards)

9/10 June, 1944; ETAMPES: This was a 5 Group attack, led by Mosquito Pathfinders, on the railway junction at Etampes, south of Paris. It had rained for most of the day across Lincolnshire with the dull overcast bringing visibility down to 1 mile. But in the evening, shortly after 21.00hrs, a force of 108 Lancasters took to the air including 21 Lancasters from Fiskerton, all bound for France once again.

Over the target marking was accurate but late, causing the Lancasters to orbit. During this dangerous period many aircraft were seen to go down in flames. P/O Cornish (LM541) and crew claimed to be the first a/c to bomb. W/Cmdr Crocker (ME787) and crew, who were forced to orbit the target eight times, were attacked by a fighter shortly after bombing; his two gunners, F/Sgt Carr and P/O Creighton claimed their attacker as a 'probable'.

Bombs started to spread from the junction into the town, and sadly over 400 houses were destroyed before the 'Master of Ceremonies' could halt the attack. Five minutes after leaving the target, F/O Hill's (ME675) aircraft struck a parachute; the pitot head was taken away and perspex was damaged. One cannot begin to imagine the final few moments of that hapless airman dangling under his parachute as the four-engined bomber thundered towards him.

Back at base, it soon became clear that two of the aircraft seen being shot down in flames, may have been from 49 Squadron; P/O Thomas Smiley (JB714) and crew were all killed in K-King and are buried in Morginy-Champigny Cemetery. The other crew missing was piloted by F/O Bryan Bell (ND533); they too are buried in France, but records show that the bomb aimer, F/O Philip Hemmens did not die until September 1944.
Altogether six Lancasters failed to return from the raid.

FTR JB714	P/O T.S. Smiley	Pilot	(Killed)
(EA-K)	Sgt B.F. Webb	F/E	(Killed)
'A Flt'	F/S I.D. Stuart RAAF	NAV	(Killed)
	Sgt D.A. Sanderson	W/AG	(Killed)
	Sgt L.J.C. Rainbow	A/G	(Killed)
Crew on their	F/S L.A. Hinch	A/B	(Killed)
3rd operation	Sgt D.V. Blaikie	A/G	(Killed)

FTR ND533	F/O B.E. Bell	Pilot	(Killed)
(EA-M)	Sgt S.C. Holmes	F/E	(Killed)
'B Flt'	F/O D. MacFayden RAAF	NAV	(Killed)
	Sgt J. Holden	W/AG	(Killed)
	F/O H.D. Clark	A/G	(Killed)
Crew on their	F/O P.D. Hemmens**	A/B	(P.o.W.)
9th operation	Sgt J.J. Reed	A/G	(Killed)

** Died in Buchenwald Concentration Camp 27-09-44

12/13 June, 1944; CAEN: Bomber Command again dispatched large numbers of bombers to attack communication targets in support of ground forces. The 18 aircraft that departed Fiskerton were part of the 5 Group force operating against Caen. The attack was scattered due to the inability of bomb aimers to see the markers through 10/10ths cloud. Four crews from the squadron jettisoned sufficient bombs to reduce their load and brought the remainder back. There was a small amount of flak in the target area, plus searchlights, and fighters were also active around the western coast of France.

All of the night's losses came from 4 and 6 Groups, with 23 failing to return. It was for his actions on this night in a 6 Group Lancaster, that P/O Mynarski RCAF, was awarded the Victoria Cross.

ROBOT PLANES: On Tuesday 13 June, the first ten German V1 rocket bombs were launched against England; four managed to reach parts of southern England, causing the death of six people. Hitler's new 'secret weapon' was an all-metal monoplane powered by a ramjet engine (capable of 400mph). The flying bomb used a gyroscopic autopilot and pneumatic servo units to aid flight, combined with a preset compass; once the missile has flown the required distance, the elevators are fully deflected causing the V1 to dive and the engine to cut out. Because the bomb coasts to earth, it explodes near or on the surface, causing a small crater but massive blast damage. Attacks on London and the south by these 'doodlebugs' or 'buzz bombs' as they soon became known, increased dramatically over the next few months. Home-based fighters and anti-aircraft guns fought valiantly against this new threat, whilst Bomber Command and USAAF played a major role in disrupting and destroying the French launch sites.

14/15 June, 1944; AUNAY-SUR-ODON: In clear weather conditions, this proved to be a very accurate attack on German troop positions at Aunay near Caen.
49 Squadron contributed 18 aircraft including a new crew piloted by F/O Jordon (ND952).

At the post-operational interrogation, most crews gave reports of excellent bombing. The only slight damage concerned F/O Larry Pederson (ND512) and crew who received a 'bullet hole' from an unseen aircraft over the coastline. P/O Edgar (LL976) summed up the operation when he reported: *"Bombing was absolutely 'bang on', a really good effort."*
No aircraft were reported lost.

THE KING VISITS NORMANDY

On Friday 16 June, King George visited the Brtish section of the beach-head in Normandy, which by then was five miles from the front line. On the same day, the British Battleship 'HMS Rodney', in support of the ground offensive, fired a 16-inch shell which landed 20 miles inland; the shell just happened to kill the commander of the 12th SS Hitler Jugend Panzer division!

16/17 June, 1944; BEAUVOIR: In the morning's newspapers, headlines from Washington announced that on the previous day, forty-seven B-29 'Superfortresses' of the Twentieth USAAF, flying from China, had bombed the Japanese mainland for the first time. US Congress stated that the raiders had hit targets in Tokyo and other cities. This was quickly denied by Tokyo radio, saying that little damage was done and that six of the giant US bombers were shot down.

Meanwhile, on English airfields, bombers were being prepared for RAF Bomber Command's new campaign against the flying-bomb launch sites. Over 400 aircraft were to be sent against four targets in the Pas de Calais area; 49's target was at Beauvoir, and the 20 Lancasters detailed started to take-off from Fiskerton shortly after 22.40hrs.

S/L Cox (ME808) and P/O Buchanan (ND683) were operating with the squadron for the first time. The marking and bombing appeared accurate and all crews reported successful sorties although some found the anti-aircraft fire around London (a German raid was in progress) on their way out, a little disconcerting. All aircraft returned safely.

17/18 June, 1944: 10.00hrs 20 aircraft detailed for ops; at 17.50hrs operations cancelled. The following day, during Sunday morning worship, a flying bomb fell on the Guards Chapel at Wellington Barracks, only yards from Buckingham Palace: 119 servicemen and civilians were killed with another 102 seriously wounded.

21/22 June, 1944; WESSELING: There was nothing unusual about Wednesday 21 June, 1944; the weather, as with previous days remained dull and the slight northerly wind kept temperatures a little chilly.

For aircrew the morning passed slowly, whilst activity on the airfield indicated that ops were on the menu for that evening. There had been no operations for the past five days so just after lunch a small crowd had gathered as an airman pinned up the Battle Order; twenty aircraft were detailed with the main briefing at 20.00hrs. For those crews listed, the usual pre-operational routine began, then later, after a noisy meal in the Sgts' Mess and with coffee flasks filled, crews walked or were ferried over to the main site for specialist briefings and then the main briefing. The tape on the wall map showed a route ending just below the Ruhr... Germany for a change.

A force of over 130 Lancasters from 5 Group was to attack the synthetic-oil plant at Wesseling, 15 miles south of Cologne - marking would be by 5 Group Mosquitoes using the 'Newhaven' method. One by one, the various specialists gave their talks, with W/Cmdr Malcolm Crocker concluding the briefing by stating that he too would be operating, and would be taking along Mr Stevenson, a War Correspondent from the BBC. Also flying this night would be both of 49's two Squadron Leaders.

Two tortuous hours now for aircrew, as they awaited the take-off time of 23.00hrs. With oleo legs compressed by their heavy bomb loads, each Lancaster rumbled around to the active runway threshold; a flash of green from the control caravan sent the first aircraft (piloted by F/Lt Johnny Hill) speeding down the concrete strip. On this, the longest day of the year, daylight still lingered during double British summertime, even at such a late hour. As F/Lt Hill's aircraft accelerated past the ever-present group of well wishers, waves and gestures were exchanged by the smiling Lancaster crew but this was to be this particular crew's final take-off, for within just a few short hours, all seven members were to perish over Holland, victims of a deadly German night-fighter.

F/O Pederson RCAF (ND512) and crew were the next away in Bandlaw C-Charlie followed by the remaining 18 aircraft... the last clearing the runway at 23.25hrs. Soon after crossing the enemy coast, fighter flares were sighted, and a deadly running battle with night-fighters ensued across Belgium and Holland. Over the target, met forecasts of clear weather could not have been more wrong; 10/10ths cloud forced the bombers to use the reserve method of bombing by H2S. Meanwhile the night-fighters had landed to re-fuel and the air battle would soon resume on the return leg.

At 03.32hrs, combat exhausted 49 Squadron crews began landing back at Fiskerton. Their opening remarks gave the first hints of the disaster that had befallen the aircrew of 5 Group. S/Ldr Botting (ND957) and crew began first; they reported; *"enemy a/c seem to be exceedingly accurate tonight - saw several aircraft shot down."* Then, just after 04.00hrs, F/O Bill Green RNZAF (JB178) and his tired, battle-chastened crew shuffled into the interrogation room and flopped down; they then commenced to report the following: *"We saw many aircraft shot down... we were attacked twice - after the first attack our rear guns went u/s but we went on... after the second attack the port-inner engine had to be feathered and the bomb load jettisoned as we were losing height rapidly."* Later, whilst sitting back and feeling a little more relaxed as they sipped their rum laced cocoa, the pilot concluded his report by adding: *"My crew behaved exemplarily!"* For his actions this night, New Zealander F/O William Raeburn Green was awarded the DFC... sadly, within a month, Bill and his gallant crew would all lie at rest together in a French Cemetery.

P/O Allen Sullings (LL976) and crew gave a similar report; Sgt Charlie Wright, the mid-upper gunner, recalls that night: *"Doug Simmons in the rear turret shouted the first warning of a fighter attacking from the rear. I determined it as an ME210 and yelled for the skipper to 'corkscrew port'. As we dived down, both Doug and I got in good bursts as the fighter overshot our starboard wing. As we came out of the corkscrew, we could still see him as he attacked again - by this time Doug had cleared a blockage in his guns and we both scored good hits on the night fighter. The German then rolled over on his back and disappeared through the cloud."* P/O Sullings then continued to the target, bombing a cluster of 3 red TI's at 01.47hrs.

F/O Jordan (JB473) and crew were attacked twice after leaving the target; in the first attack, the gunners, Sgts Herring and Fearson, damaged an ME109; in the second attack they also hit a JU88. P/O Lacy (JB399) and crew also survived two attacks by enemy night fighters. This de-brief report, given by F/O Powell (JB702) would later prove to be extremely prophetic: *"Raid apparently a failure at great cost - number of aircraft too small to cope with the number of fighters! - flak over target moderate."*

Meanwhile, outside the intensity of the operations block... in another world... dawn was just breaking over the Lincolnshire Wolds, heralding the start of a fine new day. A corporal removed the blackouts from the windows, letting shafts of bright sunlight penetrate the stuffy smoke filled room... the sun's rays played upon the operations board, where, written in large chalk white capital letters... against the names of SIX aircraft captains were those three impassive words... *'MISSING WITHOUT TRACE'*.

The Station Commander, having just returned from his long vigil at the Watch Office, scanned the ops board in silence, still numbed by the realisation that in just one very short evening, 49 Squadron had lost 42 good men, including its Commanding Officer, and a Squadron Leader. Twenty seven year-old W/Cdr Malcolm Crocker, DFC and bar, along with his second tour crew had all perished over Germany and are buried in the Rheinberg War Cemetery; along-side them lies their intrepid passenger, Mr Kent Stevenson of the BBC.

The experienced S/Ldr Leonard Cox and crew, were also killed when their Lancaster was brought down over Belgium; they are all in the Antwerpen Cemetery. F/Lt Johnny Hill's crew all died over Holland, their Lancaster crashing to the ground near Wettenseind - Nuenen; they are buried in Eindhoven General Cemetery.

P/O Alex Ross and crew have no known grave, but are remembered on the Runnymede Memorial. The circumstances of their loss have yet to be established, but it is thought they came down in the North Sea after combat with a night fighter. The crew's flight engineer was Dennis Palmer; he had joined the RAF early in the war, and one night whilst home on leave, he and his younger brother Don, watched from the shelter of a shop doorway as Hitler's bombers ripped the heart out of their native Coventry... Dennis there and then vowed revenge, and on return from leave he immediately volunteered for aircrew. After training, he was eventually posted along with his crew to 49 Squadron, Fiskerton; Wesseling was their 8th and final operation.

P/O Alex Ross (centre front) and his cheerful crew outside their Fiskerton billet. Flight engineer, Dennis Palmer is second from the left on the back row. The crew failed to return from Wesseling 20/21-6-44; and have no known graves, but are forever remembered at Runnymede. (D. Palmer)

P/O Bert Shinn DFC and crew are known to have come down in the sea off the Dutch coast. P/O Shinn's body was washed ashore near Brouwershaven on 11 July, 1944; he is now buried at Bergan op Zoom. The body of F/Sgt Stanley Hawes was recovered from the beach at Wassenaar also on 11 July, 1944; he is buried in The Hague (Westduin) Cemetery. F/O John Stanley's body was recovered from the sea on 17 July, 1944; he rests with his skipper in Bergan op Zoom Cemetery.

Five members of F/O Les Simpkin's crew survived when their aircraft was brought down near the target. Sadly F/O Simpkin and rear gunner Sgt James Maton were killed and are both buried in the Rheinberg War Cemetery.

That fateful morning at Fiskerton, as the station slowly stirred into life, those fresh from sleep found the whole situation incredulous; six empty dispersals. A bomber base becomes hardened, perhaps almost immune to a steady loss of crews, but on that Thursday morning, at Fiskerton, Dunholme, East Kirkby and Spilsby, all were totally stunned. At Morton Hall near Swinderby (5 Group HQ), the teleprinters chattered out the Base reports:

No. 52 Base.	44 Sqdn	(Dunholme Lodge)	6 Lancasters missing
	49 Sqdn	(Fiskerton)	6 Lancasters missing
	619 Sqdn	(Dunholme Lodge)	6 Lancasters missing
No. 55 Base	57 Sqdn	(East Kirkby)	6 Lancasters missing
	207 Sqdn	(Spilsby)	7 Lancasters missing
	630 Sqdn	(East Kirkby)	5 Lancasters missing

The total casualty list from the operation was 37 aircraft missing, representing 27.8 per cent of the Lancaster force.

In Fiskerton's Sgts' Mess, the surviving crews hungrily ate their bacon and eggs, trying to ignore the empty chairs all around them. The Station Commander had meanwhile telephoned the BBC to personally give them the sad news that Mr Stevenson, their brave correspondent, had failed to return from the previous nights' air operation; any further information received would be communicated immediately. At the same time clerks in the orderly room prepared the details of 42 telegrams... all began with the words; 'Deeply regret to inform you that...'.

FTR NE128	F/O L.N. Simpkin	Pilot	(Killed)
(EA-J)	Sgt A. Ladkin	F/E	(P.o.W.)
'A'Flt	F/S T.A. Wilson	NAV	(P.o.W.)
	W/O R.S. Phillips RAAF	W/AG	(P.o.W.)
	Sgt W. Watson	A/G	(P.o.W.)
Crew on their	W/O E. O'Reilly RCAF	B/A	(P.o.W.)
11th operation	Sgt J.A.T. Maton	A/G	(Killed)

FTR ND683	P/O A.W. Shinn DFC	Pilot	(Killed)
(EA-K)	Sgt N.G.V. Pettit	F/E	(Missing)
'A Flt'	F/O J.B. Stanley	NAV	(Killed)
	F/S S. Hawes	W/AG	(Killed)
	Sgt A.E. Dicken	A/G	(Killed)
Crew on their	P/O V.C. Cully RCAF	B/A	(Missing)
10th opeartion	Sgt A. Armstrong	A/G	(Missing)
FTR ND695	P/O A.R. Ross	Pilot	(Missing)
(EA-B)	Sgt D.W. Palmer	F/E	(Missing)
'A Flt'	F/S C.G. Morton	NAV	(Missing)
	Sgt C.C. Holden	W/AG	(Missing)
	Sgt A.D. Griffin	A/G	(Missing)
Crew on their	P/O G.F. MacGregor RCAF	B/A	(Missing)
8th operation	Sgt D.W.E. Hardy	A/G	(Missing)
FTR ME675	F/L J.R. Hill	Pilot	(Killed)
(EA-R)	Sgt G.F. Witty	F/E	(Killed)
'B Flt'	F/O K.W. Jones RNZAF	NAV	(Killed)
	Sgt T.B. Whewell	W/AG	(Killed)
	Sgt T.A. Hall	A/G	(Killed)
Crew on their	F/S D.M.F. Bell	B/A	(Killed)
9th operation	F/S G.F. Wood	A/G	(Killed)
FTR ME808	S/L L.E. Cox	Pilot	(Killed)
(EA-D)	F/O J.H. Ingram	F/E	(Killed)
'A Flt'	F/O J.M. Freckleton DFM	NAV	(Killed)
	F/O W. Mather DFM	W/AG	(Killed)
Crew on their	F/O W.E. Day	A/G	(Killed)
2nd operation	F/O M. James DFC	B/A	(Killed)
with 49 Sqdn	F/O A. Hambly	A/G	(Killed)
FTR LL900	W/C M. Crocker DFC&Bar	Pilot	(Killed)
(EA-T)	F/L A.E.A. Matthews DFC	F/E	(Killed)
'B Flt'	P/O L.B. Benson DFM	NAV	(Killed)
	F/O J.R. Worthington DFC	W/OP	(Killed)
	P/O A.D. Creighton RCAF	A/G	(Killed)
Crew on their	F/O K. Dutton	B/A	(Killed)
8th operation	P/O D.H. Carr DFM	A/G	(Killed)
with 49 Sqdn	MR K. Stevenson	BBC	(Killed)

24/25 June, 1944; POMMEREVAL: For the following two nights after the Wesseling catastrophe, the squadron was stood down. On Saturday 24th, BBC radio news reported that to date, 750,000 allied troops had been landed in Normandy. But the flying-bomb threat was the main concern of Bomber Command this night; 739 aircraft were detailed to attack 7 different launch sites. Despite its grievous losses 49 Squadron was able to offer 13 crews for an attack on Pommerval. The names of three new crews appeared on the Battle Order for the first time; they were piloted by F/O Taylor (LM572), P/O Poole (ND957) and F/O McCracken (LM541).

A clear moonlit night gave ideal bombing conditions, but it also gave the German night fighters a keen advantage. In all, 22 Lancasters failed to return, and sadly one of them carried the 49 Squadron crew of F/O Taylor, on only their first operation; four crew members managed to escape with their lives, but sadly the other three (including 39 year-old F/O James Judd W/AG) did not survive and are buried in a Somme Churchyard.

F/O Powell perhaps best sums up the night when at interrogation he commented: *"Weather conditions favourable... to enemy! - half light - if orbiting had not been ordered, the force would have left the target before the fighters arrived."*

FTR LM572	F/O G.B.L. Taylor	Pilot	(P.o.W.)
(EA-P)	Sgt J.R. Sidebottom	F/E	(P.o.W.)
'B Flt'	Sgt D. Reid RCAF	NAV	(Evaded)
	F/O J.F. Judd	W/AG	(Killed)
	Sgt R. Thompson	A/G	(Killed)
Crew on their	Sgt E.A. Milligan	B/A	(P.o.W.)
1st operation	Sgt D.A. Wilson	A/G	(Killed)

27/28 June, 1944; MARGUISE MIMOYECQUES: During the morning, Herbert Morrison, the Home Secretary and minister of Home Security, told the war cabinet that since the VI attacks had started, 1,600 people had been killed and 4,500 seriously wounded. That night Bomber Command made ready to dispatch 721 bombers against 6 launch sites.

Shortly before 23.00hrs, twelve Lancasters took to the air from Fiskerton to join the throng of aircraft heading for France. S/Ldr Twiggs (ND957) and crew operated with the squadron for the first time. Bombing appeared to be accurate, with most crews confirming their attacks using Gee. Defences were light, and although fighter flares appeared near the coast, only P/O Poole (LM541) and crew saw a fighter. Three Lancasters failed to return; all 49's landed safely.

And so June 1944 drew to a close; a month that will forever be remembered in the annals of history because of D-Day. A month that had promised such high hopes of an early end to the war. But on Friday 30 June, as yet more V1s devastated more of London (one landed outside the Air Ministry in the Strand, another near Bush House in the Aldwych, killing 198 people).

JUNE 1944

The stalwart population of this embattled nation knew that there was still a very dangerous enemy to be defeated... and a whole continent still to be liberated. Crews on the bomber squadrons knew all too well, that their task had not been made any easier... sixty-four good men were missing on operations from Fiskerton during June... and 49 Squadron was not alone in suffering such losses. Now on bomber stations throughout eastern England there was little mention of French targets being 'milk runs' and such operations certainly ceased to be considered as one-third of an operation towards completing a tour.

OPERATIONAL SUMMARY - JUNE 1944

Date	Target	Desp	E/R	FTR	Remarks
2/3	WIMEREUX	17	-	-	
5/6	LA PERNELLE	20	-	-	
6	CAEN	19	-	-	D-Day/Daylight
8/9	PONTAUBAULT	21	1	-	
9/10	ETAMPES	21	-	2	F/O Bell FTR
					P/O Smiley FTR
12/13	CAEN	18	-	-	
14/15	AUNAY	18	-	-	
16/17	BEAUVOIR	20	-	-	
21/22	WESSELING	20	-	6	W/C Crocker FTR
					P/O Ross FTR
					S/L Cox FTR
					F/O Simpkin FTR
					F/O Hill FTR
					P/O Shinn FTR
24/25	POMMEREVAL	13	-	1	F/O Taylor FTR
27/28	MIMOYECQUES	12	-	-	

Total number of sorties flown	199
Failed to return	9
Total tons of bombs of all types dropped -	906.01
Operational hours flown during June 1944 -	849.45
Non-operational hours flown during June 1944 -	236.15

HONOURS AND AWARDS - JUNE 1944

F/O Jones	DFC	F/S S.E. Stevenson	DFM	F/L W.J.V. Hamilton	DFC
F/S J.J. Page	DFM	W/O T.M.E. Weller	DFC	Sgt J.A. Kirwan	DFM
P/O K.H. Blackham	DFC	F/S D. Andrew	DFM	W/C A.A. Adams	DFC
F/S V.F. Pitcher	DFM	F/S M.G. Price	DFM	P/O C. Roantree RAAF	DFC
P/O J.V. Reddish	DFC	F/S J.H. Prior	DFM		

JULY 1944

4/5 July, 1944; ST-LEU-D'ESSERENT (CRIEL): On the previous two nights operations had been cancelled during the early evening, but on Tuesday 4th, 5 Group did manage to dispatch 231 aircraft against the underground flying-bomb store at St-Leu-D'Esserent. Night-fighters were out in force once again and engaged the bombers in the target area. F/O Deacon RCAF (JB473) and crew described the scene as they approached the target: *"Three unidentified a/c ahead on starboard falling in flames and exploding on ground - cause unknown - another four-engined a/c seen on starboard quarter on fire, hit by tracer; it carried on then hit by flak it fell and exploded on the ground."*

F/O Edwards (ND787) and crew had combat with an FW 190: *"He came in from astern to attack from below; rear gunner, Sgt Payn LeSueur RCAF opened fire, and fire was returned by enemy who then broke off his attack. This combat took place just after we had been coned by 8 searchlights."*

F/O Pederson RCAF (ND512) and crew were engaged by an ME 110 just after bombing:

"The fighter attacked from the starboard quarter down. Both gunners, Sgts Petzke RCAF and Goldy started firing at 600yds and the enemy returned fire; as he broke off the fighter was hit by the Lancaster's gunners. The ME 110 came in again but after fire from the gunners he again broke away. No claims - Fishpond reacted."

Note: Presumably this means the Fishpond screen showed the attacking aircraft.

Fiskerton, summer 1944:
The Pederson crew enjoy a coffee at dispersal with driver, Dot Everett.

In the background is their usual kite ND512 (EA-C); both Lancaster and crew would survive their time on the squadron, the Lancaster eventually being passed on to an HCU.

The crew endured several combats, and on one occasion Jack Harvison, flight engineer received very serious wounds.

They are (back row l to r), Len Goldy, rear gunner; Wally Petzke RCAF, mid -upper gunner; Larry Pederson RCAF, pilot; Wally Dodkins, wireless operator. (Front row l to r), Larry Shaw RCAF, navigator; Dot Everett, driver; Jack Olsen RCAF, bomb aimer; Jack Harvison RCAF, flight engineer. (Mrs D. Smith)

F/O Brady (ND383) and crew also fought off an attack by an enemy aircraft: *"The fighter came in from the port quarter up and the rear gunner, Sgt Spicer, opened fire as the Lancaster took evasive action. Hits were seen on the enemy a/c and minutes later a small aircraft was seen to crash 10 miles to port; - no claim."*

F/O Buchanan (PB207) and crew had flown their brand-new Lancaster from the English coast all the way out on three engines. Over France they were attacked by a JU88; Sgt Greenwood, in the rear turret, opened fire at 500yds as the fighter came in from the port quarter below - there was no return fire - no claim.

The crews of P/O Poole (LM190) and P/O Rowley (ND647) both reported quiet trips! Altogether 13 Lancasters were lost from the raid, which from a bombing point of view had been a success.

Of the 17 crews that had departed Fiskerton, one failed to return. Sadly, F/O Harold Dod and crew flying a brand-new aircraft, were all killed over France, and are buried together in Romescamp Cemetery near Oise.

FTR PB195	F/O H.F. Dod	Pilot	(Killed)
(EA-P)	Sgt V.A. Keen	F/ E	(Killed)
'B Flt'	F/S N. Gordon	NAV	(Killed)
	Sgt L. Horner	W/AG	(Killed)
	Sgt B.R. Scott	A/G	(Killed)
Crew on their	F/S J.L. Cox	A/B	(Killed)
17th operation	P/O J.R. Truscott RCAF	A/G	(Killed)

7/8 July, 1944; ST-LUE-D'ESSERENT (CRIEL): 5 Group paid a second visit to the V1 storage dump at St Leu on the 7th. A slightly smaller force of 208 Lancasters led by Pathfinder Mosquitoes, accurately bombed the tunnels in which the flying bombs were stored. But the cost in men and aircraft was to be high; 29 Lancasters and 2 Mosquitoes were lost as German night-fighters again took their toll.

Shortly after 22.00hrs, 16 aircraft departed Fiskerton. Operating for the first time with 49 Squadron, were the crews piloted by: S/Ldr Lace (LM191), P/O Barrie (ED602), P/O Squibb RCAF (LM190) and P/O Cannon (ND383). After completing their sorties, the squadron's aircraft started returning to base just after 03.00hrs on Saturday morning. At de-brief as with the previous operation, crews reported several sightings of aircraft falling in flames and being engaged in deadly combat with night-fighters. S/Ldr Lace (LM191) and crew were forced to land at Woodbridge with their port-outer engine on fire after combat with a night fighter. F/Lt Powell (JB701) and crew were hit by a night fighter just before bombing:

"The eneny aircraft attacked at 01.12hrs from the starboard quarter above, hitting the rudder. Sgt Moore, the rear gunner opened fire but no results were seen - the Lancaster was corkscrewed and the e/a was lost to view. At 01.30hrs another e/a was seen starboard up - Lancaster was again corkscrewed. At 01.46hrs a JU88 sighted on the starboard beam up, which opened fire - both gunners returned fire and the enemy a/c was lost in a corkscrew."

F/O Green RNZAF (JB178) and crew witnessed the demise of a Pathfinder which exploded on the ground in a mass of green and red T.I's. The terse de-brief report given by F/O Arnold (ND473) and crew briefly describes the grim reality of the air-war being fought in the night skies over France during the summer of 1944: *"At 01.13hrs, 12,000ft, Lanc going down on fire and crashed 3miles on port beam due to fighter - 01.20hrs, 12,500ft, Lanc on fire, crashed to ground 1 mile starboard quarter due to fighter, tracer seen - 01.22hrs, 12,500ft, Lanc on fire going down, starboard quarter 2 miles; 2 parachutes seen, both on fire! due to fighter tracer."*

Shortly after bombing, F/O McCracken (PB207) and crew were hit by an ME210. Both gunners returned fire as the enemy fighter was successfully avoided in the ensuing corkscrew. F/O McCracken nursed his severely-damaged Lancaster back to Fiskerton; the following day PB207 was declared a write off!

After recording the interrogation reports, Intelligence Officers reluctantly entered the words 'missing without trace' against the names of two crews... there could well have been more. What did shock and sadden many at Fiskerton was the loss of one very experienced crew; F/Lt George Ball DFC (LM541) was flying his 30th operation, and most of his crew their 29th. Tragically they were all killed and are buried in Le Chesne Cemetery, Eure, France.

The second crew reported missing was that piloted by F/O Cyril Baker (LL976); again there were no survivors. This crew lie at rest together in Marissel Cemetery, Oise, France.

Missing LL976	F/O C. Baker	Pilot	(Killed)
(EA-A)	Sgt J.M. Moss	F/E	(Killed)
'A Flt'	W/O J.H. Stibbard RAAF	NAV	(Killed)
	Sgt W. Higgins	W/OP	(Killed)
	Sgt E.W. Everett	A/G	(Killed)
Crew on their	F/S H.H. Hewitt	A/B	(Killed)
4th operation	Sgt R.E. Nineham	A/G	(Killed)

Missing LM541	F/L G.E. Ball DFC	Pilot	(Killed)
(EA-N)	Sgt E. Wardman	F/E	(Killed)
'B Flt'	P/O G. Millar	NAV	(Killed)
	P/O J. Kernahan	W/OP	(Killed)
	Sgt J.A. Kirwan DFM	A/G	(Killed)
Crew on their	P/O G.A. Rae RCAF	A/B	(Killed)
29th operation	F/S G.J.W.Parkinson DFM	A/G	(Killed)

12/13 July, 1944; CULMONT CHALINDREY: Operations had been scrubbed at the very last moment on the previous two evenings, but on Wednesday 12, the railway target at Culmont was attacked by Lancasters of 5 Group. Fiskerton launched 14 aircraft, but F/O Rowley (ND647) and crew returned early with their port-outer engine u/s.

The remaining aircraft went on to complete successful sorties; 12 returned to base but one squadron aircraft landed at USAAF Polebrook (perhaps they had a preference for American style breakfasts... Maple syrup with everything).

F/O Edwards (ND787) and crew were the only ones to encounter trouble when 'Fishpond' picked up a JU88 patrolling the enemy coast; fire was withheld until a corkscrew was initiated, then mid-upper gunner, Sgt Chandler, opened fire as the fighter broke away - no claim was made. 5 Group suffered the loss of 2 aircraft.

SURPRISE GIFT

During the early morning of Thursday 13 July, whilst bombers were returning to their home airfields, a very unexpected visitor landed at Woodbridge in Essex.

A Brand-new JU88G-1 of 7/NJG2 fitted with the latest German electronic equipment had by accident, landed into British hands. RAF technicians soon discovered the JU88 to be equipped with Naxos-Z, SN-2 radar and most importantly a new device code named 'Flensburg'. It was discovered that 'Flensburg', was a passive homing device tuned to receive emissions from bombers fitted with 'Monica', the tail warning system. It was found that the JU88 could pick up and home in on a bomber with 'Monica' switched on, whilst it was 130 miles away.

When Harris heard of this revelation, he ordered the immediate removal of 'Monica' from all aircraft. Naxos-Z could also detect H2S, Tinsel and Mandrel; from now on, their use was forbidden until enemy airspace was reached. All of 49's aircraft were fitted with these devices, and during June/July 1944, eighteen of the squadron's aircraft were to be brought down, the majority by German night fighters.

15/16 July, 1944; NEVERS: Two railway targets were the subject of attention by 222 Lancasters; 13 aircraft from Fiskerton were part of the force bound for Nevers rail yards.
F/O Edwards (ND787) and crew lost the use of their starboard-outer engine whilst climbing for height over Lincoln; the crew decided to 'press on' and carried out a successful sortie.

Both raids were successful, for the loss of 3 Lancasters.

All 49's crews returned safely to Fiskerton, claiming good results, including the two new crews piloted by P/O Lee (LM207) and F/O Russell (LM190). At de-brief several crews reported; *"trail trace attachments seen all the way down."*

It was on 17 July, that the USAAF first used 'napalm'; it was dropped during an attack on a fuel dump at Coutances.

18 July, 1944; CAEN (DAYLIGHT): A daylight raid was scheduled for this Tuesday morning. Over 900 aircraft of Bomber Command were to bomb fortified villages around Caen in support of the British Second Army's armoured attack, Operation 'Goodwood'.

Crews were briefed and aircraft prepared during Monday as it was to be a very early take-off with the actual attack taking place just after dawn. In clear conditions, 16 of the squadron's crews, including new boys piloted by P/O Burns RCAF (JB701), completed successful sorties over the Normandy battle area. All 49's aircraft returned safely with F/O Russell (ND647) and crew being the last home, touching down at 07.36hrs. The operation proved to be highly successful, although 5 Halifaxes and 1 Lancaster were lost.

18/19 July, 1944; REVIGNY: Crews, exhausted from their pre-dawn exploits were roused from their beds to be told they were 'on' again that night.

Two railway targets at Aulnoye and Revigny in France had been selected for attack by 253 Lancasters and 10 Mosquitoes of 1,3,5 and 8 Groups. P/O Burns RCAF (JB701) and crew were the first away from Fiskerton at 22.38hrs, ahead of 14 other Lancasters from the squadron all bound for the rail junction at Revigny. F/O Pederson (ND512) and crew were coned by searchlights just after crossing the enemy coast; the pilot managed to evade the searchlights by corkscrewing his aircraft for 3 minutes. Both targets were hit, severing the rail lines to the battle front, although several bomb aimers reported confusion caused by fires burning near the Red Spot, believed to be aircraft which had been shot down.

P/O Burns and crew were held in searchlights for 4 minutes on their way in to bomb. Two Lancasters (from other squadrons) failed to return from Aulnoye, but the 5 Group attack on Revigny ran into the full fury of German night-fighters. F/O Arnold (ME787) and crew were attacked by a JU88 four minutes after leaving the target.

The gunners, Sgts Grabb and Salavaara, returned fire forcing the night fighter to break off his attack. But their Lancaster had sustained severe damage including the loss of hydraulic pressure; it was decided to make for Woodbridge emergency airfield where a safe landing was achieved.

At interrogation, crews once again reported an extremely large amount of fighter activity. A glance at Fiskerton's operation board showed 5 crews were still overdue. By 06.00hrs, news had come through that F/O Arnold and crew had safely made Woodbridge, but of the remaining four crews, nothing more was heard; 49 Squadron had received yet another sickening blow, as four crews were reported 'missing'.

New Zealander, F/O William Green DFC and crew, nearing the end of a very tough tour had sadly all been killed. They lie along-side each other in Herbisse Churchyard, Aube in France.

The crew of Australian skipper, F/O William Appleyard, were also near to completing their tour; none of the crew survived when they too were brought down over France. Their graves are in Granges-sur-Aube Churchyard near Marne.

F/O Cliff Lacy DFC, and his experienced crew including two Aussies and one Canadian, also fell victims during the savage air battle over Revigny. The two gunners, Sgt Barlow and P/O Wellein RCAF, were the only survivors and were taken to Luft 7. The remainder lie at rest in St Ouen-en-Domprot Churchyard near Marne.

Six crew members, including the skipper F/O Roy Deacon RCAF, managed to escape from Q-Queenie safely, but sadly P/O Albert Rammage RCAF, did not survive and is buried in Vassimont-et-Chapelaine Churchyard, Marne. On the return leg their Lancaster received flak damage. A prowling night fighter was attracted to the damaged bomber and came in to finish them off.

With the assistance of the French five members of the crew evaded capture; Sgt John Diley, F/Sgt Allan Harpell RCAF and Sgt Harold Sharp returned to England on 3 September 1944 followed by Sgt Don Wilson RCAF the next day. Sgt Bill Fortune also returned during early September. Their pilot, F/O Deacon escaped by parachute, but on landing broke his leg after hitting a tree.

The French tried to help him but eventually had to hand him over to the German authorities. He was taken to the Military Hospital at Chalons-sur-Marne and then later transferred to the hospital attached to the PoW camp. At the end of August, the town was liberated by the advancing Americans. 'Walking' out of the camp, Roy Deacon was handed over by the Americans to the Red Cross. On Saturday 2 September he arrived at Horsham St Faith near Norwich in a B-24 Liberator.

The pilot of this Lichtenstein SN-2 radar equipped JU88G-14 flew a reciprocal compass heading (by mistake he claimed) and landed at RAF Woodbridge on 13th July 1944.
Illustration by John Ward

A detailed account of the Deacon crew's experiences (and much more) is given in Oliver Clutton-Brock's excellent book "Massacre over the Marne" printed by Patrick Stephens Ltd. Note: 'Uncle' Will by chance met Roy Deacon during a visit to Canada in 1980. Unable to remember a thing about the raid or his crew, Roy remembers waking in a German hospital where German doctors managed to save his leg from being amputated. Whilst in hospital he was attacked by a German nurse with a pair of scissors. It seems that she had a close relative killed in allied bombing.

The squadron was stood down on the 19th. For the survivors, the luxury of a night off, but it would be back to work as usual on the 20th. By now, 1,596 AA guns had been moved to the south coast of England in an attempt to combat the V-weapons.

FTR JB473	F/O R.M. Deacon RCAF	Pilot	(P.o.W.)
(EA-W)	Sgt H. Sharp	F/E	(Evaded)
'B' Flt	Sgt W. Fortune	NAV	(Evaded)
	Sgt J.A. Diley	W/OP	(Evaded)
	Sgt D. Wilson RCAF	A/G	(Evaded)
Crew on their	Sgt A.R. Harpell RCAF	B/A	(Evaded)
13th operation	P/O A.J. Rammage RCAF	A/G	(Killed)
FTR PB231	F/O C. Lacy DFC	Pilot	(Killed)
(EA-H)	Sgt I. Shingles	F/E	(Killed)
'A Flt'	W/O L.B. Holmes RAAF	NAV	(Killed)
	F/S D.J. Ryan RAAF	W/OP	(Killed)
	Sgt W.G. Barlow	A/G	(P.o.W.)
Crew on their	F/S V. Gallagher	A/B	(Killed)
16th operation	Sgt J.C. Wellein RCAF	A/G	(P.o.W.)
FTR ND684	F/O W.D. Appleyard RAAF	Pilot	(Killed)
(EA-V)	P/O H.E. Turner	F/E	(Killed)
'B Flt'	F/S D.W. Blumfield	NAV	(Killed)
	F/S G.J. Perry	W/AG	(Killed)
	P/O E.M. Matheson RCAF	A/G	(Killed)
Crew on their	F/S G.W. Jameson	B/A	(Killed)
26th operation	Sgt R.F.H.Viollet	A/G	(Killed)
FTR JB178	F/L W.R. Green DFC RNZAF	Pilot	(Killed)
(EA-U)	Sgt F.S. Seymour	F/E	(Killed)
'B' Flt	F/S H.R. Neal	NAV	(Killed)
	F/S C. Davison	W/AG	(Killed)
	Sgt A.A. Ansell	A/G	(Killed)
Crew on their	P/O M.C. Hollard RNZAF	B/A	(Killed)
27th operation	Sgt G.E.D.Hands	A/G	(Killed)

20/21 July, 1944; COURTRAI: Over 300 Lancasters led by 15 Pathfinder Mosquitoes successfully attacked the railway yards and junction near Courtrai in Belgium. Night fighters were active and one attacked P/O Lee (JB399) and crew just after bombing; at interrogation, the pilot praised his two gunners Sgt F.W. Smith and F/Sgt Townsend RCAF for their 'good show' in seeing off their attacker.

F/O Edwards (ND787) reported that fighters pursued the bomber stream halfway into the Channel on the return leg. Fortunately, all of the 12 aircraft sent by 49 Squadron returned safely to base. Bomber Command lost 9 Lancasters.

23/24 July, 1944; KIEL: The sudden switch to a German target, plus the elaborate use of radio counter-measures caught German controllers totally by surprise. A force of over 600 bombers, hidden by a 'Mandrel' jamming screen, severely damaged the U-boat yards and naval facilities of Kiel. German rescue services had great difficulty because of the high number of delayed-action bombs, numbering around 500.

Only 4 aircraft were lost out of the total force; Fiskerton's 12 aircraft were home by 04.25hrs.

24/25 July, 1944; DONGES: Canadian Halifaxes had attacked this oil target near the mouth of the River Loire the previous night causing considerable damage. 5 Group Lancasters were required to complete the job and 104 were dispatched accordingly.

49 Squadron managed to get 14 aircraft airborne with the inclusion of three new crews piloted by P/O Mallinson (ND792), F/O Carlyle (LM649) and F/Lt Millington (LM648).

The target was completely devastated for the loss of 3 Lancasters. All 49's aircraft returned with reports of good bombing and excellent RT control.

25/26 July, 1944; STUTTGART: This was the second in a series of three heavy raids on Stuttgart in five nights. The force, consisting of 550 Lancasters and Halifaxes included 14 aircraft from Fiskerton.

On approaching the target area, F/O 'Pete' Pederson RCAF (JB701) and crew became coned by a group of searchlights. During their attempts to evade them, the crew became disorientated and were unable to confirm the target. Being over a built up area in the vicinity of Stuttgart, they bombed the centre of another group of searchlights. Having completed their sortie they arrived back at Fiskerton during daylight hours. On surveying old G-George, they found numerous flak holes in the fuselage and tail plane.

F/Lt Millington (LM648) and crew were also hit by flak; damage was sustained to the cockpit perspex, starboard rudder, port main plane, mid-upper turret, escape hatch, starboard elevator and bomb doors! Being too late to reach the target, they opted to bomb Eporenheim as an alternative. Their understated de-brief was concluded as follows: *"It was a 'rough' trip as we had no broadcast winds and no joy on H2S."*

CLOSE ENCOUNTER

Turning for home, P/O Allen Sullings (ND602) and crew experienced a very close encounter with a German night-fighter; navigator Juan Christian recalls the incident:

"At 02.50hrs having left the target area and climbed to 21,000ft as planned, we were attacked by a night-fighter."

A sudden violent impact then shuddered through the Lancaster. As P/O Sullings and Sgt Johnnie Richards, the F/E, fought for control of the crippled bomber, P/O Henderson (flying in the mid-upper turret that night) informed the pilot that they had just been hit head-on by a JU88! Charlie Wright was tail end Charlie this night. 'Chris' Christian continues:

"In the collision, the starboard-outer was ripped off which in turn damaged the starboard inner airscrew and rendered the feathering gear u/s, thus obliging us to keep that engine running.
The resultant vibration arising from the eccentric path of the damaged propeller was severe and we rapidly lost height to 17,500 feet before skipper was able to regain sufficient control to allow us to think of making it at least over France. The gunners believe the German fighter went down as the combined result of the collision and their gunfire.

We continued to lose height in spite of pushing the two port engines 'through the gate' - a condition not recommended for longer than three minutes - until the starboard inner prop fell off, much to the relief of the flight engineer (and the rest of us) at 04.30hrs and at 2,500 feet. Relieved of the strain of vibration, the aircraft began to climb on the two port engines and the skipper and flight engineer were able to throttle back to a more acceptable rev setting and we headed for home."

Now began a nerve-racking and perilous journey home. Over Etampes, the struggling bomber was coned by searchlights and flak poured up at them. Re-crossing the French coast near Caen, they headed for Manston's emergency runway. This was during a period of constant V1 attacks; the sky over the south of England was one mass of barrage balloons. Manston, having received an SOS from ND602, quickly dispatched a Spitfire out to meet the damaged aircraft. Having made a rendezvous with the crippled bomber, the Spitfire pilot then shepherded her through the maze of balloon cables into Manston, where a perfect landing was executed by P/O Sullings.

There is a yet another twist to this crew's amazing display of tenacity. At the 1995 Squadron Reunion in Lincolnshire, Juan Christian, who hails from the Isle of Man, revealed the following personal incident to the author:

"It happened three weeks after the Stuttgart raid when I was at home on leave. I travelled home on a bus with my father when he surprised me by asking if I had been in some 'trouble' as the leave seemed a bit early. I said yes, and he asked me if it had been over Stuttgart. I was taken aback at this and asked how he knew. He told me that he had heard on the radio that there had been a raid on Stuttgart on the night of 25/26 July... and then went on to ask if it happened at ten minutes to three in the morning. By now I was flabbergasted! He went on to tell me that at that precise time my mother wakened him to tell him there was something the matter with me - there was an aeroplane flying about at the time so he told her to go back to sleep and stop imagining things.

When we were struck by the JU88 and initially went out of control my immediate thought was of my parents and of how they would receive a telegram in the day to say that I was missing."

As Juan concluded... *"Tell that one to Arthur C. Clarke!!!"*

Manston soon notified Fiskerton, that the Sullings crew had made a safe landing there... but on the operations board at Fiskerton, one aircraft was still unaccounted for.

Fiskerton, summer 1944:

The 'lucky' Sullings crew, survivors of a crash landing at Syerston LFS, and a head-on collision with a JU88, they completed one of the quickest tours in 5 Group:

(Back row l to r); Doug Simmons, rear gunner; Jim Skidmore, wireless operator; Johnnie Richards, flight engineer; Charlie Wright, mid-upper gunner.

(front row l to r); Chris Christian, navigator; Alan Sullings, pilot; Eddie Haines, bomb-aimer. (J. Christian)

The following article in a French newspaper some fifty years later sheds some light on the fate of F/O Walter Buchanan and his crew:

A VILLAGE IN FRANCE

'Over fifty years ago, on 26th July 1944, a 49 Squadron Lancaster bomber was returning from a raid on Stuttgart and, according to eye-witnesses, appeared to try to make an emergency landing. The aircraft crashed into a wood near the village of Coignieres in northern France, killing all seven of the crew.

The mayor at the time gathered together a seach party and went to the crash site with the aim of retrieving the bodies, and thus preventing the Germans from having access to them. Despite warnings from the Germans that the bodies should be buried where they fell, they were brought back to the village.

The mayor, M Godot, requisitioned seven coffins and a burial service took place, conducted by the village priest. A large crowd attended, including many from other villages.
Word had got around, despite the fact that the Germans were in occupation. A memorial was erected and the Tricolour flown, again in defiance of German regulations.

Immediately after the funeral the Germans called at the mayor's house to demand the location of the crash site. Inside the house were the dignitaries from local villages who had taken part in the funeral ceremony. Whilst the mayor was trying to convince the Germans that nothing unusual was going on, and indicating very approximately the area of the crash on a map, his daughter secretly left the house to remove as many of the wreaths and flags as possible from the graves and the memorial. Fortunately the Germans did not leave by the town square, otherwise they could have seen the remains of the decorations.

The villagers took great risks in retrieving the bodies and burying them with honour, and had they been found out would have suffered the consequences.

Since that time the old Comrades Association and the town Council have ensured that the crew has been remembered as part of the May 8th and November 11th acts of remembrance.

Jacqueline Godot was the young daughter of the mayor who rushed out to remove the wreaths and flags when the Germans arrived after the funeral, and she remembers very well the aircraft flying low over the village just before it crashed. She still lives in the village today, with her husband Raymond and son Alan, and is very active as a local councillor. With her husband she played a major part of organising ceremonies in the past, and 50 years after the crash of the Lancaster, with the present mayor - Henri Pailleux, the Town Council and the Old Comrades Association organised a very special ceremony on 19th June 1994.

The ceremony was also attended by S/Ldr Weight, representing the Air Attache from the British Embassy in Paris, many people from the village, and families of the pilot and crew. These included the son, daughter and nephew of the pilot, who all live with their families in Campden, the pilot's sister, Miss D. Buchanan from Sutton in Surrey and Mrs Owen and Mrs Young, sisters of Sgt Crane from Somerset.

The whole day's programme started in the same church with the actual service that was used in 1945, a year after the event. This was followed by the placing of wreaths on the British Graves and on the grave of the mayor in 1944, M Godot. A memorial was unveiled near the crash site, and had been especially designed and made for the occasion. It is a model of a Lancaster in white stone, with a marble inscription. After speeches by the Mayor and S/Ldr Weight, there was a fly-past by a 'Flying Fortress'. It flew low over the crowd three times. A reception next to the village hall was followed by a superb feast at a nearby chateau. An emotional and eventful day ended at about 8pm, with no effort having been spared by the local people to make a most memorable day.'

Members of 49 Squadron Association are forever indebted to the Godot family and indeed all the villagers of Coignieres for the care and devotion shown towards their fallen comrades.

FTR PB250	F/O W.J.F. Buchanan	Pilot	(Killed)
(EA-J)	Sgt A. Ashby	F/E	(Killed)
'A'Flt	F/S P.M. Kitto	NAV	(Killed)
	Sgt G.W. Picker	W/OP	(Killed)
	Sgt C.J. Crane	A/G	(Killed)
Crew on their	F/S E. Shackleton	B/A	(Killed)
9th operation	Sgt E. Greenwood	A/G	(Killed)

A photograph of F/Lt Botting and crew at 1661 HCU Winthorpe in April 1944 shortly before joining 49 Squadron.
With a Short Stirling in the background they are from l to r: Unknown; F/Sgt Timms, F/Sgt Bishop; F/O Edwards; F/Lt Botting; F/Sgt Wilmot RAAF; Sgt Bennett RCAF; Sgt Denny.
Survivors of the Wesseling raid in June, the crew's skipper was promoted to W/Cdr and became CO of 49 Squadron until the end of the war. (J.A. Edwards)

26/27 July, 1944; GIVORS: The 5 Group attack on railway yards at Givors by 178 Lancasters and 9 Mosquitoes included nine aircraft from 49 Squadron. Despite 10/10ths cloud and poor visibility due to rain and haze, an accurate bombing attack took place.

Six aircraft failed to return; 4 Lancasters and 2 Mosquitoes of 627 Squadron, Woodhall Spa. Several of Woodhall's pathfinder Mossies suffered in the severe weather conditions of rain, hail, electric storms and heavy icing. One of the missing Mosquitoes (DZ534), was flown by F/O Mike Gribbon DFM, with navigator F/L Bob Griffiths RCAF.

Lightning storms had put their compass 50 degrees out, and as they flew north with Gee and the ASI u/s, fuel became critical. Their SOS was heard by Exeter, but with insufficient petrol to reach a landing ground, the pilot decided to ditch the aircraft at 04.53hrs. The US Navy picked them up 12 miles east of Cherbourg; both crew members had slight cuts and were taken to the 12th Field Hospital Cherbourg. They later returned to Woodhall, where together, they went on to complete a tour of 44 operations.

At Fiskerton, the final returning Lancaster, piloted by F/O Carlyle (LM207), touched down at 07.17hrs. All nine of 49 Squadron's aircraft had returned safely including the three new crews of F/O Furber (PB295), F/O Parkin (PB348) and F/O Pereira (JB399).

28/29 July, 1944; STUTTGART: If cloud and bad weather had caused problems on the previous raid, then the bright moon conditions that prevailed over France this night were to prove an even greater hazard to the bombers. As the force of nearly 500 aircraft headed for Stuttgart, German night-fighters were waiting, and in the ensuing air battle 39 Lancasters were shot down. Fiskerton had 12 aircraft airborne.

F/O Mallinson (ND957) and crew survived an attack by a Ju88 by slipping into cloud. Sadly, such luck did not befall the Powell crew; F/Lt William Powell (JB701) and crew were all killed when their Lancaster was brought down over France. The flight engineer and rear gunner have separate graves, but the remaining five crew members are in a collective grave; all seven rest in St Martin-sur-Oreuse Cemetery, Yonne.
The remaining 49 Squadron aircraft all returned safely to base, with P/O Sullings (ND473) and crew the last to land at 06.14hrs.

FTR JB701	F/L W.L. Powell	Pilot	(Killed)
(EA-G)	Sgt J.F. West	F/E	(Killed)
'A' Flt	F/O G.E. Franklin	NAV	(Killed)
	F/S D.C. Stephens	W/OP	(Killed)
	Sgt G.E. Kirkpatrick	A/G	(Killed)
Crew on their	F/O A.S. Cole	B/A	(Killed)
17th operation	Sgt T. Moore	A/G	(Killed)

It was reported that during the US bombing raid on Merseburg on 28th July, formations of USAAF Fortresses were attacked by Me163's, the "Komet", a rocket powered German fighter.

30 July, 1944; CAEN (DAYLIGHT): Just before 06.00hrs, on Friday 30 July, 12 of the squadron's aircraft coughed and spluttered into life, in preparation for a daylight operation. The purpose of the raid was to assist a US ground attack in the Normandy battle area. Cloud over the target caused many difficulties for the force of 662 Lancasters and Halifaxes, who had to search for the markers put down by the Oboe Mosquitoes.

Just one aircraft from 49 Squadron managed to attack; F/O Brady (ND383) and crew Bombed yellow T.Is near Cahagnes from 15,000ft. The remainder of the squadron received the 'abandon sortie' signal and told to lighten their aircraft weight and head for home. P/O Squibb (PB348) misunderstood the W/T message and landed at Squires Gate, the other 11 landed back at Fiskerton well before lunch. The raid had not been a success, and sadly 4 Lancaster crews were posted missing.

31 July, 1944; RILLY-LA-MONTAGE (DAYLIGHT): Another daylight attack, but this time take-off was at a more civilised hour (around tea time). Fiskerton was able to provide 16 Lancasters for this 5 Group attack on a railway tunnel being used as a flying-bomb store. 617 Squadron were to attack first at 12,000 feet, using their 'Tallboy' bombs to seal each end of the tunnel. Flying immediately behind them at 18,000ft would come 81 main force Lancasters, whose bombs would crater the surrounding approach areas.

The operation went well, and Fiskerton's returning crews reported the bombing to be well concentrated. All 49's aircraft were home safely before dark, with F/O Barrie (ND787) and crew the last to touch down at 22.42hrs. W/Cmdr Walker (ND473) completed his first sortie with 49 Squadron. Two Lancasters from 5 Group had failed to return. At interrogation several crews reported seeing a Lancaster being shot down over the target. It was seen to be on fire in the nose, before breaking in two as it fell to the ground; parachutes were seen.
F/O Squibb (PB348) and crew gave a slightly different account; *'Lancaster suspected hit by bomb from a/c above as no flak seen'*... they were not wrong.

The Lancaster that they had witnessed the demise of, belonged to 617 Squadron (ME557). At the controls sat F/Lt Bill Reid VC, who was holding his aircraft steady whilst the camera took a 'bombing photo' when bombs from an aircraft above smashed into them. Within seconds the Lancaster began to disintegrate. The flight engineer handed Reid his parachute but before he could make good his escape through the escape hatch above his head, the spinning aircraft broke apart and F/Lt Reid found himself floating free of the doomed bomber. The wireless operator, Dave Luker, was also thrown clear of the aircraft. Sadly, these two airmen were the only survivors; both became PoW's.

F/O Walter Buchanan and crew who failed to return from Stutttgart 25/26th July 1944 in PE250 (EA-J)

Left to right back row:
F/Sgt Kitto (Nav)
Sgt Picker (W/Op)
Unknown
Sgt Greenwood (R/G)

Front row
Sgt Ashby (F/E)
F/O Buchanan (Pilot)
F/Sgt Shackleton (B/A)

JULY 1944

OPERATIONAL SUMMARY - JULY 1944

Date	Target	Desp	E/R	FTR	Remarks
4/5	ST-LEU-D'ESSERENT	17	-	1	P/O Dod FTR
7/8	ST-LEU-D'ESSERENT	16	-	2	P/O Baker FTR F/L Ball FTR 2 a/c Woodbridge
12/13	CULMONT CHALINDREY	14	1	-	
15/16	NEVERS	13	-	-	
18	CAEN	16	-	-	Daylight
18/19	REVIGNY	15	-	4	F/O Deacon FTR F/O Green FTR P/O Lacy FTR F/O Appleyard FTR
20/21	COURTRAI	12	-	-	
23/24	KEIL	12	-	-	
24/25	DONGES	14	-	-	
25/26	STUTTGART	14	-	1	F/O Buchanan FTR 2 a/c Woodbridge
26/27	GIVORS	9	-	-	
28/29	STUTTGART	12	-	1	F/L Powell FTR
30	CAEN	12	-	-	Daylight
31	RILLY-LA-MONTAGE	16	-	-	Daylight

Total number of sorties flown	192
Failed to return	9
Total tons of bombs of all types dropped	900.04
Operational hours flown during July 1944	1060.30
Non-operational hours flown during July 1944	413.05

HONOURS AND AWARDS - JULY 1944

S/L G.P. Lace D.F.M.	D.F.C.
F/O R.L. Bienvenu	D.F.C.
P/O C. Lacy	D F.C.
P/O W.R. Green RNZAF	D.F.C.

AUGUST 1944

The severe losses suffered by 49 Squadron during the previous months (18 aircraft and crews missing in the last seven weeks) represented the night before the dawn. The squadron and indeed Bomber Command, now entered a period of a decreasing casualty rate, whilst the weight and accuracy of their attacks grew. Operations against French targets still continued, and daylight operations increased, as Bomber Command approached its peak operational performance.

The 49 Squadron 'spirit' had not diminished during this period of heavy attrition. Morale amongst those on the ground as well as the aircrew remained high, despite the terrible mauling that had been received. New crews were steadily bringing the unit up to strength, and F/Lt Botting (survivor of the Wesseling raid in June) would soon be leading the squadron as its new CO, after his promotion to Wing Commander. On 1 August 1944, the strength of the squadron stood at: 67 Officers and 452 Other Ranks. The unit held 20 Lancasters, of which 4 represented the reserve aircraft.

1 August, 1944; LA-BRETEQUE (DAYLIGHT): As with previous years, August came in wet and cloudy, but at 06.00hrs, orders rattled in from Group requiring a maximum effort. A daylight attack by 777 aircraft against various flying-bomb sites was planned.

Just before 16.00hrs, 19 of the squadron's Lancasters started taking to the air bound for France. Amongst their number were three new crews piloted by: F/O Walker(PB359), F/Sgt Galloway (PB308) and F/O Hay (PB299).

F/O Leslie Hay and crew were one of the newly arrived replacement crews and had only been at Fiskerton for a few days. After two short cross country flights, they were thrown straight into the fray as F/O Hay recalls:

"I found it very different lifting a fully laden aircraft off the runway and handling it generally with a full load of bombs and petrol. We adopted what I was later to find out to be the usual Group procedure, namely, flying to Reading where all the squadrons of the Group met, formed up in a box and set course at the time, height and speed allotted to each squadron.

We saw our first flak as we approached the French coast, interesting puffs of black smoke, but more fascinating was to see the aircraft all formed up in box formation. An awe-inspiring sight."

Whilst over France, the operation had to be aborted. Poor weather conditions made accurate bombing impossible, and French civilians would be put at risk. The controller had no option but to order 'stop bombing and return to base.'

2 August, 1944; TROSSY-ST-MAXIM (DAYLIGHT): Unlike the previous day, the visibility over Trossy-St-Maxim was clear, and a successful attack was made by 394 bombers against the flying-bomb launch site and three storage sites. 5 Group lost 2 Lancasters, but all Fiskerton's 19 aircraft returned safely.

AUGUST 1944

3 August, 1944; TROSSY-ST-MAXIM (DAYLIGHT): A force of 1,114 aircraft set out once more for the flying-bomb stores, again in clear conditions. 5 Group was sent to Trossy where they carried out what some crews reported as a 'scattered attack' on the V1 storage site.

A total of 6 Lancasters was lost, five of which were from 5 Group. 49 Squadron did not lose any of its 18 aircraft, but two were damaged by flak: F/O Mallinson (PB359) and crew received slight damage and elected to land at Wittering on return. F/Lt Millington (LM648) and crew had hydraulic pipes severed by flak, which then caught fire ... bombs were jettisoned immediately in open country, and on return an emergency landing was made on Wittering's long grass runway. The remainder of the squadron, including the new crew piloted by F/O Alty (ND792) had landed back at base by 16.32hrs.

5 August, 1944; ST-LEU-D'ESSERENT (DAYLIGHT): A large force of 742 aircraft was sent to attack the VI storage sites in the Foret de Nieppe and St-Leu areas. W/Cmdr Botting (ND957) and crew were amongst the first of 17 aircraft to take-off from Fiskerton. S/Ldr Lace (PB299) later reported that:

Just one aircraft, a Halifax, was lost on the operation, but F/Lt Millington (PB360) and crew were badly shot up by flak for the second raid in succession. S/Ldr Lace formated on the damaged Lancaster and escorted F/Lt Milliington back to Ford airfield, where both aircraft landed safely. The remainder of the squadron landed back at base by 15.43hrs.

Monday 7th August; to date, V1s had killed over 5,000 people in Britain, and destroyed 35,000 homes.

7/8 August, 1944; SEQUEVILLE: This was another major attack by Bomber Command (1,019 aircraft) in support of Allied ground forces. Five German strong-points were attacked and hit in this very carefully controlled operation. 10 Lancasters failed to return; most of the losses were attributed to night fighters. All 49's aircraft returned after successful sorties, but at interrogation F/O Geoff Poole (LM190) and crew reported that whilst bombing from 7,000ft: *"The rear of the starboard-outer engine caught fire, presumably from flak over the target."* A daylight inspection of R-Roger by the ground crew revealed the real cause; a 1,000lb bomb from a Lancaster above had smashed into the engine. If it had hit them a split second later, the bomb would have almost certainly crashed through the wing with devastating results. Another incident concerned F/O McCracken and crew as the pilot's de-brief report indicates: *"I had to do a violent diving turn to port immediately on release of bombs to avoid being hit by another Lanc!"*

9/10 August, 1944; CHATELLERRAULT: On this night 176 Lancasters and 14 Mosquitoes from 1 and 5 Groups attacked an oil storage dump. Fiskerton contributed 17 aircraft of which 16 bombed; F/O Squibb (PB348) and crew had to abort when their bomb sight went u/s.

The attack was successful with crews reporting several large explosions. All 49's aircraft were back at base by 03.31hrs. Two Lancasters were missing from the operation.

10/11 August, 1944; BORDEAUX: Oil was again the target, when 8 Lancasters took-off from Fiskerton just after 18.30hrs. Bombing from 17,000ft crews could clearly see the river and the target which was well marked. There were no fighters, although the flak over the target was quite considerable. No aircraft were lost.

10 August, 1944: Sad news concerning LAC William Morrison was received at RAF Fiskerton. LAC Morrison, who was a radar mechanic on the squadron, tragically died of meningitis at RAF Hospital Rauceby.

11/12 August, 1944; GIVORS: The railway junction and yards at Givors were attacked by 179 Lancasters with outstanding accuracy. 49 Squadron had 16 aircraft airborne, including a new crew piloted by F/Lt Gorton (LM648). Most crews returned with reports that the marking was a little scattered, but despite the light drizzle and slight haze the bombing appeared 'spot on'.

There were no aircraft losses from the force; 14 Lancasters landed back at Fiskerton, whilst F/O Sullings (ED602) landed at Downham Market, and F/O Barrie (LM653) dropped in at Mildenhall.

AUTOMATIC GUN LAYING TURRET (A.G.L.T.) CODE NAMED "VILLAGE INN"

Early in 1944, 49 Squadron had been one of the squadrons chosen to test a new weapons system code named "Village Inn". It was during testing, that F/Lt Healey RCAF and crew were killed in a flying accident (see 30 Apr 44). Lancasters equipped with the new device had now arrived at Fiskerton, and on 12th August, selected crews (those in the earlier part of their tours) began training on the new device. **Note:** Operational details concerning AGLT are covered in the September 44 section.

12/13 August, 1944; BRUNSWICK - FALAISE: During Saturday morning of the 12th, 8 aircraft were required for the evening's attack on Brunswick. All 8 aircraft were airborne and away by 21.08hrs. Moments later, Fiskerton's ops room received an urgent message from 5 Group HQ (Morton Hall) requesting any 'spare' aircraft. They were urgently needed for an attack on enemy troops and armour in support of an advance by the Allies in the Falais area. Ground crews and armourers worked feverishly through the night managing to prepare 3 aircraft ready for take-off just after midnight. S/Ldr Lace (JB399) and crew were first away at 00.33hrs, followed by F/O Carlyle (ND383) then F/O Barrie (ND473). Before the active runway lights had been doused, F/O Poole (PB299) (from the Brunswick force) requested permission to land. His starboard-outer engine had gone u/s forcing them to return before the target was reached.

Over Brunswick, a total of 379 Lancasters and Halifaxes were making their attacks without the use of Pathfinder markers. It was an experiment to establish how accurate Main Force bombers could be by using their own H2S sets to identify the aiming point. At interrogation, returning crews were pessimistic about the results of the bombing; most considered the attack to be widespread. F/O Brady (ND972) and crew (flying their 32nd operation) commented: *"Target area not well pranged at all."* Later reports showed that the bombing was spread up to twenty miles from the target. The cost had been high; 17 Lancaster and 10 Halifax crews had failed to return. Fortunately all 49's aircraft were home safely by 03.10hrs.

One hour after the Brunswick bombers had landed, the 3 aircraft from the Falaise attack were back in Fiskerton's circuit. Although cloud over the target had prevented clear observation of the bomb bursts, all three crews thought the attack had been successful; it was later confirmed by the Army as an effective raid. Bomber Command had managed to muster 144 aircraft at short notice; all returned safely.

14 August, 1944; QUESNAY (DAYLIGHT): Just after midday on Monday 14th, Bomber Command aircraft prepared to take-off, once again in support of the Allied ground forces. Over 800 Lancasters, Halifaxes and Mosquitoes were to attack seven German troop positions facing the 3rd Canadian Division in the Falaise area.

F/O Bob Walker (ND647) and crew were the first of 15 Lancasters to lift from Fiskerton at 12.07hrs; 49 Squadron's target was near Quesnay.

The entire bombing had been accurate until about half-way through the raid. Then some aircraft started to bomb a quarry which held parts of the 12th Canadian Field Artillery. The Master Bomber did his upmost to prevent this error, but it is believed about 70 bombers attacked this area. The Canadian Army lost 13 men killed and 53 injured; this was the first time such an incident had happened in the Battle of Normandy.

The mistake was later attributed to the fact that the Canadians had used yellow identification smoke to show their positions - the Pathfinder aircraft were using yellow T.Is!

Crews were back at Fiskerton in time for tea; all reported a successful raid; 'met good - no flak - no fighters - formation good no snags, a good trip!' 2 Lancasters had failed to return, both from other squadrons.

15 August, 1944; DEELEN AIRFIELD (DAYLIGHT): Bomber Command decided to blunt the effectivness of the Luftwaffe night-fighter force in preparation for a new offensive planned against Germany, by attacking their home bases. 1,004 bombers were dispatched against 9 airfields in Holland and Belgium. 49 Squadron were part of the force sent to attack Deelen airfield near Arnhem in Holland. 16 Lancasters had left Fiskerton by 09.47hrs, but shortly before midday F/O Lee (JB399) had landed back early with mechanical problems.

The remainder of the squadron, including the new crew captained by F/Lt Blaire (PB348), participated in a very accurate attack on the night-fighter airfield. Just one aircraft encountered problems; F/O Larry Pederson (ND512) and crew were hit by flak shortly after bombing. The port-inner engine had to be feathered, the nose and rear turrets were rendered u/s and the fuselage had accumulated numerous perforations.

All 49's aircraft were safely back at base by 13.47hrs, including the three-engined Pederson crew. A total of 3 Lancasters were missing from the operation.

A fine portrait of Jack Harvison RCAF, a flight engineer in Larry Pederson's crew, successfully completed his tour of operations despite on one occasion receiving serious head injuries.

16/17 August, 1944; STETTIN: This was an all Lancaster attack by 461 aircraft - 14 aircraft were prepared at Fiskerton but 1 cancelled in the early evening.

By 21.27hrs, 13 aircraft were airborne and heading for Germany, including F/O Pederson (ND512) and crew in their rapidly repaired C-Charlie. S/Ldr Twiggs (PB306) and crew were forced to return early with their rear turret completely u/s.

Conditions over the target were hazy, but the Master Bomber was doing his job and markers followed by bombs were placed in the correct areas. Reports show that much damage was done to the port and surrounding factories, as well as housing.

At de-brief most crews considered that bombing had been scattered, but Command was pleased with the results. The cost had been 5 aircraft; all 49's were unscathed.

18 August, 1944; L'ISLE-ADAM (DAYLIGHT): Operations had been planned for the 17th, but were cancelled during the afternoon. On Friday 18th, orders were received at 02.00hrs requesting 10 aircraft for a daylight attack on a German supply depot near Paris. Those crews detailed were woken early from their sleep by orderlies, and the pre-operational rituals began, culminating in take-off at 11.30hrs.

Two new crews were operating for the first time, they were piloted by; F/O Maul (ND512) and F/O McRae (PB306). The attacking force was made up of 158 Lancasters and 11 Mosquitoes, all from 5 Group. Flying in at 11,000ft, the bombing was concentrated between two smoke markers; delivery was good, and an excellent raid was the result.

When the squadron landed back at Fiskerton around 16.00hrs, several kites carried the scars of combat.

German flak especially near Rouen had been quite accurate: F/O Russell (PB295) - damaged by heavy flak north of Rouen. F/Lt Blaire (PB347) - aircraft damaged over the target area by flak. F/O Poole (PB299) - damaged by heavy flak. F/O Dickson (ND792) - slightly damaged by heavy flak over the target area. F/O Gordon Burns RCAF and crew (LM649) were also hit. Mid-upper gunner, Ted Sims remembers:

"We were badly shot up by flak north east of Rouen, and two engines were knocked out. Our skipper made a crash landing at Wittering without injury to the crew, for which he was awarded the DFC."

Fortunately all 49's aircraft had returned without casualties. 5 Group lost 2 Lancasters from the raid.

On Saturday 19th, the squadron was stood down. Aircrew had the opportunity to go into Lincoln and relax, whilst on the station, the ground crews had the task of repairing the 'peppered' aircraft from the L'Isle-Adam trip. Over the next week came a series of operations that were scrubbed at the last minute - air and ground crews alike will remember the time spent out on dispersal waiting for the off, only to be frustrated at the final moment.

A Wartime Wedding - 'cider and ham sandwiches'. The tour-expired Roantree crew gather together again for the wedding of their bomb aimer, F/Sgt John Peaker DFM. John and Joy were married in Market Harborough on Monday, August 21, 1944.
In the photograph, John and Joy, seated, have crew members, P/O Clive Roantree RAAF DFC pilot (best man) and F/Sgt Jack Grimshaw, flight engineer is left of Joy. F/Sgt Jock Lowrie, wireless operator looks out between bridesmaids and F/Sgt Ken Nelson RCAF, rear gunner is behind the bridesmaids at the back.
John and Joy now live happily in retirement in the small Lincolnshire village of Rippingale. (J. Peaker)

25/26 August, 1944; DARMSTADT: Operations recommenced on the evening of Friday 25th; 7 of the squadron's Lancasters were airborne bound for Darmstadt in Germany. This target had never received a large attack before, and 5 Group were given the task of delivering its first.

As 190 Lancasters approached the target area confusion reigned; the Master Bomber had been forced to return early and his two deputies had both been shot down. Illumination flares had been dropped too far west, and as a result the low-level marking Mosquitoes were unable to locate the target.

Scattered bombing started to take place, with a portion of the force attacking other targets and some even joining in the raid on nearby Russelsheim.

On return to Fiskerton, the most senior 49 Squadron crew operating that night, F/O Arnold's (ND473), flying their 27th operation, just about summed up the whole raid giving the following de-brief report:

"Bombing indiscriminate in general vicinity of illuminating flares. If this attack is successful, it will be a miracle!"

All 49's aircraft returned safely, but 5 Group lost 7 Lancasters and their crews.

26/27 August, 1944; KÖNIGSBERG: No 5 Group dispatched 174 Lancasters against the distant port of Königsberg in East Prussia. Lying just 100 miles from the front with the Red Army, this was a very important supply port for the Germans.

The 950 mile route took the Lancasters over Sweden where F/O Maul (PB359) reported;
"plenty of light flak."

A good raid developed over the target as the following de-brief reports show: F/O Dickson:
"Markers well placed and bombing generally concentrated. About 50 searchlights seen to cone 3 aircraft."

F/Lt Blaire (PB299):
"Being the last to bomb, the target was seen to be well pranged - our bombs hit the TI. aimed for."

F/O Sullings (ND957) with F/O Winter as 2nd dickie:
"Good fires starting which were visible 150 miles from the target."

Such are the vagaries of an English summer that on return, crews found fog covering much of eastern England. As a result those airfields equipped with the FIDO system were ordered to ignite them. All of 49's eight aircraft landed safely on Fiskerton's FIDO runway with F/Lt Blaire the last to touch down after 10hrs 34mins in the air.

5 Group lost 4 Lancasters on the raid.

29/30 August, 1944; DANZIG BAY/KÖNIGSBERG: Just 8 aircraft were detailed for operations this night. This reflects the increasing 'Village Inn' training being carried out by 49's crews. The establishment of aircraft within the squadron now showed several 'Village Inn' equipped Lancasters on strength, but as yet, not operational.

AUGUST 1944

The squadron began taking off just after 20.30hrs. Two crews were bound for minelaying in Danzig Bay; the Sullings crew (ND957) carried out a successful 'gardening' trip without any hitches, whilst F/O Arnold (ND473) and crew had their H2S set 'pack up'; the navigator and bomb aimer did a fine job of mining by executing a time and distance run from a predetermined land mark; Searchlights and flak were active. Over Königsberg, 189 Lancasters milled around for over twenty minutes whilst low cloud cleared enough for the marker aircraft to do their work. Then W/Cmdr Woodroffe, a very skilled Master Bomber, allowed the attack to commence.

It was during the delay, that F/O Maul (PB359) and crew were hit by heavy flak; the oil tank in the starboard outer engine was holed and No 2 and 3 starboard tanks and No 3 port tanks were also punctured.

The raid that developed over Königsberg proved to be one of 5 Group's most successful attacks of the war on this target of such extreme range. But the cost was high, with heavy fighter opposition over the target - 15 Lancasters failed to return.

By the time 5 Group's Lancasters crossed the Lincolnshire coast it was daylight, but below them they found the countryside wreathed in fog. For the second time in just a few days, FIDO was again called into action. Fiskerton's competent control tower staff worked extremely hard to receive numerous visitors seeking sanctuary. All of 49's aircraft returned safely to Fiskerton, including the new crew captained by F/O Daniel (PB295). There were some anxious moments with PB359 nearly an hour overdue, but just before 07.30hrs, F/O Maul called up Fiskerton control for permission to land. This crew's epic 2,000 mile round trip to East Prussia had lasted an incredible 11hrs 13mins. F/O Ed Maul and his flight engineer, Sgt Bill Cooper, had coaxed their flak ravaged, fuel starved Lancaster home with great skill and determination on this only their 3rd operation as a crew.

As August drew to a close, it found the German Armies defeated in Normandy and in retreat towards their own borders with the Allies in hot pursuit. France had all but been liberated, only the coastal bastions at Le Havre, Calais, Boulogne and Cape Griz Nez remained occupied by the Germans.

On 10.00hrs on Thursday 31 August, the squadron received orders to 'stand down'.

Picture on left shows bomb damage to starboard-outer engine of LM190 over Sequeville on 7/8 Aug. (J A Edwards)

AUGUST 1944

OPERATIONAL SUMMARY - AUGUST 1944

Date	Target	Desp	E/R	FTR	Remarks
1	LE BRETEQUE	19	-	-	Daylight
2	TROSSY ST MAXIM	19	-	-	Daylight
3	TROSSY ST MAXIM	18	-	-	Daylight
5	ST-LEU-D'ESSERENT	17	-	-	Daylight
7/8	SEQUEVILLE	17	-	-	
9/10	CHATELLERAULT	17	-	-	
10/11	BORDEAUX	8	-	-	
11/12	GIVORS	16	-	-	
12/13	BRUNSWICK	8	-	-	
	FALAIS	3	-	-	
14	QUESNAY	15	-	-	Daylight
15	DEELEN	16	1	-	Daylight
16/17	STETTIN	13	1	-	
18	L'ISLE ADAM	10	-	-	Daylight
25/26	DARMSTADT	7	-	-	
26/27	KÖNIGSBERG	8	-	-	
29/30	KÖNIGSBERG	6	-	-	
	DANZIG BAY	2	-	-	Minelaying

Total number of sorties flown	219
Failed to return	0
Total tons of bombs of all types dropped	1090.68
Operational hours flown during August 1944	1233.30
Non-operational hours flown during August 1944	273.21

HONOURS AND AWARDS - AUGUST 1944

P/O J.J. Lett	D.F.C.
P/O H.C. McKay RAAF	D.F.C.
P/O J.A. Jones	D.F.C.
Sgt G.J. Parkinson	D.F.M.
F/S H.M. Kennedy	D.F.M.
F/S J.S. Peaker	D.F.M.
P/O J.H. Simpson	D.F.C.
P/O H.R. Ewens	D.F.C.
F/O K.S. Stokoe	D.F.C.

SEPTEMBER 1944

At the beginning of September, 49 Squadron was stood down in order to commence intensive training on 'Village Inn'. The A.G.L.T. 'party' consisted of the following Officers and men: S/Ldr Oatten; F/O Johnson-Briggs; F/O Collingwood; F/O Proctor; F/O Verrier; F/O Boardman; Cpl Ross Elec/1; Cpl Hilton Inst/Rep I; AC2 Weston Inst/Rep 1 and AC1 Hughes Inst/Rep II: They had the task of not only training the aircrews in how to operate the equipment, but also maintaining and servicing it... which was not easy!

Perhaps the best way to illustrate how 'Village Inn' actually worked, is to let former Lancaster pilot F/O Leslie Hay, describe the training he and his crew carried out at Fiskerton during August/September 1944. F/O Hay recalls:

"Then a great blow was struck. The whole squadron was stood down. Instead of being able to finish our tour within the month! which we had so gleefully hoped when we had done our 3 little daylights (August 1,2 & 3), we learned that we were to be trained on the Automatic Gun Laying Turret.

This was a system to combat night fighters. The rear turret of each aircraft was fitted with a radar scanner which sent out a beam that was reflected by an aircraft at the rear up to 1,500yds. These reflections were in the form of blips which got faster as the aircraft got nearer, and were also shown on the radar screen operated by the wireless operator who could detect an aircraft up to 2,000yds. The rear guns pointed so that the apex of the cone of fire was at 700 yards. The plan was for the rear gunner to search continually with a view to picking up the night fighters, and for the wireless operator to watch his screen.

When an aircraft was engaged, the problem of being friend or foe was overcome by all aircraft to be fitted in the nose with a gadget that transmitted infra red signals of dots and dashes working opposite to morse code ("Z" equipment). These could be picked up by the rear gunner who had an infra red telescope attached to his guns. The code could be changed nightly.

The drill was for the rear gunner to pick up an aircraft in conjunction with the wireless operator and, as it came in to attack, the gunner would give the order to 'GO' port or starboard depending on the direction of attack. The pilot would then go into a corkscrew making sure the gunners knew exactly where the enemy was in the sky and how much deflection to lay off. The pilot would call out what he was doing e.g. Down port, rolling, up starboard, rolling etc: these calls and actions were made at precise pre-calculated speeds by which the gunner could assess his deflections which appeared on a glass plate.

We practiced, practiced and practiced with 'Village Inn'. At the start, we flew in daylight with Spitfires attacking from the rear. Cameras were fitted on the fighter and to our rear guns and we developed a co-ordination between the wireless operator, rear gunner and pilot. Later we flew in daylight with the rear turret blacked. Fighters came at request and, after each trip we would go back and look at the films taken by both aircraft to assess progress. It was a long tedious business, and very hot as it was mid-summer. We then worked night and day fitting in practice both bombing and cross country exercises, giving me good experience in handling the aircraft."

8 September, 1944: A junior Government minister informed the nation that attacks by V1's were virtually over. The launch sites had been captured, but a few V1's are still being air-lauched from He 111's over the North Sea. In the 80 days since the first 'Doodle Bug' had landed, 2,300 V1's had got through to London, killing 5,475 people and injuring 16,000; a total of 25,000 homes had been destroyed.

That evening at 6.45pm in the West London suburb of Chiswick, a large explosion occurred killing three people; it sounded like a double thunderclap followed by the rushing sound of an express train. To avoid panic, the population was not at first informed, that this explosion was caused by the first V2 rocket bomb to land in Britain.

During the first nine days of September, crews were detailed for AGLT, and "Z" equipment tests combined with High Level Bombing practice. A Mosquito and a Hurricane were temporarily attached to the squadron for 'fighter affiliation' exercises. Then in the early hours of Sunday 10th September, orders came down from Group detailing an operation against Le Havre; the squadron was required to supply 8 aircraft for the raid.

10 September, 1944; LA HAVRE (DAYLIGHT): Nearly 1,000 bombers were to be dispatched against 8 German strong points in the area of Le Havre.

During the morning, Fiskerton had 7 aircraft airborne doing AGLT training with a further 3 practicing on H2S. Meanwhile the hard-pressed ground crews down on 'A' Flt had been given short notice to prepare 9 (plus one reserve) Lancasters for the Le Havre trip. Their predicament was that those aircraft detailed for ops were all 'Village Inn' equipped, and most had had their rear turret perspex doped with black paint. Sgt Fitter, Trevor Simpson, well remembers the problem:

"We found that the solvent we thought could be used on the turrets just wouldn't touch the dope. But fortunately one of my riggers had a carefully hoarded can of thinners, and that did the trick. We spent a very hectic morning getting the turrets spotless."

At 15.30hrs the first Lancaster lifted away from Fiskerton. Although the 49 Squadron aircraft operating were all fitted with 'Village Inn' and their crews trained in its use, this was NOT an operational use of the equipment.

The whole raid was a success and no aircraft losses were sustained. Fiskerton's 8 Lancasters were all home by 19.04hrs with F/O Hay (PB354) the last to land. The following day, the German commander of Le Havre surrendered with his 11,300 garrison, rations for 90 days and 115 guns of various calibres.

11/12 September, 1944; DARMSTADT: The previous 5 Group operation against Darmstadt had failed, but this raid proved to be a devastating success. The awful power of the bomber was well demonstrated in this outstandingly accurate and concentrated attack.

The 226 Lancasters used the 'spokes of a wheel' method in which each aircraft was given a different direction of attack on the markers, and would then undershoot or overshoot the markers by a given number of seconds. Because of the extensive fire destruction and heavy casualties, the German authorities considered the attack on Darmstadt to be an extreme example of R.A.F. 'terror bombing'. As far as Bomber Command was concerned, this was an important railway communications target. 5 Group suffered the loss of 12 Lancasters and their crews.

For 49 Squadron, this operation was of particular importance, for it saw the first operational use of 'Village Inn'. 49, who had pioneered the development of the AGLT system were given the opportunity to be the first squadron to use it in combat. Throughout Bomber Command, all aircraft had been fitted with "Z" equipment which would transmit the infra-red 'friendly' signal to any 'Village Inn' Lancasters they might come across.

Order of Battle for the night's operation was posted just before lunch; the 9 aircraft (all 'Village Inn' equipped) detailed were as follows:

PB300 S/L Lace: PB355 F/O Burns RCAF: PB373 F/L Lee: PB361 F/O Alty:
PB361 F/O Parkin: PB700 F/O Russell: PB349 F/O Furber: PB354 F/O Hay:
PB369 F/O Mallinson:

All 49's aircraft carried out successful bombing attacks and returned to Fiskerton without loss by 02.39hrs. At interrogation it was revealed that two crews had made enemy contact using their A.G.L.T., equipment and subsequent combats with enemy aircraft ensued. What follows is a quite remarkable account, given by F/O Leslie Hay or 'Uncle Will' as he became known within the squadron, who was piloting one of these Lancasters. He describes in detail the actions as they occurred during that Monday evening in September 1944. The Lancaster concerned was a Mk III (PB354) EA-G for George.

The crew consisted of; F/O L.J. Hay Pilot, Sgt F. Green flight engineer, P/O P.W.Smith navigator, W/O H. Jenkinson wireless operator, F/Sgt A.E. French mid/upper gunner, P/O A.J. Mackay bomb aimer and F/O J.S. Hall the rear gunner. 'Uncle Will' continues:

"Briefing was particularly careful because of the circumstances surrounding the trip. Each aircraft was briefed to lag behind the bomber stream and stacked in echelon upwards as if we were late trying to catch up. These were usually the aircraft that the fighters were able to pick off. We were given individual heights to fly and I found that I was right at the back, the uppermost aircraft.

I must say that I wasn't keen on being in that position. It seemed too much like being a staked out goat waiting for the tiger, and would probably be the first to get picked up.

There was the possibility that there would be some genuine late comers -there generally were -and their infra red identification or "Z" equipment as it was called was not working. To overcome this we were briefed not to open fire this side of 3 degrees east (the other side of Paris) unless we indentified the aircraft visually as an enemy. We had to be absolutely certain that we were not shooting down our own bombers. It was a bit hair-raising as it seemed to me that we had to leave so much to chance before we could get to grips with anything that might come up. We could only wait and see what happened. "We took-off (21.02hrs) as usual, but later than the other squadrons, trailing behind by working on a time basis, to Reading then the coast - guns tested - bombs fused. Here we go!

We had hardly crossed the French coast when our wireless operator reported that his radar screen (Fishpond) showed that two aircraft were at 2,000 yards and had been there a little while. The rear gunner was unable to pick them up at that range so we just waited. They then moved closer to about 1.500 yards and the rear gunner got them on his radar, their blips sounding on our intercom, but no "Z" equipment was flashing. The night was dark, no moon, but visibility was quite good.

We had not expected two aircraft like this and were a bit apprehensive, so I climbed 1,000ft -they followed. I altered course 30 degrees -they followed. With a further alteration of 60 degrees to bring us back to track, they stayed with us. They must be enemy, but we had no visual identification as per briefing and it seemed to me that we must wait, take the first attack and try avoiding action. At least we knew they were there and we were ready for them.

We hadn't long to wait, they drew apart - difficult, whichever side we took the avoiding action we were meat for the other one - but they didn't know we knew that they were there. Wireless operator -'Coming in from starboard quarter level, 1200, 1100, 1000, 900, 800, (the blips were now rapid) 700.' I turned into the oncoming aircraft and dived. A few moments later, mid-upper said in his best Cockney accent 'I've got him -he's a 188, just gone over the top of us.' " We breathed again -now we were ready and straightened out. There was no time lost. Wireless operator reported that the other was coming astern, '1000, 900, 800, 700' I dived to port and the rear gunner opened fire and, almost immediately, the enemy dropped back to 1,500yds it seemed to me like the proverbial scalded cat. He never got near us, certainly not within 600yds and was obviously hit. The two aircraft then flew behind us, close together. (Interesting to think how they were able to locate each other -presumably using us as a reference point) we assumed their R.T. was red hot and wished that we could hear their conversation.

In time they were joined by a third fighter and all three flew in a triangle (reported by the wireless operator working on Fishpond) This was real trouble. They then spread out and proceeded to make a series of attacks on us, the wireless operator reported movements, I was working a continuous corkscrew and the rear gunner beat off every attack. It was just as we had practiced so many times over the friendly fields of Lincolnshire.

They attacked again and again, the rear guns were almost out of ammunition with only two guns left firing. I told the bomb aimer to take the ammunition from the front guns to the rear which he endeavoured to do but as he was moving about and therefore not on intercom and could not hear my commentary, he had no knowledge which way I was going to throw the aircraft. Also he was not on oxygen and the floor was strewn with spent shells, but he got the ammunition to the rear just as the fighters after making an attack from 450 yards, broke off 400 yards and abandoned the engagement.

We assessed the situation. No damage -as far as we knew - and the guns were reloaded. However, we were disappointed. Why had we not shot any down? We didn't know it then, but next day when we tested the aircraft we estimated that the probable cause was the ranges sticking due to humidity which meant that the cone of fire did not centre on the enemy.

The navigator reported that there had been ten attacks in twenty-nine minutes, and immediately gave us a new course for the target. It has ever since been a mystery to me how he did this. I had been throwing the aircraft all over the sky to evade the enemy, although it was a controlled corkscrew, to the crew it must have seemed like a matter of hanging on and the navigator must have hung on by his eyebrows as he used his hands to hold onto his maps, charts, set squares, rulers, pencils etc: I never did find out.

Darmstadt was reached on time and the raid was very concentrated. Being last in, the barrage put up was murderous. Back at base we were greeted by an eager group of radar mechs and although we were puzzled and elated, we knew that 'Village Inn' worked and it gave us great confidence.

It is now a matter of record that after the war, tests were made but the device was abandoned as not being very effective. I can vouch the inaccuracy of that and suggest that they should have tested it in actual combat -they might think otherwise!"

Records show that the combat took place between 23.00hrs and 23.29hrs on the outward leg. The Lancaster had been flying at 16,500ft; all three enemy aircraft were JU 188's.

The second AGLT contact took place just after midnight; F/O Gordon Burns RCAF (PB355) and crew flying at 16,000ft picked up an unidentified enemy aircraft on 'Village Inn' at 1,200yds astern and up.

The enemy closed rapidly to 800yds whereupon the rear gunner, Sgt Ken Robinson, opened fire. Fire was maintained until 500yds then F/O Burns put B-Baker into a corkscrew port, heading for the darker sky. The enemy aircraft followed through the corkscrew, but at 600yds it broke away to starboard and was gone.

It had been an auspicious introduction into combat for 'Village Inn'. Training within the squadron continued with extreme confidence and enthusiasm.

SEPTEMBER 1944

12/13 September, 1944; STUTTGART: If the preceding evening's highly successful raid had been on a previously untouched target, then the raid set for the evening of the 12th was quite the reverse; 204 Lancasters led by 13 Mosquitoes were heading for the familiar German target of Stuttgart.

Once again, 49 Squadron dispatched 9 Lancasters, all AGLT equipped. The Order of Battle, which included the Station Commander, Grp/Cpt 'Ginger' Weir, was as follows:

PB300	G/C Weir:	PB355	F/Lt Walker:	JB369	F/O Lee:
PB373	F/O Burns RCAF:	PB374	F/O Alty:	PB353	F/O Parkin:
PB370	F/O Russell:	PB354	F/O Hay:	PB349	F/O Furber:

Take-offs from Fiskerton started just before 17.00hrs; F/Lt Walker returned early in B-Baker with his radar equipment unserviceable.

Over Germany the visibility was clear, with no moon and very dark below the horizon. In F/O Furber's aircraft, the wireless operator Sgt Holyoak, had picked up a possible fighter on his 'Fishpond' screen. He informed F/Sgt Bangay in the rear turret, that the aircraft was at one mile on the starboard beam to the starboard quarter down. At 1,500yds, 'Village Inn' had picked it up and confirmed it as an enemy aircraft. The fighter closed rapidly and at 600yds F/Sgt Bangay opened fire whilst calling for the pilot to 'corkscrew starboard'. The combat was very quickly over, and the crew of H-Howe continued on course for Stuttgart having thwarted their nocturnal predator.

F/O Norman Alty and crew were 5 minutes out from the target and on track, when Sgt Millet in the rear turret picked up a contact on 'Village Inn' at 1100 yards -at 950yds he confirmed it as hostile and closing from the port quarter up -at 700yds both he and the fighter opened fire simultaneously - when the fighter was within 450yds the rear gunner called for the pilot to 'corkscrew port'. As F/O Alty initiated this manoeuvre, Sgt Lewis in the mid-upper turret obtained a brief visual at 300yds and opened fire. The enemy dived away to starboard and was gone. Yet another Luftwaffe victory had been denied by the skill of a well trained and disciplined bomber crew.

No claim was made by the Lancaster's gunners, but both were sure that strikes were made on the enemy. The crew of J-Jig continued on to the target and completed a successful sortie.

The attack on Stuttgart was of such concentration that a firestorm was created; most damage occurred in the northern and western parts of the centre where large areas were erased. The attacking force suffered the loss of 4 Lancasters and crews, but 49's eight aircraft were home and safe by 01.57hrs.

SEPTEMBER 1944

17 September, 1944; BOULOGNE (DAYLIGHT): A mixed force of 762 Lancasters, Halifaxes and Mosquitoes attacked the German stronghold at Boulogne in preparation for an Allied ground attack.

Take-off at Fiskerton started at 06.57hrs as F/Lt Lee (PB369) led 13 Lancasters from 49 Squadron, towards France.

All aircraft from Fiskerton dropped their bombs on target, except for F/O Alty (PB361) and crew who jettisoned after receiving the 'cease bombing' order from the controller. After receiving 3,000 tons of bombs, the German garrison soon surrendered. Two aircraft failed to return from the operation but all 49's aircraft had returned to base by 10.22hrs.

AIRBORNE ASSAULT

As Bomber Command's aircraft were returning to their home bases from Le Havre, a score of airfields in the south and central Midlands were just preparing to launch a huge air armada. The airborne assault of Holland was about to begin.

Shortly before midday on that Sunday morning, countless troop carrier and glider towing aircraft started forming up over England. From a handfull of USAAF airfields south of Lincoln, hundreds of Dakota aircraft hauled their human cargo of British and American Paratroopers into the warm September morning.

Their objectives were two bridges over the River Rhine - for the Americans at Nijmegen, for the British it was Arnhem!

18/19 September, 1944; BREMERHAVEN: Although attacked on previous occasions, and mainly by the USAAF, Bremerhaven had so far not received a heavy attack from the RAF. 5 Group was once again given the task using their own method; the result was a severely damaging raid, delivered by 206 Lancasters and 7 Mosquitoes.

49 Squadron had 13 aircraft airborne and all completed their sorties. F/O Furber (PB349) and crew had a 'near miss' when some incendiaries from another aircraft struck them, but no serious damage resulted. One Lancaster and one Mosquito failed to return.

19/20 September, 1944; MÜNCHEN GLADBACH/RHEYDT: The twin towns became the subject of attention from 237 aircraft made up from 1 and 5 Groups. G/Cpt Weir was once again airborne with 49 Squadron, as 12 aircraft departed Fiskerton just before 17.00hrs. For the crews it was a normal attack, not much fighter activity and moderate flak. From 14,000 feet the bombing seemed a little scattered although some concentrations of fires were evident.

Towards the end of the raid, some crews may have heard the Master Bomber say over the R/T *"OK chaps, thats fine -now beat it home."* How many, I wonder, knew that the Master Bomber that night was none other than W/Cmdr Guy Gibson VC.DSO.DFC., and that within an hour of that final radio transmission, he and his navigator would have perished in their burning Mosquito.

One airman who was aware that it was Gibson on the R/T this night, was air gunner Phil Alwood RAAF. Phil had been a member of the Jupp crew that carried out a tour with 49 Squadron during the second half of 1943. Trevor Jupp and Phil both volunteered to go as Pathfinders and joined 83 Squadron at Coningsby. Phil Alwood continued on with the squadron and this night saw him over the target in an 83 Squadron PFF 'illuminator' Lancaster.

During a conversation with Clive Roantree in 1996, Phil recalls: *"We heard Gibson call up on the R/T and I then saw the flash as his aircraft was hit with flak!"* The loss of Guy Gibson helped persuade Phil to terminate his own operational career... he had fostered ambitions of reaching 100 operations... but he now decided that at a remarkable 85 ops, his luck had been stretched far enough! Four Lancasters also failed to return; all 49's returned safely.

S/Ldr J.B. WARWICK D.F.C., NAVIGATOR

On Wednesday 20 September, the world learned the news that the famous 'Dambuster' leader, Guy Gibson, was missing from air operations. Days later it was confirmed that he and his navigator, S/Ldr Jim 'Paddy' Warwick were dead. Their 627 Squadron Mosquito (KB267) E-Easy, had crashed on Walcheren in Holland after the Rheydt raid on the night of the 19th.

Jim Warwick, a pleasant, gentle Ulsterman, had flown his first tour on Lancasters with 49 Squadron, Fiskerton, between June and December 1943. He and his fellow crew members, (piloted by P/O Hales) had come through operations to the Ruhr, Hamburg, Peenemunde and Berlin, and in doing so suffered more than their share of adversity. After his tour, Jim helped establish the radar navigation section at 1661 HCU, Winthorpe. Later, he transferred to 54 Base at Coningsby, where he and his girlfriend were planning to get engaged. W/Cmdr Gibson had asked Jim if he would be his navigator for just this one trip.

S/Ldr Warwick DFC., and W/Cmdr Gibson VC.DSO.DFC., rest together in Steenbergan, Holland.

23/24 September, 1944; HANDORF: Training on 'Village Inn' now followed a familiar schedule; each morning at 08.00hrs a small number of crews and aircraft would be detailed for AGLT practice. By 10.00hrs, orders from Group were received, giving details of that evening's operation, an attack on Handorf, a German night-fighter airfield near Münster.

The squadron had dispatched 13 aircraft by 18.52hrs, each 'Village Inn' equipped. All crews were well aware that enemy contacts were almost certain when disturbing the hornets' nest. Two new crews were operating, both AGLT trained; they were piloted by F/O Williams (PB374) and F/O Nowrie (PB484).

Over the target cloud hampered the bombing and most crews reported being unable to observe the results of the attack.

Some crews elected to bomb Münster as the alternative target. Flak over the target hit the aircraft of F/O Johnny Cannon (PB354) and crew; one of their engines had to shut down causing them to return on three.

As anticipated, 'Village Inn' picked up a customer: F/O Maul (PB369) and crew were flying at 18,500ft and only minutes away from bombing when Sgt Houghton, the rear gunner picked up the warning at 900yds -he let the enemy come to within 600yds before giving instructions to the pilot to put A-Able into a corkscrew. At 500yds, whilst in the corkscrew the mid-upper gunner Sgt Grimsdale, got a visual sighting and confirmed their attacker as a JU88. Visible against the lighter sky on the starboard quarter above, Sgt Grimsdale fired 40 rounds off at 450yds. The enemy aircraft broke away and was not seen again. The rear gunner did not fire blind knowing that other Lancasters would be in the target area.

F/O Maul and crew pressed on to bomb Münster using H2S. They arrived back at Fiskerton on three engines, but records do not state if this was due to their fighter combat or flak.

S/Ldr Gorton (PB519) and crew had successfully bombed Münster and were some 20 minutes into their homeward leg, when F/Sgt Tingle in the mid-upper turret reported an enemy fighter on the starboard quarter up. In the clear starlit night he had spotted an Me210 which appeared to be trying to develop a climbing attack. The rear gunner, F/Sgt John, did not receive a warning on AGLT as it appears the enemy was too far towards the beam. S/Ldr Gorton threw Q-Queenie into a corkscrew and both gunners opened fire on their assailant. The enemy disengaged and disappeared into the night possibly to seek easier prey.

The first returning squadron aircraft, piloted by F/Lt Walker (PB355) landed just before midnight. When S/Ldr Lace (PB300) joined the circuit, he put Fiskerton tower into a complete panic when he casually informed them that, owing to failure of the bomb release gear, he still had a full bomb load on board. The Squadron Leader was immediately put to the top of the stack, then when everyone else had landed, and with crash crews 'under starters orders' the pilot brought K-King in for a perfect touch down.

From the force of 117 aircraft participating in the operation, one Lancaster failed to return; all 49's came home safe once again.

26/27 September, 1944; KARLSRUHE: A total of 226 Lancasters from 1 and 5 Groups, led by 11 Mosquitoes delivered a concentrated attack on Karlsruhe, destroying a large area of the city. Fiskerton contributed 14 aircraft to the attack. Most crews reported at de-brief that as with the previous raid, the results of their own bombing could not be assessed due to the 10/10ths cloud cover. Two new crews had operated with the squadron for the first time; F/O Ken Harrop (PB349) and crew took H-Howe whilst F/O Ken Lee (PB519) and crew borrowed the CO's Q-Queenie.

In fact it was F/O Lee and crew that made the first 'Village Inn' contact of the night. As Q-Queenie approached the target at 13,800ft, Sgt Wilkinson in the rear turret suddenly obtained an AGLT contact at 500yds -it was a JU88 flying dead astern and just below in the darker sky. As the enemy got within 300yds, Sgt Wilkinson opened fire, using 400 rounds as the fighter came within 150yds. The fighter, probably startled by the gunner's reaction quickly broke away to starboard without returning fire, and was not seen again. During the action, Sgt Powell in the mid-upper turret could not bring his guns to bear on the enemy. The attack was timed at 04.07hrs. It was the second raid in succession that 'Queenie' had survived a fighter attack.

F/O Williams (PB370) and crew were on their homeward track when mid-upper gunner Sgt Crawshaw reported an Me110 coming in from the port bow at 350yds. He immediately ordered the skipper to corkscrew F-Fox to port, at the same time opening fire on their aggressor. The enemy aircraft opened fire as it slipped over the Lancaster's nose to starboard -as it passed aft the rear gunner, Sgt Anderson, managed to squeeze off a short burst. The fighter, having now angered his quarry, soon sought the sanctuary of darker sky and was not seen again.

The Lancasters returned to Fiskerton in the daylight of Wednesday morning; last to land was F/O Maul (PB354) and crew at 08.04hrs. For the second trip in a row, they were flying on three engines but this time in a different kite.

27/28 September, 1944; KAISERSLAUTERN: This 'medium size' target received its first raid from Bomber Command during the early hours of Thursday 28 September. 5 Group Mosquitoes marked the target for 217 Lancasters of 1 and 5 Groups.

49 Squadron had 15 aircraft over the target, where the bombing height was just over 4,000ft -in fact S/Ldr Lace (PB300) and crew had K-King down at 3,000ft! From these heights, most crews brought back visual confirmation of damaged buildings seen in the light of the fires. One Lancaster and one Mosquito failed to return from this operation; all 49's aircraft were unharmed.

SEPTEMBER 1944

The missing Mossie (KB366) came from 627 Squadron Woodhall Spa, and was piloted by F/O Brown RCAF and navigated by F/Lt Cowan. Their aircraft was seen to mark the target but failed to pull out of the dive, presumably hit by flak. The aircraft crashed about 600yds from the target sadly killing both crew members.

Kaiserslautern was the last operation by 49 Squadron during September; another month in which no losses had been sustained and in which the new aid to bomber crew survival, 'Village Inn' showed encouraging promise. Ground crews could be proud of the aircraft servicing record, which showed only one early return, and that was due to radar failure.

OPERATIONAL SUMMARY - SEPTEMBER 1944

Date	Target	Desp	E/R	FTR	Remarks
10	LE HAVRE	8	-	-	Daylight
11/12	DARMSTADT	9	-	-	First use of AGLT
12/13	STUTTGART	9	-	-	
17	BOULOGNE	13	-	-	Daylight
18/19	BREMERHAVEN	13	-	-	
19/20	MÜNCHEN GLADBACH	12	-	-	
23/24	HANDORF	13	-	-	
26/27	KARLSRUHE	14	-	-	
27/28	KAISERSLAUTERN	15	-	-	

Total number of sorties flown	106
Failed to return	0
Total tons of bombs of all types dropped	506.39
Operational hours flown during September 1944	558.45
Non-operational hours flown during September 1944	725.25

HONOURS AND AWARDS - SEPTEMBER 1944

F/Lt A.V. Patchett D.F.C.

A.G.L.T. (Village Inn) Just visible under the rear turret. (49 Sqdn Collection)

OCTOBER 1944

The squadron strength now stood at 107 Officers and 468 Other Ranks - there were 26 Mk III Lancasters on base, of which 6 were surplus. For the first four days of October, the squadron was stood down and A.G.L.T. training continued apace. At 18.00hrs on the 4th, Group requested 16 aircraft for a daylight operation to Wilhelmshaven the following day.

5 October, 1944; WILHELMSHAVEN (DAYLIGHT): W/Cmdr Botting (PB519) and crew led 16 Lancasters away from Fiskerton at 07.53hrs on Thursday morning. They joined 211 other Lancasters (all 5 Grp) bound for Wilhelmshaven. Two new crews were operating with the squadron, captained by; F/O Watson (PB369) and F/O Talbot (PB353).

10/10ths cloud cover was encountered just short of the enemy coast and the controller therefore ordered crews to bomb blind. Of the 16 aircraft from 49 Squadron, 14 claimed to have attacked the primary - 12 bombing on H2S, 1 on a 'time and distance' run, and 1 on a concentration of bombs.

F/O Harrop (PB349) and crew, whose H2S was unserviceable, were unable to identify the target and bombed Essen instead. Aircraft C-Charlie had to take evasive action on the bombing run to evade bombs falling from above; they bombed an unidentified village about 10 miles north west of the target.

Everyone was safely back at Fiskerton by 13.09hrs, Group lost one Lancaster and crew from the operation.

6/7 October, 1944; BREMEN: 1 and 5 Groups combined their efforts once again, when 246 Lancasters delivered a tremendous 'hammer blow' to Bremen. On a clear moonlit night, the Mosquitoes had little difficulty in marking the aiming point before calling the Main Force in to bomb. Large fires were soon started; F/O Russell (PB370) and crew reported that the glow from the fires could be seen 100 miles away. F/O Watson (PB369) stated that when over the target, the river and other features could be clearly seen.

The squadron had dispatched 17 aircraft, deciding to send five new crews on the raid. They were skippered by the following pilots: F/O Essenhigh (PB355); F/O Bromfield (PB504); F/O Beatson (PB429); F/O Winter (PB519) and F/O Milburn (PB568).

Aircraft started to request landing instructions shortly after 22.00hrs but by 22.38hrs, only 15 had landed back at Fiskerton. Into the early hours of Saturday morning, it became clear that for the first time since 28/29 July, when F/Lt Powell and crew failed to return from Stuttgart, the squadron had suffered casualties.

Two 49 crews failed to return from the operation; the 'freshman' crew of F/O Cyril Beatson plus the crew captained by F/O Ken Harrop. The Beatson crew are all buried alongside each other in the Beckligen War Cemetery at Soltau in Germany.

The crew members in F/O Harrop's aircraft have no known graves but are remembered on the Runnymede Memorial, except for their Canadian bomb aimer, P/O Ernest Russell who is buried in Risor Cemetery, 25 kilometres from Arendal in Norway.

FTR PB353	F/O K. Harrop	Pilot	(Missing)
(EA-E)	SGT J.G. McKenzie	F/E	(Missing)
'A' Flt	P/O R.D. Scott RCAF	NAV	(Missing)
	SGT J.S. McClenahan	W/OP	(Missing)
	SGT S. Hodgkinson	A/G	(Missing)
Crew on their	P/O E.A. Russell	A/B	(Killed)
4th operation	F/S T. Rees	A/G	(Missing)

FTR PB429	F/O C. Beatson	Pilot	(Killed)
(EA-)	SGT D. Harrison	F/E	(Killed)
' Flt'	F/O E. Bourton	NAV	(Killed)
	F/O L.R. McMonagle RAAF	W/OP	(Killed)
	F/O J.W. Murray RAAF	A/G	(Killed)
Crew on their	F/O J.C. King	A/B	(Killed)
1st operation	SGT A. Stephen	A/G	(Killed)

PILOTS...IN THE REAR TURRET?

For some reason, known only to the powers that be, trained pilots were recruited to become AGLT rear gunners. Fresh crews posted to 49 Squadron (and some of those already established) had to endure the wrench of losing their own rear gunners, which they had trained with since OTU. Their places were taken by the new breed of Pilot/Air/Gunners. (Not all 49 Squadron AGLT gunners were former pilots). These new bods, tempted into volunteering by the promise of early combat, soon slotted into their 'foster crews'. One such crew, operated for the first time on the 6/7 October raid to Bremen. F/O Ken Bromfield (PB504) and crew had acquired Sgt 'Pat' Walters as their new Pilot A/G.

Pat Walters gives this account of how he eventually arrived at Fiskerton to become a gunner on 'Village Inn':

"I trained in Southern Rhodesia and qualified as a pilot in June 1943 and returned to the U.K. later the same year. With what appeared to be thousands of other pilots I found myself at Harrogate, hanging around with the occasional posting to Tiger Moth refresher courses, airfield control or naval recognition courses and toughening up stunts. By the middle of 1944 I thought I was going to miss getting onto ops so this left me daft enough to volunteer for anything; 'the stupidity of youth!

OCTOBER 1944

Sometime in early September 1944, a little billet doux came round asking for volunteers from the pilot pool to join an operational squadron, but not in a pilot capacity. I showed interest and in a very few days I arrived at 49 Squadron, RAF Fiskerton, near Lincoln, along with a dozen other mugs. Again we were told we would be operating in a non-pilot capacity but at the end of the tour, our chance of becoming operational as pilots (on aircraft of our choice) would be given sympathetic consideration. We would not know the exact duties with 49 Squadron until we had accepted the offer. We all wanted single seat fighters and as far as I can remember nobody dropped out. After re-reading the official secrets act to us, we learned we had volunteered ourselves into the arse end of a Lancaster! (Operating the Automatic Gun Laying Turret).

I first flew in a Lancaster on 29th September, and one week later I flew my first operational trip... to Bremen. No OTU, no air to air firing, just plain green as grass. By the following morning, I had serious doubts about the wisdom of joining.

For my part, I fired my guns several times on 'Village Inn' contacts - never credited with any hits. Crashed once at Coltishall with bombs on board - got very near the four minute mile in all my kit. After the war in Europe, I would have been on my way to Okinawa, but the two atomic bombs stopped that.

There is a sequel to the promise given when I joined Bomber Command, about the aircraft of my choice. Some years after the war I joined the RAFVR to enjoy some nice weekend flying. However the Korean war came along and by act of Parliament some members of the RAFVR were recalled for familiarisation in comparative modern aircraft. Some VR pilots, after refreshers on Spitfires, converted onto Vampires. For my part - refresher on Oxfords and then on to a comparatively modern aircraft... Wellingtons! Still no real regrets... wouldn't have missed 49."

JUST POSTED IN

Wireless operator, Jack Shearing recorded Saturday, 7 October 1944 in his diary, for it was on this day that he and his fellow members in F/O Mellor's crew joined 49 Squadron. The crew had just finished their course at No 5 Lancaster Finishing School, Syerston. Jack wrote in his diary:

"There was another crew on the lorry, going to Bardney; we dropped them first not liking the look of that bleak camp at all. After much stooging around we found the camp, got our arrival chits to fill in and did a few routine visits including seeing the Adjutant and Wingco. He gave us all the griff; told us the losses at the squadron were very light, having no losses for the previous 30 ops except for last night when we lost 2 crews... both sprog ones!

He said they had a new gunnery device called 'Village Inn' and we were the only squadron to have it. We got our quarters allotted to us next and slept in the same beds of the bods who had gone for a burton the previous night! Jack, Eddy and me caught the bus into Lincoln, feeling cheesed off, but the town was packed and we had to line up for an hour at the pictures. The film was decent, a thriller type and it was a pity we had to leave before the end to catch the bus back."

OCTOBER 1944

11 October, 1944; VERRE (DAYLIGHT): 5 Group sent 61 Lancasters in an attempt to breach the sea walls on the island at Verre. Fiskerton had 12 aircraft airborne just after lunch including a new crew piloted by F/O Littley (PB370). W/Cmdr Botting (PB519) was operating, and the records show he took F/Lt Ken Gibson (Bombing Leader) along as a front gunner!

The red TI proximity marker was placed in position 300 yards NW of the aiming point by the time 49 Squadron came in to bomb. The weather was clear and the sea wall was visually identified and bombed. At the time, results could not be seen due to the delayed action bombs used. All the crews were home shortly after 16.00hrs. It was later confirmed that the raid was not successful; luckily no aircraft were lost.

The following day, the 12th, 15 aircraft were detailed for operations but the trip was cancelled during the afternoon. That night the film scheduled to be shown at the camp cinema was 'Flesh and Fantasy' but it was also cancelled much to the annoyance of all those gathered; instead 'Keep em Flying' with Abbott and Costello was shown.

14th October 1944; ADVANCE PARTY PROCEEDS TO FULBECK : As Bomber Command continued to expand, extra airfields were required to accommodate newly formed squadrons. The Airfields of Scampton (HQ of 52 Base), Dunholme Lodge and Fiskerton (sub-stations) were to be allocated to 1 Group, and on 2nd October, 52 Base was disbanded. The two squadrons at Dunholme (44 & 619) were sent to Spilsby and Strubby, whilst 49 Squadron had been given the former USAAF Troop Carrier base at Fulbeck, south of Lincoln. On 14th October, 49's advance party left for their new home.

HOME SWEET HOME

Again from diarist, Sgt Jack Shearing, the happenings of the 14 October are recorded:

"Got up to flights at 9 to find everyone and everything in a flap. After a lot of hanging about we finally got out to the Lanc and loaded it up; in all 19 kitbags, 5 cans, 9 bikes and umpteen smaller packs and cases. We finally took off and flew over to Fulbeck in very bumpy weather. the trip taking about twenty minutes. We left the gear in the kite while we had some grub and also went up to look at our hut and were immediately impressed, even though it was only a Nissen hut. There were only 6 beds and 4 chests-of-drawers, everything was in good condition and very clean. We got our kit after lunch by MT then speedily organised going out on scrounging raids. The result of these was: 6 chairs, 2 clothes horses, 2 large mirrors, a coal bunker and 2 coal bins, 2 tables, numerous hooks and bags of firewood. Later we found the coal compound and stocked up on coal and coke. We changed our stove for a wizard new one and soon the hut was rapidly looking quite cosy. After tea we paid the NAAFI a visit and then went back to the hut and stayed in all evening playing pontoon. I lost about 5/-, but we all enjoyed it so I have no regrets."

OCTOBER 1944

The following pages contain a list of the names of those personnel serving on 49 Squadron at the time of the move to Fulbeck. It has been compiled as accurately as possible from records but please make allowances for any omissions or any mis-spellings of names, ranks or trades etc:

MOVEMENT ORDER FROM RAF FISKERTON TO RAF FULBECK

Officer in Charge: S/Ldr Patton

F/O Talbot	Pilot	F/O Baily RAAF	Nav	F/O Mottram RAAF	B/A
P/O Berry	A/G	P/O Morony	A/G	F/O McRae	Pilot
F/O MacAulay	B/A	F/O Harford	Pilot	F/O Illingworth	Pilot
F/O Le Marquand	Pilot	F/O Mersey	Pilot	F/O Mellor	Pilot
F/O Stark RAAF	Pilot	F/L Gallagher	Pilot	F/L Thatcher	Pilot
F/O Calvert	Nav	P/O McLean	Nav	F/S Gee	Pilot
F/S Middleton	Nav	F/O Watkins	??	Sgt Crawshaw	F/E
F/S Speak RAAF	W/Op	Sgt Walker	F/E	Sgt Evans	Nav
Sgt Petch	W/Op	Sgt Garrett	P/RG	Sgt Logan	A/G
Sgt Mitchell	F/E	Sgt Bennett	Nav	F/S Findlay	B/A
F/S Shaw RAAF	W/Op	Sgt Roxby	A/G	Sgt Rix	A/G
Sgt Carter	F/E	Sgt Harding	Nav	Sgt Cooper	B/A
F/S O'Brien RAAF	W/Op	Sgt Haw	A/G	Sgt Pollington	P/RG
Sgt Wade	F/E	F/S Ransome	Nav	Sgt Bowers	B/A
Sgt Langley	W/Op	Sgt Blake	A/G	Sgt Price	A/G
Sgt McIntyre	F/E	F/S McKenzie	Nav	Sgt Boyes	B/A
F/S Reynolds RCAF	W/Op	Sgt Russell	A/G	Sgt Livesley	A/G
Sgt Edwards	F/E	Sgt Fox	Nav	Sgt Cowles	B/A
Sgt Shearing	W/Op	Sgt Morrison	A/G	Sgt Palmer	A/G
F/S Bairnsfather RAAF	B/A	F/S Yeoman RAAF	Nav	Sgt Brennan	F/E
F/S Lovatt RAAF	W/Op	Sgt Gilbert	A/G	Sgt Dickson	A/G

AIR PARTY TO FULBECK

W/C Botting	Pilot	F/L Kennedy	A/G	S/L Lace	Pilot
S/L Gorton	Pilot	F/L Ferguson	Pilot	F/O Skilton	F/E
F/L Lee	Pilot	F/L Burns RCAF	Pilot	F/L Carlyle RCAF	Pilot
F/L Blair	Pilot	F/L Reynolds	Nav	F/O Lane	B/A
F/L Ballantyne	W/Op	F/L Keene	F/E	F/L Wynyard	A/G
F/O Cannon	Pilot	F/O Parkin	Pilot	F/O Russell	Pilot
F/O Furber	Pilot	F/O Hassell	Nav	F/O Williams	Pilot
F/O Moore	Nav	F/O Maul	Pilot	F/O Galloway	Pilot
F/O Wedge	B/A	F/O Emmerson	B/A	F/O Morgan	Nav
F/O Watson	Pilot	F/O Dickson	Pilot	P/O Price	Nav
F/O Findlay	B/A	F/O Thomson	B/A	F/O Essenhigh	Pilot

OCTOBER 1944

F/O Dron	P/AG	F/O Littley	Pilot	F/O Lee	Pilot
F/O White	Nav	F/O Winter	Pilot	F/O Paul	B/A
F/O Barrie	Pilot	P/O Bassett	W/Op	F/O Squibb RCAF	Pilot
F/O Campbell RCAF	??	F/O Ellis RAAF	W/Op	P/O Miller	Nav
F/O Rowley	Pilot	F/O Hayward RCAF	B/A	P/O Deutscher RCAF	Nav
P/O Abbott	F/E	P/O Thomas	W/Op	F/O Williams	Nav
P/O Gibson	W/Op	F/O Hayward	B/A	F/O Fisher	A/G
F/O Kimber	A/G	F/O Amato	Nav	F/O Edwards	Nav
P/O Denny	F/E	P/O Bishop	W/Op	P/O Wilmot RAAF	B/A
P/O Bennett RCAF	A/G	P/O Timms	A/G	F/O Furness RCAF	B/A
F/O Kennedy RNZAF	B/A	P/O Craig	Nav	F/O Lewtas	P/RG
P/O Gordon	W/Op	Sgt Telford	A/G	Sgt Jones	F/E
Sgt Hannon	Nav	F/S Francis	B/A	Sgt Tingle	A/G
F/S John	A/G	Sgt Lusty	F/E	Sgt Picking	Nav
Sgt Williams	W/Op	Sgt Myers	A/G	W/O Salter	A/G
Sgt Stansill	F/E	W/O Everley	Nav	F/S McHeffey	B/A
Sgt Makofski	W/Op	Sgt Gascoyne	A/G	Sgt Grimsdale	A/G
Sgt Beck	F/E	F/S Mainwaring	B/A	Sgt Joyce	A/G
Sgt Reynolds	A/G	Sgt Glue	F/E	Sgt Nixon	Nav
F/S Smart RAAF	W/Op	Sgt Kean	W/Op	Sgt Durtnall	B/A
Sgt Cooke	A/G	Sgt Humble	A/G	Sgt Jenkins	F/E
F/S Gentleman	B/A	Sgt Holyoak	W/Op	Sgt Bangay	A/G
F/S Cooper RCAF	A/G	Sgt Boyce	F/E	F/S Reid RCAF	B/A
Sgt Hird	W/Op	Sgt Frost	A/G	Sgt O'Callaghan	A/G
Sgt Aspy	F/E	Sgt Mather	W/Op	Sgt Crann	B/A
Sgt Crawshaw	A/G	Sgt Anderson	P/RG	Sgt Cooper	F/E
Sgt Bolton	Nav	Sgt Williams	W/Op	Sgt Jackson	B/A
Sgt Battye	A/G	Sgt Houghton	A/G	Sgt Wilson	A/G
F/S Hawkins	Nav	Sgt Tapping	W/Op	Sgt Collins	A/G
F/S Mould	A/G	Sgt Hardy	F/E	Sgt Bolton	Nav
Sgt Randall	W/Op	Sgt Ellis	A/G	Sgt Duers	F/E
Sgt Bowers	Nav	Sgt Price	W/Op	Sgt Elliott	B/A
Sgt James	A/G	Sgt Butler	P/AG	Sgt Swanston	F/E
F/S Dart RAAF	Nav	F/S Jenkin RAAF	B/A	Sgt Field	A/G
F/S Chapman RAAF	W/Op	Sgt Faloon	A/G	Sgt Ashcroft	F/E
F/S Townsend RCAF	A/G	Sgt Trimnell	Nav	Sgt Smith	A/G
Sgt Colvin	F/E	Sgt Green	Nav	F/S Kermode	B/A
Sgt Griggs	W/Op	Sgt Sims	A/G	Sgt Robinson	A/G
Sgt Kent-Phillips	F/E	Sgt Ward	W/Op	Sgt Shakespeare	A/G
F/S Kletsky RCAF	A/G	Sgt Aldridge	B/A	Sgt Crabbe	F/E
Sgt Gatfield	Nav	Sgt Pye	W/Op	Sgt Powell	A/G
W/O Kalinski RCAF	W/Op	Sgt Wilkins	P/AG	Sgt Kenrick	F/E

OCTOBER 1944

F/S Thomson	A/G	Sgt Baxter	A/G	Sgt Moss	F/E
Sgt Walters	W/Op	Sgt Dowling	A/G	Sgt Bailey	F/E
Sgt Jenkins	A/G	Sgt Gesch RAAF	P/AG	Sgt McLaren	F/E
Sgt Shorrocks	W/Op	Sgt Dumbell	A/G	Sgt Downing	A/G
Sgt Varey	F/E	Sgt Rees	W/Op	Sgt Bourne	Nav
Sgt Moore	A/G	Sgt Callon	P/AG	F/S Christian	Nav
F/S Lewis (A.G.L.T.)	A/G	F/S Goldy	A/G	Sgt Brunton	F/E
Sgt Tarling	W/Op	F/S Roostan	W/Op	Sgt Adams	F/E
Sgt Billings	A/G	Sgt Barr	F/E	Sgt Bull	A/G
Sgt Robinson	A/G				

REAR PARTY

F/L Brady	Pilot	F/O Mallinson	Pilot	F/O Newton	A/G
F/S Kennedy	A/G	F/S Sharpe	A/G	Sgt Simmons	A/G
Sgt Le Marquand	A/G	S/S Robinson	W/Op	F/S Leedham	Nav

ON LEAVE AT THE TIME

F/O Hay	Pilot	Sgt Green	F/E	P/O Smith	Nav
W/O Jenkinson	W/Op	F/S French	A/G	P/O MacKay	B/A
F/O Hall	A/G				

SEPARATE PARTY

G/C Weir	F/L Acton	F/L Shaw	S/L Bromfield
F/O Sheppard	F/L Treece	S/L Ried	F/O Lloyd
F/L Osborne	F/L Weaver	S/L Kelly	S/L Briden
F/L Swindlehurst	F/L Martin	F/O Bishop	S/O Gillespie
F/O Thomas	F/O Stokoe	F/O Grainger	

A.G.L.T. PARTY

S/L Oatten	F/O Johnson-Biggs	F/O Collingwood	F/O Proctor
F/O Verrier	F/O Boardman	Cpl Ross	Cpl Hilton
AC2 Weston	AC1 Hughes		

GROUND PARTY

Officer I/C Road Party - F/Lt Catty NCO in charge of baggage - Air crew - Sgt McLaren NCO in charge of baggage - Ground crew - F/Sgt Shaw

Sgt Bolt	F/II	Sgt Smith	F/IIE	Sgt Nowell	F/IIA
Sgt Brailey	F/IIE	Sgt Bird	F/II	Cpl Bamforth	F/IIA
Cpl Ryall	F/IIE	Cpl Creasey	F/IIA	LAC Seward	F/ME
LAC Kerfoot	F/ME	LAC Williams	F/ME	LAC Camm	F/ME
LAC Hurrell	F/ME	LAC Parke	F/ME	LAC Livingstone	F/ME

LAC Atkins	F/ME	A/C Hannon	F/ME	LAC Wallington	F/ME
LAC Pearson	F/Ma	LAC Scott	F/Ma	LAC Robertson	F/Ma
LAC Spencer	F/Ma	LAC Allan	F/Ma	A/C Hickson	I/R2
LAC Evans	I/R2	LAC Angell	Elec	A/C Porter	Elec
LAC Jackson	Elec	A/C Vesty	Elec	A/C Dyer	M/Ast
Cpl Lorimer RCAF	R/Mec	LAC Baxter RCAF	R/Mec	LAC Toole RCAF	R/Mec
LAC Smith RCAF	R/Mec	Cpl Jackman	W/Mec	LAC Way	W/Mec
LAC Thomas	W/Mec	F/S Reed	Armr	LAC Hill	Armr
LAC Fordham	Armr	LAC Harman	Armr	Sgt Gardham	F/IIA
Sgt Robichaud	F/IIE	Cpl Yemm	F/IIA	Cpl Sheridon	Armr
LAC Mitchell	F/Ma	LAC Quincy	F/Ma	LAC Becket	F/Ma
LAC Magachin	F/ME	LAC Atmear	F/ME	LAC Brazel	F/ME
LAC Wigget	F/ME	LAC Blake	F/ME	A/C Dove	Armr
A/C Price	Armr	Cpl Townley	W/Mec	LAC McNeil	Elec
LAC Johnston	R/Mec	LAC Davis	Elec	A/C Castleton	W/Mec

MAIN PARTY - GROUND STAFF

"A" FLIGHT

W/O Phillips	F/IIA	F/S Burley	F.A.E	F/S Mangham	F/I
Sgt Roberts	F/IIE	Sgt Keen	F/IIE	Sgt Simpson	F/IIA
Sgt Flanigan	F/IIA	Cpl Proud	F/IIE	Cpl Annat	F/IIE
Cpl Outwin	F/2A	Cpl Best	F/IIA	LAC Brentnall	F/ME
LAC Broadhurst	F/ME	LAC Constable	F/ME	LAC James	F/ME
LAC Wilkinson	F/M	LAC Beesling	F/ME	LAC Hammett	F/M
LAC Greenwood	F/ME	LAC Hooker	F/M	LAC Swift	F/ME
LAC Yetman	F/M	LAC Morton	F/ME	LAC Esson	F/Ma
A/C French	F/ME	LAC Fretwell	F/M	LAC Benton	F/Ma
LAC Ward	F/Ma	LAC Jackson	F/Ma	LAC Felce	F/Ma
LAC Ryder	F/Ma	LAC Suggett	F/Ma	LAC McQueen	F/Ma
Cpl Barson	Elec/1	LAC Stephens	Elec/2	LAC Weston	Elec/2
LAC Taylor	Elec/2	Cpl Allen	IN/R1	LAC King	IN/R2
LAC Penn	IN/R2	LAC Booth	IN/R2	LAC Peeke	IN/R2
A/C Watkins	IN/R2				

"B" FLIGHT

F/S Small	F/II	Sgt Willis	F/II	Sgt Freegood	F/II
Sgt Stevens	F/II	Cpl McCormack	F/IIE	Cpl Harness	F/IIE
LAC Bishop	F/ME	LAC Millichip	F/ME	LAC Baker	F/ME
LAC Sugg	F/ME	LAC Finch	F/ME	LAC Shaw	F/ME
LAC Slade	F/ME	LAC Wiles	F/ME	LAC Latimer	F/ME
LAC Greenwood	F/ME	LAC Burley	F/ME	LAC Young	F/ME
LAC Young	F/Ma	LAC Curley	F/Ma	LAC Brailsford	F/Ma
LAC Crowdy	F/Ma	Cpl Broadbent	Elec/1	LAC Clegg	Elec/2

OCTOBER 1944

A/C Inwood	Elec/2	LAC Lowry	Elec/2	A/C Meadley	Elec/2
Cpl Clancey	Ins/R1	LAC Grossay	Inst/2	LAC Wootton	Ins/R2
LAC Williams	Inst/2	LAC Wearier	Ins/R2	LAC Paling	Inst/2
LAC Wright	F/ME	LAC Bottomley	F/ME	A/C Stacey	Armr
LAC Payne	F/Ma	Sgt House	Ach/Gd	A/C Barnett	Armr
Cpl Watts	RB/M	A/C King	Ach/Ma	A/C Pendleberry	Armr
A/C Jackson	Ach/Gd	LAC Hopkins	RB/M	Sgt Watson	Armr
LAC Jones	RB/M	W/O Tufnail	RB/M	A/C Lovejoy	Armr
Sgt Luckhurst	RB/M	LAC Collister	RB/M	LAC Lambert	Armr
LAC Mathias	RCD/M	LAC Henstock	RB/M	A/C Woodward	Armr
LAC Davies	RB/M	LAC Ockleford	RCD/M	LAC Avery	Armr
A/C Skeavington	W/MEC	LAC Gullekson RCAF	RCD/M	Sgt Miller	Armr
LAC Wetherspoon RCAF	RCD/M	A/C Dennis	Ach/Ma	Cpl Degaris	Armr
LAC Dunwin	W/Mec	Cpl Ramsey	Armr	LAC Appleby	Armr
LAC Kofman RCAF	RCD/M	A/C Pearce	Armr	Cpl Stanley	Armr
A/C Hughes	RCD/M	A/C Ross	Amr/Asst	LAC Jarrett	Armr
LAC Durrant RCAF	RB/M	LAC Smurthwaite	Armr	A/C Knowles	Armr
A/C Wynn	RB/M	A/C Courtenay	Amr/Ast	LAC Robinson	Armr
A/C Boyd	Ach/Gd	A/C Horton	Amr/Asst	LAC Pusey	Armr
Cpl Tune	Ach/Gd	A/C Bassett	Amr/Asst	LAC Rose	Armr
A/C Donnington	Ach/Gd	LAC Haytor	Armr	Cpl Wattam	Armr
LAC Thompson	Ach/Ma	LAC Wright	Amr/Asst	A/C Bayne	Armr
LAC Reid	F/ME	A/C Byrd	Amr/Asst	LAC Dodgson	Armr
LAC Clarke	DMT	A/C Collins	Armr	LAC Quick	Armr
Cpl Elliott	DMT	A/C Herd	Armr	A/W Ward	Armr
Cpl Fawcett	DMT	LAC Waumsley	Amr/Asst	A/C Bridgewater	Armr
Cpl Hopkinson	DMT	LAC Collins	Armr	A/C Rowe	Armr
LAC Riddell	DMT	A/C Joel	Amr/Asst	LAC Cooper	Armr
LAC Pidocks	DMT	A/C Creber	Amr/Asst	LAC Escott	Armr
LAC Selley	DMT	A/C Smith	Amr/Asst	LAC Phillips	Armr
A/C Wild	DMT	LAC Beet	Amr/Asst	LAC Titterton	Armr
Cpl Clark	Ach/Gd	A/C Walsh	Amr/Asst	LAC Comor	Armr
LAC Partridge	Ach/Ma	LAC Lee	Amr/Asst	A/C Dewdney	Armr
LAC Mercer	Ach/Gd	LAC Wilby	Amr/Asst	LAC Lynn	Armr
Cpl Ramsey	Clk/Gd	LAC Spence	Amr/Asst	LAC King	Armr
Cpl Greenfield	DMT	LAC Woolam	Ach/Ma	A/C Shepperd	Armr
LAC Rimmer	MTM	LAC Salter	DMT	LAC Shipley	Armr
Cpl Whitehead	DMT	Cpl Menzies	N/Ord	LAC Passan	Armr
F/S Shaw	Ach/Gd	LAC Edmunds	Ach/Gd	LAC Perry	Armr
Cpl Glover	Ach/Gd	ACH Clifton	Clk/Gd	LAC Evans	Armr
LAC Grainger	Clk/Gd	Cpl Cherry	N/Ord	LAC Hancock	Armr
LAC Boston	N/Ord	LAC Fellows	N/Ord		

OCTOBER 1944

W.A.A.F.

Cpl Whitelaw	DMT	LACW Everett	DMT	LACW Fitchet	DMT
LACW Cope	DMT	ACW Stokes	DMT	LACW Wilkins	DMT
ACW Winters	DMT				

OTHERS

F/L Newnes	ADJ	F/O Hall	Radar
F/Lt Catty	Nav/Ldr	F/L Gibson	B/Ldr

14/15 October, 1944: **BRUNSWICK** 49 Squadron had one final operation to fly from Fiskerton; a visit to Brunswick. The Order of Battle for the raid consisted of the following 18 crews and aircraft:

PB519	W/C Botting:	PB369	F/O Maul:	PB355	F/O Essenhigh:
PB373	F/O Squibb:	PB370	F/O Russell:	PB361	F/O Watson:
PB354	F/O Cannon:	PB349	F/O Furber:	PB374	F/O Barrie:
PB300	F/O Blaire:	PB432	F/O Littley:	PB484	F/O Burns RCAF:
PB504	F/O Hay:	PB383	S/L Gorton:	PB455	F/O Rowley:
PB568	F/O Winter:	PB460	F/O Nowrie:	PB571	F/O Talbot:

The squadron started to take-off just after 22.30hrs to join a total force of 233 Lancasters bound for Germany. Over Brunswick, the Controller ordered crews to bomb easterly T.I's in their sectors with 14 seconds delay. The result was that bombing spread over the desired target area, with sticks falling outward from the aiming point - as F/O Watson (PB361) and crew later reported: "The fire area in centre of city radiating out to the north like spokes of a wheel." It is thought that the main weight of bombing fell in the centre and north of the target. F/O Blaire (PB300) and crew in K-King were attacked by a twin-engined enemy fighter just before bombing but managed to escape unharmed. This forced them to be late and as they approached the target they heard the Controller order "return to base", so they did not bomb.

Brunswick did not have to receive such a strong attack by Bomber Command again. Just one Lancaster crew failed to return; all 49's aircraft came home safely. Touching down at 06.20hrs, F/O Littley (PB432) and crew had the honour of being the last 49 Squadron Lancaster to land back at Fiskerton from a bombing operation.

OCTOBER 1944

49 SQUADRON MOVES TO RAF FULBECK

On Monday 16 October, the squadron was stood down during the move to its new home at Fulbeck. 56 Base had been established on 1st October, with the base station at Syerston, and two sub stations at Balderton, which was soon to receive the newly formed 227 Squadron (Lancasters), and Fulbeck with 49 Squadron, soon to be joined by 189 Squadron in November.

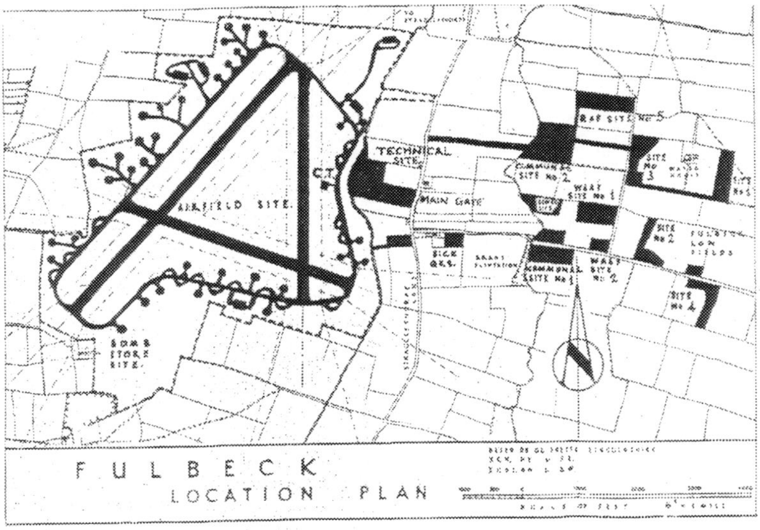

Location plan of RAF Fulbeck showing the airfield layout and the dispersed accomodation sites. Fulbeck village is located 2 miles to the east.

ROYAL AIR FORCE FULBECK

Fulbeck airfield is situated about 15 miles south of Lincoln on the western side of the Lincoln edge. Here the land flattens out as it sweeps towards Newark and the River Trent. The village of Fulbeck is situated up on the Lincoln edge about 2 miles east of the drome. Aircraft making their landing approach on the northern boundary had to very careful of the church spire just over the fields in the village of Brant Broughton.

The airfield first came into being in late 1940 as a Relief Landing Ground for RAF Cranwell. It closed in 1942 for concrete runways to be laid, and when it re-opened it housed 1485 (Bomber) Gunnery Flight, training gunners for 5 Group, with Whitleys, Lysanders, Martinets, Manchesters and Wellingtons. The airfield's true operational life began when the US Ninth Army Air Force took over the station in preparation for the D-Day operations.

As the Control Tower personnel from 49 Squadron stepped out onto the balcony of their new domain, they viewed a panorama that, just a few months earlier had witnessed the historic launch of the Invasion of Normandy.

On the evening of 5th June, 45 Dakota aircraft of the 442nd Troop Carrier Group lifted from Fulbeck's main runway to join hundreds of others, bound for France. The 442nd carried 1,937 paratroopers of the HQ and 1st Battalion, 507 Regiment, 82nd US Airborne Division to their drop zone on the Cherbourg Peninsular - 21 aircraft sustained flak damage, one dropped its stick just before crashing and one ditched in the Channel on the way home.

Then, just one month prior to 49 Squadron's arrival, Fulbeck played its part in Operation 'Market Garden' when it again acted as a springboard for an Airborne assault. This time, on Sunday 17th September, 90 Dakotas of the 440th TCG took-off from Fulbeck bound for Holland. On board were American paratroopers of the 508th Parachute Infantry and the 376th Field Artillery Battalion, 82nd Airborne Division. As British paratroopers were dropping near Arnhem, these American troops jumped near Nijmegen. The casualties suffered by the 440th included the shooting down of their CO, Colonel Frank Krebs and crew, all of whom fortunately parachuted to safety.

On each of the following two days, the 440th towed 80 'Waco' gliders filled with troops and equipment out of Fulbeck bound for the beleaguered forces on the ground in Holland. The spectacle of such a tremendous air armada as it gathered over Lincolnshire and eastern England, must have stunned all who watched. Its invasion role completed, Fulbeck now braced itself for the final stages of the bombing offensive against Germany.

19/20 October, 1944; NUREMBERG: For two days at Fulbeck, the met thwarted any attempts to fly operations, then at 10.00hrs, Thursday 19th, Group orders came through detailing a long range attack on Nuremberg.

At 17.15hrs that evening, F/O Ken Lee (PB519) and crew gunned Q-Queenie down the main runway, being the first of 19 Lancasters to take-off on operations from RAF Fulbeck. Two new crews climbed away into the murky darkness; they were piloted by F/O Harford (PB471) and F/O Dickson (PB460).

This was another exclusive 5 Group attack, in which 270 aircraft had been dispatched. Cloud cover over the target prevented the bombing from being a complete success. All Fulbeck's crews completed their sorties, with the exception of F/O Furber's (PB349) who 'got off track' and bombed the alternative target of Stuttgart.

All 49's aircraft had returned to base by 01.38hrs, but 5 Group did suffer the loss of 2 Lancasters and their crews.

A Daylight operation was planned for the 20th, but with the dawn came heavy rain and the raid was scrubbed.

OCTOBER 1944

DOWN AT THE LOCAL

With a lull in operations due to inclement weather, Fulbeck personnel took this opportunity to explore the local night life. Sgt Jack Shearing recorded this diary entry for Thursday 26th October:

"After tea, I decided to cycle down to the local at Brant Broughton with Lefty and Jack. On getting there we found both pubs shut, but heard there were two pubs open and a dance at the next village, Beckingham. The bike was running sweet and we got up a good lick. The dance was a typical village effort, a small school room being the 'floor', but there were bags of partners such as they were. Lefty fiddled three eggs out of the raffle and we also got some apples, so we were quite happy.

On getting round to our bikes however, some of the local lads had pinched our lamps, two pairs of gloves and an old mug of mine. It rained cats and dogs all the way back and we got soaked to the skin. We went into the Mess and got our eggs cooked plus some fried bread and chips which went down very well. There was a fire in the hut so we organised the clothes horses for drying our wet things - I was glad to get to bed about 2am."

28/29 October, 1944; BERGEN: Most of 5 Group had not operated for several days, awaiting clear weather in which to attack the U-boat pens at Bergen. During Saturday evening of the 28th, over 240 Lancasters took to the skies over Lincolnshire (including 18 from Fulbeck).

Although clear conditions in the target area had been forecast, when the Group arrived over the pens they found 10/10ths cloud cover; 45 Lancasters did manage to bomb, helped by 2 more from 49 Squadron. But eventually the Master Bomber conceded defeat and sent the remainder home - 3 Lancasters and their crews failed to make that return leg. All of 49's aircraft arrived back over England to find they had been diverted; 1 put down at East Kirkby, 1 at Burn, 9 at Rufforth and the remaining 7 landed at Marston Moor.

'WATCH' WHAT YOU'RE DOING!

One aircraft diverted to Marston Moor contained F/O Ken Lee (PB519) and crew. The following account is given F/Sgt John Aldridge, the crew's bomb aimer:

"The op to Bergen was aborted and on our return flight we dropped 'part' of the bomb load in the North Sea. We were diverted to Marston Moor in Yorkshire. On the last leg, I was in the bomb aimer's compartment getting my gear together and unloading the guns in the front turret. I continued to sit on the step in my compartment when we joined the circuit and prepared to land. I could see that the skipper was going to land well up the runway and expected him to go round again - but he decided against it.

With part of the bomb load aboard and a high all up weight Q-Queenie ran out of runway and carried on through the overshoot area, hit a ditch smashing off the undercart and eventually coming to a halt across a main road - I can still visualise earth appearing at my feet as I sat on the step. As we ground to a halt, there was just a moment when we all held our breath (thinking of the bombs resting on the ground in the smashed bomb bay) then someone shouted 'Let's get out of this bloody aircraft' and we in the front, pilot F/O Ken Lee, navigator Tom Gatfield and Lou Crabbe the flight engineer, went out through the top hatch like scalded cats and down the wing into a ditch to be joined by F/Sgt Pye (W/OP) and F/Sgt Powell (M/U gunner). Poor old Roy Wilkins the rear gunner came staggering along with the cocking toggle in his hand (with which he had been unloading the guns) - his turret had swung as we bumped along the ground and he had fallen out of the doors. Needless to say, the Lanc's bomb load did not go up!

There was a humorous side to this incident in that Tom Gatfield had decided to 'lose' his navigator's watch in the crash. The skipper and Tom attended a Courts of Enquiry over this - travelling to Marston to attend! -there seemed to be less concern over the loss of one Lancaster written off. Actually Q-Queenie was always used by W/Cmdr Botting, and we had flown her on three previous operations; we were never encouraged to share the CO's aircraft again. Incidentally, Ken our skipper never knew Tom had fixed the 'loss' of his watch and thought it had genuinely gone missing - that is until Tom showed it to him at a reunion several years after the war."

Author: During a conversation with Tom Gatfield regarding this incident, Tom revealed that when he exited the Lancaster, instead of going left off the port wing with the others, for some reason he turned right and tripped over the wire aerial and went 'arse over tip' down the starboard wing, landing on the run. Whilst running, Tom kept remembering the size of the crater caused by the German land mine that had bombed his family 'out' in London - in fractions of seconds Tom's mind was racing to calculate how big a crater their bomb load would make in comparison, and how far he would have to run in order to survive. At the Court of Enquiry it was also disclosed that Tom had in fact managed to jump clean over three rolls of barbed wire without even sustaining a scratch, much to the puzzlement of his rescuers. The watch... it still keeps good time today.

30 October, 1944; WALCHEREN (DAYLIGHT): 5 Group received a request to follow up the Main Force raid made on Walcheren Island two days earlier. These raids on the island's gun batteries were in preparation for a ground attack the following day.

A total of 102 Lancasters and 8 Mosquitoes of 5 Group left their Lincolnshire bases shortly after lunch. Gp/Cpt Weir (PB432) and crew were part of the 13 strong contingent sent by 49 Squadron. With a bombing height of 4,000ft, crews commented on how much flooding had been caused by the previous attack. All 49's aircraft bombed with the exceptions of F/O Dickson (PB486) and F/O Mallinson (PB568) and crews.

F/O Mallinson's Lancaster received flak hits in the starboard inner engine whilst the crew were making their 3rd orbit.

Just one aircraft failed to return, this being a Mosquito from the Marker force.

Some years after the war, Bert Weatherley, wireless operator in F/O Jack Nowrie's crew wrote the following account of their participation in the Walcheren raid:

"The squadron's effort was 13 aircraft and our loads would be 14x1000lb HE bombs. The objective of the raid was to silence the guns with accurate bombing from 4,000ft in daylight - quite a departure from our high level night bombing.

Six Lancasters led by F/O Nowrie (PB361) were to reach the target area 30 minutes before the main force and take wind speeds and direction, then report these back to base. Based on these readings, bomb sight settings were calculated then transmitted to the main force. Our 6 aircraft would then join the main force and bomb.

At briefing it was stressed, as usual, that W/T silence would be maintained but on this occasion only until a precise moment when I, as Jack Nowrie's wireless operator, would transmit in pre-arranged code, the relevant wind information. I was to transmit the group of figures through twice, followed in sequence by the other five aircraft. Then once more strict W/T silence and wait for the broadcast of the bomb sight settings.

I was very conscious of the responsibility resting on my shoulders and constantly checked the serviceability of my equipment as we headed for the Dutch coast. I felt vulnerable and naked, our night time camouflage silhouetted against the sky - six lonely Lancasters at such low level were sitting targets! The seconds on my watch were now ticking towards that vital minute and my hand was poised over the morse key. With hardly a second to spare the navigator slipped a piece of paper onto my desk, and my hand depressed the key transmitting the Base call sign. At this moment all hell broke loose! explosions, smell of cordite, and our previously level flight pattern had suddenly become a screaming dive to port. I braced myself in my seat by wedging my knees under the desk top and continued transmitting the message.

We had come within range of the very guns we had come to destroy and taken a full salvo. The starboard-inner had taken a direct hit and the captain ordered the flight engineer, Sgt Palmer, to feather it. Nobody was injured and the damage seemed confined to the wing. From our vantage point we could see the Anti-Aircraft gunners had turned their attention on Gp/Cpt Weir and shells were bursting all around him. We tagged on to the main force to bomb, but couldn't keep up on three engines. The ground gunners, seeing a lame duck concentrated their fury upon us and we were surrounded by shell bursts. One direct hit went straight through the tail plane just missing F/O Ford, the pilot/rear gunner - his report to the captain was amazingly calm.

Once away from the target we took stock of our position. We were finding it difficult to maintain height, the aircraft was handling badly, there was a stretch of the North Sea ahead of us and we were alone. Although the aircraft was not in distress, at such a low height we would have little time to send out a distress call. We therefore contacted the D/F station who told me to stay with them as they tracked my signal, periodically passing back fixes of our position and enquiring about our state of serviceability - it was very reassuring to know that if we had to ditch, the Air Sea Rescue service would be aware of our exact position.

Finally the coast was sighted and we homed on to base; 3 hours and 25 minutes from wheels up they were once more skidding along the runway and we were safely home. Those ever welcome cups of coffee were pushed into our hands by volunteers from the WAAF who, at whatever time of the day or night we returned, were always there in the briefing room to greet us."

The following morning, Tuesday 31st, as F/O Nowrie's crew drifted down to the hangar to survey the damage sustained by their faithful Lancaster, they may have noticed the 15 Halifaxes that had been diverted into Fulbeck during the night.

F/O Jack Nowrie and crew: This photograph was taken at HCU after the crew had been joined by Cliff Palmer the flight engineer, and before the rear gunner Eddie Dellow had been replaced by Freddie (Phil?) Ford (a pilot/rear gunner who was AGLT trained).

(Back row l to r) Bob Barlow, navigator; Bert Weatherley, wireless op/air gunner; Eddie Dellow, rear gunner; Peter Burridge, mid/upper gunner. (Front row l to r) Stan Goldsworthy RAAF, bomb aimer; Jack Nowrie, pilot; Cliff Palmer, flight engineer. (A.L. Weatherley)

Another month in this long war came to a close. It had been an upheaval moving base and saying goodbye to the many friends made in Fiskerton, Reepham and the surrounding area. But everyone seemed to have settled into their new surroundings quite well. Sadly, the squadron had begun once again suffering casualties and as the cold, damp November nights approached, members of 49 Squadron knew all too well that more losses were inevitable.

OCTOBER 1944

OPERATIONAL SUMMARY - OCTOBER 1944

Date	Target	Desp	E/R	FTR	Remarks
5	WILHELMSHAVEN	16	-	-	Daylight
6	BREMEN	17	-	2	F/O Harrop FTR F/O Beatson FTR
11	VEERE	12	-	-	Daylight
14/15	BRUNSWICK	18	-	-	
19/20	NUREMBERG	19	-	-	1st Op from Fulbeck
28/29	BERGEN	18	-	-	Diverted
30	WALCHEREN	13	-	-	Daylight

Total number of sorties flown	113
Failed to return	2
Total tons of bombs of all types dropped	491.14
Operational hours flown during October 1944	635.50
Non-operational hours flown during October 1944	572.00

Automatic Gun Laying Turret (A.G.L.T.) Codenamed "VILLAGE INN" (Illustration by John Ward)

NOVEMBER 1944

1 November, 1944; HOMBERG (DAYLIGHT): The Meerbeck oil plant was singled out for attention from 226 Lancasters of 5 Group. A late afternoon start, saw the force arriving over the target around dusk, where the Pathfinders (Mossies from 5 & 8 Groups) had difficulties due to the enemy jamming their VHF and W/T, plus the hazy cloud which developed in the area.

There was much orbiting and many crews elected to bomb the alternative target; but 159 Lancasters did manage to bomb the scattered markers placed around Homberg. Heavy flak in the target area damaged the Lancaster being flown by F/O Essenhigh (PB374) and crew; on the point of releasing their bombs, they found that the hydraulic system had been damaged and the bombs doors would not open. On return to England, F/O Essenhigh headed J-Jig towards Woodbridge emergency airfield and with use of the 'emergency air', the undercarriage was lowered and a successful landing accomplished. One Lancaster failed to return from the operation, but all 49's remaining aircraft returned to base, ‘U’ Uncle on 3 engines and 34 holes.

2/3 November, 1944; DÜSSELDORF: Thursday 2 November saw Fulbeck in absolute chaos and pandemonium; the new squadron, 189 was arriving on base, and on top of that, Group was requesting a big effort for the night’s raid on Düsseldorf, plus AGLT training flights were scheduled.

Eventually 13 aircraft from the squadron were airborne shortly after 17.00hrs. For some unstated reason, four crews from 49 Squadron were using 189 Squadron kites; F/O Jack Nowrie piloted ME300, F/O Le Marquand (new crew) flew LM754, F/O Leslie (Uncle Will) Hay took PB594 whilst F/O Norman Alty and crew took EE136 'Spirit of Russia', a former 9 Squadron veteran aircraft that would eventually go on to complete some 109 operations.

A total of 961 Lancasters and Halifaxes, with the aid of 31 Mosquitoes set out on a cold night with heavy frost, to deliver a heavy attack on Düsseldorf. This would be the final major attack of the war on Düsseldorf. Bomber Command lost 19 aircraft, 11 Halifaxes and 8 Lancasters; one of the Lancasters came from 49 Squadron:

F/O Peter Harford and crew, flying on only their 2nd operation, were all killed when V-Victor was brought down over Germany; they all now rest together in the Becklingen War Cemetery, Soltau Germany.

FTR PB385	F/O P.E.G. Harford	Pilot	(Killed)
(EA-V)	Sgt J.B. Mitchell	F/E	(Killed)
'B' Flt	F/S S.C. Bennett	NAV	(Killed)
	F/S W.O. Shaw RAAF	W/OP	(Killed)
	Sgt H. Roxby	A/G	(Killed)
Crew on their	F/S A.M. Findlay	A/B	(Killed)
2nd operation	Sgt J.A. Rix	A/G	(Killed)

NOVEMBER 1944

4/5 November, 1944; LADBERGEN (DORTMUND-EMS CANAL): This proved to be another successful attack by 5 Group, with both branches of the canal being breached, leaving many barges stranded. It prevented much needed smelting coke reaching important steelworks near Brunswick and Osnabrück.

2 Mosquito Pathfinders had led 174 Lancasters (including 12 from 49 Squadron). Three aircraft failed to return.

For the second raid in succession, 49 Squadron suffered the loss of a crew. F/O Derrick Talbot, a 22 year-old pilot and his crew, which contained 3 Australians, were flying on only their 5th operation together. Sadly, all were killed and are buried in the Reichswald Cemetery, Germany.

FTR PB370	F/O D. Talbot	Pilot	(Killed)
(EA-F)	Sgt S.R. Crawshaw	F/E	(Killed)
'A Flt'	F/O G.H. Baily RAAF	NAV	(Killed)
	F/S L.G. Speak RAAF	W/OP	(Killed)
	F/O W.J. Moroney	A/G	(Killed)
Crew on their	F/O H.L. Motterham RAAF	A/B	(Killed)
5th operation	F/O R.W. Berry	A/G	(Killed)

6/7 November, 1944; GRAVENHORST (MITTELLAND CANAL): No 5 Group dispatched their 'Canal Busters' once again, this time in an attempt to breach the banks of the Mittelland Canal at its intersection with the Dortmund-Ems, at Gravenhorst.

After problems finding the target, 627 Squadron Mosquitoes then had difficulty in marking the aiming point. F/O Le Marquand later reported: *"It was too dark for the markers to see; the Controller continually asked for flares and finally cancelled the attack."* One marker Mossie did find the canal accurately but his TI fell into the water and was extinguished; F/O Norman Alty (PB369) may have witnessed this event when at de-brief he reported: *"Only one red TI seen to go down but it extinguished itself before the PFF could back it up."*

Only 31 of the 235 strong force of Lancasters had dropped their bombs before the Controller ordered the raid to be abandoned. All 49's aircraft made the return journey across the North Sea with their bomb loads still intact. Unfortunately, the price of this aborted raid was high - 10 Lancasters and crews did not be return to their Lincolnshire bases.

PLEASE KEEP OFF THE GRASS

Before he volunteered for aircrew, Bernard Browning's early RAF service was as an LAC Musician. But, on a wet miserable Monday night in November 1944, he found himself over the North Sea in a Lancaster being piloted home to England by F/O Ken Bromfield (PB460).

F/O Browning (the navigator), had just been given a message from F/O Norman Wells the wireless operator, stating that they had received diversion instructions.
Bernard describes what happened next:

"We were returning from the abandoned Gravenhorst operation of 6/7 November when we were diverted to Horsham-St-Faith (a USAAF bomber base just above Norwich). Having ditched our 'cookie' in the North Sea, I was tracking our course nicely along the GEE line over Norfolk, when the skipper suddenly said 'Here it is, I can see the lights'-No! said I, carry on... we haven't reached there yet, the GEE blips don't coincide. 'I'm going down here anyway because the weather's foul... it's pouring with rain' replied the skipper. He then started to make his landing approach.

Unfortunately we could not get into radio contact with the airfield and while we were making our approach, all the airfield lights suddenly went out necessitating an overshoot! More runway lights then re-appeared but on a different heading and a new approach was made with the same result as before. Finally a third and successful landing attempt was made on a fresh heading. I then heard the skipper saying 'I can't pull her up!' The aircraft continued to career along the runway and with the added weight of bombs, the undercart collapsed smashing up into the wings. We eventually came to a sudden halt with the nose of R-Roger through the perimeter fence. Surrounded by a terrible hissing sound, seven people have never left an aircraft so fast before. Why the remaining bombs on board didn't go up, we shall never ever know... but we were forever thankful.

It transpired that we had in fact landed at the grass fighter airfield of Coltishall, and I understand that the unavailability of the first two runways that we approached, was because Mosquitoes had crashed on both of them whilst we were in the circuit."

COCKTAILS ANYONE?

F/O Leslie Hay (PB484) and crew, with F/O Len Mellor as 2nd dickey, managed to scrape into Horsham as 'Uncle Will' clearly remembers:

"On the return journey we ran into a cold front with a storm in it and I had difficulty keeping the aircraft the right way up. We were chucked all over the place and the rain, which normally didn't bother us, made visibility almost non-existent at times. The weather back at base was so bad that the question of landing there didn't arise, and we were diverted to Horsham-St-Faith in Norfolk. I thought that I would never get down on the runway as it seemed impossible to fly a straight course, let alone land, and we had a full bomb load on board. But we got down and I thought I was pretty good! No one else would be there, I was quite certain of that after the difficulties that we had experienced.

On going into the de-briefing room, I was amazed to see half of 49 Squadron standing about, partaking of refreshments as if it was a 'cocktail party' - I can tell you that my ego has never been so deflated."

Of the 12 aircraft dispatched by 49 Squadron that night, 5 managed to land at base, 6 landed at Horsham-St-Faith and one lay forlorn in a Norfolk field. The crash landing of PB460 at Coltishall was timed at 21.47hrs.

ANOTHER FLYING GAS MAIN

Friday 10 November, 1944; London: Mr Winston Churchill at last admitted to the British public, that new secret German long-range rockets called the V2's, are being launched against Britain. When the first one fell on Chiswick in September, the population was 'not discouraged' from believing that the devastation was caused by a gas explosion. To date nearly 100 have landed with as many as 8 rockets a day being launched from sites in Holland.

The 46 foot-tall V2 attains a height of nearly 70 miles and travels at 3,600mph, with a possible range of 200 miles carrying one ton of high explosives in its nose-cone. It travels too fast for the public to receive any warning. The first anyone knows is the sound of the huge explosion followed by a whooshing sound, then flames with plumes of smoke, and until now, the official explanation would have been 'a gas-main explosion'. Four rockets destroyed 2,000 houses in Croydon.

11/12 November, 1944; HARBURG: Weather over the target was clear, and much ground detail could be seen as 237 Lancasters from 5 Group passed over the oil refinery at Harburg. F/O Hay (PB504) reported: *"One stick of bombs seen to straddle the target and cause an orange explosion with clouds of grey smoke."*

Aircraft returning to England were once again confronted with poor weather conditions over Lincolnshire. Fulbeck sent 49's flock up to Carnaby in Yorkshire, where 11 had landed by 21.56hrs; F/Lt Galloway (PB432) and crew landed O-Oboe at Foulsham in Norfolk. This just left the O/C of 'B' Flight, S/Ldr Harold Gorton (PB369) and crew, flying in A-Able (borrowed from 'A' Flt), outstanding. It was later confirmed that the Squadron Leader's Lancaster was one of 7 that were lost on this Harburg operation. The pilot, along with three of his fellow crew members are buried in Hamburg War Cemetery, the other four (including 2nd pilot F/O Illingworth) have no known graves but are remembered on the Runnymede Memorial.

FTR PB369	S/L H. Gorton (O/C B Flt)	Pilot	(Killed)
(EA-A)	F/O G.E. Illingworth	2nd Pilot	(Missing)
'A' Flt	Sgt F.E. Jones	F/E	(Killed)
	F/S W.G. Hannon	NAV	(Missing)
	F/O D.A. Ellis RAAF	W/OP	(Missing)
	P/O F. Tingle	A/G	(Killed)
Crew on their	P/O L.T. Francis	A/B	(Killed)
16th operation	P/O F.E. John	A/G	(Missing)

NOVEMBER 1944

FIRST OPERATION

The Harburg raid was the first operation for F/Lt Len Mellor's crew. Once again we draw from the excellent diary of Sgt Jack Shearing, wireless operator on that crew. Jack's words, written just two days after this operation (Saturday 11 November), give a fascinating insight into a day-in-the-life on a Bomber Squadron during late 1944; Jack writes:

"Did not get called early as the daylight was scrubbed by met; went on the parade and went out to do a DI on G-George, Paddy and Harry were on the turrets. Heard, on getting back, we were on ops that night taking G-George, so the whole crew went out to do a check on her. Went to lunch after and found out that briefing was at 1300hrs. Went to signals briefing first, which proved to be quite an easy, matey, chat; we still got the gen nevertheless, Les Randall giving me a few extra tips. Went into main briefing then at 1400hrs. Heard what the target was, the oil refineries at Harburg. They told us the target would be tough as we could expect all the Hamburg defences to open up at us with 200 heavy AA guns.

We got ready and went out to the kites and did our pre flight checks. There were lashings of sandwiches out there and we tucked into these while waiting for Jack (Nav) to come with last minute gen on his flight plan. While we were running up, first S/Ldr Lace and then W/Cmdr Botting came round to see if everything was OK, and finally F/O Cannon, who usually flies G-George came out as well to wish us luck. We took-off at 16.35 and soon set course across the North Sea in the middle of a stream of 250 Lancs. We were carrying a 'cookie' 6 x 1000 pounders and 6 x 500's plus 1,500 gallons of gas. I went over to 'base' for the first 50 miles then went over to 'Group'. Our 'Village Inn' had gone u/s and tuning did not remedy it.

It soon got dark, then 20 minutes from zero hour I left Group, which was being heavily jammed and went over the W/T Controller. I picked him up OK and got the bombing winds and the instructions over the target on which T.I's to bomb. The target was well and truly pranged and was blazing and emitting huge mushrooms of black smoke. We dropped our load and set out for home. The flak was moderate but there were bags of fighter flares and scarecrows as well. We saw no fighters, but saw one kite going down over the target and we could see flak coming up from Cuxhaven and several small islands.

Group was sending out a message, but I could not make head or tail of it for some time until I deciphered it as 'Land at Carnaby'. It was a nightmare over this country for the sky was full of kites, the gunners saw 2 Lancs crash in mid-air in the funnels on one drome. We finally landed at Carnaby after being airborne for 6 hours, and rushed off to interrogation and something to drink. We found quite a lot of the other crews being interrogated. Then went in M.T. over to Lissett a satellite of Driffield as there was no accommodation at Carnaby. It was the home of 158 Squadron flying Halifaxes in 4 Group. After supper went off to bed rather tired but felt very happy and contented at the successful conclusion of my first op!"

The following day, the weather prevented the squadron from returning to Fulbeck and another night was spent at Lissett.

NOVEMBER 1944

16 November, 1944; DUREN (DAYLIGHT): Bomber Command was asked to give support to an American Army attack by bombing three towns behind the German lines. 1,188 aircraft were dispatched; 499 aircraft drawn from 1,5 and 8 Groups attacked the town of Duren, from which 3 Lancasters failed to return.

Crews from 49 Squadron had been woken up by the SP's at 07.30hrs and told that a daylight op was on. Heavy rain rattled on the nissen huts as aircrew stumbled out of bed, and all morning everyone thought it would be scrubbed. But the needs of the Army were pressing and 11 of the squadron's aircraft were airborne from Fulbeck around lunch time. Over the target, the callsign for the aiming point was "Pickwick", and as the Lancasters made their bombing runs, they heard the Controller's instructions; "bomb Pickwick plus 2 seconds" etc. One new crew was operating with 49 Squadron; piloted by F/O Stark RAAF (PB300), they completed a successful first sortie.

As the squadron returned over Fulbeck they were refused landing instructions because of decreasing visibility. Base instructed them to land over at Coningsby and 9 aircraft complied. F/Lt Mellor (PB586) landed E-Easy at Metheringham, and F/O Littley landed at Carnaby nearly an hour later.

21 November, 1944; GRAVENHORST (MITTELLAND CANAL): Whilst a 5 Group force of 123 Lancasters attacked the Dortmund-Ems Canal, 10 aircraft from 49 Squadron joined 128 other 5 Group Lancasters in bombing the Mittelland Canal at Gravenhorst.

Take-off started just after 17.30hrs and included Group Captain 'Ginger' Weir (PB300), Fulbeck's irrepressible Station Commander, piloting K-King.

The Main Force, led by 6 Mosquitoes arrived in the target area shortly before 21.00hrs. Orbiting the target, the Controller originally ordered the forces to stay at pre-briefed bombing heights, but at 20.58hrs, he then ordered the Main Force to attack from below the cloud base which was given as 4,000ft. These instructions were subjected to severe jamming of W/T which caused much confusion. The controller next ordered the crews to bomb the southern red T.I's as planned. Consequently some crews bombed through cloud and others from below, with the markers being visible through the cloud layers. In the light of photo flashes, some 49 crews did obtain visual identification and despite the communication problems, the canal was successfully breached.

49 Squadron de-briefs show that the crew's of F/Lt Len Mellor (PB373), F/O Jock Galloway and F/O Carlyle (PB484) bombed below the clouds, whilst five other crews bombed red T.I's from above. This just left the two aircraft being flown by F/O Maul (PB354) and Grp/Cpt Weir - it has been speculated that one of these two aircraft exploded after being hit by bombs or light flak, which in turn caused the other aircraft nearby, to also explode.

The only survivor from this tragic incident was the Group Captain. His own remarkable escape, in which he was forcibly blown out of an exploding Lancaster does not confirm the cause, Grp/Cpt Weir had no recollection of what happened. He remembers regaining consciousness laying on his back on the muddy bottom of the breached and drained canal, his deployed parachute trailed behind. This miraculous saving of the Group Captain's life would not have been possible but for two reasons; one, he wore a seat-type parachute and two, 5 Group's crews being successful in hitting their target and draining over 30 miles of the canal.

Flying as navigator in Grp/Cpt Weir's aircraft was S/Ldr Pat Kelly. During the early summer of 1944, whilst serving on 617 Sqdn, S/Ldr Kelly had navigated for the irrepressible W/Cmdr Cheshire, during the period when 617 were pioneering their low-level marking techniques using Mosquitoes.

F/O Edward Maul (aged 22) and crew are buried in the Reichswald War Cemetery, Kleve, in Germany, alongside those who died in Grp/Cpt Weir's aircraft. The two 49 Squadron aircraft were the only losses from the operation.

FTR PB300	G/C C.T. Weir	Pilot	(P.o.W.)
(EA-K)	F/O F.A. Wooding	F/E	(Killed)
'A'Flt	S/L P. Kelly	NAV	(Killed)
	P/O A.W. Bishop	W/OP	(Killed)
	Sgt P. Telford	A/G	(Killed)
	F/O H.W. Hayward	B/A	(Killed)
	F/O A.R. Verrier	A/G	(Killed)
FTR PB354	F/O E.C. Maul	Pilot	(Killed)
(EA-G)	Sgt W. Cooper	F/E	(Killed)
'A'Flt	Sgt S.D. Bolton	NAV	(Killed)
	P/O I.G. Williams	W/AG	(Killed)
	Sgt E. Battye	A/G	(Killed)
Crew on their	F/S A.L. Jackson	B/A	(Killed)
12th operation	Sgt J. Houghton	A/G	(Killed)

22/23 November, 1944; TRONDHEIM: Operations were on again the following night, and as crews entered the briefing room at 13.30hrs, most knew their Lancs had been given full fuel loads. The U-boat pens at Trondheim were to be the target, which meant a long stooge out over the North Sea.

Take-off was planned for 15.50hrs so it was bit of a rush for the crews; at the last minute Y-Yoke cancelled, but 9 aircraft managed to become airborne by 16.02hrs. Over the sea, crews flew at 2,000ft to keep under the weather front. After what seemed an age, 171 Lancasters from 5 Group reached the target, only to hear the controller ordering the raid to be abandoned! the time was 21.06hrs.

Evidently the target was covered by a smoke-screen and the PFF was unable to find the aiming point. Flak in the target area was substantial, and 2 Lancasters and 1 Mosquito failed to return home. After nearly 11 hours in the air, crews arrived back over Fulbeck with their bomb loads still intact; 7 landed at base, whilst F/O Watson (PB355) and crew landed B-Baker at Driffield, and a new crew piloted by F/O Jack Mersey (PB455) landed at Carnaby.

26/27 November, 1944; MUNICH: It was quite late on Sunday night 26 November, when 10 aircraft from 49 Squadron were marshalled along the peri-track with those of 189 Squadron in preparation for take-off. 'Uncle Will' (PB504) and crew were one of the last away at 23.46hrs. 'Uncle' recalls:

"It was bad weather with the cloud base between three and four hundred feet. We took off in the dark with a full load of fuel, incendiaries and a four thousand pounder. I had only just entered cloud when I saw the aircraft which had taken off ahead of us crash, then burst into flames. We learned afterwards that the aircraft taking off behind us (PB745/189 Squadron) also crashed - two aircraft gone before we had even left the vicinity of the airfield!"

The 49 Squadron Lancaster that crashed was O-Oboe, piloted by F/O Le Marquand (PB432). The aircraft came down close to the village of Dry Doddington, not far from the Great North Road. O-Oboe had only been in the air a few minutes before, laden with bombs and fuel, she sank back to earth again. Five fortunate members of the crew survived the crash landing, but sadly Norman Langley the W/Ag and Edward Blake the mid-upper gunner were both killed.

As the force of 270 Lancasters, all from 5 Group, made their way across France towards Switzerland, F/O Cannon (PB586) and crew were forced to return early on three engines; they headed for Ford, landing E-Easy at 03.16hrs.

49 Squadron aircraft were using a new navigation aid code named 'LORAN ', which acted like a long range 'GEE'.

The actual bombing appears to have gone well, with fires being observed up to 70 miles on the return leg. Just one aircraft failed to return when it crashed in France.

Once again crews received a diversion signal as they approached base. In the daylight of Monday morning, the last of the squadron's aircraft landed at Syerston by 09.55hrs. On the ground, crews were messed around terribly until transport was eventually provided to get them back to Fulbeck for de-briefing and a meal. At 08.00hrs next morning, the crews were transported back to Syerston again by road to reclaim their abandoned aircraft.

NOVEMBER 1944

Crashed PB432	F/O G.H. Le Marquand	Pilot	(Slightly injured)
(EA-O)	Sgt W.S. Wade	F/E	(Seriously injured)
'B'Flt	F/S R.E. Ransom	NAV	(Slightly Injured)
	Sgt N.I. Langley	W/OP	(Killed)
	Sgt E.G. Blake	A/G	(Killed)
	Sgt J.R. Bowers	B/A	(Slightly injured)
	Sgt T. Price	A/G	(Seriously injured)

OPERATIONAL SUMMARY - NOVEMBER 1944

Date	Target	Desp	E/R	FTR	Remarks
1	HOMBERG	15	-	-	"J" landed Woodbridge
2/3	DÜSSELDORF	13	-	1	F/O Harford FTR
4/5	LADBERGEN	12	-	1	F/O Talbot FTR
6/7	GRAVENHORST	12	-	1c	F/O Bromfield c/l
11/12	HARBURG	13	-	1	S/L Gorton FTR Rest diverted
16	DUREN	11	-	-	Daylight/diverted
21/22	GRAVENHORST	10	-	2	G/C Weir FTR F/O Maul FTR
22/23	TRONDHEIM	9	-	-	Abandoned/ 2 diverted
26/27	MUNICH	10	1	1c	F/O Le Marquand c/l Rest diverted

Total number of sorties flown	105
Failed to return	5 + 2 crash landed
Total tons of bombs of all types dropped	600.45
Operational hours flown during November 1944	570.30
Non-operational hours flown during November 1944	208.30

HONOURS AND AWARDS - NOVEMBER 1944

F/Lt G.E. Dickson	D.F.C.
F/Lt D. Brady	D.F.C.
F/Lt W.E. Edwards RCAF	D.F.C.

DECEMBER 1944

4/5 December, 1944; HEILBRONN: Nearly 300 Lancasters and Mosquitoes from 5 Group were sent to bomb the virgin target of Heilbronn. Situated on a main north-south railway line, in proximity to a river, the marker aircraft had little difficulty in dropping their yellow TI's accurately. Twelve aircraft from 49 Squadron passed over the target shortly after 19.30hrs, having left Fulbeck at 16.30hrs. The bombing height was 14,000ft and crews were easily able to identify their target visually. Within just a few minutes, over 80 per cent of the town's built-up area had been destroyed.

Lancasters started to return to their home bases around midnight, and all 49's aircraft landed safely back at Fulbeck after completing successful sorties; this included the new crew piloted by F/O MacAulay (PB361). Unconfirmed reports state that 6 of 49 Squadron's aircraft had been in fighter combats. 5 Group lost 12 Lancasters and their crews from this raid; 189 Squadron suffered the loss of PB742.

6/7 December, 1944; GIESSEN: A force of 255 Lancasters led by 10 Mosquitoes set out to attack Giessen, which lay between Stuttgart and Frankfurt. The force was divided into two parts; the larger of the two forces had their aiming point in the town centre, whilst the second wave, including the 12 aircraft from 49 Squadron, went after the railway marshalling yards.

With bombing heights of around 10,000ft, returning crews reported seeing the targets well on fire. F/O Parkin (PB586) and crew received flak damage over the target, otherwise the remainder of the squadron had returned to Fulbeck safely by 00.10hrs. As had become the usual practice by now, returning bombers, as they crossed the English coastline, fired off the 'colours of the day' giving quite a pyrotechnic display to those on the ground. 5 Group lost a further 5 aircraft and crews on this raid.

8 December, 1944; HEINBACH (URFT DAM) DAYLIGHT: Another 5 Group affair; 205 Lancasters set out just after 05.00hrs to attack the Urft Dam. Jack Shearing recorded in his diary: "As we took-off, the ground was covered with frost but the sun was shining making the countryside look beautiful." 5 Group found 9/10ths cloud over the target, which, added to the smoke created from the first Lancasters to bomb, made the task of a successful and accurate attack almost impossible. 49 Squadron had dispatched 14 aircraft which including the new crew piloted by F/O McPhee RCAF (PB586).

Arriving back over England just a few hours after they had taken off, 49 and 189 Squadrons were both diverted to Lasham, a small fighter field. With sparse facilities to cope with visitors, several crews made their way into Basingstoke during the evening in search of sustenance and beer. The following morning, as the Lancasters departed Lasham, each crew took it in turn to 'shoot up' the drome. Arriving back at Fulbeck they discovered ops were scheduled for that evening - all were much relieved when it was scrubbed just before briefing.

The following day another attempt was made on the same target, but the force was recalled without attacking.

11 December, 1944; HEINBACH (URFT DAM) DAYLIGHT: At Fulbeck, crews were awoken at 06.00hrs in preparation for yet another daylight attempt on the Urft Dam. Having had their ops meal, crews then went down to briefing only to learn that take-off had been put back 2 hours because of the weather. Everyone trooped back into the Mess and had another meal with take-off now set for 12.30hrs.

During the actual attack, carried out by 233 Lancasters, sticks of bombs were seen to hit their target but no breach was made. The Lancasters' return journey took them over France at low level, and the crews witnessed the tremendous damage done by the bombing during the summer. All 16 of 49's aircraft returned to base with the exception of F/O Mersey (PB797) and crew who landed at Manston. Group suffered the loss of one Lancaster and its crew.

FATAL WALL OF CLOUD

Loss of life amongst bomber crews was ever present even before actual operational tours were undertaken. That Saturday evening, 11 December, one such sad incident occurred. At 19.55hrs two Lancasters, flown by crews recently posted to 49 Squadron, took-off from Fulbeck. One was piloted by F/O John Branch RAAF, who recalls the tragedy:

"We arrived on squadron together with another fresh crew skippered by F/Lt Jerry Green. On the 11th, both of us were detailed to complete a cross-country and high level bombing exercise via Epperstone, Great Ormes Head, Cirencester, Norwich and finally back to base. During the flight our crew was confronted with a band of cu-nimbus cloud which I attempted to climb over.

At 29,000ft and icing up badly, we gave up and flew a reciprocal course. We eventually completed the exercise and landed safely at Fulbeck. It is my belief that F/Lt Green must have flown into that fatal wall of cloud."

F/Lt Green's aircraft and crew have never been found, and it is believed their aircraft came down in the Irish Sea; the crew are remembered on the Runnymede Memorial.

Missing PB799	F/L G.W. Green	Pilot	(Missing)
(EA-G)	Sgt A. Blanchard		(Missing)
'A'Flt	Sgt E.C. Charles		(Missing)
	F/O H.H.S. Gwyer		(Missing)
	Sgt R.W. Henson		(Missing)
	Sgt J.A. Rudd		(Missing)
	Sgt H. Stobart		(Missing)

DECEMBER 1944

DANGER MONEY

During the first two weeks of December 1944, F/O Les Hammond RAAF and crew were posted from Wigsley HCU to 5 Group's Lancaster Finishing School at Syerston. Norman Smith, navigator on the crew, remembers the period well:

"This was a short course to familiarize our crew with the Lancaster after flying Stirlings at Wigsley. Whilst at Syerston, we were sent to Fulbeck one day, to help unload bomb-lorries into the dumps and also to load containers with incendiaries. We all thought Fulbeck was a horrible place and hoped we would not be posted there at the end of our course... little did we realise!

On this day, whilst waiting for transport back to Syerston, our Skipper taught us to play 'two up'; much to his disgust we skinned him at his own native game. It also occurred to us that the lorry drivers were being paid 'danger money' for carrying bombs... I bet it was a lot more than the 13/6d per day which we were getting!

Much to our chagrin we were posted to Fulbeck, but the Skipper said he was given the choice of 1 Group or 5 Group and chose the latter... but we never regretted joining 49"

17/18 December, 1944; MUNICH: Four consecutive operations were scrubbed before 17 of the squadron's aircraft eventually got away from Fulbeck bound for Munich on 17 December. It was another exclusive 5 Group attack using 280 Lancasters led by 8 Mosquitoes. Although there was some undershooting, most crews reported the bombing to be fanning out from the sector as planned. Four Lancasters from the Group failed to return.

Back at Fulbeck, the squadron's aircraft started landing at around 02.00hrs. F/O Edward Essenhigh (PB355) and crew were overdue and reported as missing. It was established later in the day, that their aircraft had in fact crashed on Worthing beach at 17.55hrs the previous evening en route to Munich. The aircraft had blown up, luckily without loss of civilian life.

Only one crew member was found in the wreck; that of F/Sgt Gordon Callon. His body was recovered from the rear turret and at the time caused some consternation to those at the scene, as he wore pilots wings. Sgt Callon was one of the volunteer pilot/rear gunners operating the 'Village Inn' turret.

The bodies of the remainder of the crew have never been found; their whereabouts and indeed the reason for the aircraft's demise still remains a mystery. Gordon Callon is buried in Littlehampton, Sussex, whilst his fellow crew members are remembered on the Runnymede Memorial.

DECEMBER 1944

Crashed PB355	F/O E.G. Essenhigh	Pilot	(Missing)
(EA-B)	Sgt H. Varey	F/E	(Missing)
'A'Flt	Sgt L.B. Bourne	NAV	(Missing)
	F/S F.B. Rees	W/OP	(Missing)
	Sgt J.W. Moore	A/G	(Missing)
Crew on their	F/O J.A. Thomson	B/A	(Missing)
11th operation	F/S G.F. Callon	P/AG	(Killed)

18/19 December, 1944; GDYNIA: Lancasters of 5 Group were to attack German shipping and dock installations at the Polish port of Gdynia on the Baltic coast. Of the 236 Lancasters dispatched, 16 were from 49 Squadron and included four new crews captained by; F/O Smith (NG352), F/O Hytch (PB844), F/Lt Wright (NG327) and F/O Branch RAAF (PB791).

STALKING A BATTLESHIP

F/Lt Leslie Hay (PB504) and crew participated in this trip as 'Uncle Will' relates:

"At briefing, the sight of the wall map showing such a distant target brought a groan as it usually did. It was going to be a long trip and not easy. Worse still, two aircraft, F/O Milburn (PB571) and ourselves, were ordered to break from the group in the target area, join some from other squadrons and attack the pocket battleship "Lutzow" which was tied up on the South side of a mole prior to sailing into the Atlantic to attack our convoys.

The first part across the North Sea was uneventful. Some flak over Norway, token flak from Sweden, but nothing to worry about... yes there was!.. when Paul Smith our navigator switched on his radar (which he could now do as the Germans knew we were there) fire broke out in his compartment. He, with great presence of mind, reported it, grabbed his charts and went and sat on the Elsan at the rear to continue plotting as best he could.

I gave the order to put on chutes and allotted available crew members to see what they could do with the extinguishers and axes, and to open all vents (extinguishers give off phosgene, a poisonous gas). I looked over my shoulder and saw a merry little blaze going, but the bomb aimer, engineer and F/O Johnstone the 2nd Dickie were able to get it under control. The navigator returned to his burnt out compartment and quickly established our position. He now had no navigational aids but got us to Gdynia on dead reckoning which was a good show indeed.

The harbour and sea stood out as there was snow on the ground which helped identification. A smoke screen blotted out where the battleship was positioned. During our run up the master searchlight shot out and got us. I took immediate evasive action, but as the searchlight and gun crews were not as experienced as those in the Ruhr we got away without being coned. Bomb doors were opened just in case we got a glimpse - round and round again, then on the fourth run the bomb aimer reported that the smoke was clearing and a few moments later he called out 'I see her!', a joyful and excited shout, and then guided us on a pretty steady run with bomb doors open, to the target.

DECEMBER 1944

His final directions in the minutes up to bombing betrayed, for the first time in our experience with him... excitement. Almost in a whisper, as if he were stalking an animal, a shaking voice said 'steady, steady, steady left-steady, steady BOMBS GONE!' What a relief, we felt nervous wrecks but we had to fly straight and level for the photograph.

Next morning, our photo showed the mole and outer harbour well in the picture and our aiming point was right in the middle."

After the long stooge back across the North Sea, all of the squadron's aircraft landed back at Fulbeck, with F/O Hytch (PB844) and crew the last to land in D-Dog at 03.41hrs. Group suffered the loss of 4 aircraft and crews.

During the winter of 1944/45 at Fulbeck, 49 Squadron Air Bombers held a party for the squadron's armourers, photo and instrument sections. In this photograph it is difficult to put names to all those shown, but they include: LAC Starling; F/Sgt Read, F/Sgt Perfect; Cpl Tomlinson; F/Sgt Borman; F/O Goldsworthy RAAF; W/O Jenkins RAAF; F/O Stokoe; F/Sgt Westaway RAAF. (K. Gibson)

Bomb aimers party; those identified: F/Lt Gibson DFC; F/Sgt Boyes; F/Sgt Coombes; P/O Findlay; F/Sgt Crutchfield; F/Sgt Westaway RAAF; F/O Stokoe; W/O Goldsworthy; F/O Paul; W/O Jenkins RAAF; F/Sgt Pears; F/Sgt Thorley; F/Sgt Cram; F/Sgt Meade. (K. Gibson)

A priceless photograph as the Air Bombers party begins to go with a 'swing'. F/Sgt Westaway RAAF (top right) is seen in fine voice.

21/22 December, 1944; POLITZ: 5 Group sent 207 Lancasters and one Mosquito to Politz in Northern Germany to attack an oil-refinery. Instead of crossing the Danish coast, with its coastal defences and rocket ships, the force was sent via Sweden, as on the Gdynia raid three nights earlier. The squadron had 16 aircraft airborne including two new crews piloted by F/O Bolter (PB791) and F/O Johnstone (NG352). Despite the attempt to avoid the defence belts, F/O McCrae (PB349) and crew in H-Howe were hammered by flak en-route and were forced to return early, landing at Milltown.

The remaining crews experienced some difficulties in bombing within the target area due to smoke and cloud; F/Lt Wright (PB374) failed to bomb after flying through heavy rain which caused severe icing before reaching Politz. F/O Watson (ME308) and crew had to orbit three times before releasing their bombs and commented that; "marking was not up to standard."

On the return leg crews were advised that due to weather conditions over England, the squadron was diverted to Dyce near Aberdeen. After 10hrs 30mins in the air, crews started to join the circuit of the small Scottish fighter field - because of the surrounding hills the circuit height was 1,500ft instead of 1,000ft and the main runway was only 1,400ft instead of 2,000 as at Fulbeck. All of the squadron's aircraft returned safely with 'Uncle Will' (PB504) and crew the last to land at 03.08hrs. Group had lost 3 Lancasters on the operation with a further 5 crashing in England. 189 Squadron lost two aircraft.

CHRISTMAS IN THE HIGHLANDS

Bad weather had set in across the country and, with the exception of north-east Scotland, there was a complete clamp over the British Isles. This meant that the several bomber squadrons, including 49, were stuck at Dyce over the Christmas period. Aberdeen thronged with bomber crews all in battle dress - but, as one aircrew member recalls:

"The locals were embarrassingly hospitable."

Poor old RAF Dyce - this small fighter airfield was all set for the festive season, and now their noses had been put rather out of joint by these hordes of 'bomber types'. But to their credit, the staff coped very well with their visiting 'Wisemen from the East' and everyone had a merry old time.

49 Squadron crews at RAF Dyce over Christmas 1944 were:

F/O Carlyle	(ME322);	F/O MacAulay	(PB373);	F/O Hytch	(PB844);
F/O Littley	(PB361);	F/O McPhee	(PB586);	F/O Branch	(ND327);
F/O Galloway	(ME353);	F/L Hay	(PB504);	F/O Johnstone	(NG352);
F/O Milburn	(PB571);	F/O Nowrie	(PB455);	F/O Bolter	(PB791);
F/L Wright	(PB374);	F/O Dickson	(PB568);	F/O Watson	(ME308):

DECEMBER 1944

CHRISTMAS AT FULBECK

Only a handfull of aircrew (who had not been on the Politz raid) remained at Fulbeck over Christmas. How they spent their festive season is portrayed by these two following accounts; first, Norman Smith, whose crew (F/O Hammond RAAF) had only recently arrived on the station: "We spent a very lonely Christmas in the deserted Sgts Mess at Fulbeck, but were invited to the airmens mess which proved to be a lot more cheerful and we had a nice time.

"After the return of the squadron a few days later, we were taken up to Scotland to fly a repaired aircraft back to Fulbeck. It was a beautiful experience... flying back through snow covered Scottish mountains into valleys lower than the mountain tops... it was an extremely exhilarating flight, never to be forgotten. Les Hammond, our skipper, had this flight accepted as our second X-country... we were listed as 'operational' from now on."

The second account comes from diarist Jack Shearing, whose crew came back from leave on Christmas Eve. Some of them attended the Station Dance that night in the Naafi, which turned into a "beery shambles" and although the *"mistletoe was handed round freely, it still didn't feel like Christmas."* They left the dance at midnight and retired to bed. Christmas day... the last wartime Christmas is recorded in Jack's diary.

What follows, perhaps personifies more than anything, the special relationship that developed during those long years of war, between the people of Lincolnshire and their 'Bomber Boys'... they counted them out as they lay in bed at night... and in the cold grey dawn they counted them back in. They knew the losses... they saw the burnt out wrecks that littered the countryside... and they also shared the pain. There was always a welcoming open door for these young men, many far from home who nightly put their lives on the line! Jack Shearing writes:

"Got up about 11 on Christmas morning and had Xmas cake and pudding etc with Eddy and Jack. We all got ready and went down to the Mess before dinner in time to have a few drinks. The dinner was nice, pork, duck, oranges and nuts etc., but everything was in such small quantity...I came away feeling disappointed. We all went down to the hut after and then started to cycle up to Ruth's place at Normanton on Cliff. The journey was a nightmare on my bike and it took a good half hour, but we soon made ourselves at home at the Porters. Met Mum and Dad and sat talking to Ruth while Mrs P and the local school marm prepared the tea. Another guest came just after tea, Jock, a Sgt in the paratroops who had been at Arnhem and then the ten of us sat down to a wizard meal; cold ham and chicken and bags of pickled onions, followed by apricots and cream, numerous cakes and a wonderful iced Xmas cake. We listened to the wireless after...Jack Warner was very good. Then after tea had been cleared away and the ladies were ready we all set off to walk to Auntie Leena's about 3/4 of a mile on towards Grantham.

Here we met Auntie Leena and Uncle Bob (her brother), Mr and Mrs Hodgkinson, friends of their little girl...he is the station Engineer on the camp. At first we all sat around the fire and things were a little flat, but a game of darts started up, while a small crowd of us including Paddy, Ruth, Eddy, Jack and Mrs H. started a game of pontoon. There was no limit and Jock joined in and soon things began to get hectic. We went into supper and I was winning over a quid so was quite happy.

The supper was a dream, the table just groaned under the weight of the good things. We had cold ham and turkey with more pickled onions, as much as we liked and had pears and cream after, followed by mince pies etc. A wizard spread absolutely all home produced including the butter, pears and cream. We went back to the pontoon after and things got beyond all proportions...a quid on a card went unnoticed and soon I was down to my last 4/-. However, I picked up again and at the finish I was winning over £3 which was well earned after the way I sweated for it. Jack won £15 but as Jock had lost £9, Jack gave him back half his losses. It was now 4am and by the time we walked back to our bikes and rode back to camp it was past 5. We had a wonderful time and went to bed very pleased with life."

A BOXING DAY VISITOR

On Boxing Day, England remained in the grip of fog (keeping the squadron's aircraft at Dyce) although parts of Scotland remained clear. 'Uncle Will' recalls an incident that is clearly remembered by all who witnessed this unusual and almost comic event:

"On Boxing Day, we decided to take the aircraft up for a test, to keep them in running order and find any faults. We had a pleasant flight over the lovely Scottish countryside on a fine clear day. On landing, we parked the aircraft, and were standing around with other crews, waiting for transport back to the Mess. Suddenly, our mid-upper gunner's Cockney voice said 'Gor blimey, don't that look like a 109?'. I looked at an aircraft turning to make an approach to land. It was indeed an Me109, wheels down and coming in...it touched down, bounced and somersaulted onto its back close to where we were all standing.

We were just amazed... nobody thought of getting into their aircraft and bringing their guns to bear. All the crews rushed over, lifted the wings sufficiently to raise the fuselage and let the pilot, who seemed unhurt, get out. He just loosened his straps and let himself down onto the runway and we pulled him out.

The first thing that he did was to take out his comb, look in the mirror and comb his hair. He then took a parcel from a panel in the fuselage and we detained him until the Service Police came with the ambulance and took him to headquarters. What was behind it, we never knew. The amusing thing is that a few minutes later, the Station Commander's voice came over the tannoy saying that in view of a certain incident, nothing was to be said anywhere and secrecy was to be maintained... soon after this the local air raid warnings sounded, very much to our amusement."

F/O John Branch RAAF and crew also witnessed the incident; John adds:

"It turned out that this disillusioned German pilot had flown from an airfield in Denmark. The Me109 was their latest model and just off the production line... a valuable acquisition to the Allies.

My rear gunner, Sgt Warner, was one of a number who reached the aircraft before the arrival of the S.P's. It wasn't until I visited him in England many years later, that I discovered he had in his possession a well kept German pilot's issue wristwatch... his personal momento of the episode"

It is believed that more than one 49 Squadron gunner tried to claim the 109 as a "probable!"

28/29 December, 1944; HORTEN: As dawn broke on Tuesday 28th December, a reconnaissance Mosquito crossed the Norwegian coast near Boss. It was attacked by anti-aircraft fire; no hits were sustained, but the positions of the batteries were noted. The Mossie carried on towards Horten, its aim to locate the Battle Cruiser "Köln". Although marine traffic was spotted, the real target could not be located. It was presumed that the camouflage was too good for such a short investigation.

That night, a force of 67 Lancasters and 1 Mosquito all from 5 Group were sent to attack these German Naval units and merchant shipping sighted in Oslo Fjord. Each carried 8x1000 lb bombs as they arrived over the target area at around 23.30hrs to find the fjord swamped with flares and 'Wanganui' target markers dropped by the PFF. 49 Squadron had dispatched 5 crews and all returned safely after successful sorties, as the following brief accounts show;

F/O Mallinson (PB361): *"Own bombs burst alongside flak ship."* F/O Milburn (ME308): *"Made 4 runs over target and bombed ship which was heading NE approximately 2 1/2 miles from harbour."*

F/O Lee (PB374): *"First attack results not seen - second attack from 4,000 feet, own bombs seen to fall within 25 yards of large vessel which was attacked by other a/c."*

F/O McPhee RCAF (NG327): *"Ship 1 mile NE of harbour steaming south leaving a big wake - own bombs seen straddle the vessel!"*

F/L Nowrie (PB484): Bombed from 5,500ft at 23.52hrs, flak, which was coming from the position of a ship previously sighted on run up, after dummy runs. Ship thought to be the "Köln".

The results and damage caused during this raid (in which no aircraft were lost) have only recently been established.

It appears from the de-brief reports, that the crews of F/O McPhee RCAF and F/O Milburn were actually responsible for sinking a German U-boat. The following is a first hand account given by Herbert Hermann, a crew member of that U-boat, U-735 which was sunk by 49 Squadron in Oslo Fjord:

"We were at Horten, south Norway to test our new schnorkel. On the morning of 28 December 1944, we sailed for a test cruise and returned in the evening at 18.00hrs and were looking for a suitable place to drop our anchor which ultimately turned into our doom.

During the many attempts to find somewhere to drop anchor, we lost a lot of compressed air. Whilst some members went ashore, we continued to work on replacing our compressed air. This was not very successful; our Junkers compressor failed and we had to carry on with our E-compressor. That takes a long time to reach a pressure of 205 kg - at least 6 hours. It took about 3 hours to reach a reasonable pressure; this took until 21.30hrs, and then we heard the air-raid siren. Now things really became urgent. The commander ordered us to drop the anchor to save what little air we had. An order to make the diesels ready for starting was given but there was insufficient pressure. By now several aircraft were flying over the harbour of Horten.

The leading engineer managed to get the diesels started by using the compressed air from the torpedoes which used 205 kg; he reported 'diesels ready for sailing' - this took until 23.30hrs. The wireless operator reported a large number of bombers over Horten. The commander ordered the crew to sail and gun crews to their stations. At this time I was in the central control room and was able to judge everything that went on. The boat was now in the middle of the Fjord as the first bombs fell; the commander ordered a zig-zag course but one bomb fell very close to the boat. A fountain of water came over the conning tower and down the hatch.

One man on the 3.7 cm gun fell overboard and the attack diving-plane operator was told to take his place - I immediately took his place at the rudder which turned out to be for a short time only as a terrible detonation threw me against the wall. My first thoughts were that the boat must have had a direct hit which turned out to be true.

A wounded engine room mechanic came tumbling out of the engine room. It was Heinz Meior from Magdeburg. He called out 'water in the engine room!'. Pumping was impossible as the boat was already low at the stern. The commander ordered everybody on deck when he realised that there was no chance of saving the boat. Everybody jumped overboard as the boat sank very quickly; all this happened within a minute. Some tried to swim ashore but the cold water was to be their fate. This happened to all my crew members...I was the only one to be picked up by a tender and handed to a torpedo boat.

Anything else, I heard from the salvage crew - 26 bodies were recovered but 12 were not accounted for. The funeral of the 26 took place on 5 January, 1945 at the War cemetery of Eckerburg at Oslo. I had to report to the leader of U-boat East to give a detailed account."

DECEMBER 1944

THANKS... FOR SAVING OUR LIVES!

When the crew of U-682 were considering a 50 year reunion of their crewing up, Hubert Wodarz, Bosun of U-682 tried for 2 years to make contact with the men who were flying the bombers that night 28/29 December, 1944 over Horten Harbour. He succeeded in finding and making contact with three members from 619 Squadron, along with 49ers Tom Gatfield, navigator, on Ken Lee's crew and Bert Weatherley, wireless operator on Jack Nowrie's crew.

A reunion was arranged at a hotel by the River Moselle on 3/6 May, 1994, with some 30 crew members of U-682 with their wives, the sole survivor of U-735 and the 5 RAF members and their wives attending. Maps, charts, logs, intelligence reports, U-boat logs, German Admiralty reports and the log of the "Koln" were examined - this is what really did happen....

The "Köln" was camouflaged next to a promontory near to Boss and it was the "Koln" that opened fire on the Mosquito; she had not been at Horten for some time.

When the Lancasters attacked the shipping at Horten they sank an 8,000 ton oil tanker - no survivors; U-735 was sunk, 8 crew members managed to jump into the sea but at 2 degrees water temperature only one, H. Hermann survived. U-682 was severely damaged, its bow for nearly 1/3 of its length was blown out of true by some 5 degrees. This damage caused U-682 to be unseaworthy and she went to Hamburg, where, whilst in dry dock she was totally destroyed by RAF bombing in March.

Before dinner on Thursday evening, Tom Gatfield was approached by S. Theinemann (Captain), F. Shroeder (2nd Officer), H. Wodarz (Bosun) and H. Herman; after shaking hands they thanked him "For saving our lives!!"

It seemed that the morning of 28 December, 1944, a flotilla of which U-682 and U-735 were to have been a part, had been ordered to leave Norway the following day, to attack shipping in the Plymouth shallows - after the raid, the remainder did sail....all seven were sunk and there were no survivors.

In Captain Theinemanns words:

"If you had not bombed and damaged or sunk us, we too would have gone to the Plymouth shallows and would also have been destroyed - Thank you for saving our lives."

As a post-script the crew of U-682 took over U-1271, went back on duty and survived the war as did the two crews of 49 Squadron and the three from 619....which could not be said for many of the other crews who flew to Norway that night in December 1944.

30/31 December, 1944; HOUFFALIZE: A total of 154 Lancasters (including 12 from 49 Squadron) plus 12 Mosquitoes of 5 Group attacked a German supply route where it entered a narrow valley, near Houffalize.

Flying that night as W/OP in F/O Len Mellor's (PB349) crew was diarist Jack Shearing. He reveals that crews had been briefed on Saturday morning, 30 December for an attack on the Dortmund-Ems canal. This was to be the farthest the Group had ever flown in daylight, and Air Commodore Pope, who was at the briefing, told crews to expect the Luftwaffe in force even though they had an escort of 200 Spits and Mustangs.

The take-off was delayed by 2 hours, so crews had another operational meal. Then just after engines had been run up, red flares were fired from the control tower scrubbing the operation. The crews hung around all afternoon, until being told that ops were on for that night. A different target, so bomb loads and fuel had to be changed. At main briefing the trip was put back 2 hours, so it was back to the Sgts Mess for yet another operational meal. As Jack recalls:

"We had our fourth egg of the day - there was also a bit of a show on too so we all went to that, and got transport back to the flights about midnight."

The tensions during the build-up to operations during the period must have been tremendous, although this is not easily detected in Jack's writing. Jack goes on to describe his crew's part in the operation that took place 10 miles NE of Bastogne during the early hours of New Year's Eve:

"We finally got off the deck at 02.30hrs. Everything seemed unnatural and all the boys were dog tired...it was a great effort to keep awake. The trip was uneventful and there was no opposition at all. The target was covered with 8/10ths cloud and it was difficult to assess the success of the trip... in the bright moonlight you could see all the other Lancs plainly over the target.

We landed at 07.15hrs, but despite being the second kite to land we waited ages for transport and by the time we were interrogated and had our meal and another egg it was 09.30hrs before we got to bed. We got up about 17.30hrs and went down for tea and another egg and then I read the papers in the Mess. Went back to the hut and had another night indoors. I felt too tired to go to the New Year's Eve dance on the camp, and was in bed by 23.30hrs."

All of the squadron's Lancasters returned safely; Group had one Lancaster crash in France. When target changes were made at the last moment, as with the Houfflize operation, aircrew were always aware of the pressures this also put on the ground staff. Their tasks were carried out in all weather conditions, out on exposed dispersals. During the winter of 44/45 the fog, rain, snow and frost were exceptionally bad.

Much of the ground crews' work was also carried out in darkness, their only refuge being a small flight hut shared by a score of other men.

DECEMBER 1944

Sgt Trevor Simpson gives this humorous, yet so nearly fatal account of an incident that happened during this period:

"One night, I had a couple of Scots riggers working on J-Jig; one was called Andy McGowan, a bit of a Spike Milligan type character. Andy was up on the wing of the Lanc in the dark seeing to the refuelling...he was wearing gum boots and a waterproof rubber overall suit. Standing on the centre section of the wing, he suddenly slipped on the frost and slid down towards the trailing edge of the wing....as he went, he grabbed hold of the end of the refuelling hose, in an attempt to prevent himself dropping the 10 feet or so to the concrete below.

The hose broke away from its connection point and Andy slipped off the wing grasping tightly to the hose. His calls for help must have been drowned out by the sound of the bowser's pump.

Andy was now hanging from the hose, which was pumping gallons of 100 octane fuel over his head, filling up his rubber suit and gum boots. Eventually a combination of the cold and weight of fuel forced him to let go, and he dropped just a couple of feet to the ground. At this point, somebody said 'where's Andy? I can hear fuel spilling'. We rushed round to find Andy with his suit inflated with fuel, perishing with cold lying on the dispersal.

As we were quite near to the flight office, we decided to take him in there and try and get some warmth back into his body. Someone went on ahead to tell them that Andy was in a terrible state and we are bringing him in...as the flight office door was opened the coke stove was glowing red half way up the chimney...fortunately someone shouted just in time 'don't bring him in here or we'll all go up!' Poor old Andy had to be unzipped and emptied outside in the freezing cold, but happily made a sound recovery".

OPERATIONAL SUMMARY - DECEMBER 1944

Date	Target	Desp	E/R	FTR	Remarks
4/5	HEILBRONN	12	-	-	
6/7	GIESSEN	12	-	-	
8	HEIMBACH	14	-	-	Daylight/Diverted
11	HEIMBACH	16	-	-	Daylight
17/18	MUNICH	17	-	1c	F/O Essenhigh c.
18/19	GDYNIA	16	-	-	
21/22	POLITZ	16	1	-	Diverted
28/29	HORTEN	5	-	-	U-boat sunk
30/31	HOUFFALIZE	12	-	-	

Total number of sorties flown - 120
Failed to return 1c +1 missing on training flt
Total tons of bombs of all types dropped - 628.28
Operational hours flown during December 1944 922.45
Non operational hours flown during December 1944 191.00

HONOURS AND AWARDS - DECEMBER 1944

W/O L.W. Thomas	D.F.C.
F/S J. Christian	D.F.M.
P/O J.A. Castle	D.F.C.
F/S E.R. Haines	D.F.M.
F/O L.M. Pederson RCAF	D.F.C.
F/O J.C. Fleming RCAF	D.F.C.
Sgt J.A. Richards	D.F.M.
Sgt J. Skidmore	D.F.M.

F/O Galloway and crew over Deelan airfield at 15.800ft during the late morning of 15th August 1944. Bomber Command lost 3 Lancasters during the attack, but the Galloway crew in LM649 (EA-T) along with all 49's aircraft, returned safely to Fiskerton.
(L. Hay)

JANUARY 1945

1/2 January, 1945; GRAVENHORST (MITTELLAND CANAL): The early evening mist and fog was already forming over Fulbeck by the time 14 crews from 49 Squadron had been bussed out to their waiting Lancasters. A new crew, piloted by F/O Hammond (PB373) were operating for the first time; their navigator, Norman Smith recalls:

"Seeing our names on the 'Order of Battle' for the first time brought it home to me that we were at war. My thoughts were that I had had a good innings and that this might be our first and last trip. It was like going to the dentist... you have to go but don't look forward to it!"

Take off commenced at 16.28hrs when S/Ldr Wright (NG327) released the brakes on E-Easy; at 16.46hrs, Jack Nowrie (PB484) opened the 'taps' on T-Tommy and slowly accelerated down the runway; F/Lt Nowrie later reported:

"During take-off all Air Speed Indicators failed to register - I was unable to stop and took-off in the foggy conditions. At a safe height we set course for Woodbridge (emergency airfield). Control there advised us to jettison bombs in the sea, which we did, and then completed an emergency landing safely at Woodbridge."

The raid itself was carried out by 152 Lancasters and 5 Mosquitoes all from 5 Group. Breaches were made in the canal, with over half a mile of banks damaged.

Returning over England before midnight, the squadron received a diversion signal sending them to Peterhead, where everyone landed safely by 23.55hrs.
No aircraft were lost on the operation.

4 January, 1945; ROYAN: In the early hours of Thursday morning, 4 January, 347 Lancasters and 7 Mosquitoes from 1, 5 and 8 Groups dropped 1,576 tons of bombs on the German garrison in the French town of Royan. The attack was in 2 waves separated by one hour. It was thought at the time, that the French civilian population had been evacuated... sadly this was not the case and it has been estimated that up to 800 may have been killed. Since the war there have been many recriminations. As for Bomber Command's role in this very tragic event... it was immediately exonerated from any blame.

Take-off for the raid had started from Fulbeck just after midnight with 14 of the squadron's aircraft becoming airborne. All crews carried out successful sorties and returned to base by 07.54hrs. Bomber Command's losses amounted to 6 Lancasters and crews.

5/6 January, 1945; HOUFFALIZE: This was an attack on a German supply route in the Ardennes and was carried out by 131 Lancasters led by 9 Mosquitoes, all from 5 Group. Cloud over the target made it difficult for crews to assess the success of the bombing, and several crews did report that no instructions were received from the Master Bomber. Dave Hytch (NG327) and crew could not identify the target so they did not bomb as pre-briefed.

Fortunately later reports gave the target as being accurately bombed. The squadron was diverted to Croft near Darlington on return, landing around 06.00hrs. Croft was a Canadian bomber station and at de-brief, navigator, Norman Smith remembers:

"The Canadian Officer who de-briefed us kept referring to the target as 'that place that sounds like a steer'. Afterwards, he asked if we would like a smoke and then proceeded to give each of us 20 packets of Sweet Caporal cigarettes."

49 Squadron had dispatched 9 aircraft on the raid, and all returned safely with 8 landing at Croft; F/Lt Williams and crew put down at Middleton St George - Group lost 2 Lancaster crews on this operation. After a rest and snatched nap crews took-off later in the afternoon to fly back to base, only to be diverted again, this time to Balderton, only a few miles from Fulbeck. Transport ferried the aircrew over to Fulbeck, where after eating most crews went straight to bed.

7/8 January, 1945; MUNICH: Bomber Command departed from its recent Army support operations to deliver Munich's final major raid of the war. An area attack was to be carried out by 645 Lancasters led by 9 Mosquitoes.

After breakfast on the morning of Sunday 7th, the squadron's crews were again taken by road over to Balderton to retrieve their Lancasters following the diversion from the Houffalize trip, via Croft. Landing back at Fulbeck each aircraft received its daily inspection. Ground crews then prepared them for the evening's operation; 1,950 gallons of fuel, one 'cookie' plus 8 clusters. It came as a surprise when the target of Munich was revealed at briefing. After briefing, a mad rush ensued in order to meet the take-off deadline, 12 aircraft including the new crew piloted by F/O Harold Fricker RAAF (ME353) became airborne just after 17.00hrs.

IT'S DAMNED COLD DOWN THERE

John Aldridge, bomb aimer in F/O Lee's (PB455) crew remembers the operation very well!

"On this particular night we were supporting the Pathfinder Flare Force (83 & 97 Squadrons) which meant we arrived at the target at the same time, but we flew at 2,000ft below them. This attracted the flak to enable them to carry out a straight and level run.

Tom Gatfield (nav) and I had been working 'Loran' and obtained some decent fixes and we managed to keep to time, however predicted winds were all to cock that night and we arrived over Munich on time... but on our own! I remember going forward into the bomb aimer's compartment to prepare for the bomb run in our supporting role... the sky was one mass of flak bursts and we seemed to be the only aircraft around, and leaving a con trail at that. We were well and truly hammered; one piece of flak came through the front perspex and ripped the sleeve on my battle dress blouse. Searchlights also dazzled us and in taking evasive action the skipper nearly stalled the aircraft - Tom called out that the airspeed was 110 knots and falling and there was a shout of 'get the bloody nose down skip!' and thankfully he did.

We were then hit in one engine, which had to be feathered; this was the only occasion on which I removed my parachute from its stowage and laid it on the floor beside me. I remember looking down at the snow covered landscape and thinking 'it's damned cold down there' if I have to jump."

The squadron's aircraft had arrived over Munich around 20.30hrs. During the bombing run, F/Lt Hay (PB361) and crew (with F/O Gibson as second dickie) had their bomb load 'hang up'; whilst 'Uncle Will' hauled R-Roger round for a second run the bombs came away taking the bomb doors with them - the bomb aimer estimated that the bombs (and doors) fell in the northern part of the city. After attacking, all the Lancasters flew out south over Italy and around the bottom of Switzerland. Norman Smith recalls:

"We could see the lights in the villages standing out from the darkness all around."

Also visible for up to 150 miles, was the burning target of Munich. Flak and fighters had been active, and a total of 15 Lancasters with their crews failed to return. These losses included V-Victor from 49 Squadron: Sadly F/O Alec Bolter (PB586) and crew all perished when their aircraft came down in France. Their graves are in Villeneuve-St.Georges Cemetery near Seine-et-Oise, with one exception; W/O 'Dusty' Miller RAAF, a spare W/AG on the squadron, was flying with the Bolter crew this night, but does not appear to have been buried with them. His name appears in the 5 Group Roll of Honour but he still remains listed as missing.

THE TRAIN NOW LEAVING

Meanwhile, Ken Lee and crew had started their attempt to return home across the Alps on three engines; John Aldridge continues:

"We had to keep an altitude of about 14,000ft as our route home was above the Alps skirting Switzerland... we saw the lights of that neutral country. Everything went well till halfway across France (by now mostly occupied by our own troops since D-Day) when another engine started vibrating badly and shaking the whole aircraft. The skipper and Lou Crabbe our flight engineer decided to feather that engine, so now we were on two! We decided that rather than land at an airfield in France we would go for a landing at the emergency runway at Manston in Kent, entailing a short sea passage on two engines. This was managed successfully although the skipper risked unfeathering the last engine to give us trouble, to get a little more power if required.

We hoped another crew would be sent to pick us up from Manston but this was a bad winter with heavy snow and we were instructed to return to Grantham by train, where transport would collect us from the station. We travelled to London in flying boots and battle dress carrying our parachutes. In one pub where we went for a drink, Lou was actually offered £20 from a chap... we also went to the Odeon in Leicester Square where the Manager admitted us free of charge seeing us attired in flying gear.

Sleeping overnight in the Salvation Army Hostel near Kings Cross Station, we left for Grantham next morning after quite an eventful 48 hours in one way and another."

The squadron's remaining aircraft all managed to land safely back at Fulbeck.

FTR PB586	F/O A.J. Bolter	Pilot	(Killed)
(EA-V)	Sgt J. Court	F/E	(Killed)
'B' Flt	Sgt T.E. Walker	NAV	(Killed)
	W/O F.C. Miller RAAF	W/AG	(Missing)
	Sgt C.L. Atkins	A/G	(Killed)
Crew on their	Sgt J.T. Sanderson	A/B	(Killed)
4th operation	Sgt A.F. Butcher	A/G	(Killed)

A belated Officers 'Mess Christmas Party at Fulbeck in mid January 1945.

Standing to the left of the Group Captain is P/O Bert Weatherley, the most recent member to join the mess (promoted 6-1-45). (A.L. Weatherley)

13/14 January, 1945; POLITZ: For several days following the Munich trip it snowed... and it snowed. The only combats aircrew experienced were snowball fights amongst themselves. Daily inspections of the aircraft still had to be maintained despite the deep snow, and both air and ground crews alike used various modes of mechanical transport to reach their marooned Lancasters. On Friday 12th, the weather improved and a daylight operation was planned for the following day. Rain on the 13th started to wash the snow away but also brought bad visibility and the daylight trip was scrubbed. Instead a night operation was put on the programme, requiring 12 crews with briefing timed for just after lunch. The target was the oil refineries at Politz near Stettin. It was to be another 5 Group show with 218 Lancasters and 7 Mosquitoes taking part.

Each Lancaster carried a full load of fuel plus one 'cookie' and 11x500lbs of bombs as they set out across the North Sea in terrible weather. To avoid the worst of the conditions most flew across the sea below 1,500ft, only gaining height to cross the Danish coast where flak poured up at them.

The target was reached by 21.00hrs and as previously the searchlights and defences were 'stiff'. Clear conditions allowed the PFF to mark from low-level and an accurate bombing raid resulted.

15 MINUTES

With successful bombing attacks completed, crews now had to endure the return leg. Norman Smith, navigator in Les Hammond's (NG327) crew, was flying in E-Easy, but this raid proved to be anything but easy! as Norman recalls: "Before take-off a motor cyclist came round to the rear turret and told the gunner 'delay 15 minutes'. We then had difficulty in securing a top hatch which made us late on take-off, but a very fast flight over the North Sea enabled us to catch up. On arrival over Politz we saw no markers or PFF activity and then realised that the whole attack had been delayed for 15 minutes and not just take-off.

"We had a bit of flak around us then suddenly we were coned by searchlights; the skipper took evasive action and when, just as suddenly, the flak stopped and we knew fighters were coming in... Ralph in the rear turret yelled 'port go' and with that Les went into a vicious corkscrew. The fighter was seen to break away downwards and was not seen again. I then gave the skipper a course to steer back out of the area, and flying a rectangle we joined the stream 15 minutes later and bombed on time.

Our actions had depleted the fuel so I gave the pilot a course to fly out over the south of Denmark rather than the briefed route back up to Sweden. We had light flak just off the Danish coast, and the gunners spotted a JU 88 which fortunately did not see us. "With a real fear of having to ditch we started the CHAPT procedure. We just managed to scrape into Langham on the Norfolk coast with 30 gallons in our the tanks. Langham was a Coastal Command station, and we each received a healthy tot of rum which was most welcome; time in the air was 10hrs 30 minutes."

HELLO NEMO

'Uncle Will' (PB504) and crew experienced a similar fuel dilemma:

"After bombing, we were briefed to return to the tip of Denmark early to send back the wind reports to base. Instead of there being a following wind over Denmark as expected in the briefing, we encountered a very strong head wind which meant using more revs and boost to get to position on time. I well remember our Geordie flight engineer, Sgt Green, with his usual Job's comforter type voice saying 'you'll never do it Skip, you'll never get back if you keep up this speed'. (Sgt Green was actually on his last operation, having flown one operation before joining the Hay crew).

I admit that I was worried, but was not going to show it and we pressed on with the engineer complaining all the way. I was making mental calculations and considering what actions to take when we got to our rendezvous.

We made the position on time and sent the wind back to base, then I reduced our speed by less revs and boost. "From 17,000ft we made a long shallow descent towards the English coast. Watching our gauges getting lower and lower (as were the engineer's spirits), there seemed no end to the sea. Then we saw the coast - or was it cloud? difficult to tell in the darkness. The navigator had brought us back to the Norfolk coast and I circled for the bomb aimer to get a visual fix of our exact position. Precariously low on fuel, something then happened which made up my mind as to whether we should try and make base or not.

The emergency procedure for an aircraft in trouble was to orbit twice and the ground tracking stations, always on watch, would come up with a code and the difficulty could be explained. Well on this night, the listening service, always on the ball looking for customers and dying to go into action, didn't wait for a second orbit... 'Hello Nemo, Hello Nemo, do you want assistance?'

What a relief! After hours and hours of worrying... to hear the voice of an English girl eager to help. It was magnificent - our troubles were over. I asked 'Darkie' for a runway long enough to take a four-engined bomber. Lights immediately lit up to port... what a wonderful sight, better than all the illuminations ever produced. Actually the runway wasn't good, it was a wire mesh one used by a fighter squadron, but to us it was heaven and we landed there - 10 hours and 40 minutes after we had taken-off from Fulbeck."

No 5 Group suffered the loss of 2 Lancasters and their crews. All 49's aircraft landed safely back at Fulbeck, with the exception of the two already mentioned plus F/O Fricker RAAF (PB797) and crew who touched down at Grimsby (Waltham).

14/15 January, 1945; MERSEBURG: Oil was the target once again, as 5 Group joined a total force of 573 Lancasters from other Groups. This was to be a double attack, with a 3 hour separation, on a synthetic-oil plant in the Leuna region.

49 Squadron contributed 10 aircraft including three new crews piloted by; F/O Gibson (PB504) and F/O Abbott RNZAF (PB797) and F/O Binns (PB844). All 10 aircraft were airborne within 9 minutes, with the last, F/O Milburn (ME353) lifting off at 16.37hrs. The attacks on oil targets during this period were so accurate and destructive, that they had a very significant effect on the German's fighting capability; this particular raid was no exception. As expected the target was defended vigorously with the result that 10 Lancasters and crews failed to return.

BUS STOP!

Arriving back over England just after 02.00hrs, Fulbeck aircraft received a diversion signal sending them to RAF Pocklington. Tired crews were soon orbiting the Yorkshire base awaiting their turn to land. On touch down, the new boys in F/O Johnny Gibson's (PB504) crew overran the runway, smashing through the boundary hedge, coming to rest on the main road to York. Shaken but unharmed, the crew were taken to de-brief followed by a meal.

Afterwards, they returned to the scene of their mishap, and in the first light of a cold morning, they watched as ground personnel attempted to recover the stranded U-Uncle.

Peter Roberts, the flight engineer, remembers that a bus soon approached down the road and was brought to a halt by the Service Police, Peter recalls what happened next:

"The driver jumped down from his cab and began to remonstrate loudly with the first RAF bod he could find... 'Tha can't leave that bloody thing there tha knows... A've got ta get these people t'work!'; making out as if the Lancaster had been placed there on purpose, in order to prevent him."

Worlds within worlds!

16/17 January, 1945; BRUX: A combined effort by Lancasters of 1 and 5 Groups saw 231 bombers led by 6 Mosquitoes attack the distant oil target of Brux in Czechoslovakia.

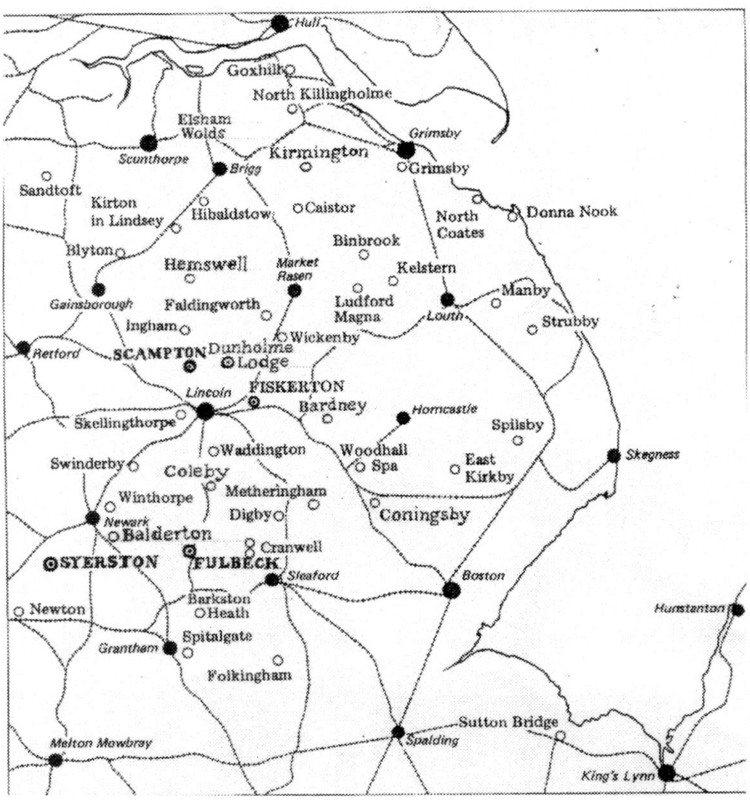

Despite the cloud cover, crews witnessed various multi-coloured explosions with columns of black smoke rising up through the clouds. It proved to be an extremely devastating raid; one Lancaster and crew failed to return.

49 Squadron had dispatched 13 aircraft, and all returned to base by 03.26hrs, having accomplished successful sorties.

The RAF Stations featured in this book are shown amidst a host of other airfields - small wonder the term 'Bomber County' was used when referring to Lincolnshire.

JANUARY 1945

SADISTIC PLEASURE

Brux should have been the 30th and final operation for F/Lt Hay and crew. But things did not go to plan as 'Uncle Will' explains:

"The usual drill... last meal, briefing, out to the aircraft, run up and check. Shut down and wait for take-off time and for the bowsers to top us up with the fuel that we had used to do the run up; about three gallons per engine. This gives an idea of how we were stretched to capacity.

We stood by at our frying pan, each with his own thoughts which we concealed from each other. We had another flight engineer, one we knew well and who did relief work. He noticed a drip, drip, drip from the glycol tank in of one of the engines. Hurriedly the ground crew rigged a scaffold and after examination decided a new tank was required... stores did not have one and our trip was cancelled. This was indeed a blow. So we went on leave next day with a forced cheerfulness, thinking 'only one more when we get back', but we were not happy.

On our way back from leave, even before we had reached Lincoln station, we met other crews who took a sadistic pleasure in telling us that a tour had been put up to 36 ops!!!"

For the remainder of January, weather prevented any further operations. Some local training flights were possible and on the 24th, 28th and 29th operations were detailed, only to be scrubbed during the afternoons. On the morning of Tuesday 30th, after it had snowed hard during the previous evening and then drifted, one very wet and bruised operational type was heard to complain: *'It makes it very difficult to ride a bike.'*

OPERATIONAL SUMMARY - JANUARY 1945

Date	Target	Desp	E/R	FTR	Remarks
1/2	GRAVENHORST	14	1	-	Diverted Peterhead
4/5	ROYAN	14	-	-	
5/6	HOUFFALIZE	9	-	-	Diverted Croft
7/8	MUNICH	12	-	1	F/O Bolter FTR
13/14	POLITZ	12	-	-	3 a/c diverted
14/15	MERSEBURG	10	-	-	Diverted Pocklington
16/17	BRUX	13			

Total number of sorties flown	84
Failed to Return	1

FEBRUARY 1945

1/2 February, 1945; SIEGEN: 5 Group once again set out in strength when 271 Lancasters and 11 Mosquitoes were dispatched against the communication target of Siegen. 49 Squadron detailed 16 aircraft for the attack including two new crews piloted by; F/O Smith RNZAF (NG327) and F/O MacAuley RCAF (PB439). F/O Jock Galloway (ME355) and crew were the first away from Fulbeck at 16.04hrs. Jack Shearing, who shared the same billet with some of Galloway's crew recorded the following in his diary:

"We D.I'ed 'Howe' and did ground runs, only to find ops were on and we were reserve crew. The petrol load was 1,600 and the load was a 'cookie' and 500's so if we hadn't been going on leave next day, we would have been cheesed to miss it. The target was Siegen near Cologne, a centre chock full of troops and equipment for the western front, and promised to be a good trip.

We went up to the caravan for the take-off and it was just like 'Derby' day as there was a big crowd up there. We waved the boys off and Galloway got a special cheer; old Les waved his arms like mad in the astrodome... a sight I shall never forget, and Ernie elevated his guns. Went up to tea after feeling rather proud and disappointed. Went to the camp cinema with Paddy and saw a film I had seen before; Deanna Durbin in 'Hers to Hold', then went up to the hut to finish packing. Heard the tour had been raised to 36 trips... a real shaker for everybody and far from a joke."

Note: Jack Shearing returned from leave to find that his close friends in Galloway's crew had been posted 'missing'.

Over cloud covered Siegen, Pathfinders had difficulty in marking accurately. A combination of high winds and dummy markers resulted in much of the bombing falling in open country, although the railway station did receive some damage. 3 Lancasters and 1 Mosquito failed to return from the operation.

F/O Binns (PB484) and crew were returning home across the sea at 4,000ft, when the gunners noticed an unidentified twin-engined aircraft coming out of cloud at 300yds to port and above. F/Sgt Pedler in the rear turret ordered his skipper to corkscrew port; the other aircraft, bearing navigation lights, followed the Lancaster down. On completion of the corkscrew manoeuvre, the unidentified aircraft then dived on the Lancaster and F/Sgt Tone in the mid upper turret opened fire immediately; their attacker did not reply, but broke away to the starboard quarter and disappeared. No claim was made by the gunners who definitely assert that the aircraft was not a Mosquito. The first contact of this action took place at 21.33hrs.

All 49's aircraft returned safely with F/O MacAuley RCAF and crew the last down at 23.35hrs.

Author's note: The one Mosquito missing from this operation came from the marker force, 627 Squadron and was piloted by F/Lt Baker RCAF (DZ637). This aircraft was seen by a Lancaster, being shot down over the target. Both the pilot and Sgt Betts his navigator did not survive and are buried in the Reichswald Cemetery.

FEBRUARY 1945

2/3 February, 1945; KARLSRUHE: Fulbeck reverberated with the sound of Merlins as 49 Squadron attempted to launch 14 Lancasters in conjunction with a further 19 from 189 Squadron. One aircraft slipped off the peri-track becoming bogged down and had to be scrubbed from the operation. This caused F/O Watson (PB349) and crew to be delayed by some 45 minutes on take-off; they were within just 40 miles of the target when the 'cease bombing' order was received. F/O McRae (ME253) and crew were forced to return early due to severe icing experienced at 4,000ft.

The raid turned out to be a failure, due mainly to the cloud conditions. 5 Group had 250 Lancasters airborne this night, of which 14, along with their crews, failed to return. Aircraft began landing back at Fulbeck just after 03.00hrs and 27 minutes later all 49's had been accounted for. But 189 had suffered the loss of 4 aircraft and crews - a shattering blow to this fledgling squadron that saw its operational losses doubled in just one night.

7/8 February, 1945; LADBERGEN (DORTMUND-EMS CANAL): No 5 Group returned once again to attack the Dortmund-Ems Canal with 177 Lancasters and 11 Mosquitoes. During the morning, 49 Squadron detailed 18 Lancasters for the trip but by the take-off time of 20.52hrs, 6 aircraft had been withdrawn. The 12 that did manage to become airborne included a new crew skippered by F/O Eltis RAAF (SW274).

Over the target, crews could not assess their attacks due to the inclusion of delayed action bombs in their loads, but most reported good visual sightings of the TI's from their bombing height of 11,500ft. Shortly before reaching the target, Sgt Hornigold, rear gunner in Harold Fricker's RAAF (PB349) crew, reported an AGLT contact at 1,400yds. At the time they were at 12,000ft in good visibility above 9/10ths cloud. As the unknown aircraft closed in without showing any identification on the "Z" equipment, Sgt Hornigold opened fire whilst calling for his skipper to corkscrew. The rear gunner fired again at 750 and 600yds but no hits were observed; the enemy aircraft soon disappeared. The crew then continued to the target, where old 'Howe' released her load at one minute past midnight.

Four minutes after midnight, and having bombed, the gunners in Ken Bromfield's (PB484) crew spotted a JU88 on the starboard beam and down (no AGLT contact). There was no moon and the Lancaster was flying 200ft above 10/10ths cloud in clear conditions at 10,000ft. On instructions from his gunners, the pilot threw T-Tommy into a corkscrew. As the enemy aircraft dived under the Lancaster to port, mid-upper gunner Sgt McLeod and rear gunner Sgt Walters reported strikes on the German's starboard wing; the enemy was not seen again. It was later determined that the JU88 had been too far on the beam during the initial contact, for 'Village Inn' to have responded.

All 49's crews returned unharmed to Fulbeck having completed successful sorties, with F/O Milburn (PB571) and crew the last to land when Z-Zebra touched down at 03.47hrs.

Group had lost 3 Lancasters and crews from the raid.

FEBRUARY 1945

8/9 February, 1945; POLITZ: The synthetic-oil plant at Politz was selected to receive a double attack by 475 Lancasters and 7 Mosquitoes from 1, 5 and 8 Groups. It was decided to send 5 Group (to get the pot boiling!) in first using their own marking method, to be followed by 1 Group using 8 Group Pathfinders.

The raid proved to be a total success with accurate bombing from both waves, which caused tremendous damage. The squadron had 15 Lancasters attacking the target, flying at between 9,000 and 11,000ft. Most crews reported large yellow and red explosions with billowing black smoke. Defences within the target area had been tough with heavy, accurate flak; 13 Lancasters failed to return. One close flak burst actually blew W/O Cluer's (SW274) aircraft over on its back. With great skill and effort, the captain managed to regain control of G-George, but tragically, during this action, the mid-upper gunner, Sgt Ron Wiggins had been killed. It is believed that he died from asphyxiation, strangled by his own communication cord during the aircraft's violent manoeuvres; the 28 year old gunner is buried in Danbury Churchyard, Essex.

W/O Cluer and crew were the last to land back at Fulbeck, touching down at 03.20hrs, which left just one 49 Squadron aircraft outstanding... Jock Galloway (ME353) and crew flying their 26th operation had failed to return. All very popular characters within the squadron, the sad loss of Galloway's crew was deeply felt by everyone: F/Lt Somerville Russell Galloway along with five fellow members of his crew have their graves in Poznan Old Garrison Cemetery, Poland. It was unknown at the time, that F/Sgt Ernie Ellis the mid-upper gunner, had managed to escape with his life.

Missing ME353	F/L S.R. Galloway	Pilot	(Killed)
(EA-Q)	Sgt H.W.J. Hardy	F/E	(Killed)
'B'Flt	F/S T.O. Bolton	NAV	(Killed)
	F/S L. Randall	W/OP	(Killed)
	F/S E. Ellis	A/G	(P.o.W.)
Crew on their	F/O G.W.A. Kidd	B/A	(Killed)
26th operation	F/O W. Dron	P/A/G	(Killed)

A SAD RETURN

During the next four days following the Politz operation, 5 Group were stood down. On Sunday 11 February, diarist Jack Shearing returned back to camp after his leave. Catching the 5.05 from Kings Cross, he got off at Newark station. During the evening of his return to Fulbeck, Jack recorded the following sentiments in his diary:

"I came up on the Cranwell bus from Newark and walked to the camp from the crossroads. On reaching the Mess, I saw Lefty and he told me the bad news that Galloway and the boys were missing... you could have knocked me down with a feather, it seemed incredible that Les, Ernie, Tom and John should have gone... we all felt it very much.

The hut seemed cold and foreboding and there was an atmosphere of death over the whole camp. The boys went down at Politz and 189 lost 4 kites at Karlsruhe, Galloway had done 26 trips, a nasty business.

Naturally everyone felt very upset, it seemed that everything had come to an end... I have not felt as miserable as this for a long time."

Postscript: After release from PoW camp, mid/upper gunner, Yorkshireman Ernie Ellis (the only survivor), visited his friends on the squadron. He gave them the following account of the night they were shot down: *"They had just done a banking search after bombing, when they were hit by a night fighter with upward firing guns. The Lancaster caught fire and the skipper gave the order to jump! Ernie opened the rear door with Les Randall W/OP, standing right behind him when he jumped; no one will ever know if the kite then blew up."*

13/14 February, 1945; DRESDEN: So much has been written about the so called controversial Dresden raid since the war, that the author does not intend adding to the already mountainous in-depth analysis. But before detailing 49 Squadron's part in the attack, it may be prudent to give the following quote from one crew member who took part in the raid; he refers to the pre-operational briefing:

"We were told this was a centre for controlling the Russian front, and that the attack would create chaos in the German command structure and communications - no mention was made of the potential civilian casualties."

49 Squadron detailed 17 aircraft for the operation, and all were airborne from Fulbeck by 18.25hrs. A force of nearly 800 Lancasters was dispatched against Dresden. The force was split into two waves; 5 Group, using its own Mosquito markers would go in first with 244 aircraft and drop over 800 tons of bombs. The second wave, three hours later, would consist of 529 Lancasters from 1,3,6 and 8 Groups, adding another 1,800 tons of bombs.

F/Lt Leslie Hay gives this detailed description of his crew's participation on this their 31st operation; 'Uncle Will' recalls:

"Dresden, right over in eastern Germany, a long way. With the enemy forces withdrawing from France the fighters and flak were more concentrated in the Fatherland. The weather forecast indicated cloud all the way with the possibility of having to bomb by H2S. That would give us cover from fighters except those vectored on to us by ground radar.

Our station 'met' man gave us his usual personal forecast which was cloud all the way, but at about 22.00hrs - the time we were due there, a break might occur some ten miles from the target. This is precisely what did happen.

The briefing was that the raid, which as sometimes happened, was to be by the whole of Bomber Command; 5 Group was to go in advance, locate and set the target alight. A few hours later, mainforce was due to arrive and use high explosives.

We took off and went straight into low cloud and stayed in it until we were some twenty miles from the target, when we ran out of it. There followed the usual pattern of marking and running up. In the first wave I saw our squadron or as much of it as the light would permit, running up almost in formation, each on their respective allotted headings. The navigation and flying had been very accurate. Hours of cloud flying without seeing anything to suddenly find that we were almost in formation... it was quite incredible. The marking was absolutely spot on; we bombed and were away. From the flying and bombing point of view, it was a classic raid."

The results of the bombing, which created a horrendous firestorm are well documented. The human casualties can never be accurately estimated due to the vast number of refugees within the town; some sources calculate it may be as high as 50,000 people. Bomber Command lost 9 Lancasters from the attack; all 49's returned safely to Fulbeck.

14/15 February, 1945; ROSITZ: Wednesday night's target was the synthetic oil plant at Rositz, between Leipzig and Dresden and was to be another 5 Group only attack. At Fulbeck, 18 Lancasters plus one possible were detailed by 49 Squadron with take-off set for 16.30hrs. F/Lt Mellor had to withdraw old 'Howe'(PB349) when the ground boys found a snag in the port inner engine; Jack Shearing the crews W/OP recorded: *"It was very disappointing particularly as we needed an op to get back in the groove (after leave). We went to tea, then on up to the hut and found a new crew in the billet. There were only three of them but it seemed sacrilege to see them sleeping in the lads (Galloway's crew) beds."*

The raid caused damage to the southern part of the oil plant for the loss of 4 Lancasters and crews out of the 224 dispatched. All 49's aircraft had come home safe and sound by 02.50hrs, including the new crew piloted by F/O Weston RNZAF who had taken PB504 U-Uncle on the trip.

19/20 February, 1945; BOHLEN: After being stood down for four days, the squadron was then alerted for another 5 Group oil strike; this time at Bohlen, again near Leipzig. Operational meal was at 18.45hrs with main briefing at 20.00rs. Norman Smith (Hammond's crew) remembers:

"I had a fright when I first heard the target name at briefing... I thought they said BERLIN! On the way to the target we passed a dummy fire, which I was able to tell the skipper to ignore. Apparently due to lack of co-operation from the Russians, the wind forecasts were wrong. I realised that the stronger winds would prevent us from reaching the target at the briefed ETA, so I cut across a right angled corner in the track and thereby gained many miles... we got to the target bang on time.

When we saw the plot of the aircraft next day, we were all on our own out front of the stream. It seems the other aircraft had settled for being late."

The target only received superficial damage from the 254 Lancasters dispatched. Just one aircraft failed to return, that of the Master Bomber W/Cmdr Benjamin DFC and Bar along with his navigator who were killed when their Mosquito was shot down by flak over the target.

20/21 February, 1945; GRAVENHORST (MITTELLAND CANAL): Crews who had returned from the Bohlen raid eventually dropped into their beds around 11.00hrs only to be woken up at 17.00hrs and told that there was still a war on! Briefing revealed that the target was the 'old faithful' Gravenhorst.

Both W/Cmdr Botting (NG352) and S/Ldr Walker (ME308) were amongst 10 aircraft from the squadron that started to take-off shortly before 22.00hrs. Each aircraft climbed up into thick cloud to be greeted by bright moonlight as they broke through at their operational height. F/Lt Williams (ME322) and crew soon experienced engine trouble and were forced to return early to Fulbeck without completing their sortie.

Unfortunately cloud in the target area caused the Master Bomber to abandon the raid, and the force of 154 Lancasters and 11 Mosquitoes turned for home without loss. 49 Squadron was diverted on return, landing at Colerne, Lyneham and Boscombe Down.

21/22 February, 1945; GRAVENHORST (MITTELLAND CANAL): A force of 165 Lancasters led by 12 Mosquitoes (all 5 Group) sallied forth once again in an attempt to breach the Mittelland Canal. This time in clear visibility the attack was successful.

The squadron had 11 aircraft airborne by 17.26hrs but shortly after 19.00hrs F/O Eltis (PB797) and crew rejoined Fulbeck's circuit requesting landing permission and requiring an ambulance. It transpired that shortly after take-off, their GEE receiver had caught fire, and in his action of putting the fire out, navigator F/Sgt Howland was badly splashed with extinguisher fluid. Not knowing the effect this would have, the crew decided to jettison their bombs and return to base.

Those crews who managed to complete their sorties started landing back at Fulbeck just before 23.00hrs. At de-brief, F/O Stark (PB373) and crew gave the following report that well illustrates the night's effort:

"Bombed from 9200ft at 20.40hrs - Green T.I. seen at the east side of the canal. 3 Red T.I's well placed near aiming point. Controller ordered to attack the northerly one. Good visibility, no cloud - attack should be successful."

By midnight three aircraft were still overdue; a phone call received from Manston in Kent revealed that Les Hammond RAAF (SW256) and crew had made an emergency landing there without compressed air brake pressure. Norman Smith recalls:

"It took all of the runway at Manston to stop, with the main wheels at the end of the concrete. When they hitched the tractor to the tail wheel it accidentally pushed the main wheels off the edges.

They had great difficulty in getting it back. A crash wagon pulled up to the door on landing and they were quite disappointed that we had no wounded. There were some horrible wrecks at the end of the Manston runway which was not very good for morale."

Of the 165 Lancasters sent to Gravenhorst, 13 had failed to return and two of those were from 49 Squadron. F/O Mallinson (PB568) and crew flying their 35th operation were posted missing... a severe blow to the Squadron's morale and coming so soon after the demise of Galloway's crew. A few weeks later, much to everyone's relief, six of Mallinson's crew were reported as being PoW's. This included the crew's bomb-aimer, F/Sgt Le Marquand whose brother was still on his tour as a pilot with 49 Squadron. The one unfortunate crew member to lose his life was F/Sgt John Gascoyne A/G; he is buried in the Reichwald War Cemetery.

The second aircraft reported missing contained F/O Ed Smith RNZAF (NG327) and crew. Tragically none of them survived this, their fourth operation. Six members are buried along with their 27 year-old skipper in the Reichswald Forest War Cemetery, whilst the bomb aimer, F/O Edwin Hook is at rest in the Durnbach War Cemetery.

FTR NG327	F/O E.P. Smith RNZAF	Pilot	(Killed)
(EA-K)	Sgt J. Corbett	F/E	(P.o.W.)
'A'Flt	F/S J. Newby	NAV	(Killed)
	P/O E.J.F. McCarthy	W/AG	(Killed)
	Sgt C.F.P. Burridge	A/G	(Killed)
Crew on their	F/O E.F. Hook	B/A	(P.o.W.)**
4th operation	P/O R.J. Simpson RCAF	A/G	(Killed)
FTR PB568	F/O R. Mallinson	Pilot	(P.o.W.)
(EA-Y)	Sgt E. Stansill	F/E	(P.o.W.)
'B'Flt	P/O H. Eberley RCAF	NAV	(P.o.W.)
	F/S N.H. Makofski	W/OP	(P.o.W.)
	P/O F.E. Grimsdale	A/G	(P.o.W.)
Crew on their	F/S Le Marquand	B/A	(P.o.W.)
35th operation	F/S J.P. Gascoyne	A/G	(Killed)

23/24 February, 1945; HORTEN: No 5 Group dispatched 74 Lancasters and 10 Mosquitoes against the German Naval base at Horten on the Oslo Fjord.

**F/O Hook was killed on 4-4-45 whilst on a 'Death March' from a P.o.W. camp. The column was strafed by fighter aircraft.

23/24-2-45 HORTEN

49 Squadron Order of Battle

ME322	Williams	SW265	Hammond	B791	Eltis		
PB844	Hytch	SW274	Johnston	PB797	McPhee		
PB ?	Lee	PB373	Littley	ME491	Weston		
PB361	Carlyle	PB484	Winter	PB537	Hay		
PB571	Binns	NG352	Walker	ME308	Watson	ME471	Fricker

Lifting from Fulbeck's main runway just after 17.16hrs, F/Lt Jack Winter (PB484) and crew were the first of 16 Lancasters from 49 Squadron to take-off bound for Norway. S/Ldr Walker (NG352), whose crew included bomb aimer F/Lt Ken Gibson (Ken had completed his very first Lancaster operation with 49 two years earlier almost to the day) was to act as controller for the attack. The Lancasters arrived in the target area just before 20.45hrs and delivered their attacks from between 8,000 and 10,000ft. By the time the final bomber departed the scene, Horten's port area was a sea of flames; F/O Littley (PB373) and crew reported later that the fires were 'still visible 100 miles away.' The results proved to be one of the most accurate bombing attacks of the war.

A PROPER JOB OF IT

The port was the main source of employment for the local population and this raid had completely destroyed their livelihoods. But an insight into the Norwegian's attitude regarding the situation may be gleaned from correspondence received by Maurice 'Chalky' White (navigator in Jack Winter's crew on the raid) in 1978. Through various coincidences, Chalky was contacted by Mr John Kaardahl, a Horten businessman. The following are extracts from a letter received by Maurice from Mr Kaardahl:

"Here in Horten people are very proud of having received the finest precision bombing during the war!! Not a single Norwegian was killed - but many Germans are probably sitting up there still wondering what hit them!

The old Naval Hospital got a direct hit - and they were almost the only bombs to fall outside the wharf-wall. The Naval Hospital was no longer a hospital but was arranged as a German Kaserne and was full of soldiers. The raid was in the evening and not a single Norwegian was inside the wharf-wall. Most of the dock buildings were destroyed - so you made a proper job of it!

The Germans were extremely busy those days - or rather evenings and nights, when all the Norwegian workers were out.

There were strong guards by the gates and rumours say that one of the biggest submarines was alongside taking-on mysterious persons and goods, but it is not possible to get this confirmed - it is thought the submarine had left the wharf just before the raid.

During the first years after the war, some people thought it was a pity that the wharf should have been destroyed so near the end - but today everybody praises it because now we have a modern shipbuilding yard and diesel factory and have been able to keep our heads above water during the bad days and now the order books are full. With the old wharf we would have been 'over and out' long ago!"

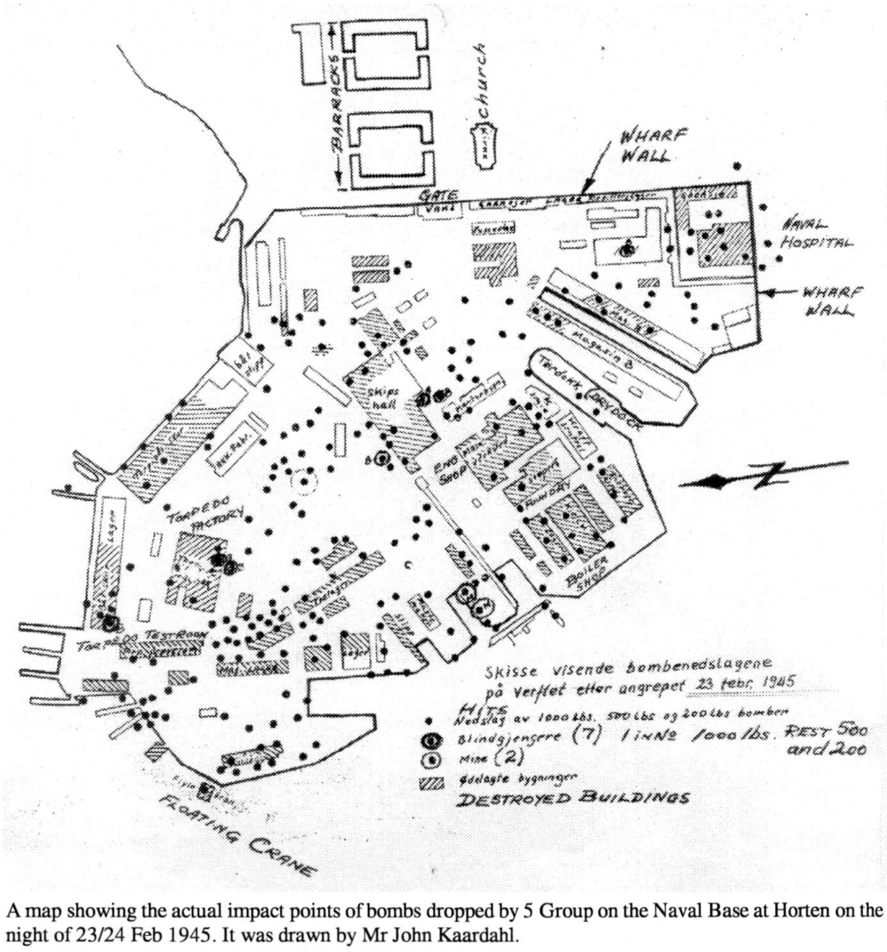

A map showing the actual impact points of bombs dropped by 5 Group on the Naval Base at Horten on the night of 23/24 Feb 1945. It was drawn by Mr John Kaardahl.

One Lancaster and crew failed to return from the force dispatched, but all 49's aircraft arrived back at Fulbeck without trouble, S/Ldr Williams (ME322) and crew the last to land at 00.50hrs.

Note: In 1940, John Kaardahl escaped from Norway on the famous 'Shetland Bus'. He served the rest of the war in the Norwegian Navy.

FEBRUARY 1945

OPERATIONAL SUMMARY - FEBRUARY 1945

Date	Target	Desp	E/R	FTR	Remarks
1/2	SIEGEN	16	-	-	
2/3	KARLSRUHE	13	1	-	
7/8	LADBERGEN	12	-	-	
8/9	POLITZ	15	-	1	F/L Galloway FTR
13/14	DRESDEN	17	-	-	
14/15	ROSITZ	18	-	-	
19/20	BOHLEN	19	-	-	
20/21	GRAVENHORST	10	1	-	Abandoned/All diverted
21/22	GRAVENHORST	11	1	2	F/O Smith FTR F/O Mallinson FTR
23/24	HORTEN	16	-	-	

Total number of sorties flown	147
Failed to return	3
Total tons of bombs of all types dropped	644.92
Operational hours flown during February 1945	1120
Non-operational hours flown during February 1945	396.20

HONOURS AND AWARDS - FEBRUARY 1945

F/Lt M.H. Fisher D.F.C.	Bar to D.F.C.
F/S D.G. Hird	D.F.M.
P/O G. Miller	D.F.C.
F/Lt T. Russell	D.F.C.

PB455 (EA-W) Flying a daylight operation during the final months of the war. (Bob Soutar)

MARCH 1945

3/4 March, 1945; LADBERGEN (DORTMUND-EMS CANAL): A force of 212 Lancasters and 10 Mosquitoes (all 5 Group) accomplished a successful attack on the Ladbergen aqueduct, putting the Dortmund-Ems Canal completely out of operation.
9 Squadron from Bardney, contributed 18 aircraft, all dropping 12,000lb 'Tallboy' bombs. But as the 5 Group Lancasters turned for home some of the Luftwaffe's 'Experten' night-fighter pilots were waiting. Airborne that night was 'fighter ace' Major Heinz-Wolfgang Schnaufer; he shot down 2 Lancasters, his 117th and 118th victims: altogether 7 Lancaster crews failed to return.

F/O Jack Mersey (PB361) and crew were unable to attack the target; whilst taking evasive action from searchlights, the pilot blacked-out. The aircraft was skilfully flown back to England by the bomb aimer, F/Sgt Boyes. Thankfully, once back over England, the captain recovered sufficiently to land R-Roger at Tilstock.

OPERATION GISELA

F/Lt 'Uncle Will' Hay, piloted PB504, one of 12 Lancasters dispatched by 49 Squadron to attack the Dortmund-Ems Canal; during the return leg he noted something rather unusual:

"Coming back from the Dortmund-Ems, I saw beacons on the Dutch coast, the type which the night fighters orbit before being vectored onto the stream. The beacons were usually single, but this was a double one and to me meant only one thing - the fighters were waiting to move in. I dropped to sea level (ignoring the bomb aimer's complaints about the sudden rush of pressure on his ears) and we came back just over the tops of the waves."

'Uncle Will's' instincts were correct; for crossing the North Sea with the returning bombers of 4 and 5 Groups, were 142 Ju88Gs of the German Luftwaffe - but here 'Uncle' (whose crew was one operation shy of their tour) luck must have been strong, for the enemy was also flying to England at wave top level.

NIGHT OF THE INTRUDERS

In the very early hours of Sunday 4 March, large scale German intruder operations were carried out over eastern England. Halifax squadrons returning to Yorkshire from operations against the Kamen Oil refinery, Special Duty squadrons landing in Norfolk and Lancasters returning to Lincolnshire from Ladbergan - all became the prey of prowling Luftwaffe night fighters in the moonlit eastern counties.

49 Squadron started letting down at Fulbeck just after midnight; F/O Les Hammond RAAF (SW265) and crew were on their final approach; navigator Norman Smith recalls what happened next:

"On return our R/T set was u/s and we could not receive messages from the control tower; so as we approached we fired a red Very light and came straight in to land. As we touched down, all the airfield lights were suddenly all switched off. Without R/T we didn't hear the 'Bograt' instructions - this was the codeword given to inform aircraft that intruders were around and that they should scram and await further orders.

The skipper turned the aircraft off the runway and just as we were getting out, an intruder 'shot up' the runway. We all dived on the deck and tried to make ourselves as small as possible... I looked up just as the intruder, a Ju88 passed overhead. Whilst all this was happening and with cannon shells ripping into the runway all around, the skipper 'walked' over to our Lancaster and switched off the navigation lights; we had left them on to warn other aircraft that may have landed behind us.

A little later we saw a flash in the distance, and thought it may have been our intruder being shot down!"

Pilot, F/O Les Hammond RAAF adds the following to his navigator's account:

We fired a red final warning on entering the funnels, and received no red from the control van. We used all the runway as the brakes were u/s and eventually turned off onto the grass at a safe distance from the runway. The crew wearily climbed out leaving the 'old girl' standing there lit up like a Christmas tree... engine noises then sounded overhead and the next thing we saw was a Ju88 on a steep turn right at us. "My first thought was the illuminated target we had given him... his aircraft was outlined by a string of horizontal muzzle flashes and we will never know where his bullets landed... there wasn't a single hole in the old kite! "This is where Smithy and I differ in our accounts; he said I walked across to our aircraft and switched the master switch off... if there had been anyone there to time me, I will wager a sizeable bet that I broke every Olympic record ever set! I don't remember how I got up through the door as the ladder had been tossed inside... I think I just flew!"

Unfortunately, the crashing aircraft that night in the fields of Lincolnshire and neighbouring counties, were nearly all RAF bombers. F/Lt Jack Winter (PB484) and crew were the final aircraft to land at Fulbeck touching down in T-Tommy at 00.27hrs... just two minutes later the carnage began:

00.29hrs. In the direction of the coast, a Lancaster of 12 Sqdn. Wickenby dived headlong into the ground at Ulceby Cross near Alford. The aircraft's engines buried themselves 10 feet into the ground; there were no survivors.

00.40hrs. A Halifax of 466 RAAF Sqdn was attacked and the crew baled out over Waddington just south of Lincoln. The crewless aircraft then flew on towards the coast but tragically crashed at Friskney near Skegness demolishing a cottage and killing three people.

00.57hrs. A Lancaster of 1654 HCU Wigsley crashed at Church Warsop near Mansfield after being shot down. The crew managed to bale out but sadly the mid-upper gunner was killed.

01.00hrs. The pilot of a 460 RAAF Sqn Lancaster had received the 'Bograt' call from his Binbrook base. Moments later they were 'Pounced' by a Ju88. F/O Warren miraculously crash landed his burning aircraft on farmland at Barfield House, Langworth, not far from the railway crossing.

The crew, who were struggling to free the injured mid-upper gunner, were the subject of the night fighter's attention still further... as they tried to make good their escape, the Nazi pilot repeatedly strafed the helpless airmen assisted by the light from the burning bomber. Fortunately the Lancaster crew survived... but for the Luftwaffe crew, who made off over Scothern heading towards Scampton, their time would soon be up for they had only a matter of few more minutes to live!... as we shall see.

01.02hrs. Another 1654 HCU Lancaster crew was attacked over their home airfield of Wigsley; the rear gunner baled out, but the pilot managed to land the aircraft at High Ercall.

01.05hrs. To the east of Fulbeck, in the direction of Cranwell, a valiant French pilot, Captain Lacou and his flight engineer, F/Sgt Le Masson, held their burning Halifax aloft whilst the rest of the crew escaped by parachute. The aircraft finally plunged to the ground near Anwick Grange, its fuel tanks erupting killing both brave airmen. At the same time, yet another Lancaster from 1654 HCU Wigsley was shot down, and dived into the ground at Stapleford Wood between Fulbeck and Newark; all the crew were killed (one of these two crashes may have been the flash that the Hammond crew witnessed).

01.05hrs. A Lancaster from 1662 HCU at Blyton near Gainsborough was attacked in the Doncaster area, but the pilot managed to land safely.

01.10hrs. Another Lancaster of 12 Sqdn. Wickenby, was shot down and fell at East Stockwith near Blyton; all the crew were killed.

01.15hrs. A Lancaster crew of 44 Sqdn Spilsby, received the 'Bograt' call and headed north away from their base... they hadn't travelled far before the intruder struck. The wreckage fell in flames into Brocklesby Park near Brigg. Sadly, none of the crew survived. A memorial plaque dedicated to this crew has been placed on a tree near where they perished.

01.18hrs. Over Norfolk, F/O Reid and crew of 189 Squadron were heading back to Fulbeck from the Ladbergen trip, when a night fighter shot them down; there were no survivors as the Lancaster dived into the nearby East Rudham Railway Station.

01.36hrs. A 76 Sqdn. Halifax crew were trying to make their Yorkshire base when a fighter caught them over Lincolnshire; the crew all managed to parachute to safety before the Halifax crashed at Cadney near Brigg.

KILLED IN THE LINE OF DUTY

Observer J.P. Kelway, was a member of L.1 Post, No 11 Group, ROC, Lincoln. Not following his usual custom of sleeping at his post prior to duty, the early morning of 4th March, saw him motoring to duty along the Welton to Hackthorn road, some 2 miles east of Scampton airfield.

Feldwebel Heirich Conze and crew (who had minutes earlier downed and strafed the Lancaster crew at Langworth) were looking for ground targets to attack. Although Observer Kelway's car lights were hooded according to regulations, there must have been just enough light to be seen by Conze. The Ju88 came streaking in at ground level aiming straight at Kelway's car when it struck telegraph wires and then the ground before hitting the car and flinging it across two fields. Kelway was instantly killed, as were the 4 man crew in the Ju88.

Observer Kelway was buried in Newport Cemetery, Lincoln, on 7 March; a large number of his fellow observers attending. He was the only member of the ROC to be killed on duty.
Note: The German crew are buried in Scampton Churchyard.

Whilst such hostilities were being enacted over Lincolnshire, many similar combats were happening over Yorkshire and East Anglia. The British defences had been taken totally by surprise; of the 5 German fighters destroyed in England, at least 3 were due to their own low level flying. Back at the German bases, 8 crews were missing, 3 more crashed, 6 crews baled out near their home airfields due to fuel shortage, and 11 aircraft crashed or were damaged when landing.

The attack had lasted just two-and-a-half hours, and during that time 13 Halifaxes, 9 Lancasters, one Fortress and a Mosquito had been shot down. Whilst over England, the Germans had strafed anything that moved on the ground; as a result 17 civilians had been killed and 12 seriously wounded.

The night had served as a timely reminder that the enemy was still a capable and deadly opponent.

5/6 March, 1945; BOHLEN: Whilst 248 Lancasters (including 49 Sqdn) supported by 10 Mosquitoes from 5 Group attacked the oil refinery at Bohlen, 760 aircraft from the main force were sent to Chemnitz - This main force attack started very badly when 9 Halifaxes crashed near their bases (due to icing) shortly after take-off; a further 22 were lost on the main operation.

49 Squadron had 19 aircraft airborne from Fulbeck including three new crews piloted by F/O Elkington (NG352), F/O Fisher RAAF (ME471) and F/O Smith RAAF (PB484).

Four Lancasters were lost from the raid, but all 49's aircraft returned to base unscathed.

Just one crew failed to attack; as F/O Elkington approached the target, the crew heard the Controller say "sky, sky", but on running over the target they saw no sign of any green or red sky markers - the Controller was then heard to order "cease bombing", so they turned for home, jettisoning their bombs in the sea.

Flying conditions had been poor both going out and coming back with most crews experiencing severe icing. Everyone was half expecting intruders again this night, but fortunately they didn't make an appearance.

WE WERE ALL 49 SQUADRON

For one crew, the raid on Bohlen was to be the final operation of their long and testing tour. F/Lt Leslie Hay 'Uncle Will', will never forget that very special trip:

"Then came our last operation, the crews 35th, and my 36th including the second dickey trip with F/O Brady. We were again quite worked up, though trying not to show it. We had seen good friends go on their 28th and 35th ops which meant that luck had a hand in it. The trip to Bohlen, was rather similar to the one that would have been our last had we finished at 30. It too was mostly cloud flying, but the Pathfinders were able to mark and we bombed without incident. Of course we were most careful on the long flight back and took no chances with fighters - flying time 9hrs 50mins.

On arrival back at base, I called up control for a landing position; 'Hello Oilgrease this is Aloft U-Uncle, permission to land please', but got no reply - I tried again and this time was given a landing number. Other crews on the circuit then broke R/T regulations to say 'good show' and 'well done!', It was very nice, and was the start of an attitude which we didn't know existed but was now to reveal itself. "I later found out that the girls in flying control kept a list of the trips done by each crew; as it had been quite a while since anyone had managed to complete a tour, they were quite excited by our return and were so busy doing a little dance in the control tower, that they omitted to answer my first call.

Now all we had to do was to get down in one piece. I suppose that I must have taken more care than usual, as I didn't feel the wheels touch the ground. Rather different from usual when you are so tired that you just drop her in. We were elated, and I seem to remember the bomb aimer kissing the ground when we got out - time was 02.55hrs in the early chilled hours of Tuesday 6th March.

Back at de-briefing everybody was coming up and shaking our hands, but it didn't end there. I discovered that nearly every section, ground crew, armourers, transport, parachutes, mess staff and stores... all, like the flying control girls, kept a record of each crew's trips and for days afterwards many personnel, who were strangers to me would stop and offer their congratulations.
It was embarrassing and certainly very touching, but a great revelation as it showed how everyone, however humble their position and job, really felt part of the squadron of which we, the flying personnel, were perhaps the image. They had all contributed to the effort in their own way ... and did it so very well!"

6/7 March, 1945; SASSNITZ: The target was a small port on the island of Rugen in the Baltic. 5 Group dispatched 191 Lancasters and 7 Mosquitoes, of which 13 Lancasters were from 49 Squadron.

F/O Les Hammond RAAF returned early in SW265 when fuel was discovered leaking, and the tank was practically dry:

"I considered that the length of trip, high air speeds, possibility of intruder activity on return and perhaps an emergency landing en route, necessitated a return to base."

Again, three new crews were operating with the squadron; they were skippered by F/O Whent (SW274), F/O Perkins (PB373) and F/Lt Babb (ME471). The attack was successful with much damage being done to the northern part of the town. At de-brief, F/O Hytch (RA531) and crew reported:

"Bombed from 8,600 feet at 23.02hrs - Red T/I's appeared to be well placed. Several ships seen in and outside the harbour; 1 large ship at southern end of breakwater - Successful."

One Lancaster failed to return - all 49's were safe.

7/8 March, 1945; HARBURG: Oil was the target, when 234 Lancasters and 7 Mosquitoes of 5 Group visited Harburg. The bombing results were good, with extensive damage being caused, but the cost was high with 16 Lancaster crews failing to return to their bases.

The squadron dispatched 18 Lancasters on the raid, F/O Littley (PB373) and crew being the first away at 17.40hrs. 49 Squadron had one aircraft fail to return plus an airman killed, and another posted missing from a second aircraft.

STILL ALIVE AND KICKING

The following is part of diarist, Jack Shearing's (F/Lt Mellor's crew) entry, regarding his crew's 17th operation; the trip to Harburg on the night of Wednesday 7 March, 1945:

"When we started our bombing run, all hell started up; we bombed and 20 seconds later we were hit by flak - the whole kite (PB349) shuddered. The run out of the target was a nightmare, we saw 5 confirmed Lancs go down, one which a parachute came out of -saw several other kites that were probables. The flak was deadly, mainly light stuff sent up in a hosepipe form and fighters were all around.

Searchlights (about 50 in all) were ineffective, but we could quite understand there being 700 guns in the target area!

We eventually got back to base; luckily the bad weather stopped the intruders, and landed after being airborne for 7 hours. On getting out of the kite, I was really shaken to see the hole in the port wing; it was mainly in the aileron but there were other holes including one through No 3 tank. I could get through the hole easily and I realise just how lucky we were.

We heard there were 5 kites missing from our station - 4 from 189 Squadron. Stark's crew was missing, which shook us all up; Johnny Yeoman, Gus Lovett, Paddy Gilbert and Fred Brennan the engineer were all wizard blokes and Starky too. After a meal we went back to the hut; 'Castille' (Ron Knight, F/O Elkington's W/OP) came in late... I woke up... he was in a terrible state (his battledress was saturated in Chesnutt's blood)... he said they were hit by flak on the way to the target and Cyril Chesnut was badly hit, dying just after (in Ron's arms) and Pat O'Keefe went out of the front hatch which was missing, but as his chute was gone and his helmet left, we presumed he baled out... although there was blood on his oxygen mask. Elkington was hit in the leg but got the kite back OK... It made us all realise the horrors of war and realise how lucky we were still to be kicking."

Australian pilot, 23 year old F/O Roussel Stark, with four of his fellow crew members were sadly killed, and are buried in Becklingen War Cemetery; the remaining three members became P.o.Ws.

FTR PB537	F/O R.W.G. Stark RAAF	Pilot	(Killed)
(EA-X)	Sgt J.F. Brennan RAAF	F/E	(P.o.W.)
'B'Flt	W/O J.C. Yeoman RAAF	NAV	(P.o.W.)
	F/S A.T.J. Lovett RAAF	W/AG	(Killed)
	Sgt R.C. Gilbert	A/G	(Killed)
Crew on their	W/O R.M. Bairnsfather RAAF	B/A	(Killed)
13th operation	Sgt J.R. Dixon	A/G	(P.o.W.)

Wireless op and diarist Jack Shearing, a lifetime supporter of Charlton Athletic! (J. Shearing)

F/Sgt Cyril Chesnut F/E aged 25, who was killed when his aircraft (ME471) was hit by flak, now rests in Torquay Cemetery. Bomb aimer, Sgt Daniel O'Keefe aged 20, (same crew) also died and is buried in Becklingen War Cemetery; their aircraft was piloted by F/O Elkington, who was wounded. Next day, Jack Shearing added to his diary:

"Got up about 11; had a pretty rough night so was glad to get up. 'Castille' (Ron Knight) seemed better for his sleep and told us all the gen about the previous night; it must have been tough for them. Went down to the mess and after lunch played darts in the ante room with Lefty. Went down to the flights on the hybrid (bike) then to the R&I hanger to see 'Howe'. Besides the big hole in the aileron, there were several others in the mainplane and they had got the tanks out already. Also saw Elkington's kite (ME471) but although it was damaged nearly as badly as ours, it was hit in more vital places."

During the afternoon, Jack should have gone to a lecture in his section, but it 'never came off'. So after tea, along with three others, he went down to Brant Broughton on his bike. There wasn't a dance on at the 'Red Lion' so they got on the dart board. A visit to the 'Generous Briton' and a chat with Auntie Clare and Edith until closing time, before cycling home to a sausage sandwich supper cooked in the hut... such was the life of the 'bomber boys', death and destruction one night followed the next by drinks and darts with the locals.

11 March, 1945; ESSEN (DAYLIGHT): After a three-day stand down, 5 Group was alerted for operations involving all the Groups in Bomber Command; a force of 1,079 bombers were being dispatched against Essen.
This constituted the largest number of aircraft sent to one target so far in the war.

But while aircrew still slumbered (awaiting their early call), over at Bridgend in Wales, 66 Germans were breaking out of their PoW camp. The escapees emerged into a ploughed field at 04.00hrs after scrambling along a 45 ft long tunnel. By nightfall, 43 had been recaptured as police, former Home Guards and Land Girls searched 100 square miles.

Later that morning, 49 Squadron was required to send 14 aircraft to Essen of which all were safely airborne from Fulbeck by 12.05hrs. The squadron arrived over a cloud-covered target around 15.20hrs and all 49's crews completed successful bombing attacks from approximately 17,000ft.

This was the last of many raids carried out on Essen by the RAF, and as the bombers turned for home they left behind a totally ruined city.

Three Lancasters failed to return from the trip, but all 49's aircraft regained Fulbeck; F/O Le Marquand (RF179) and crew were the last to touch down at 17.26hrs.

Note: 'Tommy' Thompson, mid-upper gunner in F/O Carlyle's crew (PB361), completed his second tour on this trip

12 March, 1945; DORTMUND (DAYLIGHT): Almost a repeat of the previous day's attack - but this time it was a cloud-cloaked Dortmund that received the devastation from a record 4,851 tons of bombs dropped by 1,108 aircraft.

Again, 49 Squadron had 14 Lancasters airborne; all reported successful sorties, with the exception of F/Lt Babb (NG352) and crew who aborted their attack over the target (reason un-confirmed); they jettisoned J-Jig's bomb load of 1x4000 LB HC and 16x500 LB MC's in the North Sea.

The force suffered the loss of 2 Lancasters; F/O Fisher RAAF later reported: "A/c seen going down in spiral on starboard" but all 49's aircraft had returned safely to base by 19.24hrs."

14/15 March, 1945; LUTZKENDORF: On Wednesday night, 14 March, 5 Group reverted to its solo efforts, sending 244 Lancasters and 11 Mosquitoes to attack the Wintershall synthetic-oil refinery at Lutzkendorf near Leipzig. Group requested a maximum effort, and 49 was able to provide 20 aircraft; F/O Littley (PB373) and crew were first away at 16.41hrs.

The bombers were confronted by extremely aggressive and accurate defences, with the result that 18 Lancasters failed to return (this represented 7.4 per cent of the Lancaster force). 49 Squadron did not escape the onslaught, with several aircraft receiving damage. F/O Littley (PB373) and crew were attacked by a Ju88 whilst on their bombing run; mid upper gunner Jim Field describes their brief combat:

"On his first attack, the German hit our two outer engines; the rear gunner (Sgt Fallon from Northern Ireland) shouted for the skipper to corkscrew, whilst we both opened fire on the enemy... Jack (skipper) took our Lancaster right down to the deck as we made our escape. We managed to get safely home and landed at the Pathfinder base of Wyton. At de-brief we gunners claimed the Ju88 as a 'probable'."

The returning 5 Group Lancasters received diversion orders away from their Lincolnshire bases; 49 Squadron had 10 aircraft land at Wyton, 8 at Gaydon and F/O Doug Whent (ME454) and crew dropped E-Easy in at Alconbury for an early breakfast with the Yanks. This left one squadron aircraft outstanding; F/Lt Joe McPhee RCAF (RF153) and crew, consisting of five Canadians and two British, had failed to return. Sadly, six of the crew were later confirmed as killed, whilst F/Sgt 'Corky' Corrigan RCAF (rear gunner) had escaped death and indeed custody, turning up at Fulbeck a few weeks later. The other six members of the crew are buried alongside each other in the Berlin War Cemetery.

CORKY'S MOTOR BIKE

'Corky' Corrigan was a tough looking, swarthy Canadian NCO in fellow Canadian Joe McPhee's crew. He happened to be the proud owner of a motor bike, which he kept outside his crew's hut at Fulbeck. When he failed to return from the Lutzkendorf trip, other motor bike owners on the squadron virtually stripped Corrigan's machine for spare parts.

When F/Sgt Corrigan returned 'out of the blue' back at Fulbeck, having escaped from the Germans... mysteriously all the missing spare parts suddenly reappeared on his motor cycle overnight.

FTR RF153	F/L J.N. McPhee RCAF	Pilot	(Killed)
(EA-K)	Sgt P.F. Ivett	F/E	(Killed)
'A'Flt	F/O G.A. Robinson RCAF	NAV	(Killed)
	F/S T.G.W. Dew	W/OP	(Killed)
	F/S E.G.C. Richards RCAF	A/G	(Killed)
Crew on their	F/O R.F. Thompson RCAF	A/B	(Killed)
17th operation	F/S G.K. Corrigan RCAF	A/G	(Evader)

16/17 March, 1945; WÜRZBURG: With all diverted aircraft gathered safely in, the squadron prepared to send 17 aircraft on the 5 Group attack to the virgin target of Würzburg.

The first aircraft took off at 17.53hrs, piloted by F/O Johnston (SW274). Two new crews were operating for the first time with the squadron; F/O Tommy Hawkins RAAF (PB349) and crew (who had formerly flown Stirlings in the Med) were charged with the responsibility of taking the venerable 'Howe' to Germany and back without harm. The second new crew was captained by F/O Bob Souter RNZAF (PB455); Bob had previously flown Wellingtons in the Western Desert with 108 Squadron, where he completed 39 operations; the last being over El Alamein on 1st Nov 1942.

After serving as a screen pilot at 26 OTU Wing, Bob volunteered for ops again and was posted to Balderton in 5 Group where he picked up a new crew who had lost their own skipper due to sickness. Following a long 3 months at Wigsley HCU (bad winter weather), Bob and crew eventually arrived at Fulbeck in early March, 1945.

The operation proved to be a devastating attack for Würzburg, by 225 Lancasters and 11 Mosquitoes of 5 Group. Post-war reports suggest that almost 90 per cent of the built-up area was destroyed. 6 Lancasters failed to return, of which 2 belonged to 49 Squadron:

F/O John Gibson (NG352) and crew were shot down in the target area; two members of the crew were killed, including F/O Edwards Nav, and mid/upper gunner Sgt Austin Finnerty, who died as a result of the fire inside the Lancaster.

WAR CRIME

Authors note: The details in the following account come from a newspaper cutting supplied by Peter Roberts, a fellow crew member of F/Sgt Hughes. I have not attempted in any way to elaborate or embellish the details of this cold-blooded murder; I leave the reader to reconcile this grievous crime for themselves:

> *'A third member of F/O Gibson's crew, F/Sgt Don Hughes, managed to escape from the burning aircraft successfully by parachute, landing by the banks of the River Main. In the morning he was found by two clergymen hiding in the church sacristy of Elbelstadt. He was handed over to a doctor who in turn took him to the Town Hall where he was interrogated.*
>
> *At 07.30 on Sunday 18th March, after two days in the Police cells, Don was removed from the cells by SS Kriminal-Sekretar Joseph Axt of the Würzburg Criminal Police and Obersekretar Johann Weber. He was then marched to the river, where Axt shot him in the back before throwing his body in the river; his body was recovered from the river next morning. 'Axt and Weber were charged before a military court at Iserlohn on June 11th, 1946, and both were convicted. Axt was sentenced to death by shooting, and Weber to 20 years imprisonment.'*

Peter Roberts (F/E in the crew) gives this account of his own survival and finally his repatriation:

"Most of our trips were at night, and with the Army now well into France and Holland, one thing that stands out in my memory is that you could always see the 'front line'; on the German side not a light to be seen but on our side, hundreds of lights, which we reckon were the soldiers brewing up - 'sod the shells, where's the tea?'

On the night of Friday 16 March, we arrived in the target area a little too early for the Pathfinders. I was just pouring a cup of tea out of the flask, when suddenly all hell let loose as cannon shells ripped into J-Jig. I had seen on previous raids that when fire started on a Lanc, you had about 10 seconds to get out - our Canadian bomb aimer (Sgt Henderson) was having trouble getting the front hatch open, so I went to help him... smoke and flames were everywhere!

I came down by parachute, and landed painfully on a wall. I managed to stay free for three days, frightened to death, before being found in a haystack by German Home Guard. I was taken to a village prison where I spent the night. In the morning I was marched to the Civil prison by a member of the German Home Guard who turned up in his uniform complete with spiked helmet from the First World War - quiet a shock.

I was placed in three civil prisons altogether, including Stuttgart. Finally I was sent to Stalag 5A Ludwigsberg, spending four weeks with American PoW's from the Battle of the Bulge. General Patton's Army soon swept in and liberated us - my first meal was cream of wheat cereal and '10' fried eggs with pork... talk about being ill! I was also given 3x1500 packs of 'Lucky Strike'.

At the US camp, the Americans pulled up a whole string of wagons with showers, toilets, baths etc. etc... each PoW went in at one end and came out a new man at the other! Afterwards, we were taken to Rheims in France and flown home in Dakotas."

Postscript: After the war, the controversy over the Dresden raid had a very upsetting effect on Sgt Henderson RCAF, the crew's surviving bomb aimer. He subsequently became a missionary in India; unfortunately he has since passed away.

Four members of F/O Doug Whent's (ME454) crew survived being brought down. Sadly, Sgt Frank Haylock flight engineer, and air gunner Sgt George Leeke were killed and are now buried in Choley War Cemetery, France. Sgt Bert Darbyshire has no known grave but is remembered on the Runnymede Memorial.

The remaining aircraft from the squadron were all safely back at Fulbeck by 02.11hrs, F/O Soutar and crew being the last to land.

FTR NG352	F/O J.B. Gibson	Pilot	(P.o.W.)
(EA-J)	Sgt G.P. Roberts	F/E	(P.o.W.)
'A'Flt	F/O D. Edwards	NAV	(P.o.W.)
	F/S D.J. Hughes	W/OP	(Murdered)
	Sgt A. Finnerty	A/G	(Killed)
Crew on their	Sgt R.M. Henderson RCAF	B/A	(P.o.W.)
13th operation	Sgt J. Evans	A/G	(P.o.W.)
FTR ME454	F/O D.I. Whent	Pilot	(Survivor)
(EA-E)	Sgt F.R. Haylock	F/E	(Killed)
'A'Flt	Sgt F.P. Anderson	NAV	(Survivor)
	F/S R.H. Usher	W/OP	(Survivor)
	Sgt G.C. Leeke	A/G	(Killed)
Crew on their	Sgt E.J. Sullivan	B/A	(Survivor)
4th operation	Sgt H. Darbyshire	A/G	(Missing)

20/21 March, 1945; BOHLEN: Post operational reports indicated that this had been an accurate and very effective raid by 224 Lancasters and 11 Mosquitoes, all from 5 Group. But 49 Squadron crews, who returned to Fulbeck just before breakfast on Wednesday 21 March, tended to give a less optimistic evaluation of their night's work. F/O Le Marquand (RF179) reported: *"Controller appeared to have some doubt about accuracy of the marking but called the force in to bomb the concentration of red and yellow T.I's."*

F/O Fricker RAAF (PB433) compounded the above when he stated: *"Master bomber uncertain as to accuracy of markers!"*

F/O Watson (ME308) also found that: *"The marker force had some difficulty in marking - lacked concentrated bombing."*

F /Lt Williams (ME322) concluded his de-briefing with the following: *"Marking on time but instructions were slow in coming through - some crews bombed before time. Attack not considered successful."*

The 16 crews dispatched by 49 Squadron all completed successful sorties and despite their reservations, the synthetic oil plant was put out of commission and was still inactive when captured by American ground forces several weeks later. During briefing for the operation, intelligence had informed crews that defences in the target area would consist of 118 heavy flak guns and 27 light flak guns, assisted by 25 searchlights - 5 Group lost 9 Lancaster crews.

MARCH 1945

THE RELUCTANT LANC

In the course of collecting information for this book, several unexplained events have been related by veterans when interviewed. Fulbeck may have been the home of 49 Squadron for a relatively short period of time, but it did seem to have played host to an unusual amount of strange happenings. The following mystery was revealed to me in a letter from former pilot Tom Hawkins of Melbourne, Australia; Tom writes:

"This particular day started like most others; our normal practice after breakfast was to go to the Flights and find out what the flying programme was for the day. The big question each time 'Is there a war on tonight?' closely followed by 'Are we on?' and the answer to this determined what our activities would be for the remainder of the day. As it happened, there was an operation planned for that night, and our names were down for it. So we slipped into our usual ops routine.

However, for the first time, something was niggling at me and I did not feel at ease. This feeling stayed with me during the day and by briefing time I was quite unsettled. Briefing over, we collected our gear and waited for the crew bus to take us out to our aircraft. By this time I was feeling most despondent but had not mentioned anything to my crew and do not know to this day if they were aware of it or not. On arrival at the aircraft we clambered aboard, each doing his own checks and settling in. Still with this feeling of deep foreboding, I slid open the sliding window at my left shoulder and gave the thumbs up for the ground crew to plug in the trolley acc and to stand by for starting.

Ken (Sgt Symonds F/E) and I went through the starting drill and I pressed the button for the starboard inner. The prop turned over several times but the engine would not fire. After waiting the appropriate time, I tried again and the same thing happened. As both inboard engines drove pumps for the main hydraulic and pneumatic systems and also ran a 1500 watt generator each, we next tried the port inner. This too failed to start even though the starter motor was turning the prop at normal speed. A second try also failed.

By this time, the squadron was on the move and the first aircraft were approaching the take-off point. With visions of being the last off, I signalled the ground crew that the port outer would be the next and anxiously pressed the starter.

The prop turned slowly many times but would not spring into life. A small group had gathered near the aircraft by now to watch and when the starboard outer refused to fire Ken and I looked at each other in disbelief. As I leaned out of the window to suggest another trolley acc, and try the starboard inner again, the Wingco drew up in his Hillman van and demanded to know what was going on.

From the cockpit I told him that the engines would not start and he immediately ordered us out of the aircraft and sent the fitters in. The squadron was well on its way by now and we stood in a group nearby wondering what was going on. My feelings by now were so mixed as to be beyond description and I watched in stunned silence as the ground crew attempted to start each engine in turn as we had done without success. There were no reserve aircraft that night, so the Wingco scrubbed our trip and a crew bus was called for.

To the others in the crew it was a relief not to go after such an inauspicious start, but to me I felt that an enormous load had been lifted from somewhere deep within me and it was with a considerable feeling of relief that I went to bed that night. We flew on ops the following night and apart from the usual nervous anticipation that everyone has, there was no sense of despair as on the previous night, and it never happened again.

To the best of my knowledge the reason for the failure was never officially explained and there were no problems with the aircraft on the following day, so the big question remains... why? My personal feeling is that, never having at any time experienced even one occasion during my RAAF or RAF service when an engine has failed to start... the reason for four failing at the one time must be the result of a quite extraordinary set of circumstances and this coupled with the premonition that preceded this... it points directly towards the supernatural!

I was brought up in a Christian home and know of a guiding power in peoples lives, but my lifestyle at this time was not particularly in keeping with the traditions - yet for some reason it is apparent that we were not meant to operate that night... so the engines were prevented from being started rather than they were not able to start, especially as there were no problems in the morning.

If we were spared for some reason, for some involvement in something later in life, I still do not know what it is as I have not achieved anything that I consider to be especially worthwhile in the fifty years since. Maybe it was not for me but for someone else in the crew. Oodles of possibilities but no matter which way we turn... we are still faced with the elusive WHY?"

Note: The aircraft involved has not been identified conclusively, but Tom feels it may have been SW274 G-George; the same aircraft in which mid-upper gunner Sgt Ron Wiggins lost his life in 8/9 Feb 1945. SW274 was 'given' to 619 Squadron on 4 April 45, being replaced by PB875 G-George.

Fulbeck spring 1945: Motor cycle enthusiast, F/O Tom Hawkins RAAF astride an overhead-cam Norton which he has just paid £10 for. Bought as a non-runner, a quick diagnosis found that the throttle slide was stuck open; a slight repair job and the engine roared into life. What would this classic machine be worth today? (T.C.Hawkins)

MARCH 1945

21/22 March, 1945; HAMBURG: A moderate 5 Group force of 151 Lancasters and 8 Mosquitoes made an accurate attack on Hamburg's oil refinery. The target produced 275,000 tons per year of high octane aviation fuel, much of which was held in storage tanks on site.

Using runway 23 (Fulbeck's main runway), the first of 15 aircraft from 49 Squadron began taking off at 01.04hrs on Thursday 22nd. W/Cmdr 'Buzz' Botting piloted (PB907) Q-Queenie on the operation. All 49's crews accomplished successful sorties, bombing from 15,000ft, with most crews reporting the huge clouds of black smoke. F/O Jack Winter (PB504) and crew were the last to land, slipping U-Uncle onto Fulbeck's runway threshold just after 07.16hrs.

Before take-off, crews had been pre-warned that the target would be defended by 130 heavy plus 20 light flak guns; searchlights would number about 30. In the end, 4 Lancaster crews failed to return from the trip; all 49's were safe.

23/24 March, 1945; WESEL: Wesel was an important German troop centre situated just behind the River Rhine. The British Army (under Montgomery) would start to cross the Rhine on the evening of 23 March preceded by a daylight attack by 80 Lancasters from 3 Group. Shortly before 22.30hrs another 195 Lancasters and 23 Pathfinder Mossies would again attack Wesel.

49 Squadron had 16 aircraft airborne for the second attack, including one new crew captained by F/Sgt Tolmie (SW265). The raid was carried out with success and without loss to any of the participating squadrons. F/O Lee (PB374) did report that the controller stated that bombs were falling on the west bank of the river (the British side). F/Lt Williams (ME322) confirms that he saw sticks of bombs burst on the western bank of the river.

Just one 49 crew failed to bomb; F/O Fricker RAAF (PB433) and crew nearly became a target themselves:

"One minute from the target, 3 a/c were seen at 500 feet above on the starboard beam and close quarter, closing in to directly above. I commenced a slight turn to port and thus failed to get the Red T.I's in the bomb sight graticule, so bomb aimer did not release bombs."

F/O Fricker returned to base, landing L-Love with a complete bomb load. F/O Le Marquand also returned with a one-thousand-pounder hung up. The following morning (Saturday 24), 21,000 British and American paratroopers and glidertroops (Operation Varsity) descended onto the fields around Wesel; the vanguard of Montgomery's assault by 1,250,000 Allied soldiers across the Rhine. For the remainder of March, 49 Squadron was 'stood down.'

MARCH 1945

OPERATIONAL SUMMARY - MARCH 1945

Date	Target	Desp	E/R	FTR	Remarks
3/4	LADBERGEN	12	1	-	F/O Mersey diverted
5/6	BOHLEN	19	-	-	
6/7	SASSNITZ	13	1	-	
7/8	HARBURG	18	-	1	F/O Stark FTR
11	ESSEN	14	-	-	Daylight
12	DORTMUND	14	-	-	Daylight
14/15	LUTZKENDORF	20	-	1	F/L McPhee FTR 19 a/c diverted
16/17	WÜRZBURG	17	-	2	F/O Whent FTR F/O Gibson FTR
20/21	BOHLEN	16	-	-	
21/22	HAMBURG	15	-	-	
23/24	WESEL	16	-	-	

Total number of sorties flown	174
Failed to return	4
Total tons of bombs of all types dropped	871.21
Operational hours flown during March 1945	1312.10
Non-operational hours flown during March 1945	365.15

HONOURS AND AWARDS - MARCH 1945

F/Lt G.M. Burns RCAF	D.F.C
F/S Tonkin (deceased)	D.F.M.
Sgt R.G. Robinson	D.F.M.
F/Lt G.H. Lee	D.F.C.
P/O E.F.S. Tarling	D.F.C.

Sir Archibald Sinclair visits R.A.F. Fulbeck. met by Air Vice Marshall Constantine, A.O.C. 5 Group and A/Cmdr Pope, Base Commander (Denis Orme)

Wing Commander Botting, O.C. 49 Squadron introduces Sir Archibald Sinclair to his crew. On the extreme left is G/Cpt L V Spencer. (Denis Orme)

APRIL 1945

April 1945 was to see another change of station for 49 Squadron. By Sunday 1st April, personnel were already aware that the squadron would be moving to RAF Syerston near Newark in Nottinghamshire. 49's move would take place towards the end of April, but 189 Squadron were set to leave Fulbeck on the 7th, moving over to RAF Bardney. It would appear that these proposed moves were not very popular among the personnel of both squadrons.

This was also the month in which 5 Group would launch its offensive operations before the final defeat of Hitler's Germany.

FLYING... ON THE GROUND

Being low-lying, RAF Fulbeck during the winter of 44/45 became renowned for its damp conditions. Crews returning from leave invariably found their bedding saturated from condensation and the base soon acquired the title of HMS Fulbeck! Now with the warmer spring days of April, moisture drawn from the ground in the daytime would soon turn into ground mist and fog as the temperature fell during the night.

One morning, Tom Gatfield and crew were walking around the perimeter on their way to do a D.I. and ground run on their allotted Lancaster. The mist which had formed during the previous evening still lingered just above the ground across the airfield. Suddenly one of the crew said; 'look at that Lanc... it looks as if it's flying!' - the undercarriage of this particular Lancaster as it sat at dispersal, was completely hidden by the mist, and the aircraft had the appearance of flying above cloud. As the crew passed by, another crew member was heard to remark that; 'if you ever see a Lanc that looks like it's flying on the ground - then that aircraft is fated'. Tom clearly recalls that on the following morning (after ops) that dispersal was ominously vacant!

4 April, 1945; NORDHAUSEN (DAYLIGHT): A total of 243 Lancasters led by 9 Mosquitoes (all 5 Group) attacked German barracks in the town of Nordhausen during the morning of Wednesday 4th; an attack made in support of our quickly advancing troops. From a bombing height of 16,000 feet, the target and town were both severely damaged. The squadron, led by W/Cmdr Botting, had 19 aircraft airborne including two new crews: F/Sgt Ingles (RF216) piloted J-Jig whilst F/O Westwood (PB361) and crew were last away from Fulbeck at 06.34hrs in R-Roger.

Flak or night fighter opposition proved non-existent, but one Lancaster from the force did fail to return, and it unfortunately came from 49 Squadron: F/O Arthur Fisher RAAF (ME308), aged 21, and crew were tragically all killed when their aircraft F-Fox, was seen to explode over the target. Pat Walters, pilot/rear gunner in F/Lt Bromfield's (PB484) crew had just rotated his turret in time to see the Lancaster disintegrate in a ball of flame; F/O Bob Soutar RNZAF (NX581) and crew also witnessed the explosion.

The remaining squadron aircraft landed back at Fulbeck around lunchtime, and during interrogation there was much conjecture and speculation as to the reason for the loss of F/O Fisher's crew. Some thought the aircraft had been hit by bombs from other Lancasters. Another theory was that the bomb load had been released all at once i.e. the 'Cookie' and 15x500lb bombs together, and that one of the 500 pounders may have touched the cookie. (The cookie being barrel shaped has a slower trajectory than the streamlined bombs, and should therefore always be released last).

Mustangs had escorted the force, although their presence wasn't always apparent. But Bob Soutar and crew were greatly impressed when a Lancaster on their port side developed engine problems and had to feather the prop; within a minute, a Mustang was sitting on his wing tip and escorted him back to the Rhine before disappearing again.

FTR ME308	F/O A.B. Fisher RAAF	Pilot	(Killed)
(EA-F)	Sgt D.G. Parbery	F/E	(Killed)
'A Flt'	F/S H.R. Sproston	NAV	(Killed)
	Sgt F.F. Sinclair	W/AG	(Killed)
	Sgt F. Wright	A/G	(Killed)
Crew on their	Sgt G.H. Simmonds	B/A	(Killed)
4th operation	F/S T.B. Moore	A/G	(Killed)

That evening on the base there was a Mess 'farewell' dance given by 189 Squadron. The beer and food were free, but the crews of 49 Squadron had been pre-warned of a possible daylight operation in the morning, so although the 'scoff' went down with haste, the beer was consumed only moderately. Inevitably, the following day's raid was scrubbed.

7/8 April, 1945; MOLBIS: A Force of 175 Lancasters and 11 Mosquitoes, all from 5 Group, set out for the benzol plant at Molbis just after 18.30hrs on Friday evening. The outward bound flight was carried out in the last remaining hours of daylight, and due to the rapid advances made by our ground troops, much of the flying time was spent over friendly liberated territory.

The squadron had 13 aircraft airborne; S/Ldr Walker (PB907) and crew being the first of the squadron's aircraft to arrive over the target at 23.00hrs. For the next 10 minutes, 5 Group Lancasters delivered an extremely effective attack from between 12 and 13,000 feet in clear conditions. All 49's crews carried out successful sorties. F/O Bob Perkins (RA531) and crew were the final aircraft to land back at Fulbeck, their S-Sugar touching down just after 02.47hrs. One crew later remarked what a treat it was to get through de-brief so quickly, with 189 not operating due to their move next day.

All of the squadron's aircraft had returned unscathed although F/Lt Len Mellor did receive rather a large jagged hole in H-Howe, due to 'rocket fire'. 5 Group did not lose a single aircraft from the raid, and later reports showed that the plant had been forced to cease all production.

APRIL 1945

'INSPIRED' LOW FLYING

During this period of operations, F/O Bob Soutar RNZAF remembers an incident which has left a lasting visual impression:

"On one particular trip, 5 Group had been briefed to return just above the cloud which had been forecast over southern England. The low cloud did not materialise where it should have been; instead there was ground fog, with numerous Church spires visible above it... but to the aircrew, this was cloud! and fly above it they must (as ordered). Scores of 5 Group Lancasters could be seen going round and around Church spires and anything else they could see.

No doubt we woke up most of southern England along the route, as it was just becoming daylight. It was a good excuse for some low flying... but we never had that briefing again."

8/9 April, 1945; LUTZKENDORF: 1 Group Lancasters had attacked the Lutzkendorf refinery the previous night achieving moderate success. Just after 18.00hrs on Sunday evening, 231 Lancasters and 11 Mosquitoes from Lincolnshire's 5 Group, set out to finish the job.

At Fulbeck, 49 Squadron crews assembled for the main briefing just after lunch. At the conclusion of the briefing, W/Cmdr Botting (with a piece of paper in his hand) announced that F/O Lee's crew was to stand down and that the reserve crew (F/O Cluer's) would take their place; he would tell the Lee crew the reason for their withdrawal after the squadron had taken off. John Aldridge, bomb aimer in F/O Lee's crew takes up the story:

"Roy Wilkins our pilot/rear gunner, had completed about 3 less trips than the rest of the crew (because of illness) and since the rear gunner in the reserve crew had contracted ear trouble, Roy volunteered to take his place. We all went out to the runway to see the lads take off and Roy gave us a thumbs up from his rear turret.

We reported to the Wing Co and he told us we were tour expired since the signal he had received during briefing had reduced the number of operations required from 36 to 33. That night we all went up to the 'Hare and Hounds' in Fulbeck village for a drink before rolling back into our hut. Although we never had the pleasure of knowingly flying our last op, the feeling of having finished was never the less fantastic.

Next morning, Roy's bed was still empty and we thought he may have landed elsewhere - but nothing more was ever heard of him or the crew with which he was flying."

Roy's loss was a very tragic experience for his fellow crew members coming right at the end of a long and distinguished tour. Now, every year, at least one of Roy's surviving crew mates visits the Runnymede Memorial, where on panel 273 is the name of F/Sgt R.E. Wilkins - gone but never forgotten.

FOUR LEAFED CLOVER

There is an unusual footnote to the sad loss of Sgt Roy Wilkins, and indeed F/O Cluer's crew. When John Aldridge mentioned that his crew went to wave the lads off, Sgt Pollington (the gunner with ear infection) came along with the Lee crew. Sitting on the grass on this pleasant early spring evening, awaiting F/O Roger Cluer to swing N-Nuts onto the main runway, they idly picked clover - Sgt Pollington actually picked 3 four-leafed clover in succession!!! Laughingly the Lee crew all remarked 'you lucky bas---d... it looks like your crew will get the chop tonight'. Many a true word spoken in jest!

The raid itself was a total success with the refinery being rendered inactive. The cost had been 6 Lancasters and their crews. Already mentioned was the loss of F/O Cluer's crew, but a second aircraft from the squadron also failed to return: F/O 'Polly' Perkins (RA531) and crew were brought down over Germany; there were no survivors. The crew now rest together in the Berlin War Cemetery; Sgt Bernard Manning the mid-upper gunner was only 19 years old and the rear gunner, F/Sgt Dennis Hull was just 18. Again perhaps 'fate' had been at work, for their skipper, F/O Robert Perkins, the son of a Lincolnshire farmer, had only recently confided to a fellow pilot, that he 'knew' he was not going to survive the war.

Of the 19 aircraft dispatched, the remaining 17 landed back at a misty Fulbeck just after 02.00hrs on Monday 9th. Last to land was F/O Weston's (ME491) crew in P-Peter at 02.47hrs.

FTR RA531	F/O R.G. Perkins	Pilot	(Killed)
(EA-S)	Sgt H. Prust	F/E	(Killed)
'B Flt'	F/S P.J. Warrington	NAV	(Killed)
	F/S G.R. Wall	W/AG	(Killed)
	Sgt B.C. Manning	A/G	(Killed)
Crew on their	F/S J.E. Wilkinson	A/B	(Killed)
9th operation	F/S D.R. Hull	A/G	(Killed)

FTR PB374	F/O R. Cluer	Pilot	(Missing)
(EA-N)	Sgt P. Lipp	F/E	(Missing)
'B Flt'	Sgt P.F.C. Jackson	NAV	(Missing)
	F/S J.H. McGuigan	W/OP	(Missing)
Most of the	Sgt G.A. McLennan	A/G	(Missing)
crew on their	F/O M.R. McKay RCAF	A/B	(Missing)
8th operation	F/S R.E. Wilkins	A/G	(Missing)

On the morning of Monday 9 April, a thick mist hung over Fulbeck airfield. The M/T section was in bit of a panic as the Lancasters had all been parked on different dispersals. This could have been due to the squadron returning in misty conditions the previous night and being directed into the nearest available dispersal.

The other alternative could be that whilst the squadron's aircraft were visiting Lutzkendorf, some of 49's ground crew may have obtained permission to relocate into several of 189's vacated dispersals which were positioned nearer to the main site.

11 April, 1945: During the morning of Wednesday 11th, each Lancaster received 2,000 gallons of fuel and armourers loaded them with one 'Cookie' plus 10x500 pounders. After lunch the flying programme was posted. At briefing, crews learned that their target was the great Leuna oil plant at Mersberg near Leipzig. They also received a cautionary warning that it was still heavily defended by 250 heavy flak guns. H-Hour was set for 23.00hrs so much of the outward journey would be in daylight.

With crews already out at their aircraft, pilots gave the engines a final ground run... but then just as everyone was set to go, red flares shot up into the threatening skies scrubbing the operation. As if on cue, the heavens suddenly opened and the rain came pouring down. On the 14th, the kites were bombed up yet again, only for the operation to be cancelled... on Sunday 15th, crews were in main briefing when the planned trip to Pilsen was scrubbed due to poor visibility predicted over the target.

BRIEF ENCOUNTER

The following anecdote happened during take-off for a practice flight during the spring of 1945; F/Lt Les Hammond recalls his phonetic interchange with one of Fulbeck's Control Tower WAAF's:

"I called up the tower for permission to take-off using the old word L-London... the WAAF, in a very disdainful tone answered 'Clear take-off L-Love!' with a heavy accent on Love... to which I replied, Thanks Love... taking off L for Leather!!"

F/O Tom Hawkins and crew stop to take a quick snapshot as they travel from Fulbeck to Grantham, for a night out. The photograph is taken at the junction of the A607 with the A153; the road to the left leads to Fulbeck via Carlton Scroop and Caythorpe. The road behind them heads for Sleaford via Ancaster and Wilsford. (T.C. Hawkins)

16/17 April, 1945; PILSEN: The previous day's aborted operation was on the programme for Monday 16th. Pilsen, home of the Skoda works, was to receive a visit from 222 Lancasters and 11 Mosquitoes of 5 Group. The aiming point was the marshalling yards, with H-Hour set at 04.00hrs and the bombing height around 13,000ft.

On what would turn out to be the last bombing operation flown by 49 (or any other squadron) from Fulbeck, F/Lt Len Mellor (PB349) and crew in old 'Howe' led the squadron away at 23.38hrs. Following, were 13 other aircraft:

PB559	F/L Hammond;	PB479	F/S Ingles;	PB226	F/O Eltis;		
PB875	F/O Johnson;	PB433	F/O Branch RAAF;	PB373	F/O Littley;		
PB907	F/O Westwood;	PB484	F/L Bromfield;	PB504	F/O Elkington;		
PB571	F/L Milburn;	NX581	F/O Dickson;	PB455	F/O Weston;		
RF179	F/L Wright; (new crew)						

Unfortunately, F/Lt Mellor had to abort his attack when only 50 miles from the target - the starboard outer engine started leaking oil and had to be feathered. Uncertain that he could maintain bombing height, the pilot reluctantly turned for home. Meanwhile 5 Group aircraft completed a successful attack on the railway yards in Pilsen, although some bomb aimers were hampered by smoke, which at times obliterated the markers. 'Large explosions and fires' plus 'good control' were some of the comments made at de-brief by returning crews.

DOWN ON BOSCOMBE DOWN

On the return leg, the Germans were jamming Group's frequency terrifically. At the time, squadrons were being informed that diversions to other airfields were in operation. Some crews did not receive a clear order until contacting base, by which time they were back over England. Along with 463 & 467 RAAF Squadrons from Waddington, 49 was diverted to Boscombe Down, an experimental research drome on Salisbury Plain. As could be imagined, everything was disorganised as 43 crews descended on Boscombe at breakfast time on Tuesday 17th.

Norman Smith, navigator in F/Lt Hammond's B-Baker remembers well his crew's diversion to Boscombe:

"We came over the French coast on our way home after being silhouetted against low white cloud in the moonlight. If there had been fighters we would have been sitting ducks!

At Boscombe Down I met my sister, a W/Op WAAF and introduced her to my crew. Her turnout was immaculate, shining buttons etc. - her comment to us was 'Aren't you a scruffy lot'!"

After eating a meal, crews were told to 'hang around' and be ready to fly back to their own airfields as soon as weather permitted. This gave the curious airmen a golden opportunity to go exploring! The following account was written by Jack Shearing a few days later - some 50 years later, his contemporary comments make extremely interesting reading:

There were numerous types of kites about so we roamed about ad lib... we saw many new kites and ideas. A Lincoln naturally got a lot of attention but I was very disappointed in it. It was very ugly in design and looked like a collection of scrap metal... the nose particularly looked about 15 years out of date. The fuselage was longer but hardly wider than the Lanc, but the mid upper, a huge effort housed two 20 mil cannons and there were two remotely controlled .5 cannons in the nose. The engines, Merlin 68's had a huge cowling around them which made them appear like radials from head on. It seems definite that it was produced purely for duty in the Pacific.

Amongst the other kites I looked over were the Mitchell and Boston (death traps) 2 Buckinghams, a York (for freight carrying - an enormous fuselage). All fighter types, Spits, Hurries, Tempest, Typhoon, Corsair, Mustang, Thunderbolt. Saw a Barracuda and an Avenger - also a new naval fighter still on the secret list called a Firebrand, something like a Tempest with a radial engine and a revolutionary tail plane.

Saw a Lib and a Privateer, a Halifax (civvy version), a Lanc with 2 x .5's in the mid upper turret - a very interesting walk. I hear they also had every type of bomb there including the 12,000 and 22,000 pounders. Saw a Lincoln in the air - it looked quite decent but I am still not keen to convert.

Had to fly back with the Milburn crew to camp - our starboard-outer had now seized up. Got back to find the tour down to 30 so F/Lt Milburn had finished."

The squadron's aircraft had now all returned safely to base; of the 14 dispatched, on return 2 had landed back at Fulbeck, 11 at Boscombe Down and F/O Littley had put down at Manston.

At Fulbeck, the aircrew had another meal then headed for bed. There was a station bash on that night, so some did rise from their beds later. At the dance, in order to partake of the food, each airman had to be escorted by a female partner - so in order to choose a pretty WAAF, getting there on time was of the essence. In all, despite some rather fatigued aircrew, the dance turned out to be quite a lively affair.

IT'S ONE WAY TO WASH A LANC!

On 19 April, the squadron had received a stand down, so a flying programme of training was posted. At 11.47hrs, on that Thursday morning, F/O Dave Hytch (ME357) and crew took-off in C-Charlie bound for the Epperstone Bombing Range; from there they would proceed into the Wash to practice air sea firing. For air experience, the pilot offered to take along one of the aircraft's fitters, LAC Tyler.

During the afternoon, news filtered through to flights that the Hytch crew were missing - W/O Harley and crew landed and reported seeing a 'Lanc in the water'.

It later transpired that after completing their bombing practice, Dave Hytch proceeded to the air/sea firing area. Once there, the pilot reduced height to drop the flame float during which time he momentarily blacked out! He recovered in time to level out the aircraft which however struck and entered the water - the time was 13.20hrs.

All eight crew members successfully abandoned C-Charlie, (which sank within 3 minutes) and took to the dinghy. They were sighted adrift in the Wash, by an aircraft of the USAAF and later picked up by the coaster motor vessel "Northgate". which eventually landed them at Hull. The crew had spent 1 1/2 hours in the dinghy.

Author: These are purely my own thoughts, but one finds it difficult to dispel the image of eight men bobbing about in the sea, practicing and rehearsing, until word perfect, in order for them all to 'get the story right'!

Fortunately the whole incident had a happy outcome, with all involved being safely returned to Fulbeck that evening.

Ditched	**ME357**	F/O D.I. Hytch	Pilot	(Rescued)
(EA-C)		Sgt J. Dodgson	F/E	(Rescued)
'A Flt'		F/S T.S. Harrison	NAV	(Rescued)
		Sgt K. Scott	W/OP	(Rescued)
		F/S R.H. Williams RCAF	A/G	(Rescued)
		Sgt K. Read	B/A	(Rescued)
		Sgt L. Broadbent	A/G	(Rescued)
		LAC L. Tyler		(Rescued)

The day following the Hytch ditching in the Wash, seven aircraft from 'B' Flight were detailed for a Cross-country exercise... and as some were later to conclude, intent on a little mischief, as F/O Bob Soutar RNZAF recounts:

"It all happened on Friday 20 April when we were all at bit of a loose end. It was decided therefore that seven crews should be sent on a X-country exercise with a routing Fulbeck - Dartford - Brighton - Swindon and back to Fulbeck. The aircraft detailed were: F/O Robson (PB504) U; F/O Westwood (PB455) V; F/O Littley (PB373) O; F/O Weston RNZAF (ME491) P; F/O Smith RAAF (PB361) R; F/Lt Wright PB907) Q; and myself F/O Soutar in (PB571) Z.

U,V,O,P and R took off near enough to 14.00hrs but my aircraft 'Z' was unserviceable at the time so we were late away followed by F/Lt Wright and crew in 'Q'.

Now Brighton just happened to be a P.D.C. for Australian and New Zealand aircrew who were all waiting for a boat home. So it was understandable, there being an Aussie and a Kiwi as captains of two of the aircraft that they wanted to visit some of their fellow countrymen. As I understand it, four of the aircraft did some low flying along the coast... and over the piers at Brighton. Unfortunately for them, the District Air Provost Marshal was on the sea front and began to take some interest in the happenings, and began to write down some letters. At the same time, the fifth aircraft, that of Jack Littley 'O' and crew, began dropping toilet rolls out of the flare chute along Brighton prom... some landed near the DAPM! . All five then departed in the direction of Swindon.

When my crew arrived over Brighton there were no other aircraft to be seen, but F/Lt Wright arrived soon afterwards. I did a circuit of Brighton and then also departed for Swindom accompanied by F/Lt Wright."

(Author: 49 Squadron crews obviously thought that the Aussies and Kiwis would not be supplied with enough toilet paper for their long sea journey home, and were merely trying to relieve the situation)

This episode was to have far-reaching repercussions, as we shall see later, in June, 1945.

BERCHTESGADEN - BUT NOT YET

21 April, 1945: In his diary, Jack Shearing reflects on a Berchtesgaden that so nearly happened:

"The early call came at 2am and I got down for the operational meal which was at three. F/Lt Hammond's W/OP, Moses, had stayed out all night so I volunteered to fly with him - at least he had done 17 ops and I knew his rear gunner Ralph Menhinick.

The target was Berchtesgaden and only 5 picked squadrons were on the show. 617 and 9 Sqdns were on Hitler's Eyrie itself while 106, 463 and ourselves were on the SS Barracks. It was indeed an honour our squadron being one of the selected ones out of all Bomber Command. All the boys were really keen to go, I have never seen such enthusiasm; it was the real thing, a poke at Hitler and his bodyguards. God, every man women and child in the Allied Countries would have given anything to have had the chance to go on this trip."

But Jack and the boys were to be thwarted only minutes before take-off, as reds suddenly appeared over the control tower... the trip had been scrubbed. As Jack later put it (politely):

"I was cheesed right off!"

The aircrew retired back to bed, only to be recalled at 11.30hrs and briefed for an attack on the U-boat docks at Flensburg. Yet again the op was scrubbed, this time just following the main briefing. After tea, whilst some stayed in their huts and packed (ready for the move to Syerston in the morning) others took the opportunity to indulge in some heavy drinking.

THE FULBECK TRAGEDY

It happened shortly before 10.00hrs on that fateful Sunday morning of April 22nd, as 49 Squadron's Lancasters were taking off from Fulbeck for the last time, bound for their new home at RAF Syerston.

Some aircraft had already departed, but just as F/Lt Les Hammond was about to release the brakes on B-Baker he suddenly announced over the inter-com; 'so that's how a Lanc goes!' - his crew immediately looked in the direction of the main site where a pillar of fire and smoke marked the spot where a Lancaster had just plunged into the ground. Eric Read was an eyewitness to this ghastly accident:

"I had just left Flying Control and saw the whole thing as if in slow motion - the aircraft was 'shooting up' Fulbeck and was very low; it came from my right (heading north) and as the pilot pulled up, the tail hit the MT shed, bringing the aircraft down onto a large group of ground personnel. "The clothing store was demolished along with the private car belonging to S/Ldr Brydon. The fire crew was there in seconds but to no avail; I was asked to give evidence at the court of enquiry; it was all very sad and a long time ago, but some of the shocking images still remain in my memory."

Another witness, who also had a very close call was F/O Bill Ansell DFM - Bill had previously completed a tour with 166 Squadron, 1 Group. After a spell as an instructor, he was posted to the Bomber Command Film Unit, which had been at Fulbeck and was now moving with 49 Squadron to Syerston; Bill recalls:

"On Sunday 22 April, I missed death by inches when a Lancaster crashed almost on top of me. I was standing by a truck waiting to move off to Syerston when the Lancaster hit with a horrific rending crash, the huge ball of fire seared and almost burst my eyeballs. I broke all speed records with unbelievable heat scorching my back.

Sadly all in the aircraft were killed. The truck went up in flames, together with my log book and my glorious Crombie overcoat. I have just examined the charred remains of my log book for the first time in all these years."

The aircraft involved was piloted by F/O George Elkington (PB463), who hailed from Tonbridge in Kent. There were five other crew members onboard, and all were killed. The absent crew member was mid upper gunner, F/Sgt Logan, who must have considered himself to be the luckiest man alive that day.

The unfortunate ground staff who were killed, all belonged to 5015 Works Flight; it is believed they were on parade at the time.

FULBECK PARADE GROUND DISASTER - SUNDAY 22 APRIL 1945

ROLL OF HONOUR

	AC2	G.H.	Brenchley	
	AC1	R.J.	Clewley	
	LAC	J.H.	Davies	(died 23 April 1945)
	LAC	J.	Griffin	(died 28 April 1945)
	Sgt	L.C.	Hammond	
	Cpl	H.S.	Hancox	
	LAC	T.	McKie	(died 28 April 1945)
	LAC	L.	Masterman	
	LAC	S.	Mellows	(died 23 April 1945)
	LAC	P.	Moor	(died 8 May 1945)
	LAC	F.	Plumtree	
	LAC	J.W.	Rogers	
	LAC	E.	Shaw	
	F/L	G.	Wimpenny	
	LAC	W.	Wright	
Crashed PB463	F/O	G.F.	Elkington	Pilot
(EA-Y)	F/S	C.I.	Walker	F/E
'B Flt'	F/S	L.W.	Evans	NAV
	F/S	J.W.	Petch	W/OP
	F/O	H.	Macaulay	A/B
	F/S	M.J.C.	Garrett	P/A/G

The injured survivors from 5015 Works Flight included the following:

LAC	L.R.	Hassan	Injured
LAC	J.E.	Lambourn	Seriously injured
LAC	T.	Sarling	Dangerously injured but survived
AC1	J.	Weston	Dangerously injured but survived

Later in the day over at Syerston, once everyone had found a bed, a roll call was taken to see if any extra bods had been in the Lancaster that crashed. But in wartime, life has to carry on. The immediate task was to locate all the amenities on the new base - the initial verdict was; 'grub at the Mess very good and ultra clean after Fulbeck - the Station dance was wizard and there are some wizard WAAFs here!' By 23.00hrs that night, 49 Squadron had well and truly arrived and were settled in.

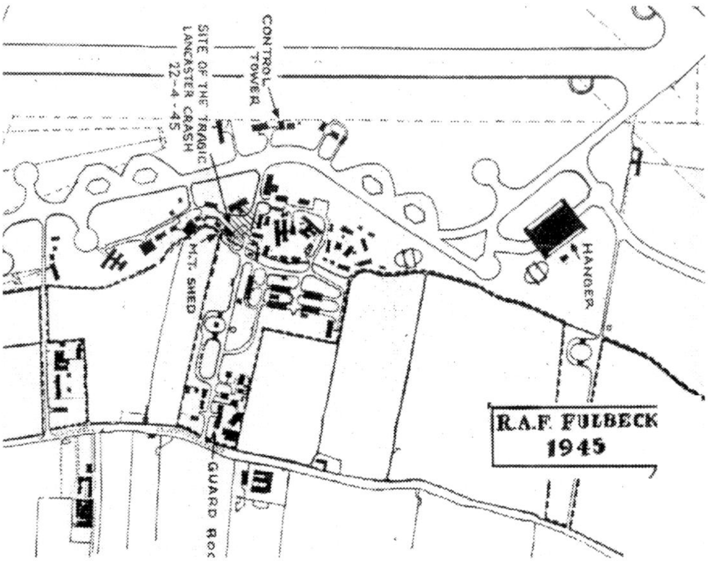

RAF Fulbeck, 1945: Site of the tragic Lancaster (PB463) crash on 22 April, 1945.

25 April, 1945; BERCHTESGADEN (DAYLIGHT): Crews had been pre-warned the previous evening of an early call for ops; in fact take-off was set for just after 04.00hrs. On what would turn out to be 49 Squadron's last bombing operation of the war (and the only bombing op flown by the squadron from Syerston) F/O Binns RCAF (PB406) and crew gunned L-Love down Syerston's main runway ahead of 11 other 49 Squadron Lancs; the time was 04.20hrs.

49 Squadron's ultimate operation was against Hitler's mountain retreat; the 'Eagles Nest' at Berchtesgaden. Seen here is just part of the 359 Lancaster stream flying over Walchen heading towards the target.
(T. C. Hawkins)

There were 359 Lancasters and 16 Mosquitoes from 1, 5 and 8 Groups dispatched against Hitler's 'Eagles Nest' and SS Barracks. Mist and snow on the ground made the targets difficult to identify, but bombing appeared to be effective. An extract from 49 Squadron's record book states: 'Wide bombing due to the difficult character of the surrounding country for map reading - it is considered that a more westerly run into the target would have been better.'

49 Squadron's Lancasters arrived over the target at 09.00hrs flying at about 14,800ft. The following are extracts from the de-brief reports given by each of the crews that took part:

F/O MacAulay (ME322): "Much bombing seen to fall to the N.NE of actual target and generally very scattered. Our own bombs straddled the barracks."

F/O Hawkins RAAF (PB559): "Explosions seen just after 09.00hrs - barracks seen - lots of smoke."

F/O Branch RAAF (PB479): "Brought bombs back - bombing very scattered. Red proximity marker not seen. Leader's speed was far too fast out of the target area causing straggling."

F/Sgt Ingles (PB383): "Unable to hit objective owing to flak hitting windscreen on point of release of bombs."

F/Lt Babb (PB226): "No red T.I's seen but saw a few overshoots. No cloud over target but it was very hazy and smoke from previous bombs covered most of the area."

F/O Johnston (PB875): "At bombing height (14,900ft) several aircraft were down below and in front of us. Bombing accurate."

F/Lt Wright (PB873): "The target was identified too late to release bombs - large numbers of bursts appeared scattered, mainly overshoots."

F/O Littley (PB373): "No red T.I's seen, bombing appeared well concentrated, but a few overshoots."

F/O Mersey: "Difficult to see target until overhead. Own bombs burst across target. 4 sticks in all seen to hit the barracks."

F/Lt Winter (PB504): "Explosions seen in woods north of the target - bombs seemed to be overshooting the barracks."

F/Lt Abbott (PB455): "No red T.I's were seen - much smoke to the west of barracks - uncertain whether from bombing or smoke screen."

F/O Binns RCAF (PB406): "Identification of target rather difficult. Bombing of barracks appeared effective. No markers seen."

Just after lunch, the first of 49's returning Lancasters entered Syerston's circuit; F/Sgt Ingles and crew in E-Easy touched down at 12.37hrs. F/O Jack Mersey and crew were the 11th to land at 12.55hrs, which left just one aircraft outstanding.

THE LAST BUS HOME

F/O Tom Hawkins RAAF (PB559) and crew had received flak damage to their starboard outer engine over Berchtesgaden. This forced them to shut the motor down, and as a result they could not keep up with the main stream. But Syerston's flying control did not have too much of an anxious wait; the overdue straggler, B-Baker, soon called up the tower requesting landing instructions, before joining the circuit on three engines. The pilot touched down perfectly at 13.20hrs and proceeded to trundle his mount around the peri-track, the warm spring sunshine glinting off the cockpit perspex. There to greet them at dispersal, as ever, was the conscientious groundcrew. B-Baker, her task completed, and with all her systems now closed down, settled back on her dispersal point, exhausted after labouring all the way back from Germany on three engines.

The disembarked crew soon lit up cigarettes and chatted with the ground boys, as Tom walked around the kite with the engine fitters to survey the damaged motor. The odour of hot oil mixed with spent aviation fuel... occasional clicks and ticks as cooling hot metal slowly contracted... the jovial banter of tension-relaxed voices... all these sounds mingled with the song of a skylark as she tunefully soared high above her nest close to the boundary fence. The tranquillity of this peaceful spring scene was interrupted only by the sound of the crewbus slowly whirring its way around the peri to the waiting crew.

The Dodge pulled up and the crew tossed their gear in the back before clambering aboard. Tommy Hawkins climbed up into the front cab with Dot; 'my crew let me know in no uncertain manner what they thought by thumping on the back of the cab all the way back to the flights!'

The great significance of this moment, could not be known to those acting it out at the time; for although during the next few days, 49 Squadron would be briefed for other bombing operations, these would all be scrubbed. Berchtesgaden had been the squadron's last aggressive action of the war... this was the last crew to come back, and they had caught the last bus home. Their driver, LACW Dot Everett braked to a halt outside Syerston's interrogation section, disgorging her cargo of boisterous young flyers... just as she had done so many times before, at Scampton, Fiskerton and Fulbeck.... For the record, the 'last crew' on the 'last bus home' comprised :

PB559	F/O	Tom Hawkins RAAF	Pilot
(EA-B)	Sgt	Ken Symonds	F/E
'A Flt'	F/S	Gubby Cable RAAF	NAV
	Sgt	Geoff Abernethy RAAF	W/OP
	Sgt	Paddy Millea	A/G
	F/S	Ron Arnold RAAF	B/A
	Sgt	Ken Reakes	A/G

Their Lancaster, B-Baker, had only recently arrived on squadron; it was part of a batch received from 460 RAAF Squadron, Binbrook. This unit had also been operating the AGLT "Village Inn" system, in 1 Group, but during the spring of 45, they surrendered all their AGLT aircraft to 49 Squadron in 5 Group.

26 April, 1945: At 09.00hrs, Squadron personnel were paraded and given a talk by W/Cmdr Botting. He mainly referred to the 'cold reception' 49 Squadron had received from the station establishment at Syerston. He also mentioned the Fulbeck crash, and said that the death toll had now reached 18, with 10 seriously injured.

Some crews were programmed for night-flying that evening, but during the late afternoon everyone was confined to camp and ops were posted for the following day.

27 April, 1945; 06.00hrs early call for operations. The aircraft were all fuelled with 1,400 gallons and loaded with 14x1000lbs of bombs; rumours were later confirmed that the target was Flensberg. At the specialist briefings, it was learnt that the squadrons were to fly out in loose gaggles; 49 Squadron was to fly its gaggle with 106 Squadron (Metheringham). On entering the main briefing crews were informed that the trip had been called off owing to the weather.

That evening, for those airmen wishing to visit the camp cinema, the main feature was 'The Desert Song'.

28 April, 1945: Another 'bullshit' parade was addressed by the Wingco, who stated that 49 Squadron was not looked upon with favourable eyes here at Syerston... and that we were to 'show them what we are made of!'

29 April, 1945: 15.00hrs - Aircrew were called to the main briefing room where W/Cmdr Botting gave a talk about VE Day, and how it would effect the squadron. He said that on the actual day (yet to be announced) everyone would be confined to camp. An announcement would then be made over the tannoy, giving details of parade timings - there will be an address by the Group Captain, followed by a Church service. In the evening, a camp dance for all ranks, and a bonfire was planned - all pistols were to be handed in!

30 April, 1945: Shortly after tea, the night-flying training was scrubbed, and all aircrew were confined to camp. The tannoy then announced that all armaments personnel were allowed out, but all those from the safety equipment section were to report for duty immediately. It was obvious to everyone on base, that the squadron was going to collect and repatriate Allied Prisoners of War.

APRIL 1945

F/O Hawkins RAAF (centre back row) and crew at Fulbeck circa spring 1945. (T.C. Hawkins)

OPERATIONAL SUMMARY - APRIL 1945

Date	Target	Desp	E/R	FTR	Remarks
4	NORDHAUSEN	19	-	1	F/O Fischer FTR
7/8	MOLBIS	13	-	-	
8/9	LUTZKENDORF	19	-	2	F/O Perkins FTR F/O Cluer FTR
16/17	PILSEN	14	-	-	12 a/c diverted
25	BERCHTESGADEN	12	-	-	**The Last Operation**

Total number of sorties flown	77
Failed to return	3 + 2c
Total tons of bombs of all types dropped	340.00
Operational hours flown during April 1945	560.15
Non-operational hours flown during April 1945	391.50

HONOURS AND AWARDS - APRIL 1945

F/Lt E. Edwards	D.F.C.
F/O D.J. Gibson	D.F.C.
F/O A.G. Squibb RCAF	D.F.C.
P/O E. Tomlin (deceased)	D.F.C.
F/O J. Barrie	D.F.C.
F/O J. Parkin	D.F.C.

MAY 1945

F/O Tom Hawkins RAAF and crew reluctantly return to dispersal after being recalled just before take-off for Exodus One. W/Cmdr 'Buzz' Botting made a late decision to go to Juvincourt and 'hijacked' their slot.

This photograph gives us an all too rare view of an AGLT equipped 49 Squadron Lancaster. (T.C. Hawkins)

The ending of hostilities in Europe was now almost a reality, and the repatriation of British and Commonwealth prisoners of war became a priority. With Transport Command still heavily involved in keeping military supply routes operating, it fell upon Bomber Command to undertake the task of bringing the boys home. Whilst 1 and 3 Groups embarked upon 'Operation Manna' (the dropping of food provisions to the population of the Netherlands) 5 Group prepared their Lancasters for troop carrying. With accommodation for up to 25 passengers, 'Operation Exodus' was put into operation at the very beginning of May.

OPERATION EXODUS

May 1, 1945: 49 Squadron detailed 10 aircraft for the first 'Exodus' trip, which involved flying to Juvincourt and returning with 'passengers' to Westcott. All 10 Lancasters became airborne by 14.45hrs. The flying programme included the following pilots and their crews:

"Q" W/C Botting	"B" S/L Walker	"G" F/O Branch	"P" F/O Binns	"U" F/O Mersey
"A" F/O MacAulay	"H" F/L Mellor	"K" F/O Fricker	"N" F/L Wright	"O" F/L Bromfield

THE WHITE CLIFFS OF HOME

Jack Shearing's diary yet again provides an invaluable insight into this operation, which many aircrew considered to be the most moving and rewarding experience of their wartime careers.

Tuesday, 1 May, 1945: *"Called at 03.00hrs and went up for our meal. Went to specialists' briefing after and got a lot of new gen. The signals procedure only differed from an op by the lack of Bombing winds and Controller. After picking up the PoW's we had to send a message to Base of ETA at Westcott and number of bods on board. After going into main briefing we heard the trip was put back so we returned to the billet for a couple of hours.*

Went up to briefing again. We heard now we were the only squadron left on!.. but it was put back another 3 hours. The Captains had careful briefing as no one had any idea what condition the boys would be in.

We got airborne and it was very bumpy; we went in low over France and saw the results of our bombing and advance. France looked very dead and desolate. The drome which had had a severe beating, was littered with wrecks of kites, and taxiing on metal strips was a bumpy business. We waited for our quota of PoW's to come along and noticed a number of Invaders (latest type of Boston) which were based there. "The boys were brought up in transport and all turned out to be Army bods, most of whom had been in Germany 5 years. One bod was captured in a Jerry Commando raid on the East Coast, the point being he was C3 (unfit for overseas). Another chap, who sat next to me, was a Channel Islander and after getting through Dunkirk was taken prisoner whilst on leave in Jersey when the Jerries invaded.

They all seemed in reasonable health and enjoyed the trip; none of them were ill. They were all very quiet and orderly, but when the English Coast came in sight the expressions on their faces as they took turns to look out, was something I shall remember all my life.
We landed at Westcott and had some 'free' tea and scoff at a YMCA canteen then came back to base. We had a meal and exchanged yarns and by then it was time to go to bed."

F/O Jack Branch RAAF (G-George) recalls:

"The ex-prisoners we collected were men of the 51st Highland Division who had been taken prisoner at Dunkirk. We made them as comfortable as possible in the aircraft. The crew kept them supplied with chocolates, and we flew low-level to keep them as warm as we could.

As we approached the coast of England, we brought as many as possible up front to see the 'White Cliffs' of Dover; it was a poignant moment which I will never forget - to see the looks on the faces of men being repatriated after so many years. It was probably the most pleasant and enjoyable experience of my flying career."

In all, the squadron had repatriated 236 ex-PoW's from Juvincourt to Westcott, before returning to Syerston; the last aircraft landed back at base at 21.02hrs. According to Jack Shearing, it would appear that 49 had achieved yet another first, in being the first squadron to repatriate PoW's.

May 4, 1945: LUNEBERG HEATH, GERMANY:

"We have won the war... Let us now win the peace."
B.L. Montgomery, Field Marshal

May 4, 1945; EXODUS 2: : After a two-day stand down, the squadron was again alerted for another Exodus operation. On Friday 4 May, 49 Squadron was detailed to fly to Melsham near Brussels, and return ex-PoW's to Wing near Leighton Buzzard. Take-off commenced at 14.50hrs, and 12 crews were on the flying programme:

"Q" S/L Walker	"A" F/L Williams	"D" F/L Hammond
"E" F/L Dow	"F" F/O Hawkins	"H" F/L Mellor
"N" F/O Soutar	"R" F/L Dickson	"T" F/O Corley
"G" F/O Eltis	"P" F/O Binns	"U" F/O Le Marquand

MAY 1945

THE CIGAR BOX

Norman Smith flew as navigator in F/Lt Hammond's D-Dog;

"We flew to Möelsbrock and picked up 25 British merchant navy men who had been captured early in the war. They were amazed at the size of the aircraft and were very pleased that we had a skipper, a port and a starboard.

One sat beside me at my table; he put a cigar box on my map and when I went to move it, he told me not to touch it... I then realised that the contents of that box had been this chap's whole world for five years... and I felt very humble."

IT'S A SMALL WORLD

F/O Bob Soutar RNZAF (PB873) and crew flew N-Nuts to Brussels; Bob recalls the following encounter which had its origins four years earlier:

"In 1941 at EFTS in New Zealand, I roomed with a chap called Frank Penman. I went to Canada for Wings training but he did his in NZ. We met again on the 'Empress of Asia' coming from Halifax to Liverpool. He went to a Wellington OTU and then ferried an aircraft out to Egypt, but was posted missing. He had crash landed out in the desert and was later picked up by some Indian troops.

FOUND AGAIN

He then went down with diphtheria and was put on the 'Laconia' bound for England along with 1,500 Italian PoW's. The ship was torpedoed in the South Atlantic by a German U-boat, and Frank was later reported as a POW. Apparently, there were a lot of survivors from the sinking, and Frank was in a lifeboat. The U-boat surfaced and helped the survivors and took Frank onto the deck. However a Coastal Command aircraft came along and the U-boat dived leaving Frank in the water.

Fortunately the U-boat returned and picked up some survivors including Frank. He was then transferred to an Italian submarine heading for Bordeaux, where Frank would become a POW. On the journey, this submarine survived another attack by Coastal Command. Frank was later to find out that the skipper of the attacking aircraft was well known to him.

On landing at Brussels, and climbing out of the aircraft, who should be stood under the nose but my old friend Frank Penman ... it's a small world."

This day, the squadron transported 288 ex-PoW's to Wing, before returning to base by 21.18hrs. Bomber Command Lancasters were able to bring back 75,000 men by May 28th. There was one tragedy, when a 3 Group (514 Sqdn) aircraft developed engine trouble shortly after take-off from Juvincourt and crashed killing all 31 on board.

---

52 YEARS AFTER EXODUS

A chance meeting at the East Kirkby Aviation Museum between Billi Watkins, an ex WAAF and wife of Association member Fred, and another member Ted Cachart brought back many vivid memories.

A letter received from Billi explains:

"When the war ended many WAAF's were sent to RAF Dunsfold in Surrey where the large aircraft were stripped out inside and were flying 'to and fro' non-stop to Germany, bringing back all the PoW's from the concentration camps. Our job was to help them down from the planes with a big 'Welcome Home' smile and big hugs, although most looked as if they might break if you hugged too tight!.

We had to take them through 'delousing' then onto the cookhouse or NAAFI to eat, and finally to stores for some decent clothing.

There were a great many tears shed over those days, especially when they each got down and kissed the ground, but I was very proud to have been chosen for that wonderful duty. And now, 52 years later, I have met and spoken with one of those wonderful brave men that landed at Dunsfold from one of those dreadful camps.

It happened at a reunion of 49 Squadron (in which my husband served). We had been listening to the roar of the Lancaster engines, one on the ground and the Battle of Britain Lanc flying low over us, a thrilling moment. We went into the tea room for a 'cuppa' when another ex-airman joined us and introduced himself as Ted and we got into conversation, during which he told us he had crashed over Germany and had been taken prisoner.

I asked him where he had landed when he was released and brought home to England but he could not remember the name except to say it was a little airfield in Kent. I asked him if it could have been Dunsfold and he immediately confirmed that it was . It was a wonderful moment to think that he could have been one of those brave men that I welcomed home".

Ted Cachart picks up the story

"I recalled how two WAAFs had grabbed me as I climbed out of the Lanc and kissed and cuddled me before leading me up to the de-lousing tent. To be honest, I don't remember very much more other than having tea and cake in a hanger served by Red Cross and WVS ladies, and then being on a train up to RAF Cosford for interrogation. What happened in-between or how long I was at Dunsfold has vanished into oblivion.

It is very possible that Billi was one of the WAAFs that greeted me, something that we will never know for certain. We can however, justifiably claim to truly represent the 'Receptionists' and the 'Repatriates' of the time., and it was a wonderful coincident meeting her like this."

MAY 1945

Note:- Extensive enquiries to the Red Cross, local Surrey newspapers, British Aerospace at Dunsfold and the Movietone News archives by Ted and Uncle Will have failed to produce any photograph of POWs disembarking from a Lancaster. There is one with POWs walking away from a Stirling, and another showing a number of Stirlings parked at Dunsfold.

Ted & Billi as they were in 1945

52 years later when they met (again?) at East Kirkby.

This picture of them together was actually taken at the Fiskerton Airfield Memorial site on Sunday 8th June 1997

VICTORY

During the early evening of Monday 7th, just after tea, it was announced over the tannoy that the following day, Tuesday 8th May was to be VICTORY IN EUROPE DAY. The European war had officially ended.

So at last, it was all over... Bomber Command had come a very long way since those early pioneer years of Hampdens, Wellingtons and Whitleys, and 49 Squadron had travelled every painful mile of that journey.

During the war, approximately 125,000 aircrew served in Bomber Command; of that number, some 55,000 lost their lives. Bomber Command ground staff also paid the price for peace with their lives; 1,479 men and 91 WAAF died whilst on duty.

If you have the opportunity, then make a pilgrimage to Lincoln Cathedral. Once there, visit The Airmen's Chapel of St Michael. Here are housed the Memorial Books containing the names of no less than 25,611 personnel who were killed flying from airfields in or near Lincolnshire... included are the names of 1,233 Canadians, 1,140 Australians, 200 New Zealanders, approximately 90 from Southern Rhodesia and 687 members of the Polish Air Force. All were members of Bomber Command.

Author: I have spent much time in quiet contemplation in this Chapel, my thoughts bathed in the many colours of the beautiful stained glass Bomber Command Memorial Window... and I still fail to comprehend the enormity of the loss and the sorrow it brought to so many families... for they too made the ultimate sacrifice.

'Do these, who help the quickened pulse run slowly,
Whose stern remembered image cools the brow-
Till the far dawn of Victory know only
Night's darkness, and Valhalla's silence now?'
John Gilespie Magee, 'Per Ardua' 1941

At Syerston, on the evening of May 7, 1945, the cost of Victory had yet to be counted; everyone just looked forward to tomorrow... and the big Victory celebrations.

VE DAY Syerston, May 1945:

8 May, 1945: Throughout this land, the Commonwealth and indeed the free world, celebration services and parties were being organised. We must concern ourselves with the happenings at RAF Syerston where 49 Squadron, along with the station personnel made ready to mark the end of the war in Europe. Again, it is to Jack Shearing's diary that we turn; Jack recorded some of the highlights of that never to be forgotten day... and night!

"Did not get up until 10, but there was nothing doing down the flight. After going to the 'YMCA heard we had to parade at the big hangar after lunch.

It was quite an impressive Do... first we had an address by the Groupie, then a service which was rather touching and finally Churchill's speech... 'In War resolution, in defeat defiance... in Victory magnanimity.' Immediately after the sports started and a wagon load of ATS came to the camp. After watching the sports, had tea and then got ready and went to the Station dance in the hangar.

The beer was cheap but there were no glasses, so Norman Warwick and I went down to the Mess to get some. At first the dance was wizard; I was with Hilda then she was seized by an officer and I did not see her for the rest of the evening.

I danced with Helen the Radar girl and found the rest of the crew Jack, Eddy and Lefty were all pretty tight. At the end things got very rowdy; everyone, particularly the erks got tight and started smashing things.

The aircrew lads started driving cars right through the hangar. They started a big fire at the end of the dance, in the middle of the parade ground and the flag pole was among the things that were burnt with great ceremony, while everyone stood round and sang to the music of two accordions."

The following day, a scratch aircrew side beat 'B' Flight at football 3-1, with Jack scoring one of the goals. The night was again rounded off with another all ranks dance.

Australian pilot, Jack Branch remembers VE day very well:

"On May 4th, we were one of three crews who went on leave for the usual 9 days, not realising at the time how lucky we were going to be. My bomb aimer, Jock Begg and I booked in at the Strand Palace, London, arriving late in the afternoon on 7th May, and were surprised at the excitement which was evident amongst the hotel staff. 'Mr Churchill is going to make an important announcement tomorrow', they told us.

We were too busy getting ready to enjoy ourselves to give much consideration to their remarks. "But next day it was a very different story - the war in Europe was over and London went mad!! And what was more wonderful, we were in the thick of it... enough to say that I only have very hazy recollections of what happened on that historic day."

During the week following VE Day, the squadron was alerted for no fewer than 5 operations (Exodus trips) but all were subsequently cancelled. On the 17th May the squadron was stood down from ops until 31st May.

OPERATIONAL SUMMARY - MAY 1945

May 1: 10 aircraft detailed to take part in operation 'Exodus' the repatriation of 236 ex PoW's. Base - Juvincourt - Westcott - Base.
May 4: 12 aircraft detailed to take part in operation 'Exodus' the repatriation of 288 ex PoW's. Base - Brussels - Wing - Base.

MAY 1945

HONOURS AND AWARDS - MAY 1945

P/O A.E. Parker	D.F.C.	P/O W.E.A. Salter	D.F.C.
F/S R.W. Norly (deceased)	D.F.M.	F/S D.J. Myers	D.F.M.
P/O N. Alty	D.F.C.	F/O J.W. Cannon	D.F.C.
W/O R.W. Petty	D.F.C.	F/O A.H. Blackmore (deceased)	D.F.C.

Syerston May/June 1945: (From l to r), F/Sgt Woodland bomb aimer; F/Sgt Menhinick, rear gunner; F/Sgt Ritchie, flight engineer; F/Lt Les Hammond, pilot; F/Sgt Smith, navigator; F/Sgt Woolsey, mid/upper gunner. (F/Sgt Moses on leave). Lancaster PA595/G came to the squadron from the Bomber Development Unit and records show she did not go on operations with 49 Squadron. (N. Smith)

A photograph showing 49 Squadron's navigators in front of the venerable 'H-Howe' (PB349). (N.C. Smith)

F/Lt Len Mellor (second left) and fellow crew members at Syerston circa May 45. Jack Shearing is standing second from right. The Lancaster forming the back drop is of note; she is still displaying a 1 Group 'yellow gas disc' on her nose, indicating former service with 460 RAAF Sqdn (AGLT equipped). Further research has revealed she is in fact PB873/G (EA-N) later becoming the Empire Air Armament School's 'THOR' which toured the Middle East, South Africa and later the Far East and Australia. (J. Shearing)

JUNE - DECEMBER 1945

TIGER FORCE

Plans were already well in advance to send a force of heavy bombers out to the Far East to participate in the war against Japan. This unit was to be called 'Tiger Force' and would come under the command of 5 Group. It would comprise 1 Mosquito and 12 Lancaster squadrons, together with Headquarters staff and various ancillary units.
The force comprised of 3 contingents each including 4 Lancaster squadrons; as follows:

No's 44, 57, 207 and 460 RAAF with their Base station at East Kirkby.
No's 83, 97, 106 and 467 RAAF plus 627 (Mosquitoes) with Coningsby as Base station.
No's 9, 49, 617, 156 or 189 made up the third contingent with Waddington as Base station.

Note:- W/Cmdr Peter Johnson (former 49 Sqdn CO in 1943) was now Commanding Officer of 97 Sqdn PFF at Coningsby. He requested several former 49 Officers to join him for their second tours, including F/Lt Tom Taylor and F/Lt Jock Simpson.
The squadrons would all be equipped with Lancaster Mk VII aircraft, with tropicalised engines and no mid-upper turrets.

49 Squadron was to dispense with their AGLT 'Village Inn' aircraft. The new aircraft were all to be fitted with FN Mk 5 front turrets and FN 82 tail turrets. They would also have the Mk XIV A bomb-sight and navigational aids would include H2S, Loran and Gee.

The island of Okinawa, south of Japan, would be the base for 'Tiger Force'. Okinawa was approximately 900 miles from Tokyo. Training units were informed that the force was expected to be resident on Okinawa and ready for operations against the Japanese mainland by 1st October, 1945.

BRIGHTON BELLES

5 June, 1945: As a result of the 'alleged' low flying over Brighton (see 20th April, 1945), 5 Group order a Courts-Martial to take place at RAF Syerston at 10.00hrs on Tuesday 5th June.

The first witness was Mr Charles Kingsley Brown of Montpelier Villas, Brighton; after being duly sworn he gave his evidence:

"I am a gardener by occupation, and am a member of the Civil Defence Observer Corps. At 15.25hrs on the 20th April, 1945, I was on duty at No.3 Observation Post, Fairways, Dyke Road, Brighton and was stationed on top of a block of flats four storeys high. This post is about 1 1/2 miles inland from the sea.

I have been a civil observer for over two years, and have considerable experience in identifying aircraft. At 15.25hrs I observed two Lancasters flying from north to south.

At 15.28hrs two more Lancasters came in the vicinity, also flying north to south. All four were flying at a height of approximately 1,000ft. All four circled the town several times gradually getting lower. Except when they disappeared from my view near the sea front all four were continually under my observation.

One after the other they circled my observation post at a distance of about 500yds from me; each flew down to a height of about 300ft above sea level. I was able to take their numbers and entered their numbers in my log. Each had a roundel between the first two numbers and the last one. The numbers of the four Lancasters were EA-P, EA-R, EA-U and EA-Z, I have no doubt whatsoever about these numbers. I checked on each one of them several times with the exception of EA-Z which I saw only once.

When they left the vicinity of my post they disappeared towards the sea front. I estimated their height of 300ft because they passed the vicinity of the chimney on the Dust Destructor which I know to be 225ft. As regards the weather at the time; the sky was mainly clear and the visibility was good."

When cross examined, Mr Kingsley confirmed that he had not observed any other Lancasters between 15.00hrs and 16.00hrs.

F/O Bob Soutar RNZAF (pilot of EA-Z) recalls the outcome of the above charges:

"It was after we had moved to Syerston that with the backing of Group, the Courts Martial were set up. Five of us were put under arrest and confined to camp! These included F/O's Robson, Westwood, Weston, Smith and myself, as all our aircraft letters had been noted - four had been noted by the DAPM and mine by the Observer Corps. Jack Littley's letter '0' was not noted by the DAPM but as I understand it, he admitted being there but not to low flying! (note it was his aircraft that was alleged to have dropped the toilet rolls). He was dealt with at Group HQ by being given a reprimand.

There were several Courts Martial as the RAAF and RNZAF accused had to have some representative of that Air Force on the Board. F/O Robson, F/O Westwood, F/O Weston RNZAF and F/O Smith RAAF were all found guilty of the charge and if my memory is correct, they lost three months seniority. That didn't worry them as they were soon going out!

In my case, with only the Observer Corps gentlemen getting my letter and coupling it with the others - when I wasn't even there; his evidence was torn to shreds by the defending officer. I had worked out that my aircraft would have had to fly at 203 knots to get there at 15.28hrs and 214 knots by 15.25hrs - no way could a Lancaster do that, especially as I was flying on 3 engines most of the way, as part of my own training!!... therefore I was found NOT GUILTY."

On the date of the incident, F/Lt Jack Winter was acting as 'B' Flight Commander and it was he , who had authorised the training X-country.

When Jack gave his evidence, he stated that the Authorisation Book had been destroyed. It was said that this happened when F/O Elkington crashed on the main site at Fulbeck... no one will ever say!

As Bob Soutar reflects:

"With our incident, the Elkington accident and Dave Hytch coming to a sudden halt in The Wash, I don't think our 49 Squadron was very popular with Group HQ. I don't know what W/Cmdr Botting's thoughts were about all this, but I don't think he ever got a gong!"

WE'LL MEET AGAIN

It was during the early part of June, 1945 that those members of the RAAF, RCAF and RNZAF began the long process of returning to their home countries. For many Australians, this homeward journey began at 9 ACHU Gamston. On arrival, these 'deportees' were handed a "Gen" letter, written and signed by the Commanding Officer, W/Cmdr French Smith. The letter contained expected references to 'reasonable discipline', 'billet inspections' and 'what are you going to do when demobbed?' The W/Cmdr tried very hard to win his new residents over... as the following shows:

"We realise that you will be 'browned off' particularly if the shipping position isn't too bright. We don't want to 'bind' you with lectures, parades etc., but are sure that your morale WILL suffer if you don't keep yourselves occupied."

The W/Cmdr was also not averse to using a little flattery in his pursuance of a 'happy ship':

"All that is expected is a fair and reasonable standard of discipline. You are a member of the RAAF, a service whose record is second to none and of which you can be proud. Demonstrate your pride by wearing your uniform properly on all occasions and behaving accordingly."

At the bottom of this 'Gen' letter is a list entitled 'Don't' - and the final don't states:

"Don't forget that saluting is not kow-towing but an expression of mutual respect between all ranks. It demonstrates smartness, pride of service and friendliness, and is a sure sign of a happy and co-operative unit."

W/Cmdr French Smith concludes with *"Help us to Help you"*... who would envy the Wingco in his daunting task.

As can be imagined, this was a highly emotional time on the squadron, for those crews with Aussies, Canucks and Kiwis in their number. After 'crewing up' at OTU, followed by months of hazardous training together, before finally going 'operational', tremendous bonds were forged. Those same bonds and strong friendships are still very much in evidence over 50 years later... whenever old bomber crews meet again!

JUNE - DECEMBER 1945

15 June, 1945: A/W/Cmdr L.E. Botting, the Squadron Commander (who had arrived on 49 Squadron in March 1944, and took command of the squadron on 23 June 1944 when W/Cmdr Crocker was reported missing from operations two days earlier) was posted to HQ Transport Command. W/Cmdr Humphreys BASO, 55 Base took over command.

16 June, 1945: W/Cmdr Humphreys was posted back to his old unit (57 Sqdn) and W/Cmdr David Balme DSO, DFC was posted in to Command 49 Squadron. W/Cmdr Balme had completed his own final bombing operation on the Berchtesgaden trip, as Commander of 227 Squadron, based at Strubby near Mablethorpe.

HONOURS AND AWARDS - JUNE 1945

F/O J.C. Atkinson	D.F.C.
W/O D. Grimley	D.F.C.
F/S S.G. Boyes	D.F.M.

Officers Mess, Syerston;
Members of the RAAF say farewell to 49 Squadron in June 1945.
The Waaf seated on Jack Branch's knee (bottom right) is believed to have been a member of the Special Operations Executive (SOE).
(J.Branch)

JULY 1945

23 July, 1945: The squadron detailed 14 aircraft for a mock operation, but shortly after take-off F/O Cliffe returned with his navigator sick.

At approximately 3 minutes before 'H'-Hour, the Controller broadcast the message "Mission abandoned". This was due to 10/10ths cloud in the target area. The aircraft then completed the route and returned to base. The Lancaster flown by F/Lt Wright developed engine trouble and the exercise was completed on three engines.

Apart from the cloud in the target area, which stopped bombing, the exercise is considered to have been fairly successful from the training point of view. Few combats were reported although numerous fighters were seen. The following crews were on the flying programme:

"B" W/C Balme	"F" S/L Glensor	"A" F/S Ingles	"D" F/O Hytch	"J" F/O Buchanan
"K" P/O McKinnon	"W" F/S Jones	"R" F/L Dickson	"S" F/L Wright	"U" F/S Robson
"T" P/O Clark	"V" F/O Cliffe	"Q" F/O Mersey	"-" P/O Stubbington	

JUNE - DECEMBER 1945

HONOURS AND AWARDS - JULY 1945

F/O J.K. Nowrie	D.F.C.

AUGUST 1945

Navigator, Norman Smith recalls the day the Atom Bomb was dropped on Japan:

"We were training hard for "Tiger Force" when we heard the news of the Atom Bomb on the radio... everyone in our room went very silent as we heard of its unbelievable power. Then when we realised this would be the end of the war we were all extremely happy!"

49 Squadron disposed of 118 tons of bombs during August 1945.

SEPTEMBER 1945

OPERATION DODGE: 5 September, 1945: 10 aircraft were detailed for operation 'Dodge'; the bringing home of servicemen from Italy; those crews detailed were as follows:

"A" S/L Glensor	"E" F/L Dow	"D" F/L Johnstone	"S" F/L Ruck-Keene
"H" F/L Mellor	"F" F/L Babb	"B" F/O Tolmie	"K" F/O Stubbington
"J" F/O Mersey	"V" W/O Robson failed to take-off due to engine trouble.		

OPERATION SPASM

On the same day as 9 aircraft from the squadron left for Italy, three other aircraft were detailed to fly to Berlin. This involved a day's stay in the German capital, specifically for those aircrew who had carried out operations against the German capital - some ground crew members, who had maintained the aircraft at that time, were also invited along.

Those named on the flying programme were as follows:

"G" W/C Balme	"W" S/L Sandison	"Q" F/L Wright
S/L Bromfield	F/L Catty	and crew
F/O Richardson	F/L Grainger	plus 5 Ground crew
F/L Thomas	F/L Tullis	
F/O Evans	F/L Kennedy	
F/O Mitchell	F/L Shepherd	
F/O Dobson	plus 5 Ground crew	
plus 5 Ground crew		

JUNE - DECEMBER 1945

A brief opportunity for some sight seeing in Italy on 6-9-45 during Operation Dodge. Members of F/Lt Johnson's crew are seen here from l to r; F/Sgt Norman Smith, navigator; F/Sgt Moses, wireless operator; F/Sgt Anderson, rear gunner; F/Sgt Livesly, mid/upper gunner; F/Sgt Woodland, bomb aimer;
F/Sgt Pedrick, flight engineer. (N.S. Smith)

7 September, 1945: Crews who had been dispatched to Italy on 5th, returned to base except for F/Lt Ruck-Keene and crew; their aircraft lost an engine (with passengers onboard) whilst in Tibenham's circuit; the pilot skilfully brought S-Sugar in safely on three engines.

11 September, 1945: 10 aircraft were detailed for another 'Dodge' trip to Bari, but only F/O Hytch and crew in F-Fox were able to get away at 07.15hrs; the remainder were prevented from taking off due to the weather.

The following day the operation was attempted again with 9 aircraft becoming airborne shortly after 07.15hrs, but again the weather intervened and they were soon recalled at 08.00hrs.

13 September, 1945: 10 aircraft detailed for operation 'Dodge' taking off just after 07.00hrs. The following crews were detailed:

"G" S/L Glensor	"A" F/O Buchanan	"B" W/O Robson
"H" F/L Wiggin	"K" F/S Ingles	"P" P/O Cliffe
"Q" F/L Wright	"W" F/O Mersey	"E" F/O Jones
"V" F/L Brown (Bomber Command Film Unit)		

F/O Jones and crew who had taken off from base at 07.10hrs, developed engine problems and landed E-Easy back at Syerston at 10.00hrs.

Later in the day, Dave Hytch and crew returned to base after completing their 'Dodge' trip to Bari.

15 September, 1945: All those aircraft which took part in the 'Dodge' operation on the 13th returned to base.

20 September, 1945: Sgt John Jones, a flight engineer on 49 Squadron, was involved in a cycling accident at Ashbourne in Derbyshire. Sadly he died of his injuries the same day in Derby Royal Infirmary. He is buried in Blackpool Cemetery.

28 September, 1945: 49 Squadron officially moved from Syerston to RAF Mepal, in Cambridgeshire.

OCTOBER 1945

7 October, 1945: 5 crews were detailed for operation 'Dodge'; all airborne as follows:

"A" F/L Philipson-Stow	at 05.50hrs
"E" F/O Bromley	at 05.51hrs
"M" F/L Ruck-Keene	at 05.59hrs
"L" F/O Littley	at 06.08hrs
"P" F/O Clark	at 06.26hrs

All aircraft arrived safely at Bari in Italy the same day.

9 October, 1945: Crews and aircraft as of 7th October, returned to Mepal, with the exception of F/L Philipson-Stow and crew in A-Able. During their flight, the pilot became sick and they landed at Marseilles.

10 October, 1945: "H" F/O Whent and crew took-off at 06.30hrs on a 'Dodge' operation (returned on 13th). "A" F/L Philipson-Stow and crew returned from Marseilles.

15 October, 1945: 6 aircraft detailed for Italy on operation 'Dodge'.

"N" S/L Sandison	"S" F/O Stubington	"M" F/L Ruck-Keene
"B" F/O Tolmie	"C" F/L Babb	"D" F/L Johnston

All airborne from Mepal and landed at Bari the same day.

16 October, 1945: 3 aircraft detailed for Italy on operation 'Dodge'.

"A" F/O Bromley	"H" W/O Ingles	"Q" P/O Robson

All airborne from Mepal and landed at Bari the same day.

18 October, 1945: Crews and aircraft as of 15th, returned to base with the exception of "S" F/O Stubington who landed at Woodbridge with engine trouble.

20 October, 1945: Crews and aircraft as of 16th, returned safely to base.

HONOURS AND AWARDS - OCTOBER 1945

W/O E.J. Thompson D.F.C.

NOVEMBER 1945

7 November, 1945: 5 aircraft took-off from Mepal for Italy on operation 'Dodge'.

"G" F/L Mellor	06.03hrs
"N" F/L Wiggin	06.13hrs
"O" F/O Littley	06.15hrs
"J" F/O Hytch	06.35hrs
"D" F/O Mersey	07.04hrs

"J" F/O Hytch returned to base at 10.20hrs with his aircraft unserviceable.
"D" F/O Mersey landed at Glatton at 07.40hrs with his aircraft unserviceable; then proceeded from Glatton in "X" at 15.42hrs.

8 November, 1945: Aircraft "X" F/O Mersey and crew returned from 'Dodge' at 13.54hrs - operation not completed.

9 November, 1945: Crews and aircraft returned to base from operation 'Dodge' as follows:

"N" F/L Wiggins	14.16hrs
"O" F/O Littley	15.33hrs
"G" F/L Mellor	15.16hrs

10 November, 1945: Aircraft "K" F/L Babb returned to base after operation 'Dodge' at 16.33hrs.

14 November, 1945: 2 aircraft detailed for operation 'Baedeker' - cancelled due to bad weather.

15 November, 1945: 2 aircraft detailed operation 'Dodge' - operation cancelled.

16 November, 1945: 4 aircraft and crews detailed for operation 'Dodge' as follows:

"C" F/L Babb "S" F/L Wiggin "G" F/O Mersey "L" F/O Littley

Aircraft to proceed to Tibenham first, but whilst taxiing, aircraft "L" had a rudder damaged - the spare aircraft "E" F/O Stubbington proceeded to Tibenham only to find the operation had been cancelled.

W/Cmdr J.H. Irvin arrived to assume command of the squadron.

23 November, 1945: After three cancelled 'Dodge' operations, 3 aircraft and crews managed to take-off:

"X" F/L Wright 06.02hrs "B" F/L Philipson-Stow 06.04hrs "Q" F/L Babb 06.09hrs

JUNE - DECEMBER 1945

29 November, 1945: 3 aircraft and crews detailed for 'Dodge' operation as follows:

"P" F/L Nicholls "C" F/L Taylor "G" F/L Karop

One aircraft "T" F/O Mason, detailed for operation 'Spasm'.

30 November, 1945: 2 aircraft and crews detailed for operation 'Spasm' as follows:

"N" S/L Sandison 09.30hrs "X" F/L Philipson-Stow 10.08hrs

HONOURS AND AWARDS - NOVEMBER 1945

S/Ldr R.E. Glensor	RNZAF	D.F.C.
F/Lt K.A. Carlyle	RCAF	D.F.C.

DECEMBER 1945

8 December, 1945: After three cancellations, aircraft and crews eventually took-off at 06.30hrs on operation 'Dodge'; they were as follows:

"X" F/L Wright "T" F/L Mason "H" S/L Woodcraft "B" F/L Philipson-Stow

30 December, 1945: Three 'Dodge' operations were cancelled on the 9th,13th and 29th, but on the 30th, F/Lt Babb (W/Cmdr Irvin as second pilot) and crew left Mepal at 07.00hrs on operation 'Spasm'.

W/Cdr David Balme DSO, DFC Commanded 49 Squadron from June to Nov 1945

MISCELLANY

DAILY WORKING - by F/Sgt Norman Smith (navigator on F/Lt Hammond's RAAF crew 1944/45):

"The call-sign for Fulbeck was 'Oil Grease' and the Squadron was 'Aloft'. I was always amused by the radio procedure when we went to Metheringham to practice fighter-affiliation; we would call up...

Hello Coffee Stall, Hello Coffee Stall this is Aloft B-Baker... may I have a playmate?.. I am at angels 12, over.'

Our hut was at the far eastern end of the site and we could walk down the lane to the pub in Fulbeck village, where we spent many an off duty evening. Being near the boundary fence we all had bikes to get up to flights in the mornings.

There was a large nissen type ablution hut near the coal store which was surrounded by a barbed-wire fence, but the coal to heat the water was always pinched for the tortoise stoves in the huts, so we all went up to the Sgts Mess to wash and shave in the hot water there.

After breakfast in the mess, cereal and tinned milk, scrambled egg or fried bread or diced kidneys or baked beans or soya links...we would go up to the flights. The navigators got a met briefing which gave a good indication of likely ops. Any up-to-date 'gen' would be given out and previous logs would be assessed and comments made by the Nav leader; during my time this was F/Lt Catty. We would then go to the crewroom and sit around the stove chain-smoking until the 'battle order' was posted on the board.

The members of the crews on ops would go down to the mess, where all the toilets were now full strangely enough... and everyone would go into the cookhouse for a pre-flight meal of bacon and egg. This would take place at anytime of the day. I can remember getting up from lunch and in a few minutes going back for my bacon and egg.

After the meal we navs would go to the briefing room where we joined the rest of the crews and the target would be announced and the route details given and noted in our logs. On some of our later raids, I had to broadcast the basic time of return so that the aircraft could adjust their speeds to spread their arrival and cut out as much stacking over the drome as possible.

We then put on our flying clothing, collected parachute and escape packs and made our way out to the aircraft in crew buses and lorries. It seemed to be the custom to say 'Have a good trip' but never 'Good luck'... just a superstition I suppose. There were quite a few superstitions... I carried a penny, the skipper had a pipe cleaner kangeroo... our rear gunner put some grass and earth in his trouser knee pocket; I only found this out when he gave me back my sidcot suit which he had borrowed... I shook it and the grass and earth fell out and I was then told what he used to do.

It was with mixed feelings that I climbed up through the aircraft and over the dreaded main spare to my seat. But once at my desk, I would get my maps out and check over the flight plan in my log. At this stage things seemed to become routine and nerves became steady.

When the engines were started and run-up I would check my GEE set when the current was sufficient and set the Air Position Indicator. On take-off I would call out the airspeed to the skipper - after take-off I would give the first course and airspeed to him. It was usual to set course away from the drome on a given heading, somewhere around 300 true and climb to half-height and then turn in the opposite direction, climbing to arrive over base at the briefed time, ready to set course to the first turning point, usually Reading, Selsy or Cromer... as far as I remember.

We did this on our first op and over base we had a near-miss with a kite doing the same thing. To avoid this in future we set course to the first turning point, climbing and flying as slowly as possible. To arrive there on time..if necessary, we would dog-leg which effectively took a third longer to cover the distance.

Using GEE, I would get fixes at 10 minute intervals; over the continent GEE was jammed by the enemy and it was a point of honour to get the most distant GEE fix. Before we lost the GEE signal, the bomb aimer would tune the LORAN set, and by comparing the fixes, he could distinguish the first sky wave, which gave the correct fix. We could get LORAN all over Europe and it was invaluable to navigation. We used H2S on only two occasions, as German night fighters could home in on it. We flew across the sea fairly low to avoid detection up to the last minute and climbed across the coast where we began to throw out 'Window' at a set rate... this was the flight engineers job.

At intervals, the skipper would check each of the crew over the intercom... silence was kept apart from technical and course instructions. Approaching the target, I would hear some exclamation describing the flak and searchlights... sometimes we would fly through a shell-burst puff and the smell of smoke came into the heating system. Before the target, the bomb aimer would go down into the nose to set up his bomb sight and distribution panel. He would call for the bomb doors to be opened and then go into his 'left left, right steady, bombs gone!' patter. He would check for hang-ups, close bomb doors and then we would dive out of the target area on a course given to the pilot just before the bomb run. But before diving away, the pilot would fly straight and level to get a photograph upon which the proof of success or failure of our raid depended.

On our return to base, we would call up and receive a message... 'you are number 2 and clear to land' etc. We would join the circuit and wait our turn to land. At dispersal we would be picked up by transport and taken to de-briefing. It may be because of the relief of getting back, but I could not take this seriously. I know the questions might be important to the powers that be, but the serious manner in which they were asked made the affair a bit like a Boy Scouts 'Kims' game.

After de-brief we went to the mess for another bacon and eggs meal and then to bed. We were allowed to stay in bed next morning, unless the tannoy announced 'Armourers to their sections' when we knew we would be 'on' again that night.

On days when there were no ops, but the squadron was not stood down, we would go to the intelligence section and look at the target photos and aircraft recognition books, or Tee-Emm....and surreptitiously play cards.

MISCELLANY

In the mess there was a scramble for the Daily Express, as the skeleton crossword was very popular. Sometimes a section of the Central Band would play 40's tunes at lunchtime. When not on duty, the mess at Fulbeck was a bit dreary so if there was no E.N.S.A. show or film in the camp cinema, we would go by cycle to Newark, or bus into Lincoln.

In Newark an evening in the 'Spread Eagle' was followed by fish and chips from the shop a few doors away. Here we met some of the local Military Police soldiers and made quite a friendship. We even got permission to take them up for a short flight, which was quite an eye-opener for them - they didn't seem as tough without their red caps and trussed up in a parachute harness!

One night my skipper and I went to Newark early to go to the cinema. We had firmly resolved not to get drunk. However we were too early for the pictures so we went to the pub... I think it was the 'Robin Hood'... just to kill time. We said to the publican that we were only going to have a half... 'why not have something special' he said... 'I have just two half pints left in this small barrel of XXXX... it's very old'.

We had a half each and agreed it was very good and thought we could manage another half. The publican managed to get two more halves out of the barrel and in the end we spent the whole evening trying to empty this barrel. We were both terribly drunk and missed the bus, but got a lift in another crew's car.

Next night we went to Harburg and I was still tight. That night I couldn't care less... I even looked out from behind my curtain, when we were over the target!

In Lincoln, we would normally go to Betty's Bar and again finish the evening with fish & chips. One had to have a ticket, obtained when going in... to be able to get on the bus coming back.

At Fulbeck, dances were held occasionally in the Village Hall and these were very pleasant. Our rear gunner once won a hare in the 'raffle'... the cook on camp said she would cook it, but first it had to be hung. It was hung in the broom cupboard in the hut and we then went on leave. The hare was very decomposed when we returned. As an operational crew, we had nine days leave every six weeks. On these leaves we were given 'Nuffield' money donated to aircrew by the Lord of that name.

In the field next to our hut, we were able to gather mushrooms. My father owned a baker's shop and so I returned to camp with dried egg powder and cake and jam. We brought bread from the mess (in our tunics) and this was toasted on the side of the tortoise stove... and on it was served mushroom omelettes made with egg powder. A certain amount of fat also found its way from the mess.

It was very cold in the nissen huts and at times one went to bed still wearing the silk and wool long johns... and long sleeved vests with your greatcoat on top of the bed and even your socks and pyjamas on after that! I remember we were issued with clean sheets at intervals from the store which was staffed by an old airman whose last three numbers were his first three."

MISCELLANY

OLD HANDS HAD BLACK CAPS!: Donald Deeley, Flight Mechanic (Engines) recalls his time at Scampton in the winter of 1941/42:

"I started my course at Kirkham near Blackpool, but half-way through I was posted to Locking. After passing out AC1 (big deal!) I was posted with two other bods to 49 Squadron, Scampton. I remember we travelled by train via London arriving at Scampton late on a cold November night in 1941.

First night we slept on the usual three boards with a mattress in one of the permanent blocks on the main camp. But next day, we were moved to a small village a few miles down a lane, as I remember, almost opposite the main gate (Welton). We slept in the half-round 'tin' huts in a field, with a stove in the middle of each, that gave off a terrible smell; we always seemed to be cold and damp. There were no cooking facilities or ablutions, so we had to eat, wash etc. in the main camp.

I was assigned to the ground crew of Hampden S-Sugar, where the lads were great, and despite the cold and snow, I felt I really belonged. My main duties were 1; Stuffing my forage cap smartly up the air intake if the engine flooded and back fired - Old hands had 'black' caps! and 2; Standing on top of a pair of steps painting a Stork carrying a large bomb in a nappy sling after the lads had found out that I'd been an apprentice draughtsman.

I remember the wireless op/air gunner of S-Sugar... not much older than me; we became friendly and he used to give me his 'sweets' to hold till he got back - whilst I was there, I am pleased to say he always collected his sweets!

I flew once in S-Sugar on circuit and bumps, much to the disgust of the lads who thought I was mad. For take-off I sat facing forward on the main spar behind the pilot. After take-off I was allowed to go down into the bomb aimers position as we flew out over the Wash, landing back after 20 minutes. I remember going into the main hangar for the first time. It contained 3 or 4 Hampdens - Oh that lovely odour of dope, oil, leather and high octane.

In April 1942 I was posted overseas to the Middle East - last in - first out! One day I intend to visit Scampton again, just to stand at dispersal and remember, and I'd love to go back to Welton again.

My time on 49 Squadron was very brief, but I am very proud to have been a member of such a fine unit."

Author's Note: On the night of 19 April 1942 (less than three weeks after Don had been posted out) Frank Slingo and crew failed to return from operations in Hampden AT217, S-Sugar.

The aircraft came down in the North Sea without any survivors - I doubt if those back at Scampton handed the sweets round.

FROSTY RECEPTION : F/Lt Leslie Hay recalls arriving back over Fulbeck from ops in the winter of 1944/45:

"We returned about 04.00hrs one cold winter's morning. Something had gone wrong (I never knew what) with nobody being given a number and we were all stacked at 500 feet spacing, orbiting the airfield. Then 'someone' (I recognised the voice) contrary to all radio procedure sang a complete verse of 'Here we go round the mulberry bush'.

Unfortunately, the Base Commander, an Air Commodore was in the control tower (in the warm) paying the station a visit and heard it. The pilots were later assembled, but of course no one knew anything about it... nor even heard it, and a suggestion that it might have been radio interference nearly resulted in a charge of 'insolence'.

After a right blasting, we were summarily and to suit the morning temperature, icily dismissed... and filed out of the Head's study - but we got our egg and sausage just the same!"

GERMAN PARAS IN THE WAAFERY?: Ex-ACW Vi Winters recalls the more humorous side of life on a wartime bomber base:

"So many sad memories, but also some good ones... like the old bikes with no brakes... how we returned from the pub in one piece I shall never know. Coming back on the ferry after celebrating my 21st birthday in Lincoln, and waking next morning to find a huge silver salver, from the 'Saracens Head' sitting on my bed-side table.

Slapping the bread on the side of the stove to toast it in the huts; enjoying the gifts of hot chocolate from the Canadians and good old spam and dried egg powder. Turning the trucks' engines over, always remembering one had to have one's thumb on the left in case it kicked back. The clothing coupons that we scrounged off the officers... the nylons of course, and who could forget the Navy Bloomers which we called 'passion killers', plus the Bra's which I'm certain were all one size... thick stockings, oh so many memories.

I shall never forget when a WAAF Officer came into our hut late at night and told us all to get out of bed and stand at the end of our huts, as we were surrounded by Germans!... I remember my friend Joan saying 'lets make ourselves look good, then maybe they will not harm us!', so there we were, striped pyjamas, pipe cleaners all over our heads, desperately trying to get them out... oh how they hurt... Of course, it was a false alarm and we never did see the Officer again."

MISCELLANY

THE LONG WALK HOME

In wartime all fighting men were heroes be it on the ground, sea or, in the air. The cream of the youth of Great Britain and Allied Countries being put in a position of danger. Before his death in September 1993 Raymond Barlow recorded the details of the crash of ED426 (Oct '43) and the subsequent events surrounding his and Don Ware's evasion from capture.

The crew:

P/O	Donald Wares,	Pilot;	Retired to Inverness	(Evader).
Sgt.	Timothy O'Leary,	Navigator,	Dublin	(Killed).
F/Sgt	Raymond Barlow.	Wop/Ag;	(Service No 1330226)	(Evader)
F/0.	Elmer Hepburn,	Bombaimer,	RCAF	(Killed).
Sgt.	Gill Attwood.	Upper Gunner,	Birmingham	(P.O.W).
F/0.	A. Fitzgerald,	Rear Airgunner,	RAAF	(P.O.W).
Sgt.	Archibald Brownlie,	Flight Engineer,	Aberdeen	(Killed).

In 1943, three members of the crew died in a crash over France, two were captured, two escaped. With this story Raymond Barlow pays tribute to his friends and dedicates this story to Elmer Hepburn, in order to let his son and daughter know the bravery of their father.

TOO LATE ON TARGET

It was 5 p.m. on 5th October 1943. After a routine kind of day our crew as well as the rest of 49 Squadron were assembled in the briefing room at RAF Fiskerton, Lincolnshire.

Now we know where we're going it's Stuttgart, the industrial centre in the south of Germany. The Briefing Officer told us the take-off time was 9.00 p.m. from RAF Dunholme Lodge and there was to be 500 bombers taking part in the raid. The target, a certain factory in Stuttgart - if we couldn't find it - we had to bring back the bombs.

An hour before take-off we arrived at RAF Dunholme Lodge, along with the other aircrews dressed in flying gear and carrying parachutes. Being the Wireless Operator and Air Gunner I also had a box of spare valves and parts for repairing the radio equipment in case of a fault or breakdown. Each of us had an escape kit, in case we needed to bail out.

We were elated and thought it was our lucky night when the C.O., told us we were going to fly a brand new Lancaster Bomber and set about doing flight checks etc., only to find out that the new plane developed engine trouble on take-off. The Ground Mechanics worked hard on the bomber trying to get the engines working but to no avail, it couldn't be put right in time.

The C.O. told us we would have to take the station's spare Lanc which had been used for many months by every Tom, Dick and Harry for practising 'circuits and bumps' and was itself, badly in need of new engines. He justified this order by saying that the Air Ministry wanted 500 planes on the mission, not 499 but 500.

The ground crew transferred the armaments from the new to the old plane and fuelled up. By this time we were getting impatient to be off, we had been hanging around for an hour after watching the others fly off towards the target and by now the mainstream would be well on their way to Germany.

Eventually, we were on our way and with it's heavy load of fuel and 10,000 lb. bomb the old plane struggled to get airborne and, in fact, just managed it at the very end of the runway. Just reaching 18,000 ft. by the time we got over the Channel. Over Holland we started 'windowing' this involved throwing bundles of strips of silver foil about 10" long and 1" wide, which gently floated downwards to confuse enemy radar and anti-aircraft guns.

It was a moonlight night and looking out of the port side window I could see the mainstream of our other bombers returning safely from their mission homeward bound for England. For them, on reaching base a luscious breakfast of bacon and eggs for which, we would be late.

My thoughts were very mixed, here we were an hour late going over enemy territory, which had by now been forewarned and were on the alert. We were sitting ducks but we wanted to keep afloat, determined to get it over with and claim our breakfast. As we approached the German town six or seven enemy fighters attacked us. Our Rear and Upper Gunners opened up with their Browning Machine Guns, you could hear the ~rat-tat-tat-tat reverberating around the plane and the night fighters soon decided to leave us alone.

The nearer we got to the target the heavier the flak and the tension built as the shells seemed to be coming up very slowly towards us and then they would flash by the 'plane at lightning speed. We seemed to be in the middle of a firework display. We were ringed all around and being the only one over the target area, we were given the full treatment and felt very vulnerable indeed, just like clay pigeons.

As we looked down at the ground below it was a mass of orange flames stretching for what seemed miles and miles. The bombers who preceded us had done a fantastic job with very accurate target bombing. The damage looked considerable and over a very wide area. Now it was time to make our contribution and Don, Tim and Elmer worked together to line up our bomber on an accurate course for the selected target. Tension was high as Elmer lay full length in the nose of the 'plane ready to drop our bomb (called 'Big Bertha') right on target. I heard Elmer shout "Bombs Away" and she was released. Next Elmer took photos of the inferno below. What seemed like hours was infact, minutes, and we couldn't wait to make a quick exit from our uneven battle. One old Lancaster bomber droning around those alien skies against the spitting anger and venom of dozens of anti-aircraft guns aiming flak, the odds were just not fair, hence our anxiety to get out.

With great relief we turned towards home and we all thought we'd got away with it and could breathe more easily. Just as we thought we were safely away, I heard a hell of a thump on the starboard side then, the 'plane reverberated and shook and my stomach turned. A shell had hit us and the starboard engine was on fire, flames were lapping around and coming out of the starboard engine. Don feathered the crippled outer engine, leaving the propeller rotating but losing power from that engine - lady luck was looking away.

We were still at 18,000 ft. and Don changed to a northerly course, returning to base on three engines. In 10 minutes the fire had spread from the outer engine to the starboard inner engine, so we had to feather the inner one leaving that useless. We all knew how serious this was but nobody voiced the fears we all had. Don was having to struggle to keep control of the 'plane and the joystick had to be held in an unfamiliar position. We were losing height, speed was dropping and with only two engines left to carry us back.

My thoughts were of ~Peggy my lovely wife of ten days and whether I would ever get back to see her smile and hear her laughter again, or .... I was snapped out of my reverie by Tim our Navigator, who came over the intercom saying we are over Northern France about 1 00 miles from Dover and at 2,000 ft. I could almost smell the longed for eggs and bacon breakfast waiting for me at base. At that minute we hit a ridge of high ground - height 2,000 ft. and all was darkness.

As I was coming too, I could hear a cacophony of sounds - a continued shushing - explosions - ~rat-tat-tat-tat of firing, what the hell was happening, where was 1? As I regained consciousness I could feel the heat, smell burning in the acrid air. The 'plane was a blazing inferno, alight from nose to tail, the extreme heat making the 10 machine guns fire their repeated ~rat-tat-tat-tat, added to the deafening roars as the oxygen bottles exploded ~(Whoomph), the noise of debris crashing everywhere just behind me. I had to get out and fast if I was going to survive.

Just above my head was the escape hatch and I tried to open it, it wouldn't budge, we had hit trees at speed, which caused the fuselage to concertina and compress, making my task impossible. Not being able to escape, I staggered forward toward Don, choking on the smoke and roasting in the heat of the flames, fear was with me, was my companion, but I had to find the others. I could not see anything of Tim the Navigator or Archie the Engineer, nothing at all of the others, they must have got out.

When I reached Don, he was slumped in his seat unconscious. I shook him, called him, shouted at him and slapped his face and, after what seemed an age, he came round to be confronted by our broiling, noisy hot pot, and of course the instinctive urge to escape from it.

On the left of Don was the slide window (used for shouting to the Ground Crew "chocks away"). After a struggle we managed to prise open the window. Not losing any time, Don was the first one out with me following hard on his heels. We landed slap-bang in the middle of burning undergrowth which had been ignited by fuel from the 'plane. We were still not free from the extreme heat engulfing the 'plane and undergrowth. Bullets from the machine guns were whizzing around our heads. This, together with the still exploding oxygen bottles still throwing debris around, all combining to create an unreal situation straight from Dante's Inferno. We had to get away and quick.

We could see no other members of the crew so we thought that they had managed to get away safely from this hell, it was imperative that we followed suit. Don and I stumbled away from the smoky wreckage of the 'plane and walked about a mile or so to hide from the Germans who, from their observation post, had spotted the flames coming from the woodland.

We had to scramble into hiding when we saw a German jeep with soldiers on board and just managed to get into the undergrowth as they passed us, heading as we thought to the crash site which, was in a very remote part of France. We had come down in woods near a small village near Commercy, and after making a distance between ourselves and the site of the crash we were exhausted. The night was chilly so we covered ourselves over with the boughs of fir trees and slept back to back to keep warm.

The following day we walked for a while, there was an autumn chill and we were feeling hungry and very thirsty. Hiding in a quarry about 10 miles from the crash, we got rid of our flying gear, tearing off the lapels and badges from our uniforms. Using the knife, which had been hidden in them, we cut away the tops of our boots. Then we had to decide which border to head for the Spanish or Swiss, on the toss of a coin it was Switzerland much to my relief, (I wasn't sure about the Franco regime) so equipped with the compass from our escape kit we struck out south for the Swiss border 400 miles away.

We skirted the towns and villages and kept to the woods as much as possible. Stealing apples and drinking from the rivers. We came across fields occupied by farmers and decided to hide in the woods until dark, then make ourselves known. They were surprised to see us but let us sleep the night in a ~shepherd's hut and we were given food and drink. We were away again before daylight. Having learned that two of our crew members were alive, with their legs and arms broken they had been captured by the Germans, at least they were alive.

We went on our way again, through the woods and fields, stealing food as we went along. The conditions were very cold and damp, but we were free and heading towards the border. We averaged about 25 miles per day. Dodging the Germans we made steady progress, whenever possible getting food from isolated farms.

Once we heard a lorry coming in the distance. We wondered whether it would stop. It did, near the woods and as it was getting daylight we could see many Germans jumping out and running into the woods. We ducked and dived and then decided to borrow the lorry to help us. By this time Don's feet were playing up and we were both suffering from upset stomachs.

We managed to get the engine started and were feeling pretty good. We travelled all of ten yards when it stopped. We tried to start it but couldn't and then found out it was running on charcoal. It was the long walk for us again and we had to make a quick exit before the Germans came back for their lorry. At one point we reached a canal thought to be St. Joan. We struggled to get over in cover of darkness. We contacted the Lock Keeper who gave us food and drink after which, we trudged through the biggest woods ever and after five hours lay down at the foot of a massive tree and slept for a couple of hours.

By this time Don was having serious trouble with his feet, so we made for a little village and stopped for food and rest. The local Blacksmith gave us food and the luxury of a bed but we had to be away by 4 a.m. before daylight because the people of the village were very frightened of the Germans. Slightly refreshed we walked about 30 miles. The grass was damp and it was too wet to sleep.

My thoughts as ever strayed and were with my wife ~Peggy. How was she coping with the news she would receive about me?

At times being pulled away from our uncomfortable situation by such pleasing memories of our times together, remembering the funny episodes when we laughed together, also, our such tender moments, only to be jerked back into reality and the need to be on the alert.

Keeping to the fields we walked most of the day stealing apples as we went along, we bought beer from a shop in a remote village. At dusk we came across another village where we asked for food and had a feast of bread cheese and wine. We tried to sleep in a mangle pit at the side of the road but were kept awake by the howling of a mad dog. We made our way again it was a wet and very miserable day. We were spotted by a German patrol and after a harrowing time of hide and seek we managed to get away in the long grass. Exhausted we reached a farm at 5 p.m. and stopped to beg for food. We were invited in given food and warm hospitality. Had my first shave in 10 days, also a soft warm bed to sleep in (bliss). In the warm comfort of the bed my thoughts once again turned to my wife and in those pleasant thoughts I drifted into a fitful sleep.

After a lovely breakfast and with kind generosity we were given coats, which served more than one purpose, cover as well as warmth. We were on our way again, it rained continually for two days and we got very wet, the sheepskin in our boots got quite soggy but we carried on. We managed to find carrots, apples or anything else edible to assuage our hunger. It was the time of year when farmers were storing the vegetables for winter so we made use of the straw they were using for warmth. At one point we came across a ditch full of snakes, I jumped away shuddering I'd never seen so many. We kept an eye out for them from then on.

Reached a village called Vanne and managed to get shelter in the loft of a barn. After leaving ~Vanne we crossed a bridge which had been blown up at the beginning of the war at a place called Soing. It was early dawn and we came across German patrol cars, we made a hasty dive into the ditch just in time and breathed with relief when they passed by without stopping. Walking all day we reached fields being tended by uniformed people so decided to hole up until dark. Under the cover of the night we reached a village called Nouvelle le Chateau, got a bed for the night, next door to some German people!

It was now 12 days after the crash and we were taken to Baron Ferons Chateau to hide until the resistance could be contacted. He was living in the basement because the Germans had stripped the Chateau of all the furniture and paintings and the walls had been used for target practice. The Baron gave us food and drink and provided us with money which, he was printing in the basement. These marvellous people made us very welcome and we spent the night in the Chateau, we were no longer on our own in a strange environment.

We met Claude a member of the resistance the next day at Velle le Chateau and a celebration was held at the local butchers - everybody invited to the party. That evening slept at a ~friend's house in the village. After three days we were still hiding at the village getting rest and plenty to eat but we were anxious to get on our way. We were visited by a French Gendarme and given identity cards etc., The Resistance was very active in this area and blew up two bridges and killed 3 of the enemy. The plans for getting us away went awry somehow, we were taken in a lorry to Versoul to hide but the Burgermaster was very scared. We stayed with marvellous people in Versoul, plenty of food, drink, and rest. We played chess and went for walks in the daytime; we saw a German camp and R. D. F. post.

We stayed in the house and were visited by a Resistance chief who promised to get news to my wife that I was safe and well. I was very worried about Peggy and could not get her out of my thoughts, otherwise everything else going well.

Things progressed well, we managed to hire a lorry and get clothes to cover our by now, dirty uniforms ready to travel to the Swiss border on the following morning. The French had managed to forge German Authorisation Papers and we were given Chemin- de-fer armbands. The lorry was slow but better than walking. On the way we passed many Germans but thankfully, nobody took any notice of us,

We saw a bombed factory at Mountbe~lliard-Su-Su works and stayed at the Post Office for the night to await the guides who were going to take us over the border. We kept out of sight of prying eyes during the daytime, We were joined by a French Diplomat who was going over the border at the same time, and we whiled away the time waiting until 8 p.m. the hour we were to set out. On the hour we set out for Switzerland, walked over fields and crept through German frontier posts. A dog barking on the German side alerted the guards that there was something going on, so we had to run for our lives over the fields and in so doing, lost our way. At last we regained the right path and stealthily crept on our hands and knees into Switzerland where we offered up a prayer of thanks.

We stayed at a Swiss Farm until 4 p.m. where I tried to persuade Don to carry on to The British Legation, but he decided to give himself up. The Police were contacted and we were put on a train for Porrentruy at Hotel Swiss where we stayed, relaxed In the sure thought of being safe for the first time since we crashed. Once in Switzerland and the formalities of interrogation completed, Don Wares with others were interned at Lugano. I was lucky and went to Berne where I was able to communicate with my wife Peggy and receive letters from her, we were apart but we were safe in the knowledge that we would see each other again.

I worked at the Swiss Embassy a few hours a day handing out clothes to personnel entering Switzerland. On one occasion meeting a chap from Nottingham my home county and we had lots to talk about. Listened to the BBC Radio and heard the news that the American and British troops had invaded Southern France.

4th October 1944 departed Lausanne at 3.30. Departed Geneva 5.30 en route to France. Caught a train to Annecy, went by car to the aerodrome. Departure was delayed.

5th October, weather no good for flying, was taken by the Marquis to see 7 Frenchmen shot for collaborating. They were buried on the spot in graves dug by Germans.

6th October, left Annecy at 10.a.m.went to Lyon by lorry. Got a Dakota and arrived at Croydon 6 p.m. Arrived London 7.30. Arrived St. Albans at 11.p.m. I was over the moon ,Peggy was waiting for me at the Station, what a sight for sore eyes. I was home! Some weeks later I was very proud to receive a Silver Boot given to evaders from the RAF Escaping Society. Demob came in June, 1945, the war had finally finished.

The two crew members taken prisoner of war were released from a camp in Poland. Don Wares went home to Liverpool . Gill Attwood returned to Birmingham, Archi Fitzgerald went to Perth, Australia, where Gill joined him at a later date.

It is regretful that the four us of never met up again. However in June, 1993 Gill Attwood came to England and we met near to the date of the 50th anniversary of the crash and talked over our experiences.

In September, 1993 Gill and I travelled to Commercy Cemetary, in France. Here we found three headstones joined to make one. We stood above the graves of our friends and paid our last respects. Later we visited the site of the remains of the AVRO Lancaster ED426P and met French newspaper men who covered our story in the local papers. We also met the policeman who went to the crash site all those years ago.

We returned to England on 9th September, with memories of nearly 50 years ago to the day.

This (re-typed for clarity) letter must have brought great relief to Ray's family.

TELEPHONE: GERRARD 9234
Extn. 3811

Any communications on the subject of this letter should be addressed to :—
THE SECRETARY,
and the following number quoted :— P.409558/4/P.4.B.3.

AIR MINISTRY
(Casualty Branch),
73-77, OXFORD STREET,
W.1.

Your Ref.............

10th November, 1943.

Confidential

Sir,

I am directed to refer to a letter from this department dated the 16th October, 1943 and to advise you that information has been received from a reliable source stating that your son, Sergeant Raymond Barlow, Royal Air Force, has arrived in a neutral country.

This information should be treated as strictly confidential and should not in any circumstances be released to the press or mentioned on the telephone.

Correspondence can be addressed to him, C/o Air Ministry A.I.1., King Charles Street, London, S.W.1. It is pointed out that as your letters will pass through enemy hands it is advisable to address your son as a civilian and not to mention service particulars.

Any further news will be immediately passed to you.

I am, Sir,
Your obedient servant,

for Director of Personal Services.

R. Barlow
Sunnyside,
Lime Avenue
Sutton-in-Ashfield
Notts.

MISCELLANY

A ONE-WAY FLIGHT THAT RETURNED 47 YEARS LATER:

Captain Arthur Whitlock, retired Airways Tristar pilot, writes of an old friend's nostalgic return to base:

"To an aviator, a one-way flight is always very bad news indeed - at best it implies a crash from which the aeroplane never returns or, far worse, that the occupants pay the ultimate price.

The RAF heavy bomber base at Fiskerton, just outside Lincoln, in the summer of 1990 was a shadow of its wartime development, when a 2- seat Cessna circled the field, then floated down from the morning sky and set down gently on a short stretch of disused runway.

Gone were 49 Squadron's long queues of 4-engined Lancaster bombers loaded with 4,000lb 'cookies', incendiaries and other assorted high explosives bound for Germany. The Cessna's pilot skilfully brought his machine to earth, avoiding numerous overhead power and telephone lines, as his wing tip brushed over rows of beehives at the side of the concrete, a perfect example of the partnership between beekeeper and the farmer who wished his crop of oilseed rape to be pollinated. A small reception committee stood waiting in a group, occasionally ducking and weaving to avoid the attentions of disturbed bees. The aircraft came to rest. The pilot stepped out and then assisted his passenger carefully from the machine, for he was a victim of past injuries and required crutches.

It was clearly obvious that the pair were good friends of long standing, such were their gestures of camaraderie. Indeed, their bond of friendship was further fortified, for above all that, they were also comrades in arms. Captain Johnny Moss and his air bomber, Len 'Brad' Bradfield, somewhat older and sadly, minus 5 members of their crew, had just landed back at Fiskerton after an absence of 47 long years. They were the only two, out of a crew of seven, who had at last made it back to base in a somewhat different aeroplane, but nevertheless by air - the way they had left.

On that long-past evening of 10 August 1943, in the gathering dusk, their 20 year old Captain of Lancaster J for Johnny had opened up his 4 Merlin engines to roaring take-off power and the huge bomber had eventually lifted off Fiskerton's main runway. Little did any of those seven crewmen know the fate that awaited them that night over Germany.

The A.O.C. Bomber Command decreed that continuous evasive action was to cease and steady flight was to be maintained over enemy territory. On their very next trip, acting on these unwelcome new orders, they were shot down. Bursts of tracer shells from two German night-fighters soon had the Lancaster a burning inferno... a hastily shouted order 'Bale out!' over the intercom and it was every man for himself. The young skipper was the last man out as the Lancaster finally exploded.

Johnny came down in open country, but there was no sign of his crew. He therefore decided to start working his way southwards across Europe without delay, pinning his hope on his RAF uniform being much the same colour as the Wehrmacht's.

On day two his luck ran out when he was surrounded by German farm workers as he crept along a hedgerow trying to get some apples to satisfy his maddening pangs of hunger. The next few years were spent in a P.o.W. camp, but were not entirely wasted - he completely mastered the German language. This came in most handy long after the war when the writer found himself in need of his Captain's help as an interpreter, while based in Berlin, for chatting up the German girls!

Johnny had been lucky not falling into the wrong hands, but air bomber 'Brad', the only other survivor, did not fare as well during his captivity. He suffered severe frostbite and the loss of some of his toes while being evacuated ahead of the advancing Russians. This permanently affected his mobility. The other five crewmen were never seen alive again. They may have fallen victims to the vengeance of civilians, who rarely spared so called 'British terror flyers' when they fell into their hands. Their names are listed in the great book kept in Lincoln Cathedral along with 25,000 other RAF airman who lost their lives operating from Lincolnshire.

In early 1945, with Germany very much on the receiving end, Johnny seized a chance to escape. He worked his way towards the advancing allied lines, and fell into the company of an American Colonel trying to rejoin his compatriots. After some nailbiting exchanges, contact was made and at last they were among friends. A celebration was called for and a bottle of brandy was produced.

The normal pint-drinking Johnny had not been anywhere near alcohol for years and after only one glass he was flat on his back, hopelessly drunk and frothing at the mouth (the brandy had reacted with recently eaten turnips and sugarbeet). Enter several burly U.S. Military Police who mistakenly took the dirty blue uniform to be German. Without hesitation, the M.P. drew out his pistol and put it to his intended victim's head and was about to fire, when a desperate shout raised; 'Hey no! This guy's a limey flyer!'

Fortunately for my old friend, a stay of execution was granted and he was eventually shipped back home to England. By all accounts of the witnesses present on that day with the Americans, it was the nearest Johnny had come to death during his war.

Today, as a bystander, watching the two veteran airmen beside their small aircraft, one supported by crutches, and the other my old friend and Dakota Captain of the post war years 37 years ago, I marvelled at how the wheel turns full circle."

Postscript: The author was also privileged to be a witness to this special occasion. To my delight, Arthur Whitlock (co-owner of the Cessna with Johnny Moss) asked if I would like a trip up in the aircraft. I jumped at the chance; and as we lifted into the air from my beloved Fiskerton airfield, for the very first time, I had a Lancaster crew's eyeview of Lincoln Cathedral, magnificent on its hilltop crest. Under the nose my childhood village of Cherry Willingham, whilst off to the south the Witham valley coursed its way into the misty city and eventually Brayford Pool. As we gained height, Arthur banked the aircraft through 180 degrees to port and the panorama of Fiskerton village and its airfield spread out before us.

"Anywhere you would like to go?" asked Arthur, to which I replied, *"How about Bardney airfield"*, *"Okay! - do you know the way?"*, again I replied, *"Yes - just follow the Witham and turn left at the sugar factory"*. *"It's all yours"* came the reply, *"Just keep the nose up and the horizon level"*. It was a dream come true - I flew steadily along the river until Bardney village came into view, then I gently banked to port and minutes later the configuration of Bardney's runways slipped below to starboard. Banking port again, I was now heading in a westerly direction, which I knew would bring us back over Fiskerton. I made an approach in line with the old main runway... by now my imagination was working overtime. As we crossed the 'drome, I could now make out several landmarks only previously studied on maps and aerial photographs.

Back to reality as Arthur regained control, and he prepared for our final approach. We passed over the former Communal site (my old primary school) and then the technical site; the old roadways were still visible. Arthur lined up on the short piece of pot-holed concrete descending slowly... delicately over the high tension cables then dropping sharply before flaring out and gently touching down... the many small stones rattling against the underside of the Cessna. It was over all too quickly. It had been such a memorable day - first Johnny and Brad making their return from that final operation, and then, without warning to go aloft above my 'field of dreams'.

I shall be forever grateful to Arthur, Brad and Johnny; they are indeed true gentlemen... and I was very proud to have been in such brave company.

GOOD FRIENDS: F/Lt Leslie (Uncle Will) Hay keeps memories:

Here 'Uncle' refers to the loss of Jock Galloway and crew (plus the Mallinson crew) in February 1945.

"The loss of experienced crews hit us very hard; Mallinson was on his 35th with only one to go! it confirmed that luck played as big a part as experience. Galloway and his crew were very friendly with us and he was very popular on the squadron. I remember several pilots volunteered to go out into the North Sea and look for them as it was said that lights had been seen 'somewhere out there'.

This of course was not allowed; it was a job, if there was one, for the air sea rescue, the experts, not us... each to his own trade.

I received a letter from Jock's fiancee, whom I had never met, asking if I could find out anything about his loss. She wrote to me as she said Jock had spoken about me, and did not know who else to contact. I should have passed the letter to the Station adjutant for formal reply, but knowing Jock so well, I really shared her distress and wrote as comforting and hopeful a reply as I could. There was always a chance that he was alive.

Now he lives in both our memories, and is only one of those who grow not old as we, who are left grow old.. ..BUT WE REMEMBER THEM. Jock now rests in Poznan Cemetery - Poland.

WHEN WE WERE YOUNG

Time has revealed numerous instances where young people have been a little economical with the truth with regards their age, when signing up to 'do their bit' for their country. Over the years, this has become synonymous with the First World War, but it has proven to be a regular occurrence during the Second World War.

We have seen in May 1945 (52 Years After Exodus) how by pure coincidence former 49er and ex-POW Ted Cachart met ex-WAAF Billi Watkins at East Kirkby, and how it is just possible that they originally met at Dunsfold in May '45 when Ted was flown back home. Again by coincidence it was revealed that they had both joined the Service 'under age'.

Billi describes how she managed *"I had just become 17 on 31st May 1942. My two friends who I worked with were both over 18 and were about to enlist in the WAAF. I so desperately wanted to go with them, so we steamed off the last stamp on my National Insurance Card and I bought a new one from the post office and replaced it (Insurance stamps went up in value when one became 18), When asked at the recruiting centre for my birth certificate, I said it had got lost in the bombing".*

After training at Bridgnorth and Morecambe, Billi went to Chigwell in Essex for Barrage balloon training. She was posted to sites in the North London around Tottenham and Finsbury Park. (Very close to where Tom Gatfield lived - did they pass in the street?) After remustering as a Flt/Mech E, Billi next went to Croughton. 1945 saw her, along with other WAAFs welcoming home returning POWs from Germany who landed at RAF Dunsfold.

Ted Cachart was even younger when he joined, being only 15 when he was sworn in and given his service number. He describes how he managed it.

"Living in Pinner, Middlesex we were just far enough away from London to avoid the 'blitz' but were close enough to be able to see the dog fights overhead during the Battle Of Britain. I think it was partly the glamour of the 'Brylcream Boys' and partly that both my elder brothers were in the army that made me decide to join the RAF when my time came. It was about March 1941 when I was cycling back home from visiting my brother who was then stationed at Mill Hill that I called into an RAF recruiting office in Edgware to find out when I could apply. The seargent told me that I could volunteer when I was 17¼ and that if I did and passed all my medicals I would be guaranteed entry into the RAF when I reached 18. He gave me an application form and some other bumf and I departed. Stopping off at Moat Farm Park I sat and read all the info and saw that volunteers under 18 had to have their parents permission but did not need to provide a birth certificate.

I decided I had nothing to lose so would 'have a go'. I cycled to Wealdstone and called on a Priest who knew my father quite well and asked him if he would act as a witness to dad's signature, explaining the application was just to make sure I got in the RAF instead of being called up into the army or navy.

I also convinced him that dad would sign it when I got home and this was accepted and he signed in the witness space. That evening I presented the form to my father using the same story and he too accepted it and next morning the application was in the post.

In April I was called to Edgware for a medical which surprisingly I passed without comment and then in May I received a rail warrant and instructed to report for Air Crew Selection at Oxford University. My parents still believed this was all just the normal preamble to ensure my entry into the service of my choice. At the Selection Board I declined a pilots course as I really did not think I would get away with that but opted to be a Wop/Ag. On May 13th I was sworn in and given my service number 1318564 and placed on the reserve list just a month before my 16th birthday.

At the end of September I received my papers and rail warrant with instructions to report to Padgate on Oct 1st. My father gave me a hard time but eventually relented believing that within a few weeks I would be begging him to get me out. (I had been evacuated to Brighton in August '39 and begged to come home in October).

After kitting out at Padgate, square bashing and morse at Blackpool, radio school at Yatesbury I passed out as a Wireless operator and put up my 'sparks badge on 13th April 1942. Due to the delays in flying training I, like many newly qualified Wops were posted to various stations to 'help out' until a course became available. I was lucky and went to 1487 Tow Target Flight at RAF Warmwell, a fighter station near Weymouth. This was a small flight of about 4 Lysanders and a Miles master.

As the only air crew trainee on the flight I was soon flying (unofficially) as a drogue operator going up almost daily in the Lizzies towing targets for the fighters and some naval gun boats out of Portland. The Polish adjutant also took me up in the Master at every opportunity as he loved to fly it and shoot up his girl friend's farmhouse.

As the flying was all unofficial it is not recorded in my log book but I had about 50 hours by my 17th birthday. September saw me posted to South Kensington for a Marconi course followed by flying training at RAF Madeley and then to Stormy Down in Wales for a 2 week gunnery course passing out as Sgt Wop/Ag on 28th April '43, 6 weeks before my 18th birthday.

A month at Wigtown (where I very nearly flew in a Botha! - was actually sitting in it with engines running when trip was scrubbed) and then OTU at Hixon, HCU at Swinderby and on 13 Oct my goal was reached when our crew was posted to 49 at Fiskerton, a somewhat cocky 'old sweat' of 18. I never regretted my decision."

Ted aged 16 whilst stationed at Warmwell
(Note the cigarette!)

49 SQUADRON MEMORIALS

A DAY TO REMEMBER

UNVEILING OF THE MEMORIAL PLAQUE - FISKERTON CHURCH

A Dedication Service and unveiling of a Memorial Plaque in memory of all those who served at R.A.F. Fiskerton, took place in Fiskerton Church on 23rd August, 1987.

HOW IT ALL STARTED:

The following account is given by Freda Styles, at the time Admin Officer of HQ No. 15 Group ROC.

"As there was no memorial to commemorate the fact that brave men and women from the two Bomber Command Squadrons which served at Fiskerton and had been part of village life from 1943 to 1945, it was felt now was the appropriate time to rectify this.

It was decided that a memorial plaque should be placed in the Church and a small committee was set up to organise this. I was selected to be committee secretary, I suppose because I have lived in the village for the last 25 years, I am a member of the Church and also Admin Officer at HQ No. 15 Group ROC. The last fact was very important because 15 Group ROC under its Group Commandant Observer, Commander Peter Jex, was to play a very important role in bringing about the Dedication Service.

Three members of the ROC were elected to the committee; L/Obs Charles Parker, Obs(W) Phyl Pyett and Obs Ron Brittain, Mr Fred Wood, an ex 49 Squadron member who made Fiskerton his home after the war, and under the enthusiastic drive of Mr Robert Walkinton, Church Treasurer, as Chairman, we got underway.

August 23rd, 1987 was the date chosen to hold the Service; at last we had a date to work towards. Sue Morrison, a Sculptress of some renown agreed to undertake to carve the memorial depicting the two squadron crests, and the words 'In Memory of all who served at RAF Fiskerton 1943-1945'. Saturday was spent decorating the Church with flowers and making certain everything was ready for our big day.

Sunday saw the small church (with an awning erected on the south side equipped with loudspeakers to accommodate the overspill), filled to overflowing. It was very moving to see squadron members meet each other after 40 years and it was amazing to hear crew members introduce the 'Skipper' as though they were still serving members of the RAF.

The moving dedication service was conducted by Canon James Day DFC, himself a former Pathfinder pilot.

Local ladies enthusiastically agreed to take care of the food for the reception at the Group HQ and what sterling work they did, the tables were laden with home cooked food and looked magnificent with swirls of red, white and blue serviettes.

49 SQUADRON MEMORIALS

The facilities made available by the ROC enabled the former squadron members and their families to mingle, reminisce and really have a most enjoyable and memorable afternoon.

Many messages and letters have been received from ex-members of 49 and 576 Squadrons thanking the local Committee and the ROC for their contribution to this memorable day.

Fiskerton village is very proud that 'their' squadrons - 49 and 576 are now permanently remembered in the little Church of St Clement's.

I feel proud - and humble - to have had the opportunity to be involved so deeply in this memorial to two brave squadrons who operated from our local airfield, where now, only our Headquarters buildings stand... they are gone but not forgotten."

Mr Robert Walkinton adds:

"Each year we have received wreaths for laying on Remembrance Sunday on behalf of both Squadrons and one from a 49 Squadron member specifically for three members of his crew."

Authors Note: Now, if you visit St Clements on Remembrance Sunday, you will find a contingent of squadron veterans and their families within the congregation... they are drawn back every year.

Left:
St. Clement's of Rome Church in Fiskerton.

Right:
The memorial stone with 49 Squadron Roll of Honour on the pedestal below and to the left.

Right: An enlarged view of the memorial stone.

49 SQUADRON MEMORIALS

THIS LITTLE BIT OF LINCOLNSHIRE

UNVEILING OF THE MEMORIAL STONE - FISKERTON AIRFIELD

A Ceremony of unveiling a stone and tree (a flowering Chestnut) in memory of all those who served at R.A.F. Fiskerton, took place on Sunday 21st May 1995.

HOW IT HAPPENED TO BE:

The 10th August 1993 was a bright sunny day, blue sky with white fluffy clouds, perfect flying weather.

"As the Cessna 150 light aircraft flew over the Lincolnshire countryside we remembered so well, much had changed, but the river and Lincoln Cathedral rising from the plain were the same. The villages had grown, Fiskerton airfield had almost disappeared back into the farmland from which it came. Part of 060 - 300 runway remained as a narrow strip of concrete through standing crops, a line of electric cables ran parallel with it, then crossed it just before the end.

Johnny Moss my skipper turned on to the circuit, the memories came flooding back - to take-off fifty years ago in 'B-Baker', a Lancaster with a crew of seven and a full bomb load, bound for Nuremburg. A few hours later everything had changed, we were shot down, five of our friends dead, Johnny and I Prisoners of War. It was if they were with us as we returned to base... mission completed.

The wind was straight down the strip minimising drift so the power line was no problem, the concrete, although overgrown, was reasonable... it was a good landing. We were met by John Ward (49 Squadron Historian), Arthur Whitlock (Johnny's post-war Co-pilot), Geoff Stuffins and his sons who farm the land, also Jim Greensmith of Yorkshire T.V., who recorded the event for the 'Calendar' programme. I was surprised at the interest our nostalgic visit generated, proving that 'Bomber County' remembers... and cares. Geoff Stuffins generously offered a site on his land for a memorial to those who had served at Fiskerton in those momentous days."

Len Bradfield, 49 Squadron.

49 SQUADRON MEMORIALS

The ceremony was conducted by Tom Gatfield, Secretary of 49 Squadron Association. The introductory address was given by Leslie Hay 'Uncle Will', Chairman 49 Squadron Association.

THE FISKERTON ADDRESS

Some 53 years ago, the people of this quiet countryside became aware of intense activity with the noise of the construction of this airfield lying between the beautiful villages of Fiskerton, from which it takes its name, and Reepham. In January 1943, 49 Squadron arrived with its Lancasters and remained until October 1944, when 576 Squadron took over and stayed until the end of hostilities. In spite of the upheaval which was inevitably created, both squadrons were well received by the local residents.

During this period, the whole area was vibrant with the activity of a Squadron on active service; not only with the noise of aircraft coming and going at all hours of the day and night, but with the constant bustle of all those ancillary sections so vitally necessary to support a bomber squadron. GROUND CREWS - just two words which embrace all the sections so necessary to supply, maintain and repair aircraft at war. To these must be added Flying Control, Transport, Parachute Section, Stores, Administration and others together with those required to house and feed all the personnel of the Station, 'each', in their own capacity, as vital as the crews who depended so much upon them-and upon them for so much.

It is through the generosity and efforts of Geoff Stuffins, who donated this piece of land, and the hard work of his sons, that we are today to witness the marking and dedication of it.

The stone, which comes from a Lincolnshire quarry, marks the site of the airfield. The tree, which annually sheds its leaves like falling aircraft, will, each spring bring new life and renewed hope for peace throughout the world, and perhaps people of the generations as yet unborn, may pause here and say -

"THIS IS HALLOWED GROUND"

On a plot of land generously donated by the local farmer Jeff Stuffins the memorial, constructed from local Ancaster stone, sits in a tree lined corner beside the remains of the main runway and the road between Reepham and Fiskerton.

In 1997 Two additional stones were erected, each containing a stainless steel plaque engraved with a poem. Listen To The Wind by Cedric Roberts (576) and Spirits In Flight by Eddy Coward (49) are both relatives of airmen who flew from Fiskerton and failed to return.

Paul Smith, 49 Squadron, then read Nöel Coward's...

'LIE IN THE DARK AND LISTEN'.

Lie in the dark and listen,
It's clear tonight so they're flying high
Hundreds of them, thousands perhaps,
Riding the icy, moonlight sky.
Men, material, bombs and maps
Altimeters and guns and charts
Coffee, sandwiches, fleece lined boots
Bones and muscles and minds and hearts.
English saplings with English roots
Deep in the earth they've left below
Lie in the dark and let them go
Lie in the dark and listen.

Lie in the dark and listen
They're going over in waves and waves
High above villages, hills and streams
Country churches and little graves.
And little citizen's worried dreams.
Very soon they'll have reached the sea
And far below them will lie bays
And coves and sands where they used to be
Taken for summer holidays
Lie in the dark and let them go
Lie in the dark and listen.

Lie in the dark and listen,
City Magnates and steel contractors,
Factory workers and politicians,
Soft hysterical little actors,
Ballet dancers, reserved musicians,
Safe in your warm civilian bed,
Count your profit and count your sheep,
Life is passing above your head,
Just turn over and try to sleep,
Lie in the dark and let them go,
Theirs is a world you'll never know,
Lie in the dark and listen.

Eddy Coward, Associate member of 49 Squadron Association, then read a poem that he had written after visiting Fiskerton airfield. It is in memory of his brother P/O Cliff Coward (and crew), a navigator of a 49 Squadron Lancaster, which failed to return 11/12 April 1944, flying from Fiskerton; they were all killed in action..

'SPIRITS IN FLIGHT'

I saw them return, seven spirits in flight,
Engines fired by the sparks of the night,
Lumbering, throbbing like a battered ghost,
So thankful for a friendly coast.

Glowing and gliding, it roars without sound,
The rubber screams, as it kisses the ground,
Perfect touch-down, on a deserted plain,
Now a cornfield, a field with no name.

Night after night, mission after mission,
Helmets, visors, masks and ammunition,
The seven Sky Warriors from long past,
All knowing tonight, could be their last.

I hear the fields, alive with noise,
Filled with brave men, some are just boys,
I see them walk, in their suits of leather,
Slowly and proudly, they walked together.

Where their planes rose, to meet the foe,
Now the larks rise, from their nests below,
Down the runway, only peace is heard,
Save for the wind, and the song of a bird.

Time passes - January to December,
From Spring to Winter, the years drift on,
Every April, Every Easter - I will remember,
Cliff, Al, Pete & John, Nick, Stan & Skipper Don.

Tom Gatfield then read an extract from the funeral oration of Pericles made in 431 BC in memory of Athenians...

> **'The brave are surely those who have the clearest vision of what is before them, glory and danger alike, and yet they go out to meet it.**
>
> **They faced the foe in the strength of their own manhood; and when the shock of battle came they chose rather to suffer the uttermost than to save lives by feeble submission.**
>
> **For the whole earth is the sepulchre of heroes; and their story is not only engraved on stone or brass in the places from which they came, their story lives on even in places far away, without visible symbol woven into the stuff of other men's lives.**
>
> **Take these men as your example. Like them, remember that posterity can only be for the free; and that freedom is the sure possession only of those who have the courage to defend it.'**

As the wind continued to blow across the old airfield, chilling the 150 plus gathering, Tom Gatfield read out Kipling's Recessional...

**"The tumult and the shouting dies;
The Captains and the Kings depart;
Still stands Thine ancient sacrifice,
An humble and a contrite heart.
Lord God of Hosts, be with us yet,
Lest we forget - lest we forget!"**

All:- **WE WILL REMEMBER THEM**

There then followed a 2 minutes silence, and during that silence... was it just me... or did others hear that distant sound of Merlin engines, winging their way back home?

**"And they thought of days that were long since by
when their limbs were strong and their courage high."**

Tom Gatfield, 49 Squadron Association Secretary and Eric Norman (576 Squadron) then unveiled the Memorial Stone, followed by Len Bradfield and Eric Norman laying wreaths to their respective squadrons. Reverend Malcom Roberts, Rector of Fiskerton Church, and Honorary Padre of 49 Squadron Association, then gave the Blessing.

The members of 49 Squadron Association and members of 576 Squadron wish to express their extreme gratitude to Geoff Stuffins and his family, for because of them, this little bit of Lincolnshire will be forever 49 and 576.

49 SQUADRON MEMORIALS

THE BRANSBY MEMORIAL

Bransby is a small hamlet between Sturton and Saxilby in Lincolnshire where Hampden AT192 (EA-O) crashed on 25th January 1942. Exactly 50 years after the crash, a special memorial service was held near the crash site in honour of all 4 members of the crew who sadly perished.

The aircraft actually came down in fields which now form part of the Bransby Home of Rest for Horses. Mr Peter Hunt, secretary of the home, helped plan the event which was conducted by Padre Andy McMullan from RAF Scampton.

Attending were relatives of the crew; Mrs Eileen Morris, sister of Albert Hibbet and Mrs Jean Lawbuary, sister of Leonard Jardine together with Eric Clark (ex-49er) who actually flew on the raid to Brest with S/Ldr Bennett. Tom Page (ex-49er) and the author were also privileged to be in attendance. A small plaque (subscribed by the directors of the home) in memory of crew members, Charles lStewart, Ken Northrop, Albert Hibbet and Len Jardine was unveiled.

On each Remembrance Day since, Eric Clark and Tom Page have laid a wreath at this memorial. Starting in 1997, this small ceremony will now be carried out by ex-49er WAAF MT driver Dot Smith (Nee Everett).

The memorial is a small wooden building which houses the plaque. The wording of the plaque is repeated here for clarity:-

IN MEMORY OF THE CREW OF A HANDLEY PAGE BOMBER WHO LOST THEIR LIVES WHEN THE PLANE CRASHED IN THIS FIELD AFTER TAKING OFF FROM SCAMPTON RAF STATION ON 25th JANUARY 1942.

SGT PILOT	CHARLES DUNCAN STEWART
SGT	KENNETH EDWARD NORTHROP
SGT	ALBERT HIBBET
SGT	LEONARD ARTHUR JARDINE

49 SQUADRON MEMORIALS

THE HAMELDOWN TOR MEMORIAL

A simple granite monolith standing on the lonely, windswept stretches of Hamel Down on Dartmoor. This memorial was first put up in 1941 to commemorate the crew of 4 of a Hampden Bomber (X3054 'S') from 49 Squadron, Scampton that crashed on the moor on the night of 21st March 1941.

It contains an equally simple inscription:-

RAF
SQDN 49
R.D.W.
R.L.E.
C.J.L.
R.B.

The crew comprised the Hon P/O Robert Wilson (Pilot), son of the Lord Lieutenant of Yorkshire's East Riding, Sgt R L A Ellis (Navigator), Sgt C J Lyon (Air Gunner) and Sgt R Brames (Wireless Operator).

They were 1 of 66 aircraft that attacked the U-Boat bases at Lorient in the Bay of Biscay. On the return journey they became hopelessly lost, possibly due to wireless failure and finally broke through cloud over the West of England instead of the sea as expected. At around 10.55 pm the aircraft flew into a hillside with the wing clipping the top of Hameldown Tor and crashed nearby.

Sgts Ellis, Lyon and Brames were all killed instantly. P/O Wilson was critically injured and taken to Moretonhampstead Hospital where he died the next day. He and the Navigator Sgt Ellis are buried in Exeter Cemetery. Sgts Lyon and Brames being buried in their respective home towns.

In 1991, 50 years after the aircraft crashed, the Torbay Aircrew Association decided to renovate the memorial as the original inscription was so badly weathered that it was almost unreadable.

The necessary permissions were obtained and around 500 people turned up for the service that was arranged. The picture on the next page shows the new inscription engraved on a plaque.

ON 21ST MARCH 1941
A ROYAL AIR FORCE BOMBER
49 SQDN SCAMPTON
CRASHED RETURNING FROM
OPERATIONS OVER FRANCE
THE 4 CREW WERE LOST

THIS MEMORIAL BEARS
THEIR INITIALS AND SQUADRON
NUMBER. COMMEMORATING
THEIR SELFLESS COURAGE
AND THAT OF FELLOW AIRMEN
WHO PERISHED ON DARTMOOR
1939 -1945
THEIR SACRIFICE HELPED US
TO MAINTAIN FREEDOM

THE AIRCREW ASSOCIATION 1991

49 SQUADRON MEMORIALS

THE FULBECK MEMORIAL

A memorial stone, with the Badges of Bomber Command and the Bomber Airfield Society and the inscription:-

IN MEMORY OF
ALL WHO FLEW FROM
R.A.F. FULBECK
NEVER TO RETURN.
1940 - 1945

The memorial, which was blessed and unveiled at a ceremony attended by Ken White's sisters in Sept 1992, is at the entrance road to the former airfield, its base in the shape of a propeller. An inscription at the foot records:

F/Sgt Ken White Memorial erected by the Bomber Airfield Society 1988.

This memorial was vandalised in 1995 and was repaired in 1996/7 by the Bomber Airfield Society assisted by ex-POW Luftwaffe airman Ben Lügering

There are other smaller memorials in France, Holland, Belgium and Denmark, tended by local people. We must always be grateful to those allies who also pay homage to our comrades who did not come home.

STAND THOSE THREE TOWERS?

(An old airman's Lincolnshire nostalgia)

Stand those three towers still a-pointing
In the dawn light, stark and clear?
Does the ghostly roar of the 'Lanc' still soar
O'er the fields of Lincolnshire?

Do the shades of Ancient Briton;
Of Roman, Saxon, Dane;
Still stand and gaze in mute amaze
On the ghosts who throng the plain?

Ghosts of the flower of England;
Of Empire and Allied Kin;
Are they still in sight in the darkening light
Each dusk as the night rolls in?

Ghosts of Geordie, Scouse and Cockney,
Of Yellowbelly and Tyke;
Do they fly again over Martin Fen;
O'er Grimsby and Boston Dyke?

And of Paddy, Jock and Taffy;
Of Aussie, Canuck and Yank.
Are they flying still over Lindum Hill,
O'er the Wash and the Humber Bank?

And the Freedom Men of Europe;
New Zealand and Afric' dark;
Do they still fly strong to the Merlin's song
And the sound of the Browning's bark?

Do those hosts of glad young warriors
Still soar and fly and toil
And fight and die in an alien sky;
Still rest in an alien soil?

Ah! Many the distant lonely cross
And many the shattered 'plane
Whose last home sight on a bombers' night
Was a view of a Lincoln Lane.

Does that lumbering bus still rumble
Those lanes from -thorpe to -by?
Does it still stop hard by the old churchyard
Where more of our brothers lie?

Sons of all the warring nations;
The plain men and the brave.
All troubles past; they've found their last
Safe home in an English grave.

While we, whom they've left behind them;
We few, as our years grow old
Still fight and fly in their battle sky
In dreams when the night is cold.

Ah! Lincoln! Our shire of memories
From the dawn to the setting sun;
Your heath and fen will live again
With us till our journey's run.

Victor Cavendish

ON MEMORIAL SUNDAY EACH YEAR WREATHS OF REMEMBRANCE BEARING A 49 SQUADRON SASH ARE LAID AT ALL THE MEMORIALS LISTED HERE BY RELATIVES, FRIENDS OR MEMBERS OF THE 49 SQUADRON ASSOCIATION.

THE LINCOLN ERA

Bomber Command's post war period, in which the Avro Lincoln played a significant role, has been somewhat overshadowed by the exploits of Lancaster crews during the Second World War. Perhaps because of this, former Lincoln crew members have themselves, been hard to locate... lying 'dormant' over the years. Fortunately, within the 49 Squadron Association, this situation is being redressed, and mainly through the efforts of Eric Newton and David Boughton, 'Lincoln' 49ers are now being found and recruited into the fold.

Unfortunately, there is insufficient space within these pages to give an adequate account of their dedicated service. Hopefully, in the near future, their interesting stories will be given more detail. But a book concerning 49 Squadron would not be complete without some mention of these post-war aviators. To this end, I am extremely grateful for the help and assistance of Eric Newton, who has provided all of the anecdotal material in this chapter... Eric remembers:

"My own arrival on 49 was in late 1951, when the first thing I noticed in the crew room was a strip of wood across the top of the dartboard. Painted on it were the white capital letters; O G P G M S T K M B M S T I K W I A T A - After a few days, curiosity got the better of me and I asked what the letters meant.

O God Please Give Me Strength To Keep My Big Mouth Shut 'Til I Know What I Am Talking About,

was the reply, to the accompaniment of guffaws all round!"

FROM LANCS TO LINCS

The squadron began to receive its first Avro Lincolns during October 1949 whilst stationed at Upwood, Huntingdonshire. For the next few months, the squadron operated both Lincolns and Lancasters, until March 1950 when 49 Squadron finally said farewell to its Lancs after a long and illustrious association with the type. In July 1952, the squadron made a further move to Waddington near Lincoln, then in August 1953 it took up residence at Wittering. It was during this period that a wave of terrorism in Kenya was reaching serious proportions.

KENYA - MAU MAU TERRORISTS

Kikuyu tribesmen were making claims on certain parts of Kenya, and they were using terrorism against the local population in attempt to further their aims. The terrorists practised a form of witchcraft and black magic which they used to influence other natives into helping them. This type of worship was called Mau Mau, and this name was adopted by East African Europeans when referring to the terrorists. Horrific acts of terrorism were being committed by the 'Mau Mau' and they were getting ever nearer to Nairobi itself.

General Sir George Erskine, C-in-C East Africa, was of the opinion that so far, the RAF operations against the Mau Mau had proved inadequate. These involved the dropping of 18lb fragmentation bombs from Harvard aircraft. The General suggested that perhaps bigger aircraft capable of dropping larger bombs would not only help destroy morale, but also flush out the gangs for the ground forces to deal with.

During November 1953, 49 Squadron was deployed on a month's 'Sunray' to Shallufa. A few days after arrival SASO Middle East made a personal visit to the CO, S/Ldr Alan Newitt DFC. After explaining the 'Kenya' situation to S/Ldr Newitt, it was decided to send 3 aircraft from the squadron to Kenya. Once there, they were to carry out a few sorties in which 1,000lb bombs would be used. It was hoped that the large 'bangs' would have the desired effect, and that the small force could then return to Shallufa. On no account were the Lincolns to drop all their bombs at once, rather to spread them out over a two week period.

Routing through Khartoum, S/Ldr Newitt (SX979) and crew (in company with two other aircraft) departed Shallufa on 10 November, bound for Kenya. After arriving at Eastleigh Airport near Nairobi, the first bomb drop took place on 18 November. A few days later, the CO was surprised by the arrival of the rest of 49 Squadron's aircraft at Eastleigh. New orders stated that the squadron would return home as soon as another replacement Lincoln squadron became available - the squadron was destined to stay in Kenya until January 1954, before returning home to Wittering.

Eastleigh Airport, some 5,500 feet above sea level, had just one main runway. Metalled at both ends, the remainder consisted of compacted red dusty soil. With few 'normal' facilities, squadron personnel knuckled down to their tasks admirably in the searing heat. With a severe lack of equipment and vehicles, ingenuity and initiative were the order of the day... in these qualities the squadron members were not found lacking.

OPERATIONS AGAINST THE MAU MAU

Now fitted with tropical sand filters over the engine air intakes, different oil and weakened coolant, the Lincoln proved an ideal aircraft for the tasks ahead. The Lincolns were able to fly at altitude without power loss, whilst still being manoeuvrable enough to cope with adverse terrain at low level. During bombing, it was considered that 2,500 feet was a safe height from which to drop the 1,000lb bombs, whilst 1,000 feet was felt safe enough for the 500 pounders.

Target information came from detailed air photography or by Piper Pacer spotter planes of the Kenya Police Air Wing, dropping smoke grenades. Individual aircraft would be used, or area bombing by up to five aircraft, with a round trip taking no longer than an hour from take-off to landing. Aircrew found themselves in the unusual situation of flying ops from a BOAC civil air terminal, then arriving home from an early sortie to enjoy a quiet coffee in the terminal lounge.

THE CRASH OF RF349

Eastleigh, November 1953:
Lincoln RF444 of 49 Squadron is seen here being prepared for a bombing strike. (E. Newton)

The Squadron's time at Eastleigh was not without incident. On the night of 17th December 1953, pilot Stuart Keay (RF349) and crew set out for Shallufa (via Khartoum). The hours were up on one of the engines and as there were no spares at Eastleigh, it had to go to Shallufa for a power-plant change.

As the Lincoln gathered speed, a CSU (Constant speed unit) failed on one of the engines causing the aircraft to 'swing'. The pilot immediately abandoned the take-off, but too late, the aircraft's undercarriage collapsed and it began slewing along on its belly. Eric Newton, in bed at the time, listened to the doomed aircraft's final moments:

"I heard the aircraft going down the runway, and it must have been close to unsticking when there was a sudden dead silence. Leaping out of bed I got to the Control Tower in less than five minutes, to find a few of my colleagues already there, gazing at the aircraft which was on its belly, with a small lick of flame on one engine.

Since the crash crew were Africans, and thought that the Lincoln contained bombs, they would not go near it! So we watched the flames spread and destroy the plane completely. The crew was uninjured but they did lose their personal kit in the fire."

Nearest the camera is Avro Lincoln RF349 of 49 Squadron. This aircraft crashed on take-off from Eastleigh on 17th December 1953. (E. Newton).

SEARCH AND RESCUE

Eric Newton recalls another incident during 49's time in Kenya, but this time the consequences were far more tragic:

"Late one afternoon at Eastleigh the standby crews were called to the operations room for a possible search and rescue sortie. A Dakota of East African Airways (EAA) was overdue at Nairobi on a flight from Dar Es Salaam, but its endurance was not yet up. The last position given by the aircraft was somewhere about fifty miles SSE of Mount Kilimanjaro 'Victor Foxtrot on top', which meant of course that he would possibly have the 19,000 foot mountain - or the cloud build up around it - in full view, although he couldn't see the ground below him. By the time any search aircraft could reach the area it would be getting dark, so the planners (included 49er Ron Houghton) decided to wait until morning.

Next day two or three Lincolns went off before dawn and we commenced searching our allotted areas. My own crew spent 9 hours on the area of the last position report received. Piper Pacers, PR Meteors and EAA aircraft were also searching the area. We were at it again the following day, again with no result. On the third day, my crew went again and this time I was given a rather large camera and told to open the back door of the aircraft so as to get oblique pictures of the forested slopes of Kilimanjaro at any point where a line through the trees might indicate where an aircraft could have ploughed in. The snag was that this was being performed too close to the tree tops for comfort, and was extremely bumpy. An army NCO was beside me and began to feel very ill... finally he tried to vomit through the open door, with the result that it came back in his face... and sprayed me from head to foot!

After a third fruitless day of searching the RAF gave it up, but EAA continued in an area where some Africans living on the mountain had reported a flash and explosion up in the clouds on the afternoon that the aircraft went missing. Of course, communication from such people had taken time. EAA were desperate for two reasons; they had already lost one aircraft mysteriously and were going to have insurance problems... and also, Mrs Sorsbie, the wife of the manager at Dar Es Salaam airport was aboard it. Eventually an EAA aircraft found the point where Captain Quirke's Dakota had slammed into the rock face of Mawenzi peak - the wreckage was many thousands of feet below... at the bottom of a ravine!"

BOMBS FROM ADEN

Two 49 Squadron Lincolns flew from Eastleigh to Khormaksar to collect loads of bombs. A signal was received at Khormaksar telling the Lincoln crews to stay there until further notice. Rains had now started at Eastleigh and the 'Marram' runway would not be safe for landing with such loads. About a week later the crews were signalled to return, but with 400 miles still to go, a long range HF W/T message informed them that the runway was still unsafe and that they were diverted to Entebbe in Uganda. A rider was added to the order, which stated that under no circumstances should the bomb-doors be opened!

THE LINCOLN ERA

The arrival of two Lincolns at Entebbe attracted a lot of interest from locals, both European and African. The crews were told to park together about 50 yards away from the front of the passenger terminal and air traffic control buildings, where many people came over to inspect the aircraft. I don't suppose that, even to this day, many of them suspected that both aircraft had full bomb loads onboard...

Eastleigh,
circa Dec 1953/Jan 1954:
Walking towards the camera are (from l to r) Ron Skinner, air gunner; Eric Newton, signaller; Sgt Donohoe, flight engineer; figure crouching unknown; Sgt Bendall, flight engineer. Lincoln RE320 has been confirmed as being a 49 Squadron aircraft.
(E. Newton)

CLUSTER BOMB TRIALS

Two Lincolns were detailed to leave Eastleigh and go to an area near Pemba Island off the East African Coast. Once there, one would drop bombs, and the second would photograph the splash patterns on the sea, then the roles would be reversed until all bombs were expended. The bonus for both crews was that when the exercise was completed both aircraft would go to Mombasa/Port Reitz airport and all would spend a couple of days as guests at the Army leave camp at Nyali Beach. S/Ldr Alan Newitt landed first; Eric Newton in the second aircraft takes up the story:

"On our approach, I heard my captain say 'Flap quarter down'. The flight engineer repeated the instruction back and made the selection. Some seconds later I heard the captain say to the flight engineer 'I said flap quarter down'. At this instant a shout came on the intercom from air gunner Stan Bartlett (later killed in a flying accident) who was by now out of his tail turret and in the crash position for landing; 'I'm being sprayed by hot hydraulic fluid!', he yelled. With no flaps, the result was a very fast landing.

It was later established that the flap jack end-cap had split. Shortly after landing I overheard S/Ldr Newitt say to my captain 'You came in rather fast, Mr Farnell'. 'Yes Sir' said Willie, 'No flaps'. 'In that case you should have gone straight back to Nairobi'. The reply went something like 'You came in for a couple of days off - I want it too'."

Eric continues:

"One day we were called to the operations room to be told that the Rabizi tribesmen were becoming belligerent around Fort Robart in Aden. Those crews detailed were to take-off before dawn, and great stress was placed on SECURITY about our planned operation.

A couple of hours later, back at the Sgts' Mess we were sorting our affairs out before departure when a 'Dhobi' boy approached my colleague - 'Bwana, can you pay me now?' he said. 'Why do you want it so soon?' asked my colleague 'you were paid last week, and it is not due for another three'. 'But you're going to Aden tomorrow, Bwana...' It seems the bush telegraph is faster than many thought!"

SECOND TOUR

49 Squadron's 'first' tour finished at the beginning of January 1954, some crews arriving back at Wittering on 4 January. They were succeeded at Eastleigh by 100 Squadron who in turn were followed by 61 Squadron and then 214 Squadron...

49 Squadron was back 'on station' in Kenya by December 1954, the first contingent arriving on 30 November. After bringing 49 Squadron up to date with the new techniques and tactics developed for round the clock all weather bombing, 214 said farewell on 10 December.

FLAG WAGGING

After each strike it was customary for aircraft to fly all over the countryside at low level, and the European farmers and families would come out to wave. One day the Farnell crew (including Eric Newton) were at low level going down the Rift Valley in a southerly direction near Naivasha, about 100 yards to the west of the north/south road, at a section where the ground fell away gently from the road. Eric continues;

"Being extremely low, we were therefore level with the road. A European car driver in front, was totally unaware that he was about to be overtaken by a rather unusual vehicle. He must have been frightened out of his wits, for when we went past him, he zig-zagged all over the road. No complaint was ever received... so the chap must have seen the funny side of it".

THE LINCOLN ERA

MUTINY... THAT NEVER WAS

Eric recalls one Saturday morning at Eastleigh, when a Station Commander's Parade was scheduled:

"We went into the Sgts' Mess for breakfast. There seemed to be no activity from the kitchen and finally we were told that the wood fires had not been lit and we would not get breakfast until late. Somebody stated that Queen's Regulations say that it is an offence to go on parade without breakfast... Mess members were getting up to go on parade anyway, and finally, only nine of us had decided, quite independently, 'No breakfast - No parade!'

When the parade was over, we were sent for and told that we were bad boys. The nine of us - eight Sergeants and one Flight Sergeant - were told to march down to the parade ground where an unfamiliar Flight Lieutenant was waiting and prepared to do his worst at being unpleasant. He was intent on making a spectacle of us, but hadn't quite thought it all through. His preliminary lecture amounted to saying that we were not just aircrew - first and foremost we were NCO's. This was funny because it had never been heard before... and we let him know it.

Then he decided to give us some drill, which caused hilarity with passing airmen. When they realised who we were, they stopped to watch the entertainment. After a time, our F/Lt 'Nice-guy" had decided to give us a final pep-talk and said 'Now come on chaps, pull your socks up'. To a man, all nine of us bent down and pulled our socks up; the audience roared with laughter, and our F/Lt nearly had apoplexy. Exasperated, he told the F/Sgt to march us back to the squadron.

When we got there we were told we were going to be charged. A knowledgeable member of our group said 'You can't do that, it's two punishments for the same crime!' and that caused some consternation with the flight commander, Ron Houghton, who was acting OC 49 Squadron in S/Ldr Newitt's absence. The upshot of all this was that they decided not to call it a mutiny; they did go through the motions of charging us, recording Admonishments with our agreement... I've often wondered whether our drill officer ever recovered from his ordeal."

An excellent view of Eastleigh airport near Nairobi, a photograph taken during 49's second tour in 1955.

Five 49 Squadron Lincolns (now sporting white spinners) can be seen in the company of a Vickers Valetta of the East African Communications Flight and five Harvards of 1340 Flight.

The Avro Lincoln parked next to the Valetta is SX984, the aircraft involved in the Githunguri tragedy
(E. Newton)

THE GITHUNGURI TRAGEDY

On 19 February 1955, the Thomas crew (49 Squadron) were visiting Githunguri police post as guests of the Kenya Police. Suddenly, the visiting crew had their attention drawn to a Lincoln (displaying white spinners) coming in on a very low approach; it was another 49 Squadron crew intent on showing those on the ground 'a thing or two'. Those on the ground threw themselves flat, thinking the aircraft was coming straight into the compound. It was during the second pass that the aircraft's tail struck the boundary fence. It then went into a severe vertical climb before stalling out onto an African 'shamba'. In the sickening carnage, four Africans and all six crew members onboard were killed.

The hero of the incident was a chap called Pierson of the visiting crew, who managed to pull Stan Bartlett from the wreckage, but sadly Stan died later of his injuries.

Crashed SX984	F/O Hunt	Pilot	(Killed)
Lincoln	Sgt North	F/Eng	(Killed)
	Sgt Hollands	Signaller	(Killed)
	Sgt Bartlett	A/G	(Killed)
	F/O King	NAV	(Killed)
	F/O Parry	NAV	(Killed)

Gradually the combination of actions by ground forces and the persistent bombing strikes had the desired effect. The emergency was drawing to a close, which inevitably led to the operational strikes being tailed off. 49 Squadron flew its last sortie against the Mau Mau on 16 July, 1955. The squadron departed for the UK on 28 July.

49 Squadron had been the first into Kenya, and were the last to be withdrawn. Their task had been completed with total success.

THE SAGA OF THE DOG

One Sunday morning at Waddington, the CO of 49 Squadron, S/Ldr Alan Newitt was in his married quarters when the doorbell rang. At the door he found two men dressed in what one could hardly call 'Sunday best', and an old van was parked at the kerb. "Good morning, Sir", they said, "Squadron Leader Newitt?" "Yes", said he. "We've brought the dog", said they. "What dog", said he. "The one we advertised", said they. "Don't know anything about it", said he. By now his curiosity was aroused so he asked for an explanation.

It seems they were joint owners of a greyhound dog which had served well during its racing life, but being no longer a match for the rest of the entrants on the racing circuit, it was time to part company. They were, however, softies at heart and, wanting to allow the animal to spend the rest of its life as a pet with a good family they placed an advert in the paper.

'Offered free, with free delivery'.

They had received one very interesting reply from someone purporting to be S/Ldr Alan E. Newitt, who had said that he was CO of 49 Squadron Bomber Squadron and, since the squadron crest had a greyhound in full flight with the motto 'CAVE CANEM', he thought it appropriate that the dog should become the squadron mascot. Rather liking the idea they had come over from the Worksop area to deliver it. The humour of all this was not lost on Newitt, so he agreed to accept the greyhound. But who could have been the perpetrator of this practical joke? (the name Wally Gill has been mentioned).

The animal was duly taken to the squadron offices on the Monday morning and introduced to all personnel. He was renamed 'Skipper' and given the honorary rank of Sgt, and an officer navigator was appointed O/IC dog. (We're not sure whether 'Wee Mac' liked the idea but he seemed to accept his responsibility with good grace).

Many were the occasions when Sgt Skipper was seen disappearing at high speed into the morning mist across the airfield, chasing a hare, with the diminutive figure of Wee Mac running after him, shouting 'Come back'... there were also rumours that other things were shouted too! Unfortunately , Skipper was killed by a lorry on the camp some months later.

STATION COMMANDER'S AEROPLANE

Group Captain Sutcliffe, a gentleman by any standards, who was station commander at Wittering, phoned 49 Squadron one day and asked for a crew and an aircraft to be placed at his disposal on a certain date and time. This was, of course, standard practice for such senior officers who needed to get away from their desks and log the requisite flying hours each month to remain qualified in rating and flying pay.

On the allotted day it became apparent that the aircraft was not going to be ready in time, and at the time the Group Captain was due to arrive there wasn't an officer to be found - none wanted to have to tell him that he couldn't have his aeroplane on time. It was left, therefore, to the servicing 'Chiefy' (Flick, I think his name was) to convey the bad news. On being told the situation, the Group Captain said *"Thank you, Chief, what time shall I come back then?"* The Officers trickled back later...

FLIGHT COMMANDER'S CHECK

At Wittering, George was an F/O pilot, and though well built was rather small in height. In fact he needed a couple of cushions to lift him up so that he could see out over the cockpit coaming of the Lincoln. He was undergoing a check one day when the cushions slipped at about 100 yards from touch-down. We watched horrified, from the squadron offices as the nose of the aircraft lifted at the worst possible time.

Fortunately the aircraft was dual control and Jack Higginbottom the Flight Commander, took over and saved the situation quite miraculously. George was taken off Lincolns and sent on a Canberra course.

NAVIGATORS ARE NEVER LOST

On an exercise over the North Sea at night, Phil, the F/O Nav plotter, was uncertain of our position. George, the F/Sgt pilot, who was captain, called and told me to get some Consol fixes for Phil, who promptly discarded all of them saying that they were no good to him.

Rowley, the F/O Nav set operator, was standing in the astrodome with the sextant getting star shots and in his inimitable whinging voice arguing the whole while with Phil, who was also throwing the star shots away. Eventually George got fed up with all this and decided that enough was enough and there was little point in carrying on, and abandoned the exercise. Turning onto 270 degrees to look for a UK landfall, he then returned to base.

Nav's log and my radio log were impounded. George and the two navigators were suspended from flying, pending high level decisions. After some weeks it was decided that George was guilty of lack of captaincy, so was posted to Swanton Morley as a staff pilot. The two officer navs were posted to Bassingbourn onto Canberra courses. Presumably they could then get lost faster...

THE ARTHRITIC LINCOLN

One aircraft on the squadron had developed a rather bad reputation for hydraulic problems. Operation of flaps and landing gear being so sluggish that captains were regularly making entries to this effect on the Form 700. The aircraft was jacked up in the hangar on at least one occasion so that operation could be observed. Nothing was detected, but then there was no airflow to make it a realistic exercise. The aircraft was put back into service only to have the same fault entered on the F700 again soon afterwards. Mounted over the main spar at the back of the Signaller, was the hydraulic accumulator which had a rather large filler nozzle with a screw cap on it. The fault was eventually traced to the fact that a person unknown had stuffed a packet of sandwiches into this filler nozzle... They cleaned out the system and everything was fine afterwards.

No. 49 SQUADRON WAS DISBANDED ON 1 AUGUST 1955

AND REFORMED ON 1ST MAY 1956.

THE VALIANTS

Much of the information in the following text comes from research carried out by ex-49er Pete Williams and is extracted from the first draft of his writings 'Teeth of the Dog'. I am indebted to Peter for his help and contributions towards this part of 49 Squadron's history.

When Britain exploded its first atomic bomb in October 1952, many assumed that the United Kingdom also had the capability to use the weapon. This was far from true... much more scientific work was required on the bomb itself, the aircraft needed to carry it was not yet available and extensive trials to marry the two systems were needed.

Designed to a 1947 specification primarily to carry Britain's proposed atomic weapons, Vickers Armstrong submitted one of the 'unsuccessful' specification bids; but further study of their design showed it could meet the requirement in almost every respect. It was simple in construction and promised to be quicker to produce. A new Air Ministry specification was written around the Vickers design in the hope that the RAF could have a four-jet bomber in service by 1955.

In the event, this target was reached - the first V-bomber squadron, No 138 at Gaydon, receiving its Valiants in January 1955. At production peak, the aircraft were produced at the rate of one per week and the last of 104 delivered was XD875 in August 1957. Eventually ten RAF squadrons were equipped: Nos. 7, 18, 49, 90, 138, 148, 199, 207, 214 and 543.

VICKERS VALIANT B1

Production Valiants were fitted with Rolls-Royce Avon RA 28 Mk 204 turbojet engines, buried in contemporary British fashion in the wing roots. The aircraft was of massive construction, a 'backbone' member along the top fuselage centre-line supported five bomb stations designed to carry either: a single 10,000 lb free-fall nuclear weapon of the 'Blue Danube' type, two 1,750 lb tactical nuclear weapons of the 'Red Beard' type, 21 1,000 lb MC Mk 15 (in clutches of five and three), or two 1,615 gall fuel tanks. The cavernous bomb-bay would also accept the 'Blue Steel' stand-off bomb, which it did for flight test purposes.

By the time the Valiant started to come off the production lines at Weybridge, stocks of the 'Blue Danube' atomic weapon had built up in the Bomber Command Armament School at Wittering and personnel training had begun. The third production Valiant B1 WP201 was allocated for bomb trials and these were carried by S/Ldr Roberts and crew, at Wisley, and from June 1955, with 1321 Flight at Wittering.

Valiant Scramble. Illustration by John Ward

THE VALIANTS

The newly re-formed 49 Squadron was the unit chosen to participate in Britain's atomic weapon tests. In February 1956, 1321 Flt became 'C' Flt of 138 Squadron (the squadron had moved to Wittering) and on 1st May this Flight became 49 Squadron. The squadron (initially three Valiant B1 aircraft and crews) was commanded by S/Ldr Roberts and from September by W/Cmdr Hubbard. It was tasked with the continuation of trials leading to a live drop of 'Blue Danube' (Operation Buffalo) and trials of Britain's thermo-nuclear megaton weapon (Operation Grapple).

OPERATION BUFFALO - MARALINGA

The two 49 Squadron Valiants designated for Operation Buffalo (WZ366 and WZ367) left Wittering early in August 1956 for the Maralinga Range in Australia. 'Blue Danube' was similar in size and shape to the 'Tallboy' HE weapon of WW2, but had an operational explosive yield of 40 kilotons. The original plan was to use a standard bomb, fused to detonate at 1,200 feet. However, should the fusing system fail, a surface burst of 40 kilotons was unacceptable so the bomb was modified to give a three kiloton yield with a burst altitude of 500 feet.

Following two tower-mounted warhead tests, the first British nuclear weapon was dropped from WZ366 on 11 October 1956. Captained by S/Ldr Flavell, the aircraft dropped the weapon from 30,000 feet, visually aimed after a radar controlled run-up. Telemetry confirmed a burst height between 500/600 feet, 100 yards to port and 60 yards short of the target. Both S/Ldr Flavell and his bomb aimer, F/Lt Stacey, were awarded the AFC.

OPERATION GRAPPLE - CHRISTMAS ISLAND

The Pacific programme of British thermo-nuclear tests, Operation 'Grapple', began in 1957. The testing of a large megaton-yield weapon had dictated that a new site be found and Christmas Island, a remote coral atoll 2 deg. north of the Equator, was chosen. The tri-Service and civilian task force for 'Grapple' was commanded initially by Air Vice-Marshal W.E. Oulton and later by Air Vice-Marshal (later Marshal of the RAF), Sir John Grandy. The Scientific Director was Mr (later Sir William) Cook. Each Service had its own Task group; No. 160 Wing was commanded by Air/Cmdr C.T. Weir (see 21 November 1944).

Although inhabited, with an economy based on the export of coconut products, the island had been largely neglected since WW2. Preparations had started the previous year to construct the support facilities and a 7,000 feet runway, 25 miles of roads, a control tower, buildings for weapon assembly and sea water distillation plant were some of the building works needed. The domestic accommodation (for personnel and the indigenous gerboa rats!) was tented but more substantial buildings were provided for recreation purposes.

Most of these works were carried out by the Army Task Group (Royal Engineers) which included a detachment of Fijian troops. To provide some relief from the somewhat primitive living conditions, the RAF contingent was entertained regularly on the light aircraft carrier HMS `Warrior`.

VICKERS VALIANT B(K)1 (GRAPPLE MODIFIED)

For Operation Grapple, 49 Squadron received eight Valiant B(K)1 aircraft... the definitive bomber version of the type, equipped for air-refuelling tanker/receiver operation. The first (XD818), resplendent in 'all white' anti-flash finish, arrived at Wittering in November 1956. In addition to the heat-reflecting finish, metal anti-flash screens were fitted to windows serving the flight deck, crew and bomb aiming positions.

Cameras were fitted in a new tail cone and on mountings within the bomb bay, and the control surfaces were reinforced. A lot of automatic strain and pressure detecting devices were fitted to the airframe and many vents and drains baffled or sealed off. The V-force standard radar navigational bombing system was replaced by a special scientific panel. The bombs to be tested during Operation Grapple were trial warheads for a proposed range of British thermo-nuclear weapons: `Short Granite`, `Orange Herald` and `Purple Granite`. For carriage on the aircraft, these trial assemblies were fitted within `Blue Danube' casing. The weapons would be released from 45,000 feet and set to explode at 8,000 feet, thus avoiding the fireball touching the surface and causing excessive radiation.

The dropping point was off Malden Island, an uninhabited atoll some 400 miles south of Christmas Island. By dusk on 14 May, scientists had made the final checks on the apparatus sited on Malden, that was designed to measure the air blast, heat and radiation levels. They withdrew and embarked on HMS `Narvik`, `Warrior` and `Messina`.

SHOT 1

The hours prior to the release of the bomb were tense and dramatic. Long before dawn on the 15 May, the Shackletons of 204 and 206 Squadrons and Canberras of 76 and 100 Squadrons had thundered off from Christmas Island on weather reconnaissance and sampling sorties - with the added duty for the Shackletons of searching the danger area to ensure that it was free of shipping. At first light, Hastings of 24 Squadron and Dakotas of 1325 Flight had left for the target area laden with observers.

'All clear' messages flashed between the task Force Commander on HMS `Narvik` and the operations room on Christmas Island, culminating in the order for XD818 to take-off. Piloted by W/Cmdr K.G. Hubbard (O/C 49 Sqdn), the gleaming white Valiant taxied out onto the runway. For the few who watched it leave, the graceful rise and climb into the morning sky was so nonchalant as to be an anti-climax.

The pilot's commentary was clear and unhurried as the Valiant made its run-in at 45,000 feet, at a speed of 0.82M. 'Bomb gone' came the brief announcement from bomb aimer F/Lt Eric Washbrook, as the 'Short Granite' round fell away. Immediately the aircraft swung in a 60-degree bank turn to port; this escape manoeuvre would take the aircraft to a position some six miles distant in the 30 seconds before detonation.

A stark, blinding flash at 8,000 feet in the Pacific sky signalled Britain's emergence as a top-ranking nuclear power. It was 10.36hrs local time, on Wednesday 15 May 1957 -six years almost to the day since the first flight of the Valiant prototype. No one saw it! No human eye could survive the hellish glare of white-hot air brought to incandescence by the fantastic heat. But those present on this historic morning, backs turned to the 'mushroom' some 30 miles away, could sense the brilliant intensity of the flash through closed eyelids. Even through thick clothing a flush of warmth penetrated the body.

SHOTS 2 AND 3

Second and third drops of weapons in the megaton yield range took place at the same location in May and June, the aircraft being captained by S/Ldr Arthur Steele and S/Ldr David Roberts (XD822 and XD823). 49 Squadron returned to the UK in June. Seven AFC's were awarded to squadron personnel in the 1957 Queen's Birthday Honours.

H-Bomber Valiant XD824 at dispersal on Christmas Island. (49 Sqdn Collection)

Dropped from Valiant XD824 by S/Ldr Millett and crew on November 8, 1957. The mushroom from this the fourth H-bomb, reached a height of 60,000 feet over Christmas Island's South East Point.
(49 Sqdn Collection)

GRAPPLE X,Y AND Z

The remainder of the Grapple tests (X, Y and Z) were conducted over Christmas Island, with an aiming point on the south-east tip of the island only 20 miles from the airfield:

GRAPPLE X 8 November 1957: S/Ldr Barney T. Millett (XD824) and crew carried out an air burst test over the ocean near Christmas Island. The height of the burst was 7,260 feet with a yield of 1.8 Megatons.

GRAPPLE Y 24 April 1958: S/Ldr Bates (XD825) and crew carried out an air burst test over the ocean near Christmas Island. The height of the burst was 8,250 feet with a yield of 3.0 Megatons.

GRAPPLE Z 2 September 1958: S/Ldr Bailey (XD822) and crew carried out an air burst test over the ocean (by ground radar) near Christmas Island. The height of the burst was 9,240 feet with a yield of 1.0 Megatons.

11 September 1958, S/Ldr O'Connor (XD827) and crew carried out an air burst test over the ocean near Christmas Island. The height of the burst was 8,580 feet with a yield of 0.8 Megatons.

MBF TO TBF

From November 1959, 49 Squadron reverted to the Main Bomber Force (MBF) role then moved to Marham in June 1961 (along with 148 and 207 Sqdns) as part of a Tactical Bombing Force (TBF) assigned to NATO Supreme Allied Commander Europe (SACEUR). In the meantime Operation Grapple was beginning to achieve results. Bomber Command received its first operational Megaton bomb (Violet Club) in 1958. The first of five of these interim 9,000 lb weapons being delivered to BCAS at Wittering in February, after spending the night stuck in a snow drift on the A1, just outside the station.

As part of the TBF, carriage by 49 Squadron of the existing UK tactical atomic weapon (Red Beard) was supplemented by the US Mk 28 lightweight (1,900 lb) bomb. The Valiant could carry two of the megaton Mk 28s as it did the later variable-yield Mk 43 -a lay-down weapon. In the early 1960's, studies showed that the V-bombers could not expect to survive against improving Warsaw Pact air defences at high altitudes; their only chance would be a target approach at low level. Accordingly, after extensive trials in Canada, Valiants converted to the low-level role. To reduce visual detection the aircraft were repainted in a camouflage scheme reminiscent of WW2. The three Marham squadrons (49, 148 and 207) all received the new camouflage finish during 1963.

The aircraft structure was now subjected to much greater air loads, causing stresses that were probably outside the design parameters. There had been two unexplained Valiant crashes in May 1964 (WZ363 and WZ396) and on 6 August WP217 of the OCU suffered a fracture of a wing spar while airborne. An inspection of the Valiant fleet revealed similar faults to varying degrees in most aircraft, a consequence of metal fatigue or of alloy age-hardening.

With a cost to repair now little short of the cost to originally build, the entire force was grounded in mid-December and aircraft disposal initiated in February 1965. Most of the aircraft were scrapped at their bases, Marham being the biggest graveyard.

HISTORIC XD818

A decision had been taken to preserve 49's historic XD818 (600 sorties and 2,560 flying hours) and although struck off charge in March 1965, it was allocated a maintenance serial 7894M and displayed at Marham; but earmarked for the proposed Bomber Command Hall at the RAF Museum, Hendon. 818 stayed at Marham for 18 years until transferred to the museum in June 1982 where it remains... the last Valiant, complete in Grapple finish.
This aircraft stands as a fitting tribute to all those conscientious men and women of the Royal Air Force, who during that period in history called the 'Cold War', as members of the British nuclear deterrent force, stood ever prepared to defend our nation's freedom.

So if one day you happen to visit the RAF Museum at Hendon and enter the Bomber Command Hall; after you have paid your due respects to Lancaster 'S-Sugar', then turn your attention to the ultra menacingly impressive 'White Lady' that is 'Megaton' Valiant XD818. Once you have walked her extensive perimeter and marvelled at her contoured beauty, then pause a while and ask yourself just one question... Was this awesome machine a 'War maker'... or a 'Peace maker'?

No. 49 SQUADRON WAS DISBANDED AT RAF MARHAM ON 1 MAY 1965.

THE SQUADRON STANDARD

Friday 5th June, 1964: On this morning the Station was closed down for all normal purposes. This followed some days of feverish activity in preparation for a visit by Her Royal Highness Princess Marina of Kent who, at a parade later in the morning, presented both 49 and 214 Squadrons with their respective Colour Standards.

49 Squadron was represented by its Commanding Officer - W/Cdr J Langston supported by Flight Commanders - S/Ldr L G Warren A.F.C., and S/Ldr H L Taylor, Standard Bearer - F/O P V Deakin, Standard Warrant Officer - W/O F C Mathers and Escorts, - Sgt R C A Tomlinson and Sgt M Dove. The march past that followed the presentation parade saw the Standard borne for the first time.

THE STANDARD AND ITS ORIGIN

The Standard, a fringed and tasselled silken banner, mounted on a pike surmounted by a Golden Eagle, was created by His late Majesty King George Vl to mark the twenty-fifth anniversary of the Royal Air Force in 1943.

Squadrons qualify for the award of a standard after twenty-five years service or for especially meritorious operations. Eight selected battle honours in scroll surround the Squadron Badge and the decorative border is embroidered with the national emblems of the United Kingdom of Great Britain.

The original use of a symbol by the Armed Forces is lost in antiquity. It is known that the Assyrians, Egyptians, Greeks and Romans all had ensigns and standards which were regarded with the greatest veneration.

They have been in use by British Forces for many centuries. It is probable that their original purpose was to be a rallying point during a confused battle.

The practice of consecrating colours is of very long standing and because of this religious significance, the Standard becomes not only an outward sign of unity, loyalty, and achievement, but also a symbol of fellowship with God.

The combination of these factors places a deep significance in the Squadron Standard. It is to be honoured as a symbol of the trust which the Sovereign reposes in the Squadron and as an emblem of its achievements. It is the shrine of our traditions, a reminder of the devotion and sacrifices of our predecessors and an inspiration to those who serve.

Note:
The photograph on the following page is regretfully in monochrome and therefore does not reflect the excellent colours and workmanship of the Standard which has to be seen to be appreciated. The Standard is retained for safe keeping at RAF Marham.

THE SQUADRON STANDARD

49 SQUADRON COMMANDING OFFICERS

Major	A.S. Barratt, MC	8 May	1916
Major	A.V. Bettington	27 Sep	1916
Major	G.L.P. Henderson MC	Feb	1917
Major	B.H. Turner	16 May	1917
Major	J.R. Gould	28 Jan	1918
Major	B.S. Benning	30 May	1918
Major	J.C. Quinnell DFC	7 Feb	1919
Flight Lieutenant	J.C. Cunningham	10 Feb	1936
Squadron Leader	W.E. Dipple	6 Jul	1936
Squadron Leader	P. McGregor- Watt	22 Nov	1937
Wing Commander	W.A.B. Bowen-Buscarlet DFC	12 Dec	1938
Wing Commander	J.S. Chick MC, AFC	27 Feb	1939
Wing Commander	W.C. Sheen	1 Dec	1939
Wing Commander	J.W. Gillian DFC, AFC	1 Apr	1940
Wing Commander	J.N. Jefferson	22 Dec	1940
Wing Commander	R.D. Stubbs DFC	17 Jul	1941
Wing Commander	L.C. Slee DSO, DFC	14 May	1942
Wing Commander	P.W. Johnson DFC, AFC	5 Mar	1943
Wing Commander	A.A. Adams DFC	1 Oct	1943
Wing Commander	M. Crocker DFC	1 May	1944
Wing Commander	L.E. Botting	23 Jun	1944
Wing Commander	H.Y. Humphreys DFC	12 Jun	1945
Wing Commander	B.M. Balme DSO, DFC	18 Jun	1945
Wing Commander	J.H. Irvin OBE	16 Nov	1945
Wing Commander	A.J. Kennedy	26 Jun	1946
Squadron Leader	R.G. Woodcraft AFC	4 Nov	1946
Squadron Leader	J.D. Mundy DFC	23 Jan	1947
Squadron Leader	L.D. Wilson DSO, DFC, AFC	19 Aug	1948
Squadron Leader	The Hon D.H.T. Dowding	26 Jun	1950
Squadron Leader	B.A. Colvin 5	Apr	1951
Squadron Leader	A.E. Newitt DFC	1 Apr	1953
Squadron Leader	D. Roberts DFC, AFC	1 May	1956
Wing Commander	K.G. Hubbard OBE, DFC, AFC	2 Sep	1956
Wing Commander	R.W. Payne AFC	15 Dec	1958
Wing Commander	A.H. Chamberlain AFC	13 Feb	1961
Wing Commander	J. Langston	17 Dec	1962
Wing Commander	D.J. Corbet	15 Dec	1964

49 SQUADRON AIRCRAFT

Main Equipment	Period in use
BE2c	Apr 1916 - Nov 1917
RE7	Dec 1916 - Nov 1917
de Havilland 4	Apr 1917 - Apr 1918
de Havilland 9	Apr 1918 - Jul 1919
Hawker Hind	Feb 1936 - Dec 1938
Handley Page Hampden	Sep 1938 - Apr 1942
Avro Manchester	Apr 1942 - Jun 1942
Avro Lancaster	Jun 1942 - Mar 1950
Avro Lincoln	Oct 1949 - Jul 1955
Vickers Valiant	May 1956 - Jan 1965

Avro Manchester Mk 1A. Illustration John Ward

NO 49 SQUADRON - BASES

DOVER, KENT	15 Apr 1916	- 12 Nov 1917
LA BELLE VUE, FRANCE	12 Nov 1917	- 27 Mar 1918
ZEAUVIS, FRANCE	27 Mar 1918	
BOISDINGHEM, FRANCE	29 Mar 1918	
PETITE SYNTHE, FRANCE	30 Mar 1918	- 3 May 1918
CONTEVILLE, FRANCE	3 May 1918	- 2 Jun 1918
FOURNEUIL, FRANCE	2 Jun 1918	- 21 Jun 1918
BEAUVAIS, FRANCE	21 Jun 1918	- 14 Jul 1918
ROZOY-EN-BRIE, FRANCE	14 Jul 1918	- 4 Aug 1918
BEAVOIS, FRANCE	4 Aug 1918	- 30 Oct 1918
VILLIERS LEZ CAGNICOURT, FRANCE	30 Oct 1918	- 24 Nov 1918
BAVAI, FRANCE	24 Nov 1918	- 29 May 1919
BICKENDORF, GERMANY	29 May 1919	- 18 Jul 1919

Disbanded - 18 Jul 1919 - Re-formed - 10 Feb 1936

BIRCHAM NEWTON, NORFOLK	10 Feb 1936	- 8 Aug 1936
WORTHY DOWN, HANTS	8 Aug 1936	- 14 Mar 1938
SCAMPTON, LINCS	14 Mar 1938	- 2 Jan 1943
FISKERTON, LINCS	2 Jan 1943	- 22 Sept 1943
DUNHOLME LODGE	22 Sept 1943	- 23 Oct 1943
FISKERTON	23 Oct 1943	- 16 Oct 1944
FULBECK, LINCS	16 Oct 1944	- 22 Apr 1945
SYERSTON, NOTTS	22 Apr 1945	- 28 Sep 1945
MEPAL, CAMBS	28 Sep 1945	- 30 Jul 1946
UPWOOD, HUNTS	30 Jul 1946	- 1 Jul 1952
WADDINGTON, LINCS	1 Jul 1952	- 1 Aug 1953
WITTERING, NORTHANTS	1 Aug 1953	- 10 Nov 1953
EASTLEIGH, KENYA	10 Nov 1953	- 22 Feb 1954
UPWOOD, HUNTS	22 Feb 1954	- 30 Nov 1954
EASTLEIGH, KENYA	20 Nov 1954	- 28 Jul 1955
UPWOOD, HUNTS	28 Jul 1955	- 1 Aug 1955

Disbanded - 1 Aug 1955 - Re-formed - 1 May 1956

WITTERING, NORTHANTS	1 May 1956	- 26 Jun 1961

Detachments to Australia and Christmas Island for British nuclear weapons trials.

MARHAM, NORFOLK	26 Jun 1961	- 1 May 1965

Disbanded - 1 May 1965

THE FINAL WORD

This book's final words are those spoken by 'Uncle' Will, the skipper of a Lancaster bomber during 1944/45:

"Well, that's it -looking back one wonders if it really ever happened, but there are times when I look at the heavens and know what they looked like when all Europe was blacked out... or when I see the full moon and clear sky, my mind goes back to similar nights over the Rhineland... and I can see fighters, the flak, searchlights and spiralling aircraft, and I know ***- Yes! it really did happen..."***

Illustration by John Ward

THE 49 SQUADRON ASSOCIATION

The birth of this association occurred a few days after V.E. day in 1945. Reg Denny collected the names and addresses of all the airmen who were at R.A.F. Syerston. In 1948 and 1949, reunions were held at the Falstaff Restaurant in London. Over 200 attended on each occasion. These 2 reunions being organised by Jimmy Edwards.

Reg Denny then took over and organised men only reunions at the Pathfinder Club in Mayfair, chat, drinks and sandwiches being the order of the day. Attendances of these gatherings being around 25 to 30 .

During the 1976 reunion, Reg Denny handed me his address book with the cryptic words *"Tom, you are the youngest here so you can arrange the reunions in future"*. I had been 'Volunteered'. Subsequent reunions were arranged (and still are at the time of publication) on the first Saturday of November.

In 1980/81 the Pathfinder Club moved to the Challoner Club in Knightsbridge. It was here that the first lady, a 49 Squadron ex-WAAF Mrs Joan Williams came as my personal guest. Later that year the "49 Squadron Association" was officially formed with a simple set of rules that permitted anyone who had served with the squadron, aircrew, groundcrew and WAAF's to become members.

During 1979, courtesy of my nephew, F/lt J Pritchard, a reunion was arranged, at R.A.F. Scampton. This was for members only, no wives or guests attending. The success of this function heralded further summer reunions, at various venues including R.A.F. stations Wyton, Scampton, Marham and at the Petwood Hotel at Woodhall Spa. In 1996 the reunion held at R.A.F. Marham allowed wives and guests to dine with us.

In 1991, with the demise of the Pathfinder Club the November reunions moved to the Union Jack Club near Waterloo station.

Between 1948 and 1997, a total of 60 reunions have been held. The attendances being around 30 in November (members only) and averaging around 100 in the summer (including wives and guests). Since 1987 our summer reunions have been honoured on 5 occasions by the Lancaster "City Of Lincoln" of the Battle Of Britain Memorial Flight flying over to salute our members, including some tight turns over the Church at Fiskerton.

The Association could not exist without the diligent researches of Uncle Will Hay who supplies information to Authors, Researchers and relatives of members, queries being received from all 5 continents with some amazing results; also to Bernard Browning, our P.R. Man whose efforts in obtaining publicity in the press, T.V. and magazines are largely responsible for our current strength of 230 with 22 associate and 6 honorary members, said to be one of the three largest squadron associations.

THE 49 SQUADRON ASSOCIATION

THE BOOK OF REMEMBRANCE

The Association sponsored and produced our "BOOK OF REMEMBRANCE".in 1992 covering the period 1939-1945. Researched by Uncle Will Hay, it contains the names and all known information (including, rank, service number, country of origin, date of loss and place of burial) of the 905 R.A.F. Personnel and 1 civilian (BBC Correspondent) who were killed in action or died of injuries sustained in the course of their duties.

The original hard backed book, laid out and printed by Ted Cachart on special archive paper designed to last at least 200 years was professionally bound and covered in Nigerian goat skin leather. This book is preserved in the safe of the Fiskerton Church but is put on view on each Memorial Sunday or when any special service is held directly involving 49 squadron.
A second copy is permanently on view in the Church for visitors to examine the entries.

Copies were presented to the National Museums of Canada (Ottawa), Australia (Canberra), New Zealand (Auckland) and several museums in the U.K. including the R.A.F Museum at Hendon.

Tom Gatfield. Secretary 49 Squadron Association.

Anyone wishing to join the Association or requiring information about any friend or relation who served with our squadron should write to:

The Secretary, Mr T Gatfield. 126 Weirdale Avenue. Whetstone. London. N20 0AH
or make contact via the Bomber Command Association. R.A.F. Hendon. London NW9 5LL

Fiskerton 1995 Association members in the sports field over the road from the 'Carpenters Arms 'as seen from the Lancaster, "City of Lincoln".

Most reunions held in Lincolnshire end with a service in Fiskerton church followed by a hearty meal in the 'Carpenters Arms'.

The Fiskerton Church is hidden by the large engine nacelle, and to its right is the Five Mile Inn (now closed) (49 Squadron)

GLOSSARY

A Flt	A Flight
A.G.L.T.	Automatic Gun Laying Turret
A/B	Air Bombardier
A/G	Air Gunner
ACC	Accumulator
ACHU	Aircrew Holding Unit
ACW	Aircraftwoman
Aloft	49 Sqdn aircraft callsign (Fulbeck)
Artichoke	Approach to Lorraine
ASI	Air Speed Indicator
B Flt	B Flight
Bandlaw	49 Sqdn aircraft callsign (Fiskerton)
Bod	Person airman etc
Bograt	Code word for intruders
Bowser	Oil tanker
Canucks	Slang for Canadians
Caterpillar Club	Anyone saving their life with Irvine Parachute
Chiefy	Slang for Flight Seargent
Coned	Caught in several searchlights
Corkscrew	Manouvre to avoid attacking fighters
D Ring	Parachute rip cord handle
D.I.	Daily Inspection
D.I. ed	Daily Inspection carried out
DAPM	District Air Provost Marshall
Darky	Emergency callsign
Desp	Despatched
DFC	Distinguished Flying Cross
DFM	Distinguished Flying Medal
Dhobi	Laundry
Dickie	Second pilot
E/R	Early Returns (aircraft returning early)
EFTS	Elementary Flying Training School
Eglatine	Approach to Heligoland
Erk	Lowest ranking airman/airwoman
Evader	Anyone avoiding capture in enemy territory
F/E (F/Eng)	Flight Engineer
FIDO	Fog Intensive Dispersal Operation (Petrol jet pipes alongside runway)
Fishpond	Radar screen showing any aircraft below
Forget-me-not	Approach to Kiel Canal
FTR	Failed To Return
Gen	Slang for news/information
H2S	Aircraft radar navigation system
HCU	Heavy Conversion Unit
HF	High Frequency
Intercom	Aircraft internal communication system
Intruders	Code name for enemy aircraft
KIA	Killed In Action

Kite	Aircraft
LACW	Leading Aircraftwoman
M.T.	Motor Transport
MC	Military Cross
Med	Mediterranean
Mossies	Mosquitoes
NCO	Non Commisioned Officer
Nectarine	Approach to Frisian Island
NFT	Night Flying Test
Nickel	Leaflets
OBFW	German NCO Oberstfeldwabel
OC	Officer Commanding
Oilgrease	Base callsign (Fulbeck)
Oleo legs	Folding hydraulic undercarriage
Ops	Operations (missions sorties)
OTU`	Operational Training Unit
P/A/g	Pilot Air Gunner
Passout	Base callsign (Fiskerton)
Peri-track	Perimeter track
PFF	Path Finder Force
Pitot head	Device measuring air pressure to indicate speed
POW	Prisoner Of War
RAAF	Royal Australian Air Force
RCAF	Royal Canadian Air Force
RNZAF	Royal New Zealand Air Force
S/Ldr	Squadron Leader
SASO	Senior Air Staff Officer
Scarecrow	Incendiary device imitating aircraft exploding
Schrage Music	German nightfighter vertical firing cannon
Screen	Experienced aircrew checking out novice
Second Dickie	Second pilot
SNCO	Senior Non Commissioned Officer
SP	Service Police
T.I.	Target Indicator
Tallboy	Codename 12000lb bomb
Tannoy	Loudspeaker (Public address system)
TEE-EMM	Name of RAF Training Manual (Phonetic)
USAAF	United States Army Air Force
VE (VE Day)	Victory (over) Europe (Day)
Village INN	Code name for Automatic Gun Laying Turret
W/Ag	See Wop/Ag
W/Cmdr (W/Cdr)	Wing Commander
W/T	Wireless Telegraphy (morse)
Window	Small aluminum strips dropped to confuse radar
Wop/Ag	Wireless Operator/Air Gunner

INDEX - Personnel Identified in Photographs

INDEX - Personnel Identified in Photographs

INDEX - Personnel Identified in Photographs

INDEX - Personnel Identified in Photographs

GROUPS AND OTHER PHOTOGRAPHS

INDEX - Aircraft

INDEX - Illustrations & Miscellaneous

ILLUSTRATIONS
(By John Ward)

MAPS

MEMORIALS

MISCELLANEOUS

SIGNATURES